D0072603

History of the American Economy

Fourth Edition

History of the American Economy

Fourth Edition

Ross M. Robertson
Late of Indiana University

Gary M. Walton
Washington State University

Harcourt Brace Jovanovich, Inc.
New York San Diego Chicago San Francisco Atlanta

Library of Congress Catalog Card Number:
78-74629
ISBN: 0-15-536504-5
Printed in the United States of America

Cover art by Joyce Kitchell

Photo credits appear on page 573.

Dedicated to my parents,
Joseph Max Walton and Lorraine N. Walton,
and to the memory of Bertha Williams Robertson
and Ross Marshall Robertson

Preface to the Fourth Edition

When Ross M. Robertson died at the age of 61 just over two years ago, the profession lost an able and gifted educator. The request by the editors of Harcourt Brace Jovanovich, Inc., for me to revise the third edition of *History of the American Economy* was both an honor and a challenge.

As a teaching assistant at the University of Washington in 1966, I used the first edition of the Robertson text; a year later, I used the second edition. A great deal of my knowledge of the details of American economic history—the names, dates, and places—was learned from these first two editions. So too was much of my interpretive understanding of our past. In short, I have enjoyed some pleasant moments of nostalgia in preparing this revision. To me, two of the major attributes of the Robertson text are its clarity and readability. Ross Robertson was adept at presenting economic and historical analyses in readable narrative, and I have labored to preserve this special quality in the Fourth Edition.

My plan for this revision was threefold. First, I felt that the third edition had become somewhat encyclopedic, largely due to the inclusion of excessive details and esoteric financial matters. I was determined to shorten the book but to maintain its chronological order, so that it would be accessible to the average student and still provide time for supplementary reading. This has been accomplished largely by deleting lengthy descriptive passages which, in my judgment, were not essential to an understanding of the underlying forces of economic change in the past.

Second, I wished to correct what I believed to be an imbalance in the book—its comparatively cursary treatment of the colonial period and economic episodes in the pre-1860 period. This edition contains a total of 30 chapters, which are evenly distributed into four main periods: the Colonial Era; the Revolutionary, Early National, and Antebellum Eras, 1776–1860; the Reunification Era, 1861–1914; and the Modern Era, 1915 to the Present.

Third, it was essential to update the Fourth Edition by including research in the field—much of which has been quantitative and at times highly theoretical—without altering the narrative style of the earlier editions. This aspect of the revision has been of special concern to me, and I hope the users of previous editions of the book will find the clarity, readability, and style of the text preserved in the Fourth Edition.

As before, included here are the findings of past and present-day scholars who are characterized by a tremendous heterogeneity of interest and by wide differences in method and point of view. In particular, the results of recent contributions in the vibrant field of American economic history are included. The reader will shortly discover what these results have been. It is fair to generalize that such recent studies have valiantly chipped away at the mythology of history and that many of the accepted "truths" of economic history have disappeared under the light of theoretical and statistical examination. Comforting as it was to think so, pre-Civil War business cycles did not result from "excessive speculation," "reckless over-banking," or "monetary overinvestment," but from sharp changes in the deficit or surplus position of the Treasury, swings in outlays for internal improvements, international forces, and factors affecting the public's confidence in banks and money. Slavery, as it turns out, was both as efficient and as profitable in the antebellum South as elementary economic analyses would suggest and was not about to "fall of its own weight" in the 1850s. The concentration of American industry, at least in the first great wave, was motivated not so much by the predatory hope of gaining monopolistic power as by the fearsome excess capacities that developed as firms first competed in a national market. To take a more recent example, the Federal Reserve did not meet the oncoming economic storm of the 1930s with easy money, but with money so tight that there were serious pressures on bank reserves until it was too late for monetary policy to save the day. Finally, a current example concerns the confusion and frustration of today's policymakers as they attempt to deal with the unique concurrence of heightening inflation and unemployment.

This and earlier editions have been sustained and supported by many individuals. I shall not relist those acknowledged by Ross Robertson in previous editions, but their influence has surely filtered through to this one. I myself am especially indebted to Hugh G.J. Aitken, Amherst College, and Paul Uselding, University of Illinois at Urbana-Champaign, who offered critical comments on the entire first draft of this revision. I am also grateful for the advise and encouragement of Duane Ball, Fred Bateman, Stuart Bruchey, Philip Coelho, Paul A. David, Lance Davis, Richard A. Easterlin, Stanley L. Engerman, Albert Fishlow, Robert W. Fogel, Robert Gallman, Claudia Goldin, Lawrence A. Harper, Robert Higgs, James Mak, Donald N. McCloskey, William N. Parker, Joseph D. Reid, Jr., R.L. Sexton, Richard Sutch, Robert P. Thomas, and Mary Yeager. My long and beneficial collaboration with James F. Sheperd again deserves special notice, as does the continued influence of Douglass C. North. I also wish to express my appreciation for the lessons I have learned from my students—most notably my graduate students, Jeremy Atack, Jeffery R. Hummel, Jack Purdum, and Austin Spencer, but also my many undergraduate students at Indiana University and the University of California, Berkeley. Their stimulation reinforced my effort to complete the task at hand.

Linda Olsen and Rose-Marie Bradley formed the editorial and production team that contributed greatly to the literary quality of the book. The index was prepared by Rose-Marie.

Of course, my greatest debt in this endeavor is to Ross, who may or may not fully approve of this unintended collaboration. I admired Ross Robertson from the outset; indeed, I first met Ross at the American Economic Association meeting in New York in December 1965. That meeting left quite an impression on me, as did our later association as colleagues for many years in the 1970s at Indiana University. I hope old friends and acquaintances of earlier editons of Ross' book will enjoy this new edition. I hope you will all find the Fourth Edition improved, and I welcome and encourage you to send me your comments and advice.

Gary M. Walton

Contents

History of the American Economy

Fourth Edition

renowned scientists debated a question that generated considerable heat: How much should be spent for civilian defense against the ravages of nuclear war? Harrison Brown of the California Institute of Technology took the position that any large-scale construction of fallout shelters would be worthless and that the hope of mankind depended on agreement between the United States and the Soviet Union on questions of disarmament. Dr. Herman Kahn of the Hudson Institute in New York City took the opposite view—that shelters would be effective against fallout and, to some extent, nuclear blast and fire. After the opening minutes of the program, it became clear to viewers that the discussion would not revolve around scientific opinion. Both Brown and Kahn had been intimately connected with developments in nuclear energy and did not differ on questions of scientific theory. Indeed, for almost an hour, the discussion was based solely on historical facts. In previous wars, they asked, how did the strategies of belligerents affect civilian populations? What was the psychological reaction of both troops and civilians to the cruel and unnecessary destruction of cities and towns? Specifically how had Confederate soldiers reacted to Sherman's march through Georgia? What were the reactions of Londoners to the blitzkrieg and of the defenders of Stalingrad to German brutality? How, in general, have civilian populations behaved under the stresses of war? Is there historical evidence of degrees of civilian fear? Would nuclear blast result in panic or in sullen, resolute resistance?

So the discussion continued for nearly an hour. As soon as the two scientists left their laboratories and began to discuss public policy, they had to resort to experience. Moreover, each scientist could assume that the other was familiar with certain recorded and more or less formal accounts of experience—in short, with history. As is often the case in literate, intelligent conversation, the search for truth ended in an appeal to history.

History, then, does more than sharpen the wits; it is a vast body of information essential to a wide spectrum of public-policy decisions. Without a history, a people would endure a kind of social amnesia as tragic as the loss of a personal past that some victims of psychic or physical shock suffer. But history does more than provide us with facts. Any historian of worth must impose some kind of organization on the facts to make them meaningful, or even comprehensible. In the chapters that follow, we will find many examples of the way the historian orders the jumble of historical events and opens the way to the solution of problems. Indeed, the historian is most useful—most "practical"—either in solving problems or in undertaking the investigations that are prerequisite to ultimate problem solving.

Yet it is easy to exaggerate the practical values of history. History repeats itself only in a limited sense, and such repetition as there is (outside the periodicity of natural phenomena) sometimes teaches us little. Moreover, it is hard to demonstrate that people profit from the mistakes of their forebears or that historians are any wiser than the rest of us. But even if history is only a frail and untrustworthy guide to prediction, it is often the only guide we have. Once again, consider how our two scientists approached the policy problem of prescribing an effective civil-defense program. Or reflect on the repeated appeals to history made by both proponents and opponents of antiballistic missile systems.

1

The Emergi
Roles o
Econom
Histor

Young people, to whom this book is largely addressed, are not easily convinced of the benefits of historical study. For the most part, the history they were exposed to in elementary and high school probably seemed irrelevant to everyday life. Too often kings and nobles, generals and wars, presidents and legislators have been arrayed into long, tiresome lists. Perhaps there was a preoccupation with explaining what happened to whom, and when, rather than how and why it happened. Perhaps, too, the past often seemed crystallized into a kind of mythology to be taken on faith and not seriously questioned.

Yet even the unenthusiastic beginner cannot escape the impression that *some* knowledge of the past is useful. We draw on history for a sense of the heritage that underlies both our rights and duties. Without history, we are separated from information that is essential to decision making, and we are deprived of the clues that help us to untangle the complexities of the world around us. In a sense, history is the source of our very identity, as the recent enthusiasm for *Roots* so clearly illustrates.[1] "In an eternal present, which is a specious present, the past is all we know. And as the past is forever slipping back, it reminds us that we too shall in time belong wholly to the past."[2]

But it is as a tool in problem solving that history is particularly useful—not just to professors and government officials, but to businesspeople, scientists, and other decision makers as well. Let's cite an example. On national television a few years ago, two

[1] Alex Haley, *Roots* (New York: Doubleday, 1976).

[2] Herbert J. Muller, *The Uses of the Past* (New York: Oxford University Press, 1957), p. 31.

1

The Emerging Roles of Economic History

Young people, to whom this book is largely addressed, are not easily convinced of the benefits of historical study. For the most part, the history they were exposed to in elementary and high school probably seemed irrelevant to everyday life. Too often kings and nobles, generals and wars, presidents and legislators have been arrayed into long, tiresome lists. Perhaps there was a preoccupation with explaining what happened to whom, and when, rather than how and why it happened. Perhaps, too, the past often seemed crystallized into a kind of mythology to be taken on faith and not seriously questioned.

Yet even the unenthusiastic beginner cannot escape the impression that *some* knowledge of the past is useful. We draw on history for a sense of the heritage that underlies both our rights and duties. Without history, we are separated from information that is essential to decision making, and we are deprived of the clues that help us to untangle the complexities of the world around us. In a sense, history is the source of our very identity, as the recent enthusiasm for *Roots* so clearly illustrates.[1] "In an eternal present, which is a specious present, the past is all we know. And as the past is forever slipping back, it reminds us that we too shall in time belong wholly to the past."[2]

But it is as a tool in problem solving that history is particularly useful—not just to professors and government officials, but to businesspeople, scientists, and other decision makers as well. Let's cite an example. On national television a few years ago, two

[1] Alex Haley, *Roots* (New York: Doubleday, 1976).

[2] Herbert J. Muller, *The Uses of the Past* (New York: Oxford University Press, 1957), p. 31.

renowned scientists debated a question that generated considerable heat: How much should be spent for civilian defense against the ravages of nuclear war? Harrison Brown of the California Institute of Technology took the position that any large-scale construction of fallout shelters would be worthless and that the hope of mankind depended on agreement between the United States and the Soviet Union on questions of disarmament. Dr. Herman Kahn of the Hudson Institute in New York City took the opposite view—that shelters would be effective against fallout and, to some extent, nuclear blast and fire. After the opening minutes of the program, it became clear to viewers that the discussion would not revolve around scientific opinion. Both Brown and Kahn had been intimately connected with developments in nuclear energy and did not differ on questions of scientific theory. Indeed, for almost an hour, the discussion was based solely on historical facts. In previous wars, they asked, how did the strategies of belligerents affect civilian populations? What was the psychological reaction of both troops and civilians to the cruel and unnecessary destruction of cities and towns? Specifically how had Confederate soldiers reacted to Sherman's march through Georgia? What were the reactions of Londoners to the blitzkrieg and of the defenders of Stalingrad to German brutality? How, in general, have civilian populations behaved under the stresses of war? Is there historical evidence of degrees of civilian fear? Would nuclear blast result in panic or in sullen, resolute resistance?

So the discussion continued for nearly an hour. As soon as the two scientists left their laboratories and began to discuss public policy, they had to resort to experience. Moreover, each scientist could assume that the other was familiar with certain recorded and more or less formal accounts of experience—in short, with history. As is often the case in literate, intelligent conversation, the search for truth ended in an appeal to history.

History, then, does more than sharpen the wits; it is a vast body of information essential to a wide spectrum of public-policy decisions. Without a history, a people would endure a kind of social amnesia as tragic as the loss of a personal past that some victims of psychic or physical shock suffer. But history does more than provide us with facts. Any historian of worth must impose some kind of organization on the facts to make them meaningful, or even comprehensible. In the chapters that follow, we will find many examples of the way the historian orders the jumble of historical events and opens the way to the solution of problems. Indeed, the historian is most useful—most "practical"—either in solving problems or in undertaking the investigations that are prerequisite to ultimate problem solving.

Yet it is easy to exaggerate the practical values of history. History repeats itself only in a limited sense, and such repetition as there is (outside the periodicity of natural phenomena) sometimes teaches us little. Moreover, it is hard to demonstrate that people profit from the mistakes of their forebears or that historians are any wiser than the rest of us. But even if history is only a frail and untrustworthy guide to prediction, it is often the only guide we have. Once again, consider how our two scientists approached the policy problem of prescribing an effective civil-defense program. Or reflect on the repeated appeals to history made by both proponents and opponents of antiballistic missile systems.

We would sell our subject short, however, if we failed to note three intangibles that in varying degrees reward those who read and write history:

1. *History is fun.* Furthermore, it becomes more enjoyable as time goes by, because the older we get the harder we try to recapture some part of our lives in nostalgic reminiscence. To be exciting, history does not have to be watered down to a fictionalized biography or a historical novel. Good history, taken straight, has a tremendous appeal to a wide variety of readers. Fortunately, in recent years, we have returned to making history important as a literary form as well as an intellectual endeavor.

2. *Like all the liberal arts, history helps us live that "nonpractical" part of our lives to which, according to John Ciardi, the poet chiefly ministers.*[3] No sane human being is exclusively practical; we all live personal lives that can be distinguished from our business or professional lives. All of us, at one time or another, find it more important to establish some order of reality in our personal lives than to determine goals in our working lives. History, like poetry or music, can help us to understand ourselves in a way that is nonintellectual—but no less real because it strikes directly at our consciousness.

3. *A sense of history is a great comfort.* For those who have no other faith, history may even be a substitute for religion. As we recall the great events of the past, we are impressed both with the shining achievements of mighty civilizations and with their ultimate catastrophes—with grandeur followed by ruin. A sense of history is really a sense of participation in these high dramas—a sense of having a part in the great flow of events that links us with those who have preceded us and with others who have yet to be born.

THE MERGING OF ECONOMICS AND HISTORY

In this book, we will be concerned with a specialized historical narrative—"a longitudinal cut through the whole fabric of history," to use Edwin Gay's expression.[4] It is often convenient to trace historical developments within a certain field of learning, such as music, science, or law. But as we will see shortly, an understanding of the economic history of the United States is more than just a convenience; it is a prerequisite to solving many of the policy problems that presently demand solution. For a moment, however, let's leave the justification of our study to look more closely at the two disciplines of history and economics and to consider how they merge.

Like any organized body of knowledge, both economics and history abstract from reality. Without such aid, the human mind cannot comprehend the complexity of our economic system. We cannot simply look at the interrelationships among economic variables and make sense out of them. It is equally apparent that history must be selective—that any attempt to record the whole

[3] Read, if you can, Ciardi's essay "An Ulcer, Gentlemen, Is an Unwritten Poem," reprinted in *Toward the Liberally Educated Executive* (New York: New American Library, 1960), pp. 66–69.

[4] Edwin F. Gay, "The Tasks of Economic History," *Journal of Economic History,* **I** (December 1941), p. 15.

of the past would be an exercise in futility. Consider, then, how economists and historians make their respective subjects manageable.

Economics

The wealth of a country consists of its resources—its people (especially their knowledge and skills), its natural endowments, and its stock of produced goods. The management of these resources is a perplexing and difficult problem, because resources are scarce in relation to unlimited human wants. Put a little differently, there is a discrepancy between the amount of goods and services that the people in any society would *like* to have and the amount that they *can* have. Just as the members of a family must choose among alternatives when spending income, so the people in a society must make choices about the use of resources.

We know from observation that the American economy operates without much apparent guidance to determine what will be produced from its resources and how output will be distributed. For example, anyone who works with young people observes their endless wrestling with the problem of choosing a career—that is, the problem of what kind of resource they want to become. Their choices, to be sure, are not determined entirely by prospects of monetary gain; a gifted college senior may aspire to be a minister rather than a business executive. Nevertheless, choices of this kind are strongly influenced by ultimate financial reward.

Similarly, we are all familiar with the problem of deciding how to spend our personal incomes. What amount should we allocate to food and to clothing? Should we spend more on a house or on entertainment and recreation? How much should we spend on present satisfaction and how much should we set aside for an uncertain future? Each family or individual who manages personal income must continuously make choices of this kind. Whether we like it or not, the act we perform almost continuously is that of *economizing*.

Economists, however, are not concerned primarily with the *individual's* problem of scarcity, although they are well aware that the choices of individuals in the aggregate affect the economy as a whole. And although economists' attentions can range from the attitudes of single human beings and the operations of individual business firms to relationships among the economies of the world, ordinarily they are chiefly concerned with the basic problem of scarcity as it is resolved by groups of people living together in various regions within a political boundary.[5]

People living in social groups economize by allocating limited resources among the vast array of alternatives that are human wants. Basically, an effective system of allocating resources must give quantitative answers to the following questions:

1. How much and what kind of productive (factor) services should be provided? Specifically, how many clerks, managers, doctors, teachers, and other workers are required to manufacture goods and furnish services?

[5] The term *economics* was not widely used until the 1870s. Before then, the expression in common use was *political economy*—a descriptive name that is once again becoming fashionable.

2. Which enterprises should obtain the different productive services?
3. How much of the total output of the economy should be relegated to households for immediate use (consumption), and how much should be added to the stock of real capital (tools, machinery, and so on) that will be needed for future productive effort?
4. How should consumer goods be distributed (rationed) among consumers, and how should additions to the stock of capital be parceled out among various enterprises?

History furnishes examples of what at first seem to be many different systems of allocating resources. Actually, there are two basic ways of directing the allocation process. One is to centrally control allocation, as in the Soviet Union, where a political commissariat decides what part of the country's productive services is to be devoted to providing consumer goods and services, what part is to be used to make capital goods, what part is to be allocated for space hardware, and so on. More detailed decisions are then made by lesser officials in the hierarchy and may or may not parallel the wishes of consumers. Although prices may be assigned to goods and services, they are mainly for the purpose of keeping accounts and informing planners.

In an enterprise economy, typified by that of the United States, the allocation of resources is accomplished by means of the price system. On one hand, households sell their services or the use of their property in markets where resources are bought and sold, thereby earning *incomes.* On the other hand, households are confronted with a battery of *prices* in the consumer market. The relationship between incomes and prices determines the levels of living both for individual households and for society. In the growing, progressing American economy, choices are continually being registered in the consumer market and telegraphed by price and quantity changes to the business sector, which responds to shifting consumer demands by changing its requirements for productive services.

It would be a mistake, however, to suppose that the price system performs its functions simply by sending impulses from consumers to business. The business sector is constantly introducing new products and innovating low-cost ways of making old ones, with resulting changes in consumer outlays. Moreover, through advertising, the business community constantly strives to sway consumer preferences among goods and services and also between making consumption expenditures and saving.

Indeed, because the choices registered by both business managers and consumers are often made *simultaneously,* it is hard to say which decisions are causes and which are effects. The important point is that through the pricing mechanism, consumer and producer choices are translated into ultimate decisions about how resources should be allocated. Because prices are so vitally important, their study and observation is the chief preoccupation of businesspeople and academic economists.

In action, the American economic system is perhaps the most exciting and complex mechanism ever devised by Western civilization. Even in its most trivial manifestations, the system ordinarily provides goods and services from all the parts of the world, as if by magic, exactly when and where they are needed. The everyday items that we all take for granted—our morning coffee and our evening newspaper, our ride to work and our television program at home, a telephone call to a friend or an airmail letter to an office in New York—require the cooperative efforts of hundreds or thousands of people and the equipment with which they work. And when we wish to describe the system in all its intricate detail, the task seems formidable to the point of impossibility.

At this point, economists, like physical scientists, must resort to theory; that is, they must abstract from the reality of the world about them to see the fundamental forces at work. In devising theories, economists encounter perplexing difficulties, because—unlike physical scientists—they cannot perform experiments in a laboratory so they are able to isolate and control certain variables. Until quite recently, economists have been unable to persuade people whose affairs have been the subject of inquiry to submit to meaningful experimentation, so they have had to fall back on the "laboratory of the mind." To get at the heart of the problems, economists set up a hypothetical model of an economy in which conditions are much simpler than they are in the real world. After they discover central tendencies that are believed to operate in the real world, they remove the simplified assumptions of the model and calculate the effect of their removal. For example, in trying to ascertain the forces that determine the price of a commodity, the theorist may assume that no extensive changes in tastes have occurred during analysis. The assumption is possibly removed from reality, but it greatly simplifies the problem. Later, to approximate reality more closely, the possibility of changes in tastes may be introduced.

As long as economists are concerned with perceiving a fundamental interplay of forces, they must construct models. Insofar as they abstract from reality to discover principles, they are theorists.[6]

But what do economists theorize about? First, they examine the workings of the principal mechanism used to allocate resources—the *pricing* system, which (1) establishes the order of priority in which producers obtain resources and (2) rations goods among consumers. For a long time, the central inquiry of economic theory was to discover how the prices and quantities of goods were determined. Since the 1930s and even earlier, another problem—the persistent and widespread unemployment of resources—has increasingly occupied the attention of economists, and a body of theory has developed to explain how unfulfilled wants can exist side by side with idle workers and idle equipment. Recently, the central problem of economic stabilization has been one of unyielding inflation, although this same theory presumably provides prescriptions for containing intractable price rises. To the classical theory of price, then, economists appended the theory of income and employment—an analysis that complements the theory of price determination by showing how unemployment and/or inflation can exist.

The broad subject of economic theory has been subdivided into a number of specialities. Some economists specialize in the theory of the firm, with its recent emphasis on problems of strategy and conflict. Others devote their full

[6]We commonly hear the expression *That's all right in theory, but it won't work in practice.* But this statement is nonsensical. If a theory is not right in practice, then the theory is wrong; that is, it fails to predict.

time to the study of monetary theory or to the perfection of social accounting systems. Still others investigate the principles by which international trade is regulated and the intricate theory of the determination of international exchange rates. But in whatever way economists specialize or break down the job of analysis, the fact remains that there are two basic theoretical questions in economics: (1) How are resources allocated? and (2) What forces determine the level of a nation's income?

Whenever a subject has a body of theory, it also has a body of applied knowledge. Thus, we often speak of "applied" or "concrete" economics. As Professor Kenneth Boulding puts it

> Any subject such as economics which is "empirical," in the sense that it is interested in the interpretation of actual human experience, must have two parts: the construction of logical frameworks (the "pure" subject) and the interpretation of reality by fitting the logical framework to the complex of empirical data (the "applied" subject).[7]

Thus, there is a part of economics that deals with more "practical" matters. The applied economist, like the theorist, can specialize in many areas. An economic statistician compiles, organizes, and interprets current quantitative information. An economic historian is concerned largely with the perception of *change* in economic phenomena. A practicing economic consultant furnishes executives who formulate policies with business forecasts to guide in their decision making.

Economists are fond of saying that economics is not an exact science.[8] But neither is it guesswork. By and large, economists rely on an almost universally accepted theoretical apparatus. Social goals are subject to debate among economists just as they are among other occupational groups. But once they are furnished with a consensus about objectives—about ends—economists can offer—within tolerable limits of error—policy prescriptions calculated to achieve those objectives. In a word, economics is a way of thinking about the "unrelated confusion" of prices, production, and incomes that makes these phenomena intelligible and sufficiently well ordered to permit scientific prediction.

Like any scientist working in an applied field, the economist must ultimately answer the question, What *action* should be taken? Here an appeal must be made both to theory and to the lessons of experience. Advisers to government officials and other decision makers cannot reason through real-world problems without some means of eliminating the least relevant facts—

[7] Kenneth E. Boulding, "Samuelson's Foundations: The Role of Mathematics in Economics," *Journal of Political Economy,* **LVI** (June 1948), p. 190.

[8] Economics, once a branch of "moral philosophy," had little claim to scientific status until the publication of Adam Smith's *Wealth of Nations* in 1776. For another century and a half, while economists were developing their theoretical propositions and giving them mathematical formulation, economics was on its way to becoming scientific. But only in the last generation or so have economists been able to attempt to empirically verify these propositions. Later we will have more to say about the similarities and dissimilarities among the social studies and the physical and biological sciences.

without applying the principles of the theoretical economist. But any adviser with good sense must inevitably return to a reading of the record. We must turn finally to economic history to check faults by reasoning and to illumine paths of action.

History

Ideally, economic historians are part economist and part historian. As historians, what problems do we encounter? What are the shackles of historical research? Are the facts of history less securely established than the facts of the experimental sciences? It is to questions like these that we must turn for a moment.

We use the word *history* almost every day, usually without being aware of the ambiguity of the term. It has come to have a double meaning. When we speak of history, we may refer (1) to the narrative of past events or (2) to the events themselves. When we say, "Oh, that's past history," we are referring to events. When we say, "History proves that dictators are cruel," we are referring to the record. The familiar saying "Mankind makes history; historians make histories" emphasizes history's dual meaning.

We could begin with the simple remark that history is the narrative statement of happenings in the past. But such an assertion does not take us very far simply because it fails to stress the burdensome obligation of the historian, who must select from the whole of the known past the material to include in the narrative. Another definition—perhaps one that is too pretentious and formal for most purposes but one that points out the problem of fact selection, is that "History is man's formal record of actual human phenomena as consecutively manifested in the past insofar as they have been ascertained to be general, important, enduring, and true, with the legitimate deductions drawn for the pleasure and education of mankind." Note the key words *general, important, enduring, true.* Obviously, history will rarely be concerned with the lives of everyday people. Rather, it will be concentrated around events that concern the community as a whole—events that have a high degree of importance in this sense. But who judges the importance of these events? The fact selectors, of course, who in the process impose their own value judgments on the reader.

So the historian, like the economist, is confronted with a jumble of facts that must be collected and molded into an intelligible, significant narrative. We can better understand the difficulty of the task when we realize that the historical event has happened in the unalterable past and can never be observed again. It can only be reconstructed from remaining evidence, chiefly in the form of documents of one kind or another, and much of the evidence is fragmentary and unreliable. But whatever difficulties historians encounter, they must collect and organize the facts, interpret them in the light of modern interests, and present them in usable form.

It has been said that there are three phases of historical procedure. With caution, so that we do not jump to any conclusions about separating the historian's work into neat compartments, we may still find it useful to consider these steps.

1. *Reconstruction of the historical facts—"the science of history."* Historical facts can be reconstructed by people who do not write history at all—basic researchers who search through attics and cellars, court houses, and business records and who publish their material in the form of collected letters, papers, memoirs, and journals. But no one has a monopoly on fact collection, and many historians who write at a highly generalized level and enlist the aid of scholars in sociology, political science, and anthropology often contribute to our knowledge of historical events.

2. *Writing the historical narrative—"the art of history."* Because the facts must be assembled to form a significant written record, the historian must make a literary effort. Sometimes this effort is so successful that the result is a high art form. Historians from Herodotus to Freeman have become famous as a result of their literary abilities as well as their substantive contributions. Macaulay is still assigned in English literature classes, and contemporary readers even today are moved by Gibbon. For some time, the nineteenth-century emphasis on literary quality in historical works may have disappeared, but in recent years, first-class historians have revived it. The monograph of a young scholar, whose aim is to exhaust a subject of limited range, can be both technical and unexciting. But general histories, including popularizations, that do not cast their spell will be quickly usurped by a TV program or the latest bestseller.

3. *Interpretation of history—"the philosophy of history."* After the facts have been gathered and the historical narrative has been written, the record should be explained in terms of the general principles that govern human conduct. Older historians sought to explain the flow of events by some grand central motivation; they exhibited an essentially *monistic* philosophy in opposition to the *pluralistic* philosophy of modern writers. The most common and best-known monistic theme was that history centered around political activity—around governments and the major phenomena of governments, such as wars, legislative acts, and changes in rulers. College students can hardly escape another monistic approach—the "great man" interpretation of Thomas Carlyle, who held that a few highly gifted people constituted the determining force in human affairs. Alternatively, in the nineteenth century, the economic or materialistic view of Karl Marx emphasized the economic determinants of the cultural, social, and political values of life. There have been many other attempts to find a single wellspring of human motivation centered on psychology, spirituality, science, or technology, the "creative mind," and geography. Gradually, however, modern historians have come to believe that the vast sweep of history cannot be explained in terms of one aspect of human activity and have adapted the pluralistic view that in a physical environment more and more shaped and dominated by people, the human race progresses or retrogresses for a variety of reasons.

But if historical writing is only the result of a drastic sifting of evidence, can we ever be sure that the history we are reading is absolutely true? To this question, we must make the qualification that we can never be certain. From a tangled web of facts, the historian must select some and discard others. Foremost historical scholars used to contend that this selection could be made on an "objective" basis. But one historian's objectivity is another historian's bias. No individual historian, however honorable or gifted, can write outside the context of his or her own experience and philosophy. We must include in our narrative those facts that we think are important in explaining changes and that in our opinion are worth explaining. Whether we like it or not, history involves implicit theorizing.

Does this argument lead us to conclude that progress in historical knowledge is impossible? Of course not! History is constantly moving toward greater clarification—toward a deeper, fuller knowledge of what has happened and how and why it has occurred. This progress is possible because a succession of historians, dedicated to the job of seeking new insights into and more logical explanations for events, endlessly rewrite history. It is this compulsion to take another look, to ask one more question, to perceive something a little more clearly, that makes history in the sense of the narrative a changing and vital subject.

ECONOMIC HISTORY AND THE ROLES OF THE ECONOMIC HISTORIAN

Economic history draws on each of the two great disciplines we have just examined—economics and history. If general historians must go through a heroic process of selecting the material to present, economic historians must winnow still further. In so doing, we are not unmindful that an understanding of our whole history is essential to a satisfactory explanation of economic development. But most men and women who are interested in economics and business do not have enough time to become historians as well. Nevertheless, they and other students of human behavior must have some clear idea of the way people have solved the age-old economic problem. Even more specifically, they may wish to know how and why Americans have allocated their resources for more than three centuries. To this question, economic history gives neither a final nor a complete answer, but it is the one special discipline that comes the closest to doing so. To the patience and imagination of the historian, the economic historian brings the discipline of economic theory and a certain expertise in dealing with quantitative information.

As we see it, economic historians are committed to four primary objectives. Some pursue only one; others are versatile enough to tackle all four. Whatever the division of labor, these four objectives must be met.

1. *The traditional assignment of the economic historian is to explain changes in the institutions that are most closely connected with the business of making a living.* In its simplest form, this work defines and describes markets, traces the behavior of sellers and buyers, and quantifies the outcome of their bargaining in statistical series that illustrate changes in prices and production over time. But this mundane labor leads to a more exciting inquiry—the question of why the present economic system, rather than some other system, is an outgrowth of the past.

The working economist knows that scarcely a day passes without people relying on the contributions of the economic historian. Several years ago, having received an assignment from the Commission on Money and Credit, Ross

Robertson stopped by the CMC offices in New York to discuss the proposed monograph. In the course of the conversation, he was asked what papers were to be furnished on the history of money and financial institutions; after all, the National Monetary Commission of two generations ago had contributed several volumes of historical material to the economist's shelves. Robertson was informed, half in jest, that "the only history the Commission is interested in is what has happened since 1950." He thought nothing more of the conversation and went to work on his monograph about the federal lending agencies.

A few months later, a telephone call from CMC's New York offices brought an urgent request for assistance. At its most recent meeting, the full commission had asked the head of one of its task forces to explain how the nonbank intermediaries had emerged. How, someone had asked, did life insurance companies, mutual savings banks, savings and loan associations, credit unions—and on and on through the whole list of intermediaries—get their start? What were the impellents to the growth of each type of institution? Did building and loan associations, for example, thrive because a few public-spirited citizens wanted to do something beneficial for small savers? Or was the profit motive responsible for the spectacular growth of these institutions in the post–World War II years? There were, of course, plenty of bits and pieces of work that touched on these matters, and in the case of one or two of the intermediaries, a full and sufficient history had been attempted. But no one had ever considered the question of the growth of the nonbank intermediaries as a whole, so Robertson was called on to construct this historical picture and analysis.

How did the performance of markets in the mid-twentieth century compare with markets in the Middle Ages? Was there ever really a kind of Golden Age of perfect competition? When did the concentration of various manufacturing firms take place and why? Despite the growth of the large firm, has competition actually changed from the day and age when there were many sellers of a manufactured product? Is it, in fact, a change in the apparatus of competition that has led to a shifting relationship between the federal government and private economic institutions? Is our "mixed economy," which depends primarily for the allocation of resources on the price system but also on government, changing its mix? It is to questions of this sort that economic historians have traditionally addressed themselves.[9]

2. *Perhaps the most fashionable subject in economics in recent years has been the study of economic growth.* The question of growth has always attracted economists, and economic historians have considered the problem central to their own efforts.

In his presidential address before the Economic History Association, Carter Goodrich wondered plaintively if the current theorists of economic growth with their elegant analysis had deemphasized history. Goodrich could quickly reassure himself. The methods of theory and of history are in this sense different: Economic theory *abstracts* from reality; economic history undertakes a

[9] For a recent attempt to explain the timing of institutional change, see Lance E. Davis and Douglass C. North, *Institutional Change and American Economic Growth* (Cambridge, England: Cambridge University Press, 1971), *esp.* pp. 3–79.

selection of variables from the complex that *is* reality. Economic theory builds models. The narrative of economic history, although admittedly a simplification, nonetheless reconstructs a world in which people live and breathe. Plainly, there are advantages of the historical method that are both intellectually satisfying and, for purposes of policy applications, more useful than pure economic theory.

For one thing, growth theorists, by focusing their attention almost exclusively on the variables that affect rates of change in a mature industrial economy, omit, for all practical purposes, the great forces of change that were at work for centuries before the "modern economies" emerged. To be sure, attention to preconditions is not infrequent. But the preconditions treated by growth theorists are almost invariably technological. Examining only science and technology, we are likely to forget the tremendous influences of legal and other human forces on the long course of economic events. More dangerous to our ultimate conclusions is the likelihood that if economic historians do not continuously reexamine the first historical interpretations, students will make all kinds of unnecessary errors.

Let's cite some examples. Growth models certainly do not provide us with a satisfactory explanation of the so-called rise of capitalism. Moreover, some historians have told us implausible stories about the emergence of modern business by making up their own history, much as economists for a century and a half made up their own psychology. Were we not told that the Renaissance was an influence on changing economies because with renaissance came interest in science and scientific application? Yet there was really no economically significant science until well after the publication of Newton's *Principia* in 1687. Renaissance was important, yes, but for the reason that the reawakening whetted avarice by demonstrating that the best things in life are by no means free. Didn't Max Weber, among others, teach that Calvinism provided capitalism with a religious rationale that at least by implication made this brand of Protestantism the most important single influence on the growth of "modern economies"? But the early Calvinists did not believe, as Weber asserted, in a concept of "calling" that made success in business evidence of God's blessing and thus of one's election. It was quite the other way around: The early Calvinists were persuaded of the irreconcilability of God and mammon, and only after a century and a half did they formulate a view of their "calling" that actually fit the capitalist spirit. But this is only to say that what promotes growth is not any positive religious faith but a *waning of faith* sufficient to permit the kind of conduct required by a powerful capitalism.[10]

In examining the problem of growth, economic history can make still another contribution that can not yet be obtained from theory. Economic growth can occur within varying social and political contexts. The forces that accelerated or retarded change are more likely to be discerned in their entirety by the historian, and even the fortuitous events that played so important a part

[10] Compare Max Weber, *The Protestant Ethic and the Spirit of Capitalism* (New York: Scribner's, 1930) with Winthrop S. Hudson, "The Weber Thesis Reexamined," *Church History* **XXX:** 1 (March 1961), pp. 88–99.

in the growth of the Western economies may be overlooked by those whose experience is largely contemporary. It would be difficult indeed to overlook the effects of World War II on such economic determinants of the postwar American economy as the rate of capital formation, the rate of saving, and the level of output. But how likely is it that young theorists today will reflect on some of the great chance happenings of the past that helped in large to promote the economic growth of the United States by forcing it to gather its mid-nineteenth century momentum?

Will they, for example, stop to think that the United States was founded after Europe had already made the change from medieval to modern times? When the American colonies were formed, many of the medieval rigidities that plague the underdeveloped countries today no longer existed in Europe and scarcely any of them were ever transplanted to the colonies. So the abundance of land not only enabled colonial Americans to feed themselves without creating huge drafts on their foreign exchange, but also made it largely unnecessary for them to throw off the shackles of feudalistic restrictions on land tenure. Or will the theorist who casts up the "fundamental equations" of growth stop to think that the United States was nurtured and sustained in its critical early years by the Napoleonic Wars, which stimulated the carrying trade of the young country, created foreign exchange to pay for capital imports, and swelled the mercantile fortunes that later sought investment outlets in one of the first American growth industries—cotton textiles?

More positively, economic history has lately progressed toward a unified, coherent historical narrative of the growth process. But now we are getting ahead of our story; we will return to this matter in Part 2.

3. *Economic history and its kindred subject, business history serve to test the propositions of economic theory.*[11] Our observations about the procedures of economic theorizing caution against expecting too much of history as a testing ground for theorems, because it is impossible to isolate only the relevant historical variables. Yet a careful and judicious observation of repeated phenomena helps us to verify or refute propositions we have reached through abstract reasoning. It is in this context that economic history can offer us its most valuable insights.

A generation and more ago, economic historians were unwilling to pass judgment of the cherished notions of the then contemporary theory. Today's historians, however, are not bashful about holding theorems up to the white light of recorded experience. In so doing, many younger people are not only testing theory—they are writing a new kind of history and bringing to their generalizations a wealth of statistically reliable data. Thus, economic history that once was expressed in such terms as "largely" and "mostly" now often contain such assertions as "60 percent" or "90 percent". The "new" economic

[11] At the moment, a digression on the nature of business history would carry us far afield. Let's tentatively assume that business history is simply a speciality that focuses on the behavior of the firm and its management and lies within the larger field of economic history. We will have the opportunity to expand on this point in later chapters, particularly when we consider the role of the entrepreneur in economic organization.

historians emphasize the use of theory and statistical analysis not only to ascertain precisely documentable fact, but also to establish the outer limits of probability and thereby provide a basis for historical judgment.[12]

4. *Like all other historians, the specialists in economic history must at last confront their noblest task—the interpretation of the records they have forged.* Recognizing that most people are unable to separate the economic system from the social whole, economic historians must nonetheless assess the performance of that system in a world of conflicting ideologies. And, finally, we must give the best account we can of the mainsprings of the process of development, because more than half the peoples of the world require and wait for this special advice.

Scholars should never be apologists for any social organization, nor can we honorably defend the demonstrable failings of the system to which we bear allegiance. By the same token, a scrupulously fair examination of a country's economic development may be the most effective testimony to the justice and worth of its total social organization.

In the pages that follow, the history of the American economy is written once again. There would be no excuse for just another recounting of the same old facts and figures, updated by a few years that all too rapidly recede into the past. There is a solid reason, though, for recasting the record to further relieve it of its mythological overburden and to bear witness to the strength of a democracy that operates within the discipline of markets.

[12] Continuing reference will be made to works of this kind. Some outstanding examples are: J.R.T. Hughes, *Fluctuations in Trade, Industry, and Finance* (Oxford: Clarendon Press, 1960); Lance E. Davis, J.R.T. Hughes, and Stanley Reiter, "Aspects of Quantitative Research in Economic History," *Journal of Economic History,* **X:** 4 (December 1960); William N. Parker (ed.), *Trends in the American Economy in the Nineteenth Century,* No. 24 in *Studies in Income and Wealth,* National Bureau of Economic Research (Princeton: Princeton University Press, 1960); Robert W. Fogel, "The New Economic History: Its Findings and Methods," *Economic History Review,* **XIX:** 3 (December 1966); Robert W. Fogel and Stanley Engerman (eds.), *The Reinterpretation of American Economic History* (New York: Harper & Row, 1971); and Lance E. Davis, Richard A. Easterlin, William N. Parker (eds.), *American Economic Growth: An Economist's History of the United States* (New York: Harper & Row, 1972).

1

The Colonial Era

2

Founding the Colonies

"For the pleasing entertainment of the Polite part of Mankind, I have printed the most Beautiful Poems of Mr. Stephen Duck, the famous Wiltshire Poet," announced "Fry, Stationer, Bookseller, Paper-Maker, and Rag Merchant, late of the City of London and now located in Boston." The advertisement, which appeared in the Boston *Gazette,* May 1–8, 1732, was not an introductory offer, for the notice continued, "It is a full demonstration to me that the People of New England have a fine taste for Good Sense and Polite Learning, having already sold 1,200 of these Poems."

No doubt Fry was anxious to please and entertain the "Polite part of Mankind," possibly at a profit. But his advertisement contained another, somewhat plainer matter that may have interested him more. It was "the common Method of the most curious merchants of Boston, to Procure their (account) Books from London," and Fry, for business reasons, took exception to the practice. He addressed the notice to all Gentlemen, Merchants, and Tradesmen. "This," he declared, "is to acquaint those Gentlemen, that I, said Fry, will sell all sorts of Accompt-Books, done after the most accurate manner, for 20 percent cheaper than they can have them from London."

That prepared "accompt" books "done after the most accurate manner" were offered for sale at such an early date should have occasioned no more surprise than that the polite part of New England was entertained by the poems of Mr. Stephen Duck of Wiltshire. *For in the beginning, the American colonies were only a small part of a greatly expanded Europe—a western frontier, so to speak.* The culture of the colonists, including double-entry bookkeeping and poetic preferences, was in many respects the culture of their former associates on the other side of the Atlantic.

Europeans migrated to the New World for many reasons. Some were hired to travel to the colonies by statesmen or entrepreneurs at home, who variously sought great riches, the extension of Christianity, or the glory of the state. Some immigrants wished to escape the political and religious disturbances of western Europe; others were motivated simply by a thirst for adventure—by a compelling desire to see and do new things. And, of course, there were the unfortunates, ranging from felons to bums and tramps, who were involuntary indentured servants or who were expelled from Europe because they were criminals.

Africa too was swept into the process of Europe's outward extension, and the African migration to the New World epitomized the harshness of the trek. Black African captives were systematically shipped to South America, the Caribbean, and to North America to pursue a dismal life of bondage and forced labor. Finally, the native peoples of the New World were greatly affected by the newcomers: they soon learned of the sting of technical and military superiority and the pains of cultural change. For them, the term "their land" soon came to have little meaning.

A full and satisfactory explanation of the forces that sent the exploring Portuguese, Spanish, Dutch, French, and English to the East and to the West and that led eventually to the discovery of America would require an extension in time and space beyond our compass. The major developments leading to European expansion during the fifteenth and sixteenth centuries are rooted deeply in the history of an earlier age. No development is limited to the evolution of a social order in a particular country or on a particular continent. The area of study that would serve as an introduction to American economic development includes, at a minimum, all of western Europe and the fringes of Africa and the Mediterranean. But we are confronted with the practical problem of compressing American economic history into a few hundred pages. Although a full treatment would require a description of the economic life of the Middle Ages, we will have to be content with only the briefest sketch of economic development before and at the time of the opening of the New World.

EUROPEAN ROOTS AND THE EXPANDING NATIONS

Shortly before America's discovery, the center of European wealth and commerce rested in the Mediterranean. That economic concentration was based primarily on long-distance trading between Asia and Europe. Because of its locational advantage and the superior commercial skills and knowledge it could provide, the Italian city-states of Milan, Florence, Genoa, and Venice dominated most of the Old World's trading for centuries. Critical to its prosperity was the maintenance of open routes to the East, because Europe had always been dependent on Asia for luxury goods and other products seemingly essential to medieval Europeans. Of course, in an age before refrigeration, spices were used with almost unbelievable liberality by medieval cooks, whose fash-

Commercial splendor: Venice (rendered here by Caneletto) was almost as much an Eastern as a Western city, and for hundreds of years, its commercial and naval power was a great sustaining force of Western civilization.

ion it was to conceal the taste of tainted meat and to embellish the flavor of monotonous food with pepper, cloves, ginger, nutmeg, and cinnamon. Where wild honey was the only local sweetener, sugar from North Africa and the Levant was in great demand. And although drugs in those times were by no means infallible (some of them probably were worse than taking nothing at all), some relief from European ailments came from Asia. Several products essential to the growing textile industries of the West—chiefly dyestuffs and chemicals for fixing colors—were imported from the East. But the most important imports were the manufactured products, far superior in quality to anything available in Europe, that made up the flow of goods from East to West. Some items, like the lovely cottons and silks from India and China and the rugs from Persia, were easy to transport; others, like the glass from Damascus and the porcelain from China, were apt to break in transit and, when they did arrive safely, were highly prized by the well-to-do of Europe.

As long as trade routes remained predominantly overland, Europe could export only a few products that could be transported safely and that sold for a high value relative to their weight and bulk: woolen textiles and certain metals and minerals, like arsenic, quicksilver, and copper. Not until sea transportation opened the possibility of further exportation from Europe to the East, could the balance of trade—the value of commodity exports compared to the value of commodity imports—begin to be achieved. For this reason, gold and silver continuously drained eastward, making the balance of trade unfavorable to Europe.

The age of discovery: Columbus reporting to Queen Isabella.

Recognizing the inexorable difficulties of transporting a sufficient variety of exports over land routes, we can see why the discovery of an all-sea route to the East was inevitable, as soon as a country emerged that was powerful enough to engineer it. But in that early period of material awakening in Europe, it was not the powerful city states that initiated the quest. Nor was Spain more than a latecomer in ocean discoveries; in many respects, it was somewhat of a historical accident that Christopher Columbus—a Genoese sailor in the employ of Spain—made the most vital of the landfalls.

Exploration and Expansion

Curiously enough, tiny, seafaring Portugal was the great Atlantic pioneer. By the time Columbus embarked, Portugal could claim more than seven decades of ocean discoveries. Under the vigorous and imaginative leadership of Prince Henry the Navigator, whose Naval Arsenal at Sagres was a fifteenth-century Cape Kennedy, Portugal—from 1415 to 1460—sent one expedition after another down the western coast of Africa. Although his sailors never found Prester John, whose mythical Christian land was as important to Enrique as gaining passage around the southern tip of Africa, the probing exploration of the Portuguese nonetheless opened new sea lanes, tapped the wealth of West Africa and its surrounding oceans and developed the caravel—a ship rugged enough to sail on any sea.

The great sea explorations from Europe took place within a little less than 35 years. In 1488, Bartolomeu Dias of Portugal rounded the Cape of Good Hope and would have reached India if his mutinous crew had not forced him to return home. In September 1522, the *Vittoria*—last of Ferdinand Magellan's fleet of five ships—put in at Seville; in a spectacular achievement, 18 Europeans had circumnavigated the globe. Between these two dates, there were two other voyages of no less importance. Columbus, certain that it was no more than 2,500 miles from the Canary Islands to Japan, persuaded the Spanish sovereigns Ferdinand and Isabella to finance his first trip. On October 12, 1492, his lookout sighted the little island of San Salvador in the Bahamas. Only a few years later, Vasco da Gama, sailing for the Portuguese, reached Calicut in India via the Cape of Good Hope, returning home in 1499. Thus, a pattern of sea travel was established: Portugal was dominant in the East; Spain, supreme in the West.

Even in these early years, other nations began to make similar efforts, and by the early sixteenth century, the wealth and commerce of Europe had shifted to the western Atlantic. The Mediterranean trades did not decline absolutely; instead, they were simply overtaken and passed by. But there were no immediate results of great importance to sea trade. Another Genoese, John Cabot, sailing for Henry VII of England, reached Newfoundland in 1497, but the English were not yet ready to profit from his discoveries. Not long after the survivors of Magellan's expedition returned home, Giovanni da Verrazano explored the waters and eastern coast of North America for France, and in the 1530s, Jacques Cartier returned to France with the first detailed information about the St. Lawrence River. But the French, like the English, were too preoccupied with affairs at home to undertake important adventures abroad before the beginning of the seventeenth century.

After a halting start, the Spaniards established colonies on the islands of the Caribbean and then began their explorations of the mainland. Within a century after Columbus returned from his fourth and last voyage in 1504, the Spaniards had conquered Central America and much of the continent of South America and had explored what is now the southern United States from South Carolina to California. After the conquest of Mexico by Hernando Cortés in 1521, American treasure flowed into Spain in ever-increasing quantities. When the Spanish king Philip II made good his claim to the throne of Portugal in 1580, Spanish prestige reached its zenith. Two great empires strong in the Orient and unchallenged in the Americas were now joined. When we reflect that no other country had as yet established a single permanent settlement in the New World, it seems astonishing that the decline of Spanish power was so imminent.

Spain was a colonizer; but Spanish attempts to settle in the Americas lacked a solid foundation. Spain was remarkably poor in natural resources in the sixteenth century and had an estimated population of only 7 or 8 million. The main interest of both the conquistadors and the rulers at home was treasure. To be sure, attempts were made to extend agriculture and to establish manufacturing operations in the New World, but the Spaniards remained a ruling caste—dominating the natives who did the work and holding them in political and economic bondage. Throughout the sixteenth century, Spain received the output of American mines and a swelling tide of other products, including copper, dyes, hides, and naval stores; the preoccupation of the home government was to assure as little American export leakage as possible. When toward the end of the century, Spain became involved in war with the English and began to dissipate its energies in a futile attempt to bring the Low Countries under complete subjection, Spain lost the advantage of being the first nation to expand through explorations in America. Even more harmful to Spain than the wars, however, was the decline in gold and silver imports that began after 1600 with the exhaustion of better-grade ores. Spain was to remain a major power for two more centuries, but the future of the New World was to lie in the hands of the Dutch, the French, and the English (see Map 2-1).

As Spanish power declined, Dutch power ascended. At first a nation of fishermen, Holland began to extend its trade routes to Scandinavia and the Baltic in the sixteenth century. Dutch exploration then turned southward, and by 1600, Holland had sent several expeditions to the East. The Dutch East India Company, established in 1602, quickly nudged the Portuguese aside in the Spice Islands. By 1650, Holland was the chief shipping, trading, and financial nation in Europe. Dutch preeminence, however, hardly lasted a century. Like Spain, Holland possessed a weak resource base at home, and its far-ranging sea captains and traders placed too much emphasis on the establishment of trading posts and too little on colonization. In the East Indies, the Dutch East India Company's ruthless exploitation of the natives resulted in fantastic profits, which for nearly two centuries bolstered Holland as a great entrepôt and money market. But the East Indian empire did not provide the strength needed in a world where, as Herbert Heaton has remarked, "coal and iron were more important than spices and herrings." Yet the Netherlands' fell from eminence not so much because they regressed but because they were overtaken by two other countries with greater resources.

As it turned out, France and England became the chief competitors in the centuries-long race for supremacy. From 1608, when Samuel de Champlain established Quebec, France successfully undertook explorations in America westward to the Great Lakes area and had pushed southward down the Mississippi Valley to Louisiana by the end of the century. And in the Orient, France, though a latecomer, competed successfully with the English for a time after the establishment of the French East India Company in 1664. In less than a century, however, the English defeated the French in India, as they would one day do in America. The English triumphed in both India and America because they had established the most extensive permanent settlements. It is not without significance that at the beginning of the French and Indian War in 1756, there were some 60,000 French settlers in Canada compared with 2 million in the English colonies.

From our special point of view, the most important feature of the expansion of Europe was the steady and persistent growth of settlements in the British colonies of North America. Why were the English so successful in their colonization? Some of the forces that impelled the English to move to the New World were the same forces that motivated the nationals of other countries.

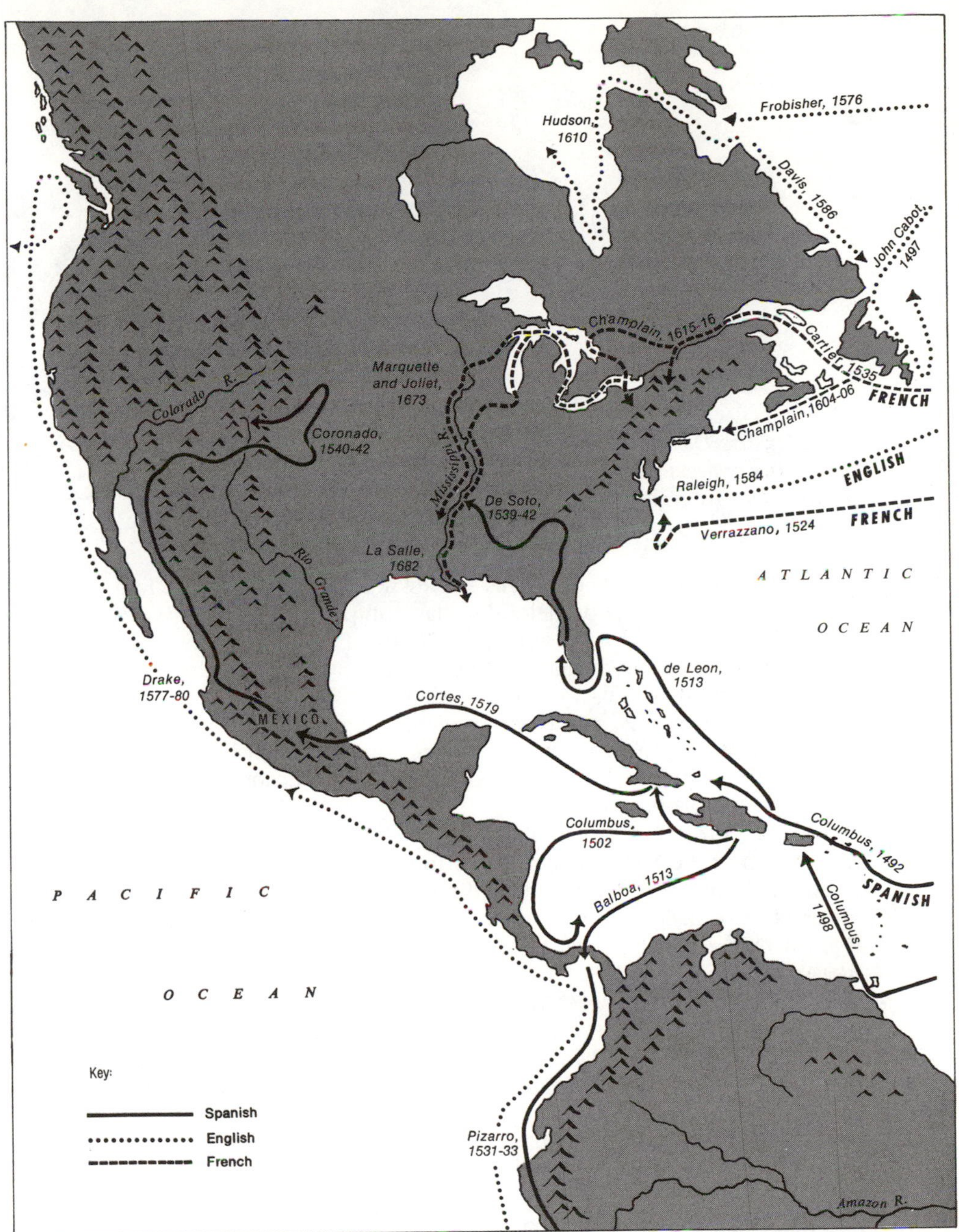

MAP 2–1

Exploration: Spain and Portugal came first; then France, Holland, and England. All of these nations explored vast amounts of territory in North America, but England's explorations gave rise to the most extensive permanent settlements in the New World.

Initially, the Dutch were active fur traders as well as shippers in early America.

There was the persistent hope that somewhere a passage to the East could be found and that it would be helpful to have outposts to serve as bases of operations while the search was going on. To the English—no less than to other Europeans—the hope of finding gold and silver in America was ever present; or if the precious metals were not to be found, then the exotic country might at least furnish spices, naval stores, wines, sugar, furs, dyes, and other commodities that England currently imported. But the English were also strongly motivated by other factors that were either insignificant to or nonexistent in the other colonizing countries.

To be sure, the English, like the French and the Dutch, coveted the colonial wealth of the Spanish and the Portuguese, and English sailors and traders acted for a time as if their struggling outposts in the wilderness of North America were insignificant. They traded in Latin America, while privateers like Francis Drake and Thomas Cavendish plundered Spanish galleons for their treasures as they sailed the Main. English venturers, probing the East for profitable outposts, gained successive footholds in India as the seventeenth century progressed. Yet, unlike the leaders of some western European countries, Englishmen like Richard Hakluyt advocated permanent colonization and settlement in the New World, perceiving that true colonies would eventually become important markets for manufactured products from the mother country. Toward the end of the sixteenth century, this consideration became especially important to England. During the 1500s, its foreign trade had passed largely from the hands of foreigners into those of English merchants. Especially lucrative had been the growing exports of English woolens, paid for by England's best customer, Spain, with gold and silver from Mexico and Peru. But Spain became an enemy, largely due to English privateering, and the resultant need for new English markets was pressing.

It was not enough, however, for merchants and heads of states to reap the advantages of the thriving colonies: Commoners had to be persuaded of the benefits to themselves and their families of emigrating to the New World. The greatest motivations to emigrate were a desire to own land—still the European symbol of status and economic security—and to strive for a higher level of living than could be attained at home by any but the best-paid artisans. These economic motivations were often accompanied by a religious motivation. Unlike the Spanish, the English did not come to these shores to convert "the heathen"; the New England settlers in particular emigrated so that they could worship as they chose, provided those around them were of similar persuasion. In their zeal, most of them became actual participants in the productive process, rather than supervisors of others. And once a cadre of able leaders arrived in America, the future settlement of New England was assured, because they fortuitously colonized the part of the New World that was to be forwarded by location and special advantages in climate and natural resources.

BRITISH SETTLEMENTS IN NORTH AMERICA

Laying the Foundations, 1606–1660

Two half brothers, Sir Humphrey Gilbert and Sir Walter Raleigh, were the first Englishmen to undertake serious ventures in America. Gilbert, one of the more earnest seekers of the Northwest Passage, went to Newfoundland in 1578 and again in 1583, but due to many difficulties, he failed to colonize the territory either time. Sir Humphrey lost his life on the return voyage to England after the second attempt. Raleigh, like Gilbert, was granted the right to settle in "Virginia" and to have control of the land within a radius of 200 leagues from any colony that he might successfully establish. Raleigh actually brought two groups of colonists to the new continent. The first landed on the island of Roanoke off the coast of what is now North Carolina and stayed less than a year; anything but enthusiastic about their new home, these first colonists returned to England with Sir Francis Drake in the summer of 1586. Undaunted, Raleigh solicited the financial aid of a group of wealthy Londoners and, in the following year, sent a second contingent of 150 people under the leadership of Governor John White. Raleigh had given explicit instructions that this colony was to be planted somewhere on the Chesapeake Bay, but Governor White disregarded the order and landed at Roanoke. White went back to England for supplies; when he returned after much delay in 1590, the settlers had vanished. Not a single member of the famed "lost colony" was ever found.

As long as the war between England and Spain continued, there was little hope of interesting the English in establishing further American colonies. But with the death of Elizabeth in 1603, the war came to an end, and Englishmen were more inclined to venture to a hemisphere that was still dominated by the Spaniards. It was not long before two companies were organized for the purpose of exploring and exploiting America. In 1606, two charters were granted—one to a group of Londoners; the other, to merchants of the western port towns, of which Plymouth was the most important. The London Company was given the right to settle the southern part of the English territory in America; the Plymouth Company was given jurisdiction over the northern part.

So two widely separated colonies were established in 1607: one at Sagadahoc, near the mouth of the Kennebec River, in which is now Maine; the other in modern Virginia.[1] Those who survived the winter in the northern colony gave up and went home, and the colony established at Jamestown won the hardearned honor of being the first permanent English settlement in America.

Virginia. As will be detailed extensively in Chapter 3, the Jamestown venture nearly failed in its first years, but with the granting of a new charter in 1609, the Virginia Company was established on a firmer basis; at least there was sufficient financial backing to enable it to secure a hold. By issuing stock, the company's promoters were able to raise "a capital." Those who agreed to emigrate to the new country as laborers were considered to have contributed the value of one share of stock (£12 10s) to the enterprise; anyone possessing special skills might have been given more than one share. It was possible for an individual to secure a wage consignment, but the greater number of colonists preferred to participate in the profit sharing. The project was to be operated on a corporate basis for the first seven years after 1609, and all the property was to be divided in equal shares at the end of the period. The affairs of the company in England were guided by a treasurer and stockholders' council; a deputy, called the governor, was to be the chief officer in the colony.

If the first emigrants hoped to strike it rich, they were quickly disappointed. Gold was nowhere to be found, and it was impossible at first to produce the products in quantity that were so much in demand in Europe. And the settlers in the first contingents were not content with the vague possibility of achieving gains in the distant future. Generally speaking, they were ne'er-do-wells, if not former criminals, and the harshest discipline produced only a minimal amount of work.

The Virginia Colony would have failed quickly if a satisfactory export commodity had not been found. Fortunately, in 1613, tobacco seed was imported from the West Indies. Tobacco was the ideal cash crop. Virginia's climate and soil were suited to its culture. It could be grown successfully with the simplest tools, even on land from which stumps had not been removed. The market for tobacco in England was strong and increasing; initially, the value of tobacco was high relative to its bulk, thereby absorbing high transportation costs. In 1617, perhaps 20,000 pounds of tobacco were shipped to England—a quantity that more than doubled the next year. By that time, a permanent settlement in America was assured; although the Virginia Company itself was not a profitable operation, trade between Virginia and England amounted to some £100,000 in 1618.

Even before the end of the period of corporate effort, it became practice to allow the colonists to own small pieces of land. In 1618, the company began to grant "headrights." Under the headright system, a person emigrating at his own expense was given title to 50 acres of land and an additional 50 acres for

[1] At this time, the name *Virginia* referred to all the territory claimed by the English on the North American continent. Early charters indicate that the area lay between the thirty-fourth and the forty-fifth parallels, roughly between the southern portion of the Carolinas and the northernmost boundary of New York.

each man, woman, or child whose transportation he paid. In the same year, the company ordered its governor to guarantee to the colonists the same protection by law accorded to Englishmen at home, and steps were taken to allow the new Americans to participate to some degree in their own government.

Persistent organizational difficulties in Virginia led to the undoing of the corporate form of control there, and the expense of added production by the company was greater than past receipts or future prospects would justify. In 1625, legal proceedings to secure dissolution were successful, and in that year Virginia became a Crown colony.

Maryland. Although it breaks the chronology of events, we must mention here the founding of Virginia's neighboring colony, Maryland. These two colonies were similar in soil and climate and in their early economic life. Maryland's colonization, however, was proprietary rather than corporate. Like Gilbert and Raleigh before him, Sir George Calvert, first Lord of Baltimore, wanted a domain of his own. Failing to establish a colony in Newfoundland, he settled in Virginia, only to be asked to leave because he was a Roman Catholic. Calvert then asked Charles I for a tract of land in Virginia—a favor that the king could grant, since the Virginia Company no longer controlled property allotments. In 1632, while the patent was being prepared, George Calvert died, but the grant was made to his son, Cecilius, the second Lord Baltimore. The tract was a huge piece of territory, originally extending from the mouth of the Potomac to New England (a later gift to William Penn reduced it). By the terms of the charter, the proprietor could dispose of the land as he chose; the only restrictions on his power were the requirements that the laws governing the colonists be in agreement with English law and that the colonists be allowed to elect a legislative body in the new country.

The first group of colonists settled at St. Mary's in 1634. Although it was originally planned that Maryland would be primarily a refuge for Roman Catholics, the rank and file of newcomers turned out to be largely Protestant. The large tracts of land were given for the most part to wealthy men of the Roman faith—a division that was to cause trouble later. As in Virginia, the staple crop was tobacco; consequently, Maryland's growth, except in the mountainous western part of the colony, paralleled that of Virginia.

Massachusetts. Perhaps the most familiar episode in American history is the story of the landing of the Pilgrims. Their movement to New England has a special appeal largely because it was precipitated by high idealism. But the profit motive played its part in the settlement of New England. In fact, the successful colonization of the unattractive northern area would have been impossible if strong economic incentives had not been present. Nevertheless, the key force was the Puritan migration.

Although the Church of England had undergone a reformation of sorts during the sixteenth century, it remained far from a "protestant" church nearly 100 years after Henry VIII had broken with Rome. As modern Episcopalians are careful to point out, the Church *in* England had simply become the Church *of* England. Certainly, no basic religious changes such as Martin Luther, John Calvin, and John Knox had wrought elsewhere had occurred. Yet many people in

England objected to the formalism of the Anglican liturgy, to the episcopal form of church government, and to the lack of concern of many parish priests for the welfare of their flocks. People in the Church of England who insisted on further reform were called Puritans. They were "puritanical," too, in the usual present-day sense of the word. In part, they wanted to change the externals of church worship, but they were also interested in changing the moral tone of English society. This could be done, they felt, only by carrying the word of God to the people through education and vigorous preaching. The zest with which these dissenters approached their task was bound to arouse the bitter antagonism of orthodox believers. Persecution of the Puritans was heightened under pious James I, the successor to Queen Elizabeth and the first of the Stuart kings. Under his son, Charles I, it became worse.

In 1608, during James's reign, one group of Puritans who found life in England intolerable moved to Leyden, in Holland. But although they found religious freedom there, life in a land of strange speech and customs was far from satisfactory. After more than ten years of exile, the group applied to the Virginia Company for permission to establish a plantation in Virginia. Although the permission was obtained, the Puritans decided for financial reasons to use the patent or public land grant of a group of English merchants, who had agreed to invest money in the venture. A joint-stock company was formed to carry out the proposed colonization, and the London merchants, who held a large part of the stock, as well as the majority of the people who sailed on the *Mayflower* had great hopes for financial success. As in the earlier settlement at Jamestown, all the property was to be held in common for at least seven years and divided into equal shares at the end of that time, thus providing a definite commercial motivation for the settlement—although not the paramount drive. The religious fervor of the Pilgrims, which provided the original impetus for the enterprise, later gave it direction and spiritual vigor.

In 1620, the little band of pilgrims inadvertently landed on the bleak Massachusetts coast, far north of their destination. Because the patent had been granted for a plantation in Virginia, it was necessary to secure another land grant through the old Plymouth Company, reorganized as the council for New England. It soon became apparent that the Puritans immediate and considerable profits would not materialize; and in 1626, the Pilgrims agreed to buy the remaining stock held by shareholders living in England.

The Plymouth Colony grew slowly and was important only as the vanguard of the New England colonists. It was to the Massachusetts Bay Company, formed in 1629, that the northern area of settlement owed its rapid and substantial growth. Under the leadership of the able but austerely devout John Winthrop, the Massachusetts Bay Colony was successful from the outset. Within a year after the receipt of its charter, the company had sent more than 1,000 people to New England. Of the 65,000 Englishmen who came to America and the West Indies during the decade of the 1630s, some 20,000 mostly Puritans, emigrated to New England.

What chiefly distinguished the Massachusetts colony from earlier colonies was its almost complete freedom from old English ties. The Massachusetts Bay Company and its charter were actually transferred to America, thereby achieving nearly complete independence from England. The governor, deputy governor, and "assistants" were elected by the stockholders in the colony, and these elected officials conducted their affairs with little, if any, interference from abroad.

We will say little now about Massachusetts economic life, but we will mention the northern system of land tenure. As the influx of emigrants became greater and greater, small groups from a particular locality in England tended to settle together. These groups would petition the General Court for a grant of land and form a "town", with a village in the center surrounded by arable fields and common woods and meadows. Such grants, sometimes for a tract as large as 40 square miles, normally lay immediately adjacent to previously settled land; in the north, the custom grew of pushing back the frontier in a regular and orderly fashion. This method of settlement, far different from the indiscriminate location of colonists in Virginia, became a permanent part of the land system of the nation to be formed a century and a half later.

Rhode Island and Connecticut. Although the Puritans left England to escape religious intolerance, they were far from being tolerant themselves in their new home. Roger Williams, the pastor at Salem, was banished by the General Court of Massachusetts in 1635 for espousing views that in essence, indicated that even the Puritans had not found the one way to salvation. After being turned away, Williams established a plantation in Providence, where he was joined two years later by Anne Hutchinson and her band of dissenters. The Hutchinson group moved on to Narragansett Bay, along with others, and a federation of the Rhode Island and Providence plantations was effected in 1644.

Meanwhile, a movement westward to the Connecticut Valley took place, and at almost the same time, a colony was established at New Haven. In 1662, Connecticut was made a Crown colony, and New England, which was to constitute a well-knit economic unit, had come into being. Indeed, for a long time, its unity had been more than economic; in 1643, Plymouth, Massachusetts, Connecticut, and New Haven had banded together in a New England Confederacy for the purposes of mutual defense.

Of great importance to both the political and economic future of the colonies was the almost complete independence of the New Englanders in these early years. They made their own laws and traded as they pleased. But where they pleased to trade was largely determined for them by the fact that the English were colonizing some distant islands that would soon become the Puritans' best customers. So, for the moment, we turn to the Caribbean.

The British West Indies. When a fleet was carrying supplies to the Jamestown plantation in 1609, the flagship was wrecked on an island in the Bermudas. Three years later, a settlement was established there, and by 1640, people from Bermuda were moving into the Bahamas, where they were joined later by adventurers from England. At about the same time, a third group emigrated from Britain to the islands that mark the eastern end of the Caribbean Sea.

The Greater Antilles—Cuba, Jamaica, Hispaniola, and Puerto Rico—were among the first American possessions of Spain (see Map 2-2). The Spanish had paid little attention to the islands east of Puerto Rico that constitute the Lesser

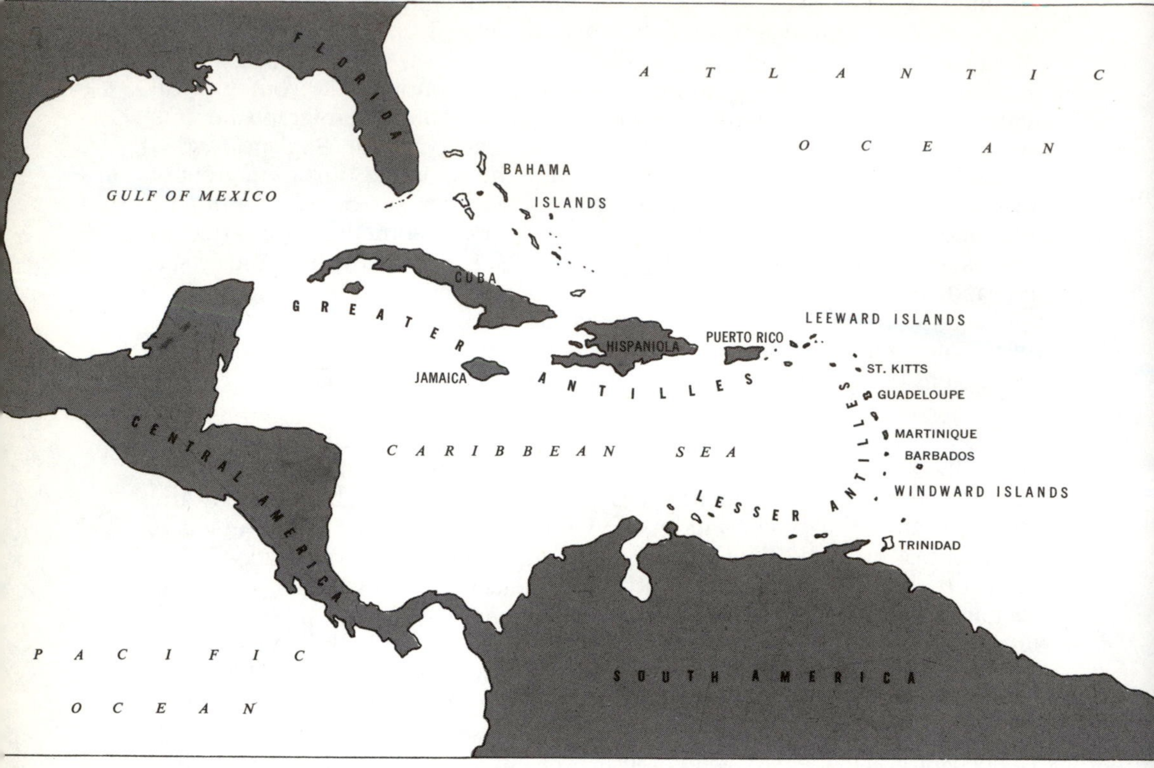

MAP 2–2

Development: Through trade, the Caribbean Islands played a significant role in the economic growth of the American colonies.

Antilles. Beginning in 1624, the English and French and, to a lesser extent, other Europeans began to gain footholds in these islands. First, the English and French took St. Kitts, each nation claiming about half of the 25 mile long island. From St. Kitts, English exploration spread to nearby islands, and a few years later, the English began to colonize Barbados at the southernmost tip of the Windward Islands. Beginning in 1635, the French took the rich islands of Martinique and Guadeloupe. By mid-century, the French and English were well established in this eastern group of islands, and the English, as a part of Oliver Cromwell's "Western Design," began to cast their eyes westward. After an unsuccessful attempt to take Hispaniola, an English fleet captured the island of Jamaica in 1655.

Land in the West Indies was incredibly fertile and especially suited to the production of sugar—a commodity in great demand in Europe in the seventeenth and eighteenth centuries and produced by African slaves. The high regard for the produce of these islands, even toward the end of the colonial period, is best evidenced by the fact that there were those who felt, at the conclusion of the French and Indian War, that England should take Guadeloupe rather than Canada. What is of immediate importance, however, is the connection that was established between the non-Spanish West Indies and the continental colonies. Specializing in the growth of tropical crops, West Indian planters imported foodstuffs, lumber, and horses—precisely the commodities the New England colonies were able to furnish. The relationship that developed between them is one we will consider in greater detail later when we describe the intricate network of trade on which the prosperity of early Americans depended.

The Later Colonies, 1661–1773

For a period of 30 years, coinciding with the English Civil Wars and Cromwell's protectorate, no new English colonies were established in America. With the Restoration in 1660, however, the English nobility again turned its attention to the possibility of making or reestablishing a fortune across the sea. (It is worth noting that all the later colonies were of the proprietary type rather than the company type.) And the desire of important nobles for great estates was by no means the only impellent to colonization in the latter half of the seventeenth century. In at least two instances, the altruistic feelings of the proprietors (Lord Penn and Lord Oglethorpe) influenced colonization considerably. In all cases, the search for new trading areas on the part of merchants and shipowners and the quest for land on the part of the commoners gave the movement its impetus. But the experiments in Virginia and New England had made it clear that a company organized for the purpose of realizing a profit within a reasonably short time could not hope to succeed financially in the long and tedious business of colonization. It is doubtful that any of the proprietors ever reaped a reward in pounds and shillings that was commensurate with their investment. Nevertheless, they intended to. Proprietors always reserved great tracts for themselves which grew in value as populations increased. There were some land sales, but even on lands given to settlers under the headright system, an annual payment known as a *quitrent* was ordinarily required. Quitrents—vestiges of feudal dues—were nominal per acre, but if properly collected they could amount to a sizeable sum on a large acreage. Then, too, owners received revenue from their own estates, which were worked by tenants. Finally, they charged license fees for the privilege of trading and even levied duties on goods coming into and going out of their province. Whatever else may have moved a Penn or a Calvert or an Ashley to action, the ultimate prospect of income was certainly not unattractive.

In the final wave of British colonization, there were two main thrusts: one into the so-called Middle Colonies; the other into the areas South of Virginia. We begin this section by picking up a thread of the narrative that runs back to the early efforts of the Dutch in America.

New York. The year after the Pilgrims landed in America, a Dutch West India Company was formed—not particularly for the purpose of colonization but to harass the Spaniards as they shipped treasure through the Caribbean. In the mid-1620s, the Dutch set up forts at key points on the present sites of Albany and Manhattan. The fort established on the southern end of Manhattan became the town of New Amsterdam—a fur-trading center and a base for Dutch ships in the area.

Contrary to the general impression, the colony of New Netherland, which lay between New France on the north and Virginia on the south, was never an outstanding success. During the early stages of settlement, the fertile lands along both sides of the Hudson were divided into huge estates and given to wealthy Dutch nobles, who operated them as feudal domains instead of trying to attract free settlers. In the area around New Amsterdam, a large number of small farms were started, but trouble with the Indians precluded a productive agriculture until mid-century. The colony was ruled in autocratic fashion by a series of governors, including Peter Stuyvesant, who lacked both honesty and ability.

Neither England nor the Northern colonies had ever been happy about what they considered to be Dutch encroachment on territory that was first discovered by the Cabots. As England and Holland drew apart in the seventeenth century, there was no longer any serious barrier to securing New Netherland by force, especially since the colony had never been sufficiently strong to defend itself. In 1664, when Charles II granted this area to his younger brother, the Duke of York, a small English fleet was able to seize it without firing a shot.

Almost a decade later, the English colony of New York reverted to Dutch rule for a year or so, but with this exception, steadily progressed toward the preeminent economic position it was to achieve within a century and a half. In 1685, with the accession to the throne of the Duke of York as James II, the colony became a royal province, thereby removing many sources of friction that had persisted when the Duke tried to exploit it for personal profit. Agriculture quickly became more important than fur trading; of greater significance, New York began to take advantage of its superb harbor and to become a center of colonial commerce.

New Jersey. The early history of New Jersey is associated with that of New York. The New Jersey territory was included in Charles II's grant to his brother in 1664. The Duke of York almost immediately deeded the area to his friends Sir William Berkeley and Sir George Carteret. When these proprietors took over, the Swedes in the valley of Delaware and the Dutch near New Amsterdam were almost the only inhabitants. But under a liberal government, colonists began to trickle in from England and, even more, from the colonies to the north. Carteret remained a proprietor, controlling East Jersey, but Berkeley disposed of his interests to the Quakers, the owners of West Jersey, until governmental rights reverted to the Crown in 1702. From the beginning, the northeastern part of New Jersey took on New York's characteristics of small industry and trade, whereas the southwestern part of the colony was at first a farming region like its neighbor Pennsylvania.

Pennsylvania. William Penn, son of the distinguished admiral who had helped restore Charles II to the English throne, accepted Pennsylvania as payment of a substantial debt that the king's brother owed to his father. The grant included all the land west of the Delaware River between the 40th and 43rd parallels—southern and northern boundaries that had been disputed by other colonies for a long time.

To the consternation of his relatives and noble friends, Penn had been converted to the Quaker faith as a young man. Quakers, it must be remembered, were considered dangerous in England in the mid-seventeenth century due in part to their pacifist beliefs and in part to their refusal to swear oaths and accept ecclesiastical supervision. But the younger Penn, a man of great personal charm, managed to stay in the good graces of his associates and avoided disinheritance by his father, and when his father died, he became immensely wealthy. Among the properties he inherited was a part of western New Jersey, which, as we have seen, was predominantly Quaker. Penn was glad to get the much larger grant from the king, because it would permit him to conduct his "holy experiment" in political and religious freedom. Although during the last two decades of the seventeenth century the Quaker sect was not actively persecuted in England or the colonies, as it had been earlier, Penn wanted to establish a colony where Quakers could settle in peace. Even more importantly, he wished to provide a place where people of *all* nationalities and religions could live together in harmony—where, in short, the Quaker ideal could be tested.

Colonization began in 1681; in the next year, Penn himself came to the new land and selected the site of Philadelphia. The combination of cheap land and the prospect of genuine liberty quickly attracted settlers, who, until 1700, were mostly English and Welsh Quakers and Germans. The colony grew rapidly, and in less than four years numbered nearly 10,000 people. The Friends tended to be colonial leaders and set the moral tone for the colony. They were usually politically supported by the Germans, who were grateful for their new-found freedom.

Delaware. We must not forget the so-called "lower counties," given to William Penn by the Duke of York in 1682. Their position was anomalous throughout most of the colonial period. They were really a part of Pennsylvania until 1703, when they obtained their own assembly. Yet this—the second smallest of the colonies—remained under the governor of Pennsylvania until the Revolution and was not called Delaware until that time.

While the Middle Colonies were receiving their first strong influx of population, colonization was taking place in a part of the great coastal area south of Virginia. Not until half a century after the settlement of Pennsylvania was well underway did the last of the thirteen colonies, Georgia, receive its first settlers, who were sent over in a final, well-intentioned experiment. We conclude our survey of the establishment of the first frontier with a consideration of these movements in the South.

The Carolinas. In the 1650s, colonists began to move from Virginia into what is now North Carolina. But the story of the Carolinas really begins with the last great proprietary grant of an English king. To eight men—among them Anthony Ashley Cooper, Sir John Colleton, and Governor Berkeley of Virginia—was given all the land on the eastern seaboard from the lower Virginia border south to Spanish Florida. In 1670, the first settlement was made at Charleston, where an excellent harbor and a fertile hinterland promised a bright future for both agriculture and commerce. Within a decade, French Huguenots joined the original English and West Indian settlers, and, oddly, a substantial colony of Scots moved into Port Royal. The colony of South Carolina first traded furs with England and naval stores with the British West Indies, but by the end of the century, production of the colony's great staple, rice, was well underway.

For many decades, South Carolina was isolated from the rest of the colonies. A wide belt of forest and wasteland separated Charleston and its environs from its companion settlements to the north. The part of the Carolinas nearest Virginia (now North Carolina) was without good harbors, and the development of this region was inhibited for a long time by the impossibility of shipping the colony's main crop—tobacco—directly to England, as required by the Navigation Laws. Virginians did not look favorably on attempts to transship a competing commodity through their ports, and the illegal tobacco trade with continental Europe, via New England, was beset with difficulties.

By the end of the seventeenth century, it was customary to distinguish between North and South Carolina. In 1719, South Carolina became a Crown colony—all governmental rights and ownership of unoccupied land reverted to England—and North Carolina assumed this status a decade later. Although the populations of these neighboring colonies were almost equal by now, North Carolina was to remain the poorer relation for a long time to come.

Georgia. Georgia was not colonized until long after the other colonies, with the possible exception of New Hampshire. Like Pennsylvania and Massachusetts, Georgia was founded to assist those who had been beset with troubles in the Old World. Together with a group of associates, Dr. Thomas Bray, an Anglican clergyman noted for his good works, was persuaded by General James Edward Oglethorpe to attempt a project for the relief of people condemned to prison for debt. This particular social evil of eighteenth-century England cried out to be remedied, because debtors could spend years in horrible prisons of the time without hope of escape except through organized charitable institutions. As long as individuals were incarcerated, they were unable to earn any money to pay their debts, and even if they were eventually released, years of imprisonment could make them unfit for work. It was Oglethorpe's idea to encourage debtors to come to America, where they might become responsible and even substantial citizens.

In addition to their wish to aid the "urban wretches" of England, Bray, Oglethorpe, and their associates hoped to prohibit slavery in the new colony. Perhaps moral repugnance to slavery was a primary motivation, but they also believed that an all-white population would provide the most secure military buffer zone between the prosperous northern English settlements and Spanish Florida. It was doubtful that slaves could be depended on to fight, and with slavery, rebellion was always a possibility.

In 1732, King George II obligingly granted Dr. Bray and his associates the land between the Savannah and the Altamaha rivers; the original tract included considerably less territory than the modern state of Georgia. By royal charter, a corporation was created that was to be governed by a group of trustees; after 21 years, the territory was to revert to the Crown. Financed by both private and public funds, the venture had an auspicious beginning. Oglethorpe himself led the first contingent of several hundred immigrants—mostly debtors—to the new country, where a 50-acre farm awaited each colonist. Substantially larger grants were available to free settlers with families, and determined efforts were made, both on the continent and in the British Isles, to secure colonists.

Unfortunately, the ideals and hopes of the trustees clashed with economic reality. Although "the Georgia experiment" was a modest success as a philanthropic enterprise, its economic development was to prove disappointing for many decades. The climate in the low coastal country—where the fertile land lay—was unhealthy. Since slavery was initially prohibited by the trustees, it was impossible to introduce the rice and indigo plantations in Georgia that were so profitable in South Carolina, and the 50-acre tracts given the charity immigrants were too small to achieve competitive levels of efficiency for commercial production.

Unable to secure the desired buffer state by attracting a sufficient number of whites without continuous subsidy and given the attractive potential profits of slave-operated plantation enterprises, the trustees eventually bowed to economic forces. By mid-century, slaves were pouring into Georgia, which was converted to a Crown colony in 1751.

3

The Conditions of Early Colonial Economic Life

PERILOUS BEGINNINGS

The misadventure of Raleigh's "lost colony" sharply accents the great perils and hardships faced by the earliest settlers of North America. Disease, starvation, Indian attack, and other calamities were commonplace, and most of the first settlers died within two years of their arrival. Clearly, migration to the New World was no routine experience.

When the London Company landed three tiny vessels at the mouth of the Chesapeake Bay in 1607, 105 people disembarked to found the Jamestown Colony. Easily distracted by futile "get rich quick" schemes, they actually sent shiploads of mica and yellow ore back to England in 1607 and 1608. Before the news reached their ears that their treasure was worthless "fool's gold," disease, starvation, and misadventure had taken a heavy toll; 67 of the original 105 Jamestown settlers died within the first year.

The few remaining survivors were joined in 1609 by 800 new arrivals, sent over by the reorganized and renamed Virginia Company. By the following spring, frontier hardships had cut their number from 838 to 60. That summer, those who remained were found fleeing down river to return home to England by new settlers with fresh supplies who encouraged them to reconsider. There can be little doubt that this was Virginia's "starving time," to use Professor Charles Andrews' label.

Inadequately supplied and untutored in the art of colonization, the earliest frontier pioneers routinely suffered and died. In 1623, a royal investigation of the Virginia experience was launched in the wake of an Indian attack that took the lives of 500 settlers. The investigation reported that of the 6,000 who had migrated to Virginia since 1603, 4,000 had died.

The heavy human costs of first settlement were accompanied by substantial capital losses. Without exception, the earliest colonial ventures were unprofitable. Indeed, they were financial disasters. Neither the principle nor the interest on the Virginia Company's accumulated investments of more than £200,000 were ever repaid. The investments in New England were less disappointing, but overall, English capitalists were heavy losers in their quest to tame the frontier.

EARLY REFORMS

Nevertheless, the lessons of these first settlements proved useful in later ventures, and colonization continued with only intermittent lapses throughout the seventeenth and eighteenth centuries. Because North America rendered no early discoveries of gold or silver mines or ancient populations prepared to exchange exotic wares, trading-post establishments characteristic of the European outposts in South America and the Far East proved inadequate. North America's frontier demanded a more permanent form of settlement. For this to result without continuous company or Crown subsidization, the discovery of "cash crops" or other items that could be produced in the colonies and exchanged commercially was essential. Consequently, the production of tobacco, rice, and the expansion of many other economy activities we will discuss in Chapter 4 proved vital in giving deep roots and permanent features to British settlement in North America. In addition, substantial organizational changes were made to increase production efficiency. The joint-stock company arrangement, which facilitated the raising of capital and which had served the British well in other areas of the world, faltered when forced to conform to the conditions in North America. Modeled after such great eastern trading companies as the East India Company, new companies—including the London Company, the New Plymouth Company, the Massachusetts Bay Company and others—must receive credit for establishing the first British settlements in the New World. But their success was limited merely to securing a colonial foothold. With the exceptions of the Hudson Bay Company (founded in 1670 and still in operation today) and the unique Georgia experiment in the late colonial period, the joint-stock company (with absentee direction from England) survived less than two decades in British North America.

The ordeals of the Jamestown experience forcefully accent the difficulties encountered and the adjustments required by the early settlers. The colony originally operated as a collective unit, in which both production methods and consumption were shared. But collectivity encouraged individuals to work less and resulted in much discontent. Unmarried men complained of working without recompense for other men's wives and children. Stronger, more able workers were embittered when they did not receive greater amounts of food and supplies than others who could or would not work as hard. In addition, common ownership stifled the incentive to care for and improve land and to introduce more efficient innovations in production.

In addition, absentee direction from England created problems, because successful production required local managerial direction. Futilely insistent demands from England for quick profits sidetracked productive effort and added to the settlers' discouragement.

Jamestown residents gained greater control over local matters in 1609 and again in 1612 when various institutional reforms were undertaken. Planter memberships were created, so that company shares became based on labor input as well as capital contributions. To generate more flexible leadership and local autonomy in that hostile environment, a deputy governor was stationed in Virginia. Steadily thereafter, direction from England became more and more decentralized.

Similarly, private land holdings swiftly replaced common ownership arrangements, and attitudes and work incentives improved as the full return for individual effort became a reality, superseding output sharing arrangements. In 1614, private land holdings of three acres were allowed. A second and more significant step toward private property came in 1618 with the establishment of the headright system. As we already noted in Chapter 2, under this system, any settler who paid his own way to Virginia was given 50 acres and another 50 acres for anyone else whose transportation he paid. In 1623—only 16 years after the first Jamestown settlers had arrived—all land holdings were converted to private ownership. The royal investigation of that year also ushered in the dissolutions of the corporate form of the colony. In 1625, Virginia was converted to a Crown colony.

Many of the difficulties experienced in early Jamestown were also felt elsewhere in the colonies. But the Puritan settlements of New England avoided some common problems faced by most settlers. For instance, because the Massachusetts Bay Company actually carried its own charter to the New World, it avoided futile direction and absentee control from England. Moreover, although considerable amounts of New England land were commonly owned, collective production and shared consumption were less forcefully imposed. Stronger social and cultural cohesion and more homogenous religious beliefs contributed to the greater relative success of communal arrangements there. Furthermore, town corporations prolonged the use of common land holdings. Nevertheless, more and more private land holdings replaced land held in common, and by 1650, privately owned family farms were predominant in New England.

GOVERNMENT AND FREEDOM

Being part of the British Empire colonists in British North America were subject to the laws of England, and they established colonial governments patterned after England's governmental organization. Within half a century of England's securing a foothold, three general types of British colonies had emerged: Crown, corporate, and proprietary. Each had an executive branch, headed by a governor, and a legislature composed of two houses, an upper house (or council) and a lower house. After 1623, Virginia was a characteristic Crown colony, and both its governor and council (the upper house) were appointed by England. But only the lower house could initiate fiscal legislation, and this body was elected by the propertied adult males within the colony. Massachusetts, Connecticut, and Rhode Island were corporate colonies, each electing its own governor and both houses of its legislature. In the proprietary colonies, including New York, Pennsylvania, and Maryland, the governor and council were appointed by the owner, but again, the important lower house was elected by propertied male colonists.

Although all laws could be vetoed by the governor and the Crown, power gradually shifted to the lower houses as colonial legislative bodies increasingly tended to imitate the House of Commons in England. The colonists controlled the lower house—and therefore the purse strings—thereby generating a climate of political freedom and independence in the colonies. Governors, who were generally expected to represent the will of the Empire and to veto legislation contrary to British interests, were often not only sympathetic to the colonists but also dependent on the legislature for their salaries (which were frequently in arrears). Consequently, the actual control of civil affairs generally rested with the colonists themselves, through their representatives.

Of course the power that permitted this state of affairs to exist rested in England, and the extent of local autonomy was officially limited. After the shift in power in England from the Crown to Parliament in 1690, the Privy Council reviewed all laws passed in the colonies as a matter of common procedure. In the process, the Council vetoed a small percentage of the legislation passed in the colonies. But even this restriction could be avoided: Time, distance, and bureaucratic apathy often permitted colonial laws to become effective long before they were even reviewed in England. If vetoed, a piece of legislation that was highly desired by the colonists could be reworded and reimplemented.

In short, day-to-day events in the colonies were influenced only modestly by British directives, and government—whether British or colonial—was a relatively minor aspect of colonial affairs. The colonists themselves held the power to resolve issues of a local nature and therefore of greatest importance to the colonies. In this way, British subjects in the New World enjoyed extensive freedom of self determination throughout most of the colonial period.

RELATIONSHIPS AMONG THE FACTORS OF PRODUCTION

In another sense, colonial economic freedoms were severely restrained—not by man-made laws or ordinances, but by the conditions of nature and the economic setting. Colonial production capabilities were determined and limited by the available factors of production—land and natural resources, capital, and labor—by the technology of the period, and by other influences such as economic organization and frontier hazards. The most distinctive characteristic of production in the colonies throughout the entire colonial period is that land and natural resources were plentiful, but labor and capital were exceedingly scarce, both absolutely and relatively. This relationship among the factors of production explains many institutional arrangements and patterns of regional development in the colonies.

Land and Natural Resource Abundance

Throughout the history of the British colonies, most people depended on the land for a livelihood. From New Hampshire to Georgia, agriculture was the chief occupation, and what industrial and commercial activity there was revolved almost entirely around materials extracted from the land, the forests, and the ocean. Where soil and climate were unfavorable to the cultivation of commercial crops, it was often possible to turn to fishing or trapping and to the production of ships, ship timbers, and naval stores. Land was seemingly limitless in extent and therefore not highly priced, but almost every colonist wanted to be a landholder. When we remember that ownership of land signified wealth and position to the European, this is not hard to understand. The ever-present desire for land explains why for the first century and a half of our history, many immigrants who might have been successful artisans or laborers in someone else's employ tended instead to turn to agriculture, thereby aggravating the persistent scarcity of labor in the New World. A shortage of workers with highly developed skills was most notable, because artisans and trained craftsmen in great demand in Europe were too content at home to be tempted even by substantially higher wages into a life of hardship at the very bounds of civilization. But all types of labor were generally scarce, because the high ratio of land to labor assured independent farmers fairly comfortable material standards of living once many of the early frontier hazards had been overcome.

Bringing in Workers

Due to the high costs of transportation, the majority of newcomers did not pay their own way to America at the time of passage, and from the beginning, the colonial labor force was heavily comprised of indentured servants, or *redemptioners* as they were called if they came from continental Europe. The *indenture contract* was a device that enabled people to pay for their passage to America by selling their labor to someone in the New World for a specified period of time. These contracts were written in a variety of forms, but law and custom made them similar. Generally speaking, prospective immigrants would sign articles of indenture binding them to a period of service that varied from two to seven years, although four years was probably the most common term. In practice, an indenture contract was originally signed with a shipowner or the owner's recruiting agent. As soon as the servant was delivered alive at an American port, the contract was sold to a planter or merchant. Indentured servants, thus bound, performed any work their "employers" demanded in exchange for room, board, and certain "freedom dues" that were received at the end of the period of indenture. This provided an active trade in human talent, and the indentured system should be viewed as an investment in migration as well as in job training (or apprenticeship).

Who were these people who came to North America as bonded servants? Abbott Smith describes them:

> Many . . . were convicts from the jails, transported instead of being hanged; a few were political and military prisoners taken in war or rebellion. There were rogues, vagabonds, whores, cheats, and rabble of all descriptions, raked from the gutter and kicked out of the country. There were unfortunate French, German, and Swiss Protestants fleeing from religious persecution, starving and unhappy Irish, rack-rented Scottish farmers, poverty-stricken German peasants

> and artisans, brash adventurers of all sorts. People of every age and kind were decoyed, deceived, seduced, inveigled, or forcibly kidnapped and carried as servants to the plantations. There were many ordinary individuals of decent substance, and a few who were entitled by the custom of the time to be called gentlemen.[1]

Most indentured servants were without skills or training. Except for convicts, who had no choice, these laborers came to America because they wished to escape their home country. Since they could raise the price of their passage—£5—6 sterling (nearly a half year's earnings) throughout most of the colonial period—in no other way, they were willing to sell themselves for a period of years. Whether the life of a servant was hard or easy depended primarily on the temperament of the taskmaster; the courts usually protected indentured servants from extreme cruelty, but the law could also be applied quickly to apprehend and return servants who ran away.

More than half of all the immigrants who settled south of New England were servants—a statistic that suggests the powerful economic force at work to make their transportation and use profitable. Colonial planters would sacrifice a great deal to secure laborers, because the labor of others made the difference between mere subsistence and affluence. The demand for colonial labor made transporting a cargo of servants a profitable venture for English merchants who sailed the trade routes to the colonies. So private interests assured the colonies of a sufficient labor supply with almost no intervention on the part of the British government.

The alternative to white servitude—slavery—did not become an important source of labor until after 1650, although slaves were imported in increasing numbers after 1620. By 1700, slavery had become a firmly established institution from Maryland southward. Slaveholding was not unknown in New England and the Middle Colonies, but it never took hold there for a number of reasons, the most important of which was climate. Whenever the labor of a person was purchased for a fixed sum of money it was necessary that he or she be idle as little as possible during the year. Rarely was a slave in the south unable to work due to the rigors of bad weather, whereas working outdoors in the North could be impossible for days at a time. Also important was the fact that tobacco, then rice, and finally indigo were the staple crops of the South. Because they required much unskilled labor that could be performed under the supervision of an overseer, these crops were especially suited to cultivation by untrained workers newly imported from a tropical land.

Yet north of South Carolina, the demand for indentured servants continued throughout the eighteenth century; not until the nineteenth century did the immigration of free workers completely remove the need for servants in the North, particularly in Pennsylvania. Only on the great southern plantations did the slave supersede the servant, and even in some parts of the Deep South, as well as in the West Indies, servants remained in demand simply because they were white and provided some security against the black uprisings. In

[1] Abbott Emerson Smith, *Colonists in Bondage* (Chapel Hill: University of North Carolina Press, 1947), p. 3.

Maryland, slaves never outnumbered indentured servants, and although slaves outnumbered servants by 1700 in Virginia, shiploads of redemptioners continued to arrive there throughout the eighteenth century.

Capital

Items of physical capital for production were in limited supply in the aggregate, especially during the first century of settlement. Particular forms of capital goods that could be obtained from natural resources with simple tools were in apparent abundance. For instance, so much wood was available that it was fairly easy to build houses, barns, and workshops. Wagons and carriages were largely made of wood, as were farm implements, wheels, gears, and shafts. Shipyards and shipways were also constructed from timber, and small ships were built in quantity from an early date.

Alternatively, metal products were especially scarce, and mills and other industrial facilities remained few and small. Work on roads and harbors lagged far behind European standards until the end of the colonial period. Capital formation was a primary challenge to the colonists, and the colonies could certainly have used much more capital than was ever available to them. English political leaders promoted legislation that hindered the export of tools and machinery from the home country. Moreover, English or colonials who had money to invest often preferred the safer investment in British firms, which were just beginning to thrive. But after all these considerations, the fact remains that residents of the developing American colonies lived better lives than people in many underdeveloped countries do today.

DEMOGRAPHIC CHANGE

Underpopulation Despite High Rates of Population Growth

As we just noted, one major fact of American economic life—underpopulation and labor scarcity—persisted throughout the entire colonial period. Another extremely important aspect of British colonization and a crucial factor in securing and maintaining Britain's hold on the North American frontier was the extremely high rate of population growth in the colonies. What generated the characteristic of apparent underpopulation was the vast amount of available land, which "thinned" the population spatially and established high population densities in only a few major port towns. This occurred despite the exceptionally high rate of growth, which was so high—the population approximately doubled every 25 years—that Thomas Malthus worrisomely referred to it as "a rapidity of increase, probably without parallel in history." Malthus and others pointed to the American colonies as a prime example of virtually unchecked population growth. Wouldn't such a rate of increase, which was twice the population growth rate in Europe, ultimately lead to famine, pestilence, and doom? Wasn't it an obvious truism that the aggregate supply of land—essential to food production—was fixed in amount?

Yes, but these European polemics were far from the minds of the colonists. Overpopulation never resulted in the colonies, despite the various methods that were used to encourage or force (in the case of African captives) population relocation to the New World. Nor did the high natural rate of population increase create population pressures in the colonies; indeed population growth was generally viewed as a sign of progress and a means of reducing the uncertainties, risk, and hazards of a sparsely populated frontier region.

Spatial Distribution of the Population

We should not forget that the period from the founding of Jamestown to the first inauguration of President Washington is about equal to the span of time from our beginnings as a nation under the Constitution to the present. It took 50 years to secure a firm hold on the new continent, and at the end of the first century of colonial history, settlement of the eastern seaboard was far from complete. By 1660, Virginia, Maryland, and Massachusetts were established commonwealths, but the first debtors did not move into Georgia for almost another 75 years. In 1640, perhaps 25,000 white people inhabited the English colonies on the mainland; by 1660, there were 80,000 colonists, and by 1690, 200,000. After 1690, population growth was spectacular. From over one-third of a million people in 1710, the white colonial population had increased to about 2.25 million on the eve of the Revolution.

Map 3-1 shows the extent of settlement as of 1660, 1700, and 1760. Before 1660, there was nothing to speak of south of Norfolk, and at the turn of the century a wilderness still separated Charleston and its environs from the major inhabited area in upper North Carolina. By 1760, the land-hungry rich and poor had spread over nearly all of the coastal plain and into the piedmont areas. As early as 1726, Germans and Scotch-Irish had begun moving into the Shenandoah Valley, and down this and the other great valleys in ever-increasing numbers, settlers sought the cheap land to the west. Through gaps in the mountains some turned east into the piedmont area of Virginia and the Carolinas; only a few years later pioneers began to trickle to the west, particularly through the Cumberland Gap into Kentucky and Tennessee.

The growth of population and the colonization of new territory were not restricted to the eastern coast of North America. During the sixteenth century, Spain had occupied northern Mexico and Florida, and while English settlement was taking place, the Spanish were moving northward into Texas, southern Arizona, and southern California. As we have already mentioned, in the seventeenth century, France established bases in the Lesser Antilles and in Canada, and from Canada, French explorers and traders pushed into the Mississippi Valley and on to the Gulf of Mexico. The three rival states were bound to clash in America, even if they had not been enemies in other parts of the world. To the general historian, we must leave the descriptions of these bitter rivalries and of the resulting complex, if small-scale, wars. Following intermittent conflict between the French and the English in the northeast and along most of the western frontier, the French and Indian War resulted in the temporary downfall of the French in North America. By the Treaty of 1763, only Spain and England

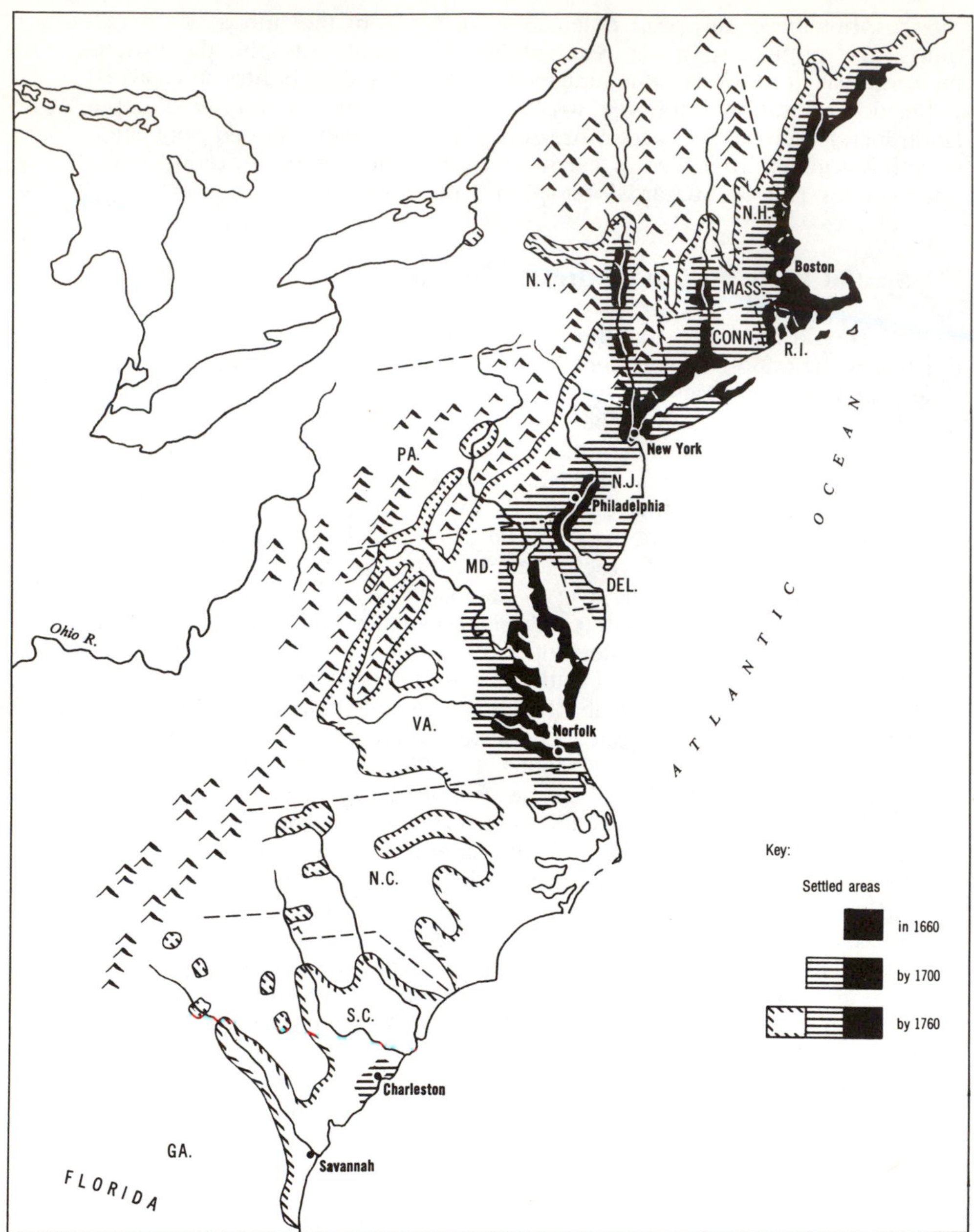

MAP 3–1

Settlement: Easily accessible coastal regions and river valleys provided the first sites for settlements, but settlers soon moved into the Piedmont areas, the great valleys of the Appalachians, and the inviting country west of the mountains.

were left in possession of the North American continent. Spain took all the territory west of the Mississippi, and England secured everything to the east, with the exception of certain fishing rights and small islands retained by the French off Newfoundland. According to this agreement, England acquired all of Florida, thereby settling perennial disputes with Spain that had long disturbed the colonies of South Carolina and Georgia. It is difficult to remember that Spain, not France, harassed the pioneers who moved out of the original thirteen colonies and into the old Southwest. Not until 1800, did France again own the Territory of Louisiana and its vital port of New Orleans, and as we know, that control did not last long.

Powering a High Natural Rate of Population Increase

Continuing rivalries among the European nation-states posed additional hazards to frontier settlers, and people of similar cultures, values, and backgrounds generally preferred to live closely to one another. Moreover, the relative size of rival populations in North America significantly influenced military ventures there. But by and large, colonists did not have children to add to the military might of the population. Large families were common primarily because economic conditions were highly favorable for a high natural rate of population growth.

The broad trends of population growth from both migration and natural causes are illustrated by region in Figure 3-1. Note that there is a remarkable similarity in the timing, rise, and levels of the total populations in New England and the upper South. The latecomers—the middle colonies and the lower South—displayed somewhat higher growth rates, which allowed them to catch up somewhat. The rate of population expansion was quite steady for the colonies as a whole.

The period of greatest absolute migration occurred in the eighteenth century—particularly after 1720, when between 100,000 and 125,000 Scotch-Irish and about 100,000 Germans arrived in North America. Most immigrants in the seventeenth century were British, and there was another strong surge of British migration between 1768 and 1775. Perhaps as many as 300,000 white immigrants came to the New World between 1700 and 1775, and a similar number of blacks came as well. Plenty of highly fertile land and a favorable climate attracted Europeans and provided motives for securing African slaves. Nevertheless, migration was the dominant source of population growth in only the first decades of settlement in each region.

In New England, natural causes were the main sources of population growth before 1650. For areas settled later, such as Pennsylvania, the forces of migration remain dominant later, but natural forces swiftly took over even there. Even the nonslave black population grew swiftly and predominantly from natural sources after 1700. On the eve of the Revolution, only one white in ten was foreign born; the figure for blacks was approximately two in ten.

Commercial successes, favorable economic circumstances, and the high value of labor powered a high rate of reproduction in the colonies. White birth rates in North America per 1,000 women ranged between 45 and 50 per year, compared to less than 30 in Europe. The colonial population was exceptionally

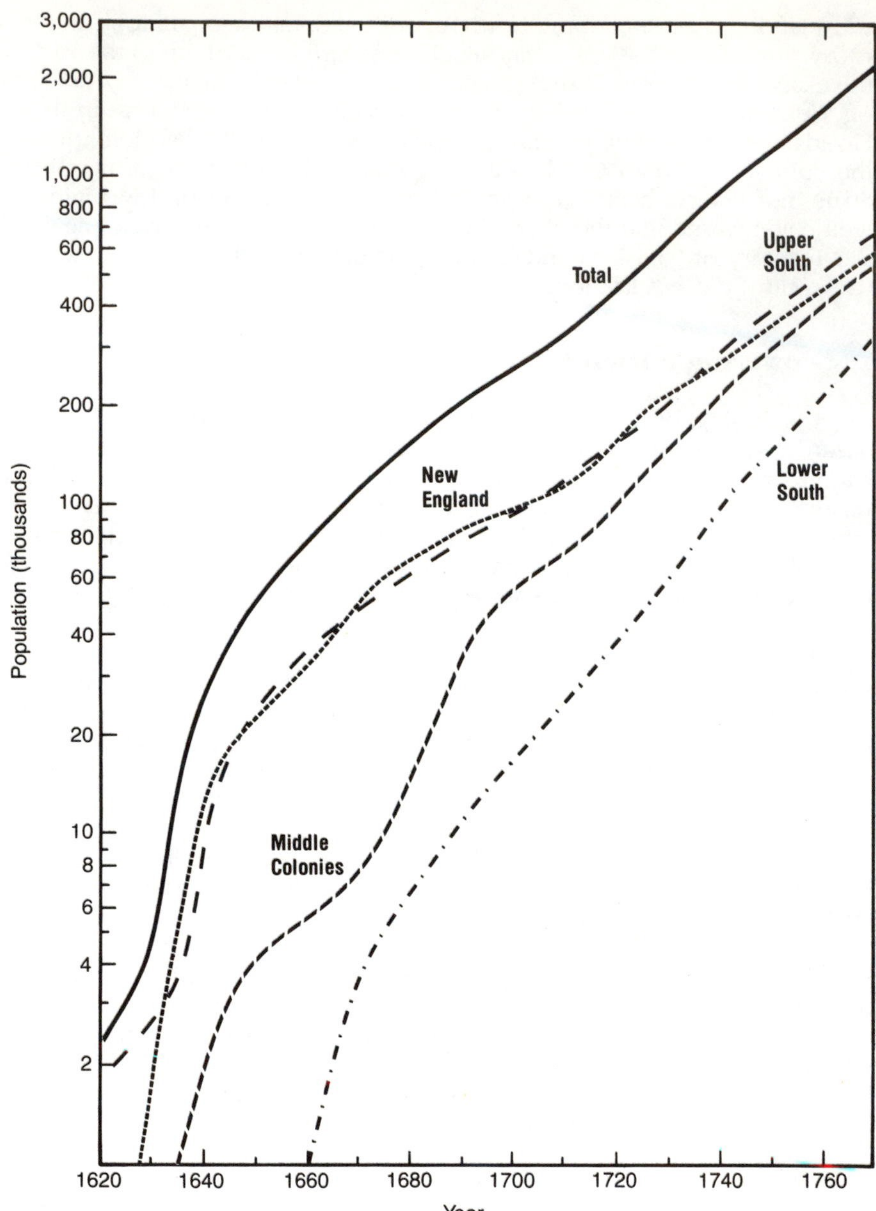

FIGURE 3–1

Colonial Population Growth, 1620 – 1770: Population growth of the thirteen colonies varied among regions, but was very similar in New England and the upper South. Overall, the rate of expansion was steady after 1650.

Source: U.S. Bureau of the Census, *Historical Statistics of the United States, Colonial Times to 1957* (Washington, D.C.: U.S. Government Printing Office, 1960), p. 756.

young, and a higher percentage of its population was of childbearing age. Typically, Colonialists tended to marry rather early—between the ages of 20 and 23, which was a couple of years younger than the average European. The cheapness of land encouraged early marriage in the colonies, and generally, it was easier for colonists than for Europeans to strike out on their own, acquire land, and set up a household. The average European marriage produced four or five children, but earlier marriages and higher proportions of mothers in their childbearing years resulted in an average colonial family of six or seven children. Greater emphasis on rural economic activity also encouraged higher birth rates in the colonies. Children were more costly to raise in urban areas, and their labor contribution tended to be less there.

Also of great significance was the fact that once the first few years of starvation had passed, the colonies experienced rather low mortality rates. The annual death rate in Europe was about 40 per 1,000 people; in the colonies, it was 20–25 per 1,000.

The lower age structure of the colonial population accounts in part for this, but the exceptionally low rate of child mortality was an even more impressive statistic. On the average, white mothers in the colonies were better fed and housed than mothers in Europe. Consequently, colonial babies were healthier. The harsh winters of North America and the inferior medical technology of the frontier were more than offset by plentiful food supplies, fuel, and housing. And because the population was predominantly rural, epidemics were rare in the colonies.

Once past infancy, white colonial males typically lived to be 60 or more. Due to the hazards of childbirth, however, the comparable age for early colonial women was slightly over 40.

The Population Profile

Natural forces, rather than migration, were also the predominant factor in the development of the black population after 1700. Because the actual number of imported slaves practically equaled the number of white immigrants, however, the proportion of the total population that was black increased significantly after 1700. In 1670, only about 4 percent of the total population was black. This proportion had increased to more than 20 percent 100 years later.

Of course, regional differences were great, and over 90 percent of the slaves resided in southern regions. As Figure 3-2 indicates, however, relatively small proportions of the total population of the mainland colonies were comprised of blacks, compared to the Caribbean islands. In the northern regions, the proportion of blacks was in the neighborhood of 5 percent. In Maryland in the late colonial years, blacks comprised 33 percent of the total population; in Virginia, 47 percent. The more limited commercial development in North Carolina, due to inadequate harbors, generated a black population proportion of only 15 percent. In contrast, South Carolina contained the largest concentration of blacks—70 percent. This especially high proportion in South Carolina resulted from the special advantages of slave labor in rice and indigo production. Consequently, the social profile of South Carolina suggested by its high

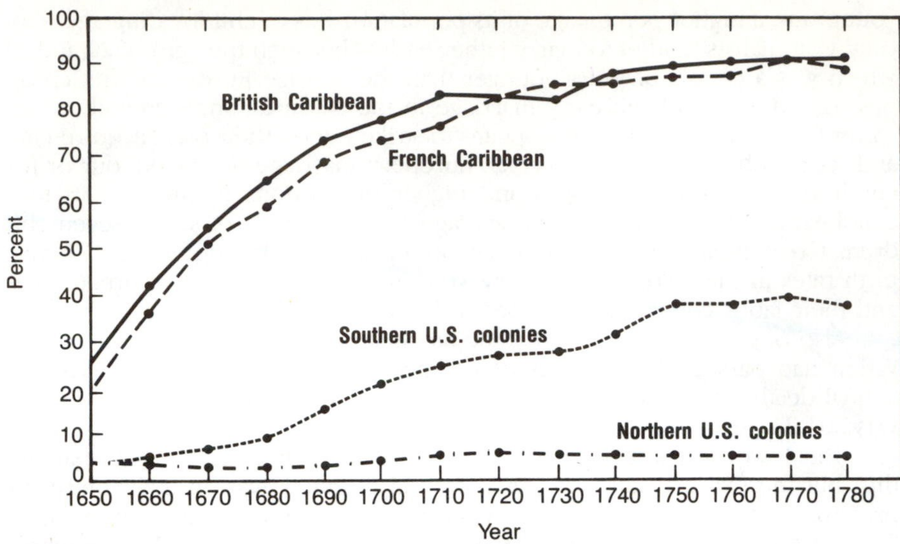

FIGURE 3–2

Blacks as a Percentage of the Total Population, 1650–1780: The population profile was much different on the North American continent than in the islands of the Caribbean. Only in South Carolina did the black population outnumber the resident white population.

Source: Robert W. Fogel and Stanley L. Engerman, *Time on the Cross,* Volume I (Boston: Little, Brown & Company, 1974), p. 21.

concentration of enslaved blacks was similar to the profiles of the British and French West Indies Sugar islands. Although Virginia's population profile did approach this proportion, South Carolina's profile of a majority of slaves controlled by a minority of plantation owners was unique among the mainland colonies. In contrast to their Caribbean counterparts, blacks typically remained a minority race on the mainland of North America.

With this profile in mind, let's examine how the colonists earned a living.

4

Colonial Economic Activity

Most production in the New World was for the colonists' own consumption, but sizable proportions of colonial goods and services were produced for commercial exchange. In time, each region became increasingly specialized in the production of particular goods and services. Areas of specialization were largely determined by the relative abundance of particular soil types, climates, and natural resources associated with the forests and the oceans. Generally, high ratios of land and other natural resources to labor generated exceptionally high levels of output per worker in the colonies.

THE DOMINANCE OF AGRICULTURE

As late as the end of the eighteenth century, approximately 90 percent of the American people earned a major portion of their living by farming. In addition to homegrown basic foodstuffs, most families ate substantial quantities of game and seafood. Clearly, where unlimited amounts of fertile land were available, it would have been foolish to import foodstuffs that could be produced domestically. There were difficulties for the farmers to overcome—especially the clearing of stubborn forests—but the costly transportation services needed to send products to markets had to be conserved for those items that could be produced in the colonies only at high cost. And almost from the beginning, many of the goods that were important to the colonies were paid for by exporting "commercial" crops from the southern and middle colonies and by the shipping services of New England.

The Southern Colonies

In terms of value of output, southern agriculture was dominant throughout the colonial period and well into the nineteenth century. The southern colonies present us with a good example of the comparative advantage that fertile new land can offer. Almost at the outset, settlers in the South grew tobacco that was both cheaper to produce and, before long, of better quality than the tobacco grown in most other parts of the world. Later the South began to produce two other staples—rice and indigo—and just after the Revolutionary War, a third—cotton. For nearly two and a half centuries, the southern economy was to revolve around a few export staples, because the soil and climate of the region provided the South with a pronounced advantage in the cultivation of crops that were in great demand in the industrial areas of the world.

It is not at all astonishing that the early colonists attempted to secure an exportable agricultural surplus. Such a surplus was the quickest way for those who had invested either capital or labor in the colonies to receive some return, and in this instance, what was good for the individual was—in the opinion of mercantilist heads of state—good for England. The southern colonies were especially important to the English. Unlike the commodities of the other colonies, very little that the South exported competed with British production, either in the Isles or in the rest of the Empire. Not that the lands and climate of Maryland, Virginia, the Carolinas, and Georgia were ideal in all respects. There was always the hope to produce more than ever materialized. For example, it was known that grapes would grow well in the South, and every effort was made to encourage the production of wines then being imported from France and Spain. But the quality of American wines was so poor that serious attempts to compete with established wine-producing areas were abandoned. Similarly, it was hoped that silk and hemp—two much needed fibers—could be produced in quantity, and bounties and premiums were offered for their production; but again, quality was inferior, and high wage rates resulted in a high-cost product.

Tobacco, as we have noted, was exported from Virginia to England within a decade after the settlement of Jamestown. The weed had been known in Europe for over a century; sailors on the first voyages of exploration had brought back samples and descriptions of the ways in which natives had used it. Despite much opposition on moral grounds, smoking had increased in popularity during the sixteenth century. It was therefore a relief to the English to find a source of supply so that tobacco importation from the Spanish would be unnecessary. Tobacco needed a long growing season and fertile soil. Furthermore, it could be cultivated in small areas, on only partly cleared fields, and with the most rudimentary implements. All this suited the primitive Virginia community. But there were two additional advantages to tobacco production in the colonies. As successive plantings exhausted the original fertility of a particular plot, new land was readily available, and ships could move up the rivers of the Virginia coast to load their cargoes at the plantation docks. One marked disadvantage that lingered for most of the seventeenth century was that the colonists had much to learn about the proper curing, handling, and shipping of tobacco, and for many years the American product was inferior to tobacco produced in Spain. Nevertheless, colonial tobacco was protected in the English market, and the fact that it was cheaper led to steady increases in its portion of the tobacco market. The culture of tobacco spread northward around the Chesapeake Bay and moved up the many river valleys. By the end of the seventeenth century, there was some production in North Carolina.

During the early years of the seventeenth century, Spanish tobacco sold in England for an average retail price of about 40 shillings per pound. When Virginia tobacco was first marketed, it commanded 4–8 shillings per pound, and until 1627 the consensus was that a price of around 3 shillings per pound could be maintained. At that price, the production of tobacco was so profitable that colonists could scarcely be persuaded to grow anything else, and a mining-camp spirit pervaded the Virginia colony.[1]

All too soon, however, the tobacco growers of Virginia encountered the problem of volatile prices that forever besets agricultural producers. By 1630, Governor Harvey complained that tobacco was fetching less than a penny a pound. And although prices in the following years had their ups as well as their downs, colonists resorted to all kinds of devices, including burning half of one year's crop, to raise their incomes.[2] An especially difficult period ensued with the increased immigration to the colonies between the outbreak of the Civil Wars and the Restoration, and only the intervention of the weather in 1667, by reducing output to nearly zero, rescued the growers from desperately low prices.

Then, as now, restrictions on production led to disappointing and frustrating results. Planters who were limited to a specific number of plants per farm responded by moving more rapidly to new and fertile fields. If Virginia tried to limit the number of pounds of tobacco exported, it was unlikely that Maryland and North Carolina would cooperate. Marketing of tobacco by consignment to merchants resulted in uncertainties about the prices to be received, and in any case, individual planters felt that they could increase their own incomes by increasing their outputs. During the latter part of the seventeenth century and the first half of the eighteenth, there were years of relative prosperity to be sure, but the days in which tobacco was a profitable crop for every producer were gone. It slowly became apparent that the competition would be won by large plantations and that if the small planters were to succeed at all, they would have to specialize in high-quality tobacco or in the production of food.

Since slaves could be worked in large numbers on a more economical scale, the large plantation unit was more efficient, and the big operator was better able to continue production despite extremely low prices. In the colonial period, slaves ordinarily produced large surpluses of tobacco in comparison to the costs of purchase and upkeep. To achieve the best results, however, a plantation owner had to have enough slaves to assure the economical use of a white manager. A plantation with less than ten slaves, although marginal, could

[1] Lewis Cecil Gray, *History of Agriculture in the Southern United States to 1860,* Vol. I (Washington, D.C.: Carnegie Institution of Washington, 1933), pp. 259–60.

[2] It should be emphasized that crop destruction would have raised incomes only if the price elasticity of demand was *inelastic;* that is, if the percentage increase in price due to the lower quantity supplied was greater than the percentage reduction in the quantity marketed.

Colonial agriculture depended heavily on such cash crops as indigo—here being processed in South Carolina from fresh-cut sheaves to final drying—and rice.

probably survive; but only larger units could earn substantial returns above cost, provided they were properly managed and were comprised of sufficient acreage to avoid soil exhaustion. Thus, the wealthy or those who were able to secure adequate credit from English and Scottish merchants attained an optimum scale of tobacco production and, in so doing, became even wealthier and improved their credit standing further. In short, bigness fostered bigness, and wealth led to wealth. We should not conclude that slaves were held only by the largest plantation owners, however; the crude statistics available today indicate that in Revolutionary times, as later, large numbers of planters owned blacks in lots of ten or less. Nonetheless, there was persistent pressure in the tobacco colonies to develop large-size agricultural units.

About 1695, the second of the great southern staples was introduced. Early Virginia colonists had experimented with rice production and South Carolinians had tried to cultivate the staple in the first two years after settlement, but success awaited the introduction of new varieties of the grain.[3] By the early 1700s, rice was an established crop in the area around Charleston, although problems of irrigation still remained. It is possible to grow rice without intermittent flooding and draining, but the quality of the grain suffers. Rice was first cultivated in the inland swamps that could be flooded periodically from the rivers, but the flooding was dependent on uncertain stream flows. Besides, such a growing method could not be used on the extremely flat land that lay along the coast itself. Before long, a system of flooding was devised that enabled producers to utilize the force of tide flows. Dikes were built along the lower reaches of the rivers, and as the tide pushed back the fresh water, it could be let through gates into irrigation ditches crossing the fields.

Proper flooding remained unpredictable because no salt water could be let in and proper drainage demanded painstaking engineering. But the heavy investment of capital was worthwhile, because proper engineering permitted the two major floodings to occur at precisely the right time and the water could be removed just as accurately. Much labor was needed, and slaves were imported at a great rate during the eighteenth century for this purpose. The "task" system of working slaves, which gave each slave a particular piece of ground to cultivate, was emphasized. The work was back-breaking and was carried out in hot, mosquito-infested swamps; although contemporary opinion held that the African was better able to withstand the ravages of disease and the effects of overexertion than the white man, the mortality rate among blacks was high. Despite production difficulties, rice output steadily increased until the end of the colonial period—its culture finally extending from below Savannah up into North Carolina.

To the profits from rice were added those of another staple—indigo. The indigo plant was successfully introduced in 1743 by a young woman, Eliza Lucas, who had come from the West Indies to live on a plantation near Charleston. Indigo almost certainly could not have been grown without the company of another staple, because its culture was demanding and the preparation of the dye required real skill. As a supplement to rice, however, it was an ideal crop, both because the plant could be grown on high ground where rice would not grow and because the peak work loads in processing indigo came at a time when the slaves were not busy in the rice fields. Indigo production, fos-

[3] Gray, p. 278.

tered by a British subsidy of sixpence a pound, added considerably to the profits of plantation owners, thereby attracting resources to the area.

In emphasizing the importance of tobacco, rice, and indigo, we are in some danger of overlooking the production of other commodities in the southern colonies. Throughout the South, there was a substantial output of hay and animal products and of Indian corn, wheat, and other grains. These items, like a wide variety of fruits and vegetables, were grown mostly to make the agricultural units as self sufficient as possible. Yet upland farmers, especially in the Carolinas and Virginia, grew livestock for commercial sale, and exported meat, either on the hoof or in cured form, in quantity to other colonies.

The Middle Colonies

The land between the Potomac and the Hudson Rivers was on the whole fertile and readily tillable and therefore enjoyed a comparative advantage in the production of food.[4] As the seventeenth century elapsed, two distinct types of agricultural operations developed there. To the west, on the cutting edge of the frontier, succeeding generations continued to encounter many of the difficulties that had beset the first settlers. The trees in the forests—an ever-present obstacle—had to be felled, usually after they had been girdled and allowed to die. The soil was worked with tools that did not differ much from the implements used by medieval Europeans. A living had literally to be wrested from the earth. But in time, a stable and reasonably advanced agriculture began to develop to the east of the frontier. The Dutch in New York and the Germans in Pennsylvania, who brought skills and farming methods that were superior to those of other peoples who came from the Old World, were encouraged from the first to cultivate surplus crops for sale in the small but growing cities of New York, Philadelphia, and Baltimore. Gradually, a commercial agriculture developed. Wheat became the important staple, and although there was a considerable output of corn, rye, oats, and barley, the economy of the region was based on the great bread grain. During the latter part of the seventeenth century, a sufficient quantity of wheat and flour was produced to permit the export of these products, particularly to the West Indies.

From the outset, New Jersey and Pennsylvania contributed heavily to wheat production, and in the years before the Revolution, Pennsylvania became the great wheat colony. The "bread colonies" not only served as a granary for their neighbors to the north and south, but also furnished a considerable output of fruits and vegetables, especially potatoes, and of quality livestock. And, as we will see shortly, this export of surplus food indirectly enabled people in the Middle Colonies to import manufactured products.

The kind of agricultural unit that evolved in the Middle Colonies later became typical in the great food belts of the midwestern United States. Individual farms, which were considerably smaller in acreage than the average plantation

[4] The Middle Colonies probably did not produce food more cheaply than the South, but it was to the South's comparative advantage to produce staples and to the Middle Colonies' comparative advantage to produce food.

to the south, could be operated by the farmer and his family with little hired help. Slaveholding was rare, because there were too many months each year when unskilled labor would be wasted due to weather conditions. It was normally preferable to acquire an indentured servant as a hand; the original outlay was not great, and the productivity of even a young and inexperienced servant was soon sufficient to return the owner's investment. Alternatively, farmers could hire itinerants to work for them, but in a country where labor was scarce, these farm hands were likely to be marginal workers who had drifted away from the seacoast towns.

New England

Vital as the agriculture of New England was to the people of the area, it constituted a relatively unimportant part of total colonial output. Generally poor soils, uneven terrain, and a severe climate led to typical "subsistence" farming, or the growth of only those crops that were necessary for family maintenance. Because it could be produced almost anywhere and because its yield even on poor land was satisfactory, Indian corn was the chief crop. Wheat and the other cereal grains, along with the hardier vegetables, were grown for family use. Due partly to climate and partly to the protection from wild predators that natural barriers furnished, the Narragansett region, including the large islands off its coast, became a cattle and sheep raising center. By the eve of the Revolution, however, New England was a net importer of food and fiber. Its destiny lay in another kind of economic endeavor; and from a very early date, many New Englanders combined farming with other work, thereby living better lives than they would have if they had been confined to the resources of their own farms.

We should mention the peculiar form of agricultural organization that persisted in New England throughout the seventeenth century. We already learned in Chapter 2 that the form of land disposition was quite different in New England than it was in the middle and southern sections; grants were made to groups of proprietors, and allotments were then made to individual New Englanders, usually on the basis of the proportion of their investments. The town became not only a political unit but, in a sense, an agricultural unit as well. The result was that for more than a century New England agriculture assumed some of the characteristics of land-use patterns in medieval Europe. The homes of the villagers normally lay close to the center of the town land. Near each house was a small parcel of land for a garden or an orchard; scattered parcels of 50–200 acres of partially arable land were ordinarily owned at varying distances from the village. Running through the center of the village would almost invariably be a common meadow to which each owner had rights and where livestock roamed freely. Often there were also a common wasteland and common fields, the latter divided into strips and allotted among the villagers. Decisions as to what crops were to be grown in the common fields were made at town meetings; individual farmers were entitled to the products grown on their own strips, but all these fields became common pasture at the end of the growing season.

In the eighteenth century, New England witnessed a movement similar to the institution of English enclosure, in which scattered holdings as well as strips in the common fields were consolidated. The movement differed from an enclosure in an important way, however; in New England, little suffering was attached to the consolidation and fencing of land that had formerly been held in common. There the process was a slow and fairly easy adjustment among free people, each of whom had sufficient land to live on after the enclosure was completed. In fact, because enclosure produced a more efficient agriculture, almost everyone benefited. In England, the lives of landlords and some free people also improved due to enclosure, but some English farmers held such small rights to the common fields and pastures that, after legal division, they were left with little land of their own on which to make a living.

This quaint and outmoded method of farm organization has left little imprint on modern American agriculture. But the systematic laying out of towns that began in New England was continued as the northern frontier progressed westward and was to have an important effect on the future land system in America.

THE EXTRACTIVE INDUSTRIES

Although most colonial Americans made their living agriculturally, many earned their livelihood indirectly from the land in what we will call *extractive* pursuits. From the forest came the furs and wild animal skins, lumber, and naval stores. From the coastal waters came fish and that strange mammal, the whale. From the ground came minerals, but only in small quantities during the early colonial years. From the various industries that were built around these products arose an output second in value only to that of agriculture.

The Fur Trade

The original thirteen colonies were a second-rate source of furs during most of the period before the Revolution, because the finest furs in any area were processed quickly and the most lucrative catches were made long before the frontier movement began. Nonetheless, farmers trapped furs as a sideline to obtain cash, although they caught primarily muskrats and raccoons, whose pelts were less desirable then, as now.

There were two centers of fur trade in the early decades of the colonies. The more important was in the North, where the chief posts were at Albany and Philadelphia for some time. Traders working through the Iroquois tapped apparently inexhaustible supplies of such luxury pelts as beaver, mink, and fox and exported them to Europe. In the South, where the less valuable deerskin was the chief commodity, Charleston and then Augusta were the base cities. Traders pushed around the southern end of the Appalachians to the Mississippi River, always dealing with the Indians, who did most of the actual trapping.

As the search for finer pelts continued into the interior, the French in both the North and the South were ever-present competitors. The English could give the Indians more goods of higher quality in exchange for furs, but the French, who had arrived first in the Mississippi Valley, long maintained excellent relations with some tribes. With the Peace of Paris in 1763, France lost its Canadian possessions and was thus removed from the rivalry. By this time, in any case, the Hudson Bay Company in Canada had secured control of most of this profitable trade.

Wood Products

The forest itself, more than its denizens, became an economically significant object of exploitation. As Map 4-1 illustrates, the colonials lived in an age of wood. Wood, rather than minerals and metals, was their chief fuel and their basic construction material. Almost without exception, the agricultural population engaged in some form of lumbering. Pioneers had to fell trees to clear ground, and wood was used to build houses, barns, furniture, and sometimes fences. Frequently, the timber was burned and the ashes were scattered, but enterprising farmers eventually discovered that they could use simple equipment to produce potash and the more highly refined pearlash. These chemicals, which were needed to manufacture glass, soap, and other products, provided much-needed cash to households throughout the colonies.

Along the fall line of the northern and Middle Colonies, small sawmills sprang up in the earliest settlements. Using stream water as both a source of power and a means of transportation, sawmill operators tended to locate in areas that boasted the best combination of virgin timber and accessible rivers. The commercial manufacture of basic wood shapes—boards, planks, cooperage materials, and so forth—began in Maine and New Hampshire and was a common occupation as far south as North Carolina by the end of the colonial period.

Some sawmills were totally devoted to the manufacture of materials for shipbuilding and ship repair. White pine was unmatched as a building material for the masts and yards of sailing ships, and white and red oak provided ship timbers of the same high quality. The pine trees that grew abundantly throughout the colonies furnished the raw material for the manufacture of so-called naval stores of pitch, tar, and resin. In the days of wooden vessels, naval stores were indispensable in the shipyard and were used mostly for protecting surfaces and caulking seams. These materials were in great demand in both the domestic and British shipbuilding industries. Considerable skilled labor was required to produce naval stores, and only in North Carolina, where slaves were trained to perform the required tasks, could these materials be produced profitably without British subsidy. Even so, English shipwrights complained that American pitch and tar were inferior to European products—a complaint never voiced against the incomparable American ship timbers.

Sea Products

Although restricted primarily to the northern colonies, the occupations of fishing and whaling were of major importance in the development of the entire early colonial economy. The sea provided New Englanders with a com-

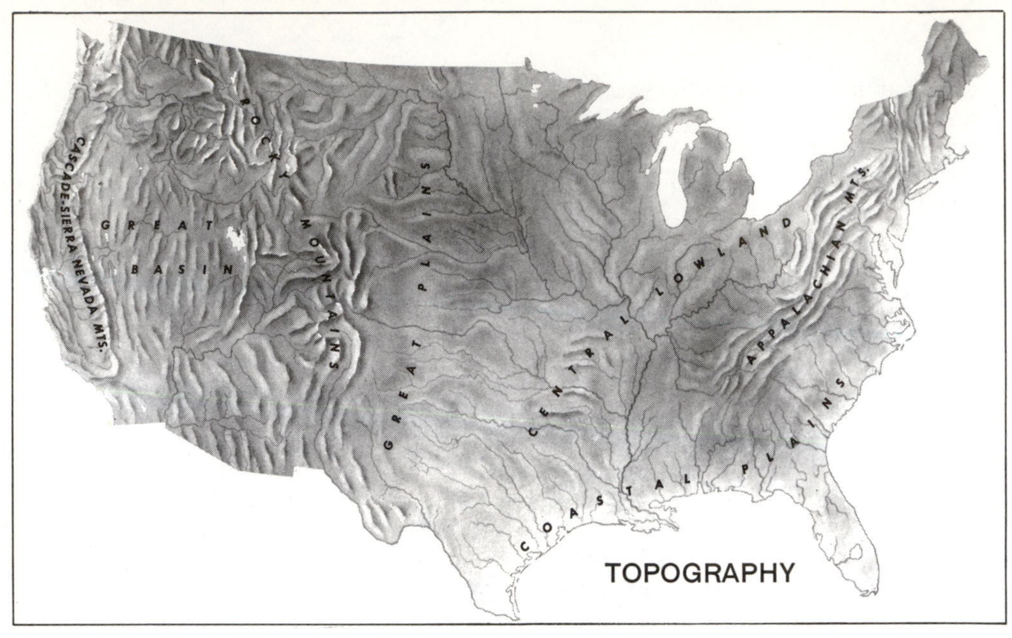

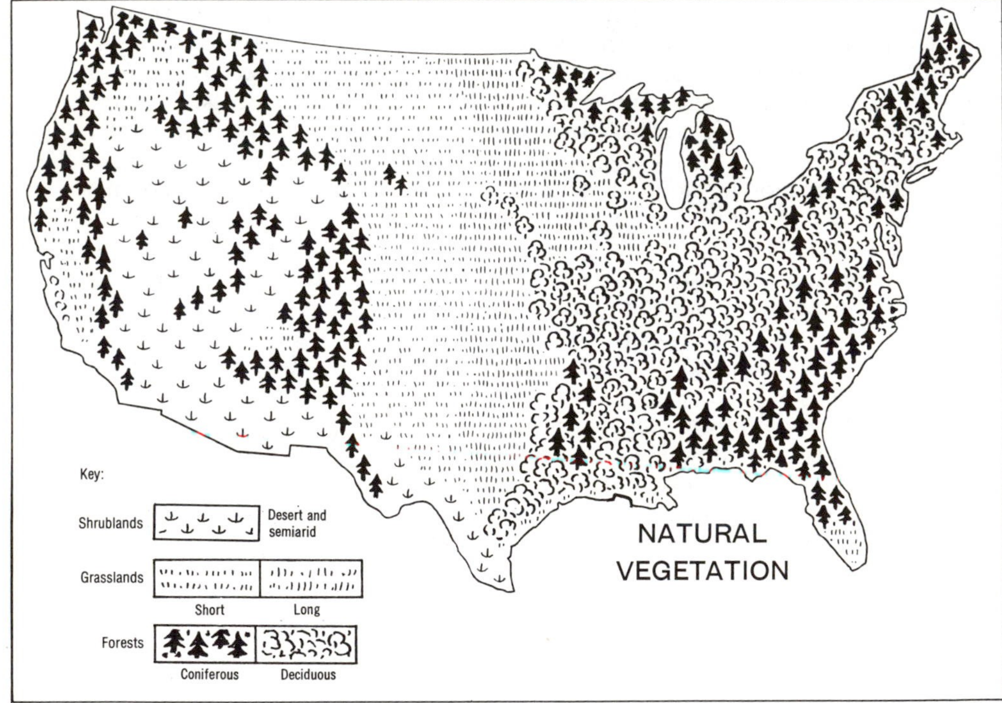

MAP 4–1

Natural Gifts: The channels of commerce and the stores of raw materials decreed by topography and natural vegetation established the initial pattern from which later economic development in America was to emerge.

Whaling was a hazardous but profitable industry in early America.

modity for which there was a ready market and also furnished a stimulus for shipbuilding. When Jacques Cartier sailed up the St. Lawrence River in 1534, fishermen from many European countries were already at work near the mouth of the river and had probably been making the hazardous journey across the North Atlantic for a long time. Originally, these pioneers had operated a "wet fishery"—that is, the catch was partly cleaned, salted down, and returned to the home country for drying. The quality of the product was much better, however, if a "shore fishery" could be established to dry fish at a nearby land base, and during the sixteenth century, fishermen from Spain, Portugal, France, and England attached themselves temporarily to the northern coastal country.

When a permanent settlement was at last made not far from the banks that extended from Long Island to Newfoundland, the settler there naturally turned to deep-sea fishing. There were many splendid harbors to house small fishing vessels and plenty of timber with which to build them. But more importantly, there was a great market for the magnificent cod. The large, fat, hard-to-cure cod were consumed at home. The best cod were exported to Catholic Europe; the poorer grades were sent to the West Indies, where they were fed to slaves. Gloucester, Salem, Boston, and Marblehead became the chief home ports for the great fishing fleets.

In colonial times, whale oil was highly prized as both an illuminant and a lubricant, ambergris, as a base for perfumes, and whalebone, as a material for stays. Whaling was therefore a profitable and vigorous, if small, industry. Before 1700, whalers operated near the New England coast, but their take was small. During the eighteenth century, however, whalers ranged far and wide, and by 1775, more than 300 vessels of all sizes sailed from the Massachusetts ports, of which Nantucket was the great whaling center.

Iron Production

The only mineral obtained by the colonials in any significant quantity was iron. A little copper and lead were found and negligible amounts of coal were mined, but in the young economy, iron was the chief metal and charcoal was the industrial fuel. For the moment, we will confine our attention to the processing of primary shapes—the "blooms" and "pigs" that were later worked into usable finished forms. This distinction may seem artificial, because at many of the ironworks established in these early years, the finishing processes were carried out—then, as now—by the same artisans who reduced the ore. But it is convenient, nevertheless, for us to consider the reduction of iron as one of the extractive industries and the finishing of iron as a manufacturing industry.

Iron, not steel, was the common product of the colonies and, for that matter, of the rest of the world. Later we will become familiar with some of the properties of steel; now it is sufficient for us to distinguish steel from wrought and cast iron. Steel is a form of iron that contains carbon in amounts ranging from about 0.1 percent to about 1.7 percent. With a greater carbon content, the product becomes cast iron. Wrought iron contains very little carbon or other impurities and can be distinguished from steel by its method of manufacture and by the presence of a certain amount of slag in the final product. Steel is malleable, very tough, and increases in brittleness and tensile strength as its carbon content becomes greater. Cast iron is extremely hard and brittle but is not malleable at any temperature. Wrought iron is tough, resists shock, does not corrode easily, and is soft enough to be worked into desired shapes. It is fairly simple to obtain wrought iron, at least in small quantities, and equally easy to obtain cast iron. The production of steel, on the other hand, is difficult, because the carbon content must be adjusted within narrow limits, and until little more than a century ago, steel was manufactured only in small quantities for special purposes.

The methods used in the colonial iron industry did not differ greatly from those developed in the late Middle Ages, although by the time of the Revolution, furnace sizes had increased greatly. In the seventeenth century, the chief source of iron was bog ore, a sediment taken from swamps and ponds. When this sediment was treated with charcoal in a bloomery or forge until the charcoal absorbed the oxygen in the ore, an incandescent sponge of metal resulted. The glowing ball of iron was removed from the forge and in a white-hot condition was hammered to remove the slag and leave a substantial piece of wrought iron. The productive output of the bloomeries was small.

Rich rock ores were discovered as the population moved inward, and during the eighteenth century, a large number of furnaces were built for the reduction of these ores. Pig iron could then be produced in quantity. A mixture of rock ore, charcoal, and oyster shells or limestone was placed in a square or conical furnace and then ignited. Under a draft of air from bellows worked by water power, the iron ore was reduced to a spongy metal, which as it settled to the bottom of the furnace, alloyed itself with large amounts of carbon thereby becoming what we call cast iron. Poured into molds called "pigs" or "sows," the resulting metal could be either remelted and cast into final form later or further refined and reworked in a mill or blacksmith shop.

These rudimentary processes provide us with an important background that will help us understand the later development of the American iron and steel industry. It is also worth noting that due to the simple processing required as well as to an abundance of charcoal, the colonial iron industry was able to compete with the British Isles in the sale of bars and pigs. There is agreement that the number of forges and furnaces in the colonies just before the Revolution probably exceeded the number in England and Wales combined, and the annual output of wrought and cast iron by then was in the neighborhood of 30,000 tons, or about one-seventh of the world's output. But the colonies remained heavy net importers of finished iron products.

THE MANUFACTURING INDUSTRIES

It is convenient for us to distinguish between the colonial extractive and manufacturing industries, even though these activities overlapped in actual practice. Included under the heading of manufacturing are the processes by which the crude or primary materials produced by the extractive industries became finished products. We should also realize that the word "industry" is ordinarily used rather loosely to describe any colonial activity, because the "firms" that comprised an industry were frequently heterogeneous units that could range from a household to a fairly large shop or mill. Nevertheless, the output of each of the major categories of commodities *tended* to be produced by only one of the three major types of colonial organizations: households, craft shops, or mills and yards.

Once again, we must remind ourselves of the proportions in which the factors of production were available to business enterprises. Land was abundant. Capital goods and labor were scarce, but capital was relatively less important to a manufacturing organization than it was to be after the Industrial Revolution. On the other hand, labor was relatively more important; the skills of artisans—not tools or equipment—were the crucial agents in the more complicated production processes. Because of labor's importance and short supply, wages rates in the colonies were sometimes nearly twice as high as they were in the home country.

Except for a relatively few gifted traders, most people of the time found the greatest hope of ultimate reward in farming and land speculation. Because they were attracted to the land, early Americans united in only a few urban settlements as their population grew, and in the rural areas—where most people lived—large quantities of goods were made in the home for home use. In the villages and towns, craftsmen tended to make those products that were in domestic demand but that required greater skill and somewhat more expensive tools to produce than the ordinary householder could provide. Finally, from mills and plants of varying sizes, came an increasing flow of goods for home trade and an even greater flow for export.

Household Manufacture

The first concerns of the colonial household were the manufacture of food and clothing. Finer items were imported, but household manufacture actually created a marketable surplus of some commodities. Animal products that we take for granted today resulted from serious efforts on the part of all members of the family at the first signs of winter. Cured or pickled meats, leather, and lard were essentials that only the well-to-do could afford to buy. Wheat, rye, or Indian corn grown on the farm was ground into flour at the local gristmill, but the women of the family made plentiful weekly rations of bread and hardtack. Jellies and jams were made with enough sweetening from honey, molasses, or maple syrup to preserve them for indefinite periods in open crocks. And we can be sure that the men of the family were rarely teetotalers. Beer, rum, and whiskey were easiest to make, but wines, mead, and an assortment of brandies and cordials were specialties of some households.

Making clothing—from preparing the raw fiber to sewing the finished garment—kept the women and children busy. There was nothing fine or beautiful about the resulting products, but it covered the body. Knit goods such as stockings, mittens, and sweaters were the major items of homemade apparel. Linsey-woolsey (made of flax and wool) and jeans (a combination of wool and cotton) were the standard textiles of the North and of the pioneer West. Equally indestructible, although perhaps a little easier on the skin, was fustian, a blend of cotton and flax used mostly in the South. Dress goods and fine suitings had to be imported from England, and even for the city dweller, the purchase of such luxuries was usually a rare and exciting occasion.

Early Americans who had special talents produced everything from nails and kitchen utensils to exquisite cabinets. Everywhere the men of the family participated in the construction of their own homes, although exacting woodwork and any necessary masonry might be done by a specialist. Specialists of widely varying abilities could be found both in cities and at country crossroads. Let's consider their work.

The Craft Shop

Much earlier than might be supposed, artisans began to ply their trades. Some of them were true craftsmen—experts in the European tradition. What distinguished workshop crafts from household manufactures was the specialization of the former. Household production was for family needs and presumably required neither the full time nor the complete attention of any member of the household. The craftsman might work at home, but the home was a craft shop if a craftsman earned his living at a trade.

The distinction between the specialized craftsman and the household worker was not always clear in colonial America. Skilled slaves on southern plantations might devote all their time to manufacture; this made them artisans, even though their output was considered a part of the household. On the other hand, the itinerant jack-of-all-trades, who moved from village to village selling reasonably expert services, was certainly not a craftsman in the European sense. Due to the scarcity of skilled labor, individual workers often performed functions more than they would have undertaken in their native country; a colonial tanner, for example, might also be a currier and a shoemaker. Furthermore, due to small local markets and the consequent geographic dispersal of nearly all types of production, few workers in the same trade were united in any particular locality. For this reason, although there were not many guilds or associations of craftsmen in the same trade as early as 1648, there were enough shoemakers in Boston to enable the General Court to incorporate them as a guild, and by 1718, tailors and cordwainers were so numerous in Philadelphia that they too applied for incorporation.[5]

Urban centers exhibited a great variety of skills at a rather early date. In 1697, for example, 51 manufacturing handicrafts in addition to the building trades, were represented in Philadelphia. As one authority puts it:

> ... that a bare enumeration of the trades that we know were plied in the colonies indicates that varied and widely diffused handicraft manufactures then existed, in the aggregate contributing largely to colonial production, but chiefly important for the leaven of knowledge, skill, and habit which they supplied for subsequent industrial development.[6]

Mills and Yards

In our discussion of the extractive industries, we observed that somewhat more complex organizations were required even for rudimentary manufacture than were required in the household or the craft shop. For want of a more precise term, we will follow common usage and speak of the mill industries. To colonials, a mill was "... either a contrivance for grinding or any machinery operated by animal power, wind, or water."[7] Thus, mills turned out the basic wood shapes and the wrought-iron bars and iron pigs. Although the finished wooden and iron articles were frequently made by skilled artisans or even household members, they were also produced in mills and furnaces. Again, the

[5] Carl Bridenbaugh, *Cities in the Wilderness* (New York: Alfred A. Knopf, 1955), pp. 43 and 191.

[6] Victor S. Clark, *History of Manufactures in the United States, 1607–1860* (Washington, D.C.: Carnegie Institution of Washington, 1916), p. 164.

[7] Clark, p. 174.

"reproductive" manufacturing might be done in connection with the primary manufacture or in a totally different location. For example, furnaces for remelting iron and refining forges for making bar iron were usually attached to smelting furnaces, whereas slitting mills and plating forges were ordinarily independent establishments.

Until perhaps the middle of the eighteenth century, most of the mills were crude affairs, run by water power that was furnished by the small streams found all along the middle and north Atlantic coast. Dam sites suitable for large power development were not in general use until after the Revolution, because operations were conducted on a small scale and owners had the means to construct dams and canals only of minimum size. Throughout most of this period, primitive mechanisms were used; the cranks of sawmills and gristmills were almost always made of iron, but the wheels themselves and the cogs of the mill wheel were made of wood, preferably hickory. So little was understood about power transmission at this time that a separate water wheel was built to power each article of machinery. Shortly before the Revolution, improvements were made in the application of power to milling processes, and the mills along the Delaware River and the Chesapeake Bay were probably the finest in the world at that time.[8] In 1770, a fair-sized gristmill would grind 100 bushels a day; the largest mills, with several pairs of stones, might convert 75,000 bushels of grain into flour annually. The highest development of this kind of manufacture was represented by the establishment of Oliver Evans, who invented devices that enabled him to achieve a continuous process of manufacture from raw material to final product. In his mill, which began operations in 1782, grain was

> . . . elevated mechanically to the top of the mill or warehouse, cleaned during gravity transmission to the hoppers, ground, conveyed by screw transmission and a second series of elevators to the top of the building again, cooled, bolted, and barreled during its second descent, without the intervention of any manual operation.[9]

Employing only six men, mostly to close barrels, the Evans mill produced 100,000 bushels of grain annually.

We can only suggest the variety of the mill industries. Tanneries with bark mills were found in the North and the South. Paper-making establishments, common in Pennsylvania and not unusual in New England, were called mills because machinery was required to grind the linen rags into pulp. Textiles were essentially a household product, but in Massachusetts, eastern New York, and Pennsylvania, a substantial number of mills were constructed to perform the more complicated processes of weaving and finishing. The rum distilleries of New England provided a major product for foreign trade, and breweries everywhere ministered to convivial needs. The gristmill, like the sawmill, was found everywhere in the colonies, but the largest ones eventually developed in Pennsylvania, Delaware, and New Jersey.

[8] Clark, p. 179.
[9] Clark, p. 179.

Largely due to their ready supplies of first-class timber and naval stores, colonial shipbuilders enjoyed an early comparative advantage in shipbuilding.

Shipbuilding

Although large-scale manufacturing was not characteristic of colonial economic activity, one important exception—shipbuilding and the busy shipyards in the colonies—deserves special emphasis. As early as 1631, little more than a decade after the Pilgrims landed at Plymouth, a 30-ton sloop was completed in Boston. During the seventeenth century, shipyards sprang up all along the New England coast, with Boston and Newport leading the way. New York was a strong competitor until the Navigation Act of 1651 (to be discussed in Chapter 5) dealt its Dutch-dominated industry a crippling blow from which it did not recover until after 1720. By this time, Philadelphia boasted a dozen large shipyards along the banks of the Delaware River, and of the five major towns, only Charleston relied on ships produced by others. In the first half of the eighteenth century, the output of colonial shipyards reached its peak.

American industry furnished the vessels for a large domestic merchant fleet and sold a considerable number of ships abroad, chiefly to the English. An uncontradicted estimate attributes nearly one-third of the ships in the British Merchant Marine in 1775 to American manufacture, and in 1700, the New England fleet exceeded 2,000, exclusive of fishing vessels.[10]

Many of the ships constructed were small. But whether they were building a square-rigged, three-masted vessel of several hundred tons or a fishing boat of ten tons, Americans had a marked and persistent advantage. As we have noted, first-quality timber supplies were readily available. A great and steady demand for vessels in England enabled American builders to sell their ships as fast as they could construct them, and the strength of this foreign demand helped them to overcome their major obstacle—that of securing anchors, cordage, shipwares, and sailcloth, which could not be produced at home in required quantities. Thus, British merchants would send over cargoes of goods to be sold in America at favorable prices. With their proceeds, they would have a ship built to order, loaded with lumber, and sent to a southern European port or to England, where the cargo and perhaps the ship as well would be sold at a high profit. Finally, the shipbuilding industry attracted skilled artisans from both England and Holland, who took pride in their work and equaled their European counterparts in every respect. Most of the artisans who came to America were second-rate, but this was not true of the shipwrights. Furthermore, a tradition of quality workmanship was handed down from father to son, so as long as the wooden sailing ship was a major factor in transportation, America's comparative advantage in its manufacture was undeniable.[11]

The Merchant Marine

Finally, as the sizable New England fleet suggests, shipping services and other distribution services associated with the transportation, handling, and merchandising of goods were important commercial activities in the colonies. The merchant marines in New England and the Middle Colonies, which employed thousands of men, were as efficient as the Dutch and English merchants in many trades throughout the world. Indeed, by the end of the colonial period, the colonies could boast of a sizable commercial sector, and as a source of foreign exchange earnings, the sale of shipping services was second only to tobacco exports. Overseas trade and these commercial activities were so important to the colonial economy that they will be given special emphasis in Chapter 5.

[10]Jacob Price, "A Note on the Value of Colonial Exports of Shipping," *Journal of Economic History* **XXXVI:**3 (September 1976).

[11]During the early colonial period, the Navigation Acts effectively subsidized both English and colonial shipbuilders. The American advantage became clear, however, soon after the beginning of the eighteenth century. See J. B. Condliffe, *The Commerce of Nations* (New York: W.W. Norton, 1950), p. 101.

5

The Economic Relations of the Colonies

ENGLISH MERCANTILISM AND THE COLONIES

Due to a highly limited and scattered domestic market, the rise of the various commercial economic activities in the colonies was largely dependent on the creation and expansion of markets in Britain, continental Europe, the Caribbean, and other distant places. But the colonies were not free to trade with any corner of the globe, and the rather extensive freedoms that the colonists enjoyed—especially regarding their own internal affairs—sharply contrasted with the many limitations and regulations imposed on their trade and shipping. The external relations of the colonies with other members of the British Empire and with other nation-states and their colonies were guarded jealously by the Crown. The British colonies in North America were settled amidst the heyday of mercantilism.

In the broader period that falls approximately between 1500 and 1800, the countries of western Europe that became nation-states were invariably influenced by a set of ideas and beliefs known as the *mercantile system* or *mercantilism.* Mercantilist doctrine was not created by a particular group of thinkers, nor was it ever set forth in systematic fashion by a "school" of economists. In fact, although there had been a massive outpouring of economic literature during this period, mostly in the form of pamphlets and small books, the first "classical economist," Adam Smith, gained attention by attacking mercantilist beliefs. Nevertheless, the ideas of mercantilism were important because they were held by practical businesspeople and heads of state who—at different times in different countries—had strongly influenced public policy.

More than anything else, the mercantilists wanted to achieve power and wealth for the state.[1] It was possible to reach these ends, they felt, by making their own country as self sufficient as possible and by doing whatever they could to weaken the power of competing states. The means toward this end were various. Perhaps the most popular was to secure a "favorable" balance of payments; Spain's experience in the sixteenth century had led most observers to conclude that an inflow of gold and silver was a potent help in attaining needed goods and services and in prosecuting successful wars. But this concept of balance of payments did not comprise the total mercantilist doctrine. Great power could be fully realized by the state only if political and economic *unity* became a fact. In a day when productivity depended so greatly on the skill and knowledge of the individual worker, it was of primary importance to keep artisans at home. If all the materials necessary to domestic industry were not available, they could best be obtained by establishing colonies or friendly foreign trading posts from which they could be imported. A strong merchant marine could carry foreign goods, thereby helping to secure a favorable balance of payments, and merchant ships could be converted for war if the need arose. Nor was the attention of mercantilist leaders directed exclusively toward relations between the home country and the rest of the world. For one thing, a self-sufficient economy implied a strong and vigorous agriculture. For another, the high rate of industrial production necessitated not only the protection of old industries and the encouragement of new ones, but also the enforcement of regulations that would provide the poor and indigent with some kind of productive activity.

Mercantilists believed that these means of achieving national power could be made effective only by the passage and reasonably strict enforcement of massive legislation directed toward regulating the whole pattern of economic life. England had begun to pass such laws by the end of the fifteenth century, but its mercantilist efforts did not fully flower until after the British, together with the Dutch, had successfully turned back the Spanish power. Indeed, it was largely a consequence of England's desire to surpass Holland—a nation that had reached the zenith of its power during the first half of the seventeenth century—that British legislation was passed marking the beginning of an organized and consistent effort to regulate colonial trade.

Adherence to mercantilist principles was, of course, implicit in the colonizing activity that began in the late 1500s. For that matter, after the first successful settlement in the New World, no one would have argued seriously that the colonies should not be regulated to benefit the Empire. Almost as soon as Virginia tobacco began to be shipped in commercial quantities to England, King James I levied a tax on it while agreeing to prohibit the growth of competing tobacco in England. Gradually, more and more restrictions were placed on cargoes shipped from the colonies in foreign vessels, and by the 1630's, foreigners were legally excluded from American trade. Furthermore, it had become well established by 1650 that certain products were to be taken to England either to be sold there or to be transshipped to other European countries. On

[1] Perhaps, as Gustav Schmoller suggested, the most important thing about mercantilism was that it sought to provide an economic undergirding for the political process of state making.

the whole, there seems to have been little objection to such rules and little feeling among the colonials that they were unjust.

During the English Civil War, which began in 1642 and ended in 1649, the British had too many troubles of their own to pay much attention to regulating trade with the colonies. In this period, Americans had slipped into the habit of shipping goods directly to continental ports, and the Dutch made great inroads into the carrying trade. In 1651, Parliament passed the first of the so-called Navigation Acts, directed primarily at prohibiting the shipping of American products in Dutch vessels. Not until after the Restoration, however, was England in a position to enforce a strict commercial policy, and it is for this reason that we usually think of the Navigation Acts of 1660 and 1663 as the first really effective ones.

The first Navigation Acts were modified from time to time by literally hundreds of policy changes. Although we will devote some attention to a few crucial changes in policy, at this point it is sufficient to note the three primary categories of trade restriction:

1. All trade between England and any of its colonies had to be carried in ships owned by English nationals or by colonials and had to be manned by crews that were at least three-fourths English or colonial.
2. All European products received by the colonies, with a few minor exceptions, had to be imported from England. This meant that any colonial imports from continental Europe first had to pass through an English port.
3. Certain commodities, called "enumerated articles," could be shipped only to England. At first, the list of articles enumerated was small, but in time, it was greatly expanded.

It is important to keep these three categories of restrictions firmly in mind. Although they were the cause of occasional protests on the part of the colonists, they probably did little harm. Largely due to widespread evasion by smuggling, these restrictions caused practically no disruption of established trade patterns during the remaining decades of the seventeenth century. When, in 1696, a system of admiralty courts was established to enforce the Navigation Acts, their impact became somewhat more pronounced. Indeed, from the beginning of the eighteenth century, all spheres of colonial activity were regulated according to what approached a unified policy.

OVERSEAS COMMERCE

The most important characteristic of colonial commerce was the predominance of the South as the producer of great staples. These staples—tobacco, rice, and indigo—in addition to naval stores, were the most desirable imports to the English under the mercantile system. If we look at the trade statistics at the beginning of the eighteenth century or just before the Revolution, we are struck by the overwhelming importance of southern exports to England compared with the exports of other colonies. In the first decade of the eighteenth century, southern exports to England were roughly four times greater than

New Amsterdam in the seventeenth century was a small but promising port city. Surrounded by relatively unproductive land, the town nevertheless combined a superb harbor with unexcelled access to the hinterland.

those of New England, New York, and Pennsylvania. Half a century later, during the 1760s, the proportion was still approximately the same, although by this time the Carolinas were exporting many more goods than they had earlier. Southern imports from England, on the other hand, were only slightly greater than British imports to the Northern Colonies in the first decade of the century. During the 1760s, imports to New England, New York, and Pennsylvania exceeded imports to the South by some £300,000 sterling.

A statistical description of trade in the late colonial period will provide us with a useful summary of the relative importance of the various trading partners of the colonies. As shown in Table 5-1 and as we just emphasized, Great Britain was the main overseas region to receive colonial exports (56% of the total) and to supply colonial imports (80% of the total).[2] Nevertheless, the West Indies and southern Europe were important trading partners, especially as markets for American exports.

Another feature of colonial trade that is revealed by the statistics in Table 5-1 is the sharp differences among the regions' ties to various overseas markets. Commerce in the southern regions was overwhelmingly dominated by the English trades. Alternatively, trade in the Middle Colonies was more evenly balanced among Great Britain, southern Europe, and the West Indies. New England's most important trading partner was the West Indies.

Colonial imports in each region arrived predominantly by way of Great Britain. Few products were imported from southern Europe, and it is also

[2] Recall that due to the Navigation Acts not all of these amounts were actually consumed or produced in the British Isles.

worth noting that commodity trade with Africa was insignificant in terms of both exports and imports.

Shipping and Trade

British ships did not completely dominate the trades of the southern colonial regions, but they did provide the lion's share of shipping services to those regions. These ships essentially engaged in a direct, shuttle-like trade with Great Britain. The major commodities, of course, were tobacco, rice, and indigo, but about 50% of the annual rice crop was shipped directly to southern Europe.

Trade in the North, unlike trade in the South, was more than the simple exchange of staple commodities for finished goods to be put to immediate use. Northern commerce has often been characterized in terms of various trade triangles. The best known of these alleged triangles began as a two-way exchange of fish, timber, livestock, and provisions, shipped from the ports of New England, New York, and Pennsylvania, for rum, molasses, and sugar from the West Indies. Molasses was converted into rum by American distilleries, and the dark, heavy liquor, together with rum already imported from the islands, was sent to the African coast in exchange for slaves. These slaves were then transported to the ports of Richmond and Charleston or to the West Indies. In a second supposed trade triangle, a ship might take a cargo from Philadelphia, New York, or Newport, exchange it in Jamaica or St. Kitts for molasses and sugar, and proceed to England to trade for textiles and ironware before returning home. A third trade triangle is said to have begun with the shipment of fish, lumber, and wheat products to Spain, Portugal, and the Wine Islands. Salt, fruits, and wine were then taken to England and exchanged for manufactured goods, which were returned to America. But southern European trade could consist of two-way transactions, since the Navigation Acts permitted the direct colonial importation of certain commodities that could be obtained in Europe.

Such triangles and other more complex patterns of northern shipping, including multilateral routes and route switching, did occur frequently. But such practices were not predominant; in fact, they were the exception (although the exceptions were numerous). Recent research has revealed that the

TABLE 5–1
The Percentage Share of Each Colonial Region's Commodity Trade to Each Overseas Area, 1768–1772 (imports are in parentheses)

	Great Britain and Ireland	Southern Europe	West Indies	Africa
New England	18 (66)	14 (2)	64 (32)	4 (0)
Middle Colonies	23 (76)	33 (3)	44 (21)	0 (0)
Upper South	83 (89)	9 (1)	8 (10)	0 (0)
Lower South	72 (86)	9 (1)	19 (13)	0 (0)
Total	56 (80)	18 (2)	26 (18)	1 (0)

Source: James F. Shepherd and Gary M. Walton, *Shipping, Maritime Trade and the Economic Development of Colonial North America* (Cambridge: Cambridge University Press, 1972), pp. 160–61.

more customary practices of shippers in New England and the Middle Colonies were to follow shuttle patterns and engage in route specialization.[3] In addition, the ships of these regions captured almost all of the coastal trades as well as the trades between themselves and the other overseas areas, especially trades to the West Indies.

The evolution of these patterns of shipping and trade dominance were determined primarily by three critical factors: the high risks of maritime trade, the problems of acquiring and responding to information about markets, and the persistence of high labor costs. Consider, as examples, why New England shippers dominated the New England–West Indies trade route and why the British captured most of the trade to the southern colonies.

In marketing their goods, New England merchants typically consigned them either to ship captains or to selling agents, called *factors,* who were stationed in overseas markets. Since these methods necessitated placing a high degree of trust in a third party, it is not surprising that colonial merchants favored colonial ship captains. After all, a greater familiarity and more frequent contact between merchant and agent lowered the risks of trade.

Due to the rudimentary forms of communication and transportation in existence at the time, geographical closeness to a market was an important advantage. For example, British shippers and merchants in the tobacco trade could acquire information about changing market conditions in the Chesapeake Bay area and in Europe more easily than New England shippers could. However, in trades to the West Indies, colonial shippers and merchants were nearer to their market and could respond more quickly to fluctuations in it. Because being close to a market reduced the cost of obtaining market information and allowed merchants to respond with more timely cargo arrivals, this also reduced the risks of trade.

Finally, the efficient use of labor time was always an important factor. It was general practice in colonial times for crews to be paid while a vessel was docked in foreign ports, and crews were normally discharged only at the end of the voyage in the home port. This meant that British crews in the tobacco trade were paid for the time they spent at sea and in southern colonial ports, but not for their port time in England. Therefore, New England shippers were at a disadvantage on this trade route, because they paid wages both in British ports and in the Chesapeake Bay. Alternatively, colonial shippers faced lower labor costs on trade routes between their home ports and the Caribbean.

These same considerations played a large role in determining the routes of trade. Although the desire to keep vessels as fully loaded as possible encouraged "tramping" from port to port to take advantage of differences in demand and cargo availability, such a practice often incurred offsetting large costs. For example, a New England ship captain in the West Indies trade, acting on behalf of his merchant, would attempt to locate the best markets for the commodities he carried. This might require several voyages among the islands before agreeing on prices, the medium of exchange, and even the question of settling past debts. Transactions were often complex even when the merchants

[3] See Gary M. Walton, "New Evidence on Colonial Commerce," *Journal of Economic History* **XXVIII:**3 (September 1968), pp. 363–89.

and captains were acquainted with one another. Of course, in unfamiliar markets, poor communications, credit limitations, and other vexatious details compounded the difficulties. For all these reasons, arrivals at strange ports often resulted in delays and costly extensions of port times; therefore, captains usually maintained regular runs between a limited number of familiar destinations. The practice of discharging crews only in their home ports further supported the growth of shuttle trade routes, because they increased the percentage of total port time that was home port (wage free) time.

Domestic Trade

We can generalize about colonial domestic commerce, but we cannot make many definite statistical estimates of its volume. Back-country people traded their small agricultural surpluses for the necessities they could not produce themselves—salt, medicines, ammunition, cotton yarn, tea or coffee, and the like. In the villages and towns, households were not as self sufficient. Although even the wealthiest homes produced some goods for everyday consumption, wherever people lived in community groups, the advantages of specialization were too obvious to be overlooked.

In the complex of colonial domestic trade, between country and town, it became common practice for the town merchant to extend credit to farmers, either directly or through the so-called country traders who served as intermediaries. Advances were made for the purposes of obtaining both capital equipment, such as tools and building hardware, and the supplies necessary for day-to-day existence. At the end of a growing season, farmers brought their produce to town to discharge their debts. In times of seriously depressed agricultural prices, farmers might be substantially in debt by the end of the year, and two or three bad years in a row could result in foreclosure and the loss of a farm with its improvements. The outcome was that many farmers gave up and moved farther west, and merchants or other propertied people who were able to withstand the vicissitudes of crop failures and wide swings in agricultural prices took the titles to these farms. As we will learn in Chapter 7, this changed the distribution of wealth in colonial times in some important ways.

A second important characteristic of colonial domestic trade was the comparatively great volume of coastwise commerce. Early in the seventeenth century, the Dutch of New Amsterdam had anticipated the profit potential in distributing European products along the coast in exchange for tobacco, furs, grain, and fish, which were then sent to Holland. After the Dutch lost power in North America, their hold on the trade declined, and New Englanders—together with enterprising merchants in New York and Philadelphia—dominated trade between Europe and North America.

The entrepôt trade started by the Dutch continued; Boston, New York, and Philadelphia, each dominant in its own trading area, became important centers in the exchange of European and colonial goods. Gradually, northern traders extended their operations southward, and although direct trade between the southern plantations and Great Britain remained the primary source of southern colonial income, a substantial amount of southern staples were exchanged

Boston's natural endowments helped the city attain a place of prominence as a trading and shipping center; but the mountains to the west inhibited access to the hinterland, and Boston ultimately fell behind New York in the commercial rivalry between these two great ports.

for northern products. Such commerce arose partly in connection with the West Indian trade. It was natural for vessels passing southern ports and plantation wharves to dock to see if they could pick up or sell some additional cargo. Perhaps more important, as time went on, were the off-season trips of Yankee fishermen. As one writer tells us

> During the winter, when there was little fishing carried on, the owners of small fishing sloops would load their craft with salt, rum, sugar, molasses, iron and wooden ware, hats, caps, cloth, handkerchiefs, and stockings, which they carried to the southern colonies and peddled from place to place, returning early in the spring with a valuable lot of pitch and tar and supplies of corn and pickled pork. These trading expeditions of the fisherman were private ventures entirely, which offered a good opportunity to secure a profit even during the winter season from the investment in fishing craft.[4]

In terms of the money value of products exchanged, coastal commerce was less than foreign trade with either Britain or the West Indies, but in physi-

[4] E. R. Johnson et al., *History of Domestic and Foreign Commerce of the United States* (Washington, D.C.: Carnegie Institution of Washington, 1915), pp. 169–70.

cal volume it was equal to each of these major trade branches. Just before the Revolution, coastwise trade comprised about one-third of the volume of total overseas trade.[5] Compared to the North, the coastwise commerce of the South was much less important, but even there it comprised perhaps one-fifth of the tonnage that entered and cleared southern ports.[6]

TRANSPORTATION AND COMMUNICATION

As we have repeatedly emphasized, communication and commerce among the important centers of colonial America during the seventeenth century were mostly by sea. At first, Americans settled near reasonably safe harbors or along navigable streams, for the obvious reason that these places were readily accessible. Before 1700, roads were little more than paths, and land travel was both difficult and dangerous. Even well into the eighteenth century, the wise traveler followed a coastal route by ship whenever possible. Even Benjamin Franklin transferred his residence from Boston to Philadelphia by sea. The schooner—a two- or three-masted, fore-and-aft-rigged ship developed in New England—made the best of adverse winds and also economized on manpower. Both the schooner and the sloop (of similar construction but with a single mast), were used in coastal trade. In certain regions, special types of crafts evolved; a typical example was the sharpie, developed in the Chesapeake Bay area specifically to traverse shallow waters.

Two factors continued to make sea travel preferable to land travel between the colonies: the excessive cost of land transportation, and the bulky nature of the commodities produced in the colonial period. But as the population increased, people were forced to move away from the waterways and into the interior, and land travel became increasingly necessary. Nearby communities—as soon as they could afford the considerable expense—became linked to one another by roads. During the eighteenth century, a road system began to emerge. By 1760, a rough road ran from Boston through Providence, New York, Philadelphia, Baltimore, and on to Charleston (see Map 5-1). Somewhat later, Forbes Road crossed Pennsylvania to Pittsburgh, and the Wilderness Road furnished a passageway through the Shenandoah Valley. Roads that were little more than trails connected the back country with strategic points along the fall line of the rivers, so that goods and passengers could be carried by boat to the ocean. From the major port towns, some reasonably good roads penetrated 50 miles into the interior.

According to contemporary descriptions, even the main roads were in a wretched condition except during the dry season. In fact, travel in some areas was easiest when heavy snow had been packed down so that it filled the worst holes and covered major obstacles. Until rather late in the colonial period, the most comfortable means of passenger travel on land was by horseback, and almost all land freight was carried by pack trains of a dozen or more horses. As the eighteenth century progressed, stagecoaches began to travel on the better

[5] James F. Shepherd and Samuel Williamson, "The Coastal Trade of the British North American Colonies 1768–1772," *Journal of Economic History* **XXXII:**4 (December 1972), pp. 783–810.

[6] Johnson, pp. 171–72.

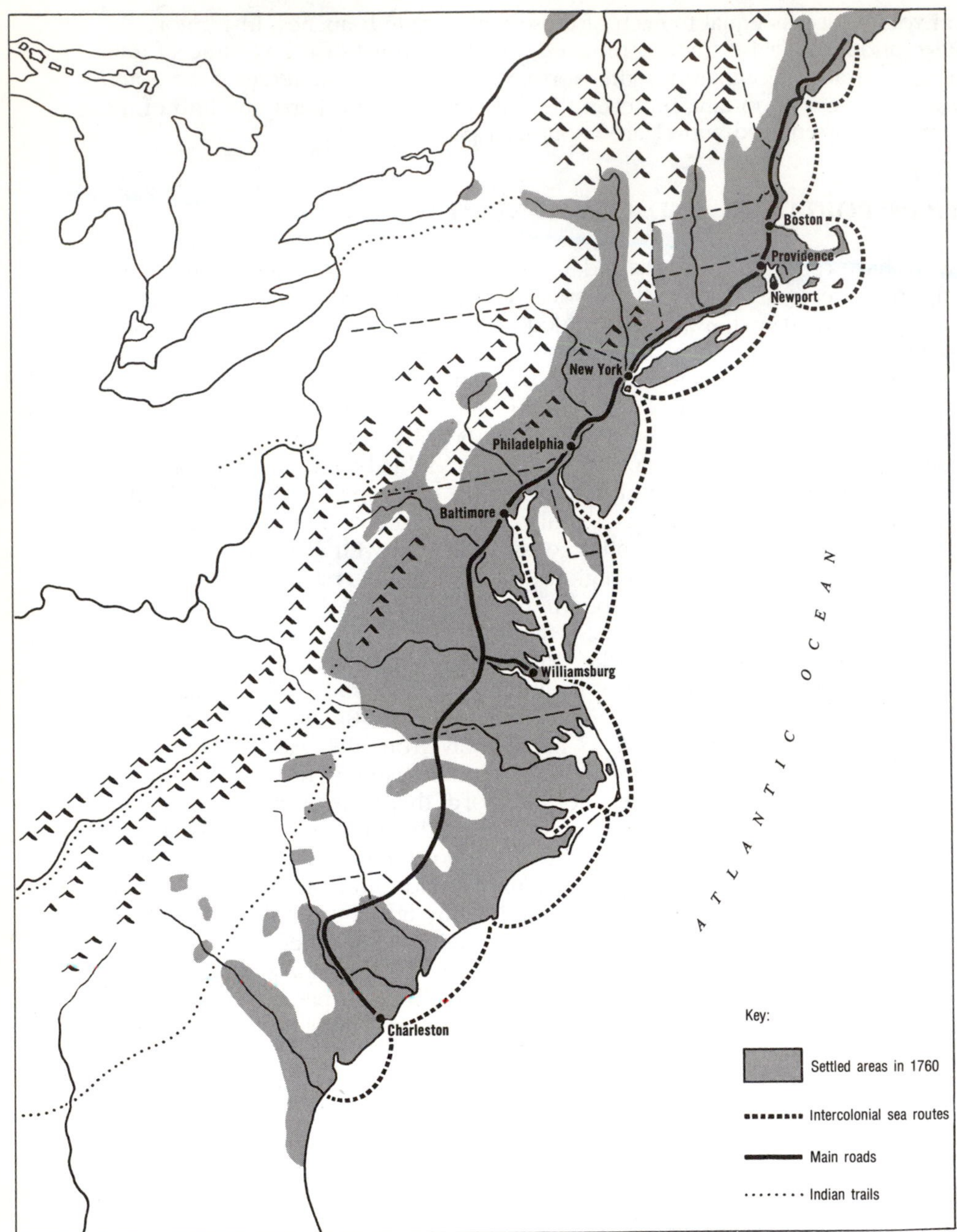

MAP 5–1

Transportation: Slow and hazardous overland travel in 1760 placed a premium on building better roads and developing alternate means of moving people and goods, particularly by waterway.

roads, and in the decade before the Revolution, it was possible to travel by stage from New York to Philadelphia in two days. For freight carriage, the Conestoga wagon—the forerunner of the covered wagon—proved reasonably efficient and reliable but, like its passenger counterpart, was limited to use on fairly level, well-kept roads.

Naturally, communication was slow and expensive at first, but by the late seventeenth century, a postal service with rates charged on the basis of weight and distance carried had been established in the main urban centers. The early mail system was under the jurisdiction of colonial governments, but in 1710, an American postal system was established under the English Post Office. During Benjamin Franklin's term as deputy postmaster (1753–1775), the American system grew and improved markedly. Post riders began to make more frequent trips and to travel both night and day. Newspapers were admitted to the mails, and postal charges were reduced, with a consequent increase in the use of the service. Even so, it took six days for a letter to travel from Boston to Philadelphia, and as late as 1760, there were only eight mailings a year from Philadelphia to points south of the Potomac River. Postal rates remained so high that letters were frequently given to travelers or to ship masters for delivery.

At the time of the Revolution, it took about three weeks for news of any importance to spread to the chief settlements throughout the colonies. Those who lived on the frontier often waited much longer to learn of major events and were almost completely isolated from reports on such mundane matters as the state of trade markets. But the postal facilities in America were not much worse than those in the Old World. Even in the highly developed economies of western Europe, communication was still slow and uncertain. Bluff-bowed sailing ships took from four to six weeks to cross the Atlantic. The colonial economy was shaped in part by the difficulties of overland travel and the slowness of communication in the New World, but these hindrances were common to all peoples of the eighteenth century world.

6

Money, Trade, and Capital

THE COLONIAL MONEY SUPPLY

An act passed by the newly elected legislature of Tennessee read:

> Be it enacted by the General Assembly of the State of Franklin and it is hereby enacted by the authority of the same, that from the first day of January A.D. 1789, the salaries of the officers of this Commonwealth shall be as follows, to wit:
>
> His Excellency, the Governor, per annum, 1,000 deer skins.
>
> His Honor, the Chief Justice, 500 deer skins.
>
> Attorney General, 500 deer skins.
>
> Secretary of State, 500 raccoon skins.
>
> Secretary of the Treasury, 450 otter skins.
>
> Each County Clerk, 300 beaver skins.
>
> Clerk of the House of Commons, 200 raccoon skins.
>
> Members of the General Assembly, per diem, three raccoon skins.
>
> Justice of the Peace fee for signing a warrant, one muskrat skin.
>
> Ministers of the gospel for marrying the people, eight mink skins.
>
> Be it enacted by the General Assembly of the State of Franklin that no citizen shall neglect the proper training of children in the schools. And be it further enacted that a fine of 20 mink skins shall be imposed on all those settlers who neglect sending their children to the nearest schoolteacher, etc.
>
> Enacted into a law this 18th day of October, 1789, under the Great Seal of the State.
>
> Witness His Excellency, John Sevier, Governor.
>
> Samuel Newel, Secretary of State.[1]

We may smile at this unsophisticated way of paying public officials, but the implicit problem it presents—establishing and maintaining an acceptable currency—was pervasive in colonial America. One of the earliest solutions—borrowed from the Indians by the first New England settlers—was to use wampum for money. These black and white polished shells, which circulated for several decades after the founding of the colonies, were legal tender for private debts in Massachusetts until 1661 and were used as money in New York as late as 1701. Throughout the colonies, almost every imaginable commodity was monetized at some time. In Maryland and Virginia, tobacco remained the principal medium of exchange long after its value had declined from three shillings to a penny or two a pound; indeed, the monetization of tobacco actually stimulated its production and thereby furthered its depreciation in value. Other colonies designated as "country pay" (acceptable for taxes) such items as hides, furs, tallow, cows, corn, wheat, beans, pork, fish, brandy, whiskey, and musket balls. Harried public officials were endlessly swindled because they received such a poor quality of "country pay," but just as serious was the cost of transporting the commodities received for taxes and loss through shrinkage and deterioration.[2] What public treasuries would accept, private merchants could not refuse. Until his death in 1764,[3] Thomas Hancock, John's uncle, in conducting business with the country merchants of New England, had to accept commodities and pass them on to reluctant creditors in turn.

Commodity money was used most extensively in the early days of the colonies and in areas where coins were especially scarce. By the end of the seventeenth century, both specie[4] and paper currencies were common in the five major seaboard cities, and by the end of the eighteenth century, commodities—particularly furs—were accepted as a medium of exchange only in communities along the western frontier.

Due to sizable trades with many overseas areas, the gold and silver coins of all the important commercial countries of Europe and their dependencies in the Western Hemisphere were freely exchanged throughout the eastern seaboard. More important than English coins, especially after 1700, were the silver coins of the Spanish mint, which were struck for the most part in Mexico City and Lima and introduced into the colonial economy via vigorous trading with the Spanish colonies. English-speaking peoples referred to the "piece of eight" (as the old Spanish peso was called) as a "dollar," probably because it was about the size of the German *thaler.* Spanish dollars were so common in the colonies that the coin was eventually adopted as the monetary unit of the

[1] Claude A. Campbell, *The Development of Banking in Tennessee* (published by the author, 1932), pp. 14–15.

[2] Charles J. Bullock, *Essays on the Monetary History of the United States* (New York: Macmillan, 1900), p. 11.

[3] A friend's comment on this passage: "What is implied as being reluctance to accept country pay by public officials and merchants was merely part of the haggling process made necessary by the less certain value of the currency." Precisely! Moreover, retailers accepting country pay were forced to look for and to maintain export outlets for a wide variety of products—a time-consuming activity.

[4] *Specie* is any monetary unit, gold or silver, whether it is in the form of bullion (bars) or coins. Oddly, the word was used by some colonials to designate country pay.

United States. The fractional coin, known as the "real" or "bit," was worth about 12½ cents, or one-eighth of a Spanish dollar, and was important in making change.[5]

The colonials complained endlessly about the scarcity of gold and silver coin, and for a century and a half they tried hard to persuade British officials to establish separate colonial mints. It would do no good, they felt, to strike colonial coins in England of English weight and fineness, because these coins would flow right back out of the colonial economy again as a consequence of the continuing favorable British balance of payments. The persistent drain of European coins convinced the colonists that they needed a special money comprised of coins that contained less metal than standard British coins.[6] For this reason, Massachusetts established a mint in 1652, striking the famed pine-tree shilling that contained only 72 grains of silver, compared with the 93 grains in the standard English shilling. But this monetary experiment proved disappointing for two reasons. First, reducing the silver content of the shilling did not give it a higher value at home than abroad, because importers simply raised the price of English goods to correspond with the reduced bullion content of the Massachusetts coin. Second, despite a ban on the exportation of the pine-tree shilling, they were dispersed anyway at approximately their actual value in silver. Although the Massachusetts experience should have been a convincing deterrent to other colonials, only heavy British opposition kept other colonies from attempting a similar remedy.

It is not surprising to learn that the colonies turned to paper to increase their meager and undependable money supply, and settlers became accustomed to paper money at an early date. The promissory notes of well-known individuals often exchanged hands for several months. Bills of exchange drawn on English merchants or various government officials in London also circulated as money. Treasurers of the different colonies began to issue promissory notes in advance of tax collection or to issue written orders to town officers requiring the payment of obligations from local stores; like other negotiable instruments, these pieces of paper were exchanged on endorsement as money.[7]

In 1690, Massachusetts issued the first bills of credit to pay soldiers who had returned from an unsuccessful military expedition. During the next 65 years, at least eight other colonies followed this example to meet financial emergencies. Bills of credit were issued with the proviso that they were to be redeemed in specie at some future date; in the meantime, they were accepted for taxes by the issuing colony. Such redemption provisions, although restricted, facilitated the free circulation of these bills as money. In some states—notably Rhode Island, Massachusetts, Connecticut, and Virginia—the bills were commonly overissued, thereby depreciating their value relative to specie. The same difficulty was encountered with the paper, of the publicly

[5] The "piece of eight" was so called in colloquial language because of the numeral *VIII* impressed on one side to indicate its value of eight *reales.* In many parts of the United States, the expressions *two bits, four bits,* and *six bits* are still used today.

[6] See Curtis P. Nettels, *The Money Supply of the American Colonies Before 1720* (Madison: University of Wisconsin, 1934), pp. 162–78.

[7] Nettels, pp. 250–51.

owned "banks" established by colonial governments.[8] These institutions, unlike anything we call a bank today, issued "loan bills," lending to individuals, usually based on the security of land or personal property. Borrowers used the bills to meet their obligations and were usually required to repay the debt, with interest, in annual installments.

A third kind of paper money, similar to the paper issued by the public loan banks, was the paper of privately owned "land banks." These organizations, about which little is known today, were associations of landowners who contributed to the bank mortgages on real property in exchange for bills, which they then passed as currency. The schemes of most private entrepreneurs were short-lived, and only in Massachusetts were repeated attempts—including the great Land Bank of 1740—made to establish a major financial institution. But private associations were formed in at least five other colonies, and it seems likely that only Parliamentary interference in 1741 forestalled the ultimate success of a private venture.

Colonial assemblies became involved in the competitive devaluation of currency early in their economic history. By raising the legal rates at which coins would pass within their own jurisdictions, they hoped to gain definite economic advantages. Colonial legislators reasoned that if the Spanish dollar were received within a colony at 5s. or 6s. (or even 7s. or 8s.), rather than at 4s. 6d., pieces of eight would be attracted to the colony and would, moreover, remain there. Furthermore, a cheaper currency would be provided for the payment of debts, because colonial laws placing values on pieces of eight made them the "lawful money" of the province, and debtors could therefore settle their obligations in fewer Spanish dollars than the amount required by the earlier and lower evaluation.

As is often true of economic panaceas, this one worked temporarily but proved defective after some time had elapsed. The colony that made the Spanish dollar relatively more valuable within its confines gained at least a temporary advantage in the competition for specie. Pirates were induced to bring their gold and silver to ports where its legal value was highest, and the colonies that most freely harbored pirates usually placed the highest value on pirate coin.[9] Unquestionably, foreign traders were attracted to the ports of Boston, Philadelphia, New York, and Charleston partly because exchange rates were sometimes relatively favorable there. But as the supply of coins increased in any locality, the prices of local products rose, so that ultimately a Spanish dollar at an arbitrarily high value would buy no more than it would have bought at its old value. Then there was always the renewed temptation to continue to increase the legal value of the dollar.

We may wonder why the English Parliament did not intervene and establish some kind of monetary uniformity in the colonies. In fact, as early as 1704, the Board of Trade did attempt to equalize the rate of exchange between the colonial shilling and the Spanish dollar by obtaining a royal proclamation making 6 s. the maximum rating of the Spanish coin. When the four leading com-

[8]Bullock reminded us that "during the entire colonial period, the word *bank* meant simply a batch of paper money." Bullock, p. 29.

[9]Nettels, p. 232.

mercial colonies defied this proclamation, Parliament passed a law in 1708 prescribing that any colonist who paid or received coin at a higher value than the proclamation rate would be imprisoned for six months or pay a fine of £10. Yet the law was flouted with impunity, and in any case, by 1720, most colonists were no longer altering the value of foreign coins as an inflationary device but were relying instead on paper money issues to achieve these objectives.

During the eighteenth century, there was continuing conflict—especially in New England—over the currency question. As in every community throughout recorded history, there were advocates of "sound" money, who took the position that efforts to increase the money supply beyond the quantity of coin in circulation were both unethical and dangerous. On the whole, however, American colonists were disposed toward "cheap" money and a rapidly increasing money stock. Primarily farmers and exporters of raw materials, Americans wanted prices to rise to increase money incomes and to provide relief from debt. Farmers clearly favored the establishment of land banks so that they could obtain money at low interest rates by offering their land as security. And many merchants, themselves debtors, joined with the agrarians to urge continuing issuances of paper. At last the Crown had to settle the controversy—largely, however, at the instigation of the English rather than the colonial merchants. The Currency Act of 1751 prohibited the New England colonies from issuing further bills of credit and from organizing new land banks. Furthermore, existing note issues were to be retired as they fell due.[10] More important, from the point of view of its ultimate political consequences, was the Restraining Act of 1764, which extended the provision of the Currency Act to all the colonies. Directed chiefly at Virginia, which had just issued £250,000 in bills of credit, the act brought loud protests from planters and merchants in all the southern colonies, while British merchants, who objected that debts due in specie were being paid in paper money issued in great quantity during the French and Indian War, nodded approval. Coming as it did during a severe postwar depression, the Restraining Act aroused much animosity.

One of the most perplexing problems to confront the founding fathers a few years later was the establishment of a uniform, efficient currency. Indeed, the conflict between the advocates of "cheap" and "sound" money has continued throughout our history and is still an important issue today.

TRADE DEFICITS WITH ENGLAND

The variety of measures implemented by the Crown to regulate trade and to generate favorable trade balances for the Empire overshadowed similar attempts at trade regulation by the colonials. Nevertheless, the continual drain of

[10] As one writer put it, the Currency Act of 1751 "did not abolish the paper money system in that area, as is sometimes supposed, but merely established rules for continuing it." But it was difficult enough to adhere to the rules. The one really liberal provision of the act permitted the New England provinces to emit bills from year to year to meet government expenses—provided that taxes were sufficient to redeem the bills within two years—thereby permitting a moderate increase in the currency. See E. James Ferguson, *The Power of the Purse* (Chapel Hill: The University of North Carolina Press, 1961), p. 2.

TABLE 6–1
Values and Balances of Commodity Trade Between England and the American Colonies (annual averages by decade in thousands of pounds sterling)

	Imports	—	Exports	=	Deficit
1721–1730	£ 509		£ 442		£67
1731–1740	698		559		139
1741–1750	923		599		324
1751–1760	1,704		808		809
1761–1770	1,942		1,203		739

Source: James F. Shepherd and Gary M. Walton, *Shipping, Maritime Trade, and the Economic Development of Colonial North America* (London: Cambridge University Press, 1972), p. 42.

specie from colonial shores and the pervasive unstable conditions of various colonial currencies were matters of grave concern in the colonies. Because European manufactured goods were in great demand in the New World, colonists faced chronic deficits, especially in their trade with England. Table 6-1 shows the size and trend of these deficits over much of the eighteenth century. As we will soon see, most of these deficits were incurred by New England and the Middle Colonies, but even the Southern Colonies frequently faced deficits in their commodity trade with England.

Benjamin Franklin's reply to a Parliamentary committee in 1760 explaining Pennsylvania's payment of its trade deficit with England was

> The balance is paid by our produce carried to the West Indies, and sold in our own islands, or to the French, Spaniards, Danes, and Dutch; by the same carried to other colonies in North America, as to New England, Nova Scotia, Newfoundland, Carolina, and Georgia; by the same carried to different parts of Europe, as Spain, Portugal and Italy: In all which places we receive either money, bills of exchange, or commodities that suit for remittance to Britain; which, together with all the profits on the industry of our merchants and mariners arising in those circuitous voyages and the freights made by their ships, center finally in Britain to discharge the balance and pay for British manufactures continually used in the province or sold to foreigners by our traders.[11]

As emphasized by the esteemed Franklin, colonial trade deficits to Britain could be paid by surpluses earned in trades to other overseas areas as well as by earnings from shipping and other mercantile services. Of course, other sources of foreign exchange, such as expenditures by the British defense forces stationed in the colonies, also affected the inflow of sterling. To determine the relative importance of these and other sources of exchange earnings (and losses), we need to assess the various components of the colonies' overall balance of payments. But more was at stake than the mere question of how the trade deficits with Great Britain were paid. The problem of chronic money

[11] Harold U. Faulkner, *American Economic History,* 8th ed. (New York: Harper & Row, 1960), p. 81.

shortages was vital to the colonists. Were colonial trade deficits with Britain offset by surpluses in other trades or by other exchange earnings? Or did overall trade cause a persistent net drain of specie from the colonies? Alternatively, were the trade deficits financed by capital inflows to the colonies and by growing colonial indebtedness to British creditors? Was indebtedness to Britain increasing, and thereby providing a possible motivation for colonial revolt? Were capital inflows sizable, and did they contribute significantly to the economic development of the colonies? Could these inflows be construed as "foreign aid," signifying extensive British subsidization of colonial development? Although somewhat complex, a study of the colonial balance of payments will shed much light on these important issues.

A BALANCE OF PAYMENTS FOR THE THIRTEEN COLONIES

Surviving information on the myriad of exchanges for the years 1768–1772 gives us a reasonably clear picture of the colonies' balance of payments in the late colonial period. A breakdown of the colonies' commodity trade balances with the major overseas areas during this period is provided in Table 6-2. These data confirm the findings presented in Table 6-1, indicating that sizable deficits were incurred in the English trade, especially by New England and the Middle Colonies. Somewhat surprisingly, even the colonies' commodity trade to the West Indies was slightly unfavorable (except for the trade of the lower South). However, trades to southern Europe generated significant surpluses (augmented slightly by the African trades) that were sufficient to raise the southern colonial regions to a surplus position in their overall commodity exchanges.

Although commodity exchanges made up the lion's share of total colonial exchanges, the colonies did have other sources of foreign exchange earnings (and losses) as well. Table 6-3 begins with colonial commodity exchanges, indictating the £1,121 aggregate deficit in that category:

TABLE 6–2

Average Annual Commodity Trade Balances of the Thirteen American Colonies, 1768–1772 (in thousands of pounds sterling)

	Great Britain and Ireland	Southern Europe	West Indies	Africa	All Trades
New England	– 609	+ 48	–36	+19	– 577
Middle Colonies	– 786	+153	–10	+ 1	– 643
Upper South	– 50	+ 90	– 9	0	+ 30
Lower South	– 23	+ 48	+44	0	+ 69
Total Colonies	–1,468	+339	–11	+20	–1,121

Notes: (1) A plus sign denotes a surplus (exports exceed imports); a minus sign, a deficit (imports exceed exports).

(2) Values are expressed in prices in the mainland colonies; thus, import values include the costs of transportation, commissions, and other handling costs. Export values are also expressed in colonial prices and therefore do not include these distribution costs.

Source: Shepherd and Walton, p. 115.

TABLE 6–3
A Balance of Payments for the Thirteen American Colonies, 1768–1772 (annual averages in thousands of pounds sterling)

	Credit	Debit
Commodities		
Exports	2,800	
Imports		3,920
Balance of trade		1,121
Ship Sales	140	
"Invisible" earnings		
Shipping earnings	600	
Merchant commissions, risk, and insurance	220	
Balance on current account from trade		160
Payments for human beings		
Indentured servants		80
Slaves		200
British collections and expenditures in colonies		
Taxes and duties		40
Salaries of British civil servants	40	
Military expenditures	230	
Naval expenditures	170	
Capital and monetary flows		
Specie		
Indebtedness	40	

Notes: See notes to Table 6-2, page 84.
Source: Table is derived from Sheperd and Walton, Chapters 6, 7, and 8.

The most important source of foreign exchange earnings to offset that average deficit was the sale of colonial shipping services. Shipping earnings totaled approximately £600,000 per year in the late colonial period. In addition, colonial merchants earned more than £200,000 annually through insurance charges and commissions. Together, these "invisible" earnings offset more than 60 percent of the overall colonial commodity trade deficit. Almost 80 percent of these invisible earnings reverted to residents of New England and the Middle Colonies. Thus, the mercantile activities of New Englanders and middle colonists, especially in the West Indian trade, enabled the colonies to import large quantities of manufactured goods from Great Britain. When all thirteen colonies are considered together, invisible earnings exceeded earnings from tobacco exports—the single most important colonial staple export.

Another aspect of seafaring, the sale of ships, also became a persistent credit item in the colonies' balance of payments. Recently, Jacob Price has suggested that colonial ship sales averaged at least £140,000 annually from 1763 to 1775,[12] primarily to England. Again, the lion's share of these earnings went to New England ship builders, but the Middle Colonies also received a portion

[12]Jacob M. Price, "A Note on the Value of Colonial Exports of Shipping," *Journal of Economic History* **XXXVI**:3 (September 1976), pp. 704–24.

of the profits from ship sales. Taken together, ship sales and "invisible" earnings reduced the colonies' negative balance of payments to only £160,000.

In contrast to these earning sources, funds for the trade in human beings were continually lost to foreign markets. An average of approximately £80,000 sterling was spent annually for the 5,000–10,000 indentured servants who arrived annually during the late colonial period. Most of these servants were sent to Pennsylvania and the Chesapeake Bay area. A more sizable amount was the nearly £200,000 spent each year to purchase approximately 5,000 slaves. Over 90 percent of these slaves were sent to the Southern Colonies, especially to the lower South in the later colonial period.

Finally, expenditures made by the British government in the colonies on defense, civil administration, and justice notably offset the remaining deficits in the colonists' current account of trade. Table 6-3 does not indicate the total amount of these costs to Great Britain. Instead, it shows how much British currency was used to purchase goods and services in the colonies and how much colonial revenue was extracted by the British government for such things as customs duties. Curiously, the cost of civil and customs administration frequently exceeded the collection of customs revenues,[13] but in Table 6-3 we have conservatively displayed these as equal amounts. In contrast, British military and naval expenditures provided a significant inflow of sterling to the colonies. During this period, the standing British army consisted of 16 regiments. At full strength, the pay and subsistence for a single regiment totaled almost £18,000 per year, but desertion, illness, and casualties normally kept military units below full strength. The total annual cost to maintain 16 regiments with an average strength of 80 percent was approximately £230,000. Undoubtedly, these soldiers spent almost all of their pay and subsistence in the colonies.

The Royal Navy's North American squadron was comprised of about 27 vessels of various sizes during this period. Taking into consideration that many of the vessels were undermanned and that sailors usually had fewer opportunities than soldiers to spend their wages ashore, the full complement of £260,000 of navy pay probably did not pour into the colonial tills. Nevertheless, it seems reasonable to presume that between £150,000 and £200,000 was spent in the colonies each year, making average annual British naval expenditures in the colonies about £170,000.

Total British defense expenditures in the colonies probably exceeded £400,000 annually in the late colonial period. If so, this inflow of funds to the colonies reduced the deficit in the colonial balance of payments to £40,000 per year or less.

Money, Debt, and Capital

The estimated remaining annual colonial deficit of £40,000 was paid either by an outflow of specie or by growing indebtedness to Britain. Temporary net outflows of specie undoubtedly did occur, thereby straining trade and

[13] For instance, one authority claims that "to collect £2,000 in customs duties in the colonies cost the British government £8,000." See John C. Miller, *Origins of the American Revolution* (Stanford, Ca.: Stanford University Press, 1959), p. 83.

prices in the colonies. But no significant part of this normal deficit could have been paid persistently with precious metals. The colonists could not sustain a permanent net outflow of specie because gold and silver mines had yet to be developed in colonial North America. Typically, then, the outflow of specie to England was matched by an inflow from various sources of colonial exchange earnings. Nevertheless, the erratic pattern of specie movement and the issuance of paper money of uncertain value caused monetary disturbances. But most colonists preferred to spend rather than to accumulate a stock of specie. After all, limited specie was simply another manifestation of a capital-scarce economy. To the colonists, it was more desirable to receive additional imports—especially manufacturers—than to maintain a growing stock of specie.

The final remaining colonial deficits were normally financed on short-term credit, and American merchants usually purchased goods from England on one-year credit. This was so customary, in fact, that British merchants included a normal 5 percent interest charge in their prices and granted a rebate to accounts that were paid before the year ended. And in Virginia, Scottish firms generally established representatives in stores to sell or trade British wares for tobacco and other products. Short-term credit was a normal part of day-to-day colonial exchanges in these instances.

The growth of short-term credit reflected the expanding Atlantic trades and represented a modest amount of increasing colonial indebtedness to Britain. Sizable claims against southern planters by British merchants after the Revolution[14] have encouraged some historians to argue that the relationship between London merchants and southern planters was disastrous at that time and even to argue that increasing colonial indebtedness to Britain provided impetus for the Revolution. But was this, in fact, so?

By adding the "invisible" earnings and ship sales to the regional commodity trade deficits (and surpluses), we obtain these rough averages of the regional deficits (–) and surpluses (+) in the colonies.[15]

New England	–£ 50,000
Middle Colonies	– 350,000
Southern Colonies	+ 240,000

Clearly, the major deficit regions were north of the Chesapeake Bay area—primarily in the Middle Colonies. The southern regions were favored with

[14] Of the approximately £5,000,000 claimed by British merchants in 1791, more than £2,300,000 was owed by Virginia; nearly £570,000, by Maryland; £690,000, by South Carolina; £380,000, by North Carolina; and £250,000, by Georgia. However, nearly one-half of these amounts represented accumulated interest on deficits that had been in effect since 1776. Moreover, Aubrey Land argues that these claims were exaggerated by as much as 800 percent, and in fact, the Americans honored only one-eighth of such claims. See Aubrey C. Land, "Economic Behavior in a Planting Society: The Eighteenth Century Chesapeake," *Journal of Southern History* **XXXII:**4 (November 1967), pp. 482–83.

[15] The regional division of shipping earnings and other "invisibles" is derived from Shepherd and Walton, Chapter 7. Because the ownership of vessels is not given separately for the upper South and the lower South, we have combined these two regions here, but undoubtedly the upper South earned the greater portion of the combined £240,000 surplus. All ship sales have been credited to the northern regions; £100,000 to New England and £40,000 to the Middle Colonies.

more than a sufficient surplus in their current accounts of trade to pay for their purchases of slaves and indentured servants.

Since British defense expenditures in the South added to colonial exchange, there can be little doubt that this area suffered no *growing* indebtedness or net specie drain in the late colonial period.[16]

Nevertheless, England's claims were real enough, although they may have been exaggerated. But remember that British merchants and their colonial representatives normally extended credit to southern planters and accepted their potential harvests as collateral. Usually, of course, the harvests came in, and the colonists' outstanding debts were paid. But with the outbreak of the Revolution, this picture changed radically. Colonial credit normally extended throughout the year was still outstanding at the end of the year, because agents or partners of British firms had retreated home before the crops were harvested and the debts were paid. But the mere existence of these debts did not indicate growing indebtedness—nor did it provide motivation for colonial revolt.

The capital inflows that did occur were rarely channeled directly into long-term investments in the colonies, and British merchants held few claims on such investments. Nevertheless, it is important to realize that because this credit was furnished by the British, colonial savings were freed for other uses: to make long-term investments in land improvement, roads, and such physical capital as ships, warehouses, and public buildings. For the purposes of colonial development, British short-term credit represented a helping hand, and its form was much less important than its amount.

However, with the highly important exception of military and civil defense, the colonies apparently were not subsidized by Britain to any great extent. For the most part, the formation of capital in the New World was dependent on the steady accretion of savings and investment from the pockets of the colonists themselves. It is impossible to determine precisely how much was annually saved and invested in the late colonial period. According to our estimates, which will be elaborated in Chapter 7, incomes probably averaged at least £15 sterling per person (man, woman, or child). Since more than 2 million people were living in the colonies on the eve of the Revolution, if we assume a savings rate of not less than 7 percent (£1 out of £15), total capital accumulation per year undoubtedly exceeded 2 million pounds at that time. Thus, the capital inflow from Britain probably contributed less than 2 percent to domestic capital formation.

Only when we consider England's civil government and defense expenditures in the colonies does the British contribution to colonial capital assume impressive dimensions (close to 20 percent). As the young nation was quickly to learn after achieving its independence, the real financial burdens of self-protection in a hostile world war were costly indeed.

[16] Further alteration of the regional deficits and surpluses would have resulted from coastal trade among the regions. Surprisingly, however, all major regions in the thirteen colonies appear to have earned surpluses in coastal trade. Florida, the Bahamas, and the Bermuda Islands and the Northern Colonies of Newfoundland, Nova Scotia, and Quebec, were the deficit areas in coastal trade. See James F. Shepherd and Samuel H. Williamson, "The Coastal Trade of the British North American Colonies, 1768–1772," *Journal of Economic History* **XXXII:**4 (December 1972), p. 803.

7

Economic Progress and Wealth

GROWTH AND CHANGE IN THE COLONIAL ECONOMY

The many local and regional economies that comprised the total colonial economy were always in a state of flux. Because they began literally as settlements in the wilderness and because war and other frontier disturbances were frequent, it is particularly difficult to systematically portray the economic growth of the colonies. Economic growth, of course, refers to the rate at which a society's material standard of living advances over an extended period of time. The yardstick of economic growth is the trend rate of growth of real per capita income. In measuring specific increments of income, we often neglect other factors that effect the quality of life, such as the amount of leisure time enjoyed, conditions of health, environment, personal attributes, even the distribution of wealth.

For the colonial period, however, these shortcomings of economic growth measure are of secondary importance. The major difficulty is the fact that historical records of colonial income and wealth for the most part are incomplete. We do not even have records of national (colonial) income or total output for a single year.

There can be little doubt, however, that total output expanded rapidly during the colonial period. The rising volume of exports and imports, the increase in shipping activity, and the rapid pace of population growth all suggest significant advances in total production. Moreover, it is obvious that the material condition of life had improved significantly from those early turbulent years of starvation and high levels of mortality. And yet determining the trend of the economic growth rate in the colonial period is somewhat of a guessing game. For instance, using statistical fragments and qualitative evidence, George R. Taylor suggests that before 1710 very little economic growth occurred in the colonies—it was "slow and irregular"—but then between 1710 and 1775 it averaged "slightly more than one percent per annum."[1] Was this in fact the case? Did such an early eighteenth century acceleration really take place, and did per capita incomes really double between 1710 and 1775 as the 1 percent rate implies? Did such economic advances continue indefinitely thereafter, or did periods of stagnation reappear? We now turn to these and other questions related to economic progress in the colonies.

Progress and Change in Agriculture

The major economic activity in the colonies was agriculture, and progress in this sector had a particularly strong bearing on total colonial production. Because agriculture was such a significant part of total output, any average gains were significantly influenced by advances (or lack of advances) in this sector. Moreover, it is important to emphasize that economic progress in real per capita terms has always stemmed primarily from human efforts to raise productivity—the increase of output relative to the input of labor, capital, and land. Therefore, we will devote particular attention to periods of change in productivity and to the causes of the agricultural improvements that were introduced.

An obvious starting point is the dominant colonial staple—tobacco. Information on tobacco prices in the Chesapeake Bay area suggests that throughout the late seventeenth century and almost all of the eighteenth century, only minor agricultural improvements were made. Most of the increases in the productivity of tobacco occurred very early in the colonial period. Ranging between 20 and 30 pence sterling per pound in the early 1620s, tobacco prices fell to almost 3 pence per pound around 1630. A second phase lasting approximately four decades followed that precipitous decline. This time the average price decreased to approximately a penny per pound. Of course, short-term periods of cyclical variations occurred, but normally tobacco prices stayed at that low level throughout most of the remaining peacetime years.

There can be little doubt that these two periods of declining tobacco prices represented major surges in productivity. Obviously, the demand for tobacco in Europe was persistently growing, and the costs of the labor and land required to produce tobacco did not decrease over these years. Since declining wages or rents cannot explain the lower costs, they must have been largely due to advances in output per unit of input, (land, labor, and capital in combination); that is, to gains in productivity. Undoubtedly, therefore, the major period of progress in tobacco cultivation was in the seventeenth rather than the eighteenth century.

This characteristic of rapid early gains and subsequent periods of relative stagnation has always been common to the growth pattern of production in firms, in industries, or even in whole economic sectors. In that early age be-

[1] George R. Taylor, "American Economic Growth Before 1840: An Exploratory Essay," *Journal of Economic History* **XXIV**:4 (December 1964), p. 437.

Additions of capital and the specialization of tasks raised the productivity per worker in colonial tobacco production.

fore widespread technological advances, productivity gains stemmed primarily from trial and error and learning by doing. In agriculture, the fruits of these efforts generally materialized within a few decades of crop introduction. Sometimes, as in the case of tobacco, the introduction of a new seed type generated a surge of crop productivity. Also, in the early phases of experimentation, the colonists found ways to combine and adjust soils, seeds, labor, implements, and other agricultural inputs to their optimum uses. In later stages of agricultural development, improvements were more gradual, due to a slower paced accumulation of knowledge about the most productive uses of available soils and resources. Of course, in some instances such as wine production and silk cultivation, these futile efforts ceased in the experimentation phase.

Similarly in grain and livestock production, gains in productivity appear to have been modest, indeed low, throughout most of the eighteenth century. At least the evidence on changes in Pennsylvania's agriculture suggests only limited progress over that century.[2]

[2] See, for example, Duane Ball and Gary M. Walton, "Agricultural Productivity Change in 18th Century Pennsylvania," *Journal of Economic History* **XXVI:**1 (March 1976), pp. 102–17.

The most visible change in Pennsylvania farms was the sharp decline in average farm size from about 500 acres around 1700 to about 140 acres at the end of the century. But this decrease did not indicate a fall in the "effective land"–labor ratio. Instead it was the consequence of population expansion and the subdivision of uncleared acres as new farms evolved. Because the amount of uncleared land per farm exceeded the minimum needs for fuel and timber, these acreage reductions had no noticeable effect on agricultural output. Because the average number of cleared acres per farm changed little, the effective input of land per farm remained almost constant over the entire eighteenth century.

Alternatively, additional implements, structures, and accumulated inventories raised the amount of capital inputs per farm. On the other hand, average family size was shrinking. Consequently, in the predominantly family farm areas such as Pennsylvania, the amount of labor per farm decreased. Therefore, both the capital–labor ratio and the cleared land–labor ratio rose. Given the increase of inputs per worker, we would expect output per worker to expand.

Indeed, the evidence reveals that output per farm was increasing. Not only were farms producing more livestock and grains (mainly wheat and maslin, a combination of wheat and rye), but by the late colonial period, a small but growing portion of farm labor time was being diverted to nonagricultural production, including milling, smithing, cabinet making, chair making, and tanning. Overall, average output per farm increased by about 7 percent between the first and third quarters of the eighteenth century. When the gain in output is compared to the change in total input,[3] it appears that total productivity advanced approximately 10 percent during these decades. Expressed in terms of rates of change, total productivity expanded 0.1–0.2 percent per year, with the most rapid change (0.3 percent) occurring in the first decades of the eighteenth century. Finally, the growth of output per worker was somewhat higher — approximately 0.2–0.3 percent per year — over the first three quarters of the century.[4]

Specific evidence as to the precise sources of these advances is almost entirely lacking. The low measured rate of advance, however, does reinforce historical descriptions. For instance, in their classic study of agriculture, Bidwell and Falconer assert that in the colonies north of the Chesapeake, "The eighteenth century farmers showed little advance over the first settlers in their care of livestock," and "little if any improvement had been made in farm implements until the very close of the eighteenth century."[5] Another study of

[3] With land per farm constant, labor per farm declining, and capital per farm rising, total input per farm changed according to the relative importance of labor and capital and the relative degree of change of each. Because labor comprised such a high percentage of total costs, total combined input per farm actually declined by a few percentage points during the eighteenth century.

[4] It should be noted that labor productivity (output per worker) increased more than total productivity (output per total combined input), because the amounts of capital and cleared land per worker increased during this period. Increases in these other inputs enabled labor to produce more.

[5] P. W. Bidwell and J. I. Falconer, *History of Agriculture in the Northern United States, 1620–1860* (Washington, D.C.: Carnegie Institute of Washington, 1925), pp. 107, 123.

Pennsylvania agriculture specifically concludes that "economic conditions throughout the century prohibited major changes and encouraged a reasonably stable and uniform type of mixed farming that involved fairly extensive use or superficial working of the land."[6] It seems reasonable to conclude that farmers were probably beginning to learn to use the soil and their implements more effectively. But there is little indication of input savings, either from technological improvements or from economies of scale in terms of larger farms. Better organized and more widespread market participation, however, may have contributed somewhat to gains in agricultural productivity.[7]

Productivity Gains in Transportation and Distribution

Although productivity advances in agriculture were slow and gradual, substantially higher gains were registered in the handling and transportation of goods. Such gains were extremely important because transportation and other distribution costs comprise a large portion of the final market price of a product. This was especially true of the bulky colonial products, which were normally low in value relative to their weight or volume (displaced cargo space). However, even the distribution costs of expensive lightwares represented a significant fraction of their value.

During the eighteenth century, the differential between English and colonial prices for manufactures shipped to the colonies was declining at a fairly steady rate. In the early decades of the century, it was not uncommon for English goods to sell for 80–140 percent more in the colonies than in England. By mid-century, prices on British wares were 45–75 percent higher in the colonies. Finally, just prior to the Revolution, this price spread had been reduced to a range of only 15–25 percent. However, as late as the 1770s, colonial staples such as pitch and other space-consuming exports were still commanding more than double their domestic price in normal English and European markets.

Evidence of improvements in the marketing and distribution of transatlantic tobacco shipments reveals the declining average differential between the

[6]James T. Lemon, *Best Poor Man's Country: A Geographical Study of Early Southwestern Pennsylvania* (Baltimore: Johns Hopkins University Press, 1972), pp. 150–51.

[7]These findings and conclusions should come as no surprise when examined in the light of agricultural developments in later periods. For instance, recent investigations indicate total productivity gains of approximately 0.5 percent per year over the nineteenth century. However, in the first half of the century, output per unit of land, labor, and capital combined advanced at a rate of 0.1–0.2 percent. In the second half of the century, the productivity rate rose to 0.8 percent. Undoubtedly, the lower-paced first half of the nineteenth century—before the transition to animal power and increased mechanization—would have been more suggestive of the eighteenth century experience. In short, agricultural progress throughout most of the late colonial period and probably all of the eighteenth century was limited and slow paced. See Robert E. Gallman, "Changes in Total U.S. Agricultural Factor Productivity in the Nineteenth Century," *Agricultural History* **XLVI:**1 (January 1972), pp. 191–210; and Gallman, "The Agricultural Sector and the Pace of Economic Growth: U.S. Experience in the Nineteenth Century," David C. Klingaman and Richard K. Vedder (eds.), *Essays in Nineteenth Century Economic History* (Athens: Ohio University Press, 1975), pp. 35–76.

Amsterdam price and the colonial price of tobacco (given as a percentage of the Amsterdam price):[8]

Years	Price Differences
1720–1724	82%
1725–1729	76%
1730–1734	82%
1735–1739	77%
1740–1744	77%
1745–1749	76%
1750–1754	67%
1755–1759	72%
1760–1764	70%
1765–1769	65%
1770–1772	51%

A series of advances in transatlantic tobacco distribution stemmed from improvements in packaging and merchandising, from declining costs of information on prices and markets, and from reductions in risk in trade. However, by far the most important improvements were in shipping. Although freight rates fluctuated and varied according to route, the long-run trend was persistently downward. During the 100 years preceding the Revolution, the real costs of shipping were almost halved. Expressed in terms of productivity gains, shipping advanced at a rate of approximately 0.8 percent per year. For that period in general—and specifically compared to changes in agriculture—these increases suggest that shipping was a strategic factor in the overall economic advancement of the colonies.

What was the cause of this improvement? Where trades were well organized and markets reasonably large and safe, economies of scale in shipping were usually realized. For instance, in such commerce as the Baltic timber trades, the use of large vessels generated labor savings per ton shipped. Although larger ships necessitated larger crews, the increased cargo capacity more than compensated for the additional labor costs. As vessels increased in size, their carrying capacity per unit of labor also increased. In other words, on larger ships, fewer men were needed to transport more goods.

Despite these possibilities; the average size of vessels employed in the western Atlantic and in the Caribbean failed to increase significantly over the 100-year period. The potential labor savings of the larger ships were offset by greater occurrences of low utilization in these waters. In fact, in those numerous small and scattered markets, the port times of large vessels were usually as much as twice as long as those for small vessels. Therefore, in colonial waters, schooners and sloops normally traveled a greater number of miles per ton than large ships or brigs did.

Nevertheless, the number of tons per man increased, because crew sizes

[8]James F. Shepherd and Gary M. Walton, *Shipping, Maritime Trade, and the Economic Development of Colonial North America* (New York and London: Cambridge University Press, 1972), p. 60.

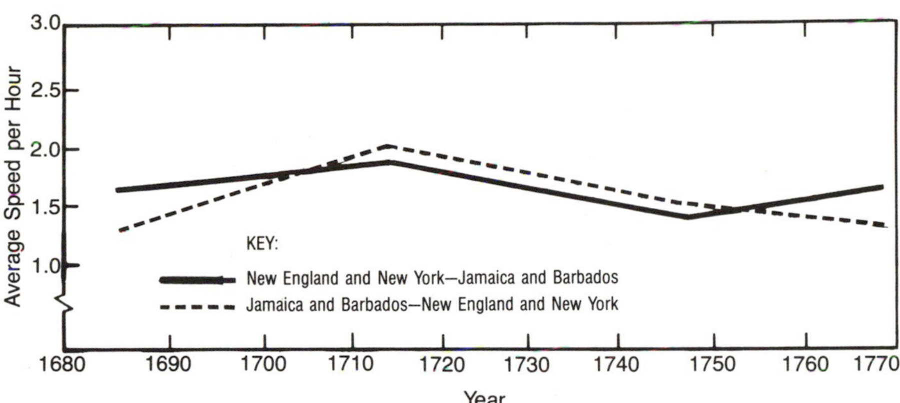

FIGURE 7–1

Average Ship Speeds

James F. Shepherd and Gary M. Walton, *Shipping, Maritime Trade and the Economic Development of Colonial North America* (New York and London: Cambridge University Press, 1972), p. 71.

decreased as vessels remained unchanged in size. For example, a Boston vessel of 50 tons employed an average of seven men early in the eighteenth century; but by the late colonial period, the same ship required only five crew members. Over this same time span, the crew size of a typical New York vessel of 50 tons decreased from eleven to seven members. Paralleling this reduction in labor was the reduction or elimination of armaments on vessels that traded in colonial waters. Guns had been commonplace on seventeenth century vessels trading in the western Atlantic, but cannons had all but disappeared on ships there by the end of the colonial period.

Although the average useful life of vessels changed little over the period, insurance rates decreased due to the declining risks in ocean travel. In contrast to earlier times, insurance rates for most one-way transatlantic passages had reached the rock-bottom common peacetime level of 2 percent by 1720. Of course, rates for voyages into pirate-infested waters were quite another matter. Between New York and Jamaica, for example, the prevailing rate of 5 percent in 1720 had dropped to 4 percent by the 1770s. On routes from New England to various other islands in the West Indies, peacetime insurance rates were halved from 1700 to 1770.

These changes were accompanied by others of similar importance. Curiously, however, faster ship speed was not a positive force in raising productivity. As shown in Figure 7-1, there was no apparent upward trend in ship speed during the last 100 years of the colonial period. Vessels from New England and the Middle Colonies that sailed to the West Indies and back showed no gains in speed on either leg of the journey over this period.

Despite the constancy of ship speed, however, round-trip voyage times declined from 1700 to 1770. As Figure 7-2 shows, with the single exception of Boston, layover times fell markedly in many key ports in the New World. Because a very large portion of a sailing ship's life was spent in port, such de-

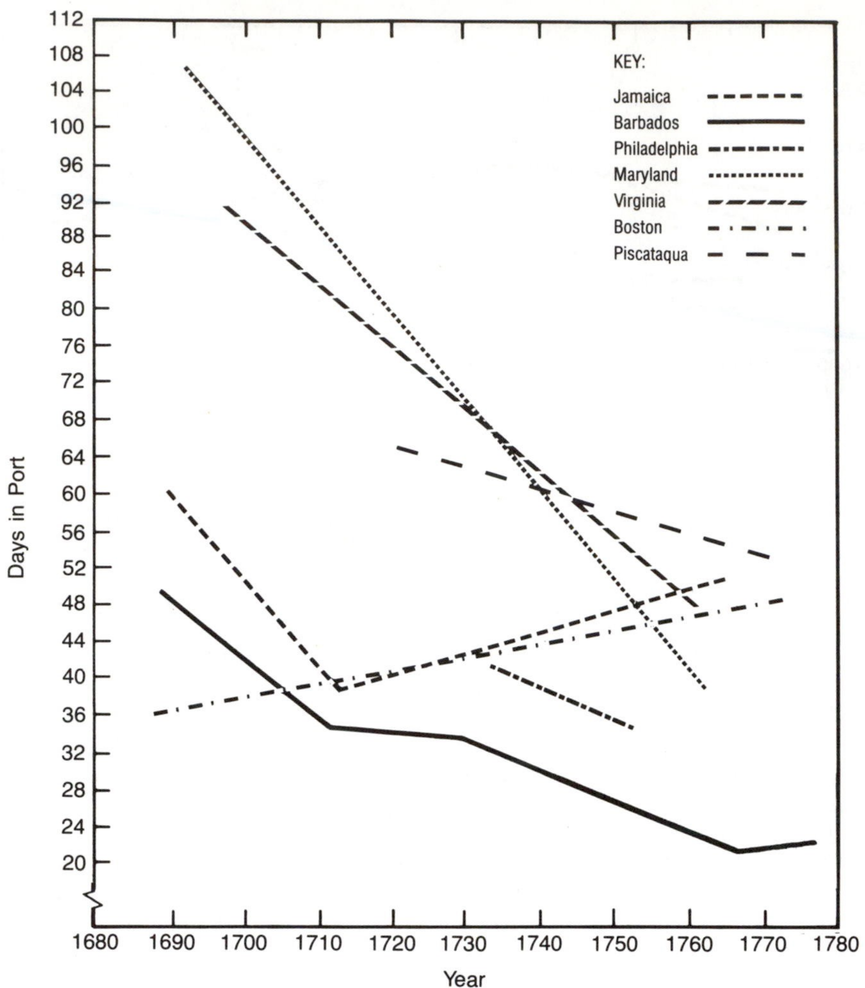

FIGURE 7–2

Average Port Times

James F. Shepherd and Gary M. Walton, *Shipping, Maritime Trade and the Economic Development of Colonial North America* (New York and London: Cambridge University Press, 1972), p. 79.

clines contributed greatly to higher productivity. For example, in the Chesapeake trade, vessels were in port more than twice as long at the end of the seventeenth century as they were in the 1760s. An important contributor to this change was the introduction of Scottish *factors* (representatives of Scottish merchant firms) into the Chesapeake Bay area after 1707. Undoubtedly their methods of gathering and inventorying the tobacco crop in barns and warehouses for quick loading significantly shortened port times in the Chesapeake Bay.

Similarly, in Barbados, port times were more than halved during this period. In the early colonial days, port times were extraordinarily long because exchanges were costly to transact. The many scattered markets were small and remote, and prices varied widely among islands and even within the same island. The shipmaster, acting on behalf of a merchant, might have to visit several islands on one trip to find the best market for his cargo. Difficulties in negotiating prices and determining the medium of exchange, as well as possibly settling past debts, all tended to lengthen the transaction period. Often bartering was practiced, but even when money was used, prices were not easy to determine because different currencies and bills of exchange (with varying degrees of risk) were afforded no set value. Finally, the problem of collecting cargoes extended port times, especially when harvests were poor. Nevertheless, long layovers in the Caribbean became less common as a more systematic market economy evolved.

It should be emphasized that decreasing port times produced savings not only in capital but also in labor costs, since crews were customarily fed and paid while they were in foreign ports as well as at sea.

Such savings more than offset other sources of cost increases. Although wages and ship repair costs remained fairly constant over the period, the costs of shipbuilding and victualing (obtaining food for the crew) increased. Overall, however, the productivity gains countervailed, and freight costs were significantly reduced.

TECHNOLOGY, PRODUCTIVITY, AND PIRACY

At this point, we might ask what part technological change in terms of advances in basic knowledge played in the reduction of shipping costs in colonial times. In general, it seems to have played a minor role. This period preceded the era of iron ships and steam, and both ship materials and the power source of ships remained unchanged. Even increasingly complex sails and rigs and the alterations of hull shapes failed to increase ship speed and, in any case, did not stem from fundamental advances in knowledge.

Of course, it might be argued that crew reductions stemmed from advances in knowledge. However, during the early seventeenth century, Dutch shipping had already displayed many of the essential characteristics of design, manning, and other input requirements that were found on the most advanced vessels in the western Atlantic in the 1760s and 1770s. In fact, the most significant technological change in seventeenth- and eighteenth-century shipping occurred in approximately 1595, when the Dutch first introduced the flyboat, or flute. The flyboat was a specialized merchant vessel designed to carry bulk commodities. It was exceptionally long compared to its width, had a flat bottom, and was lightly built (armament, gun platforms, and reinforced planking had been eliminated). In addition, its rig was simple and its crew size was small. In contrast, English and colonial vessels were built, gunned, and manned more heavily to meet the dual purpose of trade and defense. Their solid construction and armaments were costly—not only in materials but in manpower. Larger crews were needed to handle the more complex riggings on these vessels as well as their guns.

It quickly became evident that the flyboat could be used advantageously in certain bulk trades where the danger of piracy was low. However, in the rich but dangerous trades into the Mediterranean and the West Indies, more costly ships were required. In general, high risks in all colonial waters led to one of the most notable features of seventeenth-century shipping—the widespread use of cannons and armaments on trading vessels. Such characteristics were still observed in certain waters throughout much of the eighteenth century. Until around 1750 in the Caribbean, especially near Jamaica, vessels weighing more than 100 tons were almost always armed, and even small vessels usually carried some guns.

The need for self-protection in the Caribbean was self-evident:

> There the sea was broken by a multitude of islands affording safe anchorage and refuge, with wood, water, even provisions for the taking. There the colonies of the great European powers, grouped within a few days' sail of one another, were forever embroiled in current European wars which gave the stronger of them excuse for preying on the weaker and seemed to make legitimate the constant disorder of those seas. There trade was rich, but settlement thin and defense difficult. There the idle, the criminal, and the poverty-stricken were sent to ease society in the Old World. By all these conditions piracy was fostered, and for two centuries throve ruinously, partly as an easy method of individual enrichment and partly as an instrument of practical politics.[9]

Privateering also added to the disorder. As a common practice, nation-states often gave private citizens license to harass the ships of rival states. These privateering commissions or "letters of marque" were issued without constraint in wartime, and occasionally even in peacetime, they were given to citizens who had suffered losses due to the actions of subjects from an offending state. Since privateers frequently ignored the constraints of their commissions, privateering was often difficult to distinguish from common piracy.

Other government policies also tended to aggravate existing sea hazards. Adding to the supply of privateers and pirates, some of the islands were deliberately peopled with convicts. Even as late as 1718, the governor of Jamaica complained of this policy:

> Several People have been lately sent over out of the gaols [jails] in England, upon the Encouragement of An Act of Parliament pass'd the last sessions ... those people have been so farr from altering their Evil Courses and way of living and becoming an Advantage to Us, that the greatest part of them are gone and have Induced others to go with them a Pyrating and have Inveglied and Encouraged Severall Negroes to desert from their Masters and go to the Spaniards in Cuba, the few that remains proves a wicked Lazy and Indolent people, so that I could heartily wish this Country might be troubled with no more of them.[10]

[9]Violet Barbour, "Privateers and Pirates in the West Indies," *American Historical Review* **XVI** (April 1911), p. 529.

[10]Letters to the Board of Trade (September 1, 1718, C.O. 137:13, 19), printed in Frank W. Pitman, *The Development of the West Indies, 1700–1763* (New Haven, Conn.: Yale University Press, 1917), pp. 55–56.

Acts of piracy in the western Atlantic, the Caribbean, and elsewhere thrived before 1720. The long-term effects of actions by the Royal Navy to eliminate piracy were to change the characteristics of ships and reduce freight rates on ocean transport.

Earlier in 1700, Colonel Query of Virginia wrote to the Council of Trade and Plantations that "all the news of America is the swarming of pirates not only on these coasts, but all the West Indies over, which doth ruin trade ten times worse than a war."[11]

Of course, piracy was not confined to the Caribbean. Pirates lurked safely in the inlets of North Carolina, from which they regularly raided vessels trading at Charleston. In 1718, it was exclaimed that "every month brought intelligence of renewed outrages, of vessels sacked on the high seas, burned with their cargo, or seized and converted to the nefarious uses of the outlaws."[12] Local traders, shippers, and government officials in the Carolinas repeatedly solicited the Board of Trade for protection. In desperation, Carolina's Assembly appropriated funds in 1719 to support private vessels in the hope of driving the

[11] Violet Barbour, p. 566.

[12] S. C. Hughson, "The Carolina Pirates and Colonial Commerce," *Johns Hopkins University Studies in Historical and Political Science* **XII** (1894), p. 123.

pirates from their seas. These pleas and protective actions were mostly in vain, but finally the Royal Navy took action. By the early 1740s piracy had been eliminated from the western Atlantic.

The fall of piracy was paralleled by the elimination of ship armaments and the reduction of crew sizes. As such, this was a process of technical diffusion. Without piracy, specialized cargo-carrying vessels similar to the flyboat were designed, thereby substantially reducing the costs of shipping.

In summary, the main productivity advances in shipping during the colonial period resulted from (1) economies of scale in cargo handling, which reduced port times, and (2) the elimination of piracy, which stood as an obstacle to technical diffusion permitting the use of specialized low-cost cargo vessels.[13]

WEALTH AND WELL-BEING IN THE COLONIES

The evidence on advances in output relative to inputs in both agriculture and shipping indicate that the colonial economy was far from stagnant. Progress was being made—although at times perhaps haltingly. Nevertheless, we cannot precisely measure the average annual growth rate of the colonial economy. Our speculation is that over the last 100 years of the colonial period, the growth rate trend was slightly below 0.5 percent per year. This seems reasonable in light of the improvements we have already noted and also in light of England's estimated annual economic growth rate of 0.3 percent throughout most of the eighteenth century.[14]

Whatever the rate of colonial economic growth, the average levels of income and wealth per free person were extraordinarily high on the eve of the American Revolution. After years of collecting and studying colonial probate records, Alice Hanson Jones has found that the average free person held wealth in the value of £76 sterling in 1774 (see Table 7-1). Adjusting for changes in purchasing power, £1 sterling in 1774 equaled approximately $38 in 1973 prices; thus, the wealth holdings of the average free colonist were worth almost $2,860 in prices of fairly recent time. Of course, slaves and indentured servants were not free and therefore could not claim similar levels of wealth holdings. Nevertheless, such high levels of wealth holdings deserve consider-

[13] Other similar productivity gains deserve at least a brief mention here. As port times decreased, so did inventory times. This reduced the time in which a planter's capital (crop) lay idle in storage barns or warehouses. Decreased inventory times, of course, saved colonial capital. Similarly, declining risks and insurance rates reduced the costs to owners of insuring their shipments or bearing the risks of personal shipments. And there was considerable progress in packaging, as tobacco and sugar hogsheads, rice barrels, and other containers increased in size as the colonial period progressed. Although larger hogsheads and barrels demanded more input in construction, their capacity grew relatively because the surface area of such containers expanded less in proportion to their capacity. Finding the point at which increased difficulties in handling roughly offset the productivity gains from using larger containers provides us with a good example of the learning by doing, trial-and-error procedure.

[14] See Phyllis Deane and W. A. Cole, *British Economic Growth, 1688–1959: Trends and Structure* (London: Cambridge University Press, 1964), p. 80.

TABLE 7–1
Private Physical Wealth per Free Person, 1774 (pounds sterling)

	New England	Middle Colonies	Southern Colonies	Total Thirteen Colonies
Land	27	28	55	38
Servants and slaves	0	2	58	21
Livestock	3	5	9	6
Farm tools and household equipment	1	1	3	2
Crops and perishables	1	3	5	3
Consumer durables	4	4	6	5
Other	2	3	1	2
Totals	38	46	137	76

Source: Alice Hanson Jones, "Components of Private Wealth per Free Capita for the 13 Colonies by Region, 1774," in U.S. Bureau of the Census, *Historical Statistics, Colonial Times to 1970* (Washington, D.C.: U.S. Government Printing Office, 1976), Series Z, pp. 169–212, 1175.

able emphasis. After converting the wealth stocks into income flows on an annual basis,[15] Jones' findings suggest that the per capita income per free colonist was £15–25 sterling in 1774 prices, or $573–955 in 1973 prices.

These are surprisingly high standards of living for the world at that time; even today, relatively few countries enjoy average income levels that approach the earnings of the American colonists on the eve of the Revolution. In fact, more than two-thirds of the present world population live in countries where the average income is below the level of the typical free American's income 200 years ago. This is true of most people of the "Third World," including China, India, the Philippines, Korea, and large parts of Africa and South America. Relatively speaking, colonial Americans lived very well, both by today's standards in many areas of the world and in comparison to the most advanced areas of the world in the late eighteenth century. Only England and perhaps Holland generated slightly higher levels of income (or wealth) per person than the colonies.

The high levels of material well-being of the average free American in the late colonial period were not equally distributed, however. By far the richest area was the South, where average wealth holdings per free individual were more than double those in New England and in the Middle Colonies. This striking comparison was not simply the result of differences in the holdings of servants and slaves. Although Table 7-1 shows that this classification was important, two-to-one differences are also exhibited in the categories of livestock, consumer durables, farm tools and household equipment. Even the value of land holdings per free southerner was more than twice this value in New England or the Middle Colonies.

[15] Estimates of wealth stock can be converted into income flows by dividing the wealth estimates by the capital–output ratios. The relationship between capital and output (the capital–output ratio) is influenced by many different factors and varies both over time and among countries and regions. Nevertheless, under normal peacetime conditions, the capital–output ratio is seldom lower than 3 or higher than 5.

TABLE 7–2
Distribution of Physical Wealth in New England and the Middle Colonies in 1774*

Cumulative Proportion of Wealth Held by:	New England	Middle Colonies
Poorest 10%	Less than 1	Less than 1
Poorest 20%	1	2
Poorest 50%	11	23
Richest 20%	60	47
Richest 10%	40	32

Source: Alice Hanson Jones, "Wealth Estimates for the American Middle Colonies, 1774," *Economic Development and Cultural Change* **XVIII:**4 (July 1970), Part 2; and "Wealth Estimates for the New England Colonies After 1770," *Journal of Economic History* **XXXII:**1 (March 1972), pp. 98–127.

*These estimates of wealth are based on probated decedents, adjusted to the age composition of the living population for selected counties in New England and the Middle Counties. They include land, slaves, and portable physical wealth (producer and consumer durables), but exclude cash and financial assets. Of course, not all descendants left probates, especially the very poor. Therefore, these estimates understate the true inequality of wealth and income during this period.

Evidence from probate records of the times also permits us to estimate the distribution of wealth among individuals. It is widely believed that wealth and income were fairly equitably distributed until the onset of industrialization in the early nineteenth century. However, the estimates in Table 7-2 suggest that widespread inequalities of wealth and income existed.[16] For instance, the wealthiest 10 percent of all New Englanders owned 40 percent of the total wealth there. In the Middle Colonies, the wealthiest 10 percent held 32 percent of the total wealth. The poorer half of New England's population owned only 11 percent of the wealth there. In the Middle Colonies, the poorer half owned 23 percent of the total wealth. Therefore, 89 percent and 77 percent of the total wealth in these respective regions was left for the wealthy.

Trends in Inequality

The degree of inequality in the distribution of wealth in the late colonial period suggested in Table 7-2 was probably preceded by a period in which greater equality prevailed. According to Jackson Turner Main, a growing inequality in wealth and income accompanied the very process of colonial settlement and economic maturity. As development proceeded, frontier areas were transformed into subsistence farming areas and finally, in some instances, into urban areas. In Main's opinion, this increasing commercialization resulted in greater inequality in the distribution of colonial wealth and income.[17]

Other studies by James Henretta and, more recently, by Bruce D. Daniels also suggest a growth in the inequality of colonial wealth distribution over

[16]Be sure to read the footnote * to Table 7-2, which emphasizes that the figures in Table 7-2 probably understate the true degree of inequality of wealth and income in the colonies at this time.

[17]Jackson Turner Main, *The Social Structure of Revolutionary America* (Princeton, N.J.: Princeton University Press, 1965).

time.[18] Comparing two Boston tax lists, Henretta found that the top 10 percent of Boston's taxpayers owned 42 percent of its wealth in 1687, whereas they owned 57 percent in 1771. Daniels surveyed many New England probate records and therefore was able to tentatively confirm Main's contention that as economic activity grew more complex in the colonies it tended to produce a greater concentration of wealth. Apparently, as subsistence production gave way to market production, the interdependence among colonial producers generated or at least was accompanied by a greater disparity in wealth. This was true both in older and in more newly settled agricultural areas. Alternatively, large established urban areas, such as Boston and Hartford (Connecticut) exhibited a fairly stable distribution of wealth throughout the eighteenth century until 1776. These urban centers also reflected the greatest degree of wealth inequality in the colonies. Smaller towns showed less inequality, but as towns grew, their inequality also increased.

Particularly high levels of affluence were observed in the port towns and cities where merchant classes were forming and gaining an economic hold. Especially influential were the merchant shipowners who were engaged in the export–import trade and who were considered to be in the upper class of society. In addition, urbanization and industrialization produced another class group: a free labor force who owned little or no property. Obviously, occupation and property ownership were major factors in widening the gap between various social groups in the colonies. Of course, race and sex were also factors. Typically, women owned far less property than men, and women's opportunities to gain wealth were sharply restricted. Similarly, the growing use of indentured and slave labor after 1675 furthered the rise of wealth inequality in America, making it a fact of economic life long before the age of industrialization and more rapid economic growth had begun.

[18] James Henretta, "Economic Development and Social Structure in Colonial Boston," *William and Mary Quarterly* **XXII**:1 (January 1965), pp. 93–105; and Bruce D. Daniels, "Long-range Trends of Wealth Distribution in Eighteenth-Century New England," *Explorations in Economic History* **XI**:2 (Winter 1973–1974), pp. 123–35.

8

Three Crises and Revolt

THE OLD COLONIAL POLICY

The spirit and actual conditions of widespread freedom in the colonies have already been emphasized in Chapter 3. It is important to recall that the lower (elected) houses of the various individual colonial legislatures held the power of the purse. Also bureaucratic apathy on the part of the Privy Council had allowed governing power to slip steadily into the hands of the colonists, especially in the determination of local matters. The Privy Council's legislative review process established certain checks on the degree of freedom the colonists could maintain through legislative action. But time, distance, and the costs of enforcement and control permitted a climate of substantial independence to prevail in the colonies over much of the period of British rule.

The main provisions of the early Navigation Acts, which imposed the most important restrictions on colonial economic freedom, also deserve to be reemphasized here. These laws epitomized British mercantilism, and their aim was threefold: (1) to protect and encourage English and colonial shipping; (2) to insure that major colonial imports from Europe were shipped from British ports; and (3) to make sure that the bulk of desired colonial products—the enumerated articles—were shipped to England.

The first Acts of Trade and Navigation in 1651, 1660, and 1663 introduced no new concepts concerning the colonies' relationship with the Empire. Colonial settlers and investors had always been aware of the restrictions on their economic activities. Rules were changed gradually and, until 1763, in such a way that American colonists voiced no serious complaints. Articles were added to the enumerated list over a long period of time. At first, the list consisted entirely of southern continental and West Indian products, most important of which were tobacco, sugar, cotton, dyewood, and indigo. Rice and molasses were not added until 1704; naval stores, until 1705 and 1729; and furs and skins, until 1721. Whenever enumeration resulted in obvious and unreasonable hardship, relief might be granted. For example, the requirement that rice be sent to England added so much to shipping and handling costs that the American product, despite its superior quality, was priced out of southern European markets. Consequently, laws passed in the 1730s allowed rice to be shipped directly to ports South of Cape Finisterre, a promontory in northwestern Spain.

Commodities were listed because they were especially important to English manufacturers or because they were expected to yield substantial customs revenue. However, the requirements of shipping to English ports were less onerous than we might initially suppose. First, the Americans and the English shared general ties of blood and language and, more specifically, because their credit contacts were more easily established, the colonists would have dealt primarily with English merchants anyway. Second, duties charged on commodities that were largely reexported, such as tobacco, were remitted entirely or in large part to the colonies. Third, bounties were paid on some of the enumerated articles. Fourth, it was permissible to ship certain items on the list directly from one colony to another for the purpose of furnishing supplies. Finally, the laws could be evaded through smuggling, and with the exception of molasses, such evasion was probably neither more nor less common in the colonies than it was in Europe during the seventeenth and eighteenth centuries.

With respect to imports, the effect of the Navigation Acts was to distort somewhat—but not to influence materially—the flows of trade. The fact that goods had to be funneled through England probably added to costs and restricted trade. Again, however, traditional ties would have made Americans the best customers of British merchants anyway. Furthermore, hardship cases were relieved by providing direct shipment of commodities like salt and wine from ports South of Cape Finisterre to America.

If English manufacturers were to be granted special advantages over other European manufacturers in British American markets, should restrictions also be placed on competing colonial manufacturers? Many British manufacturers felt that such "duplicative production" should be prohibited and tried to convince Parliament that colonial manufacturing was not in the best interest of the Empire. In 1699, a law made it illegal to export colonial wool, wool yarn, and finished wool products to any foreign country or even to other colonies. Later, Americans were forbidden to export hats made of beaver fur. Toward midcentury, a controversy arose in England over the regulation of iron manufactures; after 1750, pig and bar iron were admitted into England duty free and the colonial manufacture of finished iron products was expressly forbidden. The fact that these were the only prohibitive laws directed at colonial manufacture indicates Britain's lack of fear of American competition.

After all, the colonies' comparative advantage in production lay overwhelmingly in agriculture and other resource-intensive products from the seas and forests. Note that the important shipbuilding industry in the colonies was not curtailed by British legislation; indeed, it was supported by Parliament. Therefore, any piecemeal actions to prevent colonial manufacturing activities appear largely to have been taken to favor particular vested interests in England, especially those with influence and effective lobbying practices.

Nevertheless, as we will emphasize later in this chapter, the laws prohibiting colonial manufactures were loosely enforced; they were restrictive and a cause of annoyance, but they did not seriously affect the course of early American industrial development or the colonial quest for independence. Also, the economic controls that England imposed on the colonies were less strict than the colonial controls other European countries imposed, and these controls were less harsh for Americans than for other colonies within the Empire. Nevertheless, we should not misapprehend the trend of enforcement of the old colonial policy. Regulation of external colonial trade was progressively strengthened. Beginning in 1675, governors were supplied with staffs of officials to aid in enforcing trade regulations; after the general reorganization of 1696, the powers of these officials were sufficient to provide considerable surveillance and commercial regulation.

The only trade law flaunted with impunity was the Molasses Act of 1733—an act that, if enforced, would have disrupted one of the major colonial trades and would have resulted in serious repercussions, especially in New England. Before 1700, New England had traded primarily with the British possessions in the West Indies. In time, however, British planters failed to provide a sufficient market for northern colonial goods, and sugar and molasses from the increasingly productive French islands became cheaper than the English staples. During the same period, British planters in the sugar islands were hurt by the requirement that cane products be shipped to England before being reexported. In an effort to protect British West Indian holdings, Parliament imposed high duties on *foreign* (predominantly French) sugar, molasses, and rum imported to the English colonies. The strict levying of these duties and the prevention of smuggling would have decreased the prices of northern staples in the British West Indies and would have seriously curtailed all trade involving rum. New Englanders appeared to have no feasible alternative, because they had to sell their fish, provisions, lumber, and rum to pay for their imports. Rather than face possible economic annihilation, they continued to trade as usual; instead of facing the issue resolutely, English officials made no serious attempts to enforce trade regulations. Some 30 years later, after the matter had been raised time after time, the Sugar Act of 1764 ruled against the American colonists in favor of the British West Indian planters. This decision, as we will see, was a key factor in helping to bring on revolution.

THE NEW COLONIAL POLICY AND THE FIRST CRISIS

The events that led to the American Revolution fall more readily into order if we keep in mind its central underlying theme: New and rapid changes in the old colonial policy that had been established and imposed on an essentially self-governing people for 150 years precipitated a series of crises and, ultimately, war. These crises were essentially political, but the stresses and strains that led to colonial fear and hatred of British authority had economic origins. Britain's "new" colonial policy was only an extension of the old, with one difference: the new enactments were adopted by a Parliament that had every intention of enforcing them to the letter of the law, thereby sharply changing the atmosphere of freedom in the colonies. Furthermore, high British officials insisted—at almost precisely the wrong moments—on taking punitive actions that only compounded the bitterness they had already stirred up in the colonies.

The series of critical events that generated the first crisis began with the English victory over the French in 1763. The Seven Years' War had been a struggle for empire, of course, but it had also been a fight for the protection of the American colonies. And the colonials had not been of much help in furnishing England with either troops or materials—to say nothing of the hurtful trade they carried on with the French in both Canada and the West Indies. The English were in no mood to spare the feelings of an upstart people who had committed the cardinal sin of ingratitude. Besides, the war had placed a heavy burden on the English Treasury, and it seemed just that American colonists be asked to contribute to the support of the garrisons that were still required on their frontier.

George Grenville, England's prime minister, decided to station a British force of some 10,000 men in the North American possessions at an estimated annual expense of £350,000. To help pay troop maintenance costs, Parliament passed two laws to generate approximately one-third of this revenue. Of the two laws, the Sugar Act of 1764 had more far-reaching implications for the colonists, because it contained provisions that served the ends of all major English economic interests and at the same time threatened American business in the colonies. But the Stamp Act of 1765, although really much less inclusive, incited political tempers to a boil that in a very real sense started the first step towards rebellion.

The most important clauses of the Sugar Act levied taxes on imports of non-British products of the West Indies. Although the duty on foreign molasses was actually *lowered* from 6d. to 3d. a gallon—a marked reduction from the rate set by the old Molasses Act—*provision was made for strict collection of the tax* in the belief that the smaller tax, if strictly enforced, would produce a larger revenue. A more important goal, however, was the protection of British West Indian planters—who were well represented in Parliament—from the competition of New England rum makers. Actually, more than half of the molasses imported by colonials was used for kitchen purposes (Boston baked beans, shoofly pie, apple pandowdy, and molasses jack—a kind of home-brewed beer). But the chief fear of the English sugar planters was that cheap molasses imports from the French West Indies would enable the New England rum distilleries to capture the rum market on the mainland as well as in the non-British islands.[1] And their concern was probably more than justified, despite the alleged inferiority of the New England product. Moreover, the Sugar

[1] For the details of this controversy, see Gilman M. Ostrander, "The Colonial Molasses Trade," *Agricultural History* **XXX**:1 (January 1956), pp. 77–84. See also Stuart Bruchery, *The Colonial Merchant* (New York: Harcourt Brace Jovanovich Inc., 1966), pp. 67–78.

Act added to the list of enumerated articles several raw materials demanded by British manufacturers, including some important exports of the Northern and Middle Colonies. Finally, this comprehensive law removed most of the tariff rebates (drawbacks) previously allowed on European goods that passed through English ports and even placed new duties on foreign textiles that competed with English products.

The Stamp Act, on the other hand, was simply designed to raise revenue and served no ends of mercantile policy. The law required that stamps varying in cost from half a penny to several pounds be affixed to legal documents, contracts, newspapers and pamphlets, and even playing cards and dice. The colonists objected loudly on the grounds that the act levied an "internal" tax, distinguished from the traditional "external" taxes or duties collected on goods imported to the colonies. When English ministers refused to recognize this distinction, the colonists further objected that the tax had been levied by a distant Parliament that did not contain a single colonial representative. And they complained that both the Sugar Act and the Stamp Act required the tax revenues to be remitted to England for disbursement—a procedure that further drained the colonies of precious specie and constantly reduced the amount of goods that could be imported to America. When it became apparent that strict enforcement would accompany such measures, severe resistance arose in the colonies. Lawyers and printers—who were especially infuriated by the Stamp Act—furnished articulate, able leadership for anti-British agitation.

The decade of trouble that followed was characterized by alternating periods of colonial insubordination, British concession, renewed attempts to raise revenues, further colonial resistance, and, at last, punitive action—taken by the British in anger at what was felt to be rank disloyalty. The so-called Stamp Act Congress met in New York in 1765, passed resolutions of fealty, and organized a boycott of English goods. "Nonimportation associations" were established throughout the colonies, and the volume of imports from Britain declined dramatically as docks and warehouses bulged with unsold British goods. A concerted effort to boycott English goods did not develop in all regions, however; the Middle Colonies—where the boycotts first centered—exhibited the greatest decrease in trade and the upper South contributed effectively to the boycott. But New England gave only slight support to these first nonimport agreements, and the lower South failed to join in the boycott. Yet overall, colonial efforts to boycott British imports were very effective. In fact, English merchants were so sharply affected that they demanded the repeal of the Stamp Act. They were joined by such political leaders as Edmund Burke and William Pitt, whose sympathies lay with the colonists. Parliament repealed the Stamp Act and reduced the duty on foreign molasses from 3d. to 1d. per gallon. Thus the first major confrontation between America and England ended peacefully.

MORE CHANGES AND THE SECOND CRISIS

Although Parliament had responded to economic pressure from America by repealing the Stamp Act, England obstinately maintained its *right* to tax the colonies. The other sugar duties remained, and a Declaratory Act affirmed the right of Parliament to legislate in all matters concerning Americans. Nevertheless, there was rejoicing in both the colonies and England, and it was generally believed that their differences would be reconciled. But even then, the Quartering Act of 1765 had been on the statute books a year, with its stipulations that the colonial assemblies provide barracks, some provisions, and part of the military transport for British troops stationed within the colonies. This law was to prove especially problematic to New York, where soldiers were to be concentrated on their way to the West. Much worse was to come, however. George Grenville had been dismissed from the British ministry in 1765, largely because King George III disliked him. He was replaced as Chancellor of the Exchequer by Charles Townshend, who in 1767, secured the passage of several measures identified with his name. Because the great English landowners were persistently clamoring for relief from their heavy property taxes, Townshend tried once again to raise revenues in America. He felt that if the colonials objected to "internal" taxes, he would provide them with some "external" duties levied on such important articles of consumption as tea, glass, paper, and red and white lead (pigments for paint).

Although they were definitely important to colonial life, the colonists might have accepted taxation on these items calmly if the British had not adopted measures to put real teeth into the law. One of the Townshend Acts provided for an American Customs Board; another, for the issuance by colonial courts of the hated general search warrants known as *writs of assistance;* and another, for admiralty courts in Halifax, Boston, Philadelphia, and Charlestown to try smuggling cases. With a single stroke, the British ministry succeeded once again in antagonizing a wide cross section of the American populace, and again resistance flared—this time in the form of both peaceful petitions and mob violence, culminating in the Boston Massacre which left five dead. Once more, the nonimportation agreements, especially effective in the port towns, were imposed. Only in the Chesapeake colonies—the one major colonial region spared of a court of admiralty—was this boycott fairly unsuccessful.[2] Nevertheless, by late 1769, American imports had declined to perhaps one-third of their normal level, and once again the English exerted pressure to change trade policy. For the second time, Parliament appeared to acquiesce to colonial demands. In 1770, all the Townshend duties except the duty on tea were repealed, and although some of the most distasteful acts remained on the books, everyone except a few colonial hotheads felt that a peaceful settlement was possible. Trade was resumed, and a new level of prosperity was reached in 1771.

THE THIRD CRISIS AND REBELLION

Reasonable calm prevailed until 1773, when resistance flared again over what now seems to have been an inconsequential matter. The English East India Company, in which many politically powerful people owned an interest, was

[2] Another contributing factor may have been that trade in the Chesapeake region was relatively decentralized, thereby reducing the possibility of blacklisting or boycotting colonial importers and others who failed to join in the effort.

experiencing financial difficulties. Parliament had granted the company a loan of public funds and had also passed the Tea Act of 1773, which permitted the company to handle tea sales in a new way. Until this time, the company, which enjoyed a monopoly of the trade with India, had sold tea to English wholesalers, who in turn sold it to jobbers, who sent it to America. There the tea was turned over to colonial wholesalers, who at last distributed it to American retailers. Overall, many people had received income from this series of transactions; besides, duties had been collected on the product when it reached English ports and again when it arrived in America. The new Tea Act allowed the East India Company to ship tea directly to the colonies, thereby eliminating the British duty and some handling costs. Consumers were to benefit by paying less for tea, the company would presumably sell more tea at a lower price, and everybody would be happy. Only everybody was not happy. Smugglers of Dutch tea were now undersold, the colonial tax was still collected (a real sore point), and most importantly, the American importer was removed from the picture, thus alarming American merchants. If the tea wholesaler could be bypassed, couldn't the businesses of other merchants also be undercut? Couldn't other companies in Great Britain be granted monopoly control of other commodities, until eventually Americans were reduced to keeping small shops and selling at retail what their foreign masters imported for them? Wouldn't just the few pro-British agents who would handle the necessary distribution processes grow rich while staunch Americans grew poor? The answers seemed clear to almost every colonist engaged in business. From

Angered colonists, disguised as Indians, invited themselves to a "tea party"—as they called it—to show the British how they felt about English mercantile policies.

wealthy merchants in Boston to shopkeepers in hamlets, there was a swift and violent reaction. Tea in the port towns was sent back to England or destroyed in various ways—the most spectacular of which was the Boston Tea Party. Many colonists were shocked at this wanton destruction of private property, but their reaction was mild compared with the indignation that swelled in Britain.

The result was the bitter and punitive legislation known as the Intolerable Acts. Passed in the early summer of 1774, the Intolerable Acts (1) closed the Port of Boston to all shipping until the colonists paid the East India Company for its tea, (2) permitted British officials charged with crimes committed while enforcing British laws to be tried in another colony or in Britain, (3) revised the charter of Massachusetts to make certain cherished rights dependent on the arbitrary decision of the Crown-appointed governor, and (4) provided for the quartering of troops in the city of Boston which was especially obnoxious to the citizens after the events of the Boston Massacre four years earlier. In the ensuing months, political agitation reached new heights of violence, and economic sanctions were again invoked. For the third time, nonimportation agreements were imposed, and the delegates to the First Continental Congress voted not to trade with England or the British West Indies unless concessions were made. By this time, however, legislative enactments were of little importance. The crisis had become moral and political. Americans would not yield to the British until their basic freedoms were restored, and the English would not make peace until the colonists relented. The possibilities for peaceful reconciliation ebbed as the weeks passed. Finally, violence broke out with the shots of April 19, 1775, which marked a major turning point in the history of the world.

Support in the Countryside

Although the events leading to the Revolution centered primarily around the conflicts between British authority and activities concerning colonial merchants, the vast rural populace played an essential supporting role in the independence movement. But how can we explain the willingness of wealthy southerners and of many poor farmers to support a rebellion that was spearheaded by an antagonized merchant class? There were certainly no apparent allied economic interests among these groups. Nevertheless, coincidentally, each group had its individual motives for resisting British authority. In rural America, antagonisms primarily stemmed from English land policy.

Before 1763, British policy had been calculated to encourage the rapid development of the colonial West. In the interests of trade, English merchants wanted the new country to be populated as rapidly as possible. Moreover, rapid settlement extended the frontier and thereby helped to strengthen opposition to France and Spain. By 1763, however, the need to fortify the frontier against a foreign power had disappeared. By this time, too, other considerations had become more important. First, the British felt it was wise to contain the population well within the seaboard area, where the major investments had been made and where political control would be easier. Second, the fur trade was now under the complete control of the British, and it was deemed unwise to have frontier pioneers moving in and creating trouble with the Indians. Third, wealthy English landowners were purchasing western land in great tracts, and pressure was exerted to "save" some of the good land for these investors. Finally, placing the western lands under the direct control of the Crown was designed to obtain revenues from sales and quitrents for the British Treasury.

For several reasons, then, many in England urged conservatism in the disposition of unsettled lands. Finally, events on the frontier forced a temporary decision. Angry over injustices—real and imagined—and fearful that the settlers would encroach on their hunting grounds, the northern Indians rebelled under the Ottawa chief, Pontiac. Colonial and British troops put down the uprising, but only after seven of the nine British garrisons west of Niagara were destroyed. Everyone knew that the "red men" would be a continuing threat unless they were pacified. Primarily as a temporary solution to the "Indian problem," the king issued the Royal Proclamation of 1763, which in effect drew a line beyond which colonials could not settle without express permission from the Crown (see Map 8-1). Governors could no longer grant patents to land lying West of the sources of rivers that flowed into the Atlantic; anyone seeking such a grant had to obtain one directly from the king. At the same time, the fur trade was placed under centralized control, and no trader could cross the Allegheny mountains without permission from England.

A few years later, the policy of keeping colonial settlement under British supervision was reaffirmed, although it became apparent that the western boundary line would not remain rigidly fixed. In 1768, the Proclamation Line was shifted westward, and treaties with the Indians made large land tracts available to speculators. In 1774, the year in which the Intolerable Acts were passed, two British actions made it clear that temporary expedients had evolved into permanent policies. First, a royal proclamation tightened the terms on which land would pass into private hands. Grants were no longer to be free; instead, tracts were to be sold at public auctions in lots of 100—1,000 acres at a minimum price of 6d. per acre. Quitrents were to be more than double their old rate. Even more serious was the passage of the Quebec Act in 1774 (see Map 8-2), which changed the boundaries of Quebec to the Ohio River in the East and the Mississippi River in the West, thus destroying the western claims of Massachusetts, Connecticut, and Virginia. The fur trade was to be regulated by the governor of Quebec, and the Indian boundary line was to run as far South as Georgia.

Not all colonists suffered from the new land policy. Rich land speculators who were politically powerful enough to obtain special grants from the king found the new regulations restrictive but not ruinous. Indeed, great holders of ungranted lands *East* of the mountains, such as the Penns and the Calverts, or of huge tracts already granted but not yet settled stood to benefit from the rise in property values that resulted from the British embargo on westward movement. Similarly, farmers of old, established agricultural areas would benefit in two ways: (1) the competition from the produce of the new lands would not be so severe, and (2) since it would be harder for agricultural laborers to obtain their own farms, hired hands would be cheaper. Moreover, many of the restrictions on westward movement were necessary, at least for a time, because of Indian resistance on the frontier.

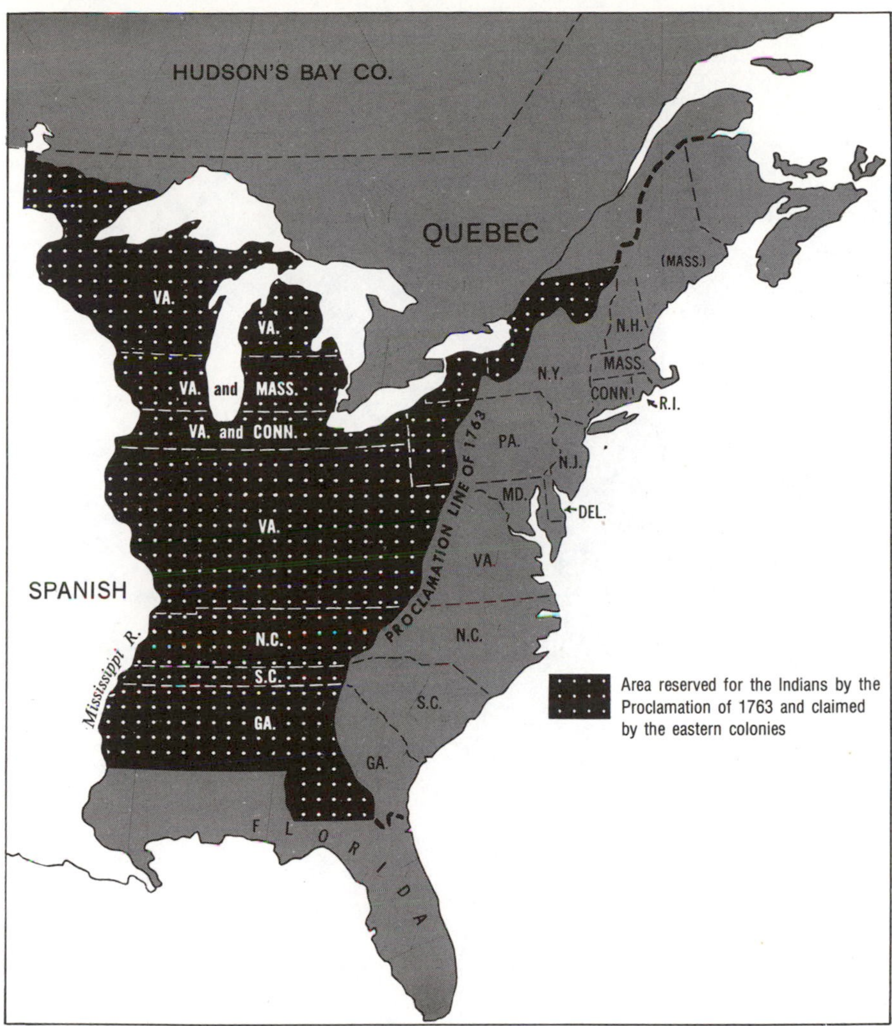

MAP 8–1

Land Claims: The colonial appetite for new land was huge, as colonial land claims by 1763 demonstrated. The Royal Proclamation of that year was designed to stop westward colonial movement.

Nevertheless, not everyone benefited from these restrictions. The withdrawal of cheap, unsettled western lands particularly disillusioned many young adults who had planned to set out on their own but now could not. Similarly, even established frontier farmers usually took an anti-British stand, because they thought that they would be more likely to succeed under a government that would be liberal in disposing of its land. Although poor agrarians did not

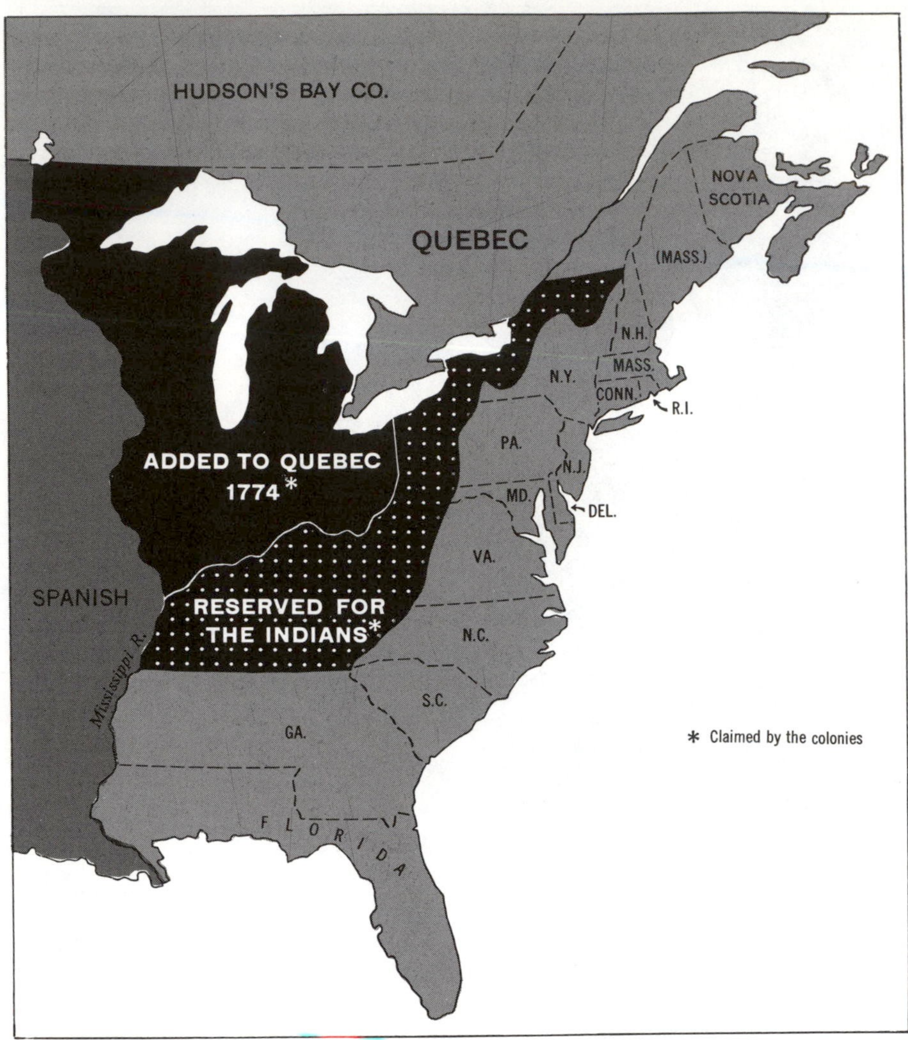

MAP 8–2

Reassignment: The Quebec Act of 1774 gave the Indians territories that had earlier been claimed by various colonies and, at the same time, nearly doubled the area of Quebec.

have dollar stakes in western lands that were comparable to those of large fur traders, land speculators, and planters, they were still affected. Those who were unable to pay their debts sometimes lost their farms through foreclosure, and a British policy that inhibited westward movement angered the frontiersmen and tended to align them against the British and with the aristocratic Americans, with whom they had no other affiliation. The Currency Act (Restraining Act) of

1764 also frustrated and annoyed this debtor group, because although prices actually rose moderately in the ensuing decade, farmers were persuaded that their lot worsened with the moderate contraction of paper money that occurred. Finally, the repeated trade stoppages that followed the nonintercourse agreements worked against the small farmers by lowering the prices of the surpluses they had to sell. As much as anything, a vague, scarcely articulated feeling that any change would be an improvement encouraged most farmers to support Revolution.

ECONOMIC EXPLOITATION RECONSIDERED

It is sometimes alleged that the American Revolution was the result of the inevitable clash of competing capitalisms and also of England's exploitation of the colonies. In long-run perspective, such conjectures defy empirical testing. After all, how can we judge whether independence or British rule offered more promise for economic progress in North America?

Of course, the short-run consequences of independence can be assessed —a task that awaits us in Chapter 9. But at this point, it is important to reconsider the question of colonial exploitation as a motive for revolt. Did British trade restrictions drain the colonial economy?

First, manufacturing restrictions had been placed on woolens, hats, and finished iron products. Woolen production in the colonies was limited to personal use or local trade, but this imposed no hardship. The colonists were quite satisfied to purchase manufactures from England at the lower costs made possible by the large-scale production methods employed there. This situation continued even after independence was achieved, and American woolens provided no competition for imported English fabrics until the nineteenth century.

A small portion of colonial manufacturing activity (predominantly New York producers) was hurt by the passage of the Hat Act in 1732. This one-sided legislation benefited London hatters by prohibiting the colonial export of beaver hats. For the overall American economy, however, the effects of the Hat Act were negligible. Similarly, Parliamentary restrictions on iron proved moderately harmless. Actually the colonial production of raw pig and bar iron was encouraged, but the finishing of iron and steel and the use of certain types of equipment were forbidden after 1750. Nevertheless, like the Molasses Act of 1733, restrictions on the manufacture of colonial iron were ignored with impunity: 25 iron mills were established between 1750 and 1775 in Pennsylvania and Delaware alone. Furthermore, the legislative freedom enjoyed by the colonists was amply displayed when the Pennsylvania assembly—in open defiance of the law—appropriated financial aid for a new slitting mill (nail factory). No matter how distasteful these British regulations were to the colonists, they were either superfluous (woolen restrictions), ignored (the slitting mill), or inconsequential (hat production).

The generally liberal British land policy was designed to encourage rapid settlement. Only after the war with Chief Pontiac and the resulting Royal Proclamation of 1763 did land policy suddenly become less flexible. When land controls were tightened again by the Quebec Act of 1774, important political issues emerged. Western lands claimed by Massachusetts, Connecticut, and Virginia were redistributed to the Province of Quebec, and land was made less accessible. Territorial governments were placed entirely in the hands of British officials, and trials there were conducted without juries.

We have already assessed the economic implications of these land policies. Some people gained; others lost. But clearly the climate of freedom changed swiftly, and the political implications of these new policies were hard for the colonists to accept. Apparently, however, those land policies were largely necessary, and the same basic restraints were prescribed and adopted by the federal government after American independence was achieved. It seems unlikely that the new government would have adopted these restraints if they had been economically burdensome on the colonists. The major issue appears to have been who was to determine the policy, rather than what the policy itself was to be.

The same thing was true of currency restrictions. After independence, the new government adopted measures similar to those England had imposed earlier. For instance, in 1751, Parliament passed the Currency Act, which prohibited New England from establishing new land banks and from issuing more paper money. A similar and supplemental Restraining Act appeared in 1764, in the wake of events in the Chesapeake area. Planters there were heavily in debt because they had continued to import goods during the Seven Years' War even though their own exports had declined. When Virginia issued £250,000 in bills of credit, British creditors stood to lose. When the planters began to use cheap money to repay the debts they had incurred in hard sterling, Britain countered by extending the original Currency Act to all the colonies. This enactment certainly hurt the hard-pressed Chesapeake region and may have stimulated its unusual support for the boycott of English imports in 1765. But the adoption of similar controls after independence indicates that the economic burden of currency restrictions could not have been oppressive overall. The real point at issue was simply whether England or the colonists themselves should hold the reins of monetary control.

It appears that only with respect to the Navigation Acts was there any significant exploitation in a strict economic sense. In the words of Lawrence A. Harper:

> The enumeration of key colonial exports in various Acts from 1660 to 1766 and the Staple Act of 1663 hit at colonial trade both coming and going. The Acts required the colonies to allow English middlemen to distribute such crops as tobacco and rice and stipulated that if the colonies would not buy English manufactures, at least they should purchase their European goods in England. The greatest element in the burden laid upon the colonies was not the taxes assessed. It consisted in the increased costs of shipment, transshipment, and middleman's profits arising out of the requirement that England be used as an entrepôt.[3]

[3]Lawrence A. Harper, "The Effect of the Navigation Acts on the Thirteen Colonies," Richard B. Morris (ed.), in *The Era of the American Revolution*, Columbia University Press (New York, 1939).

These burdens of more costly imports and less remunerative colonial exports may have amounted to as much as 1 percent of total colonial income.[4] But on the other side of the coin, the colonies were provided with bounties and other benefits such as naval protection and military defense at British expense.

In any case, the colonists had lived with these restrictions for over a century. Even those hardest hit—the producers of tobacco and other enumerated products—almost never mentioned them in their lists of grievances against England. It is especially noteworthy that *the acts of trade are not even mentioned in the Declaration of Independence.*

Rather than exploitation, it was the rapidly changing and severely administered new colonial policies that precipitated the American Revolution. Before 1763, the colonists had been free to do pretty much as they pleased. An occasional new enactment or veto of a piece of colonial legislation by Britain had caused little or no discord. After the Seven Years War, however, conditions suddenly changed. A host of new regulations were effected and strictly enforced by Britain. Then almost every colonist had a grievance: debtors objected to the Currency Act; shippers and merchants, to the Sugar Act; pioneers, to the Quebec Act; politicians, printers, and gamblers, to the Stamp Act; retailers and smugglers, to the Tea Act. As colonial resentments flared, Committees of Correspondence pressed forward to formally claim the rights they had long held de facto before 1763. In many ways, it appears that the growing economic maturity of the colonies would soon have made American independence inevitable. But was Revolution necessary to break away from the Empire: After all, other English colonies subsequently gained independence without resorting to armed warfare. By 1775, according to Charles Andrews, the colonies had reached a point where they were

> . . . qualified to cooperate with the mother country on terms similar to those of a brotherhood of free nations, such as the British world is becoming today (1926). But England was unable to see this fact, or to recognize it, and consequently America became the scene of a political unrest which might have been controlled by a compromise, but was turned to revolt by coercion. The situation is a very interesting one, for England is famous for her ability to compromise at critical times in her history. For once, at least, she failed.[5]

The nature of that "failure" is nicely summarized by Harper:

> As a mother country, Britain had much to learn. Any modern parents' magazine could have told George III's ministers that the one mistake not to make is to take a stand and then to yield to howls of anguish. It was a mistake which

[4] For an assessment of the several studies and estimates of these costs, see Gary M. Walton, "The New Economic History and the Burdens of the Navigation Acts," *Economic History Review,* 2nd Series, **XXIV** (1971), pp. 33–42.

[5] Charles Andrews, "The American Revolution: An Interpretation," *American Historical Review* **XXXI** (January 1926), p. 232.

> the British government made repeatedly. It placed a duty of 3d. per gallon on molasses, and when it encountered opposition, reduced it to 1d. It provided for a Stamp Act and withdrew it in the face of temper tantrums. It provided for external taxes to meet the colonial objections and then yielded again by removing all except one. When finally it attempted to enforce discipline, it was too late. Under the circumstances, no self-respecting child—or colonist—would be willing to yield.[6]

It would appear that the lessons they learned from their failures with the American colonies served the British well in later periods, because other English colonies subsequently won their independence without widescale bloodshed.

[6]Lawrence A. Harper, "Mercantilism and the American Revolution," *The Canadian Historical Review* **XXV** (March 1942), p. 14.

2

The Revolutionary, Early National, and Antebellum Eras 1776–1860

9

Hard Realities for a New Nation

THE WAR AND THE ECONOMY

The War of the Revolution, which began officially on April 19, 1775, dragged on for more than six bitter years. From a vantage point two centuries later, we can see that the war foreshadowed a massive upheaval in the Western world—a chain reaction of revolutions, great and small, that would transform the world. But to the embattled colonials, it was simply a conflict fought for the righteous cause of securing freedom from illegal British intervention in American affairs. Paradoxically, the Revolution was never supported by the substantial popular majority. Perhaps one-third of the colonists remained loyal to England; another third did little or nothing to help the cause, often trafficking with the enemy and profiteering by selling provisions and supplies to American troops at exorbitant prices. In varying numbers and in widely scattered theaters, foot soldiers slogged wearily back and forth in heartbreaking campaigns that produced no military gains. Although there were relatively few seamen and sea battles were for the most part militarily indecisive, it is an irony of history that the Revolutionary War was finally won with naval strength, as the French fleet under DeGrasse drove off the British men-of-war and bottled up Cornwallis at Yorktown.

Of course, maritime commerce was always an important factor in the war effort, and trade linkages were vital to the supply of arms and ammunitions. When legal restrictions were implemented by both the British and the colonists in 1775, nearly all American overseas commerce abruptly ceased. By mid-1775, the colonies faced acute shortages in such militarily essential items as powder, flints, muskets, and knives. Even salt, shoes, woolens, and linens were in short supply. Late in 1775, Congress authorized limited trade with the West Indies, mainly to procure arms and ammunitions, and trade with other non-British areas was on an unrestricted basis by the spring of 1776.

Nevertheless, the British maintained a fairly effective naval blockade of American ports, and the amounts of wartime trade were at their lowest levels in 1776 and 1777. Boston was pried open late in 1776, but most of the other major ports in New England and the Middle Colonies were tightly sealed until 1778. But as the British relaxed their grip on the North, they tightened up on the South. Savannah was taken late in 1778, as was Charleston by 1780.

Formal treaties of commerce—first with France in 1778 and with Holland and Spain shortly thereafter—stimulated the flows of overseas trade, and between 1778 and early 1782, American wartime commerce was at its zenith. During those years, France, Holland, and Spain and their possessions all actively traded with the colonies.

The Dutch actually became so active in shipping tobacco from the Chesapeake Bay area that the Dutch island of St. Eustatius became an entrepôt in the Caribbean. In fact, the lively trade there encouraged Britain to declare war against Holland late in 1780, and as the Royal Navy continued its push southward into the Caribbean, St. Eustatius fell in 1781. Trades in fish, salt, and wine between New England and Spain were maintained throughout the war on reduced levels, but Spain did serve as a center for the sale of prizes captured by American privateers. In addition, Spanish Cuba (like Holland's St. Eustatius) became an important trade center in the Caribbean, but American shippers had incurred such enormous losses there by 1782 that insurance costs and risks reached an all-time high.

As already emphasized, the wartime flows of goods in and out of the colonies were highest before 1782 but were still well below prewar levels. Smuggling, privateering, and legal trade with France, Holland, and Spain and their possessions only partially offset the drastic trade reductions with Britain. Even the coastal trades were curtailed by a lack of vessels, by blockades, and by sky-rocketing freight rates. British-occupied ports, such as New York, generated some import activity but little or nothing in the way of exports.

As a result, the colonial economy became considerably more self-sufficient. In Philadelphia, for instance, nearly 4,000 women were employed to spin materials in their homes for the newly established textile plants. There was also a sharp increase in the number of artisan workshops and a similar stimulus to the production of beer, whiskey, and other domestic alcoholic beverages in the colonies. As these facts suggest, an increasing amount of American resources was being channeled into import-competing industries, especially along the coast and in the major port cities. Only the least commercialized rural areas remained little affected by the serpentine path of war and the sporadic flows of wartime commerce.

Overall, the stringencies of war imposed a distinct economic and social hardship on the new nation. Although war had slightly lessened the degree to which the rebelling states depended on Britain, most goods had risen in cost and were much more scarce in America. Markets were greatly disrupted during wartime, making trade very uncertain. Encouraged by temporarily high prices and facing severe commercial difficulties, some investors turned from commerce to manufacturing to vent their capital. But once the trade lanes reopened with the coming of peace, even those who profited from the war were stung by the tide of imports that swept into American ports and sharply lowered prices. Although many Americans escaped the direct ordeals of war, few Americans were untouched by it—at least indirectly.

Problems, Politics, and Philosophy

In retrospect, it seems astonishing that the Americans were able to win their freedom. The British were hampered, of course, by extended lines of communication and supply, and their military leadership was marked on occasion by surpassing ineptness. Moreover, the French—not because they loved the Americans but because they hated the English—opportunistically provided the help that proved decisive. And despite serious weaknesses, the American government exhibited a persistent vitality and flexibility that surprised friend and enemy alike. Yet in the black year of 1780, only the spirit and dogged courage of those who deeply believed in independence could keep the cause alive. The next year marked the turning point of the war; after five years of noisy argument, the Articles of Confederation were ratified, and new but limited order was imposed on the administration of the nation's affairs.

To be sure, there was still disruptive division among American leaders as to what kind of government should ultimately be adopted. One group wanted no stronger central government than the Articles provided, preferring to cast its lot and fortune with the individual states. Another group, made up on the whole of less fiery revolutionaries, took the view that a strong central government, with power to coerce the states, should be quickly established. Until the end of the war, those who preferred a strong government were largely in control of the nation's affairs; but when news of a favorable peace arrived in 1783, many of the strongest leaders went home to their own pursuits, leaving the administration largely in charge of the weak-government advocates. For several years, the most able Americans seemed to be preoccupied with their own interests. Only John Jay, the Secretary for Foreign Affairs, exhibited strong leadership during this period.

But problems too great to be surmounted by the states acting individually pressed inexorably for strong rather than weak union. The great powers treated the new nation with a disdain that bordered on contempt. Britain—annoyed because Americans refused to pay prewar British creditors and to restore confiscated Tory property as provided in the peace treaty—excluded the United States from valuable commercial privileges and refused to withdraw troops from its frontier posts on American soil. Spain tried to close the lower Mississippi to American traffic. Even France refused to extend the courtesies traditionally offered a sovereign government.

Internally, the most pressing problems were financial. Fortunately for postwar Confederation officials, the money cost of the Revolutionary War had been largely written off. Between 1775 and 1781, the war was financed by the issue of paper money in amounts great enough to result in a galloping inflation—the only one ever experienced in America except in the Confederate South. Nearly $400 million in continental money, quartermaster and commissary certificates of the central government, and paper money of the states were issued to defray wartime expenses. For all practical purposes, these various issues were repudiated by the middle of 1783, the effect being that of a tax on those who held the depreciating currency while it declined in value. Only a relatively small foreign and domestic debt totaling less than $40 million remained; but the question of the responsibility for its repayment remained a thorny issue, because political leaders assumed that the political units that paid the debt would ultimately hold the balance of power. More important was the fact that Congress had no independent income and had to rely for funds on catch-as-catch-can contributions of the states that were levied roughly in proportion to their several populations. Nor were the states without their own fiscal problems. By 1786, no less than seven states were issuing their own paper, and debtor groups in the other six states were clamoring for similar issues. Although the issuing states, with the exception of Rhode Island, acted responsibly, perhaps no other course of events so frightened conservatives as the increased control of the money supply by the states.

The United States under the Articles of Confederation was by no means the weak and hopelessly inefficient organization some historians have led us to believe. Congress did manage to finance a central government through a trying period, painstakingly working to settle a multitude of obligations incurred during the war. The leadership was strong enough to effect an imaginative and nearly permanent settlement of the perplexing Western question. Barriers to trade among the states existed but were the exception rather than the rule. As early as 1783, even the supporters of a weak central government had begun to make concessions that would strengthen the power of Congress, and by 1786, most of the vehement opponents of a strong central government knew that genuine union was inevitable. Virginia called the Annapolis Convention ostensibly to settle questions of trade regulations among the states. Yet even before the delegates came to Annapolis, only to recommend to Congress that another convention be called to examine a broader range of problems, it was clear that American leadership was moving toward unity. The convention that met in Philadelphia in 1787 could ignore its instructions to amend the Articles of Confederation and create a new government instead only because the great constitutional question debated so heatedly since 1775 was at last settled in the minds of the majority. The new Constitution, which contained provisions for a great common market and a central government strong enough to assure adequate investment in social overhead capital, was a necessary condition for the unimpeded growth of the American economy.

In 1776, the Declaration of Independence rang its message of political freedom around the world. In the same year, an odd-looking Scot, whose professorial mien belied his vast knowledge of economic affairs, offered a similarly clarion rationale of economic freedom. *The Wealth of Nations* became a bestseller, and Adam Smith almost at once found himself admired and famous. Educated people everywhere, including American leaders, read his great work, marveling at the lucid language and its castigation of mercantilist constraints on economic processes. It does not deny Adam Smith's great influence to say that he was the articulate commentator on forces that existed long before he began to write. Chief among these forces were a growing regard for the advantages of private property arrangements and the abiding conviction that law and order were essential to the preservation of property rights and to the opportunity for all people to acquire the things of this world.

Equaling the political guarantees of the Constitution in their ultimate assurance of freedom were the fundamental economic guarantees of protection of private property and enforcement of contracts, assuring the stability necessary to a market economy. Smith himself could not have designed a state better tailored to his concept of an economic order directed by self-interest, of a system unshackled by governmental rules and regulations but assured the domestic tranquility and freedom from foreign interference that only a strong central government could provide.

AMERICAN INDEPENDENCE AND ECONOMIC CHANGE

The important political, legal, and institutional changes that ensued during the critical years of war and throughout the entire 1780s were paralleled and influenced by economic adjustments. That period was not a time of prosperity. Indeed, the trials and tribulations of a government functioning under the Articles of Confederation and the rising pressures that led to the ratification of the Constitution only partially convey the many painful new circumstances that the struggling young nation faced. In short, the crucial political decisions of that time were matched by challenging economic problems.

The most central problem was independence itself, because this conversion was unlike previous adjustments to peacetime. Once the young nation found itself outside the walls of the Empire, even the wartime trade alliances with France and Spain began to crumble.

In the Caribbean, U.S. ships were excluded from direct trade with the British West Indies. American merchants who tried to evade the law faced possible seizure by officials. Spain added to American woes by withdrawing the wartime privilege of direct U.S. trade with Cuba, Puerto Rico, and Hispaniola. In addition, Spain reinstituted its traditional policy of restricting trade with its possessions, permitting them to import goods only from Spain. There was an increase in U.S. trade with the French West Indies, but this was not enough to offset the other declines in commercial trade with the Caribbean Islands. Even in its lively trade with the French, the U.S. was not allowed to carry sugar from French islands, and only in times of severe scarcity did the French import American flour. In addition, the French imposed high duties on U.S. salted fish and meat, and these products were banned entirely from the British islands.

Restrictions and trade curtailments were not limited to the Caribbean. Now Americans were also cut off from direct trade with the British fisheries in Newfoundland and Nova Scotia. As a result, New England suffered severe losses in trade to the North in provisions, lumber, rum, and shipping services. To the East and into the Mediterranean, American shipping faced harassment by the Barbary pirates. The United States was no longer protected by the British flag and by British tribute to the governments of Tunis, Tripoli, and Algeria.

While American shipping rocked at anchor, American shipbuilding and the supporting industries of lumber and naval stores remained unengaged. Of course, Britain now labeled all American-built vessels as foreign, thereby making them ineligible to trade within the Empire even when they were owned by British subjects. The result was the loss of a major market for American shipbuilders, and U.S. ship production declined still further because American whale oil faced prohibitively high British duties after 1783. In fact, nearly all of the activities that employed American-built ships (cod fishing, whaling, mercantile and shipping services) were depressed industries, and New England—the center of these activities—suffered disproportionately during the early years of independence.

The Middle Colonies were also affected. Pennsylvania and New York shared losses in shipbuilding. Moreover, their trades in wheat, flour, salted meat, and other provisions to the West Indies were well below those in colonial peacetime years. By 1786, that region had probably reached the bottom of a fairly severe business cycle, but conditions began to improve in the late 1780s as these products were reaccepted into the traditional West Indian and southern European markets. Similar problems plagued the South. For instance, British duties on rice restricted planters of the lower South primarily to markets in the West Indies and southern Europe. As the price of rice declined, further setbacks resulted from the loss of bounties and subsidies on indigo and naval stores. Having few alternative uses of its productive capacity, the lower South faced special difficulties. Its overall economic future did not look bright. Similarly, the upper South faced stagnating markets for its major staple—tobacco. In Britain, a tax of 15d. sterling was imposed on a pound of foreign tobacco. In France, a single purchasing monopoly—the Farmers-General—was created to handle tobacco imports into France. Meanwhile, Spain and Portugal prohibited imports of American tobacco altogether.

Offsetting these restrictions were a few positive forces. Goods, which previously had been "enumerated," could now be traded directly to continental European ports. This lowered the shipping and handling costs on some items such as tobacco, so that American exporters and planters received higher prices. Meanwhile, the great influx of British manufactures sharply reduced prices on these goods in American ports. Although American manufacturers suffered, U.S. consumers were pleased; compared to the late colonial period, the terms of trade—the prices paid for imports relative to the prices paid for exports—had improved. This was especially true in 1783 and 1784 when import prices were slightly below their prewar level and export prices were higher. Thereafter, the terms of trade became less favorable, and by 1790, there was little advantage in the adjustments of these relative prices compared with the prewar period.

To convey these many changes more systematically and in a long-run perspective, it is essential to compare the circumstances of the late colonial period with the circumstances surrounding the time of the adoption of the Constitution. Of course, this does not entirely isolate the impact of independence on the economy, because forces other than independence contributed to the shifting magnitudes and patterns of trade and to the many other economic changes that occurred. Nevertheless, comparisons of the late colonial period with the early 1790s provide important insights into the new directions and prospects for the young nation.

In Table 9-1, we see that by 1790, the United States had taken advantage of its new freedom to trade directly with other northern European countries. Most of this trade was in tobacco to France and the Netherlands, but rice, wheat, flour, and maize (Indian corn) were also shipped there in large amounts. The emergence of this new trade pattern must be attributed largely to independence, but it should be emphasized that the lion's share of American exports continued to be sent to Great Britain, including items that were then reexported to the Continent. Many have speculated on the reasons for this renewal of American–British loyalties. Part of the explanation may be that Britain offered the greatest variety of goods at the best price and quality, especially woolens, linens, and hardwares. Moreover, British merchants enjoyed the advantages of a common language, established contacts, and a knowledge of U.S. markets. Because American imports were handled by British merchants, it was often advantageous to use British ports as dropping off points for U.S. exports, even those destined for the Continent.

In addition to these changes, new patterns of trade were emerging in the Caribbean. Before the Revolution, trade with the British West Indies had been greater than trade with the foreign islands, but by 1790 the situation was reversed, largely due to the exclusion of American shipping from the British islands. Undoubtedly, many American ships illegally traversed British Caribbean waters, and St. Eustatius remained an entrepôt from which British islands were supplied, as they had been during the war. Consequently, the statistics in Table 9-1 exaggerate this shift. Nevertheless, it would appear that U.S. trade with non-British areas of the Caribbean grew substantially during these years. This trend had been underway before the Revolution, but postwar restrictions on American shipping undoubtedly hastened that shift.

TABLE 9–1

Average Annual Real Exports to Overseas Areas: The Thirteen Colonies, 1768–1772, and the United States, 1790–1792 (thousands of pounds sterling: 1768–1772 prices)

Destination	1768–1772	Percentage of Total	1790–1792	Percentage of Total
Great Britain and Ireland	1,616	58	1,234	31
Northern Europe	—		643	16
Southern Europe	406	14	557	14
British West Indies }	759	27	402	10
Foreign West Indies }			956	24
Africa	21	1	42	1
Canadian Colonies	NA		60	2
Other	—		59	1
Total	2,802	100	3,953	100

Source: James F. Shepherd and Gary M. Walton, "Economic Change After the American Revolution: Pre- and Postwar Comparisons of Maritime Shipping and Trade," *Explorations in Economic History,* **13**:4 (October 1976), pp. 397–422.

Lastly, it is worth noting that no new trades to romantic faraway places emerged in any significant way during this period of transition. The changes in trade patterns that were effected were actually rather modest.

As trade patterns changed, so did the relative importance of the many goods traded. For instance, Table 9-2 shows that the great prewar staple—

TABLE 9–2
Annual Average Exports of Selected Commodities from the Thirteen Colonies, 1768–1772, and the United States, 1790–1792

	THIRTEEN COLONIES, 1768–1772			UNITED STATES, 1790–1792		
Commodity	Quantity (1)	Value (thousands of current pounds sterling) (2)	Value (thousands of dollars: 1790–1792 prices) (3)	Quantity (4)	Value (thousands of current dollars) (5)	Value (thousands of pounds sterling: 1768–1772 prices) (6)
Beef Pork	26,036 bbl	51	209	60,457 bbl 29,741 bbl	367 285	159
Bread Flour	38,634 tons	410	2,534	3,823 tons 63,256 tons	221 4,178	712
Cotton	29,425 lb	1	7	163,822 lb	41	8
Fish, dried	308,993 quintals	154	740	375,619 quintals	900	187
Flaxseed	233,065 bu	42	189	352,079 bu	286	64
Grain:						
Indian corn	839,314 bu	83	424	1,926,784 bu	974	191
Rice	140,254 bbl	311	1,971	129,367 bbl	1,818	287
Wheat	599,127 bu	115	654	998,862 bu	1,090	192
Indigo	547,649 lb	113	567	493,760 lb	511	101
Iron:						
Bar	2,416 tons	36	195	300 tons	24	4
Pig	4,468 tons	22	116	3,667 tons	95	18
Livestock:						
Cattle	3,433	21	63	4,861	89	29
Horses	6,048	60	240	7,086	282	71
Naval Stores:						
Pitch	11,384 bbl	5	21	7,279 bbl	13	3
Tar	90,472 bbl	34	135	68,463 bbl	102	25
Turpentine	19,870 bbl	9	42	51,194 bbl	108	24
Oil, whale	3,841 tons	46	212	1,826 tons	101	22
Potash	1,381 tons	35	134	4,872 tons	472	123
Rum, American	342,366 gal	22	132	441,782 gal	170	28
Tobacco	87,986 hhd	766	3,093	110,687 hhd	3,891	964
Wood Products:						
Pine boards	38,991 M ft	70	228	45,118 M ft	264	81
Staves and headings	21,585 M	65	275	31,554 M	401	95
Total, above commodities		2,471	12,181		16,683	3,388
All exports		2,802			19,465	

Source: See Table 9-1.

tobacco—was no longer the single most valuable export by the early 1790s, despite some recovery in the 1780s. Actually, tobacco production may have equaled or perhaps even exceeded prewar levels as early as the mid-1780s. This, along with rising tobacco prices, aided the recovery of the tobacco-producing areas of Virginia and Maryland. However, such good fortune failed to touch the other important southern staples, and the lower South in particular lapsed into more self-sufficiency. Later in the 1780s, the rising prices for rice offset the diminishing quantity exported, but indigo and naval stores both fell in value and in quantity. This decline was due, of course, to the loss of the bounties (and to increased British production of indigo in the West Indies after the war).

The most striking change of the period, however, was the increase in the export of foodstuffs such as salted meats (beef and pork), bread and flour, maize, and wheat. Of course, these accompanied the relative rise of the trades to the West Indies. Because the uptrend in food shipments to the West Indies was underway before the Revolution, not all of this shift in commodities can be attributed solely to independence.

Because of these changing patterns and magnitudes of trade, some states improved their economic well-being while others lost ground. Table 9-3 shows exports per capita for each state during this period, after adjusting for inflationary effects. Compared to prewar levels, New England had returned to about the same per-capita position by the early 1790s. The Middle Atlantic region showed improvement despite the depression felt so sharply in Pennsylvania.

As indicated in Table 9-3, the trade of the southern regions did not keep pace with a growing population. Although the South's prewar absolute level of exports had been regained by the early 1790s, its per-capita exports were significantly below those in colonial times. The lower South was the region most severely affected. However, once again, this was not entirely due to independence; it was probably due more to a decline in the growth of demand in Europe for southern staples.

The wide variety of changes among the states makes it extremely hazardous to generalize nationally. Overall, there was a 30 percent decline in real per-capita exports (per year). Total exports had climbed by 40 percent, but this fell far short of the 80 percent jump in population. Accompanying this change was a slowing in urbanization. The major cities of Philadelphia, New York, and Boston grew only 3 percent over this time period, despite the large increase in the total population of the states. Both of these adjustments—the decline in per-capita exports and the pause in urban growth—were extremely unusual peacetime experiences. Yet, as emphasized, such aggregate figures hide as much as they reveal. The southern declines were sharp; only New York and the New England states (except New Hampshire) more than fully recovered from trade disruptions.

The western movement and the persistence of self-sufficient activities cushioned the downfall of incomes per capita. Undoubtedly, per-capita internal trade also did not decline to the same extent as per-capita exports. Unfortunately, we have no statistics on domestic trade during that hectic period. Nevertheless, the external relations probably exaggerated the overall setbacks

TABLE 9–3
Average Annual Exports from Colonies and Regions of the Thirteen Colonies, 1768–1772, and States and Regions of the United States, 1791–1792 (thousands of pounds sterling; 1768–1772 prices)

	1768–1772			1791–1792		
Origin	Total exports	Percentage of total	Per-capita exports	Total exports	Percentage of total	Per-capita exports
New England						
New Hampshire	46	2	0.74	33	1	0.23
Massachusetts	258	9	0.97	542	14	1.14
Rhode Island	81	3	1.39	119	3	1.72
Connecticut	92	3	0.50	148	4	0.62
Total, New England	477	17	0.82	842	22	0.83
Middle Atlantic						
New York	187	7	1.15	512	14	1.51
New Jersey	2	—	0.02	5	—	0.03
Pennsylvania	353	13	1.47	584	16	1.34
Delaware	18	1	0.51	26	1	0.44
Total, Middle Atlantic	559	20	1.01	1,127	30	1.11
Upper South						
Maryland	392	14	1.93	482	13	1.51
Virginia	770	27	1.72	678	18	0.91
Total, upper South	1,162	41	1.79	1,160	31	1.09
Lower South						
North Carolina	75	3	0.38	104	3	0.27
South Carolina	455	16	3.66	436	12	1.75
Georgia	74	3	3.17	97	3	1.17
Total, lower South	603	22	1.75	637	17	0.88
Total, all regions	2,802	100	1.31	3,766	100	0.99

Source: See Table 9-1.

of the period. It is safe to conclude, however, that the political chaos of the Early National Era was accompanied by severe economic conditions. Indeed, the problems of government contributed to the weakness of the economy, and in turn, economic events clarified government failings under the Articles of Confederation.

These were the circumstances shortly before 1793—the year in which the Napoleonic Wars erupted and Eli Whitney invented the cotton gin. The sweeping consequences of those events could never have been foreseen in colonial times. The colonies, however, had already developed a commercial base that now would prove crucial to further development. Because of its early efforts at overseas trade, the new nation was ready to take quick advantage of the economic possibilities of a neutral nation in a world at war.

10

Economic Shocks and Early Business Cycles

WAR, NEUTRALITY, AND ECONOMIC RESURGENCE

The economic setbacks experienced by the United States throughout the late 1770s and most of the 1780s were followed by years of halting progress and incomplete recovery. Then in 1793, just four years after the beginning of the French Revolution, the French and English began a series of wars that lasted until 1815. During this long struggle, both British and French cargo vessels were drafted into military service, and both nations relaxed their restrictive mercantilist policies. Of all the nations most capable of filling the shipping void created by the Napoleonic Wars, the new United States stood at the forefront.

Due to these developments, the nation's economy briskly rebounded from the doldrums of the preceding years. The stimulus in U.S. overseas commerce is graphed statistically in Figure 10-1. As indicated, per-capita credits in the balance of payments (exports plus other sources of foreign exchange earnings) more than tripled between 1790 and the height of war between the French and English. There can be little doubt that these were extraordinary years—a time of unusual prosperity and intense economic activity, especially in the eastern port cities. It was a time characterized by full employment and sharply rising urbanization, at least until 1808. Famed entrepreneurs of New England and the Middle Atlantic region, such as Stephen Gerard, Archibald Gracie, E. H. Derby, and John Jacob Astor, amassed vast personal fortunes during this period. These and other capital accumulations added to the development of a well-established commercial sector and eventually contributed to the incipient manufacturing sector.

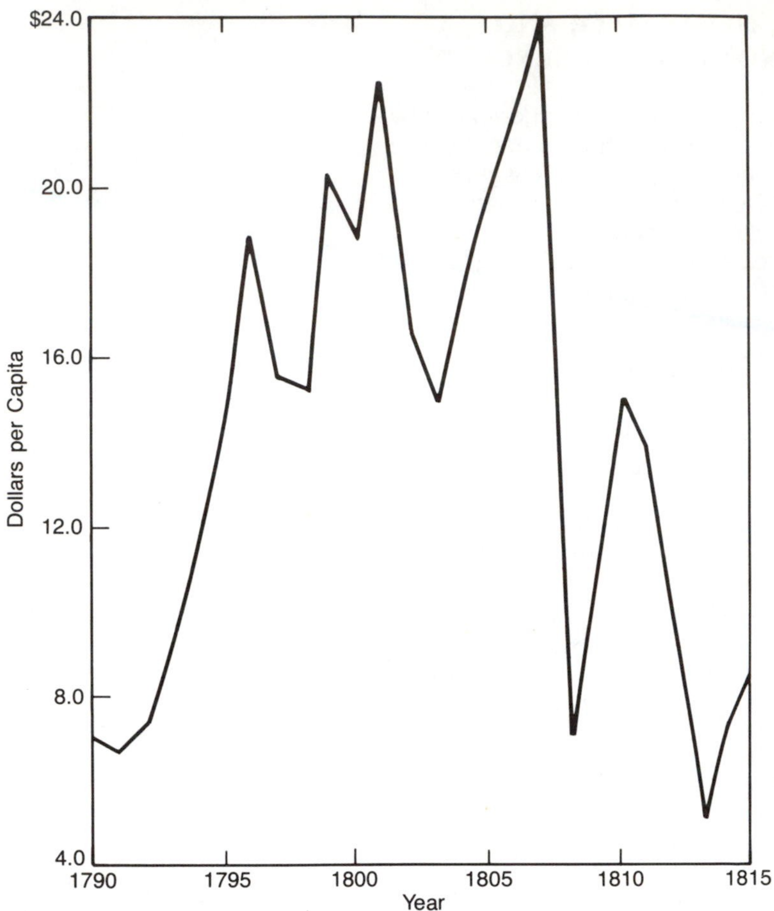

FIGURE 10–1

Per-Capita Credits in the U.S. Balance of Payments, 1790–1815
Source: Douglass C. North, "Early National Income Estimates of the United States," *Economic Development and Cultural Change,* IX:3 (April 1961), p. 390.

It is important to recognize the significance of the commercial sector of the economy as well as the role of the merchant class during these decades. The growing merchant class, of course, had played an active role in helping to spearhead the move for national independence. Now the merchant class supplied the entrepreneurial talents required to take full advantage of the new economic circumstances. As the spreading war opened up exceptional trade opportunities, the well-developed commercial sector provided the needed buildings and ships, as well as know-how. In short, both the physical and human capital were already available, and in many ways the success of the period stemmed from developments that reached back to colonial times. It was exactly that prior development that singled out the United States as the leading neutral nation in time of war. Rather than the ports of the Caribbean, Latin America, or Canada, the leading ports of the United States emerged as the entrepôts of trade in the western Atlantic.

The effects of war and neutrality on U.S. shipping earnings is shown in Figure 10-2. In general, these statistics convey the same picture that we saw in Figure 10-1, namely that these were exceptionally prosperous times for the commercial sector.

Although the invention of the cotton gin stimulated cotton production and U.S. cotton supplies grew in response to the growth in the demand for raw cotton in English textile mills, commercial growth was by no means limited to products produced in the United States. As Figure 10-3 shows, reexports comprised a major portion of the total exports from U.S. ports, especially in such tropical items as sugar, coffee, cocoa, pepper, and spices. Because their commercial sectors were relatively underdeveloped, however, the Caribbean Islands and Latin America depended primarily on American shipping and merchandising services rather than on their own.

Of course, such unique conditions did not provide the basis for long-term development, and—as Figures 10-1, 10-2, and 10-3 all show—when temporary peace came between late 1801 and 1803, the U.S. commercial boom quickly evaporated. When hostilities erupted again, the United States experienced another sharp upswing in commercial activity. This time, however, new serious problems arose with the expansion. In 1805, the British imposed an antiquated

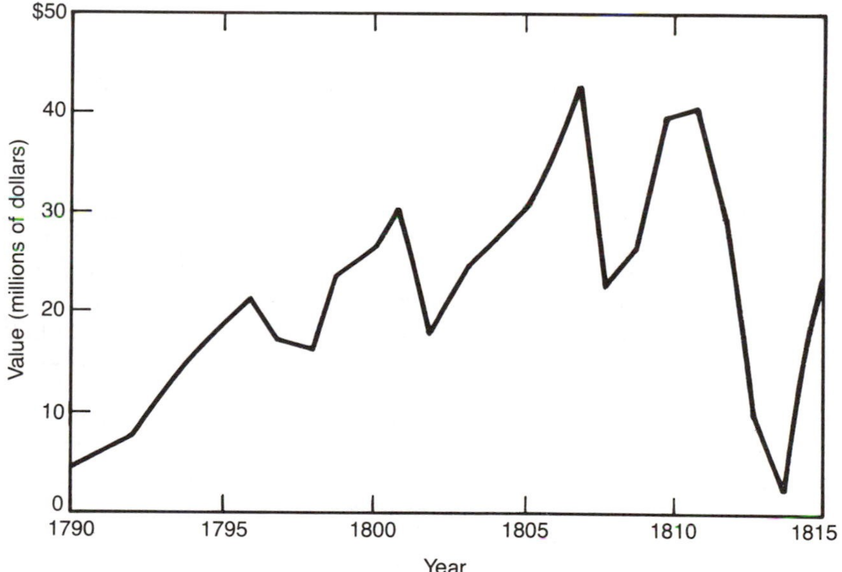

FIGURE 10–2

Net Freight Earnings of U.S. Carrying Trade, 1790–1815
Source: Douglass C. North, *The Economic Growth of the United States, 1790–1860* (Englewood Cliffs, N.J.: Prentice-Hall, 1961), pp. 26, 28.

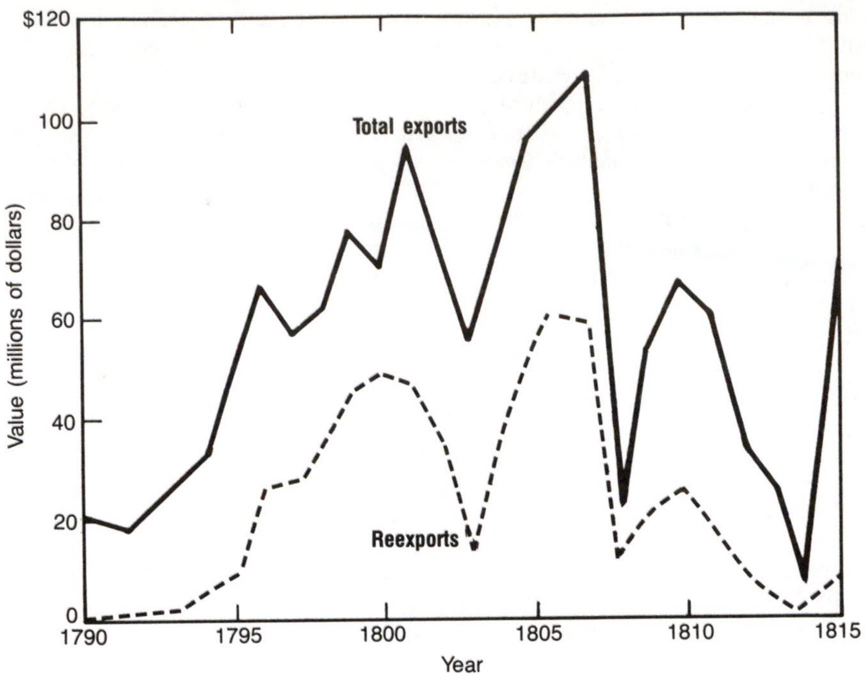

FIGURE 10–3

Values of Exports and Reexports from the United States, 1790–1815
Source: Douglass C. North, *The Economic Growth of the United States, 1790–1815* (Englewood Cliffs, N.J.: Prentice-Hall, 1961), p. 28.

ruling, the Rule of 1756, permitting neutrals in wartime to carry only those goods that they normally carried in peacetime. This ruling, known as the Essex Decision, was matched by Napoleon's Berlin Decree, which implemented a strategy of blockading Britain by sea. As a result, nearly 1,500 American ships and many American sailors were seized, and some were forcefully drafted into the Royal Navy. The Congress and President Jefferson, fearful of entangling the United States in war, declared the Embargo Act of 1807, which prohibited U.S. ships from trading with all foreign ports. Basically, this attempt to gain respect for American neutrality backfired, and as the drastic declines in Figures 10-1, 10-2, and 10-3 show, the cure was almost worse than the disease. As pressures in the port cities mounted, political action led to the Non-Importation Act of 1809. This partially opened up trade, with specific prohibitions against Great Britain, France, and their possessions.

Nevertheless, continuing seizures and other complications between the United States and Britain along the Canadian border finally led to war—the second with England within 30 years. The War of 1812 was largely a naval war, however, and the British seized more than 1,000 additional ships and blockaded almost the entire U.S. coast.

As exports declined to practically nothing, new boosts were given to the tiny manufacturing sector. Actually, stirrings there began with the Embargo of

1807, which quickly altered the possibilities for profits in commerce relative to manufactures. As prices on manufactures rose, increasing possibilities for profits encouraged capital to flow into manufacturing. From 15 textile mills in 1808, new additions raised the number to almost 90 by 1809. Similar additions continued throughout the war period, but when the Peace of Ghent in 1814 brought the war to a close, the textile industry faltered badly. Once again, British imports arrived in massive amounts and undercut prices, which were temporarily inflated by supply shortages resulting from the embargo and the war. Only large-scale U.S. concerns weathered the competitive storm, and there were few of these—most notably the Lowell shops using the Waltham system (discussed in Chapter 13) of cloth weaving. Nevertheless, these war-related spurts in manufacturing provided an important basis for further industrial expansion, not only in textiles—the main manufacturing activity of the time—but in other areas as well. This marked a time when the relative roles of the various sectors of the economy began to shift. Agriculture was to dominate the economy for most of the century, but to a lesser and lesser degree as economic growth continued.

THE FIRST AMERICAN BANKS

There is little doubt that the United States experienced its era of greatest export instability in the three decades preceding 1820.[1] Of course, as time passed, the importance of foreign trade diminished relative to the domestic economy and changing business conditions became increasingly influenced by forces that were internal to the economy. External forces were always an important factor in determining business cycles, but their almost total dominance was now beginning to wane. By the turn of the century, internal developments—especially those in the banking sector—had assumed a more pivotal role in causing economic fluctuations. As we will see at the end of this chapter, both external forces (acting through credit flows from and to overseas areas) and internal forces (acting through changes in credit availability and the money stock) came to bear on the economy during the early nineteenth century. Because the interactions of these two general forces proved critical in generating business cycles during the antebellum years, it is now time to take an in-depth look at developments in the banking sector, keeping in mind that external events were also at work.

Commercial Banks

The severing of relationships with the English during the Revolution, together with the relinquishment by the states of the right to issue bills of credit, made the establishment of modern credit-granting banks inevitable.

In 1781, Robert Morris and a few associates founded the Bank of Pennsylvania to assist in financing the Revolution. This bank so helped the harried

[1] For a statistical assessment of the United States and other experiences of export instability, see John R. Hanson II, "Export Instability in Historical Perspective," *Explorations in Economic History,* **14:**4 (October 1977).

Robert Morris (as painted by the distinguished artist and scientist Charles Willson Peale) was a prominent American who helped establish the Bank of North America in 1781 and who almost singlehandedly directed the financing of the American Revolution. Unfortunately, his speculation in land resulted in his personal ruin.

Continental Congress by facilitating the payment of troops and the purchase of provisions that after three years Morris was able to persuade Congress to grant a national charter to a new institution—the Bank of North America. The Bank of Pennsylvania soon went out of business, but many of those interested in it bought shares in the new venture. It was appropriate that the first chartered bank should be established in Philadelphia, which was to be the financial center of the country for several decades.

The first banks were "founded on specie"—that is, their capitals were subscribed for the most part in gold and silver. They received deposits, made loans, and in general functioned just as commercial banks do today. Although checks were drawn against deposits from the beginning, it was more common for people to make payments by bank notes manufactured to each bank's order by a private engraver. When a bank officer made a loan, the borrower's checking account could be credited with the amount, but the proceeds of the loan more commonly took the form of bank notes, which the borrower then put in circulation as money. In effect, the bank exchanged its more acceptable evidences of debt for the borrowers' less acceptable promissory notes.

During the years of business expansion and commercial boom, a striking number of banks were established. From merely three before 1790, there were 28 branches in the nation by 1800, and 88 by 1811—the eve of the second war with England. All except two of these banks were incorporated by special charter on the passage of a bill by a state legislature. Early charters contained few provisions restricting a bank's activities, although they frequently required that circulation be limited to two or three times the amount of a bank's capital and occasionally regulated the ratio of notes in circulation to specie reserve. The charter bills were passed only after political lobbying and, on occasion, actual bribery of the legislators. The Federalists, generally in power before 1800, granted charters to their supporters; after 1800, the friends of Democrats were more often given the valuable privilege of starting a bank. As we will see, the confluence of banking and politics was to emerge time after time in our history.

The First Bank of the United States

Shortly after becoming Secretary of the Treasury, Alexander Hamilton proposed the establishment of a semipublic banking institution that was to become the first Bank of the United States. Hamilton envisioned an organization similar to the Bank of England, which in nearly a century of operation had become a central bank, responsible for the banking business of the government and for the management of the country's monetary arrangements. Although Hamilton's idea was opposed by Thomas Jefferson and Edmund Randolph, respectively Secretary of State and Attorney General in the first cabinet, Hamilton won President Washington to his side, and approval of the bank was assured.

Hamilton's *Report on a National Bank,* in which he argued for a Bank of the United States, shows remarkable insight into both the financial problems of the young country and the economic implications of banking. Hamilton asserted that a "National Bank" would augment "the active or productive capital of a country." By this, he meant that it would increase the convertible paper money, possibly by as much as two or three times the specie base, because specie withdrawals from a bank were approximately offset by specie deposits under normal circumstances. Notes remained in circulation because of public confidence in them, and furthermore a

> borrower frequently, by a check or order, transfers his credits to some other person, to whom he has a payment to make; who, in his turn, is as often content with a similar credit, because he is satisfied that he can, whenever he pleases, either convert it into cash, or pass it to some other hand, as equivalent for it.

As important to Hamilton as the salutary effects of the proposed bank on the economy of the country was the assistance the bank could give the government by lending money to the treasury in times of stress. Moreover, the institution could serve as fiscal agent for the government by acting as a depository of government funds, making transfers of funds from one part of the country to another, and (Hamilton hoped) serving as a tax-collection agency.

The bill creating the bank followed Hamilton's report closely. There was substantial opposition to it, even in the predominantly Federalist Congress, on the grounds that (1) it was unconstitutional, (2) it would create a "money-monopoly" that would endanger the rights and liberties of the people, and (3)

One of the chief architects of the Constitution and policy makers for the new nation was Alexander Hamilton, shown here in a portrait by John Trumball.

it would be of value to the northern states but not to the agricultural South. Although the arguments of the opposition were eventually to prevail, they were unsuccessful at this time. The bill was carried on a sectional vote, and Washington signed it on St. Valentine's Day in 1791.

The Bank had a capital of $10 million—a sizable sum in those days and considerably greater than the capital of any previously existing American bank.[2] Such a large amount of capital was possible because three-fourths of the *private* subscription of $8 million were payable in U.S. bonds and only one-fourth was payable in specie, with subscriptions to be paid in four installments.[3] The United States bought one-fifth of the capital stock. Apparently, the desire of the Bank's founders to have the government share in the profits of the enterprise overcame any possible concern about the control the government might exercise through its five appointed directors. The government paid for its shares with the proceeds of a $2 million loan extended by the Bank on

[2] The Bank of North America, for example, started with a capital of $300,000, over half of which had been contributed by the government.

[3] It would have been impossible to obtain the whole $10 million in specie, and the requirement that U.S. securities be used for such a purpose strengthened the market for them. Most of the Bank stock was in fact paid for in U.S. bonds. According to Bray Hammond, "The Bank was permitted to organize as soon as $400,000 had been received from the subscribers. Whether much more was ever got from them is doubtful, though the Bank subsequently accumulated a treasure much in excess of what the stockholders were supposed to pay." Bray Hammond, *Banks and Politics in America from the Revolution to the Civil War* (Princeton: Princeton University Press, 1957), p. 123.

the security of its *own* stock; the loan was to be repaid in ten equal annual installments. At the start of operations, then, the United States participated in the earnings of a privately financed venture without contributing a penny to the original capital.

The first Bank of the United States was clearly intended to earn the greater part of its income by carrying on a regular commercial-banking business. It was run "in the main with an eye single to business and profit" and returned substantial dividends to its owners. Its earning assets consisted for the most part of short-term businessmen loans; discounts were ordinarily made for 60 days. Loans to the government were also a lucrative source of income, especially at the beginning of the Bank's existence. Indeed, the volume of such loans was probably excessive, requiring the Bank to restrict its loans to the business community and to borrow abroad.

Although the Bank was essentially a private corporation, operated for the profit of its stockholders, it performed invaluable services for the treasury—just as Hamilton had said it would. While it was not a central bank in the more fully developed sense in which its successor institution, the Second Bank of the United States, was to be, its directors showed a remarkable sense of responsibility for maintaining the stability of the banking system as a whole. In February 1805, for example, the parent board, "after duly considering the present scarcity of specie and the continued drain thereof in aid of commercial pursuits," decided it was their "indispensable duty . . . to prevent, *at this time,* the exportation of the precious metals on which the safety of our moneyed institutions principally depends. . . ."[4]

The Bank acted as fiscal agent for the government and held most of the treasury's deposits; in return, the Bank transmitted government funds from one part of the country to another without charge. After 1800, the Bank helped collect customs bonds in cities where it had branches.[5] It further facilitated government business by effecting payments of interest on the public debt, carrying on foreign-exchange operations for the treasury, and supplying bullion and foreign coins to the mint.

Relationships between the Bank of the United States and the commercial banking system are not altogether clear. It is evident that the former exercised *some* measure of control over commercial banks, particularly in restraining their note issues. The Bank's conservative lending policy made it on balance a creditor of the state banks, and it continually received a greater dollar volume of state bank notes than state banks received of its obligations. The Bank was therefore in a position to present the notes of the state banks regularly for payment in specie, assuring a moderate note issue for the country as a whole.[6] Notes of the United States Bank and its branches circulated at, or very close to, par throughout the country. At all times, the Bank held a considerable portion of the gold and silver in the country—its holdings during the last three years

[4] This quotation from the unpublished minutes of the parent board has been kindly furnished by Professor Stuart Bruchey.

[5] By 1800, the Bank had branches in Boston, New York, Baltimore, and Charleston. Branches were added in Washington and Savannah in 1802 and in New Orleans in 1805.

[6] Students of the period speak of the "friendly cooperation" of the large institution; it apparently refrained from embarrassing banks that seemed to be operating legitimately.

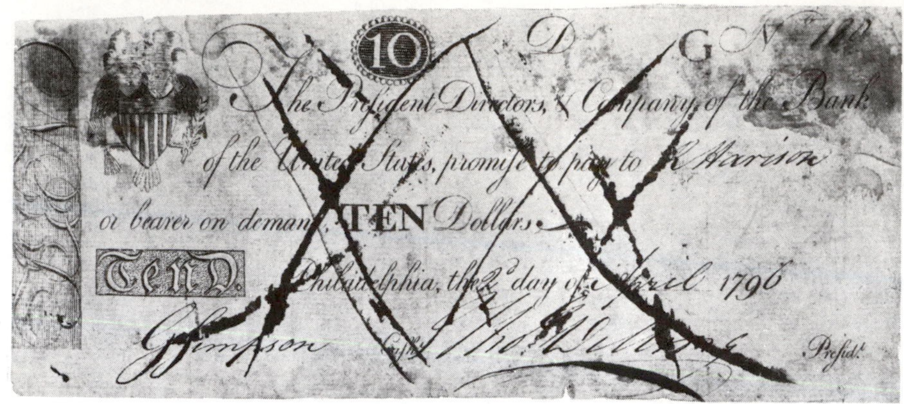

The first Bank of the United States issued these ten-dollar notes, which were canceled by inking three or four x's on their faces after they became worn.

of its existence were probably close to $15 million, which practically matched the amount held by all state banks. It made specie loans to commercial banks; the second petition for renewal of its charter asserted that the state banks generally had the use of at least one-tenth of the Bank's capital. Although there was no established custom of using deposits with the Bank of the United States as reserves and no obligation on its part, legal or customary, to assist other banks in need, in practice it became a lender of last resort. Thus, the Bank was clearly on its way to being a recognized central bank when Congress refused to recharter it.

In retrospect, the reasons for the continued operation of the United States Bank seem compelling. During the two decades of its existence, there was a well-ordered expansion of credit and a general stability of the currency; compared to the difficulties before 1791, the money problems of the 1790s and early 1800s were insignificant. The first Bank of the United States helped to give the nation a better monetary system than it had had any reason to hope for in 1791.

But arguments based on cold economic facts are rarely as effective as arguments based on appeals to human emotion and prejudice. Those who opposed the recharter of the Bank made the same points that had originally been advanced when the matter was debated nearly 20 years ago. They argued that the bank was unconstitutional and that it was a financial monster so powerful it would eventually control the nation's economic life and deprive the people of their liberties. To these contentions was added a new objection: The Bank had fallen under the domination of foreigners, mostly Britishers. Foreign ownership of stock was about $7 million, or 70 percent of the shares, but about the same percentage of U.S. bonds was owned by foreigners. Only shareholding American citizens could be directors, and foreign nationals could not vote by proxy. Nevertheless, many people felt that the influence of English owners was bound to make itself felt through those American directors with whom they had close business contacts.

The debates were not as important as the opposition of some bankers, the tactless lobbying of the Bank's supporters, and political expedients of the moment, including the pacification of frontiersmen and agrarians who were against anything called a "bank." It has often been remarked that business interests, most particularly the state banks in competition with the Bank, did not oppose it. This statement is only partly true. In areas outside the well-established financial centers, there was opposition by the state banks, which were certain to acquire new business if the big Bank were destroyed. Managers and directors who anticipated an increased volume of business and who were not impressed with the importance of the U.S. Bank as a stabilizing institution very definitely opposed it. The power of the Bank with respect to the state institutions was a major cause of enmity.

The outcome of the showdown on the issue of recharter was determined by purely political considerations. To reduce its indebtedness to the institution, which was in excess of $6 million by 1796, the government began to sell its shares, by then much appreciated in value. In 1802, the government disposed of its remaining ownership interest. Even so, the old bugaboo of unconstitutionality loomed large. On a number of occasions, Thomas Jefferson had stated his abiding conviction that the Bank was unconstitutional and a menace to the liberties of the people. Although he was no longer President when the issue of recharter arose, Jefferson's influence in Congress was tremendous. Many of his followers doubtlessly were swayed by his view. But the decisive votes were cast against the Bank as a result of personal antagonism toward Albert Gallatin, who, although a member of Jefferson's party, was a champion of the Bank. In the House, consideration of the bill for renewal of the charter was postponed indefinitely by a vote of 65 to 64. In the Senate, Vice-President George Clinton, enemy of both Madison and Gallatin, broke a 17–17 tie with a vote of nay.

Following the failure to recharter the first Bank of the United States, the number of state banks rose rapidly—from 88 in 1811 to nearly 250 in 1816. This almost threefold increase was not unexpected. There was opportunity to take over the business of the big Bank, and investors felt that without its controls bank profits would increase. The rise in the level of manufacturing activity brought about by the War of 1812 made possible the fulfillment of bank promoters' hopes for high earnings. The sharp increase in note issues, together with deficit financing by the government, led to an inflation that was stimulating to business ventures. All banks except the more conservative ones in New England and New York were forced to suspend specie payments in 1814; but suspension was considered a blessing by most bankers, for there was then no need to worry about the ratio of gold and silver reserves to liabilities. The onset of depression in 1818, which remained severe through 1819, brought about mass failures of banks in the West and South, but 300 banks still existed in 1820. During the next decade, new charters exceeded failures, and in 1830 there were 330 state banks. Four years later, more than 500 commercial banks were conducting business.

THE SECOND BANK OF THE UNITED STATES

Difficulties of financing the War of 1812, monetary confusion resulting from the rapid increase in the number of state banks, and the sharp inflation that occurred after the suspension of specie payments in 1814 convinced people of the need for a second Bank of the United States. It took two years of congressional wrangling and the consideration of no less than six separate proposals before a bill to charter such a bank was passed. Alexander Dallas and John C. Calhoun played the chief political roles in the establishment of the new bank, Dallas being especially useful in winning President Monroe's approval. Pressure from three wealthy proponents of the Bank—Stephen Girard, John Jacob Astor, and David Parish—helped to secure final passage of the act. Knowledgeable people were sure there would be a great demand for the bank stock and, consequently, for government bonds with which to pay for stock subscriptions. Since these men owned large amounts of United States securities, they were vitally interested in a charter plan that would stimulate the market for them.

The charter of the second Bank of the United States resembled that of its predecessor. The capital was set at $35 million, four-fifths of it to be subscribed by individuals, firms, or states and the remaining one-fifth by the federal government. Most of the capital was to consist of government bonds, but one-fourth of the private subscription ($7 million) was to be paid in gold or silver coin. There were to be 25 directors, 20 elected by private stockholders and five appointed by the president. The main office of the Bank was to be located in Philadelphia, and branch offices were to be established on the initiative either of the directors or of Congress.

The first president of the Bank was William Jones, an ex-merchant and an undistinguished member of the cabinets of both Jefferson and Madison. Jones was simply not competent to manage the Bank. During his presidency, branches in the West overextended loans, and outright fraud, particularly in Baltimore, led to substantial losses. In 1819, Langdon Cheves succeeded Jones to the presidency. To Cheves must be given credit for taking complete charge of the Bank and its affairs and firing the incompetent and even dishonest officers who had gotten the branches into trouble.

In 1823, there came from the Bank's board of directors to its presidency one of the notable figures in American history—Nicholas Biddle. Sophisticated, widely traveled, and well educated, Biddle typified the early American aristocrat. He had wealth, power, and a mind that enabled him to become not only a master of the business of banking but an economist as good as any in America in the first half of the nineteenth century.

It was in developing the control functions of the Bank, as distinguished from its service functions, that Biddle made his great contribution. The service functions were nonetheless important. As an agent of the government, the Bank (1) received and kept all funds of the United States, (2) transferred funds on government account from one part of the country to another without compensation, and (3) made payments to owners of government bonds and to government pensioners. On several occasions, the Bank lent money to the government on terms better than could otherwise have been obtained, although it was never put to the ultimate test in this regard because it never had to provide any war financing.

The Bank acted as a fiscal agent for the government from the outset. It also exercised limited control functions under Jones and Cheves, but only because, given its size, it could not help but affect other banks and consequently the

[7] See Fritz Redlich, *The Molding of American Banking—Men and Ideas,* Part I (New York: Hafner, 1947), p. 109.

President of the second Bank of the United States, archfoe of Andrew Jackson, and advocate of central-bank controls was Philadelphia aristocrat Nicholas Biddle. Some argued that his hauteur cost the Bank its charter; others felt that Wall Street would have done in Chestnut Street anyway.

monetary medium of the country. Under Biddle, however, there was both a full realization of the potential power of the Bank and a conscious attempt to regulate the banking system according to certain preconceived notions of what *ought* to be done.

In the first place, the Bank under Biddle soon became the lender of last resort to the state banks. State banks did not keep their reserves as deposits with the Bank of the United States, but they did come to depend on the second Bank in times of crisis, borrowing specie from it to meet their obligations. *The second Bank was able to meet such demands because it kept a much larger proportion of specie reserve against its circulation than other banks did.* The second Bank also assisted in times of stress by lending to business firms when other banks could not or would not, thereby furnishing indirect assistance in the same manner as the Bank of England. Because of these practices, many came to regard the big Bank as *the holder of ultimate reserves* of the banking system.

In the second place, as an even more important means of control, the Bank under Biddle developed a policy of regularly presenting the notes of state banks for payment. In the course of business over the years, the Bank always took in more notes from state banks than the state banks received from the Bank. This net redemption against the state banks was no accident. The Bank had to keep its own note issues (including those of its branches) within bounds, so state banks had a reciprocal influence on the institution that was presumably doing the controlling. Nevertheless, the Bank of the United States was definitely in control, and by presenting the notes of state banks for payment in specie, it kept their issues moderate. The Bank not only furnished a currency of its own of uniform value over the entire country, but it reduced to a nominal figure the discount at which the notes of state banks circulated. By the late 1820s, the paper money of the country was, for the time being, in a very satisfactory state.

Nicholas Biddle tried to affect the general economic climate of the United States by alternate expansion and contraction of the Bank's loans. Furthermore, he made the Bank the largest American dealer in foreign exchange and was able to protect the country from severe specie drain when a drain would have meant a harmful contraction of monetary reserves. Moreover, in the 1820s, the problem of making payments over considerable distances *within the country* was not much different from the problem of effecting remittances *between countries*. There was a flourishing business in "domestic exchange," and the Bank obtained a large portion of it.

By 1829, the position of the second Bank of the United States seemed secure. It had grown and prospered. It had attained a shining reputation abroad—so much so that when the Bank of Spain was reorganized in 1829, the Bank of the United States was explicitly copied. Although it had made enemies, there was a wide acceptance of the idea of a "national institution," and there was grudging admittance by those who persistently opposed "the monster" that it had been good for business. Congress had made sporadic attacks on the Bank, but they had been ineffective. Yet the apparent permanence of the Bank was illusory. Its fate had already been sealed.

In 1828, Andrew Jackson was elected to the Presidency. Beloved by the masses, Jackson had the overwhelming support of the people during two terms in office, and long ago he had decided against supporting banks in general and the big Bank in particular. A student of early Tennessee history has called attention to some of Jackson's unfortunate personal experiences with banks and bankers. As a young man, he had taken in payment for 6,000 acres of land the notes of a Philadelphia merchant that passed as currency. When he gave these notes in payment of goods for his store, he found that they were worthless because the merchant had failed. To make the notes good, Jackson consequently suffered years of financial difficulty in addition to the loss of his land. Later, he and his business partners often found themselves victims of exorbitant charges by bankers and bill-brokers in both New Orleans and the Eastern cities.[8] On one occasion, Jackson bitterly opposed the establishment of a state bank in Tennessee, and as late as 1826 he worked against the repeal of a law prohibiting the establishment of a branch of the Bank of the United States in his home state.

In his first annual message to Congress seven years before the charter of the Bank was to expire, Jackson called attention to the date of expiration, stated that "both the constitutionality and the expediency of the law creating this bank are well questioned by a large portion of our fellow-citizens," and speculated that

[8] Claude A. Campbell, *The Development of Banking in Tennessee* (published by the author, 1932), pp. 27–29.

> If such an institution is deemed essential to the fiscal operations of the Government, I submit to the wisdom of the Legislature whether a national one, founded upon credit of the Government and its revenues, might not be devised which would avoid all constitutional difficulties and at the same time secure all the advantages to the Government and country that were expected to result from the present bank.

We have the great Democrat's word for it that his statement was toned down by his advisers. It was the beginning of the "Bank War."

We are forced to omit the detailed story of that war. It must be said that Biddle tried to win Jackson's support, but Biddle's efforts were unsuccessful. Henry Clay, charming and popular presidential candidate of the National Republicans (Whigs), finally persuaded Biddle to let him make the question of recharter a campaign issue in the election of 1832. In the summer of that year, there was enough pro-Bank power in the Congress to secure passage of a bill for recharter—a bill Jackson returned, as expected, with a sharp veto message prepared by presidential advisers Amos Kendall and Roger Taney. In that political document, the President contended that (1) the Bank was unconstitutional, (2) there was too much foreign ownership of its shares, and (3) domestic ownership was too heavily concentrated in the East. A central theme ran through the message: The Bank was an instrument of the rich to oppress the poor; an institution of such power and so little responsibility to the people could undo the democracy itself and should be dissolved. Agrarians of the West and South needed no assurance of their leader's sincerity. But wily Martin Van Buren, whose banker friends in New York had so desperately sought his aid in moving the money center from Chestnut Street to Wall Street, must have enjoyed an ironic smile at the President's tender concern for the poor.

After a furious campaign, Jackson emerged the victor by a substantial margin. He considered his triumph a mandate from the electorate on the Bank question, and the acclaim he was receiving due to his masterful handling of the problem of nullification[9] strengthened his resolve to restrict the Bank's activities at once. In the fall of 1833, the government discontinued making deposits with the Bank, and Editor Greene of the Boston *Post* was moved to write its epitaph: "Biddled, Diddled, and Undone."

But Biddle was not through. Beginning in August 1833 and continuing into the fall of 1834, the Bank contracted its loans sharply and continued its policy of presenting the notes of state banks for payment in specie. Biddle maintained that his actions were necessary to prepare the Bank for liquidation, although there was doubtlessly a punitive motive in the vigor of his actions. In any case, his actions contributed significantly to the brief but definite panic of 1834.

The administration remained firm in its resolve to end the Bank, which became a state bank chartered under the laws of Pennsylvania in 1836. Although stripped of its official status, the United States Bank of Pennsylvania

[9] The principle of nullification, first enunciated by John C. Calhoun in 1828, was that any state could refuse to be bound by a federal statute it considered unjust until three-quarters of the states had agreed to the statute. South Carolina tried to apply the principle in 1832–1833 during a dispute over a tariff bill. Jackson's strong stand defeated the attempt.

GENERAL JACKSON SLAYING THE MANY HEADED MONSTER.

In this cartoon, Andrew Jackson (left) attacks the many-headed serpent (the second Bank of the United States) with his walking stick (his veto). The largest head is Nicholas Biddle, the Bank's president. The remaining heads represent other officials of the Bank and its branches. Jackson is assisted by Martin Van Buren (center).

remained the most powerful financial institution in America for a few years. With its resources alone, Nicholas Biddle could still engineer a grandiose scheme to support the prices of cotton and other agricultural staples in a heroic effort to cure the nation's economic troubles of 1837 and 1838. But this last convulsive effort started a chain of events that led to the Bank's failure in 1841, not two years after Biddle's retirement.

ECONOMIC FLUCTUATIONS AND THE SECOND BANK

During the time of Biddle's reign, the economy followed a relatively smooth course with no deep recessions or periods of significant inflation. As shown in Figure 10-4, during the 1820s, the price level slipped downward as the amount

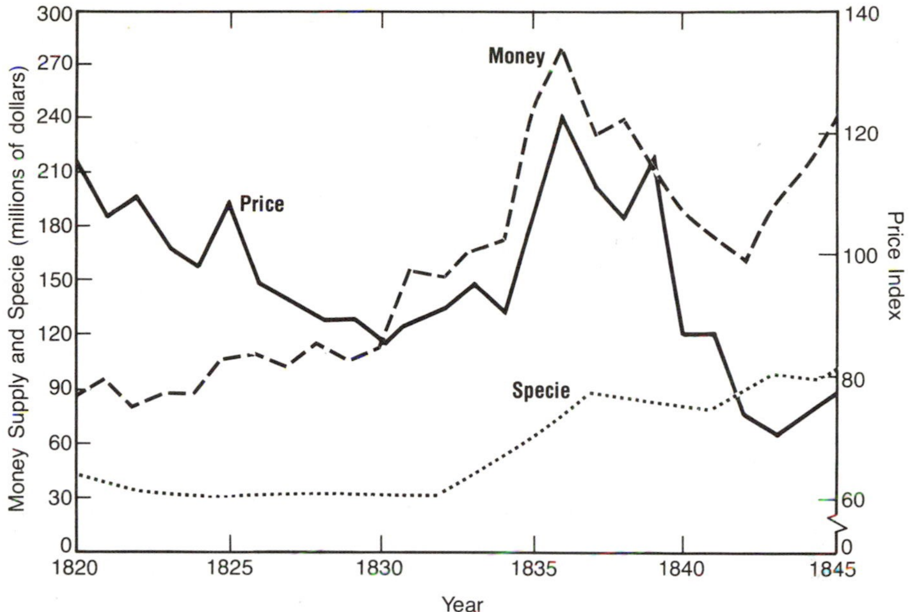

FIGURE 10–4

U.S. Prices, Money, and Specie, 1820–1845

Source: Hugh Rockoff, "Money, Prices, and Banks in the Jacksonian Era," in R. W. Fogel and S. L. Engerman (eds.), *The Reinterpretation of American Economic History* (New York: Harper & Row, 1971), Table 1, p. 451.

of specie in the economy remained roughly constant and the amount of money in the economy rose modestly. Undoubtedly, the growth in the stock of money was less than the growth of the volume of goods exchanged.

Then entirely new conditions began to prevail, and many historians believe the demise of the second Bank ushered in the inflationary bursts of the mid-1830s and ultimately the great depression of 1839–1843. Certainly, the increases in the money supply and in the price level at that time suggest that the absence of the second Bank may have unleashed irresponsible banking practices. Shortly after Jackson's veto, he began withdrawing government funds from the second Bank and placing them in so-called "pet banks." Allegedly, as Biddle's powers ebbed, many "wildcat banks" began to take advantage of the new opportunities to expand credit and their paper note issues recklessly. Did the demise of the second Bank precipitate the economic fluctuations of the period? Did Jackson's politics ultimately lead to the depression of 1839–1843?

The answer to both of these questions is only a partial or qualified yes. It must be remembered that the United States was still heavily involved in the international economy. The U.S. economy was still greatly influenced by external events. Coincidentally, at the time of the demise of the second Bank, the United States began to import substantial amounts of silver from Mexico, whose increasingly productive mines added to the stock of specie. These and other flows into the United States from England and France sharply raised the amount of specie in the United States. As shown in Figure 10-4, there was a tremendous jump in specie between 1833 and 1837. Since banks generally held specie on reserve and only in fractional amounts of their paper-note issues, as the specie amounts increased, the amount of paper money expanded by a multiple. Therefore, to a considerable extent, the influx of specie explains much of the money increase and inflation. Clearly, then, external forces were very influential in instigating the business cycles of the period.

In addition, the banking sector does not appear to have acted irresponsibly during the 1830s, even after Jackson's veto. For instance, the ratio of bank-held reserves to credit outstanding (bank notes) did not increase. On the whole, banks remained fairly cautious and did not "wildcat," as some have claimed.

Nevertheless, the influence of the second Bank, or its absence, was also important. During Biddle's reign throughout the 1820s and early 1830s, people placed an increasing trust in banks, largely perhaps because of the leadership and sound banking practices of the second Bank. As a result, the proportion of money that people normally held in specie form declined. Their confidence in paper money reached unusually high levels in the late 1820s and early 1830s. Then events changed. First came Jackson's veto in 1832. This was followed by the Specie Circular in 1834, which required that most federal land sales must be paid in specie. As prices rose and people's confidence in paper monies waned, more and more people returned paper for specie at their banks. When large numbers of depositors attempted to do this, the banks were unable to make the exchanges and banking panics occurred. The final result was a sharp, but temporary, recession in 1837 and finally what may have been the worst depression of the century in 1839–1843.[10]

Although many escaped the ravages of unemployment, failing businesses, and lost savings, the number of people involved in the market had grown tremendously since colonial times. Only remote areas of rural America were left untouched by the depression. Both the external events that altered specie flows in and out of the country and the internal events that altered people's confidence in specie, banks, and their paper issues contributed to the ups and downs of the period.

[10] In addition, the Bank of England, concerned over the continuing outflow of specie to the United States, began to call in specie (sell back bonds) in 1837 and thereafter.

11

Land and the Early Westward Movements

THE ACQUISITION AND DISPOSAL OF THE PUBLIC DOMAIN

The United States began with a solid mass of land extending from the Atlantic coast to the Mississippi River and from the Great Lakes to, but not including, Florida and West Florida. Except for some unimportant reserves, the seven of the original thirteen states with land claims west of the Appalachians more or less reluctantly yielded these claims to the central government. Between 1802, when Georgia, the last of the states to cede, relinquished its rights to western land, and 1898, when the formal annexation of Hawaii occurred, the United States very nearly assumed its present physical form as the result of eight main acquisitions (shown in Map 11–1):

1. The Territory of Louisiana, acquired in 1803 by purchase from France.
2. Florida, acquired in 1819 by purchase from Spain. A few years previously, the United States had annexed the narrow strip of land that constituted west Florida.
3. The Republic of Texas, annexed as a state in 1845. The Republic of Texas had been established nine years previously after the victory of the American settlers over the Mexicans.
4. The Oregon Country, annexed by treaty with Great Britain in 1846. Spain and Russia, the original claimants to this area, had long since dropped out. By the Treaty of 1818, the United States and Great Britain agreed to a joint occupation of the Oregon Country and British Columbia; the Treaty of 1846 established the dividing line at the forty-ninth parallel.

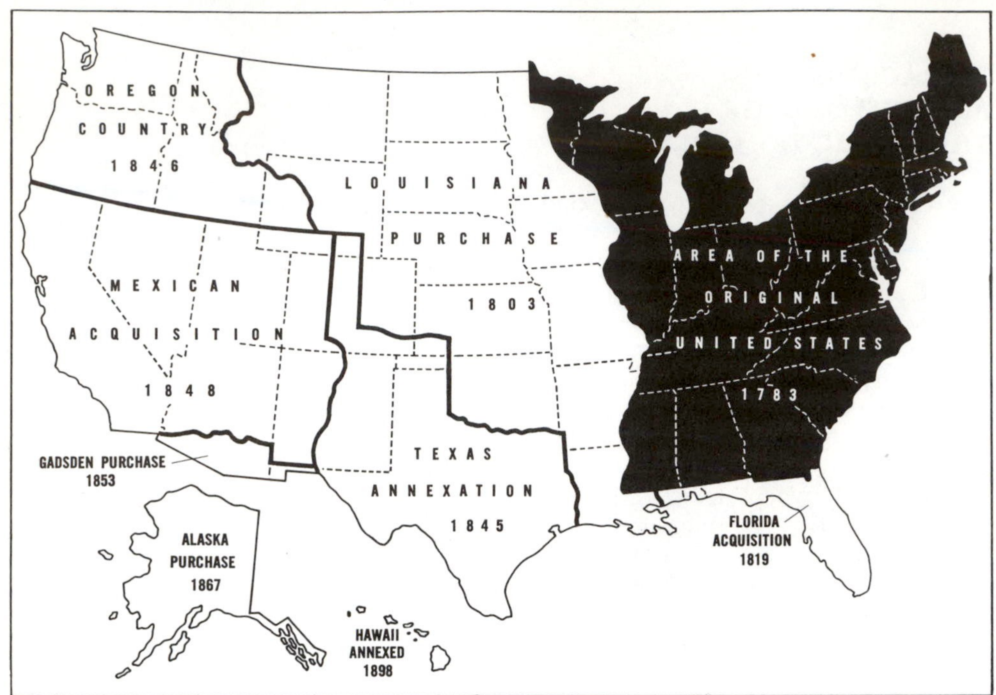

MAP 11– 1

Land Growth: The purchase of Louisiana marked the beginning of the continental expansion of the United States, which culminated in the purchase of nonadjacent Alaska in 1867 and the annexation of Hawaii in 1898.

5. The Mexican Cession, acquired by conquest from Mexico in 1848.
6. The Gadsden Purchase, acquired from Mexico in 1853.
7. The Alaskan Purchase, acquired from Russia in 1867.
8. The Hawaiian Annexation, formally ratified in 1898.

In half a century, the United States obtained a continental area of 3 million square miles, of which 1.4 billion acres, or 75 percent, constituted the public domain.[1] In 1862, two-thirds of this vast area was still in the possession of the government, but the method of disposal had been agreed on long before. The decisions of our forbearers regarding federal land policy have their consequences in the present.

The Land Ordinances of 1785 and 1787

After victory in the Revolution, the Congress of the Confederation had to make three decisions regarding the disposal of public land:

[1] In addition, Alaska contains more than 586,400 square miles, most of it still in the public domain, and Hawaii added 6,423 square miles, none of it in the public domain.

1. Was the New England or the southern land system to prevail?
2. Should the government exact high revenues from the sale of land, or should cheap land be made available to everyone?
3. What was to be the political relationship between newly settled areas and the original colonies?

Two major land systems had developed during the colonial period. The New England system of "township planting" provided for laying out townships, for the subdivision of townships into carefully surveyed tracts, and for the auction sale of tracts to settlers. In the eighteenth century, it was usual to establish townships, which often were 6 miles square, in tiers. The opening of new townships proceeded with regularity from settled to unsettled land, gaps of unsettled land appeared infrequently, and no one could own land that had not been previously surveyed. In contrast, the southern system provided for no rectangular surveys. In the South, a settler simply selected what appeared to be a choice plot of unappropriated land and asked the county surveyor to mark it off. Settlers paid no attention to the relationship of their tracts to other pieces of property, and the legal description of a tract was made with reference to more or less permanent natural objects, such as stones, trees, and streams.

Two fundamentally different points of view emerged about the terms on which land should be made available, and a debate ensued that was not to end for several decades. Those who advocated a "conservative" policy were in favor of selling the public lands in large tracts at high prices for cash. The proponents of a "liberal" policy were in favor of putting land within the reach of everyone by making it available in small parcels at low prices on credit terms.

As is nearly always the case when economic questions are discussed, arguments were advanced on two planes: the plane of unselfish, public interest and the plane of selfish, private interest. On the higher, national-interest plane, the conservatives contended that natural resources ought to be disposed of in a way that would yield substantial revenues—revenues that would be spent to further the interests of the people as a whole. The liberals argued that every person had a right to a piece of land and that the spirit of democracy could best be preserved by affording everyone who wished it an opportunity to own land and to farm for a living. Liberals believed that Americans could never be economically oppressed if the poor could avoid oppression by moving to the West. On a lower level, the conservatives argued, not always for publication, that a ragtag population in the West would be a continuing spawning place of political unrest. Furthermore, the values of real property in the East would tend to be weaker if land were readily available in the West, and the level of wages in the East would be persistently higher if a part of the labor force were forever escaping to a new life. Needless to say, the liberal forces were also composed largely of people who were more interested in furthering their personal interests than in preserving democracy. The western settler, the eastern laborer, and the land speculator stood together to support cheap land because they stood to gain financially from cheap land.

Problems of land disposal could not be divorced from politics. The decision regarding the status of areas to be settled in the future also involved a great political principle. Were these areas to remain in colonial dependence, subject to profitable exploitation by the original thirteen states? Or were they to be admitted into a union of states on a basis of equality? The answers to these questions would test the foresight and selflessness of Americans, who had themselves escaped the dominance of a ruling empire.

There was no pressure on the Congress of the Confederation to provide a system for regulating public lands until 1784, by which time Virginia and New York had relinquished their claims to the southern part of the territory lying northwest of the Ohio River. In that year, a congressional committee of five, headed by Thomas Jefferson, proposed a system based on a rectangular survey. It is noteworthy that three of the five members were southerners who, despite their origins, recognized the value of the New England method of settlement. No action was taken in 1784, but a year later another committee, composed of a member from each state, reworked the report from the previous year and offered a carefully considered proposal. With minor changes, this proposal was passed as the Land Ordinance of 1785.[2]

Insofar as the ordinance set a *physical* basis for disposing of the public lands, its effects were permanent. Government surveyors were to establish on unsettled land horizontal lines called *base lines* and vertical lines called *principal meridians.* The first of the principal meridians was to be in what is now the state of Ohio, and the first surveys covered land north of the Ohio River that was not included in the "reserves." Eventually, all the land in the United States was included in the survey except the original thirteen states and Vermont, Kentucky, Tennessee, parts of Ohio, and Texas. As the survey moved westward, other principal meridians were established, the second in what is now Indiana, the third in what is now Illinois, and so on. Map 11–2 indicates the other principal meridians and the base lines perpendicular to them. The insets show how tiers of townships, called *ranges,* were laid out to the east and west of a principal meridian. The ranges were designated by a number and a direction from the meridian, and the townships within each range were numbered north and south from the base line. Each township, being 6 miles square, contained 36 square miles numbered as shown in Map 11-2. In the Ordinance of 1785, a square mile was called a *lot,* but in later acts the term *section* was used.

The ordinance reflected the prevalent conservative view that public land should be a major source of revenue. Provisions relating to minimum size of tracts, prices, and terms were severe. Alternate townships were to be sold as a whole; the other half of the townships were to be sold by sections. All sales at public auction were to be for a minimum price of $1 per acre in cash. Thus, the smallest possible cash outlay was the $640 necessary to buy a section—an expenditure beyond the means of most pioneers. Moreover, a square mile of land was more than the small farmers wanted; they could barely clear and cultivate 10 acres or so in their first year, and a quarter-section was the most a settler could handle without the aid of grown children. Only individuals of means and land companies formed by large investors could purchase land under the first law.

Two years later, the Congress addressed the problem of establishing the *political* principles under which the settlement of the West was to take place.

[2]*Journals of the Continental Congress* (Washington, D.C.: U.S. Government Printing Office, 1933), **XXVIII,** p. 375.

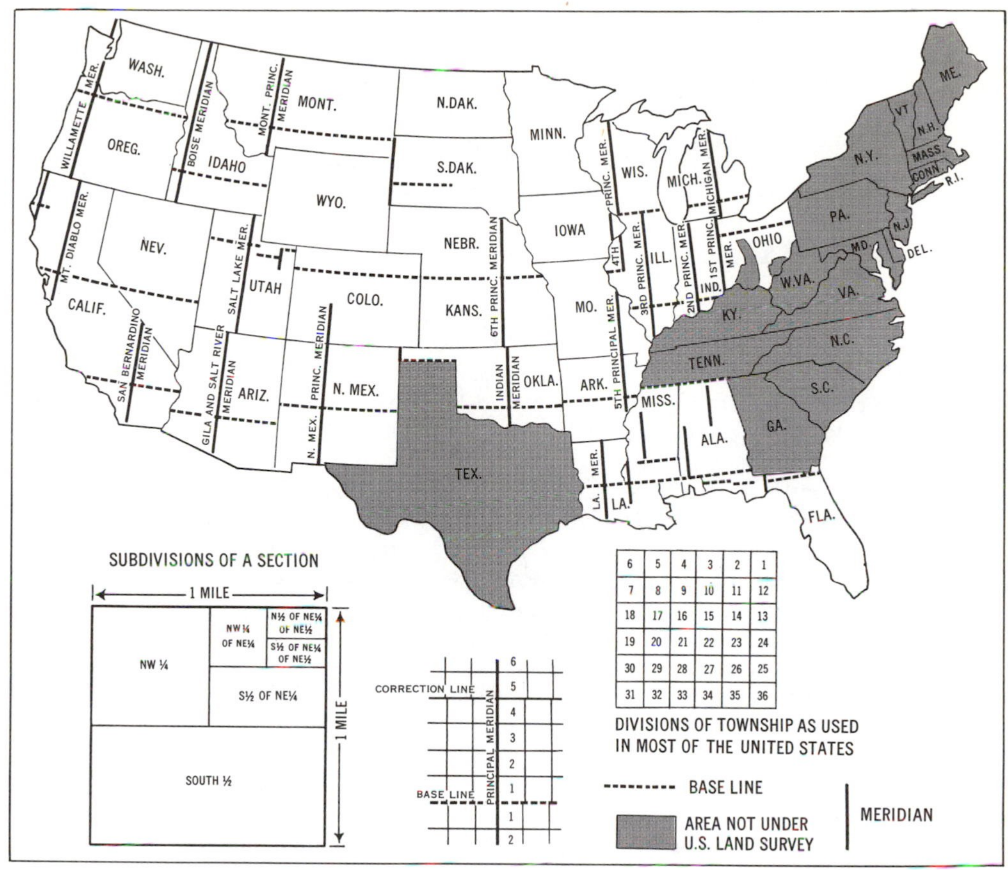

MAP 11–2

Land Survey: Principle meridians and base lines made possible precise apportioning of newly opened territories into sections and easily described subdivisions of sections, thus simplifying later property transfers.

The Ordinance of 1787 provided that the Northwest Territory should be organized as a district to be run by a governor and judges appointed by the Congress.[3] As soon as it contained 5,000 male inhabitants of voting age, a territorial legislature was to be elected and a nonvoting delegate was to be sent to the Congress. At least three and not more than five states were to be created from this territory; when any one of the established divisions of the territory contained a population of 60,000 inhabitants, it was to be admitted to the Union as a state on a basis of complete equality with the older states. Contained

[3]*Journals of the Continental Congress* (Washington, D.C.: U.S. Government Printing Office, 1933), **XXXII**, p. 314.

in the ordinance were certain guarantees of civil and religious liberties, together with a prohibition of slavery in the territory. *The main principle, however, was the eventual equality of status for the new areas.* The age-old source of trouble between colony and ruling country was thus removed by a simple, although unprecedented, device—making the colonies extensions of the empire that would be allowed to become socially and politically equal.

The Land Acts, 1796–1862

For a decade after the passage of the Land Ordinance of 1785, pioneering in the area north of the Ohio River was restricted by Indian trouble as well as by the high price of government land. The British, who persisted in maintaining posts on American territory in the Northwest, for years incited the Indians to make war on American settlers. By a treaty of 1794, the British agreed to evacuate the posts in the Northwest, and in August of that year "Mad Anthony" Wayne and his forces defeated the Indians at the Battle of Fallen Timbers. A peace treaty signed with the Indian braves in 1795 gave the white man the area in the southeastern corner of the territory and certain "islands" of land around fortified outposts. The time was now ripe for the establishment of a land policy by the Congress of the United States.

The Land Act of 1796 represented another victory for the conservatives. A system of rectangular survey substantially the same as the one established by the Ordinance of 1785 was made permanent. The minimum purchase allowed by the Act of 1796 was still 640 acres, but the minimum price per acre was raised to \$2—the only concession to the cheap-land advocates being a credit provision that permitted half of the purchase price to be deferred for a year. Only a small amount of land was sold under this act before Congress changed the minimum acreage to 320 in 1800 and permitted the buyer, after a cash payment of one-half the value, to pay one-fourth the value in two years and the final fourth in four years. A law of 1804 further lowered the minimum purchase to 160 acres. In 1820, the minimum purchase was reduced to 80 acres and the price per acre to \$1.25, but the credit provisions, which had resulted in losses to the government, were repealed. By 1820, the liberal forces had clearly won the battle. Twelve years later, the minimum purchase was reduced to 40 acres, so in 1832 a pioneer could purchase a piece of farmland for \$50. By this time, pressures for *free* land, which had been exerted from the first, were beginning to produce legislative results.

The settler who was brave enough to risk his own life and the lives of his family in a pioneering venture was not usually deterred from action by legal niceties. From the beginning, pioneers tended to settle past the areas that had been surveyed and announced for sale. As the decades passed and the West became "crowded," this tendency to pick a tract in an unopened area increased. Unauthorized settlement, or "squatting," resulted from the attempts of the pioneers to find better soils and the hope that they could settle on choice land and make it a going proposition before they were billed for it.

Squatting was illegal, of course, but it was an offense that was hard to combat. Moreover, there were those who argued that by occupying and improving the land, a squatter gained the rights to it—"cabin rights" or "corn rights" or "tommyhawk rights," as they were variously called on the frontier. At first, federal troops tried to drive squatters from unsurveyed land, but successes were only temporary. Gradually, the government came to view this pioneer lawbreaking less and less seriously. Against those who would purchase the squatter's land when it became available for public sale, informal but effective measures were taken by the squatters themselves, who formed protective associations as soon as they settled in a particular locality. When the public auction of land in that locality was held, the members of the protective association let it be known that there was to be no competitive bidding for land preempted by them. The appearance of well-armed frontiersmen at the auction ordinarily convinced city slickers and big land buyers that it would be unwise to bid. Even in places where there was no organized action, squatters who found their farms bought out from under them could often charge handsomely for the "improvements" they had made, and frontier courts were inclined to uphold their "rights."

As early as 1820, Congress began to give relief to squatters, and scarcely a year went by after 1830 in which preemption rights were not granted to settlers in certain areas. In 1841, a general Preemption Act, called the "Log Cabin Bill" by its proponents, was passed. This law granted to anyone settling on land that was surveyed, but not yet available for sale, the right to purchase 160 acres at the minimum price when the auction was held. No one could outbid the settler and secure the land, provided the squatter could raise the $200 necessary to buy a quarter section. Technically, squatting on *unsurveyed* land was still illegal; because of this and because there was still no outright grant of land, the westerner (and anyone else who could make money by buying land and waiting for it to rise in value) was not satisfied. Nevertheless, the land policy of the country was about as liberal as could be consistent with the demand that the public domain be a continuing source of revenue.

Pressure remained on Congress to reduce the price of "islands" of less desirable land that had been passed over in the first surges to the West. In 1854, the Graduation Act provided for the graduated reduction of the minimum purchase price of such tracts, to a point where if the land remained unsold for as long as 30 years, it could be purchased for as little as 12½ cents an acre. Settlers quickly purchased these pieces of land, attesting to the fact that people were willing to gamble a little on the probable appreciation of even the most unpromising real estate.

In the 1850s, as agitation for free land continued, it became apparent that the passage of a homestead law was inevitable. Southerners, who had at one time favored free grants to actual settlers, became violently opposed to this as time went on. The 160-acre farm usually proposed by homestead supporters was not large enough to make the working of slaves economical, and it seemed obvious to southern congressmen that homesteading would fill the West with antislavery people. On the other hand, many northern congressmen, who would normally have had leanings toward a conservative policy, joined forces with the westerners because they also knew that free land meant free states.

In 1860, a homestead act was passed, but President Buchanan, fearing that it would precipitate secession, vetoed it. Two years later, with southerners out

In the nineteenth century, wagon trains like these brought a steady stream of migrants to western America and its expansive lands.

of Congress, the Homestead Act of 1862 became law. Henceforth, any head of a family or anyone over 21 could have 160 acres of public land on the payment of small fees. The only stipulation was that the homesteader should either live on the land or cultivate it for five years. An important provision was that settlers who decided not to meet the five-year requirement might obtain full title to the land simply by paying the minimum price of $1.25 an acre.

Although much land was to pass into private hands under the Homestead Act of 1862, it was not the boon that it was expected to be. Most of the first-class land had been claimed by this time. Furthermore, it was so easy to circumvent the provisions of the law that land-grabbers used it, along with the acts that still provided for outright purchase, to build up great land holdings.

By 1862, the frontier had reached the edge of the dry country, where a 160-acre farm was too small to provide a living for a settler and his family.

THE MIGRATIONS TO THE WEST

In discussing the colonial period, we noted that pioneers were moving across the Appalachian Mountains by the middle of the eighteenth century. By 1790, perhaps a quarter of a million people lived within the mountain valleys or to

MAP 11–3

Moving Frontier: Census data from 1800 onward chronicled the constant westward flow of population. The "frontier," its profile determined by natural attractions and a few man-made and physiographic obstacles, was a magnet for the venturesome.

the west, and the trickle of westward movement had become a small stream. There were two eighteenth-century routes to the West. The more important one passed through the Cumberland Gap and then into either Kentucky or Tennessee; the other ran across southern Pennsylvania to Pittsburgh and on down the Ohio River. Even as the movement to the West was gaining momentum, pioneers were still settling in Pennsylvania and New York and to the north in Vermont, New Hampshire, and Maine.

The frontier, as technically defined in the census reports, was any area in which there were more than two and less than six people per square mile. In Map 11–3, the frontier lines for 1800, 1820, 1840, and 1860 have been drawn from census data. The line for 1800 indicates a wedge driven into the West, with its point in western Kentucky. Sixty years later, the line ran in a southerly direction from a point in the middle of Minnesota, with a noticeable bulge into the Nebraska and Kansas territories and a definite drift into Texas. At the moment, we are interested in seeing *how* the frontier line was pushed into the shape and general position it had assumed by 1860, but in addition to tracing the paths of this movement, we will learn *why* the westward thrust was made.

The Southern Migration

At the time of the Revolution, the three great traditional staples had given the Southern Colonies an unquestioned economic superiority in the new land. But the war with Great Britain and the separation from the empire had produced serious consequences. Markets were lost or seriously impaired during the hostilities, and some of them were never regained. Indigo production was worst hit, because Britain turned to the West and East Indies for supplies and, of course, no longer paid a bounty on the American product. Rice output remained nearly constant until around 1820, when it began to increase in importance; its culture was limited, however, to a small coastal area and could not be significant in southern development. The great blow was the decline in tobacco production. During the 1790s, tobacco continued to be near the top of the list of American exports in dollar value, but the turn of the century marked the beginning of serious difficulties. The Embargo Acts and the War of 1812 enabled the product of both the West Indies and the East Indies to gain a place in world markets; meanwhile, high duties imposed by European countries encouraged tobacco production in Europe, where the great demand was. World prices fell so drastically that tobacco could be grown profitably in America only on virgin lands, and production moved westward—to Tennessee, Kentucky, Missouri, and even into southern Ohio. Not until the 1850s were North Carolina and Virginia to regain something of their old importance as tobacco-producing states.

In cotton lay the hope or, if you wish, the tragedy of the South. Obtaining their supplies of raw cotton from the Far East, the English had turned to the manufacture of cotton cloth in the late seventeenth century. The inventions that came 100 years or so later—the steam engine, the spinning jenny, the water frame, the spinning mule, and the power loom—all gave rise to an enormous demand for cotton fiber. The phase of the Industrial Revolution that made it possible to apply power to textile manufacturing occurred at just the right time to stimulate and encourage the planting of cotton wherever it could be grown profitably. In the southern United States, the conditions for a profitable agriculture based on cotton were nearly ideal. Only some way of separating the green seed from the short-staple "upland cotton" had to be devised. One of the contributions of Yankee genius Eli Whitney was the invention of a gin that enabled a good hand to clean 50 pounds of cotton a day. With the application of power to the gin, there was no limit to the amount of fiber that could be produced.

On the humid coasts of Georgia and South Carolina, planters who had grown indigo turned to cotton: Even some rice fields were recultivated to produce the new staple. The culture moved up to North Carolina and Virginia and over the mountains to the beautiful rolling country of middle Tennessee. In the early 1800s, the piedmont of Georgia and South Carolina became the important cotton center, and these states were vying for first place by 1820, with South Carolina slightly in the lead.

Beginning with the end of the War of 1812, the really important shift in cotton production was to the West (see Map 11–4). Almost unerringly, the

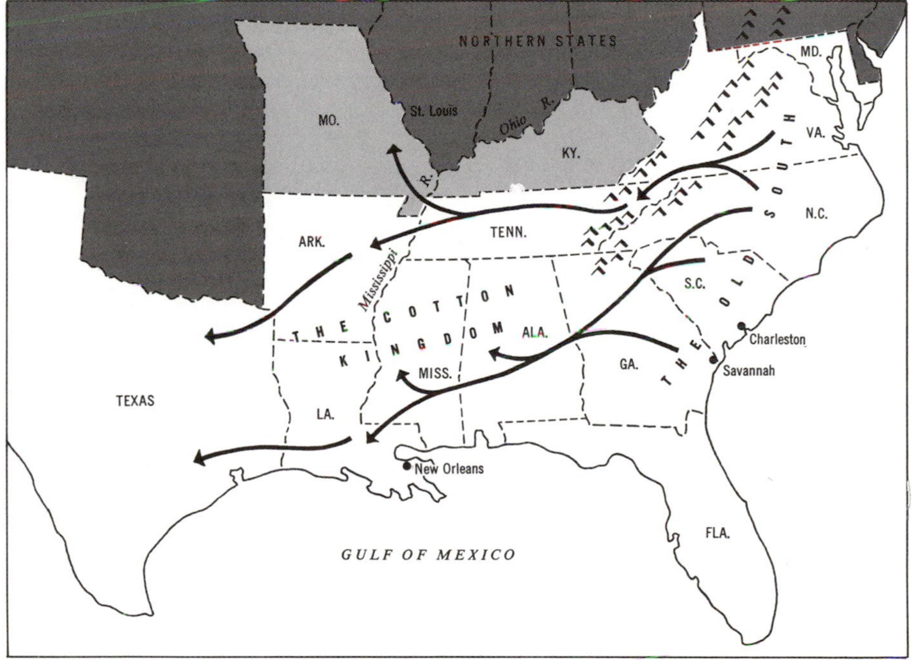

MAP 11–4

Shifts in Cotton Cultivation: The tremendous growth of the world demand for cotton propelled the westward movement of cotton civilization after the War of 1812 and up to the onset of the Civil War.

settlers first planted the loamy, fertile soils that extended in an arc from Georgia through Alabama into northeastern Mississippi. A second major cotton-growing area lay in the rich bottom land of the lower Mississippi River and its tributaries. In this extremely fertile soil, the cotton even tended to grow a longer fiber. The culture spread into western Tennessee and eastern Arkansas. A jump into Texas then foretold the future trend of cotton production.

By 1840, the early cotton-producing states had been left behind. In 1860, Alabama, Mississippi, and Louisiana were far in the lead, with Mississippi, then in the number one position, producing more cotton than Georgia and South Carolina combined. This shift in the realm of King Cotton was to have the most far-reaching consequences on the economy of the South.

Just before the Civil War, there could be no doubt that cotton was indeed king. As Douglass North has remarked,[4] it is difficult to exaggerate the role of cotton in American economic growth between 1800 and 1850. The great staple accounted for more than half the dollar value of U.S. exports—a value nearly ten times as great in U.S. foreign trade as its nearest competitor, the wheat and wheat flour of the North. At home, cotton planters furnished the raw materials for textile manufacturers in the North, who by 1860 were selling half again as much cotton cloth as wool cloth. The amount of the national income generated by cotton manufactures was greater at this time than that generated by the iron industry. It was not surprising that aristocratic southerners could scarcely envisage a North, or even a world, without their chief product.

There was both a slight push and a major pull to the new lands of the South. The push had begun in colonial times, as tidewater lands began to lose the natural fertility the staples grown there required. The small farmer, impelled by hardship, had moved into the piedmont. The shift had been especially pronounced in Virginia and North Carolina, from which struggling families tended to sift through the Cumberland Gap into Tennessee and Kentucky. The frontiersman—the professional pioneer—was then pulled into the rich new cotton country, mostly from Georgia and South Carolina, but partly from Tennessee and even from Kentucky. Following closely, came the yeoman farmer; almost simultaneously—and this is what clearly distinguishes the southern migration—came the planter, the man of substance, with his huge household establishment and his slaves. It was of course the expected return on cotton that brought the great, irregular surges of movement into the southwest, and as shown in Figure 11-1, there is a close correlation between the price of cotton on one hand and the volume of public land sales in Alabama, Florida, Louisiana, Mississippi, and Arkansas on the other.[5] The planter had sufficient means to acquire large acreages, and the small householder could compete in the best agricultural areas only with difficulty. The rich were at an obvious advantage in the public land auctions; the pioneer and the farmer with a slave or two were continually tempted to sell out to the plantation owner, because the price the latter could offer netted a profit for "improving" the land.

A farmer class of some numerical importance nevertheless developed in the South, even though many farmers sold out to planters and moved on across the Mississippi River, sometimes going north as well as west. Some of

[4] See Douglass C. North, *The Economic Growth of the United States 1790–1860* (Englewood Cliffs, N.J.: Prentice-Hall, 1961).

[5] North, pp. 124, 129.

the least able retreated to the mountains or drifted into the barren pine belts that constitute much of the land area in the deep South. But it was the plantation owner, so unimportant numerically and so very important as the aristocratic determiner of southern economic development, who was to take charge of the South's destiny.

The Northern Migration

The first settlements in Ohio were made by people who came down the Ohio River from Pittsburgh. They were joined by pioneers who, having stopped for a while in Tennessee and Kentucky, moved north and west into

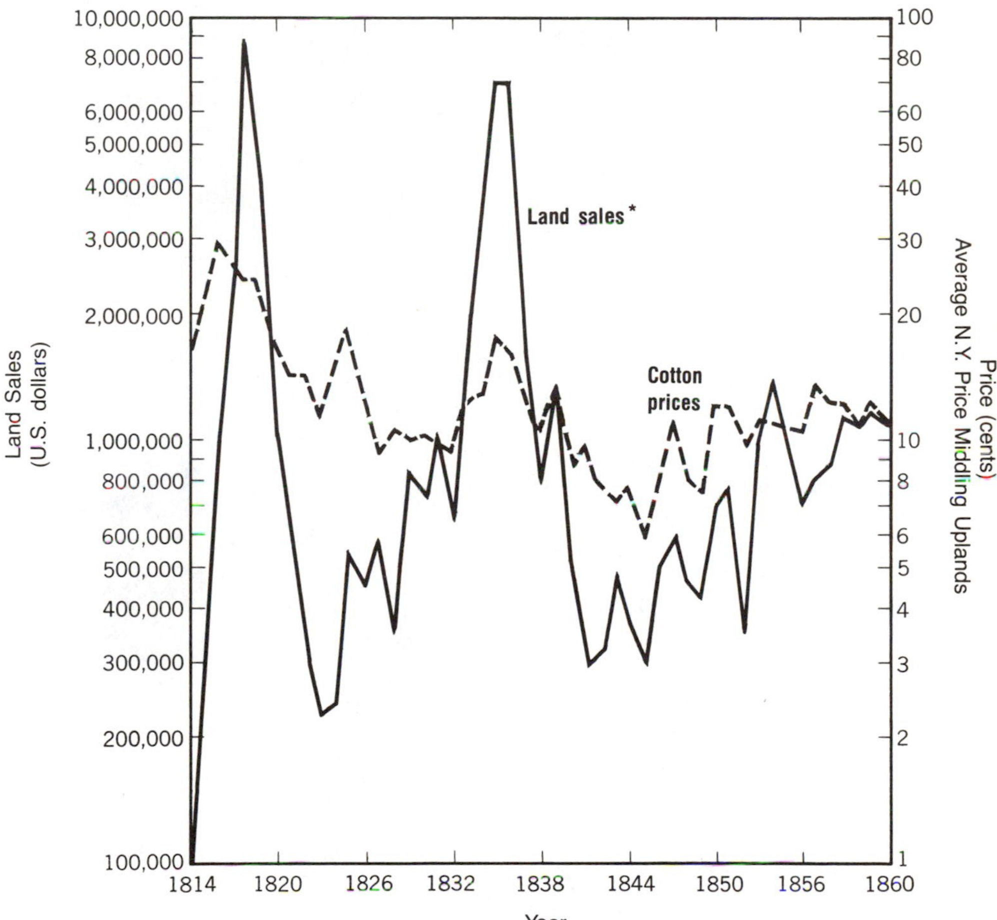

FIGURE 11–1

U.S. Public Land Sales and Cotton Prices, 1814–1860

Source: Douglass C. North, *The Economic Growth of the United States, 1790–1860* (Englewood Cliffs, N.J.: Prentice-Hall, 1961), p. 124.

Ohio, southern Indiana, and southern Illinois. The northern parts of these states did not attract southerners, who filled in the valleys of rivers that ran into the Ohio River. While the movement from the South was going on, the exodus from New England began, at first into northern New Hampshire and Vermont and then into western New York, where pioneers from Pennsylvania and New Jersey were also settling.

During the early 1800s, the movement across the top of the country gained momentum, and at the quarter-century mark, people from the New England and Middle Atlantic states were pouring into the northern counties of Ohio and Indiana and into southern Michigan. By 1850, lower Michigan was

Land speculation — "holding for a rise" — became a lively offshoot of the westward population surge. Here, a Kansas land office provides a center for speculative activity.

The morning of the opening of the Oklahoma land rush.

fairly settled, and the best lands in northern Illinois and southern Wisconsin had been claimed. On the eve of the Civil War, pioneers were pushing the northwestern tip of the frontier into central Minnesota, most of Iowa was behind the frontier line, and the handsome country of eastern Kansas was being settled. Only in Texas did the frontier line of 1860 bulge farther to the west than it did in Kansas. By this time, California had been a state for a decade, and Oregon had been admitted the year before, but the vast area between the western frontier and the coast was not to be completely settled for another half-century.

Southerners, then, moving across the Ohio River, were the chief influence in the lower part of the old Northwest. New Englanders, when the Erie Canal made transportation easy, were dominant in the Great Lakes region, but they were joined by another stream that originated in the Middle Atlantic states. For the most part, families moved singly, although sometimes as many as 50–100 would move together. As the frontier pushed westward, the pioneers on the cutting edge were frequently the same people who had broken virgin soil a short way back only a few years ago. Or they were the grown children of men and women who had once participated in the conquest of the wilderness.

Throughout this early period of westward expansion, there was an ever-increasing influx of land-hungry people from abroad. From 1789 to the close of the War of 1812, not more than 250,000 people immigrated from Europe. With the final defeat of Napoleon and the coming of peace abroad, immigration resumed. From 500,000 people in the 1830s, the flow increased to 1.5 million in the 1840s and to 2.5 million in the 1850s. For the most part, the newcomers were from northern Europe; Germans and Irish predominated, but there were many immigrants from England, Scotland, Switzerland, and the Scandinavian countries. Of these peoples, the Germans tended more than any others to go directly to the lands of the West. They provided a fairly well-educated and extremely able population that was to have a pronounced effect on the economic life of the states of the northwest and of Iowa and Missouri. Some immigrants from the other groups entered into the agricultural migration, but most of these were absorbed into eastern city populations.

Whatever may have been the place of origin of the pioneer, his older way of earning a living was probably easier than the new one he chose. Early nineteenth-century life in the West was hard, and the difficulties to be surmounted were the same ones that had confronted the American colonists. For the firstcomers there could be little more than a bare existence. Housing was cramped and drafty, clothing was crude, and there was little social life. Isolation may have protected pioneer families against contagion, but once illness struck, there was little to do but let nature take its course. The arduous work of clearing the land was slow; at first, wild plants and animals had to supplement the food brought along for subsistence, and it might take a generation to clear the land for a 160-acre farm. Only gradually did the pioneer homestead begin to produce a surplus for sale; meanwhile, with the help of neighbors, the homesteader could convert timber into a livable house and useful barn, and it was not hard to build a livestock herd. The proportion of the family's work leading to immediate consumption was limited by the necessity of providing for the future; but clearing, building, and fencing were considered an investment, and there was a sense of "building up the place." It became a part of early American folkways to keep an eye on the market for homesteads and to have in mind a price at which to sell and move on. As John Ise used to remark, the farmer more than anyone else relied for a living on the unearned increment—on the appreciation of capital values as the population increased. Eventually, the settler could choose between selling and realizing an investment or staying on a workable, money-making farm.

Settlers might have thought that when the prairies were reached, land cultivation would be easier, but the problems were still enormous. As a matter of fact, the first settlers, thinking that land on which trees did not grow was infertile, tended to skirt the grasslands of Indiana and Illinois. After 1845, with substantial rises in the world prices of grain and with railroad communication established to the east, pioneer farmers undertook the difficult task of plowing the thick and heavily matted prairie sod. Wood for buildings, fences, and fuel was scarce, but it was less expensive to break sod than to fell trees and remove stumps.[6] A sod house was probably more comfortable in both winter and

[6] See Martin L. Primack, "Land Clearing Under Nineteenth Century Techniques: Some Preliminary Calculations," *Journal of Economic History;* **XXII** (December 1962), pp. 484–97. Primack

summer than a log cabin; but the treelessness of the plains resulted in an exposure to the elements that the settlers in the river bottoms and forested areas did not have to suffer.

The North, like the South, had its staples—wheat, corn, and livestock. Animals were the first important cash product of the Northwest. Early in the 1800s, hogs were driven overland from Ohio to the urban centers of the East or were sent south by boat for sale to the plantations. Cattle, too, were driven in great herds to the East, where they were sold for immediate slaughter or for further fattening. But it was not long before pioneer farmers could market their hogs fairly close to home. Slaughtering and meat-packing centers arose in the early West, and by the 1830s Cincinnati was the most important pork-processing city in the country. Cured beef, unlike cured pork, is not as good to eat as the fresh meat; consequently, cattle drives to the East continued until mid-century, when adequate railroad service brought an end to them.

Hog raising required corn growing. For a while, hogs were allowed into the forest to forage on the mast (acorns and nuts that fell from the trees). But feeding is necessary to produce a good grade of pork, and corn is the ideal feed crop. Corn can be grown almost anywhere, provided there is adequate rainfall. It had been cultivated in all the original colonies and throughout the South. As late as 1840, Kentucky, Tennessee, and Virginia were first in corn production. But within 20 years, it was apparent that the states to the northwest would be the corn leaders, although the Corn Belt as we know it today was not yet clearly defined.[7] On the eve of the Civil War, Illinois, Ohio, Missouri, and Indiana led in corn production, and it appeared that Iowa, Kansas, and Nebraska would one day rank ahead of Kentucky and Tennessee, then in fifth and sixth place.

Wheat was to be the great commercial crop of the North. As in the case of the South and cotton, the major determinant of the pace of westward expansion in the North was the profitability of the major staples—in this case, wheat and corn. Periodic surges to the West were invariably in response to the increased profitability of these products; whereas increased returns in part resulted from cost reductions, changes in wheat and corn prices similar to cotton prices affected the pace of the westward movement most directly (see Figure 11-2).

The attraction of new lands for this basic cereal was tremendous. Wheat could not come into its own, however, until facilities were available for transporting it in quantity to the urban centers of the East, and as late as 1850, Pennsylvania and New York ranked first and third, respectively, in its production. Ohio, which had become a commercial producer in the 1830s, was second.[8] During the next decade, the shift of wheat production to the West was

---

estimates a median cost of clearing land of 33 man-days per acre in forested areas versus a median cost of 1.5 man-days per acre in unforested areas in the 1850s.

[7] For the advantages of corn growing to the western pioneer, see Paul W. Gates, *The Farmer's Age: Agriculture, 1815–1860* (New York: Holt, Rinehart & Winston, 1960), p. 169. Only a peck of seed corn, yielding as much as 50 bushels, planted an acre and could be transported far more easily than two bushels of seed wheat, weighing 120 pounds, that might bring in only 15 to 18 bushels to the acre.

[8] North, p. 136.

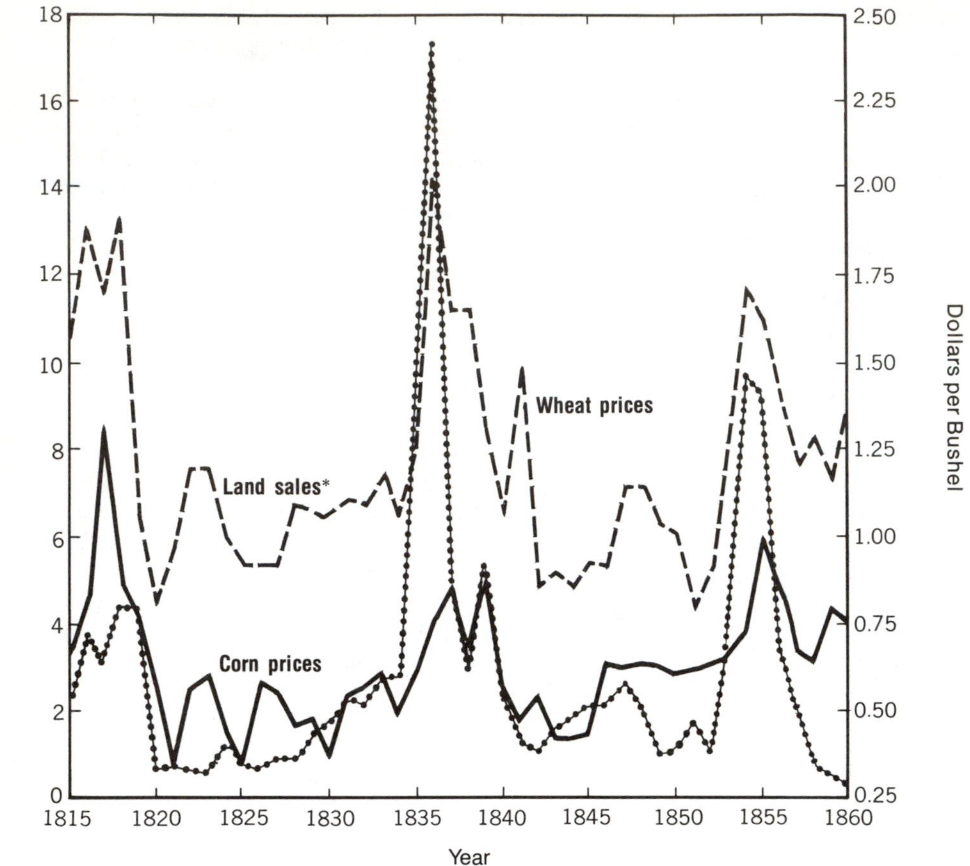

FIGURE 11–2

U.S. Public Land Sales in Several Western States* and Wheat and Corn Prices, 1815–1860

Source: North, *The Economic Growth of the United States, 1790–1860,* p. 137.

*Ohio, Illinois, Indiana, Michigan, Iowa, Wisconsin, and Missouri.

remarkable. By 1860, Illinois, Indiana, and Wisconsin were the leading producers, and the five states carved from the Northwest Territory produced roughly half the nation's output of the bread grain. The major wheat-growing areas were still not finally established; however, further shifts to the West in the production of this important crop were yet to come.

The northern migration forced changes on the agriculture of the northeastern states. For a quarter of a century after the ratification of the Constitution, agriculture in New England, except in a few localities, was exceptionally primitive; the individual farm unit produced practically everything needed for the household. With the growing industrialization of New England after 1810, production for urban markets became possible, and the result was a great improvement in the farmer's lot. Between 1810 and 1840, farmers in the Middle Atlantic states continued to grow the products for which their localities had traditionally been suited, and Pennsylvania and New York remained major wheat producers until mid-century. But the opening of the Erie Canal in the 1820s and the extension of the railroads beyond the Alleghenies in the 1840s meant that products of the rich western lands would flow in ever-increasing amounts to the East.

These and other critical developments in transportation will be analyzed in depth in Chapter 12, and their effects on patterns of regional trade and on economic specialization will be examined at length in Chapter 13. At this point, it will suffice to note that western competition caused the northeastern farmer to reduce grain cultivation, and only dairy cattle remained important in animal production. Specialization in truck garden and dairy products for city people and hay for city horses came to characterize the agriculture of this region, and those who could not adapt to the changing demand moved to the city or went west.

12

Transportation and Technology

The ratification of the Constitution in 1789 joined the thirteen states into a nation. The impact of political unification would be felt in the economic life of the people, and, in turn, the new country would be truly welded together only as it developed a unified economy. Of first importance were the new relationships among the states in matters of commerce and transportation. Establishment of tariff barriers by the states was forbidden, and regulation of commerce among the states and with foreign nations was vested in the federal government. In 1789, trade among the colonies was of much less consequence than trade with western Europe, but the uneasy bonds among the isolated settlements of America would soon strengthen. The commercial stirrings of the United States impelled extensions of colonial transportation routes and facilities.

At first, these extensions were slow and far from sufficient to lay the foundation of a modern industrial economy. Indeed, not until the close of the War of 1812, which established once and for all the basic political relationship between the United States and Great Britain, did the transportation revolution begin in earnest. Steamboats on western waters and canals pointed the way to more efficient and cheaper methods of moving goods and people. In fact, until the mid 1840s, the development of natural waterways, with the aid of canals, was the predominant force in promoting the growth of commercial farming and of interregional trade between the Atlantic seaboard and the interior. Together, the steamboat and the canals lowered transportation costs in America more significantly than the railroad in its turn.[1]

[1] Albert Fishlow, *American Railroads and the Transformation of the Antebellum Economy* (Cambridge: Harvard University Press, 1965), p. 55.

By the 1850s, however, the definite—but by no means indispensable—advantages of the railroad were eclipsing the canals and eroding the continued but slower growth of steamboats. Whereas in 1840 the nation had 3,326 miles of canals and 2,818 miles of railroads, at the end of the decade, only 400 more miles of canal had been built, compared to nearly 5,000 additional miles of railroad.[2] In the decade of the 1850s, more miles of canal were abandoned than were built, and nearly 22,000 miles of railroad track were completed. By 1854, it was possible to travel from New York to Chicago in less than three days (instead of the more than three weeks required five years earlier), and St. Louis, Missouri, as well as Dubuque, Iowa, were accessible by train.

After 1846, the ocean-going steamship and the telegraph joined the railroad as standard means of transportation and communication. As early as 1818, with the inauguration of the celebrated Black Ball Line, square-rigged sailing packets provided regular, scheduled service between New York and Liverpool. Just 30 years later, on January 1, 1848, Samuel Cunard began the first steam-packet service on the "Atlantic Shuttle" between New York and Liverpool. Thereafter, the use of iron hulls and screw propulsion increased the size, speed, and efficiency of steamships, and by 1860 they had taken over the best-paying mail, passenger, and other time-saving runs. Nevertheless, Americans clung to the romantic clipper ship, which was still efficient and competitive in shipping freight, especially on long hauls. Before 1860, sailing tonnage far exceeded steam tonnage in ocean travel.

Improvements in the movement of people and goods were paralleled by advances in communication, and it is difficult to exaggerate the revolutionary effect of the telegraph, which within a few years provided almost instantaneous communication among the well-populated areas of the country. With government support, Samuel F. B. Morse had built the first experimental telegraph line between New York and Washington in 1844, and within three years the commercial development of the telegraph began. The physical extension of lines paralleled that of the railroad, since the railroad provided a convenient right of way for telegraph lines and the telegraph made train operation safer and immensely more efficient. Because telegraph poles and lines were easier to build than railroad tracks, the telegraph actually outdistanced the railroad in the race to cross the country, and by 1860, more than 50,000 miles of line provided telegraphic communication from coast to coast and to most inhabited areas in between.

TRAILS, TURNPIKES, AND TOW PATHS

Although the least expensive means of travel usually was by water, not every place could be reached by boat. As the growing nation spread back from the coastal area, transportation to settlements that were not on waterways was of necessity by pack train—a business that employed thousands of people. Carrying goods by horseback was prohibitively expensive unless the commodities

[2] Alfred D. Chandler, Jr., *The Railroads* (New York: Harcourt Brace Jovanovich, Inc., 1965), p. 3.

were high in value relative to their weight, such as furs and whiskey. The exorbitant cost of pack-horse transportation led to the improvement of trails, so that wagons could be used where distances were not too great.

In addition to the country roads which led from farm to village, there were longer overland roads connecting the larger centers of the East with one another and with the growing settlements of the West (see Map 12-1). By 1816, Maine and Georgia were joined by a single route. To the west, crossing the mountains, ran other through roads and trails. These highways of emigration, settlement, and commerce usually followed the old Indian hunting and war paths, which in turn had followed the stream valleys providing the easiest lines of travel. One of the most important was the Wilderness Road, pioneered by Daniel Boone. Penetrating the mountain barrier at Cumberland Gap, near present-day Middlesboro, Kentucky, it then went north and west into the Ohio Territory. Over this road, which in many places was only a marked track, poured thousands of emigrants.[3] Other trails west of the mountains followed the Holston and the Watauga rivers as they flowed from their Appalachian sources into the Tennessee. Thus, geography in part directed the flow of emigration to the Southwest. As a rule, both transport and migration routes followed the natural drainage basins and the easiest, least obstacle-ridden paths overland.

Although most of the overland roads turned into quagmires in the rainy season and into billowing dust clouds in the dry season, some of them were well constructed and well maintained through portions of their length. The most notable surfaced highway was the Cumberland Road, or "National Pike," built by the federal government after much controversy. Begun at Cumberland, Maryland, in 1811, the road was opened to Wheeling on the Ohio River in 1818 and was later completed to Vandalia, Illinois. At a cost of $10,000–$13,000 per mile (quite high for the time), the road was constructed with a foundation of crushed stone 15 inches thick and a 30-foot macadamized strip in the center. The quality of the work is evidenced by the fact that the stone bridges of the road, built more than a century before, could still accommodate modern automobile traffic until the highway itself was largely replaced by Interstate 70.

The national government did not repeat its success with the Cumberland Road. As early as 1808, Albert Gallatin had proposed a plan for a system of federal roads, and progressive, enlightened people generally urged a comprehensive program of internal improvements. Opposition was based ostensibly on the assertion, repeated endlessly, that federal participation in such an activity was unconstitutional. Actually, sectional rivalries prevented the much-needed construction. The West persistently and loudly called for a national road system. At first, the Middle Atlantic states were inclined to agree, but after

[3] This same type of road or marked track appeared during the overland migration to the West Coast. The Oregon Trail, over which travel began in the early 1840s, was 2,000 miles long and carried settlers to the Pacific Northwest and to California. The Mormon Trail, broken by Brigham Young in the late 1840s, paralleled the Oregon Trail along the south bank of the Platte for some distance. Earlier trails marked by the Spaniards, such as the Santa Fe Trail into present-day New Mexico and Arizona and *El Camino Real,* or the King's Highway in California, were valuable to early explorers and traders.

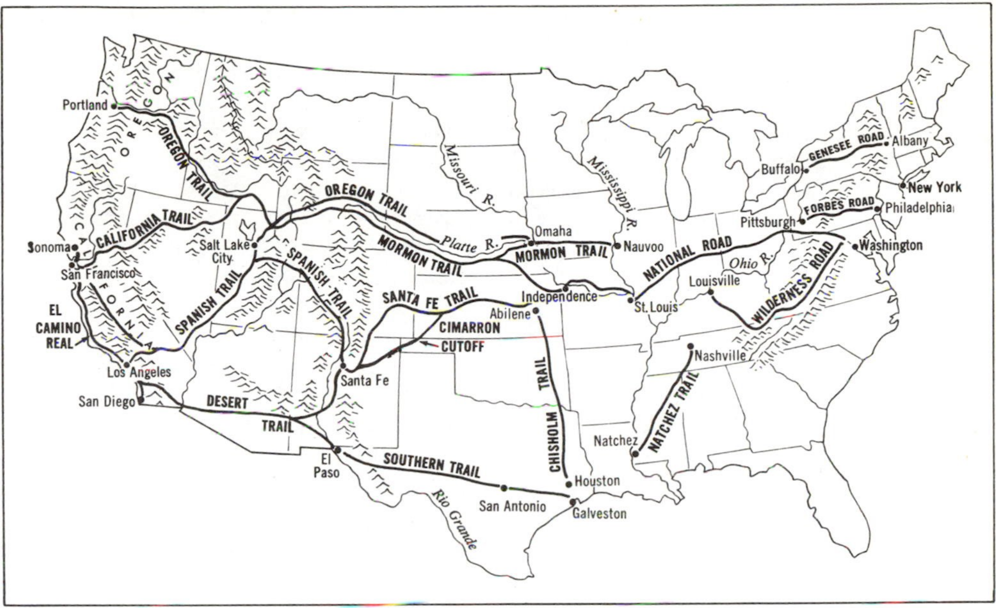

MAP 12–1

Westward Travel: The massive physical barriers faced by the pioneers could be circumvented by following such famous routes as the Oregon Trail and the Santa Fe Trail.

New York and Pennsylvania developed their own routes to the West, they did not wish to promote federally financed competition. New Englanders, with fairly good roads of their own, were even less inclined to encourage further population drains or to improve the commercial positions of Boston's rivals. The South, although mired in the mud, was bitterly antagonistic to any program that would add to the government's financial needs or facilitate access to nonslave portions of the West. Despite all the opposition, Congress could not avoid appropriating increasing sums for post and military roads, but sectional rivalries over the geographic allocation of internal improvements permitted an incredibly primitive road system to survive well into the twentieth century.

Turnpike Companies

When for some reason a unit of government refused to undertake construction, roads were often built by private turnpike companies, which then collected tolls for their use. Gates consisting of pikes or spears were turned or lifted to let the tollpayer pass to and from the road at selected points. The turnpike era began in 1789 with the construction of the Philadelphia and Lancaster Turnpike; it ended about 1830, after which date only a few private highways were attempted as business ventures. During the period, Pennsylvania chartered 86 companies that built over 2,000 miles of road. By 1811, New York had 1,500 miles of highways constructed by 135 companies, and in New England by this date, some 180 companies had been granted the right to build turnpikes. Few of the companies that constructed roads for public use were profitable ventures; in fact, it is doubtful that even one earned close to the going rate of return on its capital. Teamsters avoided the tolls if at all possible, and the receipts were pocketed by dishonest gatekeepers. But the chief difficulty—one unforeseen by most promoters—was that the only long-distance trade the roads attracted was stagecoach passengers and emigrants. Freight would not, for the most part, stand the cost of land carriage over great distances, and without freight traffic, turnpikes simply could not earn a profit. They were eventually faced with extensive competition from steamboats, canals, and railroads, but this competition did not appear until returns on invested capital had already proved disappointing. Some turnpikes were abandoned and later acquired by the states for the rapidly growing public road system; others were purchased by local governments and made into free highways.[4]

Plank Roads

Another kind of toll road, the plank road or "farmer's railroad," developed shortly after the decline in turnpike construction. Plank roads were built by laying wide, heavy planks or "rails" on stringers or ties placed in the direction of travel. The first plank road in the United States was built at Syracuse in 1837; within the next 20 years or so, several thousand miles of plank roads were in use throughout the country, the heaviest concentration being in the Middle Atlantic states. So important did they seem that some were subsidized by the states, although most were privately financed.

There were several reasons for their widespread construction. Plank roads cost far less than a macadamized highway or turnpike. A team of horses could draw much heavier loads on smooth plank roads than on a highway. They were ideal for short-haul, farm-to-market travel. Yet few plank roads were financially successful because upkeep was high. The stringers and planks were exposed to the elements at all times, and preservatives such as creosote were not available to prevent deterioration. Estimates made in Ohio showed that with the best hardwood available the life span of a plank road was about seven years.

STEAMBOATS AND THE NATURAL WATERWAYS

By comparison to the limited progress in land transportation in the early nineteenth century, developments in the natural waterways were revolutionary.

[4]A few private roads continued into the twentieth century, but all that now remains of them is the name *turnpike* given to some important arteries of the highway system. These throughways differ from the older turnpike in that the modern enterprises are owned by public corporations. As we will see in Chapter 29, toll roads are once again disappearing as they are absorbed into the Interstate and Defense Highway Systems.

Plank roadways proved essential wherever heavy military or commercial traffic was concentrated.

Before the coming of the steamboat in the West (the present-day Midwest), river travel was especially difficult and hazardous. The simplest sort of craft was a raft of logs with a shed for the protection of crew and cargo and steerage provided by huge sweeps or oars. An improvement on the raft was the flatboat or "ark," a boxlike, flat-bottomed vessel built of planks with a cabin or house covering part of the deck. Both the raft and the flatboat were broken up and sold for lumber at the destination, which in the West was usually New Orleans. Then the crews, who were ordinarily the owners of boat and cargo, made their way home overland on foot or horseback.

The keelboat, with its finer lines and keel, made journeys upstream possible. Keelboats were operated by ten or twelve crewmen who pulled the oars, manned push poles in shallow water, and occasionally went ashore to drag the boat through swift currents in the manner of a canal boat. The physical prowess and reckless attitude of the keelboatmen elicited the description "half-horse, half-alligator." Dangerous currents, shallows, or floods, attacks from Indians who still roamed the river-bank forests, and the depredations of river pirates caused frequent losses of men, vessels, and cargo. Obviously, raft, ark, and keelboat freight charges were high, but the demand for service kept them plying their hazardous trade.

Characteristic of other early experiments and innovations, the first attempts at the mechanical propulsion of boats failed to achieve commercial

Bustling inland shipping points like Cincinnati soon became major markets for an increasing variety of goods and services.

success. In 1807, Robert Fulton, with the assistance of Robert R. Livingston, built the steamboat *Clermont,* which completed a historic voyage up the Hudson River from New York to Albany, a distance of 150 miles, in 32 hours. Following the initial trip, regular passenger service from New York to Albany was inaugurated and the dependability of the steamboat was quickly demonstrated. A new era of transportation on the rivers of America had begun.

Fulton's experiment was conducted on a river that emptied into the Atlantic Ocean and provided the most favorable conditions for both navigation and traffic. The trials experienced by other vessels on other coastal rivers convinced skeptics that the steamboat would find a permanent place in inland navigation. But not until the steamboat was put into service on the "western waters"—the Mississippi, the Ohio, and the Missouri Rivers and their tributaries—could its full potentialities be judged.

This beginning in the West came at the northern terminus of Pittsburgh, which is situated where the junction of the Allegheny and the Monongahela forms the Ohio River. Plentiful supplies of timber and the local iron industry were the basis for a flourishing shipbuilding industry there, and it was at Pittsburgh that the first steamboat to ply the inland waters was constructed by Nicholas Roosevelt under the Fulton–Livingston patents. Named *The New Orleans,* it left Pittsburgh on October 20, 1811, and completed its voyage to the Gulf, despite an earthquake at New Madrid, Missouri, in a little over two and one-half months. Six years passed before regular service upstream and downstream was established, but by 1819 the tonnage of steamboats in operation on the western rivers already exceeded 10,000 and this figure grew to almost 200,000 tons by the late 1850s. The periods of the most rapid expansion were the first two decades following 1815, but significant gains occurred throughout each decade. It was not until the 1880s that steamboating in western rivers registered an absolute decline.

The appearance of the steamboat on inland waterways did not, by any means, solve all problems of travel. Variations in the heights of the rivers still made navigation uncertain, even dangerous. Ice in the spring and sand bars in the summer were ever-present hazards, and snags, rocks, and sunken vessels continually damaged and wrecked watercraft. In addition to these problems, the steamboat exposed westerners to some of the earliest hazards of industrialization; high-pressure boilers frequently exploded, accidentally killing thousands over the decades. This prompted the federal government to intervene; in 1838 and again in 1852, some of the first U.S. laws concerning industrial safety and consumer protection were legislated. Although these laws were widely evaded, steamboat designs eventually were improved, and better boilers and engines produced safer vessels. Also, the federal government sporadically engaged in the removal of snags (trees lodged in the rivers) and other obstacles from the rivers.

Competition, Productivity, and Endangered Species

One of the most significant characteristics of western river transportation was the high degree of competition among the various craft. This meant that the revolutionary effects of the steamboat, which were critical to the early settlement of the West, were transfused through a competitive market. Fulton and Livingston attempted to secure a monopoly via government restraint to prevent others from providing steamboat services at New Orleans and throughout the West. These and other associations failed to limit supply and block entry, however, and without government interference, the modest capital requirements needed to enter the business assured a competitive market.

From the early period of bonanza profits on the major routes, a normal rate of return on capital of about 10 percent was common by 1820. Only on the remote and dangerous tributaries, where trade was thin and uncertain, could such exceptional returns as 35 or 40 percent be obtained.

Because the market for western rivercraft services was generally competitive, the series of productivity-raising improvements ushered in by the steamboat were passed on to producers and consumers alike. And the cost reductions were significant, as the evidence in Table 12-1 illustrates (see page 176).

Of course, a major cause of the sharp decline in freight costs was simply the introduction of steam power. However, the stream of modifications and improvements that followed the maiden voyage of *The New Orleans* provided greater productivity gains than the application of steam power. The decrease in

TABLE 12–1
Average Freight Rates (per 100 Pounds) per Decade Between Louisville and New Orleans, 1810–1860

	Upstream	Downstream
Before 1820	$5.00	$1.00
1820–1829	1.00	0.62
1830–1839	0.50	0.50
1840–1849	0.25	0.30
1850–1859	0.25	0.32

Source: Erik F. Haites, James Mak, and Gary M. Walton, *Western River Transportation: The Era of Early Internal Development, 1810–1860* (Baltimore and London: Johns Hopkins University Press, 1975), p. 32.

rates after 1820 was greater, both absolutely and relatively, than the decline from 1811 to 1820, especially in real terms.[5]

Major modifications were made in the physical characteristics of the vessels. Initially like seagoing vessels, steamboats evolved to meet the shallow-water conditions of the western rivers. These boats became increasingly lighter in weight, with many outside decks for cargo (and budget-fare accommodations for passengers), and their water depth, or draft, became less and less, despite increased vessel size. Consequently, the amount of cargo carried (per vessel ton) greatly increased. In addition, the season of normal operations was substantially extended, even during shallow-water months. This, along with reductions in port times and passage times, greatly increased the number of round trips averaged each year.[6] Lastly, as noted earlier, government activity to clear the rivers of snags and other natural obstacles added to the time of normal operations and made river transport a safer business, as evidenced by a decline in insurance costs over the decades.

On reflection, it is clear that most of the improvements did not result from technological change. Only the initial introduction of steam power stemmed from advances in knowledge about basic principles. The host of modifications evolved from the process of learning by doing and the restructuring of known principles of design and engineering to fit shallow-water conditions. In effect, they are a tribute to the skills and ingenuity of the early craftsmen and mechanics.

In sum, the overall record of achievement gave rise to productivity advances that averaged more than 4 percent per year during the period 1815–1860. Such a rate exceeded that of any other transport medium over an equal length of time in the nineteenth century.[7]

[5] In the purchasing power of 1820 dollars, the real cost decline upstream on the New Orleans–Louisville run was from $3.12 around 1815 to $2.00 in 1820 to $.28 in the late 1850s. Downstream, the real cost changes were from $.62 around 1815 to $.75 in 1820, to $.39 in the late 1850s.

[6] Because the steamboat's contribution was greatest on the upriver leg, the decline in passage times was only partially due to faster speeds. Primarily, this decline resulted from learning to operate the boats at night. Also, shorter stopovers at specified fuel depots instead of long periods spent foraging in the woods for fuel contributed as well.

[7] See Haites, Mak, and Walton, pp. 60–63.

The labor-consuming keelboat felt the strongest sting of competition from the new technology and was quickly eliminated from the competitive fray on the main trunk river routes. Only on some of the remote tributaries did the keelboat find temporary refuge from the chugging advance of the steamboat.

Surprisingly, quite a different destiny evolved for the flatboat, which showed a remarkable persistence throughout the entire antebellum period. Because the reductions in downstream rates were more moderate, the current-propelled flatboat was less threatened. In addition, spillover effects from steamboating aided flatboating. First, there was the tremendous savings in labor that the steamboat generated by providing quick upriver transport to returning flatboatmen. Not only were they saved the long and sometimes perilous overland journey, but access to steamboat passenger services led to repetitive journeys and thus to the acquisition of skills and knowledge. This resulted in the adoption of larger flatboats, which economized greatly on labor per ton carried. Because of these gains, there were more flatboats on the western rivers near the middle of the nineteenth century than at any other time.

In combination, these western rivercraft gave a romantic aura to the drudgery of day-to-day freight haulage and commerce. Sumptuously furnished Mississippi riverboats were patronized by rich and poor alike. Yeomen farmers also contributed their adventuresome flatboating journeys. However, such developments were regional in character, and on the waterways of the East as well as on the Great Lakes, even the steamboat never attained the importance that it did in the Midwest. Canals and turnpikes furnished alternative means of transportation, and the railroad network had an early competitive start. Steamboats in the East were primarily passenger carriers—great side-wheelers furnishing luxurious accommodations for people traveling between major cities. On the Great Lakes, contrary to what might be expected, sailing ships successfully competed for freight throughout the antebellum years. Where human comfort was a factor, however, the steamship gradually prevailed. Even so, the number and tonnage of sailing vessels on the Great Lakes in 1860 were far greater than those of steamboats.

THE CANAL ERA

Although the natural waterways provided a substantial web of transport facilities, many productive areas remained regionally and economically disconnected until the canals were built and other internal improvements were made to link them together. The first major undertaking began in 1817, when the New York legislature authorized the construction of the Erie and Champlain canals, and work was begun shortly thereafter. With powerful DeWitt Clinton as the guiding spirit, the Erie Canal was promoted with enthusiasm, and sections were opened to traffic as they were completed. It quickly became apparent that the canal would have great success, and even before its completion in 1825, "canal fever" seized promoters throughout the country. In the tremendous building boom that followed, canals were constructed to link three types of areas. Some ran from the "back country" to the tidewater regions; some traversed, or attempted to traverse, the area between the older states and the

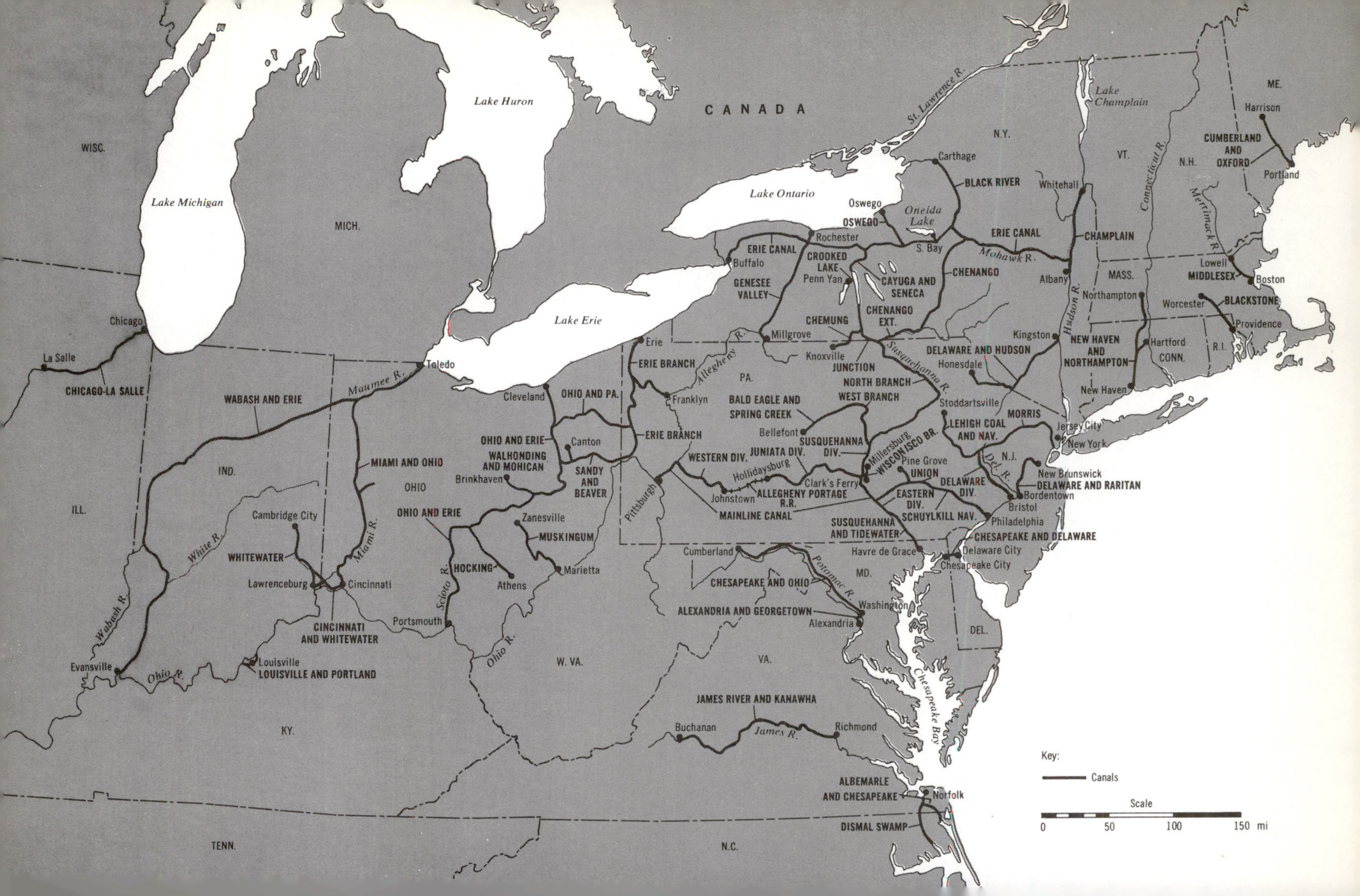

CANADA
Lake Michigan
Lake Huron
Lake Ontario
Lake Erie
Lake Champlain
Oneida Lake
Chesapeake Bay
St. Lawrence R.
Connecticut R.
Merrimack R.
Hudson R.
Mohawk R.
Susquehanna R.
Allegheny R.
Del. R.
Potomac R.
James R.
Ohio R.
Scioto R.
Miami R.
White R.
Wabash R.
Maumee R.
WISC.
MICH.
ILL.
IND.
OHIO
KY.
TENN.
W. VA.
VA.
N.C.
MD.
DEL.
PA.
N.J.
N.Y.
VT.
N.H.
ME.
MASS.
CONN.
R.I.
Harrison
Portland
CUMBERLAND AND OXFORD
Lowell
MIDDLESEX
Boston
Worcester
BLACKSTONE
Providence
Northampton
Hartford
New Haven
NEW HAVEN AND NORTHAMPTON
Whitehall
CHAMPLAIN
Albany
Kingston
DELAWARE AND HUDSON
Honesdale
Stoddartsville
Carthage
BLACK RIVER
ERIE CANAL
Oswego
OSWEGO
S. Bay
CHENANGO
CAYUGA AND SENECA
CHENANGO EXT.
Rochester
CROOKED LAKE
Penn Yan
Buffalo
GENESEE VALLEY
CHEMUNG
Millgrove
Knoxville
JUNCTION
NORTH BRANCH
WEST BRANCH
BALD EAGLE AND SPRING CREEK
Bellefont
SUSQUEHANNA DIV.
JUNIATA DIV.
WESTERN DIV.
Hollidaysburg
Millersburg
WISCONISCO BR.
Clark's Ferry
ALLEGHENY PORTAGE R.R.
Johnstown
MAINLINE CANAL
Pittsburgh
Erie
ERIE BRANCH
Franklyn
Pine Grove
UNION
DELAWARE DIV.
EASTERN DIV.
SCHUYLKILL NAV.
SUSQUEHANNA AND TIDEWATER
LEHIGH COAL AND NAV.
MORRIS
Jersey City
New York
New Brunswick
DELAWARE AND RARITAN
Bordentown
Bristol
Philadelphia
CHESAPEAKE AND DELAWARE
Delaware City
Chesapeake City
Havre de Grace
Cumberland
CHESAPEAKE AND OHIO
Washington
ALEXANDRIA AND GEORGETOWN
Alexandria
JAMES RIVER AND KANAWHA
Buchanan
Richmond
ALBEMARLE AND CHESAPEAKE
Norfolk
DISMAL SWAMP
Cleveland
OHIO AND PA.
OHIO AND ERIE
Canton
SANDY AND BEAVER
WALHONDING AND MOHICAN
Brinkhaven
Zanesville
MUSKINGUM
Marietta
HOCKING
Athens
Portsmouth
Toledo
WABASH AND ERIE
MIAMI AND OHIO
Cincinnati
CINCINNATI AND WHITEWATER
Lawrenceburg
WHITEWATER
Cambridge City
Louisville
LOUISVILLE AND PORTLAND
Evansville
Chicago
La Salle
CHICAGO-LA SALLE
Key:
Canals
Scale
0
50
100
150 mi

MAP 12–2 (Opposite)

Principal Canals of the Antebellum Period, 1800–1860
Source: Carter Goodrich (ed.), *Canals and American Economic Development* (New York: Columbia University Press, 1961), pp. 184–85.

Ohio Valley; and some—the western canals—linked the Great Lakes with the waterways running to the East. The principal canals of the antebellum period are shown in Map 12-2.

The Erie was the most important of the early canals, although it was by no means the only profitable one.[8] It was a massive undertaking. Beginning at Albany on the Hudson River, it traversed the state of New York westward to Buffalo on Lake Erie, covering a distance of 364 miles. The work cost approximately $7 million and took about nine years to complete. The builders overcame countless difficulties, not the least of which was their own ignorance. Hardly any of the engineers had ever worked in canal construction, and much experimentation was necessary in the process. Some sections of the canal did not hold water at first and had to be lined with clay after work had been completed. The locks presented a special difficulty. But ingenuity and the timely discovery of water-resistant, or hydraulic, cement led to the solution of the problems of lock construction.

The Erie system, in its final form, reached a fair portion of New York state. The Cayuga and Seneca, the Chemung, and the Genesee extensions connected important territory to the south with the canal. A branch to Oswego provided access to Lake Ontario, and the Champlain Canal gave access to the north. The system not only furnished transportation to much of the state but tapped the Great Lakes areas served by the St. Lawrence route and the vast Ohio Territory as well. Beginning about 1835, a large part of the traffic from the West that had formerly traversed the Ohio and Mississippi rivers to New Orleans was diverted over the Erie Canal to the port of New York. Lumber, grain, and meat products were the chief commodities to move eastward; textiles, leather goods, machinery, hardware, and imported foods and drugs went west in exchange. Passengers, too, rode the horse-drawn boats in great numbers, with speeds of 100 miles in a 24-hour day compensating in part for the discomfort of cramped and poorly ventilated cabins.

Pennsylvania's answer to the competition of the Erie Canal was the Main Line of the Pennsylvania Public Works—a system of railroads *and* canals chartered in 1826 by the state legislature. The terrain traversed by the Erie to reach the western frontier was difficult enough for canal construction, although at its highest point it rose only 650 feet above the Hudson at Albany. But the terrain of western Pennsylvania proved to be insurmountable by canal. The Main Line crossed the mountains, lifted passengers and freight to an altitude of over 2,000 feet, and deposited both travelers and goods, westbound from Philadelphia, at Pittsburgh some 400 miles away. All this was accomplished by as fantastic a combination of transport as the country had ever seen. From Philadelphia, at tidewater, to Columbia, 81 miles westward on the Susquehanna River, a horse-

[8]This system still exists in an expanded and improved form as the New York Barge Canal.

This painting shows the junction of the Champlain Canal and the Erie Canal—an important point on the trade route that was to become the preeminent link between Midwest and East Coast urban centers.

drawn railroad carried both passengers and freight.[9] At Columbia, the railroad joined the Juniata, or Eastern Division of the Pennsylvania Canal, from which passengers and freight were carried up a river valley by canal 173 miles to the Portage Railroad at Holidaysburg. Here intrepid passengers saw their boat separated into front and rear sections, which were mounted on cars and run on underwater rails into the canal. A 36-mile trip on the Portage Railroad then began. The inclined tracks, over which cars were pulled by stationary steam engines winding cables on drums, accomplished a lift of 1,399 feet on the eastern slope to the summit and a descent of 1,172 feet on the western slope to another canal at Johnstown. From Johnstown to Pittsburgh, a distance of 105 miles, the water journey was comparatively easy.

The completion of this colossal work in 1834 was heralded by a celebration at Liberty Hall in Philadelphia. An old print depicts one of the halfboats decked with bunting and flags being drawn away from the hall by teams of prancing horses. In the sense that it carried all the traffic it could, the Main Line

[9] Although the steam locomotive was not employed in the United States until 1829, rails to permit smooth haulage had been used in both America and Europe for several years.

was successful, but the bottleneck of the Portage Railroad plus the fact that the system had twice as many locks as the Erie kept it from becoming a serious competitor for western business. Over the years, the Main Line carried 5–10 percent of the traffic volume of the Erie Canal, to the great disappointment of the people of a state that had spent more on waterways than any other.

Other states expended large sums of money on canals to draw the trade of the new West. The Chesapeake and Ohio Canal was projected up the valley of the Potomac to Cumberland, Maryland, and on to the Ohio River. The canal company was chartered by the state of Virginia with the assent of the Maryland legislature, and the federal government contributed heavily to the venture. But, despite the political blessings of two states and the federal government, the generous financial backing of all three, and the aid of some local governments, due to technical difficulties the project was completed only to Cumberland.

The financially successful canals in the East were those that facilitated the carriage of anthracite coal from the fields to the tidewater. In the West, the most important canals were the two that contributed to the development of Ohio: the Miami and Ohio Canal, which connected Cincinnati on the Ohio River with Toledo on Lake Erie, and the Ohio and Erie Canal between Portsmouth on the Ohio River and Cleveland on Lake Erie. These canals traversed from north to south the western and central sections of the state and provided access both to the Great Lakes for eastbound traffic and to the Ohio–Mississippi river system for westbound and southbound traffic. Both canals, well built and soundly financed, did a good business and unquestionably helped to start the great flow of agricultural products to the East via the Erie Canal. On the other hand, Indiana's experience with the Wabash and Erie was frustrating. The longest canal in the United States, it was completed too late to operate for more than a few years free of rail competition.

Although most of the canal investments were not financially rewarding, they did support the natural waterways in opening up the West. Some that have been considered preposterous mistakes might have turned out to be monuments to human inventiveness if the railroad had not developed at almost the same time. The canals posed problems, it is true. The limitations on horse-drawn vehicles for cargo transport were great except with regard to a few commodities. Canals were supposed to provide a *system* of waterways, but as often as not the boats of larger canals could not move through the smaller canals. Floods and droughts often made the movement of the barges uncertain. Yet the chief reason for the eventual failure of the canals was the railroad, which could carry a wide variety of commodities at a much greater speed—and speed was requisite to a genuine transportation revolution.

THE IRON HORSE

The genesis of the railroad illustrates technical innovation by small steps. The two main elements of the railway—rails and locomotives—were developed separately in England over a period of many years. In the coal fields of Durham and Newcastle, as early as the last quarter of the seventeenth century, wagons with unflanged wheels were being drawn over roadbeds of planks. In the middle of the eighteenth century, flanged rails of cast iron were introduced to hold "flat" wheels more securely, and shortly afterwards experiments were begun with flanged wheels and a dumbbell-shaped rail. Cast-iron wheels and rails were so brittle that they broke easily, especially in cold weather, and malleable wrought-iron rails came into use early in the nineteenth century. By 1820 or so, a rather advanced type of rail was employed by the horse-drawn tramways.

The initial contribution of the steam engine to land transportation was to supply power for tramways, which consisted of rails on which cars were drawn by a cable wound on a drum.[10] But to improve overland transport significantly, the steam engine had to be mounted so that motive power could be transmitted to the wheels. Then the vehicle would be locomotive, or self-propelled. Attempts to combine the steam engine with a wheeled carriage had been made as early as 1769 by the Frenchman Cognot, but the first commercial employment is attributed to the Englishman Richard Trevithick, who in 1801 used a steam locomotive to pull carriages on rails into and out of a Cornish mine.

It remained for the Stockton and Darlington Railway Company—the first public railway company in England—to operate the first steam-powered vehicle manufactured for public use in 1825. George Stephenson, designer and builder of the locomotive, was also the engineer.[11] Four years later, Stephenson won the prize of £500 sterling offered by the directors of the Liverpool and Manchester Railway for developing a locomotive engine that would cost a maximum of £500 and would run at a minimum speed of 10 miles per hour. The *Rocket,* built by Stephenson and his son Robert for the Liverpool and Manchester competition, is generally recognized as the earliest practical steam locomotive. Weighing approximately 5 tons, it was able to draw a load three times its weight at a speed of 12½ miles per hour; with only a carriage and passengers, its speed could be increased to 24 miles per hour.[12]

The interest shown in England and on the Continent in the use of steam engines for propulsion was not without its counterpart in America. As early as 1786, Oliver Evans had unsuccessfully petitioned the legislature of Pennsylvania for a monopoly to operate steam wagons on the highways. In 1820, John Stevens, a New Jerseyite who had previously built a steamboat called the *Phoenix,* demonstrated a narrow-gauge steam railway near Hoboken. Yet it was an English locomotive, the *Stourbridge Lion,* that made the first trial run on the tracks of an established American company in 1829. The locomotive, one of three ordered from Foster, Rastrick and Company of Stourbridge, England, was

[10] The inclined planes of the Main Line of the Pennsylvania Public Works might be regarded as a sort of tramway, although tramways are generally associated with mines or quarries.

[11] George Stephenson (1781–1848) began his career in the mines of Scotland. Carefully studying the crude pumping engines used at the mines, he taught himself the principles of steam power and mechanics. Stephenson's observations led to improvements on stationary engines and locomotives, and due to his experience with tramways and rails, he was employed by various railway companies in England. He was an ardent advocate of flat grades and curves of long radius. Many engineers were opposed to these theories, but Stephenson's methods are presently applied by railroads here and abroad. It is the modern view that George Stephenson's chief claim to fame lies in his contribution as a civil engineer.

[12] In 1837, the *Rocket* carried the results of a political contest a distance of 4 miles in 4½ minutes. See Samuel Smiles, *Life of George Stephenson* (New York: Harper, 1868), p. 327.

tested over the gravity railway of the Delaware and Hudson Canal Company. The test was considered a failure because the engine was too heavy for rails and trestles that were designed to support only loaded cars.

The *Tom Thumb* was the first American-built steam locomotive. Manufactured to demonstrate the feasibility of steam power, it was given a short trial run in 1830 but was never used in commercial service. The *Peter Cooper* (named after the designer of the *Tom Thumb*), the *York* of the Baltimore and Ohio, and the *Best Friend of Charleston* of the Charleston and Hamburg were the best known of the early steam locomotives. After the practicability of steam locomotion had been proved in America by these vehicles, others were built and put into regular service; the speed and tractive power of this new means of hauling freight and passengers far surpassed any other then known.

Yet for nearly 20 years after the opening of the two pioneer railroads, the natural waterways remained the primary means of transportation. Besides the stiff competition of water transport, an important hindrance to railroad development was public antipathy, which had its roots in ignorance, conservatism, and vested interest. People thought that speeds of 20–30 miles per hour would be physically harmful to the passenger. At least one city in Massachusetts directed its representatives in the state legislature to prevent "so great a calamity to our town as must be the location of any railroad through it." Many honestly believed that the railroad would prove to be impractical and uneconomical and would not provide service as dependable as that of the waterways.

Railroad Construction 1830–1860

Unsurprisingly, the most vigorous opposition to railroads came from groups whose economic interests suffered from the competition of the new industry. Millions of dollars had been spent on canals, rivers, highways, and plank roads, and thousands of people depended on these transportation enterprises for their livelihood. Tavern keepers feared their businesses would be ruined, and farmers envisioned the market for hay and grain disappearing as the "iron horse" replaced the flesh and blood animal that drew the canal boat and pulled the wagon over turnpike and plank road. Competitive interests joined to embarrass and hinder the railroads, causing several states to limit traffic on them to passengers and their baggage or to freight hauled only during the months when canal operations ceased. One railroad company in Ohio was required to pay for any loss in canal traffic attributed to railroad competition. Other railroads were ordered to pay a tonnage tax to support the operation of canals.

Despite the opposition of those who feared the railroads, construction went on. In sections of the country where canals could not be built, the railroad offered a means of cheap transportation for all kinds of commodities. In contrast to the municipality that wished to exclude the railroad, many cities and towns, as well as their state governments, did much to encourage railroad construction. At the time, the federal government was restrained by the prevailing political philosophy from financially assisting and promoting railways. It did, however, make surveys to determine rights of way and provided tariff exemptions on railroad iron.

By 1840, railroad mileage in the United States was within 1,000 miles of the combined lengths of all canals, but the volume of goods carried by water still far exceeded that transported by rail. Furthermore, most of the rail construction was restricted to New England and the Middle Atlantic states. But the decade of the 1840s was one of expansion, and over 9,000 miles of railroads had been built by 1850. The Western and Atlantic line was completed by the state of Georgia to provide better transportation for the towns of the Georgia piedmont, the Georgia Railroad connected Atlanta with the Charleston and Hamburg at Augusta, and Chattanooga was linked with both Savannah and Charleston. In Ohio, a through line was completed from the Ohio River to Lake Erie. By 1850, the eastern railway network was well on its way to taking shape. Through routes were established from Boston to Albany and from Boston to New York, and Baltimore was nearly linked with Wheeling. The Erie Railroad, which for more than a decade had been extending a line westward from New York City across the southern counties of New York, would reach Dunkirk on Lake Erie in another year, and Philadelphia capitalists were working to overcome the difficulties of reaching Pittsburgh by rail.

With the more than 20,000 miles of rails added to the transportation system between 1850 and 1860, total trackage approached 30,000 miles at the end of the decade, and the volume of freight traffic equaled that of canals.[13] All the states east of the Mississippi were connected during this decade. The eastern seaboard was linked with the Mississippi River system, and the Gulf and South Atlantic states could interchange traffic with the Great Lakes. Growing trunk lines like the Erie, the Pennsylvania, and the Baltimore and Ohio completed construction of projects that had been started in the 1840s, and combinations of short lines provided new through routes. By the beginning of the Civil War, the eastern framework of the present rail-transportation system had been erected, and it was possible to travel by rail the entire distance from New York to Chicago to Memphis and back to New York.

But the United States was still a long way from establishing an integrated railroad system. Although the "Stephenson gauge" of 4 feet 8½ inches was preponderant in 1860, its final selection as the "standard gauge" for the country was still a quarter-century away. A multitude of gauges prevented continuous shipment, as did the lack of agreement among companies on such matters as the interline exchange of rolling stock, through bills of lading and passenger tickets, the division of through rates, and standard time.[14] Moreover, an efficient system required considerable technological improvement to develop more powerful locomotives to pull larger trains with standardized braking and coupling devices over steel (not iron) rails—to say nothing of the need for bridges across major rivers.

The outbreak of the Civil War drastically reduced railroad construction in the North and temporarily halted it in the South, as the efforts of both sections were diverted from internal improvements to internal destruction. Not until

[13] Railroads had won from canals almost all passenger business, except that of poor immigrants coming across New York state, and the carriage of nearly all light, high-value goods.

[14] George Rogers Taylor and Irene Neu, *The American Railway Network, 1861–1890* (Cambridge: Harvard University Press, 1956), pp. 6–7, 12–14.

the question of secession had been settled could promoters continue their efforts to complete the railway network and make it a standardized, interconnected system.

OCEAN TRANSPORT

Besides the many developments in internal transportation, great strides were being made in the long-traditional merchant marine. As we mentioned earlier, the Black Ball line of New York instituted regularly scheduled transatlantic sailings in 1818. Beginning with just four ships, a vessel sailed from New York bound for Liverpool, in the first week of each month, and a ship began the Liverpool–New York passage at the same time. Considerable risk was involved in pledging ships to sail "full or not full," as the line's advertising declared, because a ship might make three round trips a year (instead of the usual two made by the regular traders) with its hold far from full.[15] But by specializing in passengers, specie, mail, and "fine freight," the packets managed to operate successfully for more than 100 years. In the 1820s, the Black Ball line increased its trips to two a month each way, and other packet lines between New York and European ports were soon established. Henceforth, passengers could count on sailing at a particular hour on a given day, and merchants could book freight with something more than a vague hope that it would arrive in time to permit a profitable transaction.

The transatlantic packets fully established New York as the predominant port in the United States. Coastal packets, running primarily to New Orleans, but also to Charleston, Savannah, and Mobile, brought cotton to New York for eastbound ocean shipment and carried southward a considerable portion of the European goods brought from England and the Continent. In fact, trade between the cotton ports and New York was greater in physical and dollar volume than the ocean trade during most of the antebellum period.[16] These packets significantly complimented developments in the western rivers, which funneled produce from the interior through New Orleans.

Between 1820 and 1860, remarkable design changes in sailing ships led to increases in tonnage and efficiency. From an average of 300 tons in the 1820s, American sailing ships increased to 1,000 tons in the 1850s, and vessels of 1,500 tons burden were not uncommon. There was a marked increase in length-to-beam ratios and spread of sail for the ordinary packet ship, and the centuries-old practice of making the widest part of the vessel forward of the center was abandoned. Borrowing from French designers, Yankee shipbuilders produced a special type of ship that was to dominate the seas for the three decades before the Civil War. This was the famed clipper ship, which, at some sacrifice of carrying capacity, attained unheard-of speeds. The clipper was a graceful ship with three masts, square-rigged but equipped with abundant

[15] Robert Greenhalgh Albion, *The Rise of the New York Port, 1815–1860* (Hamden, Conn.: Archon Books, 1961), p. 4.

[16] Robert Greenhalgh Albion, *Square-Riggers on Schedule* (Princeton: Princeton University Press, 1938), pp. 49–50.

New York's rapid ascendancy as a port city is captured in this picture of the South Street Pier in 1850.

fore-and-aft sails that gave it a great advantage going into the wind, thus increasing its speed. Manned by fewer hands than vessels of foreign register, a clipper was to be driven 24 hours a day, not put to bed for seven or eight hours at night.

The first American, or "Baltimore," clipper was the *Ann McKim,* launched in 1832. Her builder, Donald McKay, became a legendary figure, and some ships of his design bore names that are remembered even now: the *Flying Cloud,* the *Sovereign of the Seas,* the *Great Republic,* and the *Lightning* were spectacularly beautiful, with concave sides and bow and sail towering 200 feet above the deck. On its maiden voyage across the Atlantic, the *Lightning* logged a record 436 miles in one day for an average speed of 18 miles an hour. Even today, many ocean vessels do not approach this speed.

Clippers were designed for the express purpose of carrying passengers and high-value cargo long distances. On the Atlantic runs, they were not profitable due to their limited capacity. But they dominated the China trade, and after 1849 they made fortunes for their owners by carrying passengers and freight in the gold rushes to California and Australia. On the New York– San Francisco trip around Cape Horn, a distance of 16,000 miles, the *Flying Cloud* set a record of just over 89 days, when a little over 100 days was about par for the clipper voyage. This meant a time saving over ordinary ocean travel of up to three months, for which some merchants and travelers would pay a good price.

Clippers, however, were not the only vessels in the American merchant fleet. Broad-beamed and full-bowed freighting ships, much slower vessels than the clippers, were the backbone of the nation's merchant marine. Officered by men to whom seafaring was a tradition and a career of considerable social prestige, manned by crews of Americans bred to the sea, and owned by merchants of vision and daring like Stephen Girard of Philadelphia, the cheaply and expertly built ships from the marine ways of New York, Boston, and the Maine coast were the great ocean-freight carriers until the Civil War.

In the meantime, the British were making technical advances that enabled them to challenge American maritime supremacy and finally to overcome it. The major British innovation was the adaptation of the steamboat, originally invented for use on rivers and protected waters, to navigation on the open sea. The two principal changes made by the British were the use of iron instead of wood for the hull and the employment of the Archimedean screw principle for propulsion instead of paddles. Iron hulls were necessary to transport the heavy machinery of the early steam era safely, but they also had greater strength, buoyancy, and durability than wood. From the 1830s on, the British rapidly solved the problems of iron-ship construction. The composite ship—with a frame of iron and a hull of wood—was tried for a while, but the acid in the oak timber corroded the iron. Once the British had perfected the techniques of riveting and working with sheet iron and steel, they had an absolute advantage in the construction of iron ships—as great an advantage as the United States had enjoyed in the making of wooden ones.

The inefficiency and slow speeds of the early steam engines were a source of unending difficulty. For a long time, steamships had to carry a greater weight of coal than of cargo, and low engine speeds made the inefficient paddle wheel necessary despite its theoretical inferiority.

After nearly 20 years of development, however, transatlantic steamships were making six voyages a year—twice as many as their sailing-packet competitors. Ten years later, Samuel Cunard's success in starting a line service was not entirely fortuitous; by 1848, engines were designed that could maintain higher speeds. The screw propeller was then rapidly adopted, and fuel consumption was cut greatly. During the 1850s, both the number and registered tonnage of steamships increased by leaps and bounds, and they almost entirely captured the passenger and high-value freight business.

In 1860, sailing ships still carried the greater part of the world's international freight. Yet by this time the shape of the future was clear to all except diehard American entrepreneurs, who—unable to comprehend the rapid obsolescence of their beautiful wooden ships—failed to take vigorous steps to compete with Britain. Although government subsidies to American steamship builders began as early as 1845, they were both insufficient and poorly administered. Under the most favorable circumstances, however, builders in the

United States could scarcely have competed on a cost basis with the vastly superior British iron industry. The signs were there for those who chose to read them. During the 1820s, American ships had carried close to 90 percent of the foreign trade of the United States; by the 1850s, this figure had declined to about 70 percent. The times had changed, and fortune's hand was laid on other shoulders.

13

Market Expansion and Industry in First Transition

The Transportation Revolution of the first half of the nineteenth century is generally viewed in terms of its technological aspects. Equally revolutionary, however, were the far-reaching effects of diminishing costs for transport that linked together many isolated places and regional markets. Improvements in transportation played the main role in increasing regional specialization, and in many ways transportation developments were instrumental to economic unification. What made them all the more remarkable is that the westward movement, the rise of King Cotton, and industrialization were all unfolding simultaneously. Inexpensive transport, more than any other force, was responsible for moving the domestic market to center stage and giving it the position of prominence that it occupies today.

THE PATTERN OF DOMESTIC TRADE

By 1860, the East or, more specifically, the New England and Middle Atlantic states had achieved about the same relationship to the rest of the United States that England had borne to the colonies a century before. As the nineteenth century progressed, eastern manufacturers turned out a growing list of goods to meet the demands of the West and the South, and the finer wares still imported into the United States passed through the ports of New York, Boston, Philadelphia, and Baltimore. In the meantime, towns located at key points on the western lake and river system became commercial cities. Pittsburgh, Cincinnati, and Louisville were the great ports on the Ohio, and Cleveland, Toledo, and Detroit became major distributing centers on the Great Lakes. Between 1820 and 1850, Cincin-

The port of St. Louis in 1854. Strategically located on the Mississippi River and providing a natural gateway to the West, St. Louis then seemed destined to become the largest city in the Midwest and perhaps even in the nation.

nati had no equal in the western trade, but as the westward movement progressed, it appeared that St. Louis and Chicago would be the final rivals for midwestern supremacy.

A century before, its citizens did not doubt that St. Louis, located near the confluence of the Missouri and the Mississippi, would be the principal city of the Midwest, if not of the country. Providentially situated where the trade of the upper Mississippi River terminated and that of the lower river began, St. Louis occupied a strategic economic position. It was the northern terminus for the large steamboats of the lower river and the southern terminus for the smaller steamboats of the upper river, and it was here that cargoes were unloaded and reloaded for further shipment. There seemed little doubt that the commerce of the Mississippi Valley would continue in a predominantly north–south direction and that it would hinge on St. Louis. Moreover, it appeared that the future physical expansion of the United States would take place with St. Louis—a natural gateway to the West and the Southwest—as a base of operations.

St. Louis's hope of primacy disappeared, however, as technological change removed the great obstacle to the development of Chicago. Possessed with facilities for water transportation eastward, Chicago's problem was tapping the rich territory to the West. The advent of the railroad meant that Chicago, with its more favorable location for east–west rail traffic, would one day break the commercial hold of St. Louis on the upper Mississippi Valley.[1] And as early as 1850, although St. Louisans did not realize it, the trade from east to west had surpassed the trade from north to south in volume.

The great east–west intersectional trade was made possible by the opening of the western section of the Erie Canal in 1825, but not until 1832, when the Ohio Canal was completed, did east–west trade begin in earnest. After 1835, lumber, grain, and livestock products flowed in an ever-increasing stream through Buffalo to the East, where they were consumed or passed on for export. For a time, low ton-mile rates on Mississippi River freight kept western products moving in unabated volume to New Orleans. By 1846, however, Buffalo was handling more wheat and wheat flour than New Orleans. A few years later, the Ohio Valley was sending nearly all its grain via the canals, although whiskey and meat products still went preponderantly south. During the 1850s, the volume of western products funneling through St. Louis was stable at a high level, but the relative importance of this commerce declined steadily as New Orleans relied more and more on the southern staples for its trade.

As late as 1860, New Orleans was the leading export city in the country and New York was second. The southern ports of Mobile, Charleston, and Savannah followed in that order, reflecting the economic dependence of the South on the sale of cotton to foreign countries. But the South also provided, through the great coastal trade, raw materials and food for the industrial Northeast. Cotton for the flourishing textile industry of New England led the list of commodities; sugar and molasses, naval stores, timber, rice, and tobacco were also exchanged in quantity for the manufactured articles of the North. Traffic from the South to the Northwest and the West, which was never as great as the downstream flow, became insignificant in the decade before the Civil War.

These commodity flows attested to differences in comparative advantages of production among the regions, and the degrees of regional specialization changed and became more apparent as transportation costs decreased and the market widened. Of particular concern here is the rise of industry or, more specifically, manufacturing activity. Growth of manufacturing occurred first and primarily in the Northeast, but the production of manufacturing was also spreading ever westward with the population. These regional aspects and patterns of industrialization will be treated later. First, we will focus on "how it all began"[2] — in the United States.

PRIMITIVE METHODS OF ORGANIZING PRODUCTION

Household Manufacture

Household manufacture, after a decline in the two post-Revolutionary decades, revived in the years of international upheaval between 1805 and 1815. By 1815, products made in the home had probably reached a peak in both

[1] See Wyatt Winton Belcher, *The Economic Rivalry Between St. Louis and Chicago* (New York: Columbia University Press, 1947).

[2] We freely acknowledge borrowing this phrase from W. W. Rostow, *How It All Began: The Origins of Modern Economic Growth,* (New York: McGraw-Hill Book Company, 1975).

volume and total value. Various estimates indicate that as late as 1820 two-thirds of the textiles used in American homes were made by American families. No doubt an even greater proportion of food processing was done in the home. Although home production was primarily for home consumption, much of it was for general sale.

By 1830, there was a marked decline in household manufacture in the East, but that decline was just about offset by an increase in home production on the frontier. From 1830 on, however, household manufacture tended to disappear in all but the most inaccessible places; the only exceptions were food processing and garment making in the home, which were common everywhere until the Civil War. The major cause of the decline of household manufacture was the development of industrial organization and modern means of transportation. Wherever steamboats ran or canals, highways, and railroads were built, home manufacture declined quickly. Even on the frontier, most households had access to the products of domestic or European factories after the middle of the nineteenth century. How important transportation was is illustrated in Map 13-1. The shaded areas in the two maps of New York show the third of the counties in the state having the highest per-capita output of woolen goods made in the home in two different years—1820 and 1845. Note that in 1820 no county lying along the Hudson below Albany was in the top third. In 1845, the counties lying along the Erie Canal had similarly dropped in amount of home manufacture. But V. S. Clark reports that as late as 1865, nearly all the country people of Tennessee, especially those living in the mountain areas, wore clothing made at home.

MAP 13–1

Canal Impact: Household manufacture of woolen cloth (an index of isolation from commercial routes) underwent a drastic change between 1820 and 1845 along the Erie Canal. The shaded areas indicate the one-third of the counties with the highest home production of woolen goods during this period.

Source: Arthur A. Cole, the American Wool Manufacture, **I** (Cambridge: Harvard University Press, 1926).

The Craft Shop and the Putting-Out System

Until approximately 1850, the substantial increases in manufacturing output were effected by craftsmen operating independently or in a craft shop. The former did "bespoke" work, making commodities only to order, maintaining the highest standards of quality, and selling through their own small retail outlets. But the production of independent craftsmen declined rapidly after 1815. More important at that date and for some time afterward was the craft shop run by a master who employed several journeymen and apprentices. Sometimes, as in the case of the hatters of Danbury, Connecticut, an agglomeration of craft shops sold a quantity output to merchant wholesalers for distribution over wide market areas.

The putting out or domestic system cannot be readily classified. In some ways, it is a unique form of organization, and yet it cuts across the categories of both household and craft production. For example, before 1830, the enterprising merchant frequently distributed cotton yarn among families for hand looming but employed skilled craftsmen to loom the yarn for finer fabrics in their shops. Until somewhat later, woolen yarn might be spun in a mill and put out to households for hand looming; the finishing processes of bleaching and dyeing were finally carried out by workmen assembled under one roof. In the boot and shoe industry, the leather might be cut under the supervision of a merchant, the pieces distributed to craft shops for sewing, and the nearly finished shoes returned to the shop for final processing. As people who bought ready-made shoes became more exacting in their demand for quality and fit and as machinery was developed for making a better product in quantity, the industry slipped easily into factory methods. Straw hats and galluses, on the other hand, were made by women and children in the home and sold by enterprising merchant employers in a wide market up to 1860.

Mill Industries

As in colonial days, the small mill was to be found everywhere from 1815 to 1860. In nearly all localities, a restricted but profitable market existed for the processed products of agriculture, forest, and mine. The census of 1860 reported nearly 20,000 sawmills and 14,000 flour mills in the country. With few exceptions, tanneries, distilleries, breweries, and iron forges also produced for local markets. The decentralization of American industry before 1860, favored by high transportation costs and the use of water power, produced small firms that often constituted effective local monopolies.

Before 1860, some mills had achieved large-scale production, using methods of manufacture typical of the factory. Furthermore, large mills in two industries tended to concentrate in certain rather well-defined areas. The flour-milling industry, which even in colonial days had been attracted to the Chesapeake area, continued to cluster there as farmers in Maryland and Virginia substituted wheat for tobacco. As cities grew larger and the demand for building materials increased, it became profitable for large lumbering firms to exploit timber areas located some distance from the markets; typical were those situated by 1850 on the upper reaches of streams flowing through New England, New York, and Pennsylvania.

THE DEVELOPMENT OF FACTORY PRODUCTION

Not until after 1845 did it become clear that the methods of production we have just described would soon be outmoded. At mid-century, no one could have foreseen that tragedy, in the form of civil strife, would hasten the process of change. Yet the developments of the 1850s were such that even the most casual contemporary observer could not fail to be impressed now by the rapid evolution of the "factory system."

Prerequisites to Factory Production

The Industrial Revolution that had already begun in England by no means guaranteed the immediate establishment of the factory system in America. In fact, the English sought to prevent dissemination abroad of the details of the new inventions, and their efforts possibly accounted for a time lag of some years in the introduction of the machines to the United States. On the other hand, the new techniques could in any case be imported only as American entrepreneurs with sufficient capital became aware of the possibilities of employing them profitably.

Largely because of the relatively high cost of labor in the United States, American managers always tended to use the most nearly automatic machines available in a particular application. More importantly, they successfully innovated new ways of organizing production that saved labor expense per unit of output. Their chief contributions—the two basic ideas that led to American preeminence in nineteenth-century manufacturing—were interchangeable-parts manufacture and continuous-process manufacture. Both advances were inevitably allied with the development of machine tools and with changes in techniques of applying power.

The idea of standardizing a product and its various parts originated in Sweden in the early eighteenth century and before 1800 had been tried at least once in France, Switzerland, and England. Through standardization, the parts of one product could be interchanged for the parts of a like product, facilitating manufacture and repair. The first permanently successful application of the idea in a nontrivial use was made in the American armament industry. At the turn of the nineteenth century, Eli Whitney and Simeon North almost simultaneously obtained contracts from the government to manufacture firearms by the interchangeable-parts method. Records suggest that North was using the "uniformity principle" as early as 1807 in making his pistols. It has long been customary to credit Whitney with the first successful manufacture by interchangeable parts, but the evidence does not substantiate his claim to priority. Perhaps the first application of the idea in a modern sense was made by John H. Hall, inventor and engineer at the Harper's Ferry Armory, who by 1817 was installing his system using metal-cutting and woodworking machines.[3] In any case, it took more than two generations to make the essential innovations in the arms industry. Captain Hall's pattern-turning greatly reduced the number of man-hours needed to shape unsymmetrical rifle stocks. Drop-forging with dies was successfully introduced about 1827. By 1855, Samuel Colt, who had long since invented his six-shooter, could establish an armory in which machine work of a high degree of accuracy was accomplished by skilled operators. From approximately mid-century on, the ultimate tool of precision was no longer the hand file.

Continuous-process manufacture—production in which the plant is so arranged that the manufacture is done with facility and as nearly in order as possible—probably had its first successful application in the mills, but milling processes did not require assembly operations. Continuous-process manufacture in its most significant present-day form, with motor-driven moving assembly, was an outgrowth of the successful interchangeable-parts production of firearms, clocks and watches, sewing machines, and agricultural implements. In the 1850s, agricultural-implement companies actually used conveyor belts to assemble the parts of major subassemblies in sequence, thus foreshadowing "mass production" techniques of the early twentieth century.

Machine tools, rather than hand tools, were necessary to the manufacture of interchangeable parts, which had to be produced within strict limits, or "tolerances." Furthermore, ways of measuring the precision with which parts were machined had to be developed, and as the years passed it became imperative to make such tests with dispatch. It should not be inferred that machine tools are important only as an aid in making interchangeable parts. It is the function of machine tools to plane or grind, cut or bore, so that smooth, accurate surfaces may be obtained. Castings, forgings, or rolled pieces nearly always have to have their surfaces finished to a certain size and smoothness if they are to fit as a part of a mechanism. Every kind of highly intricate mechanism must be made with machine tools or with a machine constructed with their help. They are essential to all industrial production that has passed the hand stages.[4]

Borrowing and Adapting Technology

Britain's head start in making machines and the more advanced stage of its iron-working industry gave the British a great advantage in the manufacture of

[3]See Robert S. Woodbury, "The Legend of Eli Whitney and Interchangeable Parts," *Technology and Culture,* **II**:1 (1960), pp. 235–53. In Professor Woodbury's view, interchangeable-parts manufacture involves four elements: (1) precision machine tools, (2) precision guages or other measuring instruments, (3) uniform measurement standards, and (4) techniques of mechanical drawing.

[4]Metal-cutting and metal-shaping machines existed long before anyone invented a generic term for them. The earliest allusion that we have found to tools that are at the same time machines appears in a report of a select committee of the British House of Commons in 1841. The first U.S. Census designation of "machine tools" is found in the Eighth Census (1860) as "machinists' tools." See Ross M. Robertson, "Changing Production of Metalworking Machinery, 1860–1920," *Output, Employment, and Productivity in the United States After 1800,* Studies in Income and Wealth, **XXX** (New York: Columbia University Press, 1966), p. 480.

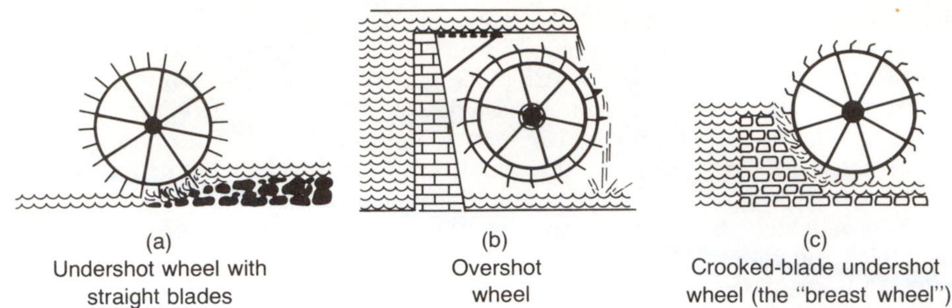

(a)
Undershot wheel with
straight blades

(b)
Overshot
wheel

(c)
Crooked-blade undershot
wheel (the "breast wheel")

FIGURE 13–1

Water Wheels Used to Power Textile and Woodworking Machinery: The three main engineering designs of waterwheels that powered early textile and woodworking machinery are displayed here.

heavy machine tools. The United States either imported machine tools or copied them from English models. Yet for their light manufactures, Americans independently developed light machine tools of such quality that in 1855 a British Parliamentary Committee visited the United States to determine the secret of the success of the "American System."

Until it was possible to work *accurately* in metals, the inventions of the late eighteenth century could not be fully effective. The *vernier caliper*—an inexpensive tool that permitted a worker to measure to thousandths of an inch—came from the shops of Brown and Sharpe in 1851. By 1854, the firm of Robbins and Lawrence was making turret lathes for general sale. Before 1860, William Sellers and Company, and Bement and Dougherty—two Philadelphia firms—were producing heavier, higher-priced machines, most of which were in the metal-forming category. The output of machine tools in 1860 must have exceeded $1 million in value.[5] From this date, growth of the machine-tool industry was rapid, and its products steadily increased in complexity and precision.

Equally important were changes in the techniques of applying power. During the period we are considering, chief reliance was placed on water, and water wheels furnished most of the motive power until the 1840s. Wheels were replaced soon after 1840 by water turbines, which gained favor during the next two decades. Despite a major reliance before 1860 on water as a means of propelling machinery, it had become apparent by that year that the steam engine would shortly become a chief source of power.

A water wheel is always placed in a vertical position on a horizontal shaft and is moved at a comparatively low speed by direct action of the water. Wheels are classified by the way water is applied to turn them (see Figure 13-1). The kind used in colonial times and for a while thereafter in frontier areas was the *undershot* wheel, which was placed in the stream so that its blades were moved by the water passing underneath it. The undershot wheel,

[5] Robertson, *Output, Employment, and Productivity,* p. 489.

although easy to install, was inefficient, transmitting no more than 40 percent of the power applied to it. The *overshot* wheel was moved by water running from a flume across the top of the wheel into buckets covering its surface; the weight of the water in the buckets moved the wheel in the direction of the stream flow. The overshot wheel was more efficient, easy to install, and satisfactory wherever there was a good head of water, but the power it developed was not great enough for heavy industrial purposes. Consequently, the large manufacturing concerns almost invariably used the *breast* wheel. This type, too, was equipped with buckets, but the water struck the wheel short of its highest point so that it rotated in an upstream direction; both the impulse of the water and its weight in the buckets enabled the wheel to utilize up to 75 percent of the power applied to it. Installed in multiples, the breast wheel developed a sufficient horsepower to serve the largest early nineteenth-century industrial firms. The machinery of the Merrimack Manufacturing Company, for example, was run by eight breast wheels, each 30 feet in diameter with buckets 12 feet long.

The slow-moving and cumbersome water wheels could develop several thousand horsepower, but they had marked disadvantages. Power from a wheel was transmitted by wooden shafts and cogwheels and was limited by the strength of the entire mechanism. Furthermore, industrial location was restricted to stream sites, and the problem of finding sites, especially in industrialized areas, became a serious one. The first difficulty was partially overcome by making wheels and transmission parts of metal; the second, by the improved engineering of dams and canals. The water turbine, which revolved on a vertical shaft, was much more efficient than a wheel and by the 1850s was adding rapidly to the power potential of the country.

But what about the steam engine as a source of industrial power? Why did it not win as ready acceptance before 1860 in industry as in transportation? Actually, there are several reasons. In the beginning, the steam engine was extremely costly to operate. Breakdowns were frequent, and expert repair technicians were rare. In transportation, the steam engine could pull such heavy loads at such increased speeds that these disadvantages were more than offset, but in industry water power remained cheaper than steam power for a long time. It has been estimated that in 1812 only 11 engines of the high-pressure type developed by Oliver Evans were in use in this country.[6] During the next two decades, steam engines became more common in the South and West, but most of them were used in ironworks and glass factories that required fuel for other purposes or in mills that could not conveniently be located near water. Around 1840, manufacturers in New England and the Middle Atlantic states estimated the annual cost per horsepower for steam to be five or six times that of water. Within the next 20 years, improvements in metalworking technology lowered the cost of steam engines and improved both their efficiency and reliability. By the 1850s, steam engines were replacing water wheels in the heat-using industries and wherever stream flows were highly variable as they were along the Ohio River. In New England, steam en-

[6] Victor S. Clark, *History of Manufactures in the United States, 1607–1860* (Washington, D.C.: The Carnegie Institution, 1916), p. 409.

gines were being installed to power textile mills due to the serious lack of adequate power sites. As of 1860, water was still the chief source of power, but the years of the water wheel were clearly numbered.

There is one further question regarding the technological changes leading to the rise of factory methods. How were the revolutionary improvements in manufacturing processes, largely brought over from England, applied in this country?

1. The American *textile industry* was almost completely mechanized by 1860. As might be surmised, the most rapid change occurred in the manufacture of cotton goods. By 1815, the Boston Manufacturing Company had installed power looms that performed satisfactorily in its Waltham plant. Between 1815 and 1860, the inventions of the earlier years were improved, chiefly in the areas of increased automaticity and greater speed. The *woolen industry* lagged as it had in England, largely because of the greater technical difficulties experienced in each of the four stages of textile manufacture. (It was a problem, for example, to obtain woolen warps that were strong enough to stand the strain of power looming.) After 1840, the innovations necessary to complete the mechanization of the woolen industry were introduced. Home manufacture of woolens lingered on the frontier, however, as did the carding and fulling mills of earlier times, and fine woolens were still imported from England. But the American industry was adequately equipped by Civil War times for making coarse materials, including flannels and carpets.
2. In discussing the *iron industry* of colonial days, we noted the two major stages of smelting and refining. Pig iron from the small blast furnaces was further refined in forges, usually under the weight of water-driven hammers. The resulting wrought-iron "merchant" bar or plate was then ready to be worked into finished products—by the village blacksmith at one end of the scale and by the manufacturer of steam engines and iron rails at the other. The domestic demand for iron was mostly for agricultural equipment, and this remained true during the first half of the nineteenth century. There was also a demand for cast-iron articles—kettles and pots, great pans and skillets, fireplace hardware, and the like, which were often produced in connection with the original smelting process. But not until the decade of the 1850s did industrial demand assume the proportions that would determine the size and character of the industry.

   Between 1815 and 1850, three British innovations were introduced into the United States. In 1817, the rolling of bars and plates began to replace the ancient method of hammering. Shortly thereafter, ironmasters began to refine pig iron by "puddling" it in a furnace that kept molten metal from contact with the fuel. More metal could then be worked at one time, and coal, which left impurities in the iron when burned with it in refining, could be used instead of charcoal. Probably the most important improvement, however, was the delayed introduction of coal into the smelting stage, a change long since made by the English because of their growing scarcity of timber. In America, where wood was plentiful, charcoal was more expensive than coal, but charcoal-iron was more malleable and more easily welded and thus suited the small operators who served the agricultural market.

Even more important deterrents to the rapid adoption of new British blast-furnace technology were the high sulfur content of known deposits of the bituminous coal required for coking, which led to poor quality pig iron, and the fact that bituminous deposits were located west of the Alleghenies, a costly transportation distance from the country's population centers.[7] Industrial requirements, which first made themselves seriously felt in the 1840s, led to the initial use of anthracite (1839) and then bituminous coal and coke as the reduction fuel.

3. During the first two decades of the existence of the Patent Office, 77 *patents* were issued annually on the average. During the 1850s, the number exceeded 2,500 annually. Even allowing for the eccentric nature of many of the patents, this figure indicates the growing inventiveness of Americans. One invention was the sewing machine, patented first by Elias Howe in 1846. With improvements by Isaac Singer and Allen B. Wilson, quantity output of these machines was possible by the early 1850s, and they became the first household appliance to gain wide acceptance. More importantly, they enabled both the shoe and garment industries to become mechanized and to increase the attractiveness of their products. By the late 1840s, the rubber industry, capitalizing on Charles Goodyear's invention of the vulcanization of rubber in 1839, was turning out its first crude but wondrous products—overshoes, buskins, and sandals. In food-processing, Americans, importing French and English ideas, "put up" items ranging from vegetables to seafood. Glass jars were used at first, and handmade tin cans made their appearance about 1820. Modern canning factories were not established until well after the Civil War, but the principles of sterilization and handling were generally known by 1860. Gail Borden's method of canning evaporated milk, for which a patent was sought in 1853, was another step toward emancipating housewives from a dependence on fresh food.

Developments like these were inextricably linked with the emergence of the factory, as we will see in the following section.

The Emergence of Factories

The word *factory* has been used customarily to designate manufacturing units with the following characteristics:

1. A substantial output of a standardized product made to be sold in a wide, rather than a strictly local, market.
2. Complex operations carried on in one building or a group of adjacent buildings. Implied is a considerable investment in fixed plant, the mechanization of processes, and the use of power.
3. An assembly of workers under a definite organizational discipline. All the factors in the combination except the workers—plant, machinery, tools, and

[7] Nathan Rosenberg, *Technology and American Economic Growth* (New York: Harper & Row, 1972), pp. 79–80.

Calico printing (above) and power-loom weaving (below) in the 1850s, as demonstrated in these prints from the Memoirs of Samuel Slater, *illustrate the complexity of mechanized factories and the substantial economies of scale related to them.*

land—are owned by the "capitalist," who has, for this reason, always assumed the role of boss.[8] The factory system is unique in the kind of personal relationships it establishes between employer and employee.

Even if we agree that these are the essential characteristics of factory organization, we may have some difficulty in concluding whether a particular firm of the pre-Civil War period fell in the category of "mill industry" or "factory." Perhaps the distinction is not important, as long as we are aware that an evolution did take place. Certainly it did not occur evenly in any one industry or at approximately the same time in different industries. Let us examine an example or two.

The factory developed first in the cotton-textile industry. Due to the unusual nature of its founding, we think of the mill of Almy, Brown, and Slater, in operation by 1793, as the first American factory. Moses Brown and William Almy were men of wealth in the New England mercantile tradition. Like many other American enterprisers, they had tried and failed to duplicate English spinning machinery. In 1790, there came to Rhode Island a young mechanical wizard, Samuel Slater, who had worked for years in the firm of Arkwright and Strutt in Milford, England. Having memorized the minutest details of the water frames, Slater emigrated to the United States, where he hoped to obtain a fortune for his information. Getting in touch with Almy and Brown, Slater agreed to reproduce the equipment for a mechanized spinning mill. Although small, the enterprise served as a training ground for operatives and as a pilot operation for managers.

Located on the Blackstone River in Pawtucket, Rhode Island, the Almy, Brown, and Slater mill was producing yarn by late 1790. By 1793, carding, roving, and spinning operations were all mechanized, and workers were assembled in a single "factory house" under central supervision. Almy and Brown began pushing their markets northward from Providence into Connecticut, Massachusetts, and Maine, and by 1801 they were shipping yarn into New York City, Philadelphia, Baltimore, and even farther south to meet a burgeoning demand.

A number of small mills like the Slater mill were started, but most of them failed by the turn of the century because their promoters did not aim for a wide market. Not until the Embargo Act of 1807 and the consequent scarcity of English textiles stimulated demand for domestic manufactures did spinning mills become numerous. Between 1805 and 1815, 94 new cotton mills were built in New England, and the mounting competition led Almy and Brown to push their markets south and west. By 1814, 70 percent of all consignments were to the Middle West via Philadelphia. Only two decades after Arkwright machinery was introduced into this country, the market for yarn was becoming national and the spinning process was becoming a true factory operation as it was in England.

[8] The term *capitalist,* of course, can mean anything from the individual entrepreneurs of the nineteenth century to shareholders and executives of today's vast corporate entities.

But two events forestalled these changes. One was the successful introduction of the power loom into American manufacture; the other was the organization of production so that *all four* stages of the manufacture of cotton cloth could occur within one establishment. After closely observing the workings of textile machinery in Great Britain, Francis Cabot Lowell, a New England merchant, gained sufficient knowledge of the secrets of mechanized weaving to enable him, with the help of a gifted technician, to construct a power loom superior to any that had been built to date. It was as an enterpriser, however, that Francis Lowell made a more significant contribution: He persuaded other men of means to participate with him in establishing a firm at Waltham that had all the essential characteristics of factory production. This was the famed Boston Manufacturing Company, the forerunner of several similar firms in which the so-called Boston Associates were interested. Specializing in coarse sheetings, the Waltham factory sold its product all over America. Consolidating all four steps of textile manufacture in a single plant lowered production costs. A large number of specialized workers were organized into departments and directed by executives who were not necessarily technical supervisors. The factory, by using power-driven machinery, produced standardized commodities in quantity.

At Lowell, where the Merrimack Manufacturing Company followed the Waltham pattern, and at Manchester and Lawrence, the factory system gained a permanent foothold. In the other great center of New England textile manufacture—the Providence–Pawtucket region—there was a similar trend, although the factories there were fewer and smaller. The third great district, located about Paterson and Philadelphia, contained mainly small mills that performed a single major process and turned out finer weaves. But by 1860, New England's industry had nearly four times as many spindles as the Middle Atlantic industry and accounted for nearly three-fourths of the country's output of cotton goods. The factory had demonstrated its superiority in the textile field.

It was simply a matter of time until other industries adopted the same organization. For reasons already mentioned, the production of woolen cloth tended to remain in the small mill longer than cotton production did. But after 1830, woolen factories began to adopt the characteristics of the Waltham system, and by 1860 the largest textile factories in the United States were woolen factories.[9] Again, New Englanders far surpassed the rest of the country in combining factors of production in large units; two-thirds of America's woolen output in 1860 was made in New England.

In most other industries, the decade of the 1830s was one of expansion and experimentation with new methods. In the primary iron industry, establishments by the 1840s dwarfed those a quarter-century earlier, and even in the pre-steel era, some of them had passed beyond what we have called the mill stage. By 1845, the Brady's Bend Iron Company in western Pennsylvania owned

> nearly 6,000 acres of mineral land and 5 miles of river front upon the Allegheny. It mined its own coal, ore, limestone, fire-clay, and fire-stone, made its own coke, and owned 14 miles of railway to serve its works. The plant itself

[9] Clark, *History of Manufactures,* p. 453.

> consisted of 4 blast furnaces, a foundry, and rolling mills. It was equipped to perform all the processes, from getting raw materials out of the ground to delivering finished rails and metal shapes to consumers, and could produce annually between 10,000 and 15,000 tons of rails. It housed in its own tenements 538 laboring families. This company, with an actual investment of $1,000,000, was among the largest in America before the Civil War, though there were rival works of approximately equal capacity and similar organization.[10]

In the anthracite region to the east, factory operation of furnaces and rolling mills had been achieved by 1850.

By the 1850s, factories were manufacturing arms, clocks and watches, and sewing machines. How one industry could adopt new methods as a consequence of progress in another industry is shown by the fact that, as the sewing machine was produced on a quantity basis, the boot and shoe industry developed factory characteristics. Carriages, wagons, and even farm implements were eventually produced in large numbers. Finally, where markets were more extensive, where there was a substantial investment in fixed plant, and where workers were subjected to formal discipline, some firms in the traditional mill industries other than the textile and iron industries achieved factory status. The great merchant flour mills of Baltimore and Rochester fell into this category, as did some of the large packing plants in New York, Philadelphia, Baltimore, and, after 1840, Cincinnati.

THE STATUS OF MANUFACTURE IN 1860

What were the leading industries of the country in 1860 and how did they rank? To answer this question we must accept the figures of the *Eighth Census of the United States: Manufactures,* shown in Table 13-1 on page 204, remembering that both the techniques of census taking and the concepts of the census takers were far from refined.

First, Table 13-1 shows the leading industries ranked by *value added by manufacture.* (There is a close correspondence between this ranking and the one by *value of total product,* but note that flour and meal were ranked fourth in value added although they accounted for the greatest value of total product. However, we are interested primarily in showing the importance of actual value and production as measured in money terms.) Cotton manufacture, with New England leading the way, ranked first, having grown from infancy in 50 years. Lumbering was a close second; moving from its old seat in the New England and Middle Atlantic states to the West and the South, it was the most important processing activity in these new areas. Of the first ten industries, the milling of flour and meal was the only other one in the West and South with a significant output. Iron manufactures were underrated due to the narrow definitions of the census; if all iron products and machinery had been combined in a single category, they would have formed the most important group of manufactures. Between 1850 and 1860, the doubling of the output of pri-

[10]*Ibid.,* p. 446.

TABLE 13–1
United States Manufactures, 1860

Item	(1) Number of employees	(2) Cost of raw material	(3) Value of total product	(4) (3)–(2) Value added by manufacture	Rank by value added
Cotton goods	114,955	$ 52,666,701	$107,337,783	$54,671,082	1
Lumber	75,595	51,358,400	104,928,342	53,569,942	2
Boots and shoes	123,026	42,728,174	91,889,298	49,161,124	3
Flour and meal	27,682	208,497,309	248,580,365	40,083,056	4
Men's clothing	114,800	44,149,752	80,830,555	36,680,803	5
Iron (cast, forged, rolled, and wrought)	48,975	37,486,056	73,175,332	35,689,276	6
Machinery	41,223	19,444,533	52,010,376	32,565,843	7
Woolen goods	40,597	35,652,701	60,685,190	25,032,489	8
Carriages, wagons, and carts	37,102	11,898,282	35,552,842	23,654,560	9
Leather	22,679	44,520,737	67,306,452	22,785,715	10

Source: *Eighth Census of the United States: Manufactures,* 1860.

mary iron products and machinery forecast the shape of America's industrial future.

The sectional figures in Table 13-2 testify to the primacy of the East in early manufacturing. Because the census counted the smallest sawmills and gristmills as "manufacturing establishments," the West and the South showed a large number of these establishments. By any other criterion, New England and the Middle Atlantic states were the leading sections; their importance as employers of labor and producers of high value-added products was unmistakable. The figures for the Midwest reflect in part the rapid antebellum industrial growth of the Ohio Valley and the burgeoning of the Chicago area.

During the period 1810–1860, total value of manufactures increased from about $200 million to just under $2 billion, or roughly tenfold. Capital invested increased from perhaps $50 million to $1 billion, or twentyfold—a substantial increase in the capital–output ratio over the 50-year period. These figures are expressed in current (1860) dollars, which are less reliable than the dollars available after 1870, but it is obvious that manufacturing had made tremendous gains in the decade and a half before the Civil War. Farming was still in first place as a means of earning a livelihood, because the value added by manufacture in 1860 was markedly less than the value of America's three major crops—corn, wheat, and hay—and total capital investment in industry was equal to less than one-sixth the value of farm land and buildings. But the United States was even then second only to Great Britain in manufacturing and would soon be the industrial leader of the world.[11]

[11] The *Twelfth Census of the United States,* quoting Mulhall's *Industries and Wealth of Nations,* placed the United States in fourth place after Great Britain, France, and Germany. But see Douglass C. North, *The Economic Growth of the United States, 1790 to 1860* (Englewood Cliffs, N.J.: Prentice-Hall, 1961), p. v.

TABLE 13–2
Manufacturing, by Sections, Census of 1860

Section	Number of establishments	Capital invested	Employment: Male	Employment: Female	Annual value of products	Value added by manufacture
New England	20,671	$257,477,783	262,834	129,002	$468,599,287	$223,076,180
Middle Atlantic	53,287	435,061,964	432,424	113,819	802,338,392	358,211,423
Midwest	36,785	194,212,543	194,081	15,828	384,606,530	158,987,717
Southern	20,631	95,975,185	98,583	12,138	155,531,281	68,988,129
Pacific	8,777	23,380,334	50,137	67	71,229,989	42,746,363
Territories	282	3,747,906	2,290	43	3,556,197	2,246,772
Totals	140,433	$1,009,855,715	1,040,349	270,897	$1,885,861,676	$854,256,584

Source: *Eighth Census of the United States: Manufactures,* 1860.

THE QUESTION OF PROTECTION

It will be recalled that after the peace of 1814, imports of English manufactured goods reached alarming proportions from the viewpoint of American businesses. Before 1814, duties on foreign goods had been set at rates that, although originally intended to protect, maximized governmental revenues in a hit-or-miss fashion. Growing protectionist sentiment in the Northeast gained enough support from the West and South to secure passage of the Tariff Act of 1816, which established the philosophy that was to guide framers of the tariff acts of 1824, 1828, 1832–1833, 1842, 1846, and 1857.

Ironically, John C. Calhoun was a leading advocate of the passage of the tariff of 1816, which levied ad valorem duties of 20–25 percent on most manufactured goods and 15–20 percent on raw materials. In general, the level of duties on manufactures did not prevent the entry of many goods at that time, although cheap cottons were shut out of the home market by specific duties (that is, duties of so much per yard). Moreover, the tax on raw materials, particularly raw wool, lowered the expansion potential of some domestic industries.

From 1816 until 1832, the protectionist tide rose; cottons, woolens, glass, and iron products received the greatest favors, with raw wool and hemp garnering their share. However, the tariff enthusiasm of southerners began to abate shortly. They saw that the American market for southern staples, especially cotton, would not soon replace the European market damaged by a high U.S. tariff; industrialization simply could not take place fast enough. Meanwhile, the terms of trade would weigh heavily against the South, who would have to buy dear and sell cheap. Offsetting the defection of the South, however, was the growing tendency of the New England merchant class to align itself with the manufacturers in favor of taxes on imports.

The political shenanigans leading to the high tariff of 1828—the Tariff of Abominations—precipitated agitation in the South and necessitated a compromise within only a few years. In fact, a severe threat to the Union was South Carolina's Nullification Ordinance, which was legislated even after downward revisions in import duties had been made in 1832. The Compromise Tariff of 1833 provided that all duties would be reduced to a maximum of 20 percent ad valorem within a decade. But only two months after the 20-percent maximum level was reached in 1842, the Whigs passed a bill in which rates reverted to about the protective level of ten years before, and President Tyler, a Southerner, accepted it because he felt this action would provide more revenue for the government. With the return of the Democrats to power, more moderate tariffs were rapidly secured, and the Walker Tariff of 1846 set an example that was followed until 1861. The principle of protection of domestic industry was maintained, but the classification of commodities, the removal of specific prohibitive duties, and the introduction of a system of warehousing of imports until duties were paid all indicated a more liberal attitude toward tariffs by the United States.[12] The good times of the 1850s and the consequent increase in imports so swelled the revenues from tariffs that the government achieved great surpluses. The piling up of cash in U.S. Treasury vaults led to a general reduction in rates and many items were placed on the free list. Just before the Civil War, it appeared that the United States might join the United Kingdom as a free-trade country. In 1860, tariffs averaged less than 20 percent of the value of dutiable imports and 15 percent of the value of all imports—levels that had only moderate protective significance.

It is hard to estimate the effects of tariff legislation on the economy of a country, for strands of causality are not easily separated. Yet most writers on the period agree on certain points. First, during the years 1816–1832, when the protectionist sentiment was waxing, duties on cheap cottons and woolens reserved the American market for the Americans. But finer textiles continued to be imported from England, and after 1825, instead of selling coarse textiles to American consumers, England sold textile machinery to U.S. manufacturers. After 1833, the reduction of import duties lightened the burden on importers and, in turn, on the American consumer. In the depressed early 1840s, as in the 1820s, tariffs probably kept industrial output and employment from declining as much as they would have in a free market. On the other hand, the high tax on imported raw wool, together with the inferiority of the American product, accounts in large part for the failure of American woolen manufacturing to develop before 1860. In sum, however, American manufactures were stimulated and the dollar value of foreign commerce was reduced by tariffs. Second, the South suffered insofar as tariffs cut American imports and therefore the amount of American exports that foreigners, particularly the English, could buy. Southerners were probably also bothered by the higher prices of imported implements, hardware, housewares, and cheap clothing for slaves. But when all was said and done, southern planters were prosperous during the period de-

[12] By classifying dutiable articles into a number of schedules, Secretary of the Treasury Walker wished to discriminate among imports according to luxuries, semiluxuries, necessities, and so on. Brandy, for example, was placed in a schedule carrying a 100-percent duty, whereas most raw materials were in a schedule carrying a 5-percent duty. Schedule C, the main category, levied an ad valorem tax of 30 percent on iron and other metals, metal manufactures, wool and woolens, and manufactures of leather, paper, glass, and wood. Cotton manufactures, in Schedule D, were taxed at 25 percent. The warehousing provision enabled importers to keep goods in a government warehouse up to one year without having to pay duties until goods were withdrawn for sale.

spite protective tariffs. What people ***think*** is bad, though, may frequently lead to trouble, and the question of the tariff was one of the minor causes of eventual civil strife.

One fact is clear: Receipts from customs constituted the major source of income for the federal government before the Civil War. But to the question "Did tariffs alter the course of early industrial and commercial development?" our reply must be "Not much," because there is little evidence that tariffs seriously changed the direction of investment. Some industries, like the iron industry, refused to grow up and remained inefficient infants for a long time, protected as much by high transportation costs into the interior as by duties on English iron. But the *rate* of growth of the manufacturing industry was probably stimulated by tariffs, and in that sense the economic progress of the country was thereby hastened.[13] However, tariffs did alter the distribution of income in favor of owners of industrial property and to the disfavor of consumers. We leave it to the student to judge whether or not that constituted economic progress.

THE RISE OF CORPORATE ORGANIZATION

We must finally consider the change that was taking place in the legal concept of the business firm—the change from sole proprietorship and partnership organization to corporate organization. The corporation gained prominence chiefly because some businesses required more capital than one person or a few people could provide. By 1810, the corporate form was commonplace for banks, insurance companies, and turnpike companies, but in ensuing decades, canals and railroads could be financed only by tapping various sources of funds from small merchants and professionals along proposed routes to English capitalists thousands of miles away.

The corporation, a legal entity with privileges and responsibilities distinct from those of the people associated with it, evolved over centuries. In England, corporations followed two major lines of development. Municipalities and universities were established under corporate charters granted by the sovereign, and the great trading companies, formed for the purpose of exploiting foreign lands, were organized as "joint-stock associations" that borrowed many of the features of the corporation.

So the development of the corporation was in reality the transformation of an instrument of communal service to accommodate the demands of a new industrial age. It is a convention of economic historiography to begin the corporate cycle with Chief Justice Marshall's *Dartmouth College* opinion, reading into it the legal foundation of modern capitalism. It is true that Marshall implied as much when he made Dartmouth's royal charter a contract between the college and New Hampshire and, as such, placed it beyond the constitutional

[13] For a careful presentation of the complexities of tariff analysis, see Paul A. David, "Learning by Doing and Tariff Protection: A Reconsideration of the Case of the Antebellum United States Cotton Textile Industry," *Journal of Economic History,* **XXX**:3 (September 1970), pp. 521–601. David tentatively concludes that after the Tariff of 1824, tariffs implied blanket subsidies for cotton textile manufacturers and offered them a means of redistributing income in their favor.

power of that state to repeal or amend. Nevertheless, this was only an implication; Marshall's explicit references concerned only municipal bodies and private charities. It is in Justice Joseph Story's concurring opinion that we find the principle extended to business enterprises. Contemporary opinion, both pro and con, recognized Story's analysis as novel and significant.

This creative revisionism, as a few historians have noted, produced a radical change in traditional analysis. The mere fact that a public authority had granted a charter meant that the corporation had, in some sense, a "public" purpose; taken at face value, this characteristic suggested the ability of the chartering authority to regulate, revise, or even revoke the privilege it had granted. But Story discarded purpose and substituted property as a starting point, achieving a two-fold division in result: on one hand, private corporations holding private property and, on the other, public corporations charged with government or administration. The state could regulate the latter group without restraint; the state could approach the former group only with the deference due vested right and private interest.

An equally significant development was Story's grafting of the ancient law of trusts onto the emerging form of business enterprise. Here the consequence was a separation of ownership and control. Under this division, the capital of a corporation became a trust fund for the successive benefit of creditors and stockholders, the directors became trustees, and the corporation itself increasingly assumed a character and personality distinct from the persons who had provided its resources. The end result was an ideal apparatus of capital formation that involved both permanent contributions of resources and transferable, judicially protected claims.

When it first appeared in the United States, the corporation lacked many of its present-day characteristics. Charters were granted by special acts of legislatures, and the question of the liability of stockholders was far from settled. Nevertheless, the corporation had a number of advantages over the sole proprietorship and the partnership, and its legal status came to be better defined than that of the joint-stock company. Of its unquestioned advantages, the most notable—in addition to the obvious one of attracting greater numbers of investors—were permanence and flexibility. The partnership and the sole proprietorship have one inescapable drawback: If one partner or the proprietor dies, the business is dissolved. The business can go on, of course, under a new partnership or proprietorship, but continuity of operation is contingent on the lives of particular individuals. Furthermore, a partnership is dissolved when one partner's interest is sold. But the shares of a corporation can be transferred, and investors, whether small or large, can enter and leave the business without destroying the structure of the corporation.

Early corporations did not have certain advantages that corporations have today. Take the question of liability, for example. What the liability of the shareholders for the debts of the corporation should be was difficult to determine. Stockholders of the English joint-stock companies had finally come to assume "double liability"—that is, the stockholders were liable to the extent of their investment plus a like amount—and some states experimented with charters specifying either double liability or unlimited liability. After 1830, however, statutes were passed in various states providing for limited liability, and by

1860 this principle was generally accepted. Under limited liability, stockholders could lose, on the failure of a corporation, only the money they had invested in the venture.

The early requirement that incorporators of banks, insurance companies, canals, and railroads obtain their charters by the special act of a state legislature was not always a disadvantage. For those who had political connections, this involved little uncertainty and expense, and there was always the possibility of obtaining a charter with exceptionally liberal provisions. Nevertheless, the politically unfavored could spend years lobbying futilely for corporate charters. As early as 1800, those who looked on incorporation by special act as "undemocratic" were agitating to secure "general" acts of incorporation—laws making it possible for any group, provided it observed and met prescribed regulations and requirements, to obtain a charter. Others, fearful that the corporation would spread too rapidly if their elected representatives did not pass on *each* application for charter, opposed general acts. In 1837, Connecticut passed the first general act that made incorporation the right of anyone.[14] From that date, *permissive* general acts (acts allowing, but not requiring, incorporation under their provisions) were gradually placed on the statute books of most of the chief manufacturing states, and before 1861 the constitutions of thirteen states *required* incorporation under general laws. In those states where permissive legislation had been enacted, incorporators continued until about 1870 to obtain special charters, because they enabled the incorporators to secure more liberal provisions than they could under general laws.

After 1837, mercantile and manufacturing firms were organized as corporations with growing frequency. There was, especially during the 1850s, a rapid increase in the number of manufacturing corporations. *Yet in 1860, the greater portion of resources devoted to manufacturing was under the control of proprietorships and partnerships.* At that time, a rolling mill of the most modern design could be built for $150,000, and the largest textile factory did not require an investment beyond the means of a single very wealthy person. The course of commerce and industry would not have been very different before 1860 if the privilege of incorporation had been given only to financial and transportation firms. Nonetheless, contemporary observers were aware that the corporate form would be inseparable from the enterprise of the future; bigness obviously lay ahead. For technical reasons alone, the size of the firm had to become larger, and, as the railroad companies had already demonstrated, enterprisers had to choose the corporate type of business organization when huge capital outlays were required.

[14] In 1811, New York had passed a law that permitted incorporation, without special act, of certain manufacturing concerns with capitalizations of under $100,000.

14

Labor's First Stirrings and Economic Change

Although before 1860 the greater part of the U.S. population was rural and self-employed on farms and in craftshops, the rapid industrialization, urbanization, and technological and organizational changes of the preceding decades foreshadowed a massive transformation in the way people earned their livings. The change to working for an employer had serious consequences, and the depersonalization of relations between employer and employee created tensions that would one day lead to serious disruption. But before the Civil War, most workers were disposed to know and keep their places, even while the more venturesome stirred the beginnings of the "labor movement." To relate to these developments, we must study the early American workers at work.

But before we do that, it is necessary to briefly reassess the economic background in which labor's first stirrings began in the United States.

ECONOMIC BACKGROUND: CYCLES AND TRENDS

Of course, periods of prosperity or hardship for the worker were effected both by short-term fluctuations and by the secular trend of economic progress. Sometimes reinforcing the secular trends and sometimes running counter to them were cyclical fluctuations ranging in duration from several months to several years. It should be recalled from Chapter 10 that in the period from the end of the Revolution to the end of the War of 1812, oscillations were frequent and wide, reflecting the changing fortunes of the European belligerents and the vagaries of international politics. The 1816–1847 period contained two crises of great severity; the panics of 1818 and 1837. Each crisis was followed by years of deflation and distress.[1] Yet the boom of 1834–1837, with its rapidly rising incomes, full employment, inflation, and speculation (in land rather than in securities), foreshadowed the recurrent upward surges of activity that characterized the growth of the economy. In 1843, a long period of prosperity began, marred by a brief crisis in 1854 and a short, nasty depression from 1857 to 1858. These years just preceding the Civil War nevertheless provided evidence of the kind of sustained forward movement of which the economy was capable.

Contrary to the beliefs in many quarters and as popularized by the writings of W. W. Rostow, the American economy did not experience one single acceleration or "take off" in the first half of the nineteenth century. Rostow argued that the "take-off" of the American economy began in 1843 and ended in 1860, when the "sustained drive to maturity" began.[2] But Rostow based his propositions about the stages of economic growth largely on statistical evidence compiled from twentieth-century rather than nineteenth-century experience. So many economic historians protested vigorously against labeling the years following 1843 the period of the U.S. "take-off" that serious doubts were cast on the validity of the concept.[3]

The hypothesis that the rate of growth did not jump suddenly in the 1840s but instead displayed other accelerations between 1790 and 1860 certainly required verification or refutation. Thanks to the path-breaking study of Paul A. David, tentative verification of the hypothesis has been made.[4]

After reviewing the adverse comments on earlier studies in capsule summaries, David could find no consensus on the rate at which per-capita product had actually increased during the half-century after 1790. The earlier estimates, he remarked, "have been banished from sight, but since no specific figures have replaced them, an afterimage of a more or less stagnant level of per-capita product before 1840 lingers on. This impression and the explanations advanced in its favor are, I suggest, barely more substantial than the Cheshire cat's smile."[5]

David offers substantial and persuasive evidence to show that real gross domestic product (GDP) "neither declined nor remained stagnant" over the 1800–1840 period but increased during these years at an average annual rate of close to 1.3 percent for the period 1800–1835 and the period 1835–1855, as well as for the entire interval between 1790 and 1860. By 1840, per-capita

[1] After the contraction of 1837–1838, there was a substantial recovery that peaked in 1839 and then disappointingly vanished.

[2] W. W. Rostow, *The Stages of Economic Growth* (Cambridge: Cambridge University Press, 1961), esp. pp. 7–10, 36–58.

[3] The journal literature both supporting and attacking Rostow's ideas on the stages of economic growth is too voluminous for detailed quotation. For a sense of its content, see Henry Rosovsky, "The Take-Off into Sustained Controversy," *Journal of Economic History,* **XXV:**2 (June 1965), pp. 271–75.

[4] Paul A. David, "New Light on a Statistical Dark Age: U.S. Real Product Growth Before 1840," *American Economic Review,* **LVII:**2 (May 1967), pp. 294–306, and "The Growth of Real Product in the United States Before 1840: New Evidence, Controlled Conjectures," *Journal of Economic History,* **XXVII:**2 (June 1967), pp. 151–97.

[5] David, "The Growth of Real Product," p. 154.

real GDP was probably 60 percent greater than it had been at the turn of the century. To be sure, growth in per-capita income did not proceed steadily during these years. As Douglass North has maintained, per-capita incomes increased substantially from 1793 to the embargo of 1807, fell somewhat, and then at least regained their 1800 levels by the depression of 1818–1819. From 1820 to the middle 1830s, per-capita real GDP may have grown at an average rate of 2.5 percent, only to fall to an average rate of 0.6 percent per annum from the middle 1830s to the middle 1840s. Thus, the acceleration of per-capita income that began about 1843 "was part of a broader pattern of recurring variations of the per-capita product growth rate and had been anticipated by a similar, possibly more pronounced surge of growth which came to an end in the mid-1830s. . . . When this approach is adopted, very serious doubts arise regarding the occurrence of any 'sharp break in the trend,' let alone an 1843–1860 'take-off,' or the putative upward shift 'not very long before 1839.' "[6]

In any case, the overall progress of labor during this period was largely the result of the many diverse forces that propelled economic growth and raised the standard of living and the conditions of work and employment.

THE EMERGENCE OF A LABORING CLASS

As we have seen, the wages of American workers during the colonial period were remarkably higher than those of contemporary English workers. When American industry started to develop at the turn of the nineteenth century, the money wages of unskilled adult laborers were still much higher than they were in England, perhaps by as much as one-third to one-half.[7] The differential was attributable to the fact that a floor under the remuneration of labor in industry was set by rewards in agriculture. Well into the 1800s, there were no insuperable obstacles, either of distance or expense, to obtaining a fertile farm. Output per worker in agriculture was relatively high, and the course of agricultural technology in the early nineteenth century tended to increase output per person rather than output per acre, as was the case in England. Moreover, farmers in America, who ordinarily owned their own land, received, in addition to their own wages and those of their families, elements of rent and profit that in England went to the landlord and the tenant farmer, as distinguished from the agricultural laborer. Finally, American farmers always stood to gain from appreciation in land values as the country's population moved westward.

However hard the lot of antebellum laborers by today's standards, workers in the United States continued to be well off compared to workers in England. Sharp increases in immigration during the 1830s and 1840s, along with the

[6] David, "The Growth of Real Product," p. 156. For another recent treatment of the problem of growth in post-colonial years, see Lance E. Davis, Richard E. Easterlin, and William N. Parker, et al., *American Economic Growth* (New York: Harper & Row, 1972), esp. pp. 19–35. Over the period 1710–1840, the authors conclude, "performance of the American economy, as measured by per-capita product, was probably increasing at a rising rate."

[7] See H. J. Habakkuk, *American and British Technology in the Nineteenth Century* (Cambridge: Cambridge University Press, 1962), p. 11. The following passage draws heavily from Professor Habakkuk's useful book.

drift of settlement opportunities ever farther from the urban East, led to a narrowing of the wage differential between British and American labor; even so, the floor for industrial wages was, by consensus of voluminous testimony, relatively high up to 1860. During the first decades of the nineteenth century, as in the colonial period, the premiums paid for artisan skills in America were apparently less than those paid in England, but the differential declined as the century progressed.[8]

The craftsman—that is, the artisan or "mechanic"—was not seriously affected by machine techniques until at least the middle of the nineteenth century. In a few trades, like shoemaking, the position of craftsmen was weakened as both demand and mechanization increased, and they found themselves making standardized products for general sale. First in craft shops and then in factories, output was for sale in ever larger markets, and pressures were great to achieve volume at the expense of artistry. In this way, skilled workers in a few industries might be replaced and the status of some craftsmen might be reduced.[9] On the whole, however, the services of skilled workers were scarce in antebellum America, and only during severe business slumps was the artisan in danger of unemployment.

The Factory and the Wage Earner

In the industries affected, the change from craft-shop artisan to factory worker was made gradually. Specialized operatives were needed to do some of the work of the factory, and workers as highly skilled as artisans were required to repair machines and to devise and construct machine tools. But much factory work consisted of machine-tending, making simple adjustments, carrying materials, starting materials in the machines, and taking finished goods out of the machines. This work required no great physical strength, no specialization, and only simple skills. Yet it was difficult for employers to hire even unskilled male laborers. There had been no enclosure movement in the United States comparable to that in Great Britain, and such a movement as did occur in New England threw few agrarians off the land to shift for themselves. Unlike English entrepreneurs, Americans had to *attract* a labor supply from farms and shops—a hard task, because mills and factories often stood beside streams and were removed from centers of population.

Mill and factory owners in the textile industry solved employment problems in two ways. Under one system, called the Rhode Island system, they hired whole families, assigned father, mother, and children to tasks suitable to their strength and maturity, and housed the families in company-constructed tenements. South of Boston, the Rhode Island system was used almost exclu-

[8]By "premiums," we mean the extra compensation above wages to unskilled labor; hence, skilled workers in the United States earned more than their counterparts in England, but their ratio of wages was less than the ratio of the wages of unskilled Americans to the wages of unskilled English workers. The relatively low premium paid for skilled labor in early nineteenth-century America resulted particularly from such causes as the greater pulling power of agricultural expansion on unskilled labor and the higher proportion of skilled British migrants entering the United States before mass migration began. For other reasons, see Habakkuk, pp. 23–24.

[9]John R. Commons, "American Shoemakers," *Quarterly Journal of Economics,* **XXIV** (November 1909), pp. 39–81.

sively, partly because child labor was first introduced there in imitation of English methods, and partly because the mule-spinning typical of the area required both heavy and light work. Francis Cabot Lowell and the Boston Associates introduced the Waltham system, under which women in their late teens and early twenties were brought together to form the nucleus of a labor force for large factories. Housed in dormitories—or boarding houses—they remained under the careful supervision of matrons who kept any taint of disreputability from the girls.

What about the conditions under which these early factory people worked? Hours of work were unbelievably long. A 12-hour day was not considered at all unreasonable, and half an hour off for meals was standard. From sunrise to sunset, it was possible to operate machinery without artificial light, and in wintertime candles furnished enough illumination to permit operation on into the evening. Because of the slow speeds of the early machines, the work pace was not great; for this reason women and children could work a 72-hour week without physical breakdown. By mid-twentieth-century standards, wages were pitifully low, but a family under the Rhode Island system earned enough to keep alive and enjoy a few creature comforts.

Young women under the Waltham system were better off; they spent half their weekly wage of $2.50 to $3.00 on room and board and were able to save money. Both families and single people worked under a paternalistic regime in which the concern of the employers was largely for the morals and behavior of the workers. As long as the level of living kept workers reasonably efficient, it was considered proper, and in the interests of strengthening character, to keep luxuries and leisure time to a minimum.

The life of a New England textile worker was tiresome and drab, although it was no worse than the life of a poor New England farmer, whose dawn to dusk regimen left little time for pleasure or intellectual growth in the household. Young women might find escape from the boredom and isolation of farm life by going to work in a factory; or they might join their mothers in hand-weaving or making straw hats, palm-leaf hats, or shoes. The domestic system provided part-time or even full-time work for both villagers and farmers of the Northeast right up to the end of the 1850s. Pay was low, sometimes only $.25 a day or less, but the work was leisurely, and the income kept many families from penury. Also, work was done at home, so the sociological strains of taking the young out of the home were avoided.

New England factory workers generally escaped the harshness to which their English counterparts were subjected during the first decades of the factory system. Undoubtedly, this was largely because American manufacturers were compelled to maintain a certain standard of decency to attract and hold the labor they required. Nor does evidence show that American factory owners were cruel to children, as some English employers were.

The first signs of the ugly urban society that was to come appeared after the early 1840s. City workers, who led impoverished lives, bore the brunt of early industrialization. Under the domestic system, city employees fared less well than country people; unable to eke out an existence by farming or fishing in the cities, they were subject to the artful exploitation of merchant

The factory labor force—as these drawings suggest—was in significant part comprised of women and children. Judging from the expressions on their faces, the prospect of such work was no reason to rejoice.

employers.[10] "Sweated" workers slaved 14–16 hours a day in the garment industries of New York, Philadelphia, and Boston, and common laborers sold their services for a pittance to transportation companies and urban building contractors. Factory and mill workers found themselves in an unenviable position as competition from immigrant labor retarded the growth in real wages.[11] Whatever the long-run benefits of immigration, its immediate effect was to dilute the gains American workers had obtained from rapidly increasing industrial productivity.

Population Changes and Immigration, 1790–1860

Between 1790 and 1820, the population of the United States increased from nearly 4 million to 10 million people. Almost the entire increase resulted from the remarkable birth rate of Americans (and their low death rate); not more than 250,000 new settlers came from abroad during these 30 years, and half of these arrived after the War of 1812. During the decade of the 1820s, the influx of foreigners was less than 150,000. As Figure 14-1 shows, immigration grew substantially in the 1830s and early 1840s, leading to the great movement that began about 1845.

Nationals of three countries constituted the overwhelming majority of newcomers. A steady stream of immigrants from England flowed into the United States until a decade after the Civil War. After 1830, the Irish and the Germans came in ever-increasing numbers, repelled by conditions at home and attracted by economic opportunities in a new land. The tragic potato famine of 1845–1847 precipitated the heavy Irish emigration that lasted well into the 1850s. Fleeing starvation and the oppression of hated absentee landlords, the Irish found employment as common laborers and factory hands. The census of 1850 reported nearly 1 million Irish in the United States, 40 percent of them in large cities, where their "shanty towns" became the notorious slums of the era. The Germans came only a little later, following the failure of the democratic and nationalistic revolutions of 1848. Within fifteen years, 1.3 million had arrived. Most Germans, having a little capital, settled on farms in the Midwest, but almost one-third of them swelled the populations of booming cities like Cin-

[10] The word *exploitation* is one commonly used in socialist writing, and there is some point in making its technical, economic meaning clear here. Workers are said to be "exploited" when they do not receive, in any time period, an amount equal to the "value of their marginal product"; that is, a worker is exploited when he or she does not receive wages equal to what he or she, in combination with the other agents of production, contributes to the value of the output. This contribution can be determined by holding all the conditions of employment constant, removing the worker from the combination, and observing how much output (and consequently, its value) declines. To Marxians, of course, the word is more sinister, meaning the failure of labor to receive the combined product of *all* the factors.

[11] Necessarily rough estimates indicate that real hourly earnings grew at an average rate of less than 0.5 percent per annum in the two decades before the Civil War. See W. S. Woytinsky et al., *Employment and Wages in the United States* (New York: Twentieth Century Fund, 1953), p. 46. Average annual increases in the productivity of labor (output per man-hour) certainly exceeded this figure during the period.

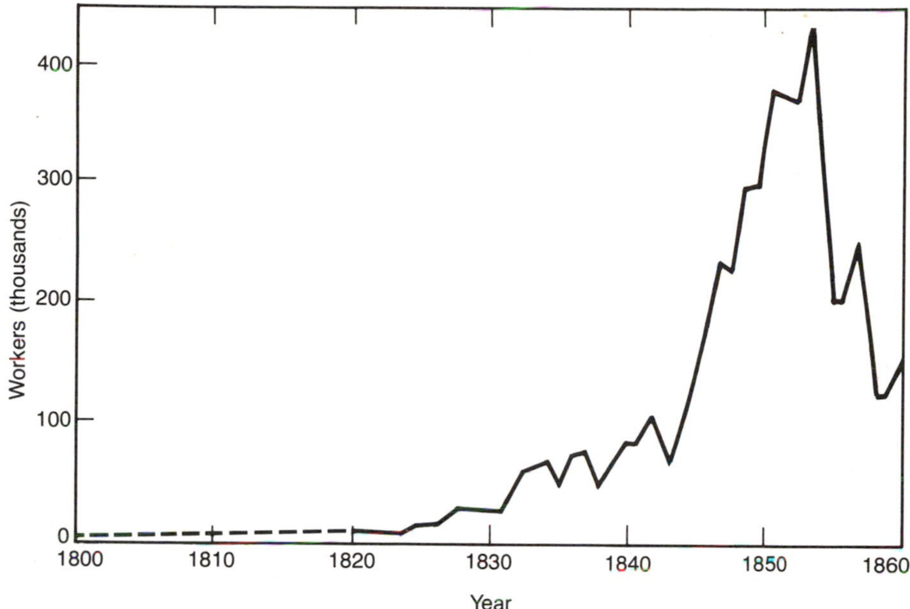

FIGURE 14–1

Additions to the U.S. Labor Force from Migration, 1800–1860: Laborers came in huge numbers during the post-1848 period to a nation rich in land and rapidly increasing its stock of capital. Famine in Ireland and domestic unrest in Germany sent millions of immigrants across the ocean to America.

cinnati, Chicago, Milwaukee, and St. Louis. Between 1820 and 1860, the population of the country tripled to 31.5 million. The density of the population—only four and a half persons per square mile in 1790—was almost eight persons per square mile in 1850.

It is impossible to glean data from the early censuses that is comparable to any of the modern censuses of the Bureau of Labor Statistics. Concepts and definitions were crude. The Superintendent of the Census, as he was then called, took more pains with his rhetoric than with his figures, placing undue emphasis on counting the lame and the halt, the deaf and the blind, the insane and the idiotic. But if we remember that in both 1850 and 1860 the Census of Manufactures included every establishment "producing . . . of any kind of manufactured article the amount annually of five hundred dollars," we can extract some informative labor statistics. The census excluded "the very large aggregate of mechanical productions below the annual value of five hundred dollars," as well as "carpenters, bricklayers, painters, and the members of other mechanical trades not classed as manufacturers." People employed in trade, commerce, and the transportation industries were also excluded. By 1850, within these limits, there were just under 950,000 people of all ages employed in manufacturing industries, approximately one-fourth of whom were females.

We have no way of knowing how many children were employed. In the early 1830s, as many as half the operatives in some cotton-textile factories were children. In the next two decades, the percentage of children employed in the industry decreased, but the absolute number rose. At mid-century, women were dominant in textile manufacture; about twice as many females as males worked in cotton fabric manufacture, although males exceeded females in woolen manufacture. About one-third of the 225,000 females who had jobs in industry worked in textile factories. The rest were, for the most part, home workers under the domestic system.

By 1860, the number of "hands" in industry had risen to 1,385,000. Women now constituted only one-fifth of the manufacturing labor force, indicating the lessening *relative* importance of textile manufacture and the competition of cheap immigration labor, most of which was male. Like today, this was a period of significant change in women's social roles, but then the trend was toward domestic pursuits. The cotton-textile industry still employed the most females (many of whom were children), and the clothing and boot and shoe industries were second and third in this respect, ahead of woolen textiles. The Superintendent of the Census estimated that each person employed in manufacturing maintained, on an average, 2½ other persons; thus, nearly one-sixth of the population was directly supported by manufactures.[12] Another sixth of the population may have been supported by other nonagricultural pursuits. These figures remind us that the people of the United States in 1860 were still predominantly agrarians, two-thirds of them gaining their livelihood directly from the land. But urban workers had achieved a numerical importance that made them a force to be reckoned with. Let us see how they acquired a unifying sense of class consciousness.

THE EARLY LABOR MOVEMENT

Economists like to say that the modern labor problem springs from the separation of workers from their tools.[13] Like most generalizations, this one has its uses, but it may lead the unwary interpreter to make false inferences. The Industrial Revolution placed great numbers of laborers in a position of uncertainty and insecurity, making them dependent on the vagaries of economic fluctuations and the mercy of employers. Yet the first impetus to a genuine labor movement was furnished by craftsmen who were by no means separated from their tools. The ever-increasing numbers of factory workers became articulate and powerful only with the passage of time. At first, factory workers were little more adept at organizing than were day laborers, and their bargaining strength was slight. In the first half of the nineteenth century, factory operatives, except for the influence they could exert at the polls, served labor's cause chiefly by demonstrating how rising industrialism might create permanent class distinctions.

[12] *Preliminary Report on the Eighth Census,* p. 59.

[13] Artisans, no matter how inexperienced, had always owned the customary implements of their trade. When the artisans became factory workers, the capitalists furnished their equipment.

Organization: Economic Motivation

In colonial days, craftsmen of the same trade banded together in benevolent and protective associations, but until just before the Revolution there seem to have been no organizations that could be called unions. Beginning in the 1790s, craftsmen in Philadelphia, New York, and Boston founded the prototypes of the modern unions. Most of the societies were established in the vain hopes of securing increases in real wages (that is, of pushing up money wages faster than the prices of consumer goods), although attempts were made to gain shorter working hours, to establish and maintain a closed shop, and to regulate the conditions of apprenticeship. Invariably, there was some fraternal motivation; people who made a living in the same way easily forged a social bond. In nearly all the major cities, shoemakers (cordwainers) and printers were among the first to form "workingmen's societies," and carpenters, masons, hatters, riggers, and tailors also found it worthwhile to organize.

The early craft societies were transitory. Many of the unions of the 1790s were established to meet particular objectives and, succeeding or failing, passed quickly out of existence. Apparently, the Philadelphia cordwainers, who maintained a union from 1794 to 1806, were the first to keep their organization in operation for more than a few years. Two influences worked against permanence. One was the cyclical nature of economic activity; the other was the unfavorable attitude of the courts, which before 1850 were uniformly hostile toward union activity.

Union membership always rose rapidly during prosperous periods and declined just as rapidly with the onset of depression. On the economic upswing, everything was favorable to organizing endeavors. Price rises in commodities, and increases in rents and wages, invited collective action. Nor did workers fear the wrath of employers due to union activity, because when jobs were plentiful, employer tolerance was high. On the downswing labor's advantage was undone. As general unemployment prevailed, those fortunate enough to have jobs accepted wage cuts rather than go hungry. Attempts by unions to resist wage reductions were met by the counterefforts of belligerent employers, who themselves frequently banded together. Union members, when called on to strike rather than take lower wages, usually withdrew from the society, because they knew the employer could hire nonunion labor to break the strike.

In good times as well as bad, there was always the threat and sometimes the actuality of court action to hinder and thwart organizational efforts. Conservative judges, in their instructions to juries, contended that union action per se was illegal. Societies of workers were considered conspiracies under English common law, a conspiracy being defined as "a confederacy of two or more, by indirect means to injure an individual or to do any act, which is unlawful or prejudicial to the community." A doctrine developed in England during the late Middle Ages was thus applied some 500 years later to restrict the unionization of craftsmen. In the famous case of the Pittsburgh Cordwainers in 1815, the judge contended that both the master shoemakers *and* the journeymen were coerced:

> No shoemaker dare receive one who worked under price; or who was not a member of the society. No master workman must give him any employment, under the penalty of losing all his workmen." Moreover, "a conspiracy to prevent a man from freely exercising his trade, or particular profession, in a particular place, is endictable. Also, it is an endictable offense, to conspire to compel men to become members of a particular association, or to contribute towards it.[14]

The jury in this case agreed that the master shoemakers, the journeymen, and the public were endangered by the association of journeymen and returned a verdict of guilty of conspiracy, although the court fined the defendants only $1 each and the prosecution costs. Judgments against unions were not severe, and the climate remained favorable for unions until 1818. It took the depression of 1819–1820 to wipe out most of the societies.

From 1824 until 1837 there was a gradual resurgence of craft unions. Gathering momentum after 1833, the movement reached substantial proportions, and had it not been for the devastating severity of the economic slump that began in the late 1830s and extended well into the 1840s, American labor might have attained a position at mid-century that, in fact, it was not to reach until around 1900. Aside from the political gains made in these years, unions progressed in two directions:

1. *The technique of bargaining collectively was learned, and fighting unions began to use the weapons of the strike and boycott with skill and daring.* The *closed shop*—an agreement whereby membership in a recognized union is made a condition of employment—was soon tested as an instrument for maintaining union security. The benevolent and protective aims of labor organizations tended to disappear, and militancy replaced early hesitance and reluctance to act.
2. *The rapidly increasing number of individual societies began to coalesce.* Local federations and then national organizations appeared. In 1827, unions of different crafts in Philadelphia federated to form a "city central" or "trades' union"—the Mechanics' Union of Trade Associations. Six years later, the societies in New York established a General Trades' Union. In the next three years, city centrals were formed in several major cities—not, as might be supposed from the modern functions of such organizations, to exchange information or engage in political activities, but for the more pressing purpose of aiding individual unions engaged in battle with employers. Attempts at organization on a national scale followed. In 1834, the General Trades' Union, New York's city central, called a national convention of these city federations, that resulted in the foundation of a National Trades' Union. At the same time, some of the craft societies began to see the advantages to be gained from a national organization along strict craft lines, and in 1835 and 1836 no less than five national unions of this type were established. The strongest of these were formed by the shoemakers and the printers.

[14] From Commons' *A Documentary History of American Industrial Society,* Vol. 4 (Glendale, Calif.: Arthur H. Clark Co.), pp. 82, 83.

However remarkable these early gains were, labor's minority elite, the craftsmen, were the primary beneficiaries. *Factory workers and home workers under the domestic system were almost completely outside the union movement.* So too, of course, were all slaves, domestic workers such as housewives, and most other workers. There are records of occasional organizations of factory hands in the textile industry, but these embryonic unions were unstable. Spontaneous strikes occurred from time to time, even in the absence of formal organization, but they were easily broken. It was hard for a factory worker or a laborer and family if the wrath of an employer were incurred. The "blacklist," which was to have a long and dishonorable future, contained the names of those known to be disruptive influences, and its circulation in an area precluded the employment of those who were listed.

The shock of the long depression that began in 1837 brought to an abrupt end the trend toward unionism of the preceding ten years. As unemployment spread, city centrals and national organizations disappeared. So did all but the hardiest locals. For several years, there were only sporadic efforts to revive the unions, and activity was confined to the urban centers of the East. By the early 1840s, it looked as if the energies spent in bringing American trade unionism to some degree of maturity had been wasted.

As unions gathered strength toward the mid-1830s, people of property and their natural allies in the professional classes looked with alarm on what seemed to them a dangerous growth of labor's power. The courts concurred in this view. Two cases reminiscent of the older conspiracy trials were important in checking the union movement. The first was the trial of the Geneva Shoemakers. The journeymen shoemakers of Geneva, New York, had agreed not to work for any master who did not hire union workers. One master hired a nonunion member at below union rates, and the other workers in the shop promptly struck. For refusing to work, the journeymen were indicted and convicted for criminal conspiracy. The case was appealed to the State Supreme Court, and Chief Justice Savage upheld the conviction on the grounds that such union action was harmful to trade. "It is important to the best interests of society," he said, "that the price of labor be left to regulate itself. . . . Competition is the life of trade." Meantime, in New York City, the Society of Journeyman Tailors had secured an increase in wage rates for its members only to have them later reduced by a combination of master tailors. A strike, accompanied by much strife, ensued. "Dungs," as scabs were then called, were hired by the masters to break the strike, with violent results. After Justice Savage handed down his decision in the Geneva Shoemakers case, the master tailors charged 20 of the journeymen with conspiracy. Again, the strike was the offense. The judge followed Justice Savage in his charge to the jury, and the journeymen were convicted and fined heavily. As a result of the trial judge's contention that American "trades and tradesmen" had hitherto flourished without the aid of combinations and that the unions must therefore have been "of foreign origin . . . and upheld by foreigners," there was much indignation among labor supporters over the outcome of the trial. In two similar cases, union members were acquitted, but the legality of union activity was still very much in question.

A definite turning point came in the now famous case of *Commonwealth v. Hunt.* In the fall of 1840, Hunt and other members of the Boston Bootmakers' Society were hauled into municipal court for attempting to enforce a closed shop. Again, after a strict charge from a judge who felt that such union activities could lead only to a "frightful despotism," the accused were convicted. The case was appealed to the Supreme Court of the Commonwealth of Massachusetts, and in 1842 Chief Justice Lemuel Shaw handed down a monumental decision that set a precedent on one point and opened the way to more liberal decisions on another. First, he held that a combination of union members was not criminal unless the object of the combination were criminal; the mere fact of organization implied no illegal conspiracy. Second, he asserted the doctrine that union members were within their rights in pressing for a closed shop and in striking to maintain union security. Justice Shaw was not a radical, nor was he particularly sympathetic with labor's cause, but he was well aware of the economic realities that were pressing labor to act collectively. This decision did not mean that trade unions were free from further court confrontations, but there were no more serious efforts to make the mere fact of organization a criminal offense, and there would henceforth be some reticence about presuming that the use of any and all weapons of the trade unions were socially harmful.

After a tentative revival in the mid-1840s, workingmen's societies made a strong comeback during the 1850s. From 1850 to 1854, the rapidity with which craft unions organized was comparable to that of 20 years earlier, with inevitable retardation accompanying the depression of 1854. Another setback occurred in 1857, but the end of the period showed signs of definite growth. City centrals were back, as were national craft unions, and there were signs that the federations could do more than discuss matters of "mutual interest." Individual unions acquired members who were disposed to greater militance. Funds were accumulated to assist in the successful prosecution of strikes, and serious attempts were made by the stronger crafts to bargain with *all* employers in a particular locality.

Leaders who viewed the labor movement as a whole still had to face the problem presented by the growing masses of workers who had no particular skills. People who worked in factories had always been hard to organize. As the uneducated Irish, largely with agricultural backgrounds, swelled the ranks of industrial workers, the problem became increasingly difficult to solve. Yet the English and Germans were not without a tradition of labor solidarity, and they would be a source of strength in years to come.

Organization: Political Motivation

Anyone concerned with modern labor problems must be aware of a certain artificiality in distinguishing between the economic and political aspirations of labor. The two classes of ends merge and blend into one another and are indistinguishable at times. Yet there always have been certain goals that could be reached through the collective action of workers who make their living in the same way, and there have been others that could be achieved only through political processes. Many of labor's demands 100 years ago were for rights that today are considered matters of common decency. But these rights were then objects of desperate striving, and the struggle for them was carried on in an atmosphere of hostility and vindictiveness hardly imaginable today.

Labor's political awakening did not come until toward the end of the 1820s, and this awakening was not by mere chance. We do not disparage the founding fathers when we remark that most of them were not democrats. The Constitution was not designed to give great power to the masses, and state governments also favored people of wealth and property. During the first decades of our hisstory as a republic, there was a persistent demand by the people for a greater voice in political affairs. The most significant gain in this regard was a broadening of suffrage. Requirements that a person own a minimum amount of real property or pay a certain amount of taxes were modified. The struggle for voting privileges took place in the original thirteen states; only four of the new states entering the Union placed property or tax-payment qualifications on the right to vote. By the late 1820s, suffrage had been extended sufficiently to enable working people to participate in the elections of the populous states. First to disappear was the property-owning requirement; by 1821, only five states retained it. Five states still set a tax-paying restriction 30 years later, but it was purely nominal.[15] Generally speaking, by 1860 white male citizens of the United States could vote, black males could vote in New York and New England, and aliens could vote in the agricultural Northwest.

In the 1820s, leaders of persuasive powers and genuine conviction came into prominence who were able to stir laboring people to a sense of political destiny. Robert Owen, a Scot, was too impractical to gain a widely enthusiastic reception, but his countrywoman and disciple Frances Wright took firm hold of the imaginations and passions of a large segment of the laboring population. She fulminated against reactionaries on the bench and among clergy of all denominations and insisted on a rational program for improving material welfare. Fanny Wright and other ardent leaders of the workingmen's movement strove hardest for reforms in education. Except in New England, children of the poor received little or no education, and in New England the early training was of poor quality and exhibited a religious slant that was obnoxious to egalitarians. Fanny Wright and her followers proposed that the state establish boarding schools for the education of rich and poor children alike, where class distinction would be eliminated.

Other proposals of the workingmen's movement were less radical than this state-guardianship system of education; indeed, many supporters of Fanny Wright broke with her to propose a simple plan of free public schools. Some of the movement's intellectuals believed that hard money (*literally*—a money supply made up of gold and silver coins) was necessary to the economic salvation of the worker; they were convinced that ruin for the common laborer would result from giving money-creating power to the state banks. In the minds of the working people, the most needed reform, next to that of the educational system, was the abolition of imprisonment for debt. Thousands of citizens were jailed annually for failure to meet obligations of a few dollars,

[15] Comparing the votes for President with the total population, we find that there were two large jumps in the electorate: from 1824 to 1828 (3.2 percent to 9.3 percent) and from 1836 to 1840 (9.6 percent to 13.6 percent).

and there was understandably fierce resentment against this injustice. The unfairness of the militia systems of the several states, which favored the rich, rankled in the hearts of the poor who were faced with the alternatives of a term in the service or a term in jail. These and other objectives—removing the competition of convict labor and obtaining the right to file liens on the property of employers for back wages—inflamed the spirits of great numbers of laborers, small businessmen, and professional people with a high degree of social consciousness.

But flaming spirits accomplish little unless they have organizations through which to work. In Philadelphia in 1827 and shortly thereafter in New York City, independent workingmen's parties were formed to do battle at the polls. Similar political groups sprang up in most of the northern states and were more or less successful in their own localities. Supported by about 50 newspapers and by voluminous pamphlet literature, tickets of workingmen's parties frequently ran well in local elections. But these independent labor parties were short-lived; they tended to be absorbed into the Democratic party, where they formed a radical wing sympathetic to Jacksonian principles. The heated national election of 1832 hastened this process; American labor learned early that it had to take on the aura of respectability and orthodoxy of a major party if more than local success was to be gained at the polls.

The first political movement had borne fruit. Some progress had been made in the educational field. The militia system had become less onerous, mechanics' "lien laws" were passed in many states, and imprisonment for debt was outlawed in most jurisdictions. But this first movement lost momentum after 1832, as labor turned its energies during the ensuing period of prosperity to advancing the cause of unionization. The onset of depression in 1837 dashed the hopes of those who looked for victory in the economic sphere. Out of the frustration and disillusionment that accompanied the breakdown of the economic mechanism came a second wave of political activity—this time with vaguer goals and the even greater support of intellectuals and reformers.

The 1840s were characterized by the utopian schemes of idealists and the mundane agitation of those who looked to specific movements for relief. Of the utopian notions, the associationism of Charles Fourier and the land reform of George Henry Evans were the chief contenders for the interest of workers. Fourierism (associationism) advocated the division of society into "phalanxes" or communities of 1,600 producing members. Residing in a common building (a phalanstery), members of the community would occupy themselves primarily in agricultural pursuits, but they were divided into a sufficient number of groups to permit a wide variety of activities, including menial domestic service. To avoid monotony, people could change jobs, but division of the total product was to be made according to a formula that took into account each individual's contribution of labor, "talent," and capital. No matter what contribution was made, however, each person was assured a certain minimum livelihood, and it was hoped that everyone would live together in peace and classless harmony. Between 1840 and 1850, perhaps 40 phalanxes were established in the United States. Of these, Brook Farm near Boston was the most famous due to the association with it of well-known New England literary figures. Differing somewhat from Robert Owen's earlier socialist experiment at New Harmony,

Indiana, the phalanxes nevertheless came to the same quick end. The chief trouble was that Fourierism did not accept the growing industrialism of the nineteenth century. Instead, the doctrine suggested a withdrawal of uneconomically small groups back into the agricultural and craft society from which the nations of the western world were emerging.

The agrarianism of George Henry Evans looked backward, too. Evans believed that the root of the worker's plight was in technological change. Machines, he felt, would continue to displace human labor, resulting in chronic unemployment and low wages. The remedy lay in free grants of land from the public domain to groups of farmers and craftsmen who would form self-sufficient townships on the frontier. After a flurry of acceptance by isolated groups, Evans' land-reform effort faded. It had no lasting results and little influence, except that it added to the clamor for a homestead law and strengthened the arguments of those who demanded free land for any worker who wanted it.

The common laborer's selfish interest was for a time captured by proposals for cooperation. Both producers' and consumers' cooperatives were advocated, the latter gaining a rather impressive acceptance. Co-ops of both kinds had been started in the 1830s and had failed in the depression years. Revived in the mid-1840s, they reached a peak during the early 1850s and declined almost as suddenly. Producers' co-ops were started by craftsmen in many cities as attempts to provide steady and permanent employment for those who combined to set up the cooperative shop. Sharing the expenses of a retail establishment, workers hoped to provide a marketing outlet that would enable them to *share* profits instead of allowing a capitalist to take them. Consumers' co-ops were aimed at reducing the living costs of the workers by rebating to them their share of the profits of a store on the basis of their patronage. Some success was attained in New England, where member stores of the New England Protective Union did a retail business of $4 million in one year. The success of consumer cooperatives in America has always been limited by the necessity of operating on a shoestring capital, by meager managerial talent, and by lack of loyalty among members. Co-ops temporarily vanished just before 1860.

Only one movement of the period gained quick relief for workers—the struggle for the 10-hour day. Why the 10-hour day was a goal of labor reform is not entirely clear; perhaps to the people of the time it seemed a great improvement and one that was within reach. The goal was set as early as 1835, but there was then no serious prospect of attaining it. Hope rose in 1840 when Martin Van Buren set a 10-hour day for federal employees. Craftsmen in some trades already worked no longer than 10 hours, but factory operatives still labored 12–14 hours a day. In the mid-1840s, New England factory workers added to the agitation for shorter hours. In 1847, the New Hampshire legislature passed the first regulatory law setting a 10-hour upper limit for a day's work, but there was a loophole in it. The law provided that if workers *agreed* to work longer hours, the 10-hour limit might be exceeded. Threatened with discharge if they did not agree, factory hands found themselves no better off. Statutes passed by other state legislatures followed the same pattern, except that laws limiting the workday of children to 10 hours did not contain the hated "contract" clause. Perhaps the most important effect of the agitation for regulatory acts was the pressure of public opinion thereby exerted on employers. Many large factories voluntarily established 11-hour days. By 1860, a 10-hour day was standard in all the craft trades, and already a new standard of eight hours was being timorously suggested.

When we reflect on the temper of the era, this shortening of the workweek seems a notable advance. Labor had argued that acceleration of the working pace made a reduction in work hours mandatory and that a shorter workday would improve employee health and efficiency. To a considerable extent this was true. Given a long work week of, say, 60 hours, a modest reduction in hours worked per week did not lead to a proportionate decline in output. Reductions in hours, then, were partly offset by a greater intensity of work per hour. Of course, employers did not always agree or consider hour reductions profit-enhancing, but competition for workers forced them to comply with labor's demands for a shorter workweek. It is a credit to the American laborers of more than a century ago that increased time for self-improvement was part of the progress of the period. This brief sketch has left some questions unanswered about the status of labor after nearly 75 years of our national history. In many respects, the results of organizational effort were disappointing. Craft unions were stronger in 1860 than they had ever been. A certain realism in the best sense of the word had crept into their endeavors. Objectives were clearer, and the techniques of attaining them had been learned. Yet employees of the factory and domestic systems for the most part remained outside the union movement. On balance, immigrants weakened the position of organized labor and prevented solid and unquestioned gains. It was difficult to strike effectively against an employer who could turn for unskilled and unspecialized help to an endless supply of job-hungry foreigners.

There were impelling reasons for a struggle to secure union privileges and protection for the whole labor force. The worker–employer relationship was being depersonalized; due to the separation of private morality and business morality, most laborers no longer were protected by friendly, *personal* relations with the boss. What the owner of a craft shop or a small mill would never have countenanced, due to scruples of conscience, the manager of an urban factory thought nothing of doing. Nor was the increasing use of the corporate form, with an increasing divorcement of ownership and control, likely to mitigate the workers' plight. Protection could come from government, but government would be slow to guarantee a climate in which the laborer could earn a daily living and a little more without having to spend a whole life doing it. Meantime, labor had to rely on its own efforts.

One series of congressional acts had already helped labor's cause. The victory of the liberal land forces provided occupational alternatives for some workers. As we have seen, during the first half-century of our history under the Constitution, opportunities in agriculture set a floor under industrial wages. If land for settlement had not been available, many immigrants who came directly to the West would have looked for work in the cities of the East instead and worsened labor conditions. Those who would escape the hopelessness of life at a bare level of subsistence on an unproductive farm in New England, New York, or Pennsylvania could move to the frontier; or if they could not stand the rigors of pioneering, they could settle on improved land short of the frontier—at least until about 1840.

After 1840, the "safety valve" of the system was an unreliable mechanism, as factory workers and common laborers began to constitute a larger proportion of the workforce. Factory workers who lived in a manufacturing town were not prepared for agricultural pursuits, even if they preferred a sod house to a tenement, and unlike the craftsmen they could not make a living at a trade. Financing a trip to the frontier for self and family became more expensive as the frontier moved farther away, and once there, an increasingly substantial outlay of cash had to be made for land and the expenses of initial settlement. That the frontier itself did not attract many working people directly has been conclusively demonstrated; laborers, when they did migrate, went only a short way west to take jobs much like the ones they had previously held. All this notwithstanding, the West did drain off failing eastern farmers who might have swelled the industrial labor supply and forced wages downward—a fact attested to by the vigor with which manufacturers in the old states opposed liberal land laws.

15

The Entrenchment of Slavery

CONSTITUTIONAL LIMITATIONS

In 1780, the enslaved populations in the United States equaled nearly 575,000 blacks. Nine percent of these resided north of the Chesapeake; the remainder lived in the South. As part of one of the great constitutional compromises, the nation's forefathers agreed in 1787 not to allow the importation of slaves after 20 years. In 1807, therefore, pursuant to the authorizing Constitutional prohibition, Congress prohibited the foreign slave trade, effective the next year. In this way, the growth of slavery in the United States was limited, at least partially. Of course, the smuggling of human cargo was not uncommon, especially during years in which slaves brought high prices, and various estimates suggest as many as a quarter of a million blacks were illegally imported before 1860. But, illicit human importation was only a minor addition to the total numbers held in bondage, and foreign-born blacks comprised a small percentage of the enslaved population in 1860. Natural sources of population expansion were predominant in increasing the number of slaves, and in 1863 their number equaled almost 4 million—all residing in the South.

NORTHERN EMANCIPATION

Even before the writing of the Constitution, some states were progressing toward the elimination of slavery. Between 1777 and 1804, the eight northeastern states individually passed measures to provide for the emancipation of their resident slave populations. In Vermont, Massachusetts, and New Hampshire, vague Constitutional clauses left the matter of emancipation to the courts. Unfortunately, little is known about the results of this process, but in any case, these three states domiciled only a very small fraction of the northern blacks—probably 10–15 percent in 1780. As shown in Table 15-1, Pennsylvania, Rhode Island, Connecticut, New York, and New Jersey each passed laws of emancipation well before the year prohibiting slave importations.

The process of emancipation used in these states is interesting. The living population of slaves was not freed. Instead, newborn babies were emancipated when they reached adulthood.

Due to the form of the emancipation legislation it is apparent that many—perhaps most—of those who were politically dominant were more concerned with the political issue of slavery than with the slaves themselves. Besides not freeing the living slaves, there were no agencies in any of these states to enforce the enactments. In addition, the enactments themselves contained important loopholes, such as the possibility of selling slaves to the South.

The emancipation process, however, did recognize the issues of property rights and costs. These "gradual emancipation schemes" imposed no costs on taxpayers, and owners were not directly compensated financially for emancipated slaves. But curiously enough, owners were almost entirely compensated for their free slaves. This was accomplished by maintaining the free-born in bondage until they had repaid their owner for their rearing costs. In most cases, these slaves were freed when they reached their mid-20s. In the first several years after birth, a slave's maintenance cost was in excess of the value of his or her services (or output). Near the age of 10, the slave's output usually just about matched the costs of food, clothes, and shelter. Thereafter, the value of output exceeded maintenance costs, and normally by the age of 25 or 26 the slave had fully compensated the owner.

Most of the political rhetoric of the period was concerned with the problems of suddenly turning an uneducated and unskilled minority out into the world at large, as the ages in Table 15-1 suggest. But results and intentions are

TABLE 15–1
Slave Emancipation in the North for the Free-Born

State	Date of Enactment	Age of Emancipation	
		Male	Female
Pennsylvania	1780[a]	28	28
Rhode Island	1784[b]	21	18
Connecticut	1784[c]	25	25
New York	1799[d]	28	25
New Jersey	1804[e]	25	21

[a] The last census that enumerated any slaves in Pennsylvania was in 1840.
[b] All slavery was abolished in 1842.
[c] The age of emancipation was changed in 1797 to age 21. In 1848, all slavery was abolished.
[d] In 1817, a law was passed freeing all slaves as of July 4, 1827.
[e] In 1846, all slaves were emancipated, but apprenticeships continued for the children of slave mothers and were introduced for freed slaves.

Source: Robert W. Fogel and Stanley L. Engerman "Philanthropy at Bargain Prices: Notes on the Economics of Gradual Emancipation," *The Journal of Legal Studies,* **3:**2 (June 1974), p. 341.

two quite different things. Perhaps the intentions of the legal designers were noble; perhaps they were not. In any case, we do know that the slaves themselves bore the lion's share of the costs of emancipation in the North. Newborn slaves who were eventually freed fully paid back their owners for their rearing costs. Owners of males who were born before the dates of enactment suffered no wealth loss. Owners of females who were born before the enactments and who could or eventually would reproduce incurred some minor wealth losses in that they lost the value of their slaves' offspring. About 10 percent of the value (price) of a young female slave was due to the value of her offspring, and perhaps as many as 30 percent of the total enslaved population was comprised of females in their fertile or prefertile years.[1] If so, only 3 percent (10 percent of 30 percent) of the total slave wealth was lost to northern owners by abiding by these enactments, but the percentage was probably much closer to zero because of the loopholes of selling slaves to the South, working the slaves harder, and reducing maintenance costs.

COMPLEMENTARY FACTORS TO SLAVERY IN THE SOUTH

Despite the constitutional restrictions on slave imports and the "gradual emancipation schemes" of the northern states, slavery did not die. The primary reason for this was the rapid expansion of cotton growing in the South and the gains in efficiency offered by the plantation system. In combination with food crops, cotton production kept workers busy almost all year. Cotton was planted in April and required careful and persistent cultivation during most of the growing season. The bolls did not ripen all at once, and picking, which began in September, might not be completed until late December or early January. During the winter months, the field hands could be worked in gangs to clear new land, build fences, and do general repair work.

Continuous utilization of the slave workforce was further encouraged by the mild climate of the Deep South. There were few winter days in which cold weather enforced idleness. Southern summers, while unpleasantly humid and persistently and uncomfortably warm, were not characterized by the high maximum temperatures of the Midwest and Southwest. Except along the rice and sugar coasts, there were no serious health hazards, and blacks lived in an environment that was less enervating than equatorial Africa. The soft climate required owners to outlay only minimal housing and clothing to maintain the physical well-being of the slaves. The profitability of slavery, then, was largely a function of latitude[2] and the comparative advantages in production derived from heavily utilizing relatively low-skilled labor and particular soils and climates.

There was considerable variation in the number of acres required to keep a slave busy. If we count garden land and woodlands in addition to arable

[1] Female slaves of all ages comprised 37 percent of the total slave population.

[2] In considering the "profitability" of slavery, writers have always argued the question from two points of view—that of the slave trader or owner and that of the South as a geographic unit. But profits are earned by the firm—by the entrepreneur who ventures capital. The greater problem of economic gain or loss to the South is a separate one and cannot be discussed in terms of net revenue to the agricultural units. See Harold D. Woodman, "The Profitability of Slavery: A Historical Perennial," *Journal of Southern History,* **XXIX** (August 1963), pp. 303–25.

fields, the number of acres per field hand varied from 15 to 40, depending on the quality of the land. Poor Alabama pine land might require 35–40 acres per hand, whereas 15 acres of clear Mississippi alluvium would be more than the very best workers could handle.[3] By 1850, the rule of thumb was established that on land of good quality 10 acres of cotton and 10 acres of corn would keep an average slavehand fully occupied.

Slaves were employed in agricultural units of all sizes, but it was the plantation, as distinguished from the farm, that provided the economic basis of the slave system.[4] U. B. Phillips has suggested that a plantation was a unit that worked a minimum of 20 field hands—the smallest number of slaves over which it would be profitable to put an overseer. If we estimate that a slave could work 20 acres of arable land, a cotton plantation would contain at least 400 acres under cultivation. Waste and woodland would add to the total acreage, so that the smallest plantation would scarcely be smaller than 700–800 acres. At the other extreme, there were huge units, especially in the cane-growing region of southeastern Louisiana, containing 20,000–40,000 acres and worked by 500 or more slaves.

It will be noted from Table 15-2 that in 1850—almost at the height of the plantation's economic importance—almost half of the slaveholding families had four slaves or less. This group of slaveholders owned only 10 percent of the slaves. If we consider a unit employing 20 or more slaves to be of plantation size, it is a reasonable estimate that about one-half of the slave population lived on these large units. Roughly one-fourth of the slaves belonged to the substantial farmers and small planters who owned between 10 and 19 slaves.[5]

PLANTATION EFFICIENCY

In the heyday of King Cotton, the growth in the number and size of plantations in the South was dramatic. Of course, many small family farm units produced cotton and their related items for market. But the really distinguishing characteristic of southern agriculture in the antebellum period was the plantation.

[3] For further detailed estimates, see Alfred H. Conrad and John R. Meyer, "The Economics of Slavery in the Antebellum South," *Journal of Political Economy,* **LXVI** (April 1958), pp. 100–101.

[4] The word *plantation* has long been used, and is still used, to denote any large-scale agricultural unit employing a great number of workers under the systematic control of a single manager. In this broad sense, plantations are not confined to any particular region or period, nor is it essential that the workforce be unfree or limited to the people of a particular race. For example, plantations existed in seventeenth-century America with a workforce composed of indentured servants, and plantations are operated today under a sharecropping system or using the labor of migrant workers. But the large units of the antebellum South remain the archetype of the plantation. For a full treatment of these matters, see Paul S. Taylor, "Plantation Agriculture in the United States: Seventeenth to Twentieth Centuries," *Land Economics,* **XXX:**2, pp. 141–52.

[5] Interested students wishing to pursue the matter further should refer to the *Compendium of the Seventh Census* (Washington, D.C.: A. O. P. Nicholson, Public Printer, 1854), pp. 82–95. The table giving the percentage distribution of slaveholding families according to number of slaves held was computed directly from Table XC, p. 95, of the *Compendium.* Figures showing number of slaves by size of holding unit can be derived only after assuming an average number of slaves were owned by each unit. The approximations given here do not contain serious errors.

TABLE 15–2
Percentage Distribution of Slaveholding Families According to Number of Slaves Held, 1790 and 1850

	Percentage of families	
Number of slaves	1790	1850
1	24.5	17.4
2–5	30.5	29.5
5–10	22.0	24.4
10–20	14.3	17.4
20–50	6.4	9.1
50–100	1.0	1.7
100–200	0.2	0.4
200–300	[a]	0.1
300 or more	[a]	[a]
Unknown	1.0	

[a]Less than one-tenth of 1 percent.
Source: *Compendium of the Seventh Census* (Washington, D.C.: A. O. P. Nicholson, Public Printer, 1854), Table XC, p. 95.

Based on forced labor, the plantations represented both the economic grandeur and the social tragedy of the southern economy.

Although most of the condemnation of slavery was confined to moral and social issues, some of the damnation was extended to strictly economic aspects. In some instances, the forced labor of blacks was condemned as inefficient, either on racial grounds or because slavery per se was considered economically inefficient and unproductive. For example, the contemporary observer Cassius M. Clay noted that Africans were "far less adapted for steady, uninterrupted labor than we are,"[6] and another contemporary, Frederick L. Olmsted, reported that "white laborers of equal intelligence and under equal stimulus will cut twice as much wood, split twice as many rails, and hoe a third more corn a day than Negroes."[7]

Were plantations worked by masses of slaves more or less efficient than free family farm units? Did the South face increasing economic peril as slavery became more and more entrenched? Before addressing the second question, we should carefully assess the evidence pertaining to the first.

Of course, due to their size, plantations produced more cotton and other goods and foodstuffs than the southern free family farms. But when comparing output per unit of input (capital, labor, and land in combination), it is clear that the large plantations were considerably more productive than the small or slaveless farms. Table 15-3 shows these productivity comparisons for southern farms and plantations as well as for plantations worked by different amounts of slaves. By far the most efficient units were those using 50 or more slaves. Small-scale farming was less productive per unit of input employed, and there

[6]C. M. Clay in H. Greeley (ed.), *The Writings of Cassius Marcelius Clay: Including Speeches and Addresses*, (*The New Yorker*, 1848) p. 204.

[7]F. L. Olmsted, *The Cotton Kingdom*, A. M. Schlesinger (ed.), (The New Yorker, 1953), pp. 467–68.

TABLE 15–3
Comparisons of Efficiency in Southern Agriculture by Farm Type and Size
(Index of fall–summer farm = 100)

Number of slaves	Indexes of output per unit of total input
0	100
1–15	101
16–50	133
51 or more	148

Source: Robert W. Fogel and Stanley L. Engerman, "Explaining the Relative Efficiency of Slave Agriculture in the Antebellum South," *American Economic Review,* **67**:3 (June 1977), Table 7, p. 285.

was little difference in efficiency between southern free family farms and small farms employing only a few slaves. Therefore, it appears that racial factors had an insignificant effect on productivity. Black workers with their complementary but white-owned capital and land were about as productive in small units as white workers on single-family farms. Alternatively, plantations with sizable numbers of slaves were extraordinarily efficient. Clearly economies of scale, or some other sources of productivity gains, provided advantages for large-sized plantations.

Final answers to why such differences existed still elude us, but variations in land quality, location, crop mix, and length of workday (and workyear) have already been accounted for in Table 15-3. By and large, the main difference appears to be in the organization of slaves into production units called gangs, the careful selection of slaves by skill for particular uses, and in the intensity per hour with which the slaves were worked.

In many ways, the large antebellum plantations were more like factories than farms. Their organization of slave labor resembled that of assembly-line workers. Even contemporary reports stress these characteristics:[8]

> The cotton plantation was not a farm consisting, as the farm does, in a multiplicity of duties and arrangements within a limited scope, one hand charged with half a dozen parts to act in a day or week. The cotton plantation labor was as thoroughly organized as the cotton mill labor. There were wagoners, the plowmen, the hoe hands, the ditchers, the blacksmiths, the wheelwrights, the carpenters, the men in care of the work animals, the men in care of the hogs and cattle, the women who had care of the nursery . . . the cooks for all . . . [n]o industry in its practical operation was moved more methodically or was more exacting of a nice discrimination in the application of labor than the Canebrake Cotton plantation.

[8] These quotations by contemporaries are in reference to the Canebrake Plantation and the McDuffis Plantation, respectively. See Jacob Metzer, "Rational Management, Modern Business Practices, and Economies of Scale in Antebellum Southern Plantations," *Explorations in Economic History,* **12**:2 (April 1975), pp. 134–35 for complete citations and other examples.

> When the period for planting arrives, the hands are divided into three classes: 1st, the best hands, embracing those of good judgment and quick motion; 2nd, those of the weakest and most inefficient class; 3rd the second class of hoe hands. Thus classified, the first class will run ahead and open a small hole about seven to ten inches apart, into which the 2nd class [will] drop from four to five cotton seeds, and the third class [will] follow and cover with a rake.

Therefore, the efficiency gains stemmed primarily from worker–task selection and the intensity of work per hour. In fact, slaves on larger plantations typically took longer rest breaks and worked less on Sundays than their white counterparts did. Indeed, these conditions were needed to achieve the levels of work intensity imposed on the slaves. It is apparent that these productivity advantages were not voluntary. Essentially, they required slave or forced labor. No free-labor plantations emerged during the period. And as we will see, there was a significant reduction in labor participation and work intensity and organization after emancipation.

ECONOMIC EXPLOITATION

It hardly needs to be stressed that black slaves were exploited. They had no political rights, and the law of the plantation and the whim of the taskmaster

A busy cotton plantation on the Mississippi.

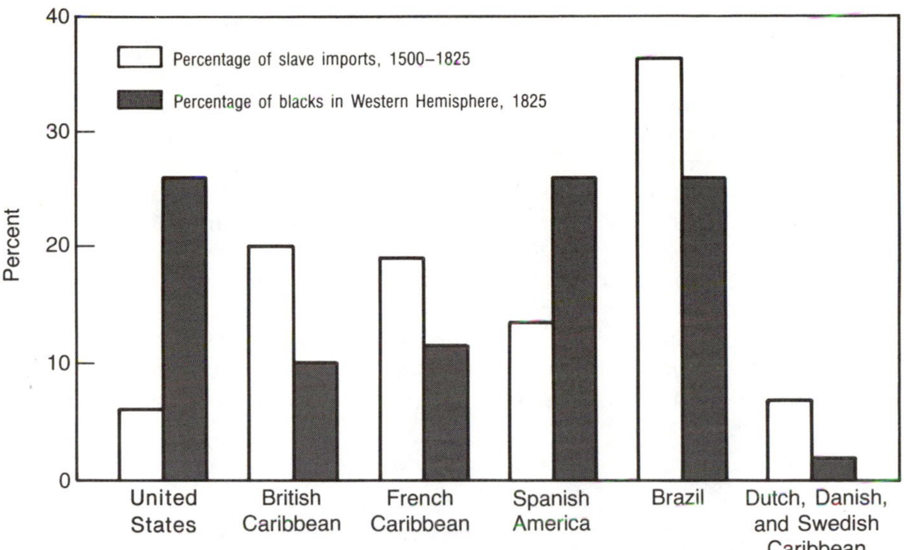

FIGURE 15–1

The Distribution of the Black Population (Slave and Free) in 1825 Compared to the Distribution of Slave Imports, 1500–1825

Source: Robert W. Fogel and Stanley L. Engerman, *Time on the Cross: The Economics of American Negro Slavery* (Boston: Little Brown, 1976), Figure 8, p. 28.

was the web of confinement the slave directly faced. Owners did not carelessly mistreat their slaves for obvious reasons. A prime male field hand was worth nearly $45,000 in today's (1979) prices.

Various forms of punishments and rewards, however, pressured slaves to be obedient workers. Few failed to witness or feel the sting of the lash, and their lot was far from pleasant, as these photographs attest. Part of the reason for this, of course, was their relatively low standard of living, which certainly would have been considerably higher if the value of their total output had been returned to them. However, because the property rights to their labor and their product resided with the white owner, their output accrued to the owner.

Under approximate conditions of competition, workers tend to be paid amounts that are equal to what they contribute in terms of output. An additional worker adds a certain value of output. Any difference between what the worker adds and what he or she receives may be reasonably termed economic exploitation. For the average slave, this difference (the value of output added minus maintenance costs) divided by the value of the output added was at least 50 percent and may have been as high as 65 percent.[9]

[9] For further elaboration, see Richard Vedder, "The Slave Exploitation (Expropriation) Rate," *Explorations in Economic History,* **12:**4, (October 1976) pp. 453–57. As Vedder notes, in New England cotton textile mills (a sample of 71 firms) in 1820, the comparable exploitation calculation was 22 percent; for iron workers in 1820 (101 firms), the rate was 28 percent (p. 456).

Yet, we should not overlook the fact that the American slave fared well in some aspects. A superior environment reduced the incidence of disease, and a hearty, but dull, diet sustained a healthy and growing population. A southern slave's life expectancy at birth in 1850 was as high as a free person's in Holland or France and was well above the life expectancies in most other parts of the world, civilized or savage.

The conditions of American bondage were harsh, but compared to conditions of forced labor elsewhere they were favorable. Figure 15-1 shows the percentage of slave imports to various parts of the Western Hemisphere (1500–1825) compared to the location of slaves in percentage terms in 1825. Note the drastic declines in population, relatively, in the Caribbean and in Brazil. There conditions were especially brutal. By comparison, the southern United States offered treatment that was life-sustaining. Slaves in the antebellum South experienced standards of material comfort that were low by today's

The technological breakthrough that revitalized the plantation economy was the cotton gin—a product of the innovative genius of Eli Whitney, a New England schoolmaster.

standards, but they were well above those of the masses in many parts of the contemporary world.

OTHER CHARACTERISTICS OF SLAVERY

Although the slave system proved efficient on the plantation, its economic advantages were not widely applicable elsewhere. As a result of this and other factors—especially its overwhelming comparative advantage in agriculture—the South experienced little structural change during the antebellum years. For instance, the South was slow to industrialize, partially due to the slave system. However, in pre-Civil War days, some slaves did become skilled craftsmen, and slaves were employed in cotton factories, coal mines, ironworks, lumber mills, and railroads. But there was no point in incurring the costs of training slaves

The somberness of this group of slaves suggests their ill fortune.

for industrial occupations on a large scale when they could readily be put to work in agriculture.[10]

In addition, the South experienced very little immigration from Europe or elsewhere. It was not the South's "peculiar institution" that kept European migrants away, because immigration did not increase after emancipation. Europeans tended to settle in the latitudes where most of the incoming ships set them down and where the climate was not unlike that of their former home. But the main deterrent to locating in the South was that outsiders perceived the lack of opportunity; the immigrant feared that he or she would become a "poor white." By 1860, only 3.4 percent of the southern population was foreign-born, compared with a foreign-born population in the central states of 17 percent and in New England of 15 percent.

Despite the living conditions of slaves and "poor whites," it would be an error to conclude that the South was poor or backward in the antebellum period. As we will see in Chapter 16, incomes per free person in the South were actually higher than in the North, and the wealthy cotton belt area of the West South Central area was the richest region in the country in per-capita terms (for an average of blacks and whites). Nor was the South internally stagnant. Incomes per capita were increasing rapidly and approached the national average in the antebellum years. In addition, internal migration from the older southern states to the new cotton belt areas was on a large scale. The Southern economy did show signs of flexibility.

Lastly, there seems to be little doubt that plantation slavery was profitable throughout the South. Extremely high net returns in parts of the cotton belt and rewards at least equal to those of alternative employments of capital in

TABLE 15–4
Estimated Average Slave Prices in Georgia, 1828–1860 (selected years)

Year	Average price of prime field hands
1828	$ 700
1835	900
1837	1,300
1839	1,000
1840	700
1844	600
1848	900
1851	1,050
1853	1,200
1859	1,600
1860	1,800

Source: U. B. Phillips, "The Economic Cost of Slaveholding in the Cotton Belt," *Political Science Quarterly,* **XX**:2 (1905), p. 267.

[10]The literature on slavery and the plantation system is voluminous. For two elegant treatments of social and political as well as economic variables, see Stuart Bruchey, *Cotton and the Growth of the American Economy: 1790–1860* (New York: Harcourt Brace Jovanovich, Inc., 1967), and Kenneth M. Stampp, *The Peculiar Institution* (New York: Alfred A. Knopf, 1963).

The blacks shown in this photograph taken in the 1880s—more than 20 years after emancipation—had scarcely improved their lot since slave days.

most areas of the Deep South were the rule. Nor were there economic forces at work making the slave economy self-destructive. There is simply no evidence to support the contention that slave labor was overcapitalized, and slaves clearly reproduced sufficiently to maintain a growing workforce.

Yet from the moral, social, and political viewpoints, the slave system imposed a growing source of self-destruction on the American people. The system epitomized a great barrier to human decency and social progress which was contrary to deeply felt ideals in many quarters. With almost religious ferver, abolitionist elements grew in strength and national disunity grew proportionately. It was highly unlikely that southerners would voluntarily free their own slaves. Without hope for compensation and fearing the social consequences of sudden emancipation, the South's oligarchical slave power stood firm. Meanwhile, the costs of emancipation to slave owners soared. As Table 15-4 illustrates, the value of slaves continued to increase, primarily in response to the rising productivity of forced labor profitably employed in cotton and other staples. Steadily, the entrenchment of slavery grew.

Slavery could only be ended by a significant political adjustment or by military force. As we know, it was a national tragedy that the political alternative was not found.

16

The Civil War Experience

TENUOUS COMPROMISES AND REGIONAL CONFLICT

Neither northern emancipation nor federal prohibition of the foreign slave trade removed slavery as a major political and economic issue in the United States. As the country continued to grow and expand, the issue of slavery became more and more pressing, particularly in the western territories. Anti-slave forces in the North wanted to limit slavery to the South as a first step toward complete emancipation. But the South successfully maintained equal voting power in the Senate throughout the first half of the century. In this way, southerners won a series of compromises that enabled them to extend the institution of slavery and counter abolitionist threats.

In 1819, the political balance in the Senate was even; there were 11 slave and 11 free states. By the Missouri Compromise of 1820 (see Map 16-1), Missouri was admitted as a slave state and Maine as a free state, on the condition that slavery should thereafter be prohibited in the territory of the Louisiana Purchase north of 36° 30′. For nearly 30 years after this, states were admitted to the Union in pairs, one slave and one free, and by 1850 there were 15 free and 15 slave states. As of that year, slavery had been prohibited in the Northwest Territory, in the territory of the Louisiana Purchase north of 36° 30′, and in the Oregon Territory—vast areas in which an extensive slave system would not have been profitable anyway. Violent controversy arose over the basis of admission for prospective states contained in the area ceded to the United States by Mexico. The terms of the Mexican Cession required that the territory remain permanently free, yet Congress in 1848 had rejected the Wilmot Proviso, which

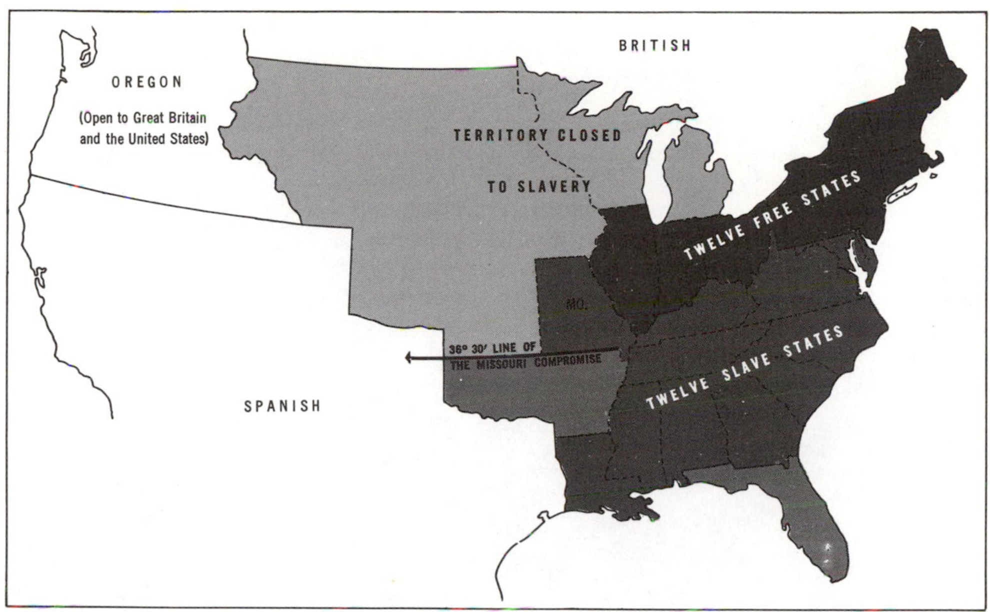

MAP 16–1

Missouri Compromise: After this 1820 enactment, growing sectional acrimony was supposed to be a thing of the past. For a time, a truce did prevail.

would have prohibited slavery in the Southwest, where its extension was economically feasible. In the end, California was admitted as a free state in 1850. The territories of Utah and New Mexico were organized, and slaveholding was to be permitted there; the final decision was to be made by the territorial population on application for admission to the Union.

Further events of the 1850s for a time appeared to portend ultimate victory for the South in the matter of slavery extension. The Kansas–Nebraska Act of 1854 (see Map 16-2) in effect repealed the Missouri Compromise by providing for "popular sovereignty" in the hitherto unsettled portions of the Louisiana Purchase. The Dred Scott decision of a states' rights Supreme Court went even further and declared that Congress could not prohibit slavery in the territories. And during this, Southerners, desperately eager to inhibit the movement of small farmers into territories where slavery could not possibly flourish, successfully resisted passage of a homestead act.

Yet legislative successes could be achieved only as long as Democrats from the North and Northwest were willing to ally themselves with the South. Toward the end of the 1850s, the antislavery movement in the North became irresistible. In large part, the movement was led by those who opposed the servitude of anyone on purely ethical grounds, but altruistic motives were reinforced by economic interests. Northwest farmers resisted the extension of the plantation system because they feared the resulting competition of large units with their small ones. And as transportation to eastern centers improved, the

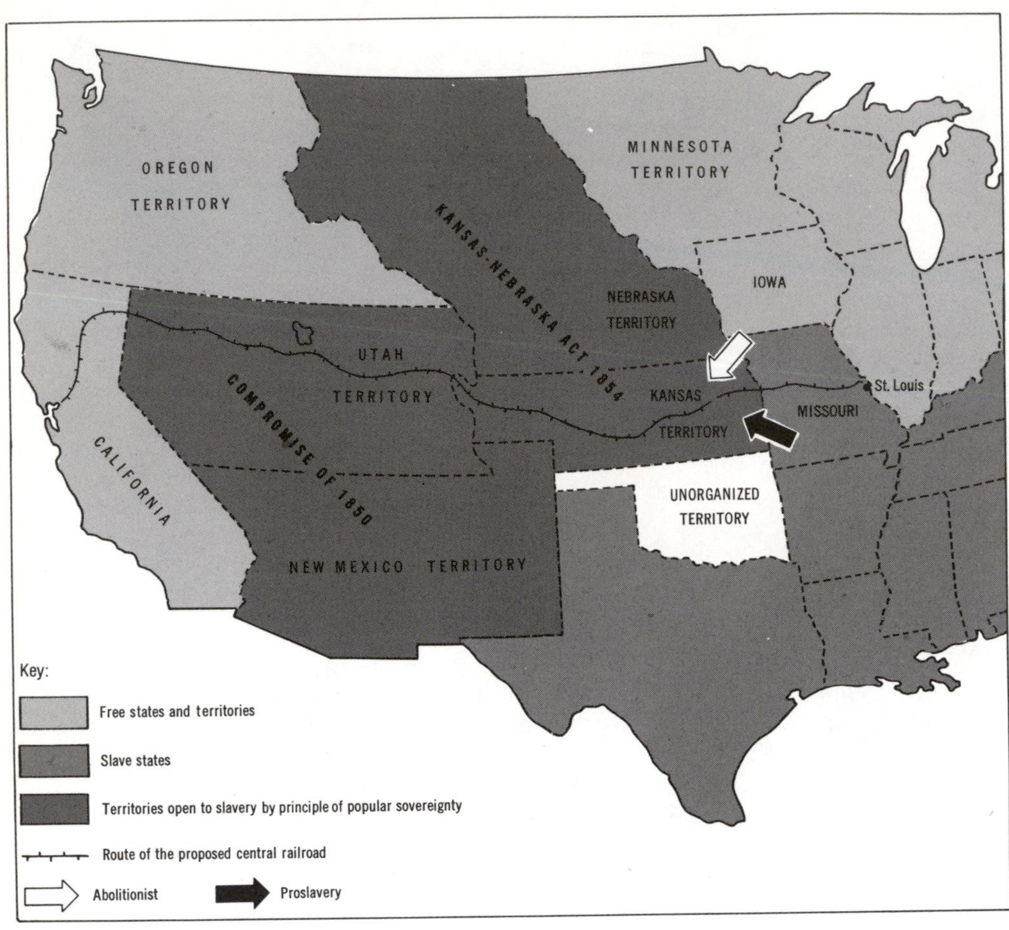

MAP 16–2

New Settlements: The Compromise of 1850 and the Kansas–Nebraska Act of 1854 were further attempts to keep sectional strife from erupting into warfare. The concept of "popular sovereignty" introduced in this act led to conflict in Kansas.

products of the Northwest increasingly flowed into the Middle Atlantic states and Europe. In this way, the people of the Northwest found their economic and other interests more closely tied to the eastern industrialist than to the southern planter. The Republican Party, founded in the mid-1850s, capitalized on the shift in economic interests. As old political alignments weakened and ebbed, the Republican Party rapidly gained strength, chiefly from those who opposed the extension of a slavery into the territories.

In Abraham Lincoln's opening speech in his sixth debate with Stephen A. Douglas on October 13, 1858, in Quincy, Illinois, he elaborated on slavery:

President Lincoln's military actions to preserve the Union ultimately led to the legal emancipation of slaves in the United States. The weight of his office and the difficult negotiations with his generals show vividly on Lincoln's face.

> We have in this nation the element of domestic slavery.... The Republican party think it wrong—we think it is a moral, a social, and a political wrong. We think it is a wrong not confining itself merely to the persons or the State where it exists, but that it is a wrong which in its tendency, to say the least, affects the existence of the whole nation.... I suppose that in reference both to its actual existence in the nation, and to our constitutional obligations, we have no right at all to disturb it in the States where it exists, and we profess that we have no more inclination to disturb it than we have the right to do it.... We also oppose it as an evil so far as it seeks to spread itself. We insist on the policy that shall restrict it to its present limits.... We oppose the Dred Scott decision in a certain way.... We propose so resisting it as to have it reversed if we can, and a new judicial rule established upon this subject.

From the southern perspective, the election of Lincoln in 1860 presented only two alternatives: submission or secession. To a wealthy and proud people, submission was unthinkable. To Lincoln, alternatively, the Union had to be preserved. The holocaust that maintained the Union cost the country more lives and human suffering than any war in the history of the United States. Although initially emancipation was not an objective of the northern war effort, it became, as we know today, a celebrated outcome matched only by the preservation of the Union itself.

TABLE 16–1
Per-Capita Income Before the Civil War in 1860 Prices

	Total Population		Free Population	
	1840	1860	1840	1860
National Average	$ 96	$128	$109	$144
North	109	141	110	142
Northeast	129	181	130	183
North Central	65	89	66	90
South	74	103	105	150
South Atlantic	66	84	96	124
East South Central	69	89	92	124
West South Central	151	184	238	274

Source: Robert W. Fogel and Stanley L. Engerman, "The Economics of Slavery," in *The Reinterpretation of American Economic History* (New York: Harper & Row, 1971), Table 8, p. 335.

Regional Per-Capita Income Comparisons

There should be no doubt that the South chose secession out of strength rather than weakness. The politically dominant slaveholders feared the northern abolitionist threats and the uncertainty of Lincoln's Presidency, but they definitely anticipated a continuation of their social order. The southern economy was not diversified and other signs, such as a lack of urbanization, suggested degrees of backwardness. But the levels of income per free person in the South were actually higher than those in the North. Moreover they were increasing at a more rapid rate.

Table 16-1 shows these figures for various regions according to different population characteristics. Note the relative wealth position of the West South Central region, where King Cotton reigned supreme. This was by far the wealthiest region in the country. Such an economic footing instilled confidence in the South to say the least.[1] And these high relative standings remain whether or not slaves are included in the population figures. When the incomes per capita of only the free population are compared, even the older, less wealthy southern areas show levels that were quite high. There can be little doubt, that on the eve of the Civil War, the south was a very rich area indeed.

THE ECONOMICS OF WAR

The South

Although there was ample southern income, pride, and talent, the South was woefully unprepared for a lengthy war. Tied to a limited range of production alternatives, it strained to shift its resources out of agriculture and into manufacturing and the production of war goods. But these efforts had only

[1] Recall the prewar scene from *Gone With The Wind* when anxious southern warriors were predicting a short war and a decisive southern victory. Rhett Butler, alone, cautioned to the contrary.

limited results, and the trade policies of the South also tended to counter needed preparation for war.

The northern naval blockade of the South was developed early, but it did not become really effective until 1863 and 1864. For nearly two years of the hostilities then, it was feasible for the South to produce and export specialty crops like cotton to England in exchange for needed munitions and manufactures. However, the Confederate government discouraged exports in the hope of forcing England to support the southern effort, and only 13,000 bales of cotton from the 1861–1862 crop of 4 million bales were exported. Also the southern government imposed a strict ban on cotton trade with the North. With the advantage of hindsight, it is clear that such policies weakened the southern war effort and helped to maintain a situation of inadequate supply.

Besides production and trade problems, the South also faced financial difficulties. For the most part, foreigners were unwilling to lend sizable sums to the Confederacy, especially in the final years when the North's naval blockade was effective. Primarily, the South's war materials and support were accrued by inflationary finance—by paper note issues.

Indexes of money and prices in the South are given in Figure 16-1, and clearly the final years were ones of hyperinflation. Whereas the stocks of money grew from an index of 100 in early 1861 to 2,000 by April 1865, the price level jumped from an index of 100 to 9,200. Once people developed

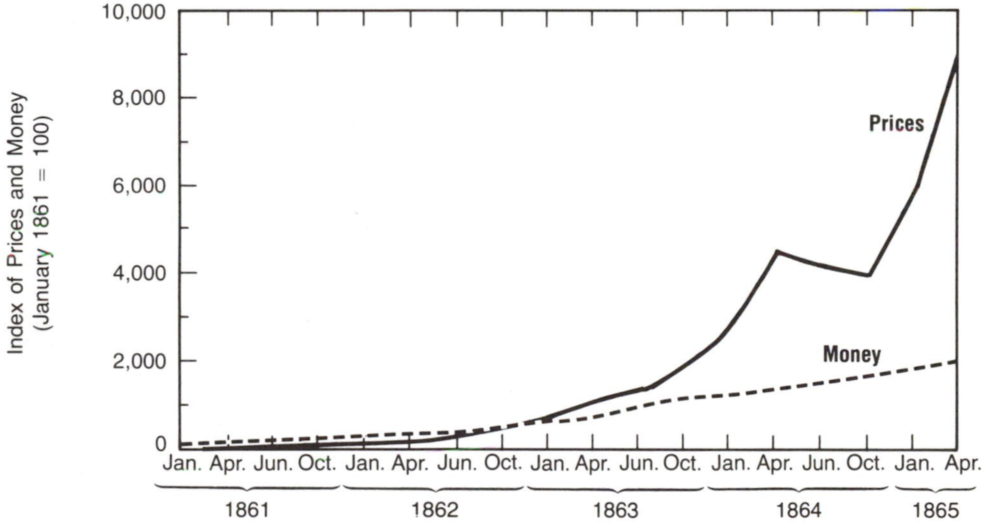

FIGURE 16–1

Inflation in the Confederacy: The rate of inflation was not very great in the beginning of the Civil War, but the value of a Confederate dollar had depreciated to about 1 per cent of its original value by the end of the war.

Source: E. M. Lerner, "Money, Prices, and Wages in the Confederacy, 1861–1865," *Journal of Political Economy,* Vol. 63 (February 1955), p. 29.

expectations about price increases, they routinely spent more money (and spent it faster). This, of course, fueled the inflation. And once a Union victory appeared likely, the value of Confederate notes declined sharply. This precipitated the astronomical rates of inflation experienced in the final months of the war.

Valiant as the Confederate forces were, they could not prevent the southern economic base from being whittled away. By late 1861, Union forces controlled Missouri, Kentucky, and West Virginia. Union amphibious forces later took New Orleans in the spring of 1862. This strategic move cut off the major southern trade outlet. By 1863, the entire Mississippi was under Union control, and Sherman's march through Georgia in 1864 splintered the Confederacy.

The North

The economic strain of the war on the North was not as severe as it was on the South, but the costs of the war were extremely high even there. A substantial portion of the labor force was reallocated toward the war effort, and the composition of production also changed. At the outset, in 1861, a sharp financial panic ensued and banks suspended payments of specie. With the federal treasury empty, the government quickly raised taxes and sold bonds. The tax changes included the first introduction of a small income tax, but the most significant increases were in tariffs and excise taxes. Yet bond sales brought in nearly three times the revenues of taxes. However, even these measures were inadequate, so the Union government also resorted to inflationary finance. Paper notes, termed "greenbacks" because of their color, were issued by the federal government. Unbacked by gold and silver, but based on the government's promise to redeem them, they fluctuated in value. In 1864, one gold dollar was worth 2½ greenbacks. Moreover, the northern price level in 1864 was twice what it had been in 1860.

By and large, the new dimensions of output in the North were modest adjustments in the various sectors. There were no major shifts or sharp adjustments that called for special notice. In fact, the most startling aspect of the war years was the minute stimuli to manufacturing. Iron production for small arms increased, but iron production for railroads declined. Although the demand for clothes and boots for servicemen stimulated manufactures, the loss of the southern market more than offset this. For example, in Massachusetts—the major state of boot and shoe production—employment and output in that important industry decreased almost one-third during the war period. Similarly, without raw cotton, the textile mills were underutilized. Nevertheless, the enlistment and conscription of men ameliorated the unemployment problem, and speculation offered opportunities for enrichment for a select few. Overall, however, expenditures by the federal government did not spur rapid industrialization or economic expansion. They were primarily a shifting of resources from the private sector into the war effort. This was a costly transfer.

The outcome of the war was what knowledgeable observers would have predicted, although few could have foreseen the prolonged civil strife that resulted from the ineptness of northern military leaders and Lincoln's strange inability to find competent commanders. The North was clearly superior to the South in every major category of economic resource. In 1860, the population of the North was 22 million compared with the South's 9 million, more than a third of which were slaves. Perhaps 90 percent of the country's manufacturing capacity was located in the North, and a similar percentage of the skilled workforce lived there. Moreover, in the specific business of providing armaments, the South was hopelessly outweighed; V. S. Clark has remarked that in 1861 the only important engineering works in the Confederacy were at Richmond, and southern emergency efforts to produce war materiels were limited and all too quickly undone by invading troops. The northern railway network was not only substantially larger but much better designed for the direct connection of major centers. Only in the number of farm units was the South comparable to the North.

The Alleged War Stimulus

It is sometimes contended that the decade centered on the Civil War was a major watershed in U.S. history—not only in political and social terms, but in economic terms as well. Of course, in terms of political change, the shifts were momentous. Charles Beard and Louis Hacker have emphasized the transfer of power from the southern agrarians to the northern industrial capitalists. With new powers, the northerners passed legislation intended to propel the process of industrialization forward, including the establishment of the National Banking system, the issuance of greenbacks, the increase of tariffs, the adoption of contract labor law, and the grants of land to transcontinental railroads. We will discuss some of these in this chapter and the remainder in Part 3; it is sufficient to note here that when the quantitative evidence is surveyed, it is clear that this war-torn decade was far from an industrial renaissance.[2] Indeed, rather than being marked by rapid advances in industrialization and overall production, the Civil War decade was a definite departure from the trends in output, income, and productivity that had previously existed.

Perhaps this is less surprising when we realize that nearly 1 million men—or almost 15 percent of the labor force of 7.5 million—were normally involved in the fighting each year. Of these working-age soldiers, 259,000 Confederate men and 360,000 Union men were killed and another 261,000 southerners and 356,000 northerners were wounded. The permanent losses of labor and human capital were severe.

For these and other reasons, the growth rate of total commodity output in the Civil War decade was only 2.0 percent per year—by far the lowest of any decade of the century after 1820. For example, the trends of commodity production between 1840 and 1860 reveal average yearly rates of 4.6 percent. Between 1870 and 1900, these rates were 4.4 percent. The rates during the Civil War decade, then, were less than half those during normal times.

[2] For elaboration on this point, see the classic article by Stanley L. Engerman, "The Economic Impact of the Civil War," *Explorations in Economic History,* **3**:3 (Spring 1966), pp. 176–99.

However, the regional differences demand consideration, and the aftermath of war revealed a distinct reversal in the relative income (per-capita) positions of the South and the North. Whereas the free populations of the South averaged higher incomes than the North in 1860, the opposite was true in 1870 by a large margin. As shown in Table 16-2, from a slight southern advantage in 1860, the situation had changed in 1870 to the point that northern incomes were more than 50 percent higher than southern incomes on the average. However, this was not the result of rapid advances in the North. As noted earlier, there was less progress in the North between 1860 and 1870 than there was in the surrounding decades. The major source of the reversal in relative income positions was the dramatic, absolute decline in southern incomes during and just after the war. The Civil War decade ushered in the economic aspects of southern backwardness.

POSTWAR RECOVERY IN THE SOUTH

It would be in error, however, to believe that the southern economy remained stagnant for long. Quite the opposite is true: As the income per-capita figures in Table 16-3 suggest, southern economic growth was rapid during the 1870s. The economy of the South rebounded from the war more quickly in the area of manufacturing than in that of agriculture, and by 1870 southern manufacturing output had approached prewar levels. In addition, the South's transportation network, based on steamboats, roads, and railroads, had been completely revitalized by the late 1860s. Actually, this was accomplished with reasonable ease; little more than making repairs and modest additions of capital were required.

In agriculture, however, the prospects for southern recovery were quite different. Lincoln's Emancipation Proclamation altered the whole makeup of the agricultural society. That highly significant "once and for all" change brought about great reductions in output, especially during the immediate postwar years. In the absence of emancipation, the South's agricultural sector surely would have restored itself within a few years.[3] But due to the political, social, and economic adjustments stemming from emancipation, regenerative growth was delayed. Moreover, the decline in southern output was much deeper than that precipitated by war destruction alone.

[3] Such rapid postwar recoveries are quite common and have been noted explicitly by astute observers from the time of J. S. Mill (and perhaps earlier):

> . . . the great rapidity with which countries recover from a state of devastation. . . . An enemy lays waste a country by fire and sword, and destroys or carries away nearly all the moveable wealth existing in it; all the inhabitants are ruined, and yet in a few years after, everything is much as it was before. . . . The possibility of a rapid repair of their disasters, mainly depends on whether the country has been depopulated. If its effective population have not been extirpated at the time, and are not starved afterwards; then, with the same skill and knowledge which they had before, with their land and its permanent improvements undestroyed, and the more durable buildings probably unimpaired, or only partially injured, they have nearly all the requisites for their former amount of production (Mill, 1848, Book I, Chapter 5, Section 7).

TABLE 16–2
Commodity Output per Capita by Region

	Outside the South	South
1860	$ 74.8	$77.7
1870	81.5	47.6
1880	105.8	61.5

Source: R. A. Easterlin, "Regional Income Trends, 1840–1950," *American Economic History,* S. Harris (ed.), (New York: McGraw-Hill Book Co., 1961), pp. 525–47.

First, the highly efficient plantation system was lost forever, and attempts to resurrect plantation methods proved futile. Assembly-line characteristics and old methods of driving gangs of workers were shunned by free blacks, just as they had always been by free whites. In place of the plantations, there arose smaller units—some owned, many rented, and many sharecropped.

In addition, there was a significant withdrawal of labor from the fields, especially women and children. Undoubtedly, this reallocation of human output raised household production, but as we know, this type of production is not tabulated in our national (or regional) income accounts. With this caveat in mind, per-capita agricultural output in the South fell 30–40 percent. In total, the withdrawal of labor was by a similar percent.[4] However, this decline in labor output was not matched by similar percentage reductions in capital and land. Consequently, the output reduction due to the labor withdrawal was less than the labor reduction itself.[5] The loss of the plantation system in conjunction with the labor withdrawal, however, generated the sharpest economic decline ever experienced by a major geographic region in the history of the United States.

The effect of war destruction on output is sometimes drastic but is usually only temporary, as implied by J. S. Mill (see footnote 3). For example, the destruction of a bridge can make unusable the connecting road and other productive capital that is dependent on part of that transportation artery. The repair or replacement of the bridge will lead to a sharp jump in output. Finding and investing in such key bottleneck areas is critical to rapid economic recovery and is the underlying mainspring of regenerative growth.

The "once and for all" losses stemming from the abandonment of plantation agriculture and the withdrawal of labor returned southern per-capita incomes to levels that had been recorded decades earlier. From that new lower base, the forces of regeneration advanced the economy at a temporarily high rate that equaled the economic growth rate in the North. Both the North and South grew at an annual rate of 2.6 percent in the 1870s and 1.9 percent from 1880 to 1900, with evidence of a slowing in the growth rate during the later years. But the gap between the South and North remained a permanent feature

[4] See Roger Ramsom and Richard Sutch, "The Impact of the Civil War and of Emancipation on Southern Agriculture," *Explorations in Economic History,* **12:**1 (January 1975), p. 14.

[5] Output reduction would match labor reduction exactly only if capital, land, and labor inputs were combined in fixed and unalterable amounts.

of the economic landscape, and conversion awaited twentieth-century developments.

In conclusion, the appearance of southern backwardness in the early part of the second half of the nineteenth century and its persistence thereafter was not a result of prolonged stagnation in the South. Both the South and the North enjoyed sustained periods of economic progress throughout almost all of the nineteenth century. The Civil War decade, however, was a major economic watershed for both regions—especially for the South, which suffered drastic setbacks from the war and its aftermath.

3

The Reunification Era, 1861–1914

17

Transportation from Coast to Coast

Nineteenth-century Americans knew intuitively that a satisfactory growth rate depended on a reliable and improving transportation system. In small groups and large, from motives ranging from civic pride to selfish pecuniary interest, they were willing to invest substantially in a system that would link every community with any pretense of economic importance to every other.

Over the decades 1860–1914, railroad companies offered a service—the fast, efficient transportation of passengers and freight—for which there was an immediate and growing demand at prices that apparently covered all costs. If a group of enterprises ever seemed likely to earn a large return on invested capital, the railroads did. Yet throughout the period, most companies were at one time or another in financial difficulties, and by World War I, there was serious opinion that the system should be nationalized.

COMPLETING THE RAILROAD NETWORK

Although the expansion of railroad systems was restricted during the Civil War, technological developments during the war years resulted in greater operational efficiency and increased capacities of engines and roadbeds. The most important development was the introduction of the steel rail. First brought to this country from England shortly after 1860, steel rails were rolled in American plants a few years later. Their initial cost was high, but this disadvantage was offset by the fact that steel was far more durable than either wrought or cast iron. Steel also rapidly replaced iron in locomotives and rolling stock. Steel wheel rims, frames,

The Victorian splendor of Pullman and dining cars appealed to railway passengers. Millionaires usually traveled in their own plush private cars.

and fittings were stronger than the iron materials formerly used, and steel boilers permitted higher steam pressures with a greater margin of safety.

Not until the late 1860s, however, was progress made toward overcoming the major safety problem of stopping heavy trains. In 1868, George Westinghouse patented his first air brake, which had the defect of stopping cars in order of front to rear—to the peril and discomfort of passengers at the end of the train. More than 20 years elapsed before braking systems were developed that stopped the locomotive and the cars simultaneously. Meanwhile, after a decade of experimenting, George Pullman produced the first really successful sleeping car in 1865, and within a few years the Pullman Palace Car Company was taking the torture out of long-distance travel with cars that were indeed palatial. By using salted ice, railroads had developed the refrigeration car and were using it extensively by 1887. As trains grew in size and durability, the cost of railroad carriage decreased, and high rates no longer limited traffic to passengers and light, high-value freight.

After Civil strife ended, the nation again turned its eyes to the territory west of the Mississippi. The Gold Rush of 1849 had produced knowledge of the fabulous West Coast and exciting stories about the vast spaces that separated East from West. Hard routes to the land of opportunity were open to adventurous people in the East. Wagon trails to California and the Pacific Northwest were beset with the dangers of blizzards in winter, thirst in summer, and Indian attacks in all seasons of the year. The trip via the Isthmus of Panama, with an overland trek through malarial and pestiferous jungles to board ship on the other side, was a nightmare of suffering.[1] The third route, around "Cape Stiff," was no less dangerous; the long voyage in slow sailing ships to the Cape, the storms encountered there, and the final reach to the California coast deterred all but the bravest. Thus, when the Civil War was over and the rich goal of far western lands was contemplated, a safe rail connection with the new West was eagerly sought.

The Transcontinentals

The dream of spanning the continent by rail was almost as old as the railroad itself. The first concrete proposal is attributed to Asa Whitney of New York, a merchant in the China trade, who in 1845 proposed to Congress the construction of a railroad from Lake Michigan to the mouth of the Columbia River. By 1853, Congress was convinced of the feasibility of a road to the West Coast and directed government engineers to survey practical routes. The engineers described five. Years passed before construction began because of rivalry for the eastern terminus of the line. From Minneapolis to New Orleans, cities on the Mississippi River vied for the position of gateway to the West, boasting of their advantages while deprecating the claims of their rivals. The outbreak of the Civil War removed the proponents of the southern routes from Congress, and in 1862 the northern Platte River route through uninhabited country was selected because it was used by the pony express, stages, and freighter wagons.

By the Pacific Railway Act of 1862, Congress granted a charter of incorporation to the Union Pacific Railroad, which was authorized to build a line from Omaha, Nebraska, to the western boundary of Nevada. The Central Pacific, incorporated under the laws of California in 1861, was at the same time given authority to construct the western part of the road from Sacramento to the Nevada border. Due to the uncertainty of the revenues to be derived from the undertaking, the government had to furnish financial assistance in two ways. Ten sections of public land (five alternate sections on each side of the right-of-way) were granted for each mile of track laid.[2] The government agreed fur-

[1] The shorter sea route via the Isthmus could cut the 6–8 month trip around Cape Horn to as little as six weeks. But from Chagres, a squalid eastern port on the Isthmus, to Panama City was a five-day journey by native dugout and muleback, and at Panama travelers might have a long wait before securing passage north. For those who could afford it, the best way to California was by clipper ship, which made the passage around the Horn in 100–110 days.

[2] The land had little or no value without a means of access to it, but everyone knew that it would increase in value after the railroad was built. The fact that the companies had assets that would appreciate, in addition to the prospect of growing revenues, made private investment more attractive.

ther to lend the companies certain sums per mile of construction; the loans were to be secured by first-mortgage bonds. Because the Act of 1862 failed to attract sufficient private capital, the law was amended in 1864 to double the amount of land grants and to provide second-mortgage security on government loans, thus enabling the railroads to sell first-mortgage bonds to the public. To encourage speed of construction, the Central Pacific was permitted to build 150 miles beyond the Nevada line; later, it was authorized to push eastward until a junction was made with the Union Pacific.

Both companies had to overcome enormous difficulties. The terrain to be traversed contained mountains and desert. From Omaha, the eastern terminus of the Union Pacific, rails were laid across the flat Great Plains. Grading problems were not severe, but obtaining ties and bridge timbers was difficult because the line traversed grasslands. In the initial stages of building, procurement of supplies was complicated by lack of a railroad connection between the East and the jumping-off point at Omaha. High-cost materials and supplies were freighted to the rail terminus by wagon.

Recruiting a labor force for the Union Pacific was not easy. The expanding war economy in the urban East kept workers close to home; jobs were plentiful, and few wished to endure the hardships of railroad construction in the West. The labor problem was solved partly by hiring demobilized officers and soldiers from the Union and Confederate forces and partly by recruiting Irish immigrants who had settled on the eastern seaboard in the late 1840s and early 1850s. The Irish found the high wages of western railroad building attractive, and many were lured from Middle Atlantic cities where they had worked for lower wages at manual labor or in unskilled trades.

Procuring the necessary labor and equipment for the construction of the Central Pacific took imaginative effort. With almost no local labor market, thousands of Chinese were recruited to prepare grades, build structures, and lay ties and rails. In the West, timber was readily available for ties and bridges, and stone for ballast and structures was abundant. But the Central Pacific was even farther away from supplies of iron and steel than was the Union Pacific. From the industrial cities and seaports of the East, around Cape Horn or by transshipment across the Isthmus of Panama, came the machinery and hardware with which the western part of the first transcontinental railroad was built. Some food and other supplies also had to be imported. But the greatest difficulty confronting the builders of the Central Pacific was the terrain itself. The steeply rising slopes of the Sierra Nevada mountain range presented serious problems of grading, cutting, tunneling, and bridging. Machine-driven tools were nonexistent. Horses and mules were used to move obstacles, but turning earth and breaking rocks were largely accomplished by human effort. Blasting powder was used whenever possible, but muscle and bone did most of the work that linked the West and the East.

The last two years of construction were marked by a race between the two companies as to which could lay the most track. With permission to build eastward to a junction with the Union Pacific, the directors of the Central Pacific wished to obtain as much per-mile subsidy as possible. The Union Pacific laid 1,086 miles of track; the Central Pacific, 689 miles. The joining of the Union Pacific with the Central Pacific occurred amidst great fanfare and

At Promontory Summit, Utah, the "Rival Monarchs" nuzzled up to one another as hundreds cheered the completion of the transcontinental railroad line. The date was May 10, 1869.

celebration on May 10, 1869, at Promontory Summit, a few miles west of Ogden, Utah.[3] Two trainloads of dignitaries, one from the East and one from the West, approached the joining place of the rails. By telegraph, President Ulysses S. Grant gave the signal from Washington to drive in the last spike. The hammer blows that drove home the golden spike were echoed by Mr. Morse's telegraph to waiting throngs on both coasts. The hope was expressed that the

[3] By some strange quirk of historical writing, the meeting place of the two trains is usually designated Promontory Point. Leonard Arrington, a resident of the area, assures us that Promontory Point extends well into the Great Salt Lake, where a railroad track would be most unlikely to be built, and that the 1869 news dispatches were filed from Promontory Summit.

fruits of the toil of farmer and laborer could now be transported swiftly and cheaply from coast to coast or from the interior to either coast. The continent had at last been spanned by rail; although transcontinental train travel was not without discomfort and even danger, the terrible trials of the overland and sea routes were over.

Yet the thin rails that crossed half a continent could not carry all the traffic to and from a growing West. New lines were quickly projected, but construction, although well under way, was halted by the Depression of 1873. In 1876, southern California was opened to transcontinental traffic by a line from San Francisco to Bakersfield and Los Angeles. Next, the Southern Pacific lines reached eastward from California to El Paso. The Santa Fe and the Texas and Pacific soon provided connections from St. Louis and Kansas City to the Los Angeles area, and the Southern Pacific thrust on east from El Paso only a little later. These southerly railroads provided the second of the three major transcontinental routes. The third route was the northern one from the Mississippi to the cities of Oregon and Washington. In 1883, the Northern Pacific, chartered nearly 20 years before, connected Portland with Chicago and Milwaukee and three years later reached Seattle.

Expansion in the Settled Regions

As the first transcontinentals were pushed to completion, railroad construction and integration elsewhere continued to keep pace. The two decades following the Civil War witnessed the competition of the great trunk-line systems in the territory of the Middle Atlantic and North Central states that extended from the seaboard to Illinois and Wisconsin. Major lines strove continuously to free themselves of a dependence on competitors for connections with key traffic points; above all, they tried to secure access to New York in the East and to Chicago and St. Louis in the West. By lease, purchase, and construction, the Pennsylvania reached Chicago in 1869 and pushed southwest to St. Louis. A chief competitor, the Baltimore and Ohio, entered Chicago in 1874, but for years encountered difficulties in obtaining a connection with New York. On the more northerly routes, the New York Central achieved a through line from New York to Chicago by 1877, and the Erie did the same only a few years later. After the mid-1880s, the trunk lines filled in the gaps, gaining access to secondary railroad centers and building feeder lines in a north–south direction.

From 1864 to 1900, the greatest percentage of track, varying from one-third to nearly one-half of the country's total annual construction, was laid in the Great Plains states. Chicago became the chief railroad terminus, extending north, west, and south, but a web of rails also surrounded such cities as St. Louis, Kansas City, Minneapolis, Omaha, and Denver. Many systems—the Burlington and the Rock Island are two examples—built main lines across the prairies from Chicago to Denver and then proceeded to extend branches into small towns in the rich farm country. A few railroads—like the Chicago, Milwaukee, and St. Paul—began as regional systems and at last became transcon-

Sherman Station, Wyoming Territory, looked like this six months after the completion of the coast-to-coast railroad line.

tinentals. Throughout the midlands, competition for business led to the entry into small towns of two and sometimes even three or four roads, where one could scarcely have done a profitable business.

The Southeast and the Southwest lagged both in railroad construction and in the combination of local lines into through systems. Sparseness of population and war-induced poverty accounted in part for the backwardness of the Southeast, but the competition of coastal shipping was also a deterrent to railroad growth. The only southern transmountain crossing utilized before 1880 was the Chesapeake and Ohio, and, except for the Southern, no main north–south line was completed until the 1890s. In the early 1900s, competitive building was still taking place in Florida. Meanwhile, although the Southwest had been tapped as early as 1873 by lines running from St. Louis and Kansas City the construction of a closely knit railroad network did not begin until the 1890s, although this activity flourished until the eve of World War I.

Because the rate of growth of the railway network varied so in different regions, investment was extended over time. Railroad investment proceeded in "towering waves," cycles varying in length from 10–23 years. Annual investment in railroads rose in peaks in 1873, 1882, 1891, and 1911 and fell to troughs in 1876, 1886, 1897, and 1920.[4] Railroad construction contributed to economic instability and at the same time served as a powerful stimulus to economic growth, accounting for 20 percent of U.S. gross capital formation in

[4] Melville J. Ulmer, *Trends and Cycles in Capital Formation by United States Railroads, 1870–1950,* Occasional Paper 43 (New York: National Bureau of Economic Research, 1954), pp. 25–34.

the 1870s, 15 percent of the total in the 1880s, and 7.5 percent of the total in each of the remaining decades until 1920.[5]

Financing the Railroads

An outstanding characteristic of the railroad industry is the indivisibility of much of the fixed plant required for operation. To provide any service at all between two points, large outlays must be made on roadbeds, tracks, bridges and other structures, and rolling stock. Due to the sheer magnitude of capital needed for railroad construction, railroad builders attempted to augment capital obtained from private sources by subsidies from government units, even after the railroad had become an accepted means of transportation.

States and municipalities, competing with one another for lines they thought would bring everlasting prosperity, continued to help the railroads, but on a smaller scale than they had in the early days. They purchased or guaranteed railroad bonds, granted tax exemptions, and provided terminal facilities. Several states subscribed to the capital stock of the railroads, hoping to participate in the profits. Michigan built three roads, and North Carolina controlled the majority of the directors of three roads. North Carolina, Massachusetts, and Missouri took over failing railroads that had been liberally aided by state funds. Outright contributions from state and local units may have reached $250 million—a small sum compared to a value of track and equipment of $10 billion in 1880, when assistance from local governments had almost ceased.

In contrast to the antebellum period, subsequent financial aid from the federal government exceeded the aid from states and municipalities, although by how much we cannot be sure. Perhaps $175 million in government bonds were loaned to the Union Pacific, the Central Pacific, and four other transcontinentals, but after litigation most of this amount was repaid. Rights-of-way, normally 200 feet wide, together with sites for depots and terminal facilities in the public domain and free timber and stone from government lands, constituted another form of assistance. But the most significant kind of federal subsidy was the grant of lands from the public domain.

Congress simply invested a portion of the unsettled lands in the public domain in the railroads in lieu of money or credit. Following the precedent set by grants to the Mobile and Ohio and Ohio and Illinois Central in 1850, alternate sections of land on either side of the road, varying in size from 6 to 40 acres, were given outright for each mile of railroad that was constructed. The

[5] It is frequently remarked that railway construction was related closely to cyclical movements of business, reaching a peak either in the year before a cyclical business peak or in the peak year itself. J. R. T. Hughes suggests that the periodicity of railroad construction was an *effect* rather than a major cause of the business cycle. See his elegant and sophisticated book, *Industrialization and Economic History: Theses and Conjectures* (New York: McGraw-Hill Book Co., 1970), p. 120. Observing that railway construction was heavily dependent on finance, Hughes argues that downturns in construction were precipitated by the tight money and capital markets coincident with oncoming depressions. We concur in this view, but would insist that the consequent drop in railroad investment made the slide steeper and the trough deeper than it would have been otherwise.

ILLINOIS CENTRAL RAILROAD COMPANY

OFFER FOR SALE

ONE MILLION ACRES OF SUPERIOR FARMING LANDS,

IN FARMS OF

40, 80 & 160 acres and upwards at from $8 to $12 per acre.

THESE LANDS ARE

NOT SURPASSED BY ANY IN THE WORLD.

THEY LIE ALONG

THE WHOLE LINE OF THE CENTRAL ILLINOIS RAILROAD,

For Sale on LONG CREDIT, SHORT CREDIT and for CASH, they are situated near TOWNS, VILLAGES, SCHOOLS and CHURCHES.

For all Purposes of Agriculture.

The lands offered for sale by the Illinois Central Railroad Company are equal to any in the world A healthy climate, a rich soil, and railroads to convey to market the fullness of the earth—all combine to place in the hands of the enterprising workingman the means of independence.

Illinois.

Extending 380 miles from North to South, has all the diversity of climate to be found between Massachusetts and Virginia, and varieties of soil adapted to the products of New England and those of the Middle States. The black soil in the central portions of the State is the richest known, and produces the finest corn, wheat, sorghum and hay, which latter crop, during the past year, has been highly remunerative. The seeding of these prairie lands to tame grasses, for pasturage, offers to farmers with capital the most profitable results. The smaller prairies, interspersed with timber, in the more southern portion of the State, produce the best of winter wheat, tobacco, flax, hemp and fruit. The lands still further South are heavily timbered, and here the raising of fruit, tobacco, cotton and the manufacture of lumber yield large returns. The health of Illinois is hardly surpassed by any State in the Union.

Grain and Stock Raising.

In the list of corn and wheat producing States, Illinois stands pre-eminently first Its advantages for raising cattle and hogs are too well known to require comment here For sheep raising, the lands in every part of the State are well adapted, and Illinois can now boast of many of the largest flocks in the country. No branch in industry offers greater inducements for investment.

Hemp, Flax and Tobacco.

Hemp and flax canbe produced of as good quality as any grown in Europe Tobacco of the finest quality is raised upon lands purchased of this Company, and it promises to be one of the most important crops of the State. Cotton, too, is raised, to a considerable extent, in the southern portion. The making of sugar from the beet is receiving considerable attention, and experiments upon a large scale have been made during the past season. The cultivation of sorghum is rapidly increasing, and there are numerous indications that ere many years Illinois will produce a large surplus of sugar and molasses for exportation.

Fruit.

The central and southern parts of the State are peculiarly adapted to fruit raising ; and peaches, pears and strawberries, together with early vegetables, are sent to Chicago, St. Louis and Cincinnati, as well as other markets, and always command a ready sale.

Coal and Minerals.

The immense coal deposits of Illinois are worked at different points near the Railroad, and the great resources of the State in iron, lead, zinc, limestone, potters' clay, &c., &c., as yet barely touched, will eventually be the source of great wealth.

To Actual Settlers

the inducements offered are so great that the Company has already sold 1,500,000 acres, and the sales during the past year have been to a larger number of purchasers than ever before. The advantages to a man of small means, settling in Illinois, where his children may grow up with all the benefits of education and the best of public schools, can hardly be over-estimated. No State in the Union is increasing more rapidly in population, which has trebled in ten years along the line of this Railroad.

PRICES AND TERMS OF PAYMENT.

The price of land varies from $7 to $12 and upward per acre, and they are sold on long credit, on short credit, or for cash. A deduction of *ten per cent.* from the long credit price is made to those who make a payment of one-fourth of the principal down, and the balance in one, two, and three years A deduction of **twenty per cent.** is made to those who purchase for cash. Never before have greater inducements been offered to cash purchasers.

EXAMPLE.

Forty acres at $10 per acre on long credit, interest at six per cent., payable annually in advance ; the principal in four, five, six, and seven years.

	INTEREST.	PRINCIPAL.
Cash payment	$24.00	
Payment in one year	24.00	
" two years	24.00	
" three "	24.00	
" four "	18.00	$100.00
" five "	12.00	100.00
" six "	6.00	100.00
" seven "		100.00

Or the same farm, on short credit :

	INTEREST.	PRINCIPAL.
Cash payment	$16.20	$90.00
Payment in one year	10.80	90.00
" two years	5.40	90.00
" three "		90.00

The same farm may be purchased for $320 in cash.

Full information on all points, together with maps, showing the exact location of the lands, will be furnished on application in person or by letter to

LAND COMMISSIONER,

Illinois Central R. R. Co., Chicago, Ill

Public land granted to the railroads as a subsidy and in turn sold to settlers was a continuing source of capital funds. Ads like this one appeared in city newspapers, luring thousands of Americans and immigrants westward.

alternate-section provision was made in the expectation that the government would share in the increased land values that were expected to result from the new transportation facilities. Land-grant subsidies were discontinued after 1871 due to public opposition, but not before 79 grants amounting to 200 million acres, reduced by forfeitures to just over 131 million acres, had been given away.[6]

It should be remembered, however, that aid to the railroads was not given unconditionally. Congress required that companies that received grants transport mail, troops, and government property at reduced rates. In 1940, Congress relieved the railroads of land-grant rates for all except military traffic; in 1945, military traffic was removed from the reduced-rate category. While land-grant rates were in effect, the government obtained estimated reductions of more than $500 million—a sum several times the value of the land grants when they were made and about equal to what the railroads have received from their sale until now.[7]

Subsidies doubtlessly added to the profits and thus to the incentives of railroad builders until the early 1870s. But the great bulk of both new and replacement capital raised by the railroads came from private sources, both domestic and foreign. The benefits of railroad transportation to farmers, small industrialists, and the general public along a proposed route were described in glowing terms by its promoters. Investors responded with enthusiasm and generosity, if not with extravagance—their outlay of funds promoted in part by the realization that the growth of their communities and an increase in their personal wealth depended on the new transportation facility. Except in the industrial and urban Northeast, however, local sources could not provide sufficient capital, so promoters had to tap the accumulated wealth of eastern cities and the financial capitals of Europe.

Thus, as the first examples of truly large corporations, railroad companies led the way in developing fund-raising techniques by selling securities to sophisticated investors. Before 1860, first-, second-, and third-mortgage bonds were issued and traded, and convertible debentures and real estate bonds were introduced.[8] Preferred stocks were used to finance railroad construction, although this type of issue was not widely adopted until it was used as a substitute for bonds in the reorganizations of the 1890s. And although the common stock of the railroads was completely avoided by conservative investors, the proliferation of such issues added tremendously to the volume of shares listed and traded on the floor of the New York Stock Exchange.

The modern investment banking house appeared as an intermediary between seekers of railroad capital in the South and the West and eastern and

[6] Five great systems received about 75 percent of the land-grant acreage. These were the Union Pacific (including the Denver Pacific and Kansas Pacific); the Atchison, Topeka, and Santa Fe; the Northern Pacific; the Texas and Pacific; and the Central Pacific system (including the Southern Pacific Railroad).

[7] This comment is not intended to pass judgment on the wisdom of federal land grants to railroads but simply to suggest the magnitude of the sums involved. An estimate of the total cost to the federal government would have to include interest.

[8] For a detailed treatment of financial innovation by railroad promoters, see Alfred D. Chandler, Jr., *The Railroads—The Nation's First Big Business* (New York: Harcourt Brace Jovanovich, Inc., 1965), pp. 43–94.

European investors, who could not easily estimate the worth of the securities offered them. From the 1850s on, the investment banker played a crucial role in American finance, allocating capital that originated in wealthy old areas among those seeking it. J. Pierpont Morgan, a junior partner in the small Wall Street firm of Dabney and Morgan, joined forces in 1859 with the Drexels of Philadelphia to form Drexel, Morgan and Company. Along with Winslow, Lanier and Company and August Belmont and Company, Morgan's house grew rich and powerful through the placing of railroad securities, particularly in foreign markets.

European interests eventually owned a majority of the stock in several railroads, and English, Dutch, and German stockholders constituted important minority groups in the others. In 1876, European holdings amounted to 86 percent of the common stock of the Illinois Central, and at one time two directorships of the Chicago and Northwestern were occupied by Dutch nationals. In 1914, Europeans who were largely English owned one-fifth of all outstanding American railroad securities.

Most American and foreign investors were content to purchase securities and wait for legitimate returns in dividends and interest. But this was not true of the more unscrupulous officers and directors of the companies that were most active in post-Civil War construction. In a day when the issue of corporate securities was subject only to the cursory supervision of state authorities, promoters indulged in questionable, even fraudulent, practices. Yet ways had to be devised to promote private gain without disobeying the law. The most common method was the organization of "construction companies," which stood between the railroad corporation itself and the contractor who actually did the building.

The construction company was organized to permit the sale of stock below par value—a practice prohibited by law in some states. The railroad contracted with a construction company to build a certain number of miles of road at a specific amount per mile; payment was to be made in stocks and bonds. The contract price was set high enough to permit the construction company, when selling the stock, to offer real "bargains" to the investing public and still earn a profit.[9] Because the railroad corporation had issued the securities at par, no law was violated when they were sold at a discount by a second party, and the construction company obtained enough money from the transaction to build the road and make a profit. This method of financing, although it smacked of deceit, provided funds that might not have been obtained otherwise. It was in the "inside" construction company that the real evils of such financing were to be found. The owners of the company were often "insiders"—that is, officers and directors of the railroad corporation. It was common practice to sell railroad bonds to the general public for cash. The construction costs were then met by paying cash and issuing common stock to the construction company, in addition to passing the subsidies on to the con-

[9]Although the value of a company's assets, plus its current and potential earning power, might determine prices for more sophisticated investors, rank-and-file buyers quickly become accustomed to receiving $2,500 or more in stocks and bonds for every $1,000 they paid out in cash. For 50 years or more after 1860, it was next to impossible to convince individuals to buy common stock in a new venture without sweetening the deal with a bond or two.

struction company in the form of land grants and state and local bonds. The higher the price charged by the construction company, the greater, of course, were the profits that the railroad promoters made at the expense of the railroad company itself.

Although not all railroad construction was financed through inside construction companies, this device was common—especially during the 1860s and 1870s—and all the transcontinentals made use of it. It was not unusual for the proceeds of security issues, plus the value of the subsidies, to exceed twice the actual cost of a railroad. The most notorious inside company was the Crédit Mobilier of America, chartered under Pennsylvania statutes, which built the Union Pacific. During President Grant's second term, when Americans were far from squeamish about conflicts of interest, this company's operations caused a national scandal: Certain members of Congress were on the Union Pacific's directorate. By voting for land grants, some congressmen were indirectly voting themselves vast acreages in the western plains. Huge profits accrued to the Crédit Mobilier. A congressional committee reported in 1873 that over $23 million in cash profits had been realized by the company on a $10 million investment—and the cash take was over and above a $50 million profit in securities.[10]

The managements of many railroads dissociated themselves from the welfare of their companies in a way that is unique in American business history. Officers and directors did not try to maximize railway earnings or net worth; instead they endeavored to maximize their own wealth. Given the choice of keeping $1 million worth of land for the railroad company or transferring it to a construction company, they preferred the latter. Moreover, the inflated building costs were absorbed in the base rate, producing such high rates that the railroads were at a competitive disadvantage. Too often managements had no normal identification with their companies, and the result was to weaken the financial structures of most railroads permanently.

RAILROAD REGULATION

State Regulations

Before 1870, a railroad usually had some degree of monopoly power within its operating area. However, as the railway network burgeoned, adding more than 40,000 miles in the 1870s and a fantastic 70,000 miles in the 1880s, the trunk lines of the East and the transcontinentals of the West began to suffer the pangs of cut-throat rivalry.[11] To be sure, major companies often faced no

[10] The Crédit Mobilier scandal unquestionably turned both public and congressional opinion against further land-grant subsidy of railroads. Recent research indicates that profits from the Union Pacific and Central Pacific system were probably not much greater than necessary to induce private venturing in such high-risk projects. See, for example, Lloyd J. Mercer, "Rates of Return for Land-Grant Railroads: The Central Pacific System," *Journal of Economic History,* **XXX**:3 (September 1970), pp. 602–26.

[11] Frequently, only two lines would compete, and it was unusual for a shipper to have more than six lines to choose from on a long haul. Nevertheless, *alternative* routings became more and more common.

competition at all in local traffic and therefore had great flexibility in setting prices for relatively short hauls. But for long hauls between major cities there were usually two or more competing carriers. The consequence was a variance in the rates charged to shippers that brought increasingly noisy cries of outrage.

Railroad managers were in charge of firms with high fixed costs, so they tried to set tariffs in ways that would assure the fullest possible use of plant and equipment. Where it was possible to separate markets, they did. Tariffs were set much lower on bulk freight such as coal and ore than they were on manufactured goods. If traffic was predominantly in one direction, shipments on the return route could be made at much lower rates, because receiving any revenue was better than receiving nothing for a hauling empty cars. And lower charges for hauling carload lots than for smaller shipments were justified on the ground that it cost no more to move a loaded car than one that was half full.

Discrimination of this kind brought few complaints. Suppose, though, that three companies had lines running from a midwestern city to New York. Roughly parallel, the lines might cross each other at several points. For the full route or parts of the route, there could be competition. For portions of the route, sometimes between major shipping points, each line might have a strong monopolistic position. Discrimination arose because the same railroad was in both a *monopolistic* and a *competitive* position, allowing rates charged for equivalent distances to be anything but equal. Rates were raised for shippers who lacked alternative rail or water routes to make up for the cut rates offered to shippers who did have alternative routes to choose from. Rates also were lowered more readily for favored firms that had real bargaining power. Shippers not favored by these discriminatory rates or by outright rebates were naturally indignant at the special treatment accorded their competitors. Railroads also discriminated among cities and towns—a practice especially resented by farmers and merchants of one locality who watched those in another area enjoy lower rates for the same service. The high costs and high prices of goods received in a community and the low prices of goods shipped out of it were attributed, rightly or wrongly, to this form of discrimination.

By 1873, the railroad industry was plagued by tremendous excess capacity. One line could obtain business by cutting rates on through traffic, but only at the expense of another company, which then found its own capacity in excess. Rate wars during the depressed years of the 1870s led to efforts to stop "ruinous competition." Railroad managers responded by banding together on through traffic rates. They allocated shares of the business among the competing lines, working out alliances between competing and connecting railroads within a region. But more often than not the alliances were fragile agreements that were easily broken under the pressure of high fixed costs and excess capacity. To hide the rate cutting, shippers might pay the published tariff and receive a secret rebate from the railroad. But sooner or later, word of the rebating would leak out, with a consequent return to open rate warfare. To provide a stronger basis for maintaining prices, Albert Fink took the lead in forming regional federations to pool either traffic or profits. The first was the Southern Railway and Steamship Association, which was formed in 1875 with Fink as its first commissioner. Then in 1879, the trunk lines formed the Eastern

Trunk Line Association. But despite their careful organization and competent leadership, even the federations eventually came unglued, as weak railroads or companies run by managers unconcerned about stability broke with the pool and began price cutting.[12] Moreover, both shippers and the general public resented pooling, as well as discrimination in any form. The result was both popular and industrywide support of legislation directed toward government regulation of the railroad business.

The first attempts to regulate railroad practices took the form of charters permitting incorporation. Some charters contained maximum charge schedules; others provided a reduction in rates if the return on investment exceeded a certain percentage. Regulation by charter was not successful because the established rates were generally higher than the railroads would have charged anyway, and no provisions were made against discrimination. Another reason for the failure of regulation by charter was the difficulty of changing the provisions as conditions changed.[13] In some states, as in Massachusetts, charters expressly allowed alterations of the provisions by the state legislature, but even in these instances it soon became apparent that some kind of quasi-administrative body would have to exercise authority.

In some New England states in the 1830s and 1840s, commissions were created to regulate certain activities of railroads. Their powers were limited, however, and none of them could control rates. These commissions were charged with the enforcement of laws related to safety and were given investigative powers to determine charter violations. They also collected accounting and statistical information from the railroads.

The first comprehensive railroad regulation came in the early 1870s, largely in response to increasing evidence of discrimination against persons and places. As the decade progressed, agrarian tempers rose as incomes declined sharply in 1873. Agricultural prices, which had started to drop in the late 1860s, declined more than the prices of many commodities the farmers had to buy, and farmers in the Middle West attributed a large measure of their economic difficulties to the railroads. Many farmers had invested savings in railroad ventures on the basis of extravagant promises of the prosperity that would result from better transportation facilities. When the opposite effect became apparent, farmers, particularly in the Middle West, initiated a move for legislation to regulate rates. Prominent in the movement were members of the National Grange of the Patrons of Husbandry, an agrarian society founded in 1867. Thus, the demand for passage by the *states* of measures regulating railroads, grain elevators, and public warehouses became known as the Granger movement, the legislation as the Granger laws, and the review of the laws by the Supreme Court as the Granger cases.

Between 1871 and 1874, regulatory railroad laws were passed by Illinois, Iowa, Wisconsin, and Minnesota. Fixing schedules of maximum rates by commission rather than by statute was a feature of both the Illinois and Minnesota laws. One of the common practices that western farmers could not tolerate was

[12] Chandler, *The Railroads,* p. 161.

[13] As we have seen in the *Dartmouth College* case, the Supreme Court declared that a charter was a contract that could not be changed without the consent of both parties.

charging more for the carriage of goods over a short distance than over a longer distance in the same direction and by the same line. The *pro rata* clause contained in the Granger laws, which prohibited railroads from charging short shippers more than their fair share of the costs, was intended to rectify this alleged injustice and was the forerunner of the present-day *long-and-short-haul* clause of the Interstate Commerce Act. Both *personal* and *place* discrimination were generally outlawed. Finally, strong commissions were given power to investigate complaints and to institute suits against violators.

Almost as soon as the Granger laws were in the statute books, attempts were made to have them declared unconstitutional on the grounds that they were repugnant to the "due process" clause of the Fourteenth Amendment to the Constitution. Pleadings in the courts were based on the premise that limitations on rates and charges restricted the earnings of companies and deprived properties of their value. Six suits were brought to test the laws. The principal one was *Munn* v. *Illinois,* an action involving grain elevators. This case was taken to the U.S. Supreme Court in 1877 after state courts in Illinois found that Munn and his partner Scott had violated the state warehouse law in 1872 by not obtaining a license to operate grain elevators in the city of Chicago and by charging prices in excess of those set by state law. Although the Munn case involved grain elevators, the Supreme Court held that the principles expounded in the case also applied to the five railroad cases then before it; in each instance, the right of a state to regulate certain businesses was upheld. Chief Justice Morrison Remick Waite stated in the majority opinion that both in England and in the United States the activity of some firms had been regulated with respect to both services rendered and charges made. He remarked that while the Fourteenth Amendment was new to the Constitution, the principle (that a person could not be deprived of property without due process of law) was well established. Nevertheless, said the Court, when businesses are "clothed with a public interest," their regulation as public utilities is constitutional.[14] The Munn case settled the constitutionality of the state regulation of railroads and certain other enterprises.

Between 1875 and 1878, however, the Granger laws were repealed or modified, and the active commissions were replaced by advisory ones that had no control over rates and little control over services and discrimination. There were several reasons for the reversal in public attitudes. One was the vigorous campaign waged by the railroads that convinced people that the Granger legislation was a mistake and a burden on both business and agriculture. The obviously questionable provisions of the laws—enforcing competition by forbidding consolidations, the inflexible pro rate clauses, and the legislative determination of maximum rates—were all emphasized. Furthermore, railroad construction was brought to a halt by the panic of 1873, and economic difficulties were cited as evidence that capital was being driven away from railroad enterprises by the harsh and restrictive Granger laws. Swayed by such arguments, the legislatures of Illinois, Iowa, Wisconsin, and Minnesota took the teeth out of

[14] Associate Justice Stephen Johnson Field, in the dissenting opinion, objected to the vague language of the majority; he went on to say that the public is interested in many businesses and that to extend the reasoning of the majority might bring "calico gowns" and "city mansions" within the scope of such regulation.

their laws. These four states retained some regulatory legislation, however, and by 1890 30 other states had passed laws affecting railroad operation.

A compromise might have been delayed indefinitely if two pressures for action had not exerted themselves. First, discriminatory rate-setting put so many firms at a competitive disadvantage that business joined agriculture in demanding reform. Also important were the actions of the Supreme Court. In 1886, a decision in the case of *Wabash, St. Louis and Pacific Railway Company* v. *Illinois* made a critical delineation of the sphere of state control as distinguished from that of federal control. The state had found that the Wabash was charging more for a shorter haul from Gilman, Illinois, to New York City than for a longer haul from Peoria to New York City and had ordered the rate adjusted because it violated the pro rata clause in the regulatory statutes. The Supreme Court held that Illinois could not regulate rates on shipments in interstate commerce even in the absence of federal regulation, because such regulation would inevitably restrict freedom of commerce among the states. This view was an extension of the opinion of the Court in the Granger cases, where the contention of the railroads had been that the Granger laws interfered with interstate commerce and therefore with the powers of the U.S. government. In the absence of federal legislation, the Wabash case left a vast area with no control over carrier operation; regulation would have to come at the national level or remain hopelessly inadequate. The public-policy answer was of more than passing importance, because it marked the first massive intervention of the federal government in the private economic sector outside the field of banking.

Federal Regulations

Early in 1887, the Act to Regulate Commerce was passed by Congress and approved by President Grover Cleveland. Its chief purpose was to bring all railroads engaged in interstate commerce under federal regulation. The Interstate Commerce Commission, consisting of five members to be appointed by the president with the advice and consent of the Senate, was created and its duties were set forth. First, the commission was required to examine the business of the railroads; to this end, it could subpoena witnesses and ask them to produce books, contracts, and other documents of the carriers. Second, the commission was charged with hearing complaints that arose due to violations of the Act and was empowered to issue "cease and desist" orders if unlawful practices were discovered. The third duty of the commission was to require railroads to submit annual reports based on a uniform system of accounts. Finally, the commission was required to submit annual reports of its own operations to Congress.

The Act to Regulate Commerce seemingly prohibited all possible unethical practices. Section 1 stated that railroad rates must be "just and reasonable." Section 2 prohibited personal discrimination; a lower charge could no longer be made in the form of a "special rate, rebate, drawback, or other device." Section 3 provided that no undue preference of any kind should be accorded by any railroad to any shipper, any place, or any special kind of traffic. Section 4 enacted, in less drastic form, the pro rata clauses of the Granger legislation by prohibiting greater charges "for the transportation of passengers or of like kind of property, under substantially similar circumstances and conditions, for a shorter than for a longer distance, over the same line, in the same direction, the shorter being included in the longer distance."

Two other restraints were imposed on the railroads by this pioneer regulatory effort. One was the prohibition of the pooling agreements by which railroads apportioned among themselves the available business between competitive points; any attempt at collusion on the part of railroads was anathema to shippers, who feared the railroad monopoly. It was further provided that railroads should publish their fares or rates for the information of all concerned and that no increase in these charges should be made without a 10-day notice.

The commission soon encountered difficulties in enforcing its decisions. Although at first the railroads complied with the commission's orders in general, companies soon began to challenge certain powers delegated by Congress to the commission and compliance became spotty and uncertain. Moreover, Supreme Court decisions in the *Social Circle* case (1896) and the *Maximum Freight Rate* case (1897) affirmed only the right of the commission to rule on the reasonableness of *existing* rates. If a rate were found to be unreasonable, a maximum *future* rate could not be prescribed. In effect, these two cases deprived the commission of the power to regulate maximum rates and destroyed its effectiveness.

For the next few years, uncertainty and confusion characterized attempts to control the railroad industry. As powerful systems vied with one another in unchecked rebating, it appeared that the whole decades-long movement was doomed to frustration and failure. But increasing freight rates and discrimination that put some shippers at a great competitive disadvantage once again aroused the ire of large segments of the business community. Even some railroad executives began to argue in favor of an "orderly," competitive environment. Still more important was the developing political climate, which became more and more hostile to big business and suspicious that it represented the exploitation of small business and the public. Thus, in the first decade of the twentieth century, it became possible for Congress to pass three major laws that closed most of the loopholes of earlier railroad legislation and made control of the carriers solid and lasting.

The Elkins Act of 1903 dealt solely with the practice of personal discrimination. There is convincing evidence that the Elkins Act, and indeed the government regulation of railroads in general, represented the wishes of a large majority of the railroad companies and that it was drafted with their support, because this Act protected them from demands for rebates by powerful shippers and brought the government to their aid in enforcing the cartel prices set by the trunk-line associates. The Elkins Act stated that the railroad corporation should be liable for any unlawful violation of the discrimination provisions. Up to this time, only officials and employees of a company had been liable for discriminatory actions; henceforth, the corporation itself would be responsible, too. A second provision made the *receiver* of rebates guilty of violating the law, even though the rebate was given voluntarily by the carrier. But the most important provision of the Act dealt with the practice of departing from published rates. Until this time, the courts had overruled the commission in the enforcement of published tariffs by requiring that discrimination against or injury to *other* shippers of similar goods had to be proved. The Elkins Act made *any* departure from a published rate a misdemeanor and authorized the courts to enjoin railroads from (1) continuing to depart from published rates and (2) unlawful discriminations.

Although the Elkins Act corrected some of the more flagrant abuses, it was deemed necessary to restore the commission's powers that had been weakened by the Supreme Court decisions of 1896 and 1897. In 1904 and 1905, President Theodore Roosevelt recommended legislation to give the Interstate Commerce Commission (ICC) firm control over rates and to plug the remaining loopholes that still permitted discrimination by various means. The Hepburn Act of 1906 extended the jurisdiction of the ICC to private-car companies that operated joint express, tank, and sleeping cars. Such services as storage, refrigeration, and ventilation, furnished by railroads in connection with transportation, were also made subject to the control of the commission. The definition of a "railroad" was expanded to include spurs, switches, tracks, and terminal facilities. The extension of ICC jurisdiction over these phases of railroad transportation was necessary because the management of the railroads could use such services to discriminate among shippers in subtle fashion. Railroads normally charged for storage or refrigeration; if shippers were not charged for these services, discrimination resulted. Another blow was struck at discrimination by the insertion in the Act of a "commodities clause," aimed to keep railroads from engaging in business activities such as coal mining that were competitive with nonrailroad firms. The law prevented the railroads from moving over their own lines any commodity except lumber in which they had an interest. All these regulations were reinforced by giving the commission the strengthened authority to require regular reports and uniform systems of accounts and to inspect the books of any railroad at any time.

The most significant portion of the Hepburn Act second to the maximum-rate provision, however, was the change in the procedure for enforcement of the commission's orders. Congress was cognizant of the difficulties previously experienced by the commission in obtaining court approval of its decisions. After the regulatory authority had made a decision, it frequently had to resort to the federal courts to make the ruling stick. In practice, the courts reopened *de novo* most of the orders of the commission that were appealed to them, allowing new evidence to be introduced into the appeals and negating the authority of the commission. The commission—a representative of the government—in effect had to prove before the court the case it had adjudicated under the authority it had been granted by Congress. The Hepburn Act put the burden of proof on the carriers. Disobedience of commission orders carried a penalty of $5,000, and each day of violation constituted a separate offense. The right of judicial review was recognized, but the railroads—not the commission—had to appeal, and the presumption was for—not against—the commission. Procedural obstacles were removed in an effort to keep cases from dragging on for years in litigation.

Surely, it would seem, sufficient power to regulate in the public interest now lay in the hands of the government. One more piece of major legislation was necessary, though, before all the obvious avenues of escape from national authority were blocked. The Mann–Elkins Act of 1910 amended the long-and-short-haul clause incorporated in the original Act to Regulate Commerce of 1887. In the *Alabama Midland* case, the decision of the Supreme Court had rendered the clause practically inoperative: The Court held that the railroad—not the Interstate Commerce Commission—could determine the meaning of "under substantially similar circumstances and conditions." The effect of the Mann–Elkins Act was to return to the commission the power to determine exceptions to the long-and-short-haul clause; permission to charge less for a long than for a short haul now had to be obtained in advance. Perhaps as important in giving the commission practical control over rates was a new power to suspend proposed changes to ascertain their effect on shippers and on the roads themselves. At last, control over rates and discriminatory practices was secured by government regulation. Yet, for all its promise, regulation had not achieved economic health for the railroads, even in the days when no other modes of transportation offered serious competition.

OTHER MEANS OF TRANSPORTATION

Domestic Water Transport

Rivers and canals, which before mid-nineteenth century had furnished the chief mode of transport for both goods and people, declined greatly in relative importance after 1850. For a time after the Civil War, some of the big arteries showed substantial absolute increases in commodity flows. Freight traffic on the Mississippi below St. Louis reached a high point around 1880. Peak tonnage on the Erie Canal was not achieved until 1889, seven years after toll charges for its use had ceased. But even on these key waterways business had declined remarkably by the early 1900s. Along the Monongahela, the Allegheny, and the Ohio, where bulk cargoes related to steel production furnished most of the business, river traffic continued to flourish, but elsewhere it dropped to a small fraction of its former volume. By 1914, half of the country's canal mileage had fallen into disuse, although the Cape Cod Canal had been completed only the year before and the New York Barge Canal was not fully constructed until 1918. Only one great nineteenth-century canal would play a vital part in the transportation system of the future. This was the Sault Ste. Marie Canal—the link that made Lake Superior an integral part of Great Lakes navigation and, in particular, made its iron-ore deposits accessible for steel production on Lake Michigan and Lake Erie.

Modern industrial and commercial activity requires speed, punctuality, and dispatch. The railroads—for all their discrimination and relatively high ton-mile rates—usually met these requirements, thereby furnishing transportation that was actually cheaper per quality unit of service than the waterways. However, some bulky commodities, such as iron ore, coal, and sand and gravel, continued to be shipped on slower vessels on a "pipeline" basis. Where annual requirements were stable and easily estimated, carriers could ply slowly back and forth, continuously picking up and discharging cargo.

The obvious economic justification of inland water carriage for this kind of traffic made it easy for professional promoters to secure federal aid to improve and extend navigable channels—many of them useless but some of them so extensive and well designed as to secure an ultimate resurgence of traffic on the main rivers. The agitation first produced results in 1907, when President Roosevelt appointed an Inland Waterways Commission to propose feasible projects. The first congressional appropriation was made in 1911 for work on the channel of the Ohio River. World War I intervened to smother the enthusiasm of chambers of commerce and certain firms for this kind of subsidy, but large expenditures on river channels have been made since 1920.

While canal and river traffic was diminishing, the flow of traffic on the Great Lakes was growing phenomenally. When waterways in most sections reached their peak volumes in the 1880s, the lakes system was just getting started. During the quarter-century after 1890, annual tonnage quintupled as the size of vessels increased and mechanical devices for loading and unloading cargoes were perfected. Iron ores from the great ranges of Minnesota and Wisconsin constituted the greater part of eastward shipments, although grain, flour, lumber, and copper also moved in quantity. Coal was the chief commodity transported west to the lake ports, as various locational influences brought important units of the iron and steel industry into production there.

Other Domestic Transportation Facilities

It is easy to overlook the electric railway in an account of the development of the transportation system in the United States. The urban trolley car has nearly vanished. The "interurban," so familiar to the preceding generation, is almost extinct. Elevated railways—noisy manifestations of the need for rapid city transportation—are being torn down. Only the subway train is able to hold its own against the encroachment of the automobile.

Yet from 1865 to 1914, urban and interurban railways had an important economic and sociological impact on the nation. Pulled by horses or powered by steam before 1890, they were rapidly electrified after that date. By 1914, slightly less than 50,000 miles of track had been laid. Streetcars and interurban cars made possible the first movement of city people to suburban areas. In the same way, the trolley broadened the markets of city retailers and opened the pleasures and conveniences of the city to country dwellers. The great investments in these enterprises that occurred between 1890 and 1914 provided a major boost to the economy in those years. As in the case of the railroads, great expectations led to over-optimistic expansion, and chicanery and fraud characterized much of the promotion. Nevertheless, even if we discount considerably the $5 billion of the book value shown on the balance sheets of street railway companies by the World War I years, a remarkable amount of capital formation remains.

At the time of street railway electrification, the automobile—still a curiosity in 1900—was emerging from its status as an experimental gadget. Fairly reliable cars were available in quantity by 1910. In 1910, 100,000 automobiles were produced, well over 500,000 were manufactured in 1914, and output in

1917 was almost 2 million units. By that time, it was apparent, even to those who had little feeling for the future, that the automobile would affect the basic structure of the economy.

Thus, the highway, after being eclipsed for nearly a century by the railroad, came back into its own. Before 1910, the small mileage of hard-surfaced roads adequate to support automobile traffic was confined almost entirely to the urban East. These roads were maintained primarily in support of the "bicycle craze" of the late nineteenth century. Beginning in 1891, however, efforts were made to move control of the roads from municipalities, where it had traditionally resided, to the state level. By 1914, state highway commissions could insist on a certain minimum quality for key roads, supervise the raising of funds by bond issues, and experiment with new surfaces and types of road-building machinery. Concrete roads were laid as early as 1914, and only two years later the federal government made its first timorous financial contribution to a national system.[15] Even with these improvements, as any motorist of those years could attest, major highways could be incredibly treacherous after inclement weather, and the estimated condition of the roads was a vital consideration when contemplating a trip of any length. Final acceptance of the motor vehicle, especially as a freight carrier, was essentially a post-World War I development.

The Merchant Marine

The Civil War hastened the decline of the American merchant marine. During the war, ships were lost to privateers, and many owners took advantage of the high prices offered by foreigners to rid themselves of their obsolete vessels. A slight revival of the shipping interests after the war was short-lived.

A partial exception to the decline was coastal shipping. Protected by an old law limiting entry to vessels built in the United States and owned by Americans, the coastal and intercoastal trade increased in tonnage between 1860 and 1914. As might be expected, railroads preempted the light and more valuable cargoes, leaving ship transport to such products as coal, iron, lumber, sand, and stone. By 1914, the railroads were carrying perhaps ten times as much freight by weight as the coastal and intercoastal fleets.

The initial reason for the decline of the American merchant marine was the unquestioned technical superiority in shipbuilding that the British had achieved. Iron and then steel sailing vessels could be built more cheaply in English shipyards, and the British were probably ahead of the Americans in steam-engine and propeller design until the 1880s. But the failure of the American merchant marine to make a comeback long after these technical differences had evened out must be attributed to other causes. One was a lack of government subsidies. The United States granted nominal mail subsidies after

[15] The failure of the United States to develop a national road system in the nineteenth century meant that travel between distant points was annoyingly circuitous until well into the twentieth century. The great 1909 automobile race from New York to San Francisco was over a 4,106-mile route. The winning car covered the distance in 22 days.

the Civil War, but these did not compare favorably with the subsidies European shipowners received. After 1891, substantial mail subsidies were granted, but the investment required to be eligible for them was so great that their stimulating effect on American shipbuilding was negligible. Another cause was the regulation against the purchase of foreign-made ships. Not until 1912 could cheaper, foreign-built ships be admitted to American registry, and then they were permitted only under certain restrictions. Finally, largely due to the relatively high wages paid American seamen, profits from shipping were lower than the profits capital earned in the United States when applied to internal pursuits.

By whatever criterion we measure the decline of the American merchant marine in foreign commerce, the change was striking. Registered tonnage in foreign trade declined from about 2.5 million in the 1860s to 750,000 in 1910. A more revealing indicator, perhaps, was the change in the proportion of imports and exports carried by U.S. vessels. Two-thirds of the value of American foreign trade was carried by American ships in 1860. By 1900, this figure had dropped to one-tenth, and it remained at about this ratio until 1915. Not even the opening of the Panama Canal in 1914 could bring intercoastal trade into serious competition with the rails.

18

Agriculture and Further Strides West

THE ECLIPSE OF THE FRONTIER

Within 30 years after 1860, the area that lay between the frontier line of that year and the West Coast was totally overrun; a clearly marked frontier no longer existed. The region was not completely settled by 1890; great tracts of land were as yet unclaimed, and not until the eve of World War I was all the good agricultural land gone. But after 1890, westward settlement, except for Alaska, was essentially a filling-in process.

The final major thrust to the West was spearheaded by two occupational groups—miners and cattlemen—who gave direction and pace to the movement. For more than ten years after the discovery of gold in California, the Great Plains and the western mountains were the only barriers to be crossed by those who sought their fortunes in California or Oregon. In 1859, gold was discovered near Pikes Peak in Colorado, and a rush to this area began at once. Simultaneously the famed Comstock Lode of silver was discovered in western Nevada. The gold boom in Colorado tapered off shortly, only to be renewed when rich silver deposits were found there.[1] These fabulously successful operations stimulated prospecting all over the West. Into the territory from which Idaho, Arizona, and New Mexico would later be carved and into western Montana flocked those who hoped to strike it rich. The last great rush was in 1874 to the Black Hills of South Dakota, where Indian troubles flared as whites overran the reservations.

[1] The output of silver was so great in the next few years that by the mid-1870s the world price of silver began to decline rapidly—a fact that was to have important economic and political repercussions.

Except for the year and the locale, one might find a favorite western figure and his or her sidekicks in this 1865 picture of Main Street in Helena, Montana.

These sharp, quick moves into widely separated districts gave impetus to the settlement of the last frontier. In the wake of the miners came the first businesspeople, artisans, and early-day professionals to furnish goods and services; not far behind came small numbers of farmers and ranchers to grow food and livestock in the limited valley areas that surrounded the mining towns. This opening-up process was overlaid with a spirit of adventure and a novel standard of moral values that helped make the far West a genuinely new frontier area in America.

After the Civil War, the range-cattle industry developed in the Great Plains and became as important to this region as mining was to the territory directly to the west. Even before the war, a few Texas cattle had been sent to northern markets, but from the mid-1860s on, beef animals moved in ever-increasing numbers to the Northeast in response to high prices. Because there were no transportation facilities, the cattle were driven overland in great herds from Texas to the nearest railway point from which shipment could be made to urban centers. The first terminal point of the drives was Sedalia, Missouri, but as soon as the rails reached into Kansas, a much easier journey was possible to Abilene and Dodge City. Cattle were fattened on the natural grasslands near these towns in Kansas and to the northwest and then sent to Kansas City, Omaha, and Chicago for sale.

For 20 years after the Civil War, the range-cattle industry flourished. It reached its peak around 1885 and began a rapid decline in the late 1880s—but not before it created cattle kings from Texas to Montana whose wealth would dominate the West for generations.[2] The railroads made possible the growth of this business, and they were also instrumental in putting an end to it; they enabled land-seekers from the East to move with little difficulty into the open range and, by increasing the number of shipping points, permitted the decentralization of cattle operations. Newly invented barbed wire made it possible for farmers to fence off their own property, and eventually the long cattle drives were effectively disrupted. From this point, cattle were to be raised on ranches, and other ways of getting the animals to market would have to be used.

However important miners and cattlemen were as path-breakers, the abiding economic pattern of the West was set by the families who settled down on tracts of land. Most of the participants in the final opening of new land came from places that only a few years before had been the object of settlement. People who moved into Kansas, Nebraska, and the Dakotas, and later into Montana and Colorado, more often than not traveled only short distances to get there. They might have settled previously in Missouri or Iowa, Minnesota or Wisconsin, Indiana or Illinois. Or they might have been the sons and daughters of the pioneers of a previous generation. It was not uncommon for settlers to move from place to place within one of the new states. No matter how bitter previous pioneer experiences had been or how drab and unrewarding the life was on virgin land, the hope of better times always persisted if only new soil could be broken farther west. Joining the restless movement of people already in the West was a continuing stream of migrants from the old East and from abroad, but these newcomers were usually content to cultivate land more intensively that had already been broken and let experienced pioneers serve as the western vanguard.

Principal New Agricultural Areas

As they did in other periods, various areas specialized in the cultivation of major crops. The Midwest became the center of food and feed production, although an ever-extending agriculture knew no precise sectonal bounds (see Map 18-1).

The Wheat and Corn Belts. To the north, in western Minnesota and the Dakotas, spring wheat gained an early lead as the chief bread grain. Winter wheat cultivation spread from southern Illinois across southern Iowa and Missouri into southern Nebraska, Kansas, and Oklahoma.[3] Sandwiched between

[2] See Lewis Atherton, *The Cattle Kings* (Bloomington: Indiana University Press, 1961). Although the scions of wealthy eastern families like Richard Trimble and Teddy Roosevelt could not resist the West, the men who started from scratch and became fabulously successful were for the most part country boys from the Midwest and South or cowboys only a few years away from the hard-drinking, roistering life of Newton or Dodge City.

[3] Winter wheat is sown in the fall and harvested in late spring and early summer, depending on the latitude. Where the climate is too cold, spring wheat is grown. Modern varieties of winter wheat are hardy enough to be grown in the southern half of South Dakota at least as far north as Pierre.

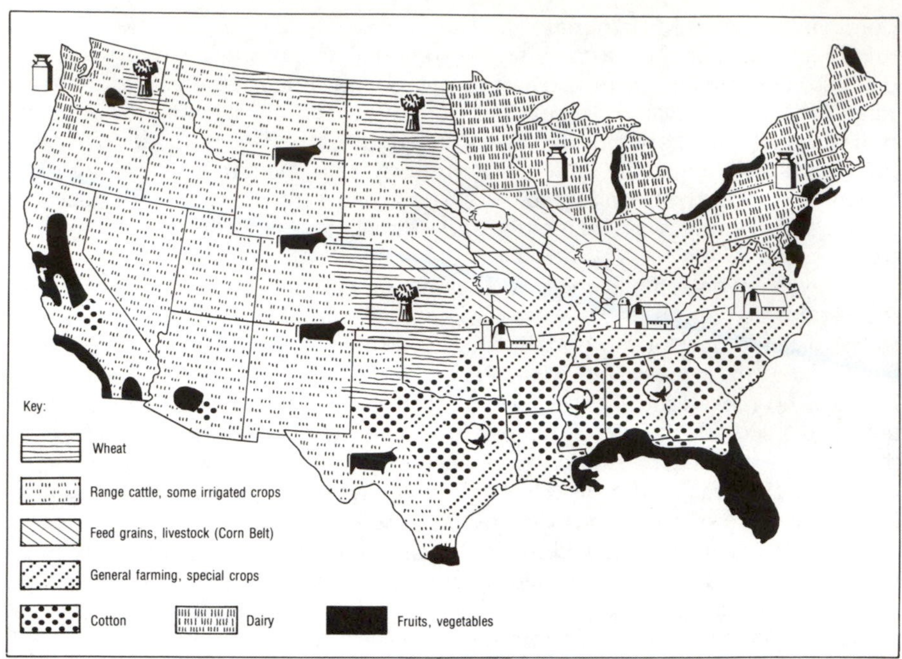

MAP 18–1

Geographic Areas of Specialization in Major Cash Crops in the United States: It should be noted that the boundaries between sections can change and that many crops are grown within various belts.

the spring wheat belt to the north and the winter wheat belt to the south was the corn belt of Indiana, Illinois, Iowa, and eastern Nebraska. Other grains—oats, barley, and rye—were also grown, but their production could not compare with that of wheat and corn. Between 1860 and 1915, annual corn production increased from 800 million to nearly 3 billion bushels. In the same period, the yearly output of wheat increased from 173 million to a little over 1 billion bushels.[4]

Cotton. From 1860 to 1914, cotton production approximately quadrupled, although there were large annual variations in output. By 1870, cotton had recovered from the disruption of the Civil War, and the trend from then on was persistently upward. The 1914 crop reached a new high of over 16 million bales, and the total acreage harvested exceeded 35.5 million acres. During this period, the preeminence of the cotton states east of the Mississippi River disappeared. By 1900, Texas was first in cotton production, harvesting in that year a crop equal in size to the annual production of the entire South just before the Civil War.

[4] For detailed production statistics, see U.S. Bureau of the Census, *Historical Statistics of the United States, Colonial Times to 1957* (Washington, D.C.: U.S. Government Printing Office, 1960). For specific figures on corn and wheat production, see pp. 296–97.

Wheat harvesting in South Dakota, shown in this drawing, suggests the scale to which American agriculture had grown by the late 1800s and the innovative methods that were increasing farm productivity.

Tobacco. While cotton was moving westward, tobacco was firmly maintaining itself as the second crop of the old South. Like cotton, tobacco was hit hard during the 1860s, but by 1880 total annual production had recovered to something less than half a billion pounds and by 1910 output had doubled to 1 billion pounds. The old tobacco states of Maryland and Virginia gave way to Kentucky, Tennessee, and North Carolina, and Kentucky remained the chief producer until the end of World War I. Even the smallest operators in the border states cultivated some tobacco, and in the mid-South it increasingly became the important cash crop.

Milk and Milk Products. Dairying, too, moved westward to form a "belt." Farmers in New England and New York had begun to specialize in dairy products for urban markets as western competition forced down the prices of cereal grains. Similarly, as the wheat and corn belts began to take shape, farmers in states around the Great Lakes found it profitable to produce less cereals and more milk products for the growing cities nearby. The soil and climate of central and southern Michigan, Wisconsin, northeastern Iowa, and large parts of Minnesota were ideal for the growth of hay and forage, and the Scandinavians, Germans, and eastern Europeans who settled there could continue to apply a type of agriculture with which they were familiar.

Fruits and Vegetables. Farmers strategically located with respect to the cities in the Northeast specialized early in the production of fruits and vegetables. As the center of the population shifted westward, this kind of specialization spread. Specific local advantages of soil, climate, and market helped innumerable small areas to become famous for a particular product. In places favored with fertile soil and a warm climate, it was possible to produce fruits and vegetables for the year-round consumption of people who lived in the North. With the introduction of the refrigerated railroad car in the late 1880s, California began to rise to a position of importance in American agriculture. Florida and the warmer states in the South entered into the cultivation of fruits and vegetables somewhat later but by 1920 were established competitors with California for the eastern markets.

GROWTH AND INSTABILITY IN AMERICAN AGRICULTURE

Technological Change in Agriculture

Technological change in agriculture has been transmitted largely through mechanization and through the application of the discoveries of pure science. Mechanization and scientific applications are not entirely independent of each other; scientific discovery may affect the invention of machines, and a certain level of mechanical development must be attained before some scientific applications can be made. Nevertheless, the distinction is useful in helping us to analyze changes in American farming.

Mechanization. In the mechanization of American agriculture, there have been three more or less clearly distinguishable but overlapping periods. The first was a period of basic invention, extending from about 1830 to 1880. The second, covering the half-century from 1860 to 1910, was a period of the extensive use of machines that depend on animal power. The third began about 1900 and continues into the present—the period of the innovation of power-driven machinery, typified by the rapid introduction of the internal combustion engine.

Until the 1830s, grains were invariably harvested with hand tools. The sickle and, in some areas, the cradle were used to harvest small grains. The most significant of the many agricultural inventions in the years before the Civil War was the mechanical reaper. By 1830, Cyrus McCormick had built a working reaper, but Obed Hussey secured the first reaper patent on December 31, 1833. Moving his main implement plant to Chicago in 1848, McCormick was strategically located to capture a large share of the reaper market, but not without facing some competition from other smart innovators. Scarcely less important if less impressive, were improvements in that prosaic instrument, the plow. Beginning in 1819 with Jethro Wood's perfection of a cast-iron plow with replaceable parts, new types and patterns of plows developed by 1850. But cast-iron plows generated too much friction in the tough prairie soils of the

High horsepower became almost a logistiscal problem before the advent of steam and gasoline-powered tractors, as this scene indicates.

Midwest, and they would not polish or scour. A solution to the problem lay in the introduction of a steel plow; by 1857, John Deere was producing 10,000 steel plows annually at his plant in Moline, Illinois. Seed drills, cultivators, mowers, rakes, and threshing machines were in common use before 1860.

These newly invented farm implements effected a surprisingly small saving of labor: Reapers of the 1850s reduced the number of workers required for harvesting by only about one-third. But wheat prices were high from 1853 on, and harvest hands cost a dollar a day. By 1860, 80,000 reapers had been sold,[5] and further impetus was given to their adoption by the manpower shortages that resulted from the Civil War. Also, steady improvements, such as the various attachments and gadgets devised for harvesting machinery, increased the reaper's usefulness. Early reapers, which threw the cut grain onto a platform from which it was raked by hand, were improved by the addition of a mechanical raker that raked the grain from the platform and dropped it to the ground

[5] Paul W. Gates, *The Farmer's Age: Agriculture, 1815–1860* (New York: Holt, Rinehart & Winston, 1960), p. 287.

in sheaves that were then bound by hand. A further improvement—the Marsh harvester, which was first used in the mid-1860s—enabled two or three workers to ride on the platform and bind the grain as it was raked.

Finally came the binding mechanisms. The first binders, manufactured in the 1870s, used wire that was dangerous to harvest hands; moreover, the wire often broke into small pieces that sometimes became mixed with the threshed grain. A Marsh-type harvester, with John Appleby's twine binder attached, was sold in the 1880s as the Deering harvester and quickly outstripped its rivals. The combined harvester–thresher or "combine," which had developed over many decades, began to be used in the 1880s in dry, level wheat-growing regions. Late-century combines used a steam engine to power the thresher, but 30–40 horses had to pull the huge outfits.

By 1900, the list of farm implements was almost as varied as it is today; the gang plow, the spring-tooth harrow, the disc harrow, and the lister were well known. Specialized equipment, from corn binders to fertilizer spreaders, was being marketed. Total animal power available on farms in the United States had reached a little over 18.5 million horsepower—roughly three times what it had been in 1850. Steam engines accounted for about 3.5 million additional available horsepower. It is a curious fact, however, that the horsepower available *per agricultural worker* in 1900 was only 2.2 compared with 1.8 per worker in 1850, both the number of workers and the amount of animal power having almost tripled in the half-century.[6]

About 1905, the gasoline tractor was introduced, and by the outbreak of World War I, it was apparent that tractors would one day supersede draft horses. In 1920, there were only a quarter of a million tractors on farms, but this number was to increase phenomenally from then on. In addition, "power on the farm" would include trucks, automobiles, and, with electrification, fractional horsepower motors.

Applications of Science. Before 1914, mechanization was more important than scientific application in the development of agriculture. Not until about 1890 was there a general awareness of the importance of the contributions of the sciences. "Book farming" was derided by the rank and file throughout the nineteenth century, and only the well-to-do and those pressed by rapidly deteriorating soils made serious attempts to apply it.

Despite this general lack of interest, scientific improvements were made during the nineteenth century. Many modern animal breeds had been imported before 1860, and after the Civil War these breeds were rapidly improved. Plant importations, mutations, and natural hybridizations were continually changing the characteristics of plants, and farmers began to select their seeds carefully. Standard fungicides and insecticides were developed and came slowly into general use. By 1890, much was known about the chemistry of soils, and the combination of essential plant foods in artificial fertilizers enabled producers in older regions to compete with farmers in newer regions.

[6] See Erich W. Zimmermann, *World Resources and Industries, Rev. Ed.* (New York: Harper & Row, 1951), p. 160, for a convenient table of data on agricultural power compiled from Department of Agriculture materials.

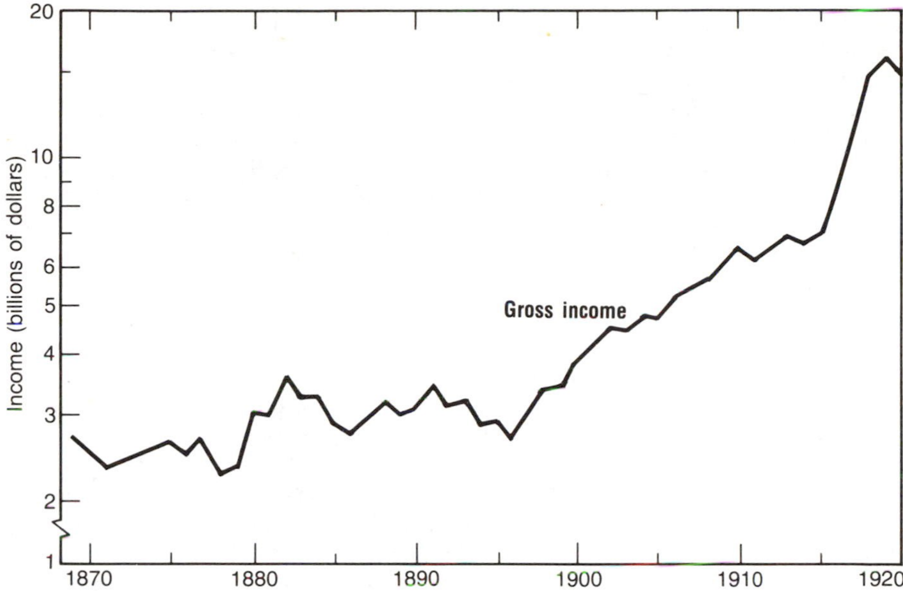

FIGURE 18–1

U.S. Farm Income, 1870–1920: Figures on agricultural revenues tell us much about political realities in the United States. During the decade and a half preceding the 1896 election, farm income languished. During the following two decades, it rebounded sharply, rising dramatically during World War I only to fall off in the postwar depression.

Source: Strauss and Bean, *Gross Farm Income and Indices of Farm Production and Prices in the United States, 1869–1937.*

The "miracles" of modern science were yet to be worked, but a firm groundwork had been laid by World War I. Methods of disseminating information had only to become more efficient for scientific applications and mechanization to move forward together.

Bad Times on the Farm, 1864–1896

The years from the close of the Civil War to the end of World War I comprise two major periods in agricultural history. The first of these, from 1864 to 1896, was characterized on the whole by great agricultural hardship, whereas the second, from 1896 until about 1920, represented a remarkable, sustained improvement in the lot of the farm population.

Let us begin our analysis of these two periods by looking at the chart of gross farm income (revenue) for the 1869–1920 period shown in Figure 18-1. Although changes in money income level are by no means the only indicator of welfare trends for a particular economic group, they are suggestive. Figure

18-1 shows that gross farm money income from 1869 to 1896 rose only slightly. Because, as the years went by, this income was divided among a rapidly growing farm population, money income per farm unit was decreasing. From 1896 on, the upward thrust of the income curve is very sharp in years of both peace and war, although the rate of increase of the farm population had slackened. Clearly, then, money income per farm family rose rapidly during this period.

From the middle 1860s to the middle 1890s, American farmers knew that their lot was hard without being shown data to prove it. Farm people were living under frontier conditions, and the utter drabness of their surroundings combined with their physical hardship was not conducive to a cheerful acceptance of the difficulties of economic life, which included declining prices and incomes, indebtedness, and the necessity of purchasing many goods and services from industries in which there was a growing concentration of economic power. Predictable of postwar deflation, the prices of commodities in general continued to decline at a greater rate than the prices of agricultural goods in particular. However, farm prices, except during the early 1870s, fell precipitously until 1878. Figure 18-2 presents an index of total farm prices, an index of total farm production, and the downward drift of prices.[7] The curve of total farm production, however, moved sharply upward, although the annual rate of increase fell from 6 percent in the 1870s to about 2 percent in the 1880s and 1890s.

One of the causes of the farmer's plight during the period stemmed from the supply of farm products, which increased at a rate that was much greater than the demand for them. Consequently, prices fell below the cost levels of many farm units. All over the world—in Canada, Australia, New Zealand, and the Argentine—fertile new lands were becoming agriculturally productive. In the United States, the number of farms nearly tripled between 1860 and 1900 (see Table 18-1). Reinforcing this trend was the increased output (per farm worker) made possible by mechanization and the application of scientific discoveries.

If the demand for farm products had been increasing as fast as the supply, there would have been little difficulty. Indeed, one favorable influence on the domestic demand for food, feed, and fiber was the rapid increase in the population. After 1870, the *rate* of population growth in the United States fell, but until 1900 it was still large. In the decades of the 1870s and 1880s, the increase was just over 25 percent, and in the 1890s, it was more than 20 percent—a substantial growth in the number of mouths to feed. But there was an offsetting factor. In 1870, the Americans spent one-third of their current per-capita incomes on farm products. By 1890, they were spending just over one-fifth of those incomes on farm products, and in the next few years this proportion tended to drop a little more. Thus, although both the money and real incomes of the American population rose during the period, the proportion of those incomes earned by farm people declined rather rapidly.

Export demand for farm products increased steadily until the turn of the

[7] Over the period 1869–1900, the average rate of decline in the Wholesale Price Index was slightly more rapid than the rate of decline in wheat and corn prices. Moreover, the real price of agricultural output remained constant or rose slightly during each decade between 1849 and 1899, except during the Civil War and the 1870s.

century, when a drift began downward until the eve of World War I. Wheat and flour exports reached their peak in 1901, at which time nearly one-third of domestic wheat production was sold abroad. Likewise, meat and meat products

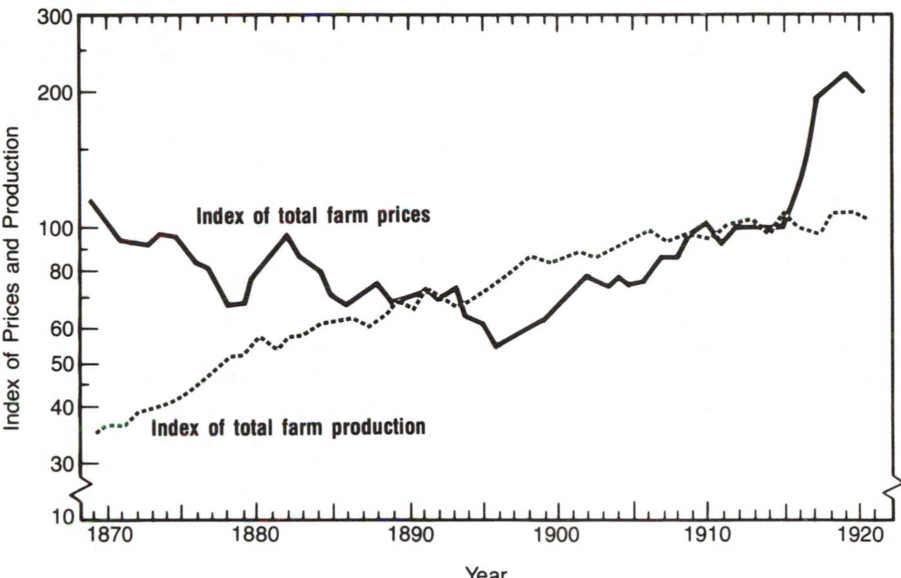

FIGURE 18–2

U.S. Production and Prices, 1870– 1920: From 1870 on, steadily improving levels of output per acre and per worker reflected great advances in agricultural technology. After more than a quarter-century of downtrending prices, a quarter-century of generally rising prices followed. The period from 1896 to 1920 is often called the "Golden Age of American Agriculture."

Source: Strauss and Bean, *Gross Farm Income and Indices of Farm Production and Prices in the United States, 1869–1937.*

TABLE 18–1
Increase in Number of Farms, 1860–1920

Year	Number of farms (100,000s)
1860	2.0
1870	2.7
1880	4.0
1890	4.6
1900	5.3
1910	6.4
1920	6.5

Source: *Historical Statistics of the United States, Colonial Times to 1957,* p. 278.

were exported in larger and larger quantities until 1900, when these exports also began to decline. The dollar value of exports from the end of the Civil War to 1896 fluctuated, and the decline in world prices during this period meant that the dollar value of farm exports did not rise in proportion to the increase in physical units sent abroad. To take a single example: the export value of crude foodstuffs (largely grains, fruits, and vegetables) was $12 million in 1860 and just under $130 million in 1896, yet in 1880 it had been as high as $266 million. Nevertheless, the value of agricultural exports rose from $297 million in 1870 to over $840 million in 1900. Exports of farm products during nearly three decades of bad times on the farms alleviated the agricultural problem, but they were far from sufficient to correct the deep-seated difficulty.

Another fundamental contribution to the discontent of this era was the entire process of commercialization. In earlier decades, farmers were relatively less involved in commercial agriculture. Reliance on the market was commonplace, but generally only on the periphery of farming activity. Most farmers marketed crops and livestock only to obtain essential tools and equipment.

After the Civil War, however, the degree of market participation soared, paralleling the rapid rise of agricultural productivity. To keep abreast of progress, the farmer needed more equipment—reapers, planters, harrows—as well as more land and irrigation facilities. This often meant greater indebtedness as extensions of credit became normal farming (business) practices. When agricultural prices fell, foreclosures or cessation of credit extensions brought ruin to many farmers. Predictably, malcontented farmers would blame the railroads, the grain elevators, or the banks for their difficulties. Such economic troubles precipitated one of the most colorful episodes in the history of American politics.

Hardship on the Farm and Agrarian Agitation

Farmers of the late nineteenth century were painfully aware of the *symptoms* of their distress. Like people of any age and time who endure such distress, they reasoned back to particular causes; having discovered these causes, they wanted to remove them, one by one, by any means available.

The rapid movement to the West that followed the Civil War was accompanied, as we have seen, by persistently falling prices. Although land could be obtained for nothing, many found it necessary to outlay money to purchase farms in better locations. Even when farmers obtained free land, it was becoming necessary to make larger capital outlays for equipment. Typically, Westerners obtained funds by mortgaging their farms, and more often than not they found themselves in the squeeze suffered by debtors in times of falling prices. Amounts owed to banks or eastern mortgage companies had to be repaid in continually appreciating dollars. If farmers lost their health or had some bad crop years, they often lost their land through foreclosure. Even if forced off their farms, they might find it psychologically easier to escape indebtedness by moving farther west or by becoming tenants on lands they had formerly owned. Such insecurity led to deep-seated frustration and bitterness. The apparent remedy, too, was plain. What the country needed was a larger and continually increasing money stock. Or, at least, so the farmers thought—and they could bring forth some good arguments to support this view.

There was another major complaint. Farmers felt that the business sector of the economy was getting more than favorable treatment under the law. For generations, there had been a strong "antimonopoly" sentiment among country people, and after the Civil War they were convinced that centralized economic power was a great evil. Agrarians wanted to take especially vigorous action against their major "oppressors"—bankers, railroads, and great landholders. But there were other oppressors. Processors of farm products, like meat packers and the great milling companies, appeared to charge monopoly prices for their products while they beat down the prices of the commodities they bought from the farmer. There was also a hated class of "middlemen"—commission merchants, wholesalers, and speculators on the recently organized commodity exchanges. Again, the solution to the broad problem was clear enough—regulatory action on the part of government.

In what has been called the "Thirty Years' War" against the princes of privilege, a number of organizations, large and small, were formed to fight for the farmers. Some organizations were influenced by urban industrial labor, and many of the ideas of the agrarians originated in the urban radicalism of the East.[8] The so-called agrarian revolt was not a purely agrarian agitation. It was neither closely knit nor well organized. There were four separate and rather clearly distinguishable movements, dominated—if not entirely motivated—by farmers in the West and South.

The Grangers. The first farm organization of importance was the National Grange of the Patrons of Husbandry. Formally organized in 1867, the order grew rapidly. By 1874, it had 20,000 local branches and a membership of about 1.5 million. After seven years of ascendancy, a decline set in, and by 1880 membership had largely disappeared except in a few strongholds such as the upper Mississippi Valley and the Northeast.

Although formal political action by the Grangers was strictly forbidden by the organization's bylaws, members held informal political meetings and worked with reform parties to secure passage of regulatory legislation. In several western states, the Grangers were successful (1) in obtaining laws that set an upper limit on the charges of railroads and of warehouse and elevator companies and (2) in establishing regulation of such companies by commission, a new concept in American politics. The Grangers developed a new weapon for fighting unfair business practices. If prices charged by businesses were too high, then, it was argued, farmers ought to go into business themselves. The most successful type of business organization established by the Grangers was the cooperative, formed for the sale of general merchandise and farm implements to Grange members. Cooperatives and stock companies were estab-

[8] For a readable treatment of this matter, see Chester McArthur Destler, "Western Radicalism, 1865–1901: Concepts and Origins," *Mississippi Valley Historical Review,* **XXXI** (December 1944), pp. 335–68.

In Granger Movement meetings like this one in Scott County, Illinois, members focussed their discontentment on big-city ways, monopoly, the tariff, and low prices for agricultural products. From such roots grew pressures to organize support for agriculture.

lished to process farm products, and the first large mail-order house, Montgomery Ward and Company, was established to sell to the Granges.

The Greenback Movement. Some farmers, disappointed in the Grange for not making more decisive gains in the struggle to bolster farm prices, joined forces with a labor element to form an Independent National Party, which entered candidates in the election of 1876. This group was hopelessly unsuccessful, but a "Greenback Labor" party formed by the same people made headway in the election of 1878. To finance the Civil War, the government had resorted to the issue of fiat paper popularly known as "greenbacks," and the suggestion that a similar issue be made in the late 1870s appealed to poor farmers. The "Greenback Labor" platform, more than any other party program, centered on demands for inflationary (they would have said "reflationary") action. Although Greenback Labor candidates were entered in the presidential campaign of 1880, they received a very small percentage of the popular vote because labor failed to participate effectively. Greenback agitators continued their efforts in the elections of 1884 and 1888, but with continued indifferent success.

The movement is worth remembering for two reasons. First, Greenback agitation constituted the first attempt of farmers to act politically on a national scale. Second, the central tenets of the group were adopted by the later Populists as the most important part of their appeal to the electorate in the 1890s.

The Alliances. At the same time that the Granges were multiplying, independent farmers' clubs were being formed in the West and South. Independent clubs tended to coalesce into state "alliances," which in turn were consolidated into two principal groups—the Northwestern Alliance and the Southern Alliance. In 1889, an attempt to merge the Alliances failed, despite the similarity of their aims. The Alliances advocated money reforms similar to those urged by the Greenback parties and, like the Grangers, favored government regulation and cooperative business ventures. Alliance memberships favored actual government ownership of transportation and communication facilities. Each Alliance offered a proposal that had a highly modern ring. The Southern Alliance recommended that the federal government establish a system of warehouses for the storage of nonperishable commodities so that farmers could obtain low-interest loans of up to 80 percent of the value of the products stored. The Northwestern Alliance proposed that the federal government extend long-term loans in greenbacks up to 50 percent of the value of a farm. Due to their revolutionary nature, such ideas received little support from the voters.

The Populists. After the mild periods of prosperity of 1885–1886 and 1888–1890, there was another downturn in economic activity, and the hardships of the farmer and the laborer again became severe. In 1891, elements of the alliances met in Cincinnati with the Knights of Labor to form the People's Party. At the convention of 1892, held in Omaha, famed agrarian and formidable orator General James Weaver was nominated for the Presidency. Weaver, an old Greenbacker, won 22 electoral votes in the election of 1892. Two years later, the party won a number of congressional seats, and it appeared that greater success might be on the way.

Populism thus emerged from 30 years of unrest—an unrest that was chiefly agricultural but that had urban connections. To its supporters, Populism was something more than an agitation for economic betterment: It was a faith. The overtones of political and social reform were part of the faith because they would help to further economic aims. The old ferment against monopoly control—against the oppression of corporations, banks, and capitalists—had come to a head. Along with the key principle of antimonopolism ran a strongly collectivist doctrine. Populists felt that only through government ownership of banks, railroads, and the means of communication and through government control of the monetary system could the evils of monopoly be put down. In fact, the "yardstick" operation of firms in basic industries was advocated by some Populists, so that the government could determine whether or not monopolistic prices were being charged.

In the older areas the extreme radicalism of the People's Party alienated established farmers who had a definite conservative bias. Had the leaders of the 1896 coalition of Populists and Democrats not chosen to stand or fall on the issue of free coinage of silver, there is no telling what the future of the coalition might have been. But inflation was anathema to the property owner, and when the chips were down, rural as well as urban property owners supported "sound" money.

Attempts by farmers to improve their condition through organization were unsuccessful as far as immediate goals were concerned. But the way had been opened to legislation. We will now review the first laws passed for the benefit of agriculture.

The Beginnings of Federal Assistance to Agriculture

The land acts of the nineteenth century worked to the advantage of the farmers, but they can scarcely be considered part of an agricultural "program." Similarly, much regulatory legislation passed late in the nineteenth and early in the twentieth centuries, although originating in agrarian organizations, produced effects that were not restricted to agriculture. In speaking of federal assistance to agriculture before World War I, we refer to attempts to compile and disseminate information to help the individual farmer. Such efforts were calculated, however, to increase productivity; they were not designed to alleviate distress, as the New Deal legislation was.

The Department of Agriculture. As early as 1839, an Agricultural Division had been set up in the Patent Office. In 1862, Congress created a Department of Agriculture, but its head, who was designated the Commissioner of Agriculture, did not have Cabinet ranking until 1889.

Until 1920, the Department of Agriculture performed three principal functions. These were (1) research and experimentation in plant exploration, plant and animal breeding, and insect and disease control; (2) distribution of agricultural information through publications, agricultural experiment stations, and county demonstration work; and (3) regulation of the quality of products consumed by human beings through the authority to condemn diseased animals, to prohibit shipment in interstate commerce of adulterated or misbranded foods and drugs, and to inspect and certify meats and dairy products in interstate trade. There was always pressure on the department to give "practical" help to the farmers, as evidenced by the fact that throughout this period it regularly distributed free seeds. In retrospect it seems that the chief contribution of the Department of Agriculture in these early years lay in its ability to convince farmers of the value of "scientific" farming.

Agricultural Education. Attempts to incorporate the teaching of agricultural subjects into the educational system began locally, but federal assistance was necessary to maintain adequate programs. Although colleges of agriculture had been established in several states by 1860, it was the Morrill Act of 1862 that gave impetus to agricultural training at the university level. The Morrill Act established "land-grant" colleges in the several states and these colleges gradually assumed statewide leadership in agricultural research. The Hatch Act of 1887 provided federal assistance to state agricultural experiment stations, many of which had already been established with state funds. The Hatch Act also provided for the establishment of an Office of Experiment Stations in the Department of Agriculture to tie in the work of the department with that of the states. After 1900, as the quality of work accomplished by the agricultural colleges reached a university level, interest began to develop in secondary-school work. The Smith–Hughes Vocational Education Act of 1917 provided funds to states that agreed to expand vocational training at the high-school level in agriculture, trades, and home economics.

Government and Land Policy

Congress passed the Homestead Act of 1862 as the frontier line approached the hundredth meridian. First-class land remained untaken in western Iowa and western Minnesota and in the eastern parts of Kansas, Nebraska, and the Dakotas, but it was soon claimed. Most of the unclaimed land then lay west of the hundredth meridian, either in the Great Plains (an area of light annual precipitation) or in the vast mountain regions.

In both plains and mountains, the 160-acre homestead provided by the Act was impractical economically, because the land was suitable only for the production of livestock, which require much larger acreages. Moreover, mining companies and land speculators wanted to expand their holdings with as little outlay as possible. At the behest of special-interest groups in the West, Congress then passed four more principal land acts. These were:

1. *The Timber-Culture Act of 1873.* This law, passed ostensibly to encourage the growth of timber in arid regions, made available 160 acres of free land to anyone who would agree to plant trees on 40 acres of it.
2. *The Desert Land Act of 1877.* By the terms of this law, 640 acres at $1.25 an acre could be purchased by anyone who would agree to irrigate the land within three years. (The serious defect of this Act was that there were no clearly defined stipulations as to what constituted irrigation.)
3. *The Timber and Stone Act of 1878.* This statute provided for the sale at $2.50 an acre of valuable timber and stone lands in Nevada, California, Oregon, and Washington.
4. *The Timber-Cutting Act of 1878.* This law authorized residents of certain specified areas to cut trees on government lands without charge, with the stipulation that the timber be used for agricultural, mining, and domestic building purposes.

There were other ways of transferring public lands into private hands, including purchases at public auctions under the Preemption Act, which continued to be enforced until 1891. Furthermore, huge acreages granted by the government as subsidies to western railroads and to states for various purposes were in turn sold to settlers.[9] Nearly 100 million acres from the Indian territories were opened for purchase by the Dawes Act of 1887 and subsequent measures.

[9]As late as 1891, an individual could buy a maximum of 1,120 acres at one time under the public land acts. Unlimited amounts of land could be purchased from railroad companies and from states at higher, although still nominal, prices.

Under the first administration of Grover Cleveland, steps were taken to tighten up on the disposition of public lands, but Congress did not pass any major legislation for several years. In a single bill, the General Revision Act of 1891, several loopholes were closed. The Preemption Act was repealed, and to the Desert Land Act of 1877 were appended definite provisions regarding the irrigation of land secured under this law. The Timber-Cutting Act of 1878 was repealed, removing from the books one of the most flagrantly abused of all the land laws. Finally, the President was authorized by the 1891 Act to set aside forest preserves—the first step in the conservation movement that was shortly to gain popular support.

After the turn of the century, the Homestead Act itself was modified to enable settlers to obtain farms of economically practical size. After 1904, a whole section could be homesteaded in western Nebraska. A few years later, the Enlarged Homestead Act made it possible to obtain a half-section in many areas free of charge. Still later, residence requirements were reduced to three years, and the Stock-Raising Homestead Act of 1916 allowed the homesteading of 640 acres of land suitable only for grazing purposes.

From the findings of a commission that reported to President Theodore Roosevelt on the pre-1904 disposition of public lands, we may take data for a recapitulation of U.S. land policy. The total public domain in the United States from 1789 to 1904 contained 1,441 million acres. Of this total, 278 million acres were acquired by individuals through cash purchase and 273 million acres were granted to states and railroads. Lands acquired by or available to individuals free of charge (mostly via the Homestead Act) amounted to 147 million acres. The rest of the public domain, aside from miscellaneous grants, was either reserved for the government (209 million acres) or unappropriated (474 million acres). Between 1862 and 1904, acres homesteaded exceeded cash sales by the government to individuals. If, however, we count purchases from railroads and states, ultimate holders of land bought twice as much between 1862 and 1904 as they obtained free.

After 1904, U.S. land policy became less generous, but by that time nearly all the choice agricultural land, most of the first-rate mineral land, and much of the timberland located close to market centers had been disposed of. Between 1904 and 1920, about 100 million acres of land was homesteaded in the dry and mountainous country. During this same short period, the government reserved about 175 million acres. Of the original public domain, 200 million acres of land that were yet to be disposed of were "vacant" in 1920.[10]

The outstanding feature of American land policy was the rapidity with which valuable agricultural, mineral, and timberlands were put into private hands. During the nineteenth century, the goal of making a piece of ground available to anyone who wanted it was largely achieved. In the process, great tracts of land fell into the hands of corporations and wealthy individuals. In the case of railroad grants, the disposal of land to powerful business interests was considered public policy. Large grants to the states for educational purposes

[10]Homestead entries were substantial in the 1920s and 1930s. Since 1940, they have decreased until they are practically nonexistent, although just over 159 million acres of the public domain remained technically vacant at the end of 1970. In Alaska, there is presently some homesteading on federal and state-owned lands.

could be justified, even though the politically favored often purchased them advantageously. But much good land was obtained fraudulently by mining and lumber companies and by speculators. Aided by the lax administration of the land laws, large operators could persuade individuals to make a homesteading entry or a purchase at a minimum price and then transfer the title for a song. With the connivance of bribed land officials, entries were made for people who did not even exist. Some chiseling was inevitable, however, and although the injustice of it rankles, it is not on a basis of fairness to individuals that we can decide whether American land policy was good or bad. Rather we must focus on the direct effects of American land policy on economic efficiency.

For at least the last half-century, the emerging consensus among American historians has been that federal land policy was economically inefficient. Moreover, because people of all sorts and conditions settled on the land, there was a high rate of failure among the least competent, who lost their holdings and became either poor tenants or low-paid farm workers. More importantly, the rapid distribution of the public domain, it is alleged, laid the groundwork for modern agricultural problems by inducing too much capital and labor into agriculture. As a consequence of this excessive allocation of resources to agriculture, after the Civil War, the new West began to produce its commercial crops at such a rate that they could not be purchased from domestic and foreign markets at prices that covered their costs to most farmers. The result was a 30-year period of secularly falling prices and languishing income per farm unit.[11]

CONSERVATION OF NATURAL RESOURCES: THE FIRST STAGE

Due to the rapid rise of the conservation movement at the turn of the present century, there is a tendency to think of it as the result of a sudden awakening to the fact that private exploitation of the land is not necessarily consistent with the public good. The political charm of one man—Theodore Roosevelt—was the chief influence in convincing the nation of the necessity for conservation. Yet from the very inception of the nation, some citizens had urged a prudent land policy because it seemed to be a good business practice and because they felt posterity deserved some consideration. As early as the 1880s, there were

[11] A 1970 study by Fogel and Rutner suggests that the orthodox view of the efficiency effects of federal land policy may be based on insufficient and statistically unreliable evidence. See Robert William Fogel and Jack Rutner, *The Efficiency Effects of Federal Land Policy, 1850–1900: A Report of Some Provisional Findings,* Report 7027, Center for Mathematical Studies in Business and Economics, University of Chicago, 1970.) The authors concluded *provisionally* that national income was not necessarily lower in the post-Civil War years than it would have been if land had remained in the public domain for a longer time and if the capital and labor introduced into agriculture had instead remained in nonagricultural pursuits or languished in unemployment. Fogel and Rutner contend that the data, when carefully scrutinized, indicate that American agriculture between 1866 and 1896 was earning returns to capital and labor comparable to those earned in manufacturing, except in the older sections of New England and the South, where late nineteenth-century land policy was not directly relevant.

strong pressures for reform from scientific organizations and major periodicals.

The first major step toward reform of the land system—the General Revision Act of 1891—has already been mentioned. This law repealed measures that had been an open invitation to fraud and made it more difficult for corporations and wealthy individuals to steal timber and minerals. Prevention of theft scarcely constitutes conservation, but one section of the 1891 Act, which empowered the President to set aside forest reserves, was a genuine conservation measure. Between 1891 and 1900, 50 million acres of valuable timberland were withdrawn from private entry despite strong and growing opposition from the western states. Inadequate appropriations made it impossible for the Division of Forestry to protect the reserves from forest fires and from depredations of timber thieves, but a start had been made.

When Theodore Roosevelt succeeded to the Presidency in 1901, there was widespread concern, both in Congress and throughout the nation, over the problem of conservation. During both his terms, Roosevelt, with imagination and fervor, sought legislation to provide a consistent and far-reaching conservation program. By 1907, he could point to certain major achievements:

1. National forests comprised 150 million acres, of which 75 million acres contained marketable timber. In 1901, a Bureau of Forestry was created, which became the United States Forest Service in 1905. Under Gifford Pinchot, Roosevelt's able chief adviser in all matters pertaining to conservation, a program of scientific forestry was initiated. The national forests were to be more than just locked-up preserves; the "crop" of trees was to be continually harvested and sold so that ever-larger future crops were assured.
2. Lands containing 75 million acres of mineral wealth were reserved from sale and settlement. Most of the lands containing metals were already privately owned, but the government was able to retain large deposits of coal, phosphates, and oil.
3. There was explicit recognition of the future importance of water-power sites. A policy was established of leasing government-owned sites to private firms for a stipulated period of years, while actual ownership was reserved for the government.
4. The principle was accepted that it was a proper function of the federal government to implement a program of public works for the purpose of controlling stream flows. Specifically, storage dams and irrigation works were to be constructed for the benefit of western settlers. The Reclamation Act of 1902 provided for the use of receipts from land sales in the arid states to finance the construction of reservoirs and irrigation works, with repayment to be made by settlers over a period of years. In this way, the idea of "reclamation" entered into the broader concept of conservation.

To the student of the 1970s who is concerned with contemporary problems of the environment, such achievements seem modest enough. But in the first decade of the twentieth century, many bitterly opposed any interference with the private exploitation of the remaining public domain. The controversy became a matter of the East versus the New West. Westerners argued that settlers in the older parts of the country had once had *their* feet in the trough and that the same principles should apply in the West until settlement was complete. Easterners rejoined that the West was full of wicked people who would not rest until they had despoiled the land. Westerners contended that without free access to natural resources, the development of the new states would come to an end; easterners had hard things to say about the harm that was being done to generations as yet unborn. And there were divisions within the sections. The large western timber interests, for example, were in favor of conservation. The withdrawal by the government of supplies of timber from the market meant higher lumber prices, and large companies were in a favorable position to buy trees from the national forests. In the East, on the other hand, some people had misgivings about government ownership of reclamation projects, fearing that such doctrines might some day be applied to easterners.

Theodore Roosevelt was aware of these deep-seated differences. As he neared the end of his second term, he feared that without stronger popular support, his conservation program might eventually disintegrate. For this reason, Roosevelt called a conference of state governors in Washington in May of 1908. "The object of the meeting was to create a uniform public sentiment looking to the conservation of all natural resources and their ultimate complete utilization in the manner which would yield the most profit with the least waste, so that these resources might be passed down to future generations unimpaired save by unavoidable wear and tear."[12] The conference received wide publicity and led to the creation of the National Conservation Commission, with Gifford Pinchot as chairman. Early in 1909, the findings of the commission were published in three volumes, furnishing a wealth of material in support of the conservation cause. Roosevelt enlisted widespread voter support, even among westerners, but more importantly, he secured the active cooperation and assistance of leaders in many fields.

The achievements of the Roosevelt Administration were not undone by the anticonservationists in the years that followed. In fact, halting forward steps were taken in the Taft and Wilson administrations. By the Withdrawal Act of 1910, all known coal, oil, gas, and phosphate lands remaining in the public domain were reserved, and the practice of creating Naval Oil Reserves began in 1912. The Weeks Act of 1911 empowered the federal government to *purchase* forest lands in the Appalachian and White mountains, ostensibly for the purpose of protecting watersheds to maintain the navigability of streams. Henceforth, the East was to be included in conservation programs, and the power of the government to extend its conservation activities beyond the lands in the public domain was established. During the Wilson Administration, the chief controversy centered on the disposition of public power sites. A Supreme Court decision of 1917 affirmed the right of the federal government to do with these sites as it saw fit, and the argument was temporarily concluded with the passage of the Federal Power Act of 1920. This law provided that private companies could lease land containing water power sites for a period not to exceed 50 years; at the end of the period, the government could renew the lease or purchase any plant and equipment of the leasing company.

[12] Roy M. Robbins, *Our Landed Heritage* (Princeton: Princeton University Press, 1942), p. 355.

It seems sensible that the government should have taken steps to prevent the unnecessary waste of its dwindling resources at the end of the nineteenth century. There is little question, however, that the early conservationists overstated their case. They failed to see that technological advances would enable industrialists to use old materials more efficiently and new materials to the eventual exclusion of the old. They did not realize that the estimated reserves of some minerals, especially petroleum, would be raised again and again. Nor did the conservationists of an earlier day direct sufficient attention to more serious kinds of resource depletion—soil erosion, the pollution of air and water, and drastic ecological disturbance. A different emphasis would come with the inauguration of a second Roosevelt, but not for two generations would the problem of the conservation of resources erupt in all its perplexing and frightening dimensions.

19

Industrial Expansion

During the half-century that lay between the end of one great war and the beginning of another, the American economy assumed most of its modern characteristics. The most impressive change was the shift from an agricultural to an industrial economy. Until the decade of the 1880s, agriculture was the chief generator of income in the United States. The census of 1890 reported that manufacturing output was greater in dollar value than farm output, and by 1900 the annual value of manufactures was more than twice that of agricultural products. Relative to the rest of the world, American gains in manufacturing output were phenomenal. In the mid-1890s, the United States became the leading industrial power, and by 1910 its factories poured forth goods of nearly twice the value of those of its nearest rival, Germany. In 1913, the United States accounted for more than one-third of the world's industrial production.

Industrialization and its concomitant, urbanization, have been the persistent and readily measurable characteristics of the process of American economic growth for well over a century. As a measure of the increasing importance of industrial output, we can compare the changing shares of the two chief commodity-producing sectors—agriculture and industry—in the income generated by the two sectors.[1] Table 19-1 shows, for the period 1859–1919, the steady and inexorable rise in industry's share of value added by commodity production. Industry's share moved from 38 percent in 1859

[1] As time has progressed, services, as distinct from commodities, have become an increasingly important part of national output. However, the comparison made in Table 19-1 gives a good picture of the pace of industrialization up to 1920.

to 65 percent in 1919, while agriculture's share dropped from 62 percent to 35 percent over the same period. In only one of the decennial intervals, 1899–1909, was the persistent rise in industry's share arrested.

Of course, the question arises: To what degree did the decline in agriculture's share of value added result from price trends that were favorable or unfavorable to the agricultural sector? The figures in the Constant Prices column are revealing. Once price changes are taken into account, the final conclusions are essentially the same. Yet the interesting finding emerges that relative prices moved in such a way as to *moderate* the decline of agriculture, especially after 1899.[2]

Europeans were no less concerned than Americans about developing a solid foundation of manufactures, but American experience differed in two respects from that of the older nations. First, the industrial products of the United States were sold primarily in the home market; not until late in the nineteenth century did most American manufacturers aggressively seek major outlets in foreign countries. Their own nation provided an expanding free-trade area protected by high tariffs, and within it enterprisers found more than satisfactory markets except in times of prolonged depression. Second, and perhaps more important, was the fact of considerable national self-sufficiency. In large part, western European countries brought raw materials from overseas to workers steeped in a tradition of fine craftsmanship. In contrast, "the industrial progress of the United States was the result of carrying labor to raw materials."[3] It might be added that the labor brought to the raw materials was, on the whole, unskilled and unspecialized.

TECHNOLOGICAL CHANGE AND THE INCREASING SIZE OF THE FIRM

Mechanization and Changes in Processes: Nondurable Consumer Goods

As we learned in Chapter 13, widespread substitution of machines for hand methods was underway by the mid-1850s. Indeed, invention and innovation continued throughout the nineteenth century.

We will now pick up a thread of the previous narrative by considering the textile industries, because it was in the processing of fibers that machines first proved themselves. In no other field had power-driven machines been so successful before the Civil War, and improvements during the latter part of the nineteenth century were in the direction of achieving greater automaticity. Ring spinning, which had been invented about 30 years before the Civil War, was perfected and as early as 1870 became the dominant type of spinning in

[2] Robert E. Gallman and Edward S. Howle, "Trends in the Structure of the American Economy Since 1840," in *The Reinterpretation of American Economic History,* Robert W. Fogel and Stanley L. Engerman (eds.), (New York: Harper & Row, 1971), pp. 25–27.

[3] V.S. Clark, *History of Manufactures in the United States,* Vol. II (New York: McGraw-Hill Book Co., 1929), p. 2.

TABLE 19–1
Shares of Value Added in Agriculture and Industry, 1849–1919, Current and Constant Prices (percentage)

	1849	1859	1869	1879	1889	1899	1909	1919
Current Prices								
Agriculture	61	62	57	53	39	37	38	35
Industry	39	38	43	47	61	63	62	65
Constant Prices								
Agriculture	64	61	57	53	41	35	26	22
Industry	36	39	43	47	59	65	74	78

American cotton mills. Ring spindles made it possible to draw, twist, and wind yarn simultaneously, making processing continuous. A major advantage of the rings was that they could be operated by unskilled or semiskilled labor, whereas mules (machines that both spun the yarn and wound it onto spindles) were run by skilled workers. Moreover, unskilled ring operators were less likely to form strong labor unions than skilled mule spinners, and American textile manufacturers detested union organization. Finally, automatic looms required the stronger yarns produced by ring spinning, and manufacturers who wished to introduce automatic weaving were almost certain to opt for ring frames.[4]

The outstanding development in the textile industries was the commercial success of the Northrup automatic loom in 1895. For decades, power looms had been in general use, and operations had become smoother as time passed. Yet two considerable difficulties remained after nearly a century of practical use. When the shuttle ran out of yarn, operations had to cease while a weaver inserted a new bobbin, and when a warp thread broke it was necessary to stop the loom by hand. Automatic looms, such as the Northrup loom, were provided with devices that ejected empty bobbins and inserted fresh ones during the split-second interval in which the shuttle rests between movements across the loom. Furthermore, these looms stopped automatically when a thread broke, so that constant surveillance by a weaver was not necessary. After 1900, further strides were made toward automaticity. Of special importance were the tying-in and drawing-in machines that made possible the mechanical attachment of new warp threads to those already in the loom.

Many other changes took place simultaneously in the clothing industries, or "needle trades." We saw earlier how the sewing machine led to some factory production of clothing in the 1850s. During the Civil War, mechanization of the men's branch of the clothing industry increased rapidly. Standardized sizes were derived from measurements for soldiers' uniforms taken by the Army, and the problem of achieving approximate fit was solved. Beginning in the 1870s, rotary cutting machines and reciprocating knives made it possible to cut several thicknesses of cloth at once. By 1895, sewing machines had been im-

[4] For an intriguing discussion of economic influences on technological change, see Lars G. Sandberg, "American Rings and English Mules: The Role of Economic Rationality," *Quarterly Journal of Economics,* **LXXXIII**:1 (February 1969), pp. 25–43.

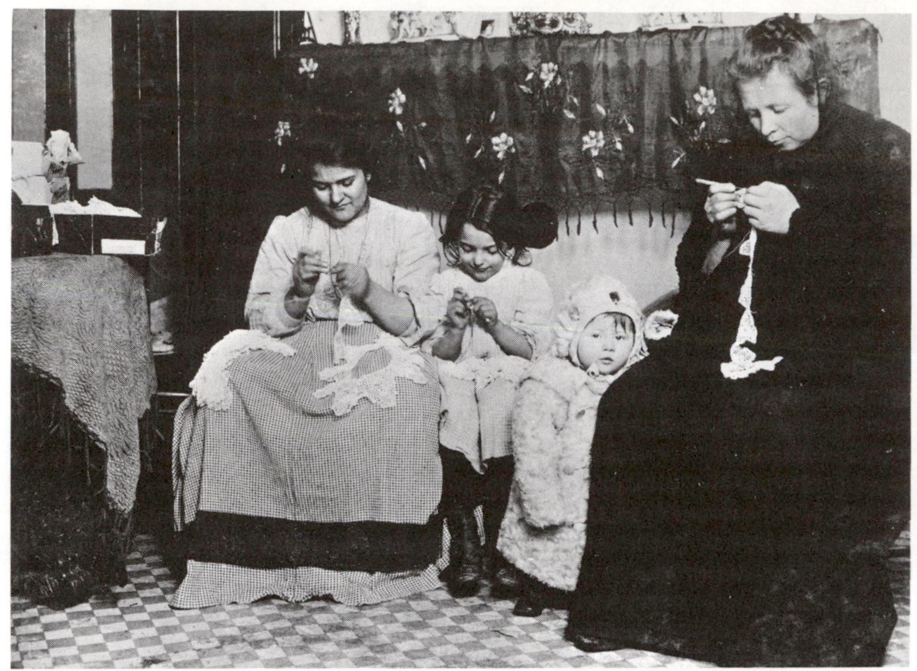

Although mechanization in the clothing industry was well advanced by the turn of the twentieth century, many hand operations and home-production methods remained, as this photograph by Lewis Hine, circa ***1900, illustrates.***

proved to the point that, power driven, they could operate at speeds of 1,600, 2,200 and 2,800 stitches per minute. Well before World War I, pressing machines were replacing hand irons. Because of style considerations, women's dresses were usually made in the home or by a dressmaker until the very end of the nineteenth century, but by 1900 coats were made in factories, as were hosiery and underwear. Even after mechanization, many hand operations were still required in the making of outer garments. As late as 1920 only half the workers in the garment industries were machine operators or helpers.

The subject of apparel leads us to mention leather and shoe production. During the half-century before 1860, the shoe industry had passed from the craft shop into the merchant–employer stage and was moving rapidly into factory production. It was only in the decade or so before the Civil War that manufactured shoes were shaped for the left and the right foot; consequently, ladies and gentlemen had their footwear custom made and continued to do so for a long time. Manufacturers, however, eventually realized that design, finish, and attention to size and fit were necessary to secure a broad market for factory-made shoes. In 1875, they introduced the Goodyear welt process, which enabled soles to be attached to uppers without allowing nails and stitches to penetrate the inside of the shoe. Within the next 20 years or so, machines were devised to do the work of lasting, eyeleting, heeling, and so on. By 1914, the industry was highly mechanized.

In the food industries, changes were unspectacular but persistent and important. Innovations in food processing, plus rapid urbanization, led to the removal of much food preparation from the home. Consider the flour-milling industry. Even in colonial times, some of the great mills were almost completely mechanized and were the earliest examples of continuous-process manufacture. Until after the Civil War, there was little change in methods or techniques. Thereafter, technological changes were rapid and were followed by increases in the size of mills. Greater size enabled the mill to draw its supply of wheat from a large area, so that many types of wheat could be blended to obtain a flour of uniform quality. For the little baker's shop, a standardized flour was not crucial; for the commercial baker, it was.

The cracker and biscuit division of the industry was mechanized earlier than the bread-baking division and before the turn of the twentieth century had begun to expand rapidly. By 1910, it was apparent that the bread-baking division would shortly begin to perform the arduous work previously accomplished in the kitchen. During World War I, the trend away from bread baking in the home was rapid, but the commercial unit remained characteristically small. Advances in mechanization and therefore in the size of bakeries have been post-1920 developments.

At the same time that bread made outside the home became obtainable for most consumers, a steady, safe supply of meat entered city markets. Cured pork had long been furnished to the eastern market by western packers, but fresh beef and pork were supplied by local packers, and even they had to confine their slaughtering to cold months because of spoilage. The West had a great cost advantage in the production of meat animals, but livestock could be transported to major markets only with prohibitive weight losses. Clearly, some practical means of refrigerating, both in slaughterhouses and in railroad cars, had to be devised before western beef could be transported economically to eastern markets. By 1870, slaughterhouses had rooms refrigerated by ice, and shortly thereafter a Swift employee, by circulating air in an iced boxcar, made possible the long-distance shipment of perishable fresh beef. The bitter opposition of local packers could only briefly delay the advent of a cheaper and more reliable source of meat. By 1880, the rise to dominance of the great national meat packers was well underway. With the opening of national markets, the large houses increasingly utilized the output of by-products, thereby reducing meat costs. The technique of the assembly line (operating in reverse) had its first great acceptance in the relatively simple process of preparing meat animals for market.

By 1920, city people could find a large number of staple items in cans on the grocer's shelves; indeed, except for meat specialties, the variety of canned goods was about as great at the close of World War I as it is today. The Civil War experience of Union soldiers had done much to gain acceptance for canned milk and the commoner fruits and vegetables. By the late 1880s, consumers of modest means could obtain over a counter nearly all of the commodities that only 25 years before they had laboriously "put up." The canning industry, thus firmly established, rapidly improved its operations along two main lines. More was learned about making canned foods safer and more palatable—from the chemistry and bacteriology of processing to the temperature and pressure at which different foods should be cooked. Important in bringing about typical factory production was the introduction of machine-made cans, the automatic soldering of can tops, and machines for filling cans. By the turn of the century, even the process of getting vegetables and fruits ready for canning had been mechanized.

Mechanization and Changes in Processes: Producer Goods

Iron and Steel. It will be recalled from Chapter 13 that between 1815 and 1850 three innovations in iron manufacture were adopted: the rolling of bars and plates, the "puddling" of pig iron (to make merchant bar), and the use of anthracite coal and then coke in the reduction process. By the middle of the nineteenth century, tough, fibrous, malleable, noncorrosive wrought iron and hard, brittle, nonmalleable cast iron were available in quantity to machine makers. The wrought iron was too costly for many uses, and, although suitable for agricultural implements, it lacked tensile strength and could not withstand the stresses and strains that the greater speeds and heavier structures of industry were beginning to require. The brittleness of cast iron, on the other hand, ruled it out for most purposes. There was an obvious need for a cheap, multipurpose metal with high malleability and toughness and the ability to withstand strain without distortion.

For centuries, producers knew how to make steel in small quantities. As late as 1850, high-carbon steel, used chiefly in the manufacture of cutlery and certain tools, was a scarce and expensive commodity. It was made in a crucible or pot by melting wrought iron and then carefully adding carbon. The steel of the future was to be a relatively low-carbon product made by the so-called *indirect* process—indirect in the sense that the iron is first reduced in a blast furnace and then refined or converted into steel in a second step.

The first successful method of making steel in quantity was invented almost simultaneously by an Englishman, Henry Bessemer, and by an American ironmaster, William Kelly. There is reason to believe that Kelly may actually have been the first to conceive the concept, but the fame and fortune fell to Bessemer. In the Bessemer–Kelly process, hot air is blown through molten pig iron, so that the oxygen in the air ignites and burns out the chief impurities, carbon and silicon. Although Bessemer presented his idea in a paper read in 1856, several years of experimentation followed before commercial production was possible. And almost as soon as the first operations began in 1864, Bessemer was denounced as an imposter by some manufacturers who found that the method did not work.

Only a little while after Bessemer and Kelly invented substantially the same process, the open-hearth method reached experimental status. Inventors were trying to find a way of making cheap steel without infringing on Bessemer's patents. They were also trying to overcome some of the deficiencies of Bessemer's process—including the fact that the method was so quick there was not sufficient time to test the steel for carbon content, so that the manufacturer could never be certain for what purposes a given batch would be suitable. The best work in this new direction was accomplished by William and Friedrich Siemens in England and Émile and Pierre Martin in France. By 1868, the main features of the open-hearth or Siemens–Martin process had been developed. Instead of a cylindrical converter that could be tipped like a huge kettle, the open-hearth method employed a furnace with a shallow, open container holding a charge of molten pig iron, scrap iron, limestone, and even some iron ore.

Several considerations made the open-hearth process more economical than the Bessemer process. A large charge required about 12 hours compared to 10–15 minutes for a Bessemer "blow," but during the long refining period open-hearth steel could be sampled and its chemical composition could be adjusted to exact requirements. The open-hearth furnace also had a cost advantage over the Bessemer converter in that scrap iron and iron ore could be charged with the more expensive molten pig iron. The regeneration principle, by which the open-hearth furnace made use of hot gases drawn from nearby coke ovens or blast furnaces to melt and refine the charge, was highly efficient.

Increases in size of furnace and efficiency of operation followed these changes. In 1860, good blast furnaces produced 7–10 tons of pig iron a day; 25 years later, 75–100 tons a day was the maximum, and by 1900 a daily output of 500 tons or more, with markedly less coke consumption, was common. During these years, methods of handling material improved greatly, regenerative heating of the blast was developed, blowing equipment was strengthened, and coke entirely superseded anthracite and bituminous coal as a fuel.

Perhaps the major accomplishment of the industry during that period was the integration of processes that led to great savings in heat. Coke ovens were eventually placed close to blast furnaces to avoid heat loss. Blast furnaces, in turn, were placed near steel furnaces (either Bessemer or open hearth), so that molten pig iron could be delivered directly to them. Finally, converters and open hearths were situated near the roughing mills, so that the first rolling could be accomplished as quickly as possible with a minimum of reheating. There were, to be sure, other economies resulting from integration—the most notable being a savings in the handling of materials and in the administration of the entire process.

Although introduced shortly after the Bessemer method, the open-hearth steel method actually lagged far behind until the 1890s, since Bessemer steels were eminently satisfactory for rails, which constituted the first great demand for the new product. Eventually, however, as the engineers grew familiar with the characteristics of steel, they became convinced that plates and structural shapes made of Bessemer steel contained defects that did not appear in the open-hearth product. The consequence of this preference was that some rolling mills had to build open-hearth furnaces to meet the new demand. Furthermore, the costs of open-hearth processing were much lower than these costs of the Bessemer process, not only because scrap could be used but also because small operators could build and operate plants far smaller than those needed for a Bessemer operation. Moreover, small owners did not have to fear being "held up" by the large companies that controlled the Bessemer ores. By 1910, the open hearth had clearly won out over the Bessemer converter; of the 26 million tons of steel produced in that year, the open-hearth process ac-

Steel manufacture required unprecedented amounts of capital in the form of great furnaces and mechanical aids as well as skilled workers who were able to judge when the time was ripe to tap Bessemer converters like these.

counted for 63 percent and the Bessemer process for only 36 percent; from this time on, the annual output of the Bessemer method decreased steadily.[5]

The second major development before World War I was the increasing use of alloy steels. Nothing compared to the volume of output during and after World War II was achieved, but the end of World War I saw the United States as the global leader in ferroalloy production. Like nearly all the principal innovations in the technology of steelmaking, the idea of obtaining great hardness by bringing other metals into the composition of steel originated in Europe. Chrome steel was known by 1821, and a process for making nickel steel was patented in France in 1876. Ten years later, the Bethlehem Steel Works purchased patent rights for the latter process, and in 1890 the company was making nickel steel plates for the Navy. The decade of the 1890s saw the steady introduction of alloy steels in the making of gear wheels and die castings, and by 1900 Bethlehem was producing tool steel. Besides chrome and nickel, tungsten, molybdenum, manganese, vanadium, titanium, and other metals—all familiar to the modern layman—were in use by 1905; five years later, over 500,000 tons of alloy steel were produced annually. To satisfy the growing demands of the machine-tool and automobile industries, large amounts of the ferroalloys were also imported, but World War I forced American manufacturers to meet most of these requirements themselves.

Nonferrous Metals. Other metals quantitatively far less important than steel have played a vital part in the growth of the capital goods industries. Of the nonferrous metals, copper and aluminum rank after steel in tonnage and fulfillment of essential functions.

Copper played no major role in the life of Americans until late in the nineteenth century. Then, due to its property of electrical conductivity, copper became an essential material to U.S. industry when electricity was developed as a major source of power.

Deposits of pure copper were quickly exhausted; the chief sources in modern times have been ores containing copper oxides and copper sulfides. Unlike iron ores, which may contain as much as 60 percent iron, copper ores are "rich" if they are as much as 7 percent copper. The sulfides, which since 1910 have been the principal ores, contain 1 percent or less of copper. Because of the low copper content of the available ores, a process of "concentration" must precede reduction, and it was the discovery, around 1914, of a new way of concentrating—by the "froth flotation" method—that made it practical to use previously unexploited low-yield reserves.

A striking and significant development in metals technology took place when aluminum was made available for industrial purposes. The most common of the metallic elements, aluminum long defied efforts to separate it from the minerals with which it is found. Aluminum was first obtained in a pure form early in the nineteenth century, but for many decades it remained in the "precious" metals class, and was obtainable only in the scientific laboratory. European scientists worked first on chemical rather than electrolytic processes

[5] For details of iron and steel output changes, see Peter Temin, *Iron and Steel in Nineteenth-Century America* (Cambridge, Mass.: M.I.T. Press, 1964).

of separating the pure aluminum. Their first major step toward success was the extraction of aluminum oxide, or alumina, from the ore, bauxite. As so frequently happens when a number of minds turn seriously to the solution of a problem, two men almost simultaneously discovered an economic method of reducing alumina. In 1886, Charles Martin Hall, a student at Oberlin College, and Paul Hiroult, a young Frenchman, successfully separated the aluminum by passing an electric current through a mixture of cryolite and alumina. The electrolytic process made it possible to produce the light metal in quantity, and the rise of commercial output in the 1890s paralleled the availability of cheap electricity on a large scale. This is another important example of the interdependency of technological advances.[6] At first confined to the manufacture of trinkets and cooking utensils, by the twentieth century aluminum, sometimes alloyed with steel, was gaining acceptance as a structural material and as cable for power transmission. The advent of the automobile increased the demand for aluminum and adumbrated the growing need for light metals. But it was not until the expansion of aircraft production in World War I, that aluminum began to take its place in the economic sun.

Metalworking Machinery

Improvements in metals processing made possible rapid advances in the design of metalworking machinery. For some years after the Civil War, Great Britain led in the production of such machinery, and the French and the Germans largely copied their efforts. Until at least 1900, the English maintained their superiority in heavy machinery manufacture, whereas Americans excelled in making light machine tools.

Metalworking machinery consists of two main types of power-driven machines: (1) shaping or forming machines, which press, forge, hammer, and the like, and (2) machines that cut metal, such as gear-cutting, grinding, and milling machines. The latter are called machine tools. Except for a few expensive toys produced by do-it-yourself addicts, metalworking machines are pure capital goods that are always sold in the producer-goods market, and fluctuations in the output of these products that are so essential to modern manufacturing are remarkable.

During the period under consideration, progress was made toward greater accuracy, uniformity, and simplicity of design of metalworking machinery. Particularly during the 1890s, there were two major technical advances: (1) Machine tools became automatic or semiautomatic and (2) compressed air and electricity were used to drive high-speed cutting tools and presses. The demands of the automobile industry and of the armament and aircraft industries during World War I brought the machine industry to maturity. V.S. Clark reports that between the end of the Civil War and the end of World War I, precision in metalworking increased from a tolerance limit of 0.01 inch to 0.001 inch, and tolerances of 0.0001 inch had been achieved, although

[6] Hall spent three years improving his process and raising the capital necessary for the venture. The Pittsburgh Reduction Company (later the Aluminum Company of America) was formed in 1889, and Hall was made vice president of the company in 1890.

not in quantity production. By 1919, metalworking machinery had increased greatly in power as well as in precision. Great electrically driven shears could cut steel slabs 12 inches thick and 44 inches wide, and huge presses could stamp out parts of automobile bodies rapidly enough to make "mass" production possible. Moreover, the industry played the central role in *diffusing* technical knowledge from its point of origin to other sectors of the economy that encountered similar problems. As Nathan Rosenberg has so cogently observed:

> The machine-tool industry, then, played a unique role *both* in the initial solution of technical problems and in the rapid transmission and application of newly learned techniques to other uses. In this sense, the machine-tool industry was a center for the acquisition and diffusion of the skills and techniques uniquely required in a machinofacture type of economy. Its role was a dual one: (1) new skills and techniques were developed here in response to the demands of specific customers, and (2) once acquired, the machine-tool industry served as the main transmission center for the transfer of new skills and techniques to the entire machine-using sector of the economy. A wide range of metalworking industries were continually being confronted with similar kinds of problems which urgently required solution and which, once solved by the machinery-producing sector, took their place in short order in the production of other metal-using products employing similar processes.[7]

Sources of Power

Between 1860 and World War I, there was a remarkable transition from reliance on the power of wind and water and the physical exertion of humans and animals to other sources of energy. The transition had begun only in the first half of the nineteenth century. In 1850, more than three-quarters of all power was furnished by animal energy, and human energy produced more power than machines did. As late as the eve of the Civil War, water power was far more important than steam power in the United States.

In Chapter 13, we discussed the difficulties encountered in the introduction of steam engines. Throughout the 1850s, there was much disagreement as to the relative costs of steam versus direct power, but by the end of the Civil War the argument was settled. Sites on streams large enough to power early mills and embryonic factories were scarce, and the ones available were frequently too distantly located to be economical for industrial concentration. Furthermore, as the forests were cleared, stream flows became more and more variable and less reliable. Sometime during the decade of the 1870s, steam surpassed water as a source of power. Then two major additional influences hastened the final phasing out of the ancient water wheel and the more recently developed water turbine. These were (1) the ever-increasing efficiency of the steam engine, along with the increased safety of high-pressure boilers, and (2) the opening up of vast and apparently inexhaustible supplies of coal as

[7] Nathan Rosenberg, *Technology and American Economic Growth* (New York: Harper & Row, 1972), p. 98.

a result of the transportation revolution. This instance portrays the interdependence of resource availability and technological advances. By 1890, relatively few factories—mostly in the textile and paper industries—used direct water power, although gristmills and sawmills were still powered by this source.

But another way of utilizing the force of water flow was to be devised. At the time when steam engines had gained an unquestioned ascendancy, electricity appeared on the scene as a form of power. Like steam, electricity was not a new energy *source;* it was a new *means* of using energy generated either by the flow of water or the burning of fuel. But electricity brought about a remarkable improvement in the utilization of the older sources of energy. Because electric power is flexible and divisible, the power plant could be separated from the manufacturing establishment by long distances, and the cumbersome devices required to change the to-and-fro motion of the steam engine into rotary motion and then to transmit this motion were no longer necessary. Furthermore, the energy required to turn either a small motor or a large one was readily "on tap."

Electric power could be generated by the manufacturing, mining, or transportation company that uses it, or it could be bought from a company that specializes in the generation of electricity. The construction of Edison's central power plant in New York in 1882 is rightly considered a monumental event, yet on the eve of World War I less than half the electric motors in use were driven by power purchased from a central plant. By the end of the war, however, a trend from nonutility to utility power was unmistakable. One-third of the nation's industrial power was then provided by electricity, far more than in any other country. Nearly one-half of all urban dwellings had electric lights, although more than 98 percent of all farm families were burning kerosene lamps after dark.

The growing importance of electricity should not, however, divert our attention from the fundamental *sources* of energy. Before World War I, the machines that generated power, whether electrical or not, were run either by the flow of water or by the burning of mineral fuels. In 1890, coal was the source of 90 percent of the energy furnished to industry; in the years just before 1920, coal remained the source of at least 80 percent of all industrial energy. But petroleum was rapidly growing more important, and hydropower was recovering. Within 25 years, petroleum and natural gas would become strategic fuels, but the transportation and manufacturing industries were planted squarely in the age of coal as late as 1920.

Two New Ideas: Mass Production and Scientific Management

No outline of the developments in American industry between the Civil War and World War I would be adequate without some account of two new approaches to production. These closely related developments—known popularly as *mass production* and *scientific management*—had such a pronounced impact on the American economy that even the average citizen quickly became aware of them. *Mass production* has become an almost magical expression that embraces all the characteristics of modern American industry; *scientific management* implies the use of business procedures that have a laboratory-like exactness.

Mass production is something more than quantity production. It implies two procedures: continuous-process manufacture and interchangeable-parts manufacture. Mass production further implies a high degree of mechanization, application of power, accurate machine tools, and uniform quality of materials. During the nineteenth century, American industry was acquiring these attributes, and certain industries, notably those engaged in the manufacture of farm implements and bicycles, approached the modern notion of mass production. Yet something still was lacking. Physically, it was necessary to devise a mechanical means of systematically transporting materials from one stage of production to another. Intellectually, detailed planning and ordering of the assembly process by the managers was required. It was essential that management's goal be the minimization of the time consumed by workers in assembling a complex product.

During the century or more that followed Oliver Evans' attempts at continuous-flow milling, entrepreneurs moved toward the ideal of minimizing processing time. The concept of stationary assembly was applied in the manufacture of carriages and railroad cars. It remained for the automobile to offer the ultimate challenge and for Henry Ford to accept it unhesitatingly. When, in 1908, Ford decided to produce a low-priced car designed to furnish cheap transportation and nothing more, he devised the first progressive line production of an automobile. Under Ford's first "stationary" system, subassemblies were constructed at several stations, but no provision was made for continuous movement from station to station. Beginning in 1913, the Ford plant adopted the "moving assembly" that had long been used in the manufacture of simple products. Pulled along by a windlass, subassemblies were produced in a series of operations. In 1914, a chassis, which had formerly been assembled in 12 hours, could be put together along a 250-foot line in a little over 1½ hours. Before 1920, motor-driven conveyors were moving motors, bodies, and chassis at optimum heights and speeds to workers along greatly lengthened lines. By this time, the moving assembly had spread throughout the automobile industry, the electrical industry, and the budding household-appliance industry, as well as to food processing and cigarette manufacture.

With increases in size of plant and complexity of layout, the problems of efficiently handling a large labor force became apparent. Frederick W. Taylor, ultimately the most famous contributor in this regard, argued that worker efficiency could be improved by (1) analyzing in detail the movements required to perform a job, (2) carrying on experiments to determine the optimum size and weight of tools and optimum lifts, and (3) offering incentives for superior performance. From such considerations, Taylor went on to develop certain principles pertaining to the proper physical layout of a shop or factory, the correct routing of work, and the accurate scheduling of the production of orders. In brief, it was Taylor's idea, with which numerous associates and followers concurred, that in planning production old rules of thumb should be replaced by principles determined after careful analysis and measurement. In this sense, guiding operations would no longer be haphazard, and management could become "scientific."

In 1911, famed attorney Louis D. Brandeis gave great publicity to the concept of "scientific management" when he argued before the Interstate Commerce Commission that what the railroads needed was not an increase in rates but an intelligent ordering of operations in accordance with scientific principles. By this time, entrepreneur Henry Ford, who probably had no thought of being scientific, had put these principles into practice. And soon the demands for increased output in World War I unquestionably motivated many managers to test procedures they might otherwise have scorned as useless theory.

Laborers could not escape the conviction that they were being driven to inhuman limits of effort. But increasing productivity and the tendency of real wages to move upward left them with the uneasy feeling that there might be some merit to "scientific management" after all. Having the materials flow faster did not necessarily force a person to work faster. With improved methods, workers did not have to move as far to handle materials; they made smaller personal expenditures of energy and were better protected against physical discomfort and industrial accidents. In any case, by 1920 nineteenth-century attempts to drive the worker were disappearing in industries experiencing rapidly increasing output.

THE CONCENTRATION OF INDUSTRY AND INCREASING FIRM SIZE

From the foregoing, we might conclude (and correctly) that pressures of technological change would lead to an increase in the size of the firm. A trend toward bigness was indeed unmistakable after the Civil War. During the decade of the 1870s, the number of manufacturing establishments remained nearly constant, but the capital invested in them increased by about two-thirds and the value of their output increased by more than one-half. Nevertheless, except in a handful of industries, there was no startling growth in the size of the firm during this decade. But beginning around 1880, initiated by forces that were not entirely technological and continuing for nearly a quarter of a century, a change occurred in the structure of American industry that was awesome in its manifestations and far-reaching in its consequences. This change has borne many labels, none of which has been properly descriptive. At the time, the change was referred to as the "rise in the trusts." Later writers have called it the "combination movement" or the "merger movement." Whatever we call it, the trend toward bigness—toward the concentration of economic power—demands our careful attention.

Ways of Achieving Industrial Power

One concept of the firm that economists find convenient is that of "optimum" size—that is, the most efficient (lowest cost) firm in the long run. With reasonably free entry into and exit from an industry and with no legal limits placed on size, the individual firm can become quite large. It may grow large *horizontally* by acquiring a number of plants that turn out approximately the same product, or it may integrate *vertically* to control a sequence of processes. In some industries, on the other hand, the typical firm may be small and may remain so for generation after generation. Bigness brings many advantages. A large firm can normally hire more skilled managers, set up a more effective marketing department, finance itself easily and cheaply and (up to a point, at least) better withstand the vagaries of the economic climate. Moreover, a large firm can readily achieve the technological economies resulting from division of labor, integration of processes, the use of large machines, and substantial research facilities. But there is a limit to the reductions in cost that can be derived from increases in scale. If nothing else, the pressure on management at last brings diseconomies. One person must finally make crucial decisions, and an organization can become so vast that human capabilities are insufficient to guide complicated operations efficiently.

It was to be expected, then, that the size of the business unit, in manufacturing and mining industries at any rate, would increase. But there was another reason why firms aspired to bigness: They wanted to gain some degree of monopoly control over the sale of their products. And now we have used a common word that requires some explanation, because "monopoly" can mean many things to many people.

Strictly speaking, a monopoly is a firm that is the sole seller of a product for which there is no close substitute. But examples of pure monopoly are hard to find. In the entire history of the United States, there have been no more than a dozen monopolies of important products sold in a nationwide market. A more meaningful term, which describes a common market structure in our economy, is "monopoly power." Without having the market control of a single seller, a firm may nevertheless obtain such a large portion of the total sales of a good or service that it can effectively influence—or even determine—the price at which the good or service sells. For example, if a large firm produces one-third of the total output of a good, smaller firms may be so fearful of aggressive action on the part of the large firm that they simply "follow" the big firm in matters of price and production policy. Or half a dozen firms, each of such a size that by varying output it can affect price, may produce nearly the whole of an industry's output; in such a market (an "oligopoly" in economic terms), *even without collusion among the sellers,* the price charged the consumer may be monopolistic.[8]

A firm or a small group of firms may become dominant in an industry in many ways. The least spectacular route to monopoly power is the simple expansion of the original firm over time.[9] Financing itself by reinvesting its own profits or with new funds from outside the company, a firm *may* achieve

[8] The problem of pricing when there are few independent sellers is a stubborn one. Whenever a firm controls such a large portion of an industry's output that it can, by varying its output, influence price, it will take into account the *reactions* of rivals to any intended price-cutting. As soon as sellers realize that price cuts will almost certainly be followed by the retaliatory cuts of rivals, the industry may well become stable with respect to price and production policy. Firms then tacitly agree to assure themselves a share of the monopoly profits they would obtain by collusion.

[9] The Aluminum Company of America (ALCOA) achieved its pre-World War II market dominance in this way.

monopoly power without resorting to any of the devices we will presently name. To do so, however, a firm must possess some special advantage conferred on it by law, such as a patent or a special license to operate, or it must control the whole supply of a necessary factor of production, most likely a raw material. Once a firm has achieved considerable size, it can be protected from the competition of rivals because of "good will" or because the size of fixed plant necessary to efficient operation has become so large that no entrepreneur can, without undue risk, become a full-fledged competitor.

During the first half of this century, except for the decade of the 1920s, the type of growth just described has been common. Between 1880 and 1905, however, the process of achieving bigness was hastened by the efforts of existing firms to combine. The devices by which combination was achieved were numerous, but they can be classified into three categories: (1) devices for bringing together the managements of firms to "share the market"; (2) devices for bringing together the managements and linking the financial structures of firms; (3) devices for bringing together the managements, financial structures, and physical properties of firms so as to create a single *new* firm.

The first attempts at combination were through the relatively simple devices in the first category. In the years immediately following the Civil War, the so-called "gentleman's agreement" was common—and not ordinarily successful for very long. Such agreements were informal, verbal arrangements chiefly made for the purpose of setting and maintaining prices, but they might also serve for adopting common policies regarding extension of credit, cash discounts, and the like. When restriction of output was desired, the stronger and formal (that is, written) contract known as the "pooling agreement" earned favor, because it was difficult to agree informally on such restrictions. The pool corresponded to the European cartel; it differed from its European counterpart chiefly in the fact that, as a heritage from the English common law, such agreements were considered illegal in this country and were not enforceable in the courts. But the purpose of the pool was the same as that of the cartel. By the means of a pool, sellers could divide a market and assign each seller a portion. The market could be divided on the basis of output, (each producer to sell so many units) or on a territorial basis (each producer to be free to sell within his own protected area). Or sellers could form a "profits pool," whereby net income was paid into a central fund and later divided on a basis of percentage of total sales in a given period. Although pools were formed even before the Civil War, they did not come into their own until after 1875. During the 1880s and 1890s, strong pooling arrangements were made in a number of important industries; producers of whiskey, salt, coal, meat products, explosives, steel rails, structural steel, cast-iron pipe, and certain tobacco products achieved great success with pooling agreements, as did the railroads in trunk-line territory.

Both gentlemen's agreements and pools "worked," at least temporarily. In fact, they were employed all throughout the period under discussion, and they are probably with us today (even though they are punishable offenses under the antitrust laws). But there were serious disadvantages in these "loose" forms of collusion. First, insofar as they were successful in raising prices and achieving a "monopoly" profit, they encouraged new firms to enter the field. Second, one of the major objectives of collusion was the maintenance of prices in deflationary periods; yet it was in times of declining business activity that the temptation to violate business agreements was strongest. The very freedom allowed the several firms, although usually an advantage, made it possible for individual managers to exceed their assigned outputs or encroach on another's territory when the going was rough, and there was no legal recourse against violators. Inevitably, smart operators sought a foolproof method of achieving the same ends by linking the financial structures of firms as well as their managements—the second category of devices by which combination was achieved.

The first of these stronger forms to find favor was the trust—a perversion of the ancient fiduciary device whereby trustees held property in the interest of either individuals or institutions. Under a trust agreement, the stockholders of several operating companies formerly in competition with one another turned over their shares to a group of trustees and received "certificates of trust" in exchange. The trustees therefore had voting control of the operating companies, and the former stockholders received dividends on their trust certificates. This device was so successful as a means of centralizing control of an entire industry and so profitable to the actual owners of stock that trusts were formed in the 1880s and early 1890s to control the output of kerosene, sugar, whiskey, cottonseed oil, linseed oil, lead, salt, rubber boots and gloves, and other products. But the trust form had one serious defect: Agreements were a matter of public record. Once their purpose was clearly understood, such a clamor arose that both state and federal legislation was passed outlawing them, and some trusts were dissolved by successful common-law suits in the state courts.

Alert corporate lawyers, however, thought of another way of linking managerial and financial structures. Occasionally, special corporate charters had permitted a company to own the securities of another company, such provisions having been inserted to allow horizontal expansion. In 1889, the New Jersey legislature revised its *general* incorporation statutes to allow any corporation so desiring to hold the securities of one or more subsidiary corporations. As trusts were declared illegal in several states, many of them simply obtained charters in New Jersey as "holding companies." The prime objective of centralizing control and at the same time leaving individual companies free to operate under their several charters could therefore be achieved by a relatively simple device. Theoretically, the holding company had to own more than 50 percent of the voting stock of its several subsidiaries. In practice, especially as shares became widely dispersed, control could be maintained with a far smaller percentage of the voting stock. The holding company was here to stay, although it would have to resist the onslaughts of Justice Department attorneys from time to time.

Yet it already seemed clear to many ambitious promoters that an outright consolidation of interests (in the technical sense) was preferable to any other form of combination. Strictly speaking, a consolidation takes place when two or more operating companies unite to form a *new* corporation. Some writers on corporate finance still insist on calling this kind of combination an *amalgamation* as distinguished from a *merger,* which refers to the acquisition by an existing corporation of the assets or voting stock of one or more other corporations. In the case of a technical consolidation (amalgamation), a new corporate name results from the joining together of two or more companies; in the case of a merger, the ensuing corporate name is that of the company that purchases the assets or securities of the firm or firms that are absorbed. In either case, the physical properties of two or more previously existing entities are brought together, either by an exchange of old securities for new or by a cash purchase. The result is the third type of combination listed in our earlier classification—that of the managements, financial structures, and physical properties of the firms.

THE TWO PHASES OF THE CONCENTRATION MOVEMENT

Whatever the path to combination and whatever the form of organization finally selected, the large firm was typical of American manufacturing industry by 1905. Why was bigness inevitable? How can we account for the major transformation that occurred in the last few decades of the nineteenth and the early years of the twentieth centuries? We have suggested that one reason for the concentration of industry was a natural movement, encouraged by competitive pressures, toward "optimum" size and that another reason was a conscious aiming for monopoly power. We now have to examine the forces that impelled entrepreneurs toward the control of a large part of the output of many major industries, for it is clear that a rapacious, overweening desire for monopoly profits did not suddenly sweep American entrepreneurs into great combinations.

We find a clue to the motivation toward combination in the reflection that the movement occurred in two major phases. The first was the predominantly *horizontal* combination (1879–1893) of industries that produced the old staples of consumption. The second was the predominantly *vertical* combination (1898–1904) of the producer-goods industries for the most part but also of a few consumer-goods industries that manufactured new products for growing urban markets.[10]

Phase One

As late as the 1870s, America's major industries served an agrarian economy. Except for the few companies that provided metal parts and rails for the rapidly expanding railroad industry, firms in most industries simply processed

[10]The following analysis is based closely on the path-breaking work of Alfred D. Chandler, Jr., to whom we are indebted for a new interpretation of the concentration movement. For the Chandler thesis at various stages and in alternative sources, see "The Beginnings of 'Big Business' in American Industry," *Business History Review,* **XXXIII:** 1 (Spring 1959), pp. 1–31; "Development, Diversification and Decentralization," in *Postwar Economic Trends in the United States,* Ralph E. Freeman (ed.), (New York: Harper & Row, 1960), pp. 235–88; and *Strategy and Structure* (Cambridge, Mass.: M.I.T. Press, 1962).

agricultural products and sold them in the still small cities to the farmers who had provided the raw materials. These firms were small, they usually bought raw materials locally and sold finished goods locally, and their markets were protected by some distance from the plants of competing manufacturers by high costs of transportation. When, as in the case of the textile industry, firms competed in a national market, they bought and sold through commission agents, who also handled the business of other firms in the same industry.

During the 1870s and 1880s, as the railroads bonded the country together into a national market, existing small firms in the consumer-goods industries first experienced a phenomenal increase in the demand for their products, followed by an expansion of facilities to take advantage of the new opportunities. Then, shockingly and distressingly, came the realization that there was great excess capacity, with consequent "overproduction," and prices persistently dropped below the production costs of most firms. To protect themselves from insolvency and ultimate failure, many small manufacturers in the

John D. Rockefeller, archetype of the nineteenth-century businessman, brought discipline and order to the unruly oil industry, parlayed a small stake into a fortune estimated at more than $1 billion, and lived in good health (giving away some of his millions) until 96 on a regimen of milk, golf, and riverwatching.

leather, sugar, salt, whiskey, glucose, starch, biscuit, kerosene, and rubber boot and glove industries (to name the most important) combined horizontally into large units.[11] They then systematized and standardized their manufacturing processes, closing down the least efficient plants and creating purchasing, marketing, finance, and accounting departments to service the units that remained. By 1893, consolidation and centralization were well under way in those consumer-goods industries that manufactured staple household items that had long been in use. Typical of the large firms created in this way were the Standard Oil Company of Ohio (after 1899, the Standard Oil Company of New Jersey), the Distillers' and Cattle Feeders' Trust, the American Sugar Refining Company, and the United States Rubber Company.

Of the firms that became large during the first wave of concentration, the most spectacular was the Standard Oil Company. Today it is hard for us to think of petroleum as primarily a consumer good, but the fact is that until well after the turn of the twentieth century an illuminant—kerosene—was the chief petroleum product. Beginning in 1854, kerosene was manufactured from a soft bitumen called cannel coal; by 1859, there were 34 small companies, ranging in a great semicircle from St. Louis to Portland, Maine, that made "coal oil." Edwin L. Drake's successful oil strike at Titusville, Pennsylvania, in the late summer of 1859 spelled doom for the coal-oil industry; kerosene could be extracted much more simply from liquid petroleum.

From its beginnings in 1860, the petroleum-refining business was characterized by a large number of small firms. By 1863, there were more than 300 firms in the industry, and although this number had declined by 1870 to perhaps 150, competition was vicious and the industry was plagued by excess capacity. "By the most conservative estimates," write Williamson and Daum, "total refining capacity during 1871–1872 of at least 12 million barrels annually was more than double refinery receipts of crude, which amounted to 5.23 million barrels in 1871 and 5.66 million barrels in 1872. At the same time, total demand approximated crude production at $4 per barrel.[12] An industry with investment in fixed plant and equipment that can turn out twice the volume of current sales is one inevitably characterized by repeated failures (usually in waves on the downswing of the cycle) and highly variable profits in even the most efficient firms. In the oil industry, the Rockefeller firm—organized in 1869 as the Standard Oil Company of Ohio—was perhaps the best managed, with two great refineries, a barrel-making plant, and a fleet of tank cars.[13]

Exactly when John D. Rockefeller made the decision to bring order to the petroleum industry is not certain. But Standard's holdings grew steadily during the 1870s, largely through the acquisition of refineries in Pittsburgh, Philadelphia, and New York, as well as in Ohio. Demanding and receiving rebates on

[11] As we have already observed, in the various industries, pools and other loose forms of organization often preceded combination into a single large company.

[12] Harold F. Williamson and Arnold R. Daum, *The American Petroleum Industry* (Evanston, Ill.: Northwestern University Press, 1959), p. 344.

[13] John D. Rockefeller got his start in business at the age of 19, when he formed a partnership with Maurice B. Clark to act as commission merchants and produce shippers. Moderately wealthy even before the end of the Civil War, Rockefeller entered the oil business in 1862, forming a series of partnerships before consolidating them as the Standard Oil Company.

oil shipments (and even drawbacks on the shipments of competitors), Standard had made considerable progress in reducing independent refining competition by the end of 1876. By 1878, Standard either owned or leased 90 percent of the refining capacity of the country. The independents that remained were successful only if they could produce high-margin items, such as branded lubricating oils, that did not require high-volume, low-cost manufacture.

To consolidate the company's position, a trust agreement was drawn up in 1879 whereby three trustees were to manage the properties of Standard Oil of Ohio for the benefit of Standard stockholders. In 1882, the agreement was revised and amended; stockholders of 40 companies associated with Standard also turned over their common stocks to nine trustees. The value of properties placed in the trust was set at $70 million, against which 700,000 trust certificates (par value $100) were issued. The agreement further provided for the formation of corporations having the name Standard Oil Company in New Jersey and New York as well as in other states. When the Supreme Court of Ohio ordered the Standard Oil Trust dissolved in a decree of 1892, the combination remained effective for several years by maintaining closely interlocking directorates among the major refining companies. Threatened by further legal action, company officials changed the Standard Oil Company of New Jersey from an operating to a holding company, increasing its capitalization from $10 million to $110 million, so that its securities might be exchanged for those of the subsidiaries it held. All the advantages of the trust form were secured, and, at least for the time being, no legal dangers were incurred. Thus, as the American Sugar Refining Company had done in 1891, Standard went from a trust to a holding company after successful combination had long since been achieved.

Phase Two

The severe downturn in economic activity that began in 1893 brought combinations of all kinds almost to a standstill. The return of prosperity beginning in late 1896 marked the advent of a new movement toward industrial concentration so pronounced that it caused earlier historians to overlook the significance of the first wave of combinations we have just designated "phase one." Over the span of years 1898–1905, more than 3,000 mergers were effected, according to U.S. Department of Commerce figures, and many acquisitions of smaller firms were probably not even recorded. Yet the changing characteristics of the second wave of combinations impressed contemporary observers with its startling dimensions.

In part, urbanization led to changes in both the demand for and the ways to supply consumer goods. Whereas in 1860 20 percent of the population resided in cities (or towns of 2,500 and more), by 1900 the figure was 40 percent; by World War I it was almost 50 percent. This changing proportion, coupled with population growth, raised the numbers of city dwellers from 6.2 million in 1860 to 54.2 million in 1920.

As a consequence, there emerged a new kind of consumer-goods industry that produced *new* products (or old products in novel ways) for growing markets composed of city dwellers. Firms in these industries formed large organizations that were vertically integrated, except for the raw-material stage, to achieve economies of production and marketing. These industries were comprised of producers of fresh meat, cigarettes, and high-grade flour, as well as manufacturers of sewing machines and typewriters. Thus, Gustavus F. Swift and his brother Edwin, after experimenting with the shipment and storage of refrigerated meat, formed a partnership in 1878 that grew over the next two decades into a huge, integrated company. Its major departments—marketing, processing, purchasing, and accounting—were controlled from the central office in Chicago. Other meat packers, like Armour and Morris, built similar organizations, and by the late 1890s the meat-packing industry was dominated by a few firms with highly centralized, bureaucratic managements. In a similar manner, James B. Duke set out in 1884 to establish a national, even worldwide, selling organization to market his machine-made cigarettes. In 1890, he merged his company with five competitors to form the American Tobacco Company. Less than 15 years later, American Tobacco, after a series of mergers, achieved a monopoly in the cigarette industry.

But an even more spectacular result of the growth of the cities was the increased demand for producer goods and the consequent stimulation of output in the heavy industries (steel, copper, power machinery, explosives, and so on). Beginning in the 1840s, municipal authorities were shocked to discover what immense outlays were required to lay mains for water and sewer systems, which until then were provided by private companies only for the wealthy. The post-Civil War mushrooming of the cities meant a continually growing demand for such public-health facilities, which was followed by an expanded demand for gas lighting, telephone lines and exchanges, complex electrical lighting equipment, power lines, and street and elevated railways, to say nothing of construction materials to build the steel-skeletoned skyscrapers that made their first appearance in the late 1880s. These demands led in turn to the formation of large firms that emphasized vertical integration and highly centralized control over vast operations, extending from the mining of raw materials to the purveying of finished products.

In steel, the Carnegie Company had by the early 1890s consolidated its several manufacturing properties into an integrated firm that owned vast coal and iron deposits. As the Carnegie interests grew, other businesspeople were creating powerful steel companies. In 1898, the Federal Steel Company was formed under the auspices of J.P. Morgan and Company. Its integrated operations and products greatly resembled those of the Carnegie Company, but it had the further advantage of having a close alliance with the National Tube Company and the American Bridge Company, producers of highly finished products. The National Steel Company, created by W.H. Moore, was the third largest producer of ingot and basic steel shapes and was closely connected with other Moore firms that made finished products—the American Tin Plate Company, the American Steel Hoop Company, and the American Sheet Steel Company. When Carnegie, strong in coal and (through his alliance with Rockefeller) iron ore, threatened to integrate forward into finished products, he precipitated action toward a merger by the Morgan interests. The result was the United States Steel Corporation, organized in March 1901 with a capital stock of over $1 billion and, by a substantial margin, the largest corporation in

Andrew Carnegie, the central figure in this photograph, dominated any scene. A great salesman, he built an integrated steel firm that combined with the Morgan and Moore interests to form the United States Steel Corporation in 1901.

the world. Controlling 60 percent of the nation's steel business, United States Steel owned, in addition to its furnaces and mills, a large part of the vast ore reserves of the Lake Superior region, 50,000 acres of coking-coal lands, more than 1,100 miles of railroad, and a fleet of lake steamers and barges. While protecting its position in raw materials, the corporate giant was now able to prevent price warfare in an industry typified by high fixed costs.

In copper, Guggenheim's Philadelphia Smelting and Refining Company began a huge integrated operation that was soon imitated by Amalgamated Copper and the American Smelting and Refining Company. In the explosives industry—after more than a generation of effective control of prices and production through the Gunpowder Trade Association—E.I. Du Pont de Nemours and Company bought a large number of independent companies in 1902 and consolidated them into a single, well-knit organization with centralized accounting, purchasing, engineering, and traffic departments. We could trace similar combinations with similar motives through a long list of "Americans," "Nationals," and even "Internationals", among them, American Locomotive, American Can, National Packing, and International Harvester.

How should we sum up this discussion of the concentration of American industry? One way is to ask how many really important large firms were created during this early period of combination. A well-known study notes that 328 major combinations were formed during the years 1888–1905, 156 of which were large enough to have a degree of monopoly control in their general industries.[14] Some of these were failures, but a large proportion are major concerns that exist today. As to the degree of dominance attained by these firms at the turn of the century, we are less well informed. The accepted estimate is that by 1905 roughly two-fifths of the manufacturing capital of the country was controlled by 300-odd very large companies with an aggregate capitalization of over $7 billion. Perhaps four-fifths of the manufacturing industries contained at least one representative of the 328 large firms.

And what about the period from 1905 to 1920? During this decade and a half, the trend toward industrial concentration slowed greatly. Prosecution under the 1890 Sherman Act resulted in spectacular dissolutions of the Standard Oil Company of New Jersey and the American Tobacco Company, but 30–40 new combinations of a size comparable to those of the 1888–1904 period were effected. The considerable growth of two firms in the automobile industry indicated that companies producing durable consumer goods might become large. Thus was foreshadowed a resumption of widespread efforts to achieve market dominance in new industries—efforts for which promoters of the 1920s were to become notorious.

Clearly, our explanation of the concentration movement has centered on the evolution of great, impersonal economic forces. We have not touched on the personal and institutional influences that made the years 1860–1920 such an exciting, dangerous, and critical period of history. Where, we might ask, is an account of that strange and potentially terrible oligarchy, the Robber Barons, which, after all, masterminded the rise of the large business firm? Our contention is that the concentration movement would have occurred about the time it did, no matter who engineered it. Of course, the demand for social control of industry focused on the leading business figures of the time—the agents of the great impersonal forces at work—rather than on the economic forces alleged to be at work. That and the struggle that ensued between the seekers of economic power and the people are issues we will consider in the following chapters.

[14] See Shaw Livermore, "The Success of Industrial Mergers," *Quarterly Journal of Economics*, **L**:4 (November 1935), pp. 68–96.

20

America's New Labor Consciousness

THE CHANGING STATUS OF AMERICAN LABOR

Post-1860 growth in the size of plant, firm, and industry changed the lives of American workers. As factories grew larger and more and more firms combined, the relationship between owner and worker took on new dimensions. The emergence of corporate organization replaced the owner–managers of former years with a class of professional executives. Hired executives felt less personal concern for the welfare of workers, and, by the same token, workers found old loyalties to the employer dissolving.

Employer and employee could have gotten along well enough in the absence of mutual affection or loyalty if another emotion had not become a part of the daily life of all but the most highly skilled or especially favored workers. Fear was omnipresent. Workers were afraid of many things. They were afraid of unemployment, which could result from technological change or from seasonal and cyclical swings in economic activity. They were afraid of the physical danger involved in most occupations in a day when little was known about the prevention of industrial accidents, when insurance was almost nonexistent for poor families, and when neither society nor industry felt responsible for any harm that befell the worker either on or off the job. And many immigrant workers, of whom there were millions, felt lost and insecure simply because they were strangers. But most of all, laborers were afraid of a lack of bargaining power. As economic units grew larger, the individual became a less and less important part of the productive process.

There might be strength in union, but workers often ran the gravest sort of risk whenever they participated in union activities. It was a rare thing to find a management that was not violently opposed to the collective action of labor. Union leaders or "agitators" found themselves blacklisted and were unable to secure employment. Companies often summarily discharged anyone who joined a union and even insisted that prospective employees sign "yellow-dog" contracts, or agreements not to join a union. Employers hired labor spies—detectives in the guise of workers—to furnish complete lists of union members and to report union plans and strategies in detail. Often when employees threatened to strike, an employer would immediately close his plant, "lock out" the workers, and wait for hunger and the pressures of angry households to bring them to submission. Thus, between 1860 and World War I, unions operated in a political and social climate of incredible hostility.

Business and professional people felt that the working masses would be content if they were not stirred up by a few misguided and power-hungry rabble-rousers. Employees who worked hard, did what they were told, and saved their money could always rise to the top, they thought. To grant security to unions in the form of, say, a closed shop was an unconscionable interference with the rights of both the employers and those laborers who wanted to remain rugged individualists.

State and federal governments stood firmly on the side of business against labor unions. It was considered a legitimate use of police power to call out troops to break strikes. Such actions were condoned by the state and federal courts, which proved to be invaluable allies of management in the struggle to suppress collective action on the part of the laboring class. Especially effective as a device for restraining union action was the injunction. Employers could go to court to have labor leaders enjoined from calling or continuing a strike. Failure to comply with an injunction meant jail for the offenders, and "government by injunction" proved to be one of the strongest weapons in the anti-union arsenal.

Despite these odds, labor made progress as a class between the end of the Civil War and the end of World War I. Nothing like adequate standards of Social Security for the majority were attained by 1920, but the laborer's workweek was shorter and earnings were greater than they had ever been in the past. And these benefits were accomplished in the general absence of unions.

Wages and Hours

Until quite recently, the least satisfactory economic statistics for the years between the Civil War and World War I were those for wages, earnings, and hours of labor. Five basic data sources have long been available: the Aldrich Report (1893), the Weeks Report (1880), Bulletin 18 of the U.S. Department of Labor (1898), the First Annual Report of the Commissioner of Labor (1886), and the Dewey Census Report for 1890. But until these materials were subjected to formal scrutiny and analysis, historians could reach only tentative conclusions from them. Fortunately, Clarence D. Long has done the long-awaited job.[1]

[1] Clarence D. Long, *Wages and Earnings in the United States, 1860–1890* (Princeton: Princeton University Press, 1960). See especially pp. 3–12 and 109–18.

What changes occurred in the hours that constituted a workweek? How did wage rates and earnings vary? In 1860, the average number of hours worked per day in nonagricultural employment was close to 10.8. By 1890, according to Long, the average workday in manufacturing was 10 hours—a decline of about 7 percent—and people normally worked a six-day week. There were, of course, variations from the average. Skilled craftsmen in the building trades worked a 10-hour day in 1860 and probably no more than an average of 9.5 hours per day by 1890. On the other hand, in the textile mills outside New England, 12–14-hour days were still common in 1890, and workers in steel mills, paper manufacturing, and brewing stayed on the job 12 hours a day, seven days a week.

Both daily wages and annual earnings in manufacturing increased by about 50 percent between 1860 and 1890. Prices rose so rapidly during the Civil War that real wages fell drastically between 1860 and 1865. But from then on, the cost of living declined, not steadily but persistently, eventually returning the dollar to its prewar purchasing power.[2] The consequence was that *real* wages and earnings in 1890 also increased by about 50 percent. Daily wages in manufacturing rose from just over $1 in 1860 to $1.50 in 1890, and annual earnings increased from slightly under $300 in 1860 to over $425 in 1890. In the building trades, both real wages and real earnings rose a little higher, perhaps by 60 percent. It should be realized that wage differentials among industries were great in both 1860 and 1890: The highest-wage industry paid 2–2½ times more than the lowest. If we take into account the shortening of the workweek by about 7 percent, the net increase in hourly money or real wages over the 30-year period was about 60 percent, or 1.6 percent compounded annually.[3] Despite the tremendous immigration during these years, American workers made substantial gains.

Similarly, in the decades between 1891 and 1920, real wages marched upward. The real earnings of manufacturing workers advanced 37 percent—or an annual compound rate of 1.3 percent—between 1890 and 1914.[4] Further gains were made during the war years, so that the annual rate between 1891 and 1920 was only slightly less than that recorded during the preceding 30 years.

During the second 30-year period, there was continued gradual improvement in the standard workweek. By 1910, it was 55 hours in all industries; by 1920, it had dropped to about 50. A widespread weekly work pattern was comprised of five 9-hour days and 4–5 hours on Saturday morning; the Saturday noon siren still blows today in many small towns. Again, the skilled trades fared better, having achieved a 44-hour week by 1920. Unskilled laborers, on the other hand, were still working 9-hour days, six days a week, and the 12-hour day persisted in the metal-processing industries.

In summary, we can make two generalizations about wages and hours:

1. For 30 years after the Civil War, despite frequent setbacks, labor made definite and substantial gains in real income. However, traditions regarding the

[2]Long, p. 109.

[3]Long, p. 109.

[4]Albert Rees, *Real Wages in Manufacturing, 1890–1914* (Princeton: Princeton University Press, 1961), pp. 3–5.

length of the working day were hard to break down, except in the skilled trades where they showed signs of weakening.

2. Between 1890 and 1920, the increase in real wages and earnings was about the same as that in the previous period, and labor made considerable gains in the form of markedly shorter workdays and workweeks.

Other Measures of Progress

American wage earners have always stressed gains in the form of higher wages and shorter hours as the proper criteria for judging progress. But since the early years of the nineteenth century, labor has also striven to achieve welfare gains through political activity, and by World War I, after a century of effort, some of these gains were finally realized.

Before 1920, there was a reversal of the upward trend in the employment of children that had resulted from post–Civil War industrialization. In 1880, 1 million boys and girls between the ages of 10 and 15 were "gainfully occupied," and the number had risen to a high of nearly 2 million by 1910. In 1910, one-fifth of the youngsters between 10 and 15 had jobs, and they constituted 5.2 percent of the workforce. But in 1920, the total number employed in this market was again less than 1 million, children made up only 2.6 percent of the workforce, and only one-twelfth of the 10–15-year age group was at work.

Since hours were long and working conditions were unsatisfactory, if not positively harmful, the decrease in the employment of children represented a social improvement. This improvement was primarily attributable to the successes of humanitarian groups in obtaining protective legislation at the state level. Massachusetts had a long history of ineffective child-labor legislation. The first stringent regulation did not appear until 1903, when Illinois passed a law limiting child labor to an 8-hour day. State laws limiting hours of work, requiring minimum wages, and setting age limits were common by 1920, but a further remedy was still required—especially in the cotton belt of the South and in certain industrial states in the mid-South and East.[5] Efforts by Congress to place federal restrictions on the use of child labor were declared unconstitutional by the Supreme Court on two occasions before 1920.

The role of women in the labor force had also changed dramatically by World War I. The number of women gainfully employed increased remarkably after 1880. In that year, 2.5 million women, constituting 15 percent of the gainfully employed, were at work outside the home. This number doubled by 1900, when women comprised 18 percent of the workforce. By 1920, 8.5 million women, comprising one-fifth of the gainfully employed, were involved in some pursuit other than homemaking.

As with child labor, statutes prescribing maximum hours and minimum wages for women were common by 1920. There was growing legislative concern with the physical surroundings in which work was performed, but in the mill towns of the South and the industrial cities of the North, women gained further protection under the law.

[5] In these states especially, the fight against child labor was waged indirectly through increases in compulsory education ages.

When publicized, bad working conditions like these among very young slate pickers in Pennsylvania at the turn of the century won middle-class sympathy for labor's cause.

In the absence of strong legal measures, the slow but inexorable forces of competition operated to open more pleasant and more lucrative occupations for women. The typewriter and other office equipment became generally accepted before the turn of the century, and young women found a new field in which they faced no employment disadvantages. Sales work in city stores became a more attractive occupation than degrading domestic service. As the ancient notion that females were intellectually inferior to males began to dissipate, parents educated their daughters for professional work. Finally, World War I caused the greatest shake-up in hiring policies as employers, urged to employ women as replacements for men lost to the armed services, discovered that women performed a wide range of occupations as satisfactorily as men and that in some jobs their performance was often superior.

To gauge the progress of labor, we should note developments in the field of social insurance. In an industrial society, workers are vulnerable to loss of income from industrial accidents, prolonged and serious illness, old age, and unemployment. Before 1920, only the problem of insurance against loss from industrial accidents received legislative attention. Until World War I, the idea of protecting employees against the hazards of sickness, superannuation, and economic fluctuations was preposterous to most Americans—even though Europeans since the 1880s had begun to make systematic provisions for alleviating the suffering that resulted from these foreseeable causes.

By the end of the nineteenth century, it was apparent that simple justice required that the laborer be protected against the frightful hazards of accident. We can only guess how many industrial accidents occurred annually in the years before 1900, but the estimates of insurance companies show that after 1900 there were 25,000–35,000 deaths annually and more than 2 million serious injuries from accidents on the job. Some occupations were more dangerous than others; mining, metal processing, railroading, commercial fishing, and stevedoring were notoriously risky. Under English common law (which had developed in a society in which the handicrafts predominated), workers did have recourse against an employer in the event of an accident but under conditions that made it unlikely that they would win compensation. To receive compensation for injuries, employees had to file suit against their employer, and they could not win unless they could prove negligence on the part of the employer—a difficult thing to do. Furthermore, if employers could show (1) that the employee was aware of the hazardous nature of the job when hired or (2) that an accident was the result of the negligence of the employee or a fellow worker (the "fellow-servant" rule), they could present a good defense. And, of course, many workers had neither the means nor the knowledge to take the steps necessary to bring legal action.

Two remedies were possible. One was to pass laws providing safer working conditions in hazardous occupations. The second was to abrogate the common-law rules that practically freed the employer of responsibility and to require that the employer compensate workers for their injuries. Since most employers did not have sufficient resources to guarantee indemnities, the second remedy required some form of insurance, either with a state fund or with a private insurance company. In Germany in 1884 and in England in 1897, the concept of insurance was put into practice successfully, and in the United States the first workmen's compensation act was passed by Maryland in 1902. Like other early laws, it was declared unconstitutional, but in 1914 New York and New Jersey succeeded in framing statutes that stood up under court tests. Meanwhile, Congress, acting under its power to regulate interstate commerce, passed an Employers' Liability Act in 1908, which protected railroad workers by abrogating the "fellow-servant" rule. In 1916, the federal government provided compensation laws for its civilian workers. With the tremendous acceleration of industrial activity during the war, other states hastened to establish similar insurance plans, and by 1920 the great majority of the states had compensation laws in effect. During the war years, the merits of other kinds of social insurance were debated, but no important extensions were considered seriously by Congress.

IMMIGRATION AND THE LABOR FORCE

In 1860, two-fifths of the labor force was engaged in nonagricultural pursuits and three-fifths was engaged in agricultural pursuits. By 1890, these proportions had been reversed, and by 1920 three-fourths of the labor force was engaged in some form of nonagricultural employment and one-fourth worked in agriculture. No other single statistic is as accurate an indicator of the profound change that took place in the economy over these 60 years. (Looked at another way, these figures show that although the labor force as a whole increased fourfold during the period, the number of people in nonagricultural employment increased sevenfold.)

The striking growth in the total workforce in great part reflected the tremendous pulling power of America for Europeans. Between 1865 and 1880, more than 5 million immigrants found permanent or temporary homes in the United States, and between 1880 and 1920, the number swelled to 23.5 million. Of course, there were considerable variations from year to year: The number of immigrants rose in good times and fell in bad times. Peak years of inflow coincided with or immediately preceded the *onset* of severe depressions. In times of rising economic activity and employment, the tug on immigrants increased tremendously; as depressions ensued and jobs disappeared, the attractiveness of American opportunity receded. Peaks were reached in 1873, 1882, 1892, 1907, and 1914. For obvious reasons, immigration declined greatly during the prosperous World War I years.

In the 1880s, there was a decreasing influx of people from northern and western Europe and an increasing influx from southern and eastern Europe. It is usual to speak of the immigration from Great Britain, Ireland, Germany, and the Scandinavian countries as the "old" immigration, as distinguished from the "new" immigration composed of Hungarians, Poles, Russians, Serbs, Greeks, and Italians. In the 1870s, more than 80 percent of the immigrants came to America from northern and western Europe; by 1910, 80 percent of the total was arriving each year from southern and eastern Europe. It is reckoned that 1896 marked the point at which a majority of those arriving annually were no longer of the "old" nationalities.

Much was once made of the presumed economic significance of these geographic shifts in the sources from which new Americans were drawn. In ethnic characteristics, the Swedes and Germans of the old immigration were not unlike the Anglo-Saxons who colonized America. Slovaks and Magyars, on the other hand, along with Russians and Italians and other peoples from the new areas, had unfamiliar customs and spoke odd languages—and they looked different. To native-born citizens of turn-of-the-century America, the new immigrants seemed inferior in skills, in cultural background, and in potentiality.

The great source of cheap labor was immigration. Densely packed ships brought millions of unskilled workers to America, often under contracts that specified no wage increases during the first year of employment.

Even their late arrival on U.S. shores appeared to indicate a certain lack of energy and aggressiveness.[6]

The new immigrant supplanted the old for two reasons. As economic opportunity grew in England, Germany, and Scandinavia, America became less attractive to the nationals of these countries. Also important was the rapid improvement in transportation during the 1860s and 1970s. The steamship put the Mediterranean much closer to America, and railroads from the interior of eastern Europe to Mediterranean ports gave mobility to the southeastern Europeans. There was a vast difference between the economic opportunities

[6]*Each* immigrant group in its period of peak arrivals looked inferior; the "shanty Irish" and "dumb Swedes" of a previous generation were scorned as much as the "crazy Bohunks" who came later. But twentieth-century Americans seized on the assumed "inferiority" of southern and eastern Europeans as an argument for excluding them.

offered an American laborer — even an unskilled one — and those available to the European peasant at home. The suction created by the removal of transportation barriers was irresistible; railroads, steamship companies, and American mill and factory managers hastened the movement by promotional advertising and financial assistance.

It is probably true that immigrants after 1880 were less skilled and educated than earlier immigrants had been. It may be that their different political and cultural history made their assimilation into American democracy and their organization into labor unions more difficult. Nevertheless, the economic effects of the old and the new immigrations were roughly the same. New arrivals, whatever their national origins, usually filled the ranks of unskilled labor. Slovaks, Poles, and Italians replaced Irish, Germans, and Swedes in the coal fields and steel mills and, like their predecessors, took the lowest positions in the social strata.

What was the impact of these foreigners on the American economy? Although 28 million people arrived between 1865 and 1920, the ratio of foreign born to the total U.S. population remained *fairly constant at around 14 percent.*[7] But at the end of the period, more than one-third of the employees in manufacturing industries and almost one-half of the miners were foreign born. Moreover, the great majority of immigrants entered the labor markets of New England, the Middle Atlantic states, and the states of Ohio, Michigan, and Illinois, where they concentrated in the great industrial cities. Working for low wages in crowded factories and sweatshops and living in unsanitary tenements, immigrants complicated such urban social problems as slums, crime and delinquency, and municipal corruption. But their difficulties were not the result of discrimination in hiring or in wages. The relative earnings of native and foreign-born workers were almost equal.[8]

American business profited greatly from an inexhaustible supply of unskilled and semiskilled workers. The steamship companies that brought these immigrants to America and the railroads that took them to their destinations were the first to benefit. But manufacturing and mining companies profited most; immigration enabled them to expand their operations to supply growing markets without any increase in the costs of low-grade labor. Moreover, the influx of immigrants meant more customers for American retailers, more buyers of cheap manufactured goods, and a greatly enlarged market for housing.

The rapidly increasing supply of unskilled labor kept wage levels for great numbers of workers from rising as fast as they would have otherwise. Therefore, insofar as established American workers could not escape from the unskilled ranks, they were adversely affected. But supervisory jobs and skilled jobs were given to native white Americans, and the number of better jobs available increased as the mass of unskilled new immigrants grew. Moreover,

[7] This rather curious fact is explained by the high rate of increase in the native population plus substantial *out*migration during periods of depression.

[8] Martha Norby Fraundorf, "Relative Earnings of Native and Foreign-Born Women," *Explorations in Economic History,* **15** (1978), pp. 211–18. Peter J. Hill, "Relative Skill and Income Levels of Native and Foreign-Born Workers in the United States," *Explorations in Economic History,* **12** (1975), pp. 47–60. Peter R. Shergold, "Relative Skill and Income Levels of Native and Foreign-Born Workers: A Re-examination," *Explorations in Economic History,* **13** (1976), pp. 451–61.

An inevitable consequence of the urban crowding of workers was the appearance of slums. This photograph shows the litter and filth on Orchard Street in New York City, sometime between 1907 and 1915.

the wages of those craftsmen engaged in making equipment to be used by the unskilled and semiskilled masses doubtlessly rose. And native American labor gained from the lower-priced manufactured products made possible by cheap labor.

Management was convinced that unrestricted immigration was necessary to the growth of American industry. Labor was equally certain that the influx of foreigners continually undermined the economic status of native workers.

From the Civil War to the end of World War I, there was a constant struggle between the proponents and adversaries of immigration restriction. In 1864, at the behest of the manufacturing interests, Congress passed the Contract Labor Law, which authorized contracts made abroad to import foreign workers and permitted the establishment of the American Emigrant Company to act as an agent for the American business sector. The Contract Labor Law had the practical effect of bringing in laborers whose status could scarcely be distinguished from that of indentured servants, their cost of passage being repaid out of their earnings in the United States. Wage earners fought this law until its repeal in 1882, after which there was a continuing struggle to restrict immigration in general.

The first to feel the effects of the campaign for restriction were the Chinese. The influence of the Chinese on the labor market was localized in California, where the Workingman's Party (the "sand lotters") urged the exclusion of all Orientals. By the Chinese Exclusion Act of 1882, the first victory of the restrictionists was won. Successful in their first major effort, the restrictionists pressed on to make illegal the immigration of anyone who could neither read nor write. Acts requiring literacy tests passed Congress, but President Cleveland, and later President Taft, vetoed them. For many years, labor had to be content with whittling away at the principle of the free movement of all immigrants who came into the United States. After the Chinese exclusion, the next success was to outlaw the importation of "contract" workers. In succeeding laws, further restrictions were imposed on the immigration of the physically and mentally ill, vagrants, and anarchists. In 1917, Congress finally passed a literacy requirement—this time over President Wilson's veto—and permanent bars to the free flow of migrants into the United States were soon to be erected.

THE ACHIEVEMENT OF PERMANENT ORGANIZATION

The outbreak of the Civil War, at once disruptive and stimulating to the economy of the North, was a blow to union efforts that had begun to flower in the years immediately preceding. Labor received bad publicity, too. Its loud objections to the conscription law that allowed men who could pay a $300 commutation fee to escape military service left an impression of disloyalty in the public mind—an impression deepened by isolated riots fostered by northerners who sympathized with the southern cause, the Copperheads. The fortunes of organized labor ebbed to the point of apparent hopelessness.

The recovery of business from the initial adverse effects of the hostilities was not long delayed. As war contracts were let and the stimulating effects of deficit financing were felt throughout the economy, output and incomes rose. By the middle of 1862, the depression of the early months of the war was over. During the summer, the prices of consumer goods began to increase and, as almost always happens, wages lagged behind the cost of living. The reduction of real incomes became severe. Due to the extreme labor scarcity that developed as men were called into the army, the time was ripe for a renewed union effort. The few unions that had managed to stay alive through 1860 and 1861 gained in memberships rapidly, and new unions sprang up even outside the established industrial areas. Strikes were used so successfully to obtain wage concessions that organization became progressively easier. The unsuccessful strikes were mainly those called in protest against technological innovations that threatened to destroy jobs. During the Civil War, labor became convinced that it was futile to struggle against the inevitable mechanization of industry. A great step forward was taken when its leaders realized that time could not be rolled back.

Craft unions increased so markedly in numbers and strength that employers began to become concerned. By December 1864, there were about 300 local unions with a membership of 200,000 concentrated in the industrial states of New York, Pennsylvania, and Massachusetts. City centrals reappeared, as did national unions organized along craft lines. At least 11 national unions, some of them having a continuous history down to the present, were formed by 1865.

Business activity slackened after the war, and labor's position was weakened further by the return of soldiers to their jobs. Moreover, the downward pressure exerted on wages by immigrants—their numbers swollen by the Contract Law—was not relieved by the westward movement stimulated by the Homestead Act. But the economy (except for agriculture), after hesitating, moved on to good years in the early 1870s. By 1873, there were 41 national craft unions with an estimated membership of 300,000–400,000.

A type of craft union had always been advocated by conservative labor leaders, who were concerned primarily with wages, hours, and working conditions. These men knew that national organization was essential, for the great improvements in communication and transportation had given labor a mobility it had never had before. There was no point in organizing in New York City if Philadelphia workers in the same trade who were not abiding by union rules could come to New York to take the jobs of the strikers. On the other hand, while they recognized the need for a national association of workers in a single craft, these leaders did not advocate an all-inclusive union seeking broad social and political ends. But the depression that followed the downturn of 1873 revealed once more, and with crushing finality, the inherent weakness of the pure national craft union. One of the first to collapse was the numerically strongest of them all—the shoemaker's association, known as the Knights of St. Crispin. Of the 41 national craft unions, only eight, greatly weakened, survived six years of hard times. Was there no way to achieve lasting labor solidarity?

"One Big Union"

Two alternative lines of action had long been urged by leaders who were disgruntled with the periodic disintegration of the job-conscious union. One course of action was to form a new political party aimed at overthrowing orthodox economic institutions and establishing a socialist government. The other course was to support whichever existing political party would further labor's goals within the institutional framework of capitalism. The success of either plan depended on the formation of a single, all-inclusive union that could unite all labor elements and bring sympathizers in business and the professions into close, active alliance with labor. The more radical movement, advocating the revolutionary establishment of a socialist government, never mustered sufficient support to be taken seriously, and the socialists furnished many leaders who later furthered the more conservative cause. The alternative approach to power, through "one big union" operating within the existing government framework, was nearly successful.

As early as 1864, a national federation of city centrals—local organizations of several craft unions—had been attempted without success. Only two years later, another federation was started that captured the imaginations of laborers and their political allies and quickly secured 500,000 members. This was the National Labor Union (NLU), noteworthy as the first manifestation of labor's yearning to present a solid front against the opposition of the business class. Originally seeking modest, purely economic objectives, this federation of city assemblies attracted a few national craft unions as affiliates. At first, the NLU proposed a moderate program, emphasizing arbitration of disputes and advocating strikes only as a last resort, which placated labor's enemies. But radical leaders gradually injected a more idealistic fervor into the spirit of the union, and the organization began to place an increasing emphasis on social reform. In coalition with agrarian reformers, the National Labor Union entered politics on a platform that proposed an increase in the money supply, a weakening of the "money monopoly" of the banks, and the establishment of producers' and consumers' cooperatives. This growing emphasis on political activity alienated the NLU's local craft membership, and it was dissolved after defeat at the polls in 1872.

Meanwhile, in 1869, the most romantic of all American labor organizations was formed as an association of poor Philadelphia tailors. Under the leadership of a Baptist preacher, Uriah S. Stephens, the Noble and Holy Order of the Knights of Labor had an inauspicious beginning. With all the trappings of a fraternal lodge, including a secret religious ritual, this group offered a new appeal to workers and sought a new type of protection for them. Besides having economic ends in common, the membership was to be held together by bonds of brotherly love. Since the bitter opposition of property owners had proved so damaging in the past, the new organization extended the protection of anonymity to its members.

The Knights of Labor grew slowly during the first ten years. Its real rise began in 1881, when its membership may have been as large as 20,000. Within five years, membership reached the unprecedented total of 750,000—a huge increase in members occurring in 1885. Although the Knights were initially opposed to strikes, it was through a series of brilliant strike victories that their great membership was won. In 1884 and 1885, the Knights were successful in a series of work stoppages against the railroads—then the most powerful business firms in the country. The acclaim accorded the union was tremendous. When, in addition, the leadership announced the attainment of an eight-hour day as the next major objective, workers rushed to join.

A peak of membership and power was reached in the spring of 1886 and was followed by a decline almost as precipitous as the rise had been. Stretching their luck too far, the Knights lost a strike against one of Jay Gould's railroads as well as much of the prestige they had gained in a victory over Gould the preceding year. When a general strike to achieve an eight-hour day failed to materialize in May 1886, members lost faith. Membership slipped to 100,000 by 1890, the year in which the growing American Federation of Labor won a showdown fight against a group backed by the Knights to organize the cigar trade in New York City. Although the Knights remained in existence until 1917, they were of no importance after 1900.

The American Federation of Labor

In 1881, the year in which the Knights of Labor began its rise to short-lived eminence, the leaders of six of the country's strongest craft unions, meeting in Pittsburgh, Pennsylvania, proposed a federation of national unions. The new organization, composed of printers, glassworkers, iron and steelworkers, molders, and cigar makers, was to be known as the Federation of Organized Trades and Labor Unions. Its leaders were Adolph Strasser, then president of the International Cigar Makers Union, and Samuel Gompers, a former radical who rose to prominence as a colleague of Strasser. The original membership of the Federation was less than 50,000 and did not begin to increase until the Knights of Labor had expended itself. In 1886, strong national unions connected with the Knights withdrew in dissatisfaction and founded the American Federation of Labor. It was then a simple matter for the two federations to amalgamate—the new organization taking the name of the American Federation of Labor (AFL). Samuel Gompers became the first president of the group that was to dominate the labor movement for half a century.

Membership grew slowly during the next 12 years, reaching 250,000 by 1898. Then the first of two pre-1920 periods of remarkable AFL growth followed. By 1904, 1,676,000 workers had enlisted in the cause. A decade of slow increase ensued, and membership numbered approximately 2 million by 1914. Then came the second period of rapid additions to the ranks; by the end of World War I, the Federation could legitimately claim 4 million workers, or 80 percent of all union members. Of the unions remaining outside the AFL, the most important were the four railroad brotherhoods, which were highly cooperative. The rest contended for jurisdiction with AFL affiliates or had disaffiliated.

Although labor leaders themselves might not place primary emphasis on the fortuitous onset of almost 25 years of good times, prosperity was a major element in the stability of the new organization. Between 1898 and World War I, economic activity on the whole was quite high, exhibiting a rapidly growing rate of industrial output. There were only three depressed periods, and the country emerged from these without experiencing serious deflation or prolonged unemployment. But credit must also be given to those who planned the strategy. After long years of trial and error, labor leaders, including men with radical backgrounds like Strasser and Gompers, had discovered the principle of pushing for concrete gains in good times and strongly supporting what legislative action could be achieved without participating in politics as a labor party.

Furthermore, their policy "to defeat labor's enemies and to reward its friends" meant that they played one major political party against another—a practice that probably maximized the number of bills favorable to labor that were passed by legislative bodies and minimized the risk of shattering defeats at the polls.

Certainly some credit for the American Federation of Labor's remarkable prewar success must be attributed to (1) its almost uncanny ability to make suitable modifications in structure without violating craft autonomy or permitting "dual" unionism, and (2) its promotion of the trade or collective-bargaining agreement as a means of stabilizing employer–employee relations.

From the experiences of the preceding 75 years, AFL leaders were convinced that stable unions had to be organized by self-governing crafts. The one unifying principle of the Federation was control of job opportunities and job conditions. This principle implied an organizational unit comprised of workers who performed the same job and who, in the absence of collective action, would compete with one another to their economic detriment. Thus the craft union could act quickly to exert economic pressure on the employer.

But craft organization also meant that there could be no more than one union to a trade. Two unions within a single craft (dualism) was unthinkable; dualism weakened solidarity and destroyed a "united front." Yet the disadvantages to rigorous adherence to the single-craft ideal became more pronounced after the turn of the century. First, there was the perplexing problem of setting the boundaries between different crafts; "demarcation" or "jurisdictional" disputes arose with increasing frequency. Second, problems of common interest to several crafts could not be solved because there was no basis of cooperative action. Finally, mechanization of industry and rapid immigration made it possible for employers to substitute unskilled for skilled workers, thereby weakening the control of single-craft unions.

To solve these problems by a wholesale turning to industrial unionism would have been to deny the principle of craft autonomy. Yet it quickly became apparent that there would have to be *some* exceptions to craft organization. As early as 1902, for example, the AFL granted a charter to an industrial union, the United Mine Workers, for it was readily apparent that the numerical superiority of noncraftsmen in mining made organization on a basis of crafts altogether unrealistic. By 1915, however, only five industrial unions were affiliated with the AFL.

The AFL tended to solve the problem of structure by the amalgamation of two or more closely allied trades. Sometimes called "material" craft unions, the amalgamated organizations unified craftsmen who worked with the same material, such as metal or glass. By 1915, an observer could count only 28 pure craft unions in the AFL compared to nearly 100 amalgamated unions.

Meanwhile, AFL affiliates were assuring their own continued existence and the general stability of the labor movement by obtaining increased use of the written trade agreement. Written trade agreements were rare before the late 1880s; after 1890, they gradually became an accepted outcome of collective bargaining, whether on a local or national level. Such recognition was a great source of strength in the decade of slow growth that followed, and the footholds thus secured made possible a second period of increase in collective bargaining during World War I.

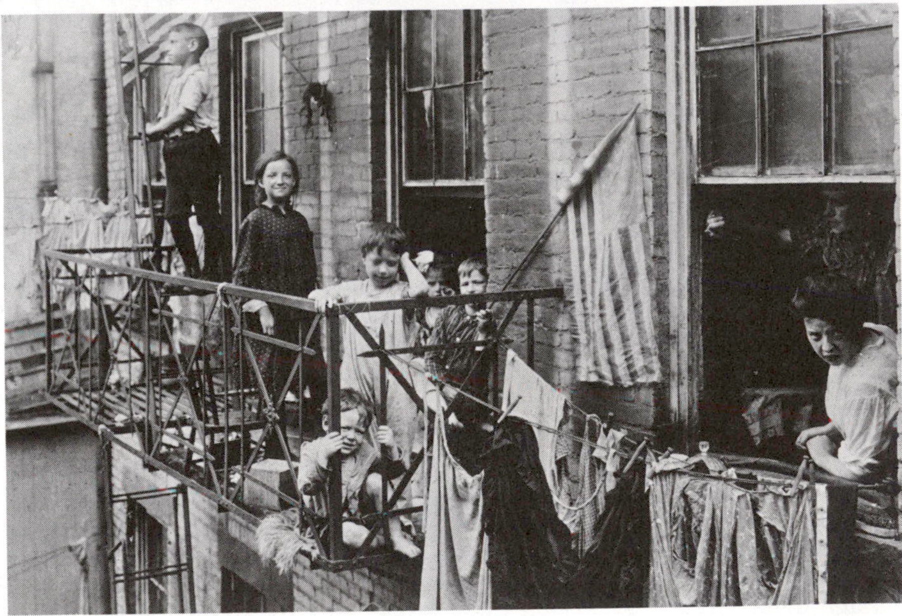

These pictures taken in New York's Lower East Side, circa *1920, change the focus from the generalities of slum dwelling to the particular poignancy of children with a fire-escape landing and a back alley for playgrounds.*

Industrial Conflict and Employer Opposition

The labor gains just recounted were not obtained without a serious and prolonged struggle that was still unresolved by 1920. Employers, supported by middle-class opinion and by government authorities, took the position that their rights and the very institution of private property were threatened by the growing strength of the unions.

The most violent conflict between management and labor occurred during the long, grinding deflation that lasted for nearly one-quarter of a century after 1873. During the depressed years of the mid-1870s, blood was shed as strikes were broken by force; a climax in the conflict was reached in the turmoil of 1877, which began with the railroad strikes in Pittsburgh and spread throughout the country. The brutality was not all on one side. In the anthracite regions of Pennsylvania, a secret society known as the "Molly Maguires" terrorized the populace and committed murder and other outrages for years while fighting employers and strikebreakers. Generally, however, it was the laborer who had to fend off the physical assaults of paid thugs, state militiamen, and federal troops.

Three incidents, purposely spaced over time to do the maximum damage to labor's cause, stand out as examples of the most severe disputes. The infamous Haymarket affair of May 4, 1886, was the tragic climax of efforts of the

Simultaneous strikes by various Chicago unions were met by strong police action, resulting in the Haymarket Riot of May 4, 1886.

Henry Clay Frick (shown here with his wife enjoying the 1915 Easter Parade in New York) obtained coking coal properties that were vital to an integrated steel firm. Frick later became Andrew Carnegie's partner and an architect of the hard line that steel leaders took with the labor unions in the bitter Homestead Mill strike of 1892.

Knights of Labor to secure a general strike of workers in the Chicago area. A bomb thrown at police officers attempting to break up a mass meeting at Haymarket Square resulted in several deaths. Four men, who were probably innocent, were executed for murder. Although the injustice of the punishment aroused great resentment on the side of labor sympathizers, anti-labor agitators used the incident as a horrible example of what radicals and anarchists would do to undermine American institutions by violence.

Six years later, just as anti-labor feeling was subsiding, the management of the Carnegie Homestead Works at Pittsburgh decided to oust the Amalgamated Association of Iron and Steel Workers, which was trying to organize the Homestead laborers. A strike was called, ostensibly because the company refused to come to an agreement on wage matters, and Henry Frick, a close associate of

Carnegie, brought in 300 Pinkerton detectives to disperse the strikers and maintain order. Turning the tables, the striking mob won a heated battle with the detectives, capturing several and injuring them severely. To restore order, the state militia was called out, and the union suffered a defeat that set the organization of labor in steel mills back several decades.

The adverse publicity received by the Homestead episode was exceeded only by that of the Pullman strike of 1894. Although the Pullman strike was led by mild-mannered Eugene V. Debs, who had not yet embraced socialist doctrines, the strife was attributed to the un-American ideology of radical leaders. Rioting spread over the entire Chicago area, and before peace was restored—this time by federal troops sent on pretext of protecting the U.S. mails—scores of people were killed and injured. Again the seriousness of the labor problem became a matter for widespread concern and the basis of much immoderate opposition to the labor cause in general. On the other hand, the Pullman strike served as a warning to conservative union leaders that violence would only disrupt unions and damage them in the public regard. Furthermore, the dispatch with which Debs and other labor leaders were jailed on contempt proceedings for disobeying a court injunction against inciting union members to strike was a sobering blow. Any long-run strategy would have to include efforts both to pacify voters and to strengthen labor's position in the courts. Pre-1920 successes along both lines were, to say the least, limited.

Beginning in 1902, employers changed their tactics. They began a serious drive to sell Americans on the benefits—to employers, workers, and the public—of the open shop. To further their propaganda, several organizations were formed. The most prominent were the National Association of Manufacturers and the American Anti-boycott Association, both of which were assisted materially by employers' trade associations. So effective were the employers' efforts that labor leaders of all shades of political belief experienced increasing pressure from their constituents to fight back.

It was inevitable that a radical, activist left should emerge. A small group of extremists advocated the overthrow of the state itself and, in their militancy, tinged the leftist movement with the threat of violence. Socialism under various labels gained small followings; doctrines ranged from the utopian idealism of Edward Bellamy to Marxist insistence on revolutionary seizure by the state of basic industries and services. Yet the only radical group that showed any signs of gaining a permanent place in the labor movement was the Independent Workers of the World (IWW), which was formed about 1905. From 1909 to 1917, it was a militant organization, preaching doctrines of intimidation and sabotage, leading successful strikes against textile firms in the East, and keeping the mining and lumber industries of the Northwest in a continual state of upheaval. But the "Wobblies" opposed World War I so vocally that they aroused public hostility and ultimately the bitter repression of police authorities everywhere. The small postwar remnant of the IWW membership apparently joined forces with the Communists.

Gompers, able young John Mitchell of the United Mine Workers, and others favored a counteroffensive against the employers through education and propaganda. Affiliating with the National Civic Federation—an association of people with an enlightened social outlook, including wealthy eastern

Labor leadership eventually became concentrated largely in the hands of Samuel Gompers who sat on the first Executive Council of the American Federation of Labor in 1881.

capitalists, corporation officers, editors, professional people, and labor representatives—AFL leaders sought to elicit a more favorable attitude from the electorate. The National Civic Federation maintained a division for the mediation and conciliation of disputes, tried to secure wider acceptance of collective-bargaining agreements, and preached the doctrine that greater labor responsibility would mean fewer work stoppages and a better livelihood for all. How much good the National Civic Federation did is hard to say. It doubtlessly served in part to offset the organized efforts of employers, but the alliance may have lulled job-conscious unionists into ultraconservatism at a time when more aggressive policies were called for. At any rate, the core of employer opposition remained almost as solid as ever, particularly among the industrialists of the Midwest.

Nor did the judiciary show signs of increasing liberality toward statutory attempts to protect the right of workers to organize. By the end of the nineteenth century, the right of labor unions to *exist* was established. Yet the right of employers to force employees to enter into anti-union contracts was upheld to the very end of the period under discussion. In the case of *Adair* v. *United States* (1908), the Supreme Court declared unconstitutional a provision of the Erdman Act that made it unlawful for any carrier in interstate commerce to discharge an employee because he or she had joined a union. In the case of *Coppage* v. *Kansas* (1912), a state law, similar to many state laws passed to outlaw anti-union contracts, was declared invalid. Coppage, a railroad employee, had been fired for refusing to withdraw from a union. Because his withdrawal would have cost him $1,500 in insurance benefits, the Kansas Supreme Court held that the statute protecting him prevented coercion and was valid. But the Supreme Court of the United States reversed this decision, holding that an employer had a constitutional right to require an anti-union contract from employees; a statute contravening this right, the Court held, violated the Fourteenth Amendment in that it abridged the employer's freedom of contract.

As late as 1917, the U.S. Supreme Court decided that anti-union or "yellow-dog" contracts, whether oral or written, could be protected by injunction. The Hitchman Coal and Coke Company, after winning a strike, had hired back miners on the condition that they could not be members of the United Mine Workers while in the employ of the company. Later, union organizers tried to convince the miners to promise that after a certain time had elapsed they would again join the union. In a U.S. District Court, the company asked for and obtained an injunction stopping further efforts to organize. The Supreme Court affirmed the decision, holding that, even though the miners had not yet joined the union, they were being induced by organizers to break a contract with the employer and that the employer was entitled to injunctive protection.

In the aggregate, union impact remained negligible throughout the entire nineteenth century. Without legal support, union membership remained small, as did the influence of organized labor. For instance, union membership in 1860 was merely .1 percent of the total labor force. This figure had jumped to 2.3 percent by 1870, but then it slumped throughout the 1880s and 1890s. By 1900, it had regained its 1870 proportions at 2.7 percent. But not until the end of World War I did union membership exceed 10 percent of the total labor force.

In 1920, labor could look back on 60 years of improvement. Real wages were up and hours were shorter. As laborers, children and—to some extent—women were protected by law. The fundamental ideas of Social Security were being more generally discussed, and clear-cut legislative victories had been won to reduce the hardships caused by industrial accidents. In addition, trade unions had become strong enough to weather future depressions without disintegrating, and they gave political support to legislated advances. For the most part, however, labor's progress was reflected in rising standards of living and work stemming from economic growth and rising productivity—not from union strength.

21

Commerce at Home and Abroad

TRADE AT HOME

Major Flows of Commerce

For 30 years after the Civil War, the currents of commerce were comparable to what they had been in the antebellum period, largely because the old regional specializations were maintained that long. New England and the Middle Atlantic states continued to send manufactured goods west and south in exchange for agricultural products and raw materials. In the 1890s, however, the composition of the flow of goods changed perceptibly as the North Central and southern states began to generate a significant amount of manufacturing output for national as well as local markets. Between 1900 and 1920, production in the industrial Northeast increased steadily, but not as fast as it did in the newer areas, which took advantage of their ready access to rich sources of raw materials and westward-moving markets to reduce transportation costs.

Ohio, Indiana, Illinois, Michigan, and Wisconsin specialized in making goods that were dependent on the basic resources of coal and steel. Until 1900 or so, the products of these newer states were typically less highly finished than the products of the eastern states. But with the growth of the automobile industry and with rapid additions to the list of household appliances, it became apparent that one day this area would be the formidable rival of the Middle Atlantic–New England region. We have already observed that agricultural processing industries flourished in the central states. The only major raw materials that had to be imported in time were lumber from the South and petroleum from the Southwest.

The South's sharp and absolute economic decline in the 1860s remained visible for at least 15 years after the Civil War, and for another half-century the South remained *relatively* backward. Progress lay in industrialization that would furnish jobs for the excess rural population so that incomes could rise sufficiently to give southerners a standard of living comparable to that of the rest of the country. Yet before 1920, southern manufacture was mostly of the low-value-added kind. The cotton-textile industry, chief among the new industries, made remarkable gains after the turn of the century. Indeed, by 1920, the South boasted almost half the spindles in cotton manufacture and probably more than half the spindle-hours operated. In addition, tobacco manufacture, production of food and related products, and furniture making had become significant southern industries by 1920. And more and more of these products began to be distributed in a westerly as well as a northerly direction.

Cities in the Midwest and the South, long established as distributing centers for the manufactures of the East, grew phenomenally as industrial workers flocked to them. Chicago and Detroit, Cleveland and Cincinnati, St. Louis and Kansas City, Memphis and New Orleans, and Atlanta and Birmingham originated shipments that went far beyond their own trade areas in all directions. By 1910, the West and the South originated half as much railroad tonnage of manufactures as the East. Meanwhile, smaller cities within the trade areas of the metropolises and cities in the thinly populated region west of the Mississippi specialized in the mercantile function. Trade eddied about these lesser centers, which distributed wholesale and retail goods over clearly marked, if overlapping, territories. As automobiles came into common use after 1910, large towns and cities gained business at the expense of small towns and villages; by 1920, retailers in urban centers were beginning to attract customers from distances which had been unimaginable during the previous decade. This change was reflected in new ways of distributing goods and in new marketing institutions.

Changes in Marketing Methods

Nineteenth-century Americans resented the middleman. This feeling was a holdover from the days when any seller of goods was suspected of chicanery and the courts adjured the buyer to beware. Something of the same suspicion is still attached to those who handle goods in the intermediate distributive processes. On hasty consideration, manufacturers' agents, wholesalers, brokers, jobbers, and even salespeople may seem unnecessary. A little reflection, however, convinces us that their contribution to the entire productive process is great. It is obvious that consumer goods are of no use if they are not somehow made available to household units.

Due to the difficulties of communication and transportation until late in the nineteenth century, wholesalers were far more powerful then than they are today. The problems to be surmounted in the assembling of wares required people who had great business ability. During colonial days and until about 1840, the wholesaling function in the United States was performed by great importing merchants and by brokers and commission agents. Importers bought from the rest of the world a variety of semifinished and finished goods that were sold to jobbers or directly to city retailers and country merchants. As the output of American factories grew in the first half of the nineteenth century, manufacturers found it convenient to let commission agents take their whole product and dispose of it in urban markets. Manufacturers were thus relieved of the necessity of selling their own products, although they frequently became overly dependent on their agents.

In the two decades before the Civil War, wholesaling institutions began to change. As an agent middleman, the commission merchant received the goods of others for sale and was accountable to the owner for the proceeds of the sale, but did not take title to the goods.[1] The full-service wholesale houses that evolved after 1840 bought goods on their own account from manufacturers and importers to sell to retailers, frequently on credit. In the growing cities of the Midwest, successful retailers began to perform some wholesale functions along with the business of selling to consumers. As these houses grew, they sometimes dropped their retailing activities altogether and concentrated on handling the output of manufacturing centers in the East. Occasionally, wholesale firms—especially those located in major distributing centers like Chicago and St. Louis—offered several lines of merchandise, but more often they specialized in a single "full line," such as hardware or dry goods.

From 1860 to 1900, full-line, full-service wholesale houses were without serious competitors in the business of distributing goods from manufacturers to retailers. But as transportation and communication facilities improved after the turn of the century, the power the wholesaler enjoyed began to shift, because some manufacturers—their financial capabilities increasing with size—could advertise their wares in great regional markets or even the national market and thus reach retail outlets directly. Wholesale houses did not decline between 1900 and 1920; in fact, their sales continued to increase, but they handled an ever smaller *proportion* of goods in wholesale channels.

In rural areas, where retail units remained characteristically small and independent, the wholesale house kept its customers. The general store was rapidly disappearing except in villages and hamlets, as retailers in towns with a surrounding trade area began to specialize in particular lines. But this specialization of retail functions did not bring about a reduction of the traditional wholesaler's business. What transpired was the development of new types of retail outlets, usually large ones, and the increasing ability of manufacturers to establish strong consumer preferences through advertising.

Department Stores. Of the new retailing organizations that gained definite acceptance by 1920, the department store ran counter to the trend of greater specialization in handling merchandise. As cities became bigger and more congested, the convenience of being able to shop for all personal necessities in a single store had an increasing appeal. Furthermore, department stores offered delivery services and credit privileges that were conveniences in an ever more complex urban existence. The early department stores in large cities

[1] After deducting the expenses of selling the goods (chiefly transportation and warehousing costs) and a commission, the commission merchant remitted the sales receipts to the manufacturer of the goods.

Manhattan residents purchased a great variety of groceries from vendors. In this photograph, an inspector is testing the accuracy of the scale of a downtown pushcart vegetable vendor in the early 1900s.

evolved after the Civil War from the efforts of dry-goods stores to replace business lost to the growing ready-to-wear trade. There was a definite division of the store into separate departments, each with its own manager, buyers, and clerks for a line of merchandise; the separation was once so distinct that departments were frequently leased to individuals or companies—a practice much less common today.

At first, department stores bought merchandise through wholesalers. However, larger stores like Macy's in New York, John Wanamaker's in Philadelphia, and Marshall Field in Chicago took advantage of their growing size to obtain price reductions by going directly to manufacturers or their selling agents. Due to the size of their operations, large stores with numerous clerks had to set one price for all customers and the old practice of haggling with

Measurements of American male sizes for Civil War uniforms marked the beginning of standardized clothing, and U.S. manufacturers of boots and shoes steadily improved the quality and fit of their product. Economies resulting from massproduction techniques drove down the cost of clothing and mail-order solicitation helped to broaden markets.

F. W. Woolworth—a pioneer in chain-store merchandising—opened his first store in 1879 in Lancaster, Pennsylvania.

merchants over the price of an article was soon a thing of the past. So successful was the department store concept that by 1920 even small cities could usually boast one. Small department stores purchased merchandise through regular wholesale channels, and their departmentalization was so indistinct that they were very similar to the general store of an earlier day.

Chain Stores. Middlemen participate in the series of transactions that makes it possible for goods to yield their services to consumers; the middleman's profit is the return received for taking risks in the performance of this function. The fact that nineteenth-century middlemen were doing a necessary job did not mean that they were doing it as efficiently as possible. It soon became apparent to some enterprisers that the costs of distributing goods in certain lines could be reduced by performing agency and brokerage functions in their own departments and by buying directly from manufacturers and processors. But to achieve the bargaining power to enable them to buy directly, enterprisers had to have retail sales of considerable magnitude. Such sales could be obtained by combining many spatially separate outlets in chains with a centralized buying and administrative authority. Additional savings could be made by curtailing or eliminating the major services of credit and delivery.

One of the early chains, still with us today, was the Great Atlantic and Pacific Tea Company, founded in 1859. From an original line restricted to tea and coffee, the company expanded in the 1870s to a general line of groceries. In 1879, F.W. Woolworth began the venture that was to make him a multimillionaire when he opened variety stores carrying articles that sold for no more than a dime. By 1900, tobacco stores and drugstores were often organized in chains, and hardware stores and restaurants soon began to fall under centralized managements. By 1920, grocery, drug, and variety chains were firmly established as a part of the American retail scene. A few companies then numbered their units in the thousands, but the great growth of the chains was to come in the 1920s and 1930s—along with innovations in physical layout and the aggressive selling practices that would incur the wrath of the independents.

Mail-Order Houses. It is difficult for the modern urban resident to imagine the thrill of "ordering by mail." Yet for many American families in the decades before World War I, the annual arrival of a catalog from Montgomery Ward or Sears, Roebuck was an event that was anticipated with pleasure. Although Montgomery Ward started his business with the intention of selling only to Grangers, he soon included other farmers and many city dwellers among his customers. Both Montgomery Ward and Sears, Roebuck & Company experienced their great growth periods after they moved to Chicago—a vantage point from which they could sell, with optimum economies of shipping costs and time, to eager midwestern agrarians and to both coasts as well. Rural free delivery and the establishment of a parcel-post system were godsends to mail-order houses. By 1920, however, farmers were readily accessible to town and could make their own purchases; if the mail-order houses were to remain important merchandisers, they would have to modify their selling methods.

Differentiation of Products

Merchants had advertised long before the Civil War. But as long as durable and semidurable goods were either made to order for the wealthy or turned out carelessly for the undiscriminating poor, and as long as food staples were sold out of bulk containers, the field of the advertiser was limited. In fact, the

Advertising helped to expand the consumer demand for new products like this all-purpose potion.

first attempts at advertising on more than a local scale were directed largely toward retailers rather than consumers. Notable exceptions were patent-medicine manufacturers—the first sellers in America to advertise on a national scale. A combination of circumstances accounted for this peculiar fact. The general health of Americans in the nineteenth century was not especially good, medical facilities were not available to everyone, and there was a universal seeking for relief from aches and pains.[2] Once a nostrum gained acceptance, competitors could make inroads on its sales only after persistent and extensive newspaper campaigns. In a field where profit margins were tremendous, rewards to successful advertisers were high.

[2] There is a suspicion that the popularity of patent medicines resulted in good part from their high alcohol content. Many, if not most, customers would not have touched liquor, and they may not have realized that the immediate sense of well-being derived from such medicines arose from alcohol instead of from other "beneficial ingredients."

Not until after the Civil War, however, did advertising on a national scale become a widely accepted business practice. With the trusts came truly national firms, whose brand names and trademarks became impressed on the minds of consumers. Where products such as tobacco, whiskey, kerosene, and rubber boots and shoes could be rationally differentiated in terms of buyer thinking, the trusts attempted a staid institutional advertising designed to reassure householders about the quality of the goods being purveyed. And as the quality of nondurables improved, particularly in the case of clothing, manufacturers of leather shoes, hosiery, underwear, and men's suits and overcoats found that a loyal, nationwide following could be won through brand-name advertising.

By 1920, advertising was a billion-dollar industry. In some fields, the increasing size of the firm in American industry was an important factor in the growth of national advertising, but advertising itself helped firms to attain large sizes.

It became a well-accepted fact that a firm had to advertise to maintain its share of an industry's sales. It was also realized that as competing firms carried on extensive campaigns, the demand for a product might increase throughout the entire industry. Yet only a beginning had been made. Two changes were to loom large in the future of American advertising. One was the radio, which within a decade was to do the job of advertising far more effectively than it had ever been done before. The second was the change in the kind of consumer durables people would buy in the future. In 1869, half the output of consumer durables consisted of furniture and house furnishings; 30 years later, the same categories still accounted for somewhat more than half of the total. But after 1910, as first the automobile and then electrical appliances revolutionized American life, the share of furniture and household furnishings in the output of consumer durables declined rapidly. Household furnishings were articles that could not be differentiated in people's minds with any remarkable degree of success, although efforts were continually made to do so. On the other hand, automobiles and household appliances could be readily differentiated and presented a wonderful challenge to the American advertising account executive.

FOREIGN TRADE

Between 1860 and 1920, the network of international trade underwent extensive changes and assumed its modern characteristics. From the new lands of the world came an ever-swelling flow of foodstuffs and raw materials to support the growing industrial populations and feed the furnaces and fabricating plants of industry. In exchange went the manufactured and semimanufactured products of the industrial countries—chiefly Great Britain, Germany, and the United States.

Two major forces dominated the great sweep of change. One was the rapid improvement in methods of communication and transportation. To take several instances: The first transatlantic cable began operations in 1866, a railroad line spanned the American continent in 1869, the Suez Canal was opened in the same year, and dramatic productivity gains in ocean transportation occurred over the last half of the nineteenth century. An extremely important improvement was the development of railroads in various parts of the world, making possible a flood of cheap grain from Canada, Australia, Argentina, Russia, and the Danube Valley, as well as from the midlands of the United States. In the late 1870s and early 1880s, refrigeration on vessels made possible the shipment of meats, then dairy products, and lastly fruits. To these were added the products of the tropics—rice, coffee, cocoa, vegetable oils, and tapioca. However, the shipment of grains was also of great importance in stimulating the worldwide distribution of foods.

But transportation was not the whole story. We have already described the second major force at work—improvements in metals processing. It was not by mere chance that Great Britain, Germany, and the United States rose to industrial supremacy during the nineteenth century: These were the countries that had coal and iron in abundance. England, which until 1875 was preeminent in manufactures, lost ground in the last quarter of the century to Germany and the United States. The volume of British trade increased, but England's chief role became that of a world financial leader. The United States forged to the front in iron and steel production; Germany and the United States quickly became leaders in the applied fields engendered by the scientific efforts—the electrical, chemical, and machine-tool industries.

During the last third of the nineteenth and the first decade of the twentieth centuries, the countries of the world became divided for at least a century into two groups—those that possessed political and economic power and those that did not. The tropical and subtropical countries of Africa, Asia, and South America, although drawn into world trade as sources of materials and (reciprocally) as buyers of cheap factory products, remained nearly stagnant at low levels of income per capita and developed little industrial power. In the temperate zones, where the Occident had reproduced itself—in the United States, Canada, Australia, New Zealand, and Argentina—population growth ran ahead of food production and income per capita rose rapidly. No other area, however, reached a stature comparable to that of the United States.

Since the period 1864–1896 was one of falling prices, the dollar values of United States foreign trade increased less than the physical volume of trade did. On the other hand, the period 1896–1914 was one of steady increases in prices, and from 1914 to 1920, price rises reflected sharp inflationary pressures. Thus, the physical volume of trade between 1896 and 1920 did not increase by anything close to the amount indicated by the dollar figures. Nonetheless, due to World War I, there was a remarkable increase in trade, especially on the export side, between 1914 and 1920. Merchandise imports almost invariably exceeded exports until 1875. From 1875 on, exports exceeded imports in every year except three; from 1894 on, there was no year in which the value of goods exported from the country did not exceed the value of goods imported into the country.

There were also major changes in the kinds of goods exchanged. On the export side, the most striking change was the decline of raw materials from three-fifths the value of exports at the end of the Civil War to less than one-fifth the value of exports by 1920. Crude foodstuffs swelled to nearly one-quarter of the total exports for the five-year period 1876–1880, reflecting the piercing of the West by the railroads, and then declined until 1915. Manufactured foodstuffs also rose to one-quarter of total exports for the period 1876–1880, held this proportion for 25 years, and then dropped in relative importance until World War I brought a small revival. A third important trend was the sustained rise of semimanufactures and finished manufactures. In the 1915–1920 period, these two categories accounted for about half the total value of exports.

We find the opposite movements, although not as marked, on the import side. Crude materials rose from one-tenth the value of imports after the Civil War to two-fifths the value of imports during the World War I years. The chief crude materials imported—those that were necessary to a great industrial structure but that could not be found in the United States—were rubber, tropical fibers, and metals such as nickel and tin. Crude foodstuffs showed uneven ups and downs, but did not change materially over the half-century, as Americans imported coffee, tropical fruits, and olive and coconut oils that could be produced domestically only at great cost, if at all. Imports of semimanufactures increased somewhat, but finished manufactures declined in importance as American productive capacity grew.

Finally, trade linkages altered as well. Although Europe became a more important customer of the United States than ever before after the Civil War, American exports to Europe began to decline about 1885. During the 1870s and 1880s, Europeans were the recipients of more than four-fifths of all U.S. exports; by 1920, this figure had dropped to three-fifths. In the meantime, the United States remained Europe's best customer. But the sharp decline in the proportion of American imports from Europe during the years 1915–1920, a result of wartime disruption, permanently injured this trade.

In the first 20 years of the twentieth century, American foreign traders found customers in Asia and Canada, and an interest in the Latin American market was just beginning. On the import side, the Asiatic countries and Canada were furnishing a great part of the crude materials that were becoming typical U.S. imports. South America had already achieved a substantial position as a purveyor of coffee and certain key raw materials to Americans.

The best way to summarize the history of American foreign trade is to examine a series of international balance-of-payments statements to see what changes occurred in the major accounts. As Table 21-1 shows, the United States had a slightly unfavorable trade balance between 1850 and 1873. Between 1874 and 1895, the balance of trade shifted to favorable, becoming markedly favorable between 1896 and 1914 and enormously favorable between 1915 and 1920. But, as we have learned, items other than merchandise enter into the international balance of payments. A persistently favorable balance of trade may be offset by "importing" the services, the securities, or the gold of other nations. It is important to understand how, as years went by, the people of the United States offset their consistently favorable balance of trade.

The Civil War and the years immediately following saw a continuation of high levels of income and a consequently high propensity to import goods and services. Moreover, U.S. firms were paying foreigners substantial sums in interest and dividends on *previous* investments by foreign nationals in American business enterprises. Table 21-1 shows that a total of $1.8 billion *net* was paid out by Americans over the period 1850–1873. Residents of the United States could enjoy this net inflow of goods and services and pay interest and divi-

TABLE 21–1
United States International Payments, by Periods
(billions of dollars)

Period	Net goods and services	Net income on investment	Net capital transactions	Unilateral transfers	Changes in monetary gold stock[a]	Errors and omissions
1850–1873	–.8	–1.0	1.6	.2		
1874–1895	1.7	–2.2	1.5	–.6	–.4	
1896–1914	6.8	–1.6	–.7	–2.6	–1.3	–.6
1915–1919	14.3	1.4	–14.1	–1.8	1.2	–1.0

Source: *Historical Statistics of the United States, Colonial Times to 1957,* pp. 562–65.
[a]A minus sign indicates an addition to the U.S. monetary gold stock. Why?

dends on existing foreign investments largely because foreign nationals continued to make *new* investments in American businesses, usually in American railroads.[3] Another balancing item during this period was the $200 million in foreign currencies brought or sent to the United States and changed into dollars by immigrants and their families. Such payments are called *unilateral transfers.*

From 1874 to 1895, the American price level declined more than price levels abroad, so exports were stimulated, while the slowly growing real incomes of many Americans kept imports down. Moreover, American agricultural commodities were available to the world market in rapidly increasing quantities. When we consider that the manufacturing industries of the United States were also becoming progressively more efficient, it is hardly surprising to find that exports increased as they did. During these years, the favorable *trade* balance was reduced by the growing tendency of Americans to use the *services* of foreigners. Even so, Americans had net credits on current account of $1.7 billion, and foreign investors poured another $1.5 billion into this country. Offsetting the credits were more than $2 billion in interest and dividend payments to foreigners, and on balance unilateral transfers began to reverse themselves as immigrants sent substantial sums back to friends and relatives in their countries of origin. To make up the balance, the United States imported a little gold.

During the prosperous years of 1896–1914, the United States came into its own as an economic power. The favorable balance of trade shot up to over $9 billion, but this figure was cut to less than $7 billion by purchases of services from foreigners. Interest and dividend payments to foreign investors, remittances of immigrants to their families, a slight reversal of the capital flow, and an inward gold flow secured a balance of payments.

Finally, World War I wrought a change in the balance of payments of the United States. The last rows of Table 21-1 show the great jump in the favorable balance of trade created by the prodigious demand for American war materials.

[3]International investment can take one of two forms: *real* investment or *portfolio* investment. Real investment occurs when a foreign company builds a plant for operation in the domestic market of another country. Portfolio investment takes place when foreign nationals buy the securities (stocks and bonds) of firms in another country.

Until the United States entered the war in 1917, European nations financed their purchases here by selling their American securities and by shipping gold. When the United States finally took its position on the side of the Allies, continued large purchases of American goods were made possible by U.S. government loans to the Allies of nearly $10 billion. At this stage in the progress of international relations, the United States did not think of *giving* assistance to its friends. It was expected that one day the loans would be repaid, but just how Europeans would earn the dollar exchange with which to repay the loans no one made clear. During the war, Americans, as private citizens, began to invest heavily in the fortunes of other countries; in these few years they received more income in the form of interest and dividends than they paid out. At last, the United States had shifted from a debtor position to the position of a major creditor. Although the capital flow reversal had preceded World War I, the effect was to involve the United States in world matters on an unprecedented scale. As we will see in the following section, to some, we appeared to be a new imperialist country.

THE ACCEPTANCE OF PROTECTIONIST DOCTRINES

In a Victorian world that paid more than lip service to the ideal of laissez faire, the untrammeled price system was allowed to allocate domestic resources more than ever before or ever since. But the United States, which—like most of Europe—had long been protectionist, became more so beginning with the Civil War. Setting up ever-higher tariff walls, Americans led the way in trying to control trade with other countries in the interests of national policy.

In 1861, maximum U.S. tariffs were not more than 24 percent and averaged about 20 percent on dutiable commodities. The national prosperity of the last 15 years before the Civil War seemed to refute protectionist arguments that a healthy economy required high duties. Yet by 1864, the trend of nearly three decades was reversed so sharply and positively as to put the United States on a high protective-tariff basis for nearly three-quarters of a century. There was no widespread demand for such a change in policy; only in the manufacturing centers were the old arguments for protection advanced with enthusiasm. To win the votes of the industrial East, the Republicans advocated higher tariffs during the campaign of 1860. After the returns were in but before Lincoln's inauguration, Congress passed the Morrill Act of 1861—the first in a long series of laws levying ever-higher taxes on imports. Thus, the first step was taken before the war, but only when the southern congressional opponents of the tariff were not in the Congress. The requirements of Civil War financing, at a time when import duties and domestic excises furnished the principal revenues, provided an excuse for raising tariffs to unprecedented highs. By 1864, the *average* level of duties was 47 percent, and protection was granted to any commodity for which it was requested.

For 25 years after the war, a few leaders in both political parties attempted to reduce the "war tariffs." In 1872, to ward off drastic downward reductions that appeared imminent, protectionist forces in Washington agreed to a flat 10-percent decrease in all protective duties. But in 1875, the earlier levels were restored, and it appeared for a time that the electorate was resigned to permanently high import rates. Yet people were increasingly persuaded that protective tariffs were, in effect, a tax that raised consumer-goods prices—and there was a growing suspicion that high levels of protection fostered the rapid growth of business combinations. During his first administration, President Grover Cleveland placed the Democrats squarely on the side of greater freedom of trade, but two Democratic assaults on the protective system produced disappointingly modest results. Cleveland's defeat in 1888 blasted hopes of genuine reform. The McKinley tariff of 1890 raised the average level of protection to 50 percent, increased the articles on the dutiable list, and reaffirmed the Republican commitment to the support of high tariffs. Following insignificant reductions during Cleveland's second term, the Dingley Act of 1897 raised duties to an average of almost 60 percent. More goods, by value, were now taxed as imports than were admitted free. As might be expected, free goods were mostly raw and semifinished commodities requiring further processing, but even some farm products, raw wool, and hides were placed in a protected category.

The prosperity of 1897–1914 made it easy to defend high-tariff policies. It was argued that the country was experiencing a high level of employment and economic activity *because* tariffs were high. Yet by 1900, American industry had obviously come of age. American manufacturers were competing in the markets of Europe; it was apparent, especially in the metal-processing industries, that most American firms needed no protection. The textile industries, which had enjoyed the benefits of high tariffs for a century, paid the lowest wages, had the highest unemployment, and suffered from the rigors of competition more than any other class of producers. Moreover, it was readily demonstrable by this time that import duties usually raised the prices of protected articles to consumers. As the populace felt the pressures of rising living costs in the first decade of the century, voters blamed the tariffs, and Democratic politicians exploited this political unrest. When the Payne–Aldrich bill of 1909 failed to bring any relief from high tariffs, there was widespread political protest.

In the campaign of 1912, the Democrats promised a downward revision of import duties—a revision that was carried out in the Underwood–Simmons bill of 1913. These reductions, while substantial, were not sufficient to satisfy everyone; however, iron and steel were placed on the free list, and duties on cost-of-living items like cotton and woolen textiles were sharply reduced. The result was a simplified tariff structure, still of protective significance, with average duties about one-half of what they had been for several decades. During President Woodrow Wilson's administration, the average level of the tariffs was just slightly more than 25 percent—almost the level that had prevailed in 1860.

From 1789 until almost the end of the period we are considering, tariff-making was a legislative matter in the United States. The executive branch of the government no longer had discretion in setting tariff rates, and the same duties applied to imports of a given class, no matter what the country of origin. Shortly after the return to protection in the 1860s, it became apparent that the increasingly complicated tariff structure would require Congress to seek technical assistance in establishing rates. Furthermore, in a world in which barriers to international commerce were increasing, someone in the executive branch would have to be granted the authority to make tariff concessions to obtain favors from other countries. And even the firmest protectionists were aware that schedules made under the political pressures continually exerted on Congress might contain serious inequities that would burden those who ultimately had to pay the tax. Both political parties at last came out in support of tariff-making on a "scientific" basis. Tariffs were presumed to be scientifically computed if they precisely offset the lower cost of production of a given article by a foreign country.[4]

From the end of the Civil War, boards and commissions were suggested to achieve these various objectives, but no steps were taken until 1916 when Congress authorized a United States Tariff Commission. The Commission was not empowered to set tariff rates, but it could investigate rates and make recommendations for change. The Commission was to be bipartisan, and its freedom from political bias was supposed to help in achieving the proper "scientific" attitudes. This body added something new to American tariff history when, in 1922, Republicans in Congress got down to the serious business of raising rates again.

THE UNITED STATES IN AN IMPERIALIST WORLD

The erection of trade barriers by European countries in the nineteenth century (Great Britain being a notable exception) marked a revival of national selfconsciousness in the Old World. One manifestation of the revived nationalism was a "new" imperialism. During most of the nineteenth century, Europeans did not seek physical expansion, because the economically and politically powerful countries were not convinced that colonies were a paying proposition. But in the early 1880s, western Europeans became obsessed with a desire to own more of the earth's surface. Africa, which before 1875 was almost entirely unexplored and unsettled, was partitioned among the major European powers. In Asia, the French took over all of Indochina, British India annexed Burma, and Britain extended its hold over the Malay states. China, although it avoided physical disintegration, nevertheless had to make humiliating economic concessions to the major European powers. By the end of the nineteenth century, there was not much of the world left to colonize.

Pressures built up by the Industrial Revolution encouraged this second expansion of Europe. By 1875, the productive output of the industries that were first mechanized was becoming very great. Industrialists and merchants thought that Asiatic and African markets would furnish an outlet for the rapidly increasing production of cheap manufactured goods. The centuries-old notion that a government ought to have command over its sources of raw materials also played a strong part in the colonization. The most important of all the economic reasons, however, was the profit seeking of those who had capital to invest; the frantic efforts to seize thinly populated and apparently worthless land were stimulated by the hope of return from the fruits of the land or from

[4]Equalization of costs, if widely attempted, would of course have nullified the gains from international specialization.

mineral discoveries. Reinforcing the purely economic motives was a desire for national glory. Private citizens took personal pride in the fact that their country owned exotic territories and dominated weak peoples. Nor could it be denied, in a day when sea power was still vital to a nation's military success, that national strength was buttressed by the ownership of naval stations in widely separated parts of the globe.

The importance of economic motives in the search for colonial possessions is suggested by the fact that the nations that industrialized first were the leaders in late colonization. Great Britain, France, Belgium, and the Netherlands obtained the prize possessions. Germany, Italy, and Japan — the last major powers except Russia to feel the full impact of the Industrial Revolution — came out of the competition with the poorest prizes.

At this time, the United States maintained its preoccupation with internal affairs. As long as great areas of unexploited land lay within its borders, there were no pressures for physical expansion; inside its large free-trade area, domestic markets developed rapidly enough to forestall concern for foreign markets. When America finally decided to expand, the decision had little to do with the vulgar profit motive. U.S. imperialistic ventures were primarily the result of (1) a strong nationalist feeling engendered by a few politicians and vociferous newspaper editors and (2) the desire to achieve an impregnable military position in the Caribbean, the Central American Isthmus, and the Pacific.

But whatever its real motives, American expansion ostensibly sprang either from pure altruism or from accidents of history. The only territory outside the continental limits that the United States acquired before 1898 was Alaska, which was presumed at the time to be almost worthless. In 1893–1894, there was agitation to annex Hawaii, but the American people would not stand for the high-handed methods proposed to depose the old Hawaiian government. Business interests generally were opposed to the needless and tragic Spanish-American War, and there was little popular enthusiasm for the conflict, despite the chauvinist campaign of the Hearst newspapers, until a martial spirit was whipped up by the destruction of the U.S. battleship *Maine* in Havana harbor on February 15, 1898. But the quick and favorable outcome of the war forced Americans to make decisions regarding expansion outside their continental borders.

The first decisions concerned disposition of the former Spanish colonies of Cuba, Puerto Rico, and the Philippines. Cuba was given nominal independence and Puerto Rico received territorial status, but the Platt Amendment of 1901 so restricted Cuban independence that Cuba, in effect, became a protectorate of the United States. Instead of granting independence to the Philippines, the United States claimed them as a colonial possession. With these islands in the Pacific (see Map 21-1) and a growing interest in trade with the Orient, the United States insisted on an "open-door" policy in China and, in general, on economic opportunities in the Far East equal to those of the European powers. By the Hay–Varilla Treaty of 1903, the United States acquired a perpetual lease of the Panama Canal Zone from the newly independent Republic of Panama, and the completion of the canal in 1914 assured a lasting American interest in the Caribbean and Central America.

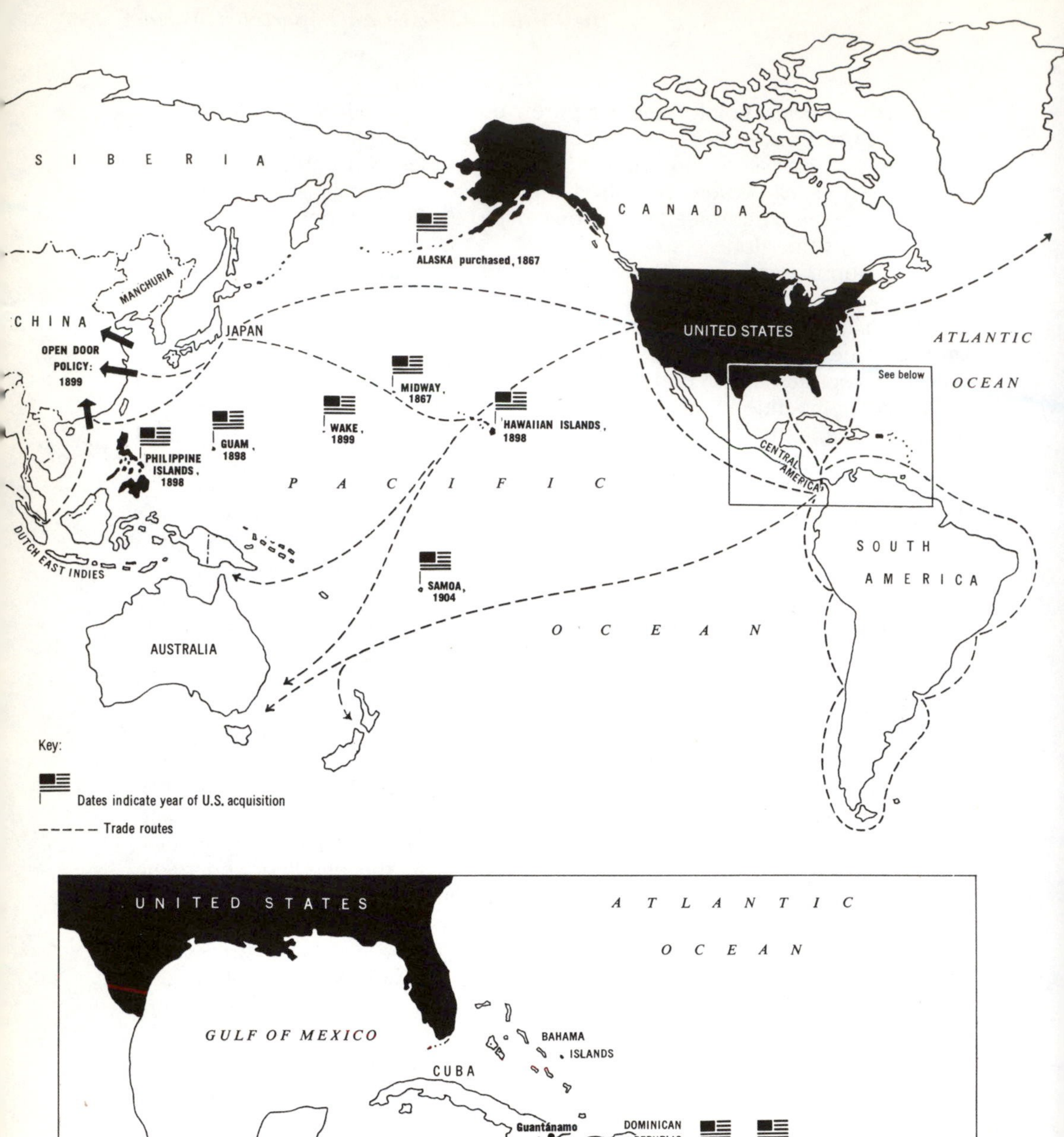
SIBERIA
CANADA
ALASKA purchased, 1867
MANCHURIA
CHINA
JAPAN
UNITED STATES
ATLANTIC OCEAN
OPEN DOOR POLICY: 1899
MIDWAY, 1867
HAWAIIAN ISLANDS, 1898
WAKE, 1899
GUAM, 1898
PHILIPPINE ISLANDS, 1898
See below
CENTRAL AMERICA
PACIFIC
OCEAN
DUTCH EAST INDIES
SAMOA, 1904
SOUTH AMERICA
AUSTRALIA
Key:
Dates indicate year of U.S. acquisition
Trade routes
UNITED STATES
ATLANTIC OCEAN
GULF OF MEXICO
BAHAMA ISLANDS
CUBA
Guantánamo
U.S. NAVAL BASE
DOMINICAN REPUBLIC
PUERTO RICO, 1898
VIRGIN ISLANDS, 1916
JAMAICA
HAITI
MEXICO
BR. HONDURAS
GUATEMALA
HONDURAS
EL SALVADOR
NICARAGUA
CARIBBEAN SEA
COSTA RICA
PANAMA CANAL ZONE, 1903
PANAMA
VENEZUELA
PACIFIC OCEAN
COLOMBIA
BR. GUIANA

Indeed, two years before construction of the canal began, the policy known as the "Roosevelt Corollary" to the Monroe Doctrine had been pronounced. In a message to Congress in 1904, President Theodore Roosevelt enunciated a principle that was to make the Monroe Doctrine an excuse for intervention in the affairs of Latin American countries. Because, Roosevelt argued, chronic weakness of a government might require some "civilized" nation to restore order and since, by the Monroe Doctrine, European interference would not be tolerated, the United States might be forced to exercise police power in "flagrant cases of wrongdoing or impotence." Europeans were not disturbed by such an assumption of international police power, but Latin Americans were. And they had reason to be apprehensive.

The United States did not take long to apply the Roosevelt Corollary. When the Dominican Republic could not meet its financial obligations, certain European states threatened to collect payments by force. Roosevelt's new doctrine required American intervention to forestall such moves. A treaty was signed in 1905 giving the United States authority to collect customs duties, of which 55 percent was to be paid to foreign creditors. In 1916, the Dominican government tried to escape American domination, and the U.S. Marines were sent in to quell the rebellion. In 1914, Haiti was made a protectorate of the United States, again with the aid of the Marines. American forces landed so often in Nicaragua that the succession of episodes became a standing joke.

After the 1910 revolution in Mexico against the old dictator, Porfirio Díaz, American and other foreign investors, who were heavily committed in railroads and oil, pressed for intervention and the restoration of order. For a time, President Wilson encouraged Latin Americans by failing to invade Mexico. But "watchful waiting" could last just so long amid the cries of outrage at the destruction of American property, and U.S. politicians were unable to tolerate these repeated affronts to American honor. Troops crossed onto Mexican soil in 1914 and 1917—the second time, under the leadership of Black Jack Pershing, to seize the "bandit" Pancho Villa. With the adoption of the Mexican Constitution in 1917, the turmoil subsided temporarily, only to begin again in the early 1920s.

The word "imperialism" has had a pejorative connotation in the American lexicon, even when the United States, flanked by the Atlantic and Pacific, was annexing such exotic places as the Philippines, Samoa, Hawaii, and the Virgin Islands, which allegedly provided essential naval bases. The years 1898–1918 were marked by an uncomfortable conviction on the part of many Americans that euphemisms, including *manifest destiny, extending the areas of freedom,* and the *white man's burden,* could not long cover up such high-handed methods as those used to wrest the Panama Canal Zone from Colombia. Nor would it be possible to maintain approval for a diplomacy that was devoted largely to promoting or protecting the private financial or commercial interests of the

MAP 21–1 (Opposite)

New Imperalism: A reluctant and sometimes uncertain America assumed colonial responsibility as a consequence of expanding world interests, wider-ranging trade, and growing industrial might.

United States. If American capital was willing to seek profits in the weak countries of Central America and the Caribbean, it should also have been willing to take the risks of venturing under unstable governments. Some Americans contended, of course, that the benighted Latins were better off with the improved sanitation, better educational facilities, and higher incomes that usually resulted from American intervention. Our friends to the south were not properly impressed, however—apparently preferring freedom to material gain.

The imperialistic ventures of the United States made the nation turn its attention outside itself and increase its military strength. Offsetting these gains were the fears and hatreds built up among natural allies in Central and South America, with whose aspirations Americans should have been in sympathy. It would take a new generation of Americans and a second world war to remove part of this emotional conflict. Even so, the harm of two decades of harsh diplomacy could not be undone. As the fires of world revolution were kindled among the disadvantaged peoples of the world, beginning in the 1950s, it was not hard to perceive the permanent injury to U.S. international relationships that was inflicted by America's experiment with imperialism.

22

Money, Banking, and Economic Fluctuations

THE MONEY SUPPLY, 1863–1914

In the last quarter of the nineteenth century, much economic hardship was imposed on some Americans because leaders in politics and finance insisted on "sound money." Following the inflation of the Civil War, prices in the United States began a decline that persisted, with brief interruptions, until a few years before the end of the century. During these years, various groups in the economy suffered at one time or another from the protracted deflation. As noted in Chapter 18, farmers of the West and the South were particularly hard hit and supported a variety of measures to reverse the long-time trend of deflation that began in the late 1860s. However, the periods of runaway inflation during Revolutionary times and in the South toward the end of the Civil War had taught American businesses a lesson they would not soon forget, and they were successful in resisting inflationary moves. To see this, we must trace the changes in the various types of currencies that made up the total money supply.

Greenbacks (United States Notes)

To meet its wartime obligations, the Treasury issued a fiat currency nicknamed "greenbacks." People were bound to accept greenbacks in payment of all debts except interest on the public debt, and the government accepted greenbacks for all payments except customs duties. Had the government been able to nationalize gold and silver and put the country on a paper basis, the problems of war financing would have been diminished. But in the 1860s, calling in gold and silver in exchange for bank deposits or greenbacks would have been an unthinkable violation of property rights. The value of greenbacks decreased to a discount compared with that of gold and silver, and two sets of prices soon were being quoted for commodities and foreign exchange. On the gold market in New York, greenbacks at one time sold at a gold price as low as 35 cents on the dollar; on August 31, 1865, 4½ months after the assassination of Lincoln, $100 in gold exchanged for $144.25 in greenbacks or checks drawn on bank deposits. Stated another way, the gold price of $100 in greenbacks on this date was $69.32. State-bank notes, which could be redeemed only in greenbacks, depreciated similarly; a serious element of instability was injected because the paper currency fluctuated violently below the gold par.

At the end of the war, there was agitation to have the greenbacks retired. Businesses wanted to return to a gold basis as quickly as possible, and most authorities agreed that gold redemption would be possible only after the paper circulation was reduced. After the close of hostilities, Congress authorized the redemption of greenbacks at a rate of $10 million per month for six months and $4 million per month thereafter. Prices began to drop, however, and Congress stopped the retirement. Later, a reissue of greenbacks was authorized; then, for the second time, a reduction was ordered. Finally, in 1878, the dollar volume of greenbacks authorized for circulation was left at just under $347 million—the amount that remains outstanding today.

The Gold Resumption Act

Although agitation to increase the amount of greenbacks in circulation was to continue for years, the question, as it turned out, had been finally settled. A second piece of legislation was to solve the problem of putting all money, including greenbacks, and other currencies on a par with gold.

A premium on gold meant that the price of a gold dollar in terms of all other money in the economy was above a dollar. To cause the resumption of specie payments, this *premium* of more than a dollar had to decrease to zero.

To achieve such a result, government policymakers first had to diagnose the problem. Between 1860 and 1865, the money stock had tripled and the price level had approximately doubled. The market price of gold had moved with the general price level, so that it was way above the mint price. Several alternative monetary policies were open to Treasury officials, but for all practical purposes two courses of action were available:

1. The general price level could be forced down by contracting the supply of paper money. The price of gold would decline with the general decrease in prices; when the mint price was reached, resumption could be proclaimed.
2. A slower and probably less painful decline in prices could be achieved by holding the money supply constant and allowing the growth of the economy to bring about a gradual decline in prices. Once again, the market price of gold would fall and ultimately reach the mint price.[1]

[1] Other alternatives included devaluation of metal dollars, abandoning the specie standard, and simply hoping and praying for a fortuitous increase in the supply of the money metals. See Richard H. Timberlake, Jr., "Ideological Factors in Specie Resumption and Treasury Policy," *Journal*

Actually, a severe policy of money contraction was initiated by Hugh McCulloch, appointed Secretary of the Treasury in the Johnson Administration, and this strategy was approved by Congress in December 1865 by passage of the Contraction Act. But the deflationary medicine was too bitter, and Congress ended contraction in February 1868. Grant's Secretary of the Treasury, George S. Boutwell, followed a much easier policy—a general *easing* of the money markets rather than a tightening of them.[2] After Boutwell's resignation in 1873, his Assistant Secretary, William Richardson, pursued a less vigorous policy that was nevertheless calculated to "grow into" resumption.

From 1868 to 1874, the Republican administration, while paying lip service to a return to gold, had taken the temperate course of not pressing for this return through severe contraction of the money stock. But when the Democrats won control of the Congress in the election of 1874, lame-duck Republicans, fearful of the antipathy of western and southern legislators toward resumption, hurriedly passed an act providing for a return to gold payments in four years. After January 1, 1879, the United States was to maintain strict interconvertibility between greenbacks and gold. Thanks to a favorable balance of trade in the latter years of the 1870s, gold stocks in this country increased at a rapid rate. The government removed the requirement that all customs duties be paid in gold to prevent discrimination against greenbacks, and on the appointed day the United States began to maintain specie payments. For a technical reason to be discussed presently, the United States was not finally and legally committed to a gold standard and would not be for another 21 years. Nevertheless, between 1879 and 1900, the government did *in fact* maintain parity of all other money forms with gold, and during these years America was on a *de facto* gold standard.

Silver and Silver Certificates

During the Civil War and for several years afterward, silver coins had gone out of circulation, having been replaced at first by ungummed postage stamps and later by fractional currency—paper notes issued by the government in denominations of 5, 10, 25, and 50 cents. It is not surprising, then, that when Congress sought to simplify the coinage in 1873, the silver dollar was omitted from the list of coins to be minted. There was no agitation over the omission at the time, because at the mint ratio of approximately 16 to 1, silver was worth more on the market than at the mint, and little silver was brought to the mint

---

of Economic History, **XXIV:**1 (March 1964). See also James K. Kindahl, "Economic Factors in Specie Resumption: The United States, 1865–1879," *Journal of Political Economy,* **LXIX:**1 (February 1961), pp. 30–48.

[2] It was Boutwell who broke the dramatic corner on gold attempted by James Fisk and Jay Gould by selling $4 million of the money metal in the "Gold Room" of the New York Stock Exchange. A good exercise in the use of materials would be a trip to the Government Publications Department of the Library to read the official telling of this episode. See *Gold Panic Investigation,* Forty-First Congress, Second Session, House Report No. 31 by the Committee on Banking and Currency, James A. Garfield, Chairman, esp. pp. 1–4 and p. 463. Alternatively, see Gary M. Walton and Roger L. Miller, *Economic Issues in American History* (San Francisco: Canfield Press, 1978), pp. 82–83.

When gold fluctuated wildly in 1869, the Gold Room of the New York Stock Exchange was the nerve-center of speculation. In its center, a bronze Cupid sprayed water quietly; on the dais, the secretary of the room had to cup his ears to hear and record transactions.

for coinage. Yet, scarcely three years later, the failure to include the silver dollar in the Act of 1873 began a furor that was to last for a quarter of a century.

The reason for the subsequent agitation over the "demonetization" of silver lay in the fact that the price of silver was falling in international markets. Increasing output of western silver mines in the United States and a shift of the bimetallic countries of western Europe to the gold standard had led to a growing surplus of silver. When the price of the silver contained in a dollar actually fell below the price of $1 that the government, under the Coinage Act of 1834, had *formerly* paid, silver producers took silver to the mint for coinage.[3] To

[3]Recall that a dollar contained 371.25 grains of pure silver, or a little over three-quarters of an ounce. The *average* bullion value of that amount of silver in 1873 was $1.00368. The next year, the value dropped to $0.98909 and fell consistently from that year on.

THE CURRENT QUESTION.
SILVER—"*You need not hold yourself so high. I'm as good as you are.*"
GOLD—"*You never were, and never will be, my equal.*"

Friends of silver saw in its monetization relief from depression but persistent grief and agony if gold continued to reign as the sole monetary metal in America.

their dismay they discovered that the government would take only as much silver as the Treasury needed for subsidiary coins. The cry that went up from the silver producers was horrendous.

A relatively small group like the silver producers would not appear to have much power in a large country like the United States. But during the 1870s and 1880s, a number of western states were being admitted to the Union, each with two U.S. Senators to represent their small populations, and silver producers acquired political representation out of all proportion to their numbers. The "reflationist" element in the West and South joined the silver producers in a clamor for the free and unlimited coinage of silver at the old mint ratio of 16 to 1. Silver advocates knew that at such a ratio silver would be brought to the mint in great quantities and that the monetary reserves of the country—and the general price level—would consequently be increased. The cry of the opposition that gold would be driven out of circulation meant nothing to the unemployed, oppressed debtors or others who wanted to raise the general price level. To the supporters of the free coinage of silver, the act that had demonetized the metal became the "Crime of '73." Even though the silver dollar had been struck from the list of coins largely because no one thought the matter was of any importance, the slogan greatly helped to stir the emotions of the electorate.

Within two years, the silver forces were able to push through Congress a compromise between the positions of the "sound-money" advocates and the free-coinage forces. This, the first of four major silver bills, was the Bland–Allison Act of 1878. The law provided for the coinage of silver in *limited* amounts. The Secretary of the Treasury was directed to purchase not less than $2 million and not more than $4 million worth of silver each month at market price.[4] The conservative secretaries in office during the next 12 years purchased only the minimum amount of silver, but by 1890 the Treasury's monetary silver (not counting subsidiary coins) amounted to almost $380 million. According to the Bland–Allison Act and an amendment passed in 1886, the Treasury could keep the actual silver in its vaults and issue silver certificates, dollar for dollar, instead. Due to the bulkiness of silver dollars, nearly everyone except westerners preferred paper currency, and silver certificates circulated more than silver dollars.

But the silver question was by no means settled. After 1888, Republicans were in control of both the administration and Congress. To secure the passage of high-tariff legislation, it was necessary to have the votes of the silver senators. In exchange for their affirmative votes on the McKinley tariff bill, the Republican leadership agreed to further silver legislation. A new bill—the Sherman Silver Purchase Law of 1890—was carefully prepared to avoid the veto of President Harrison.

The Secretary of the Treasury was directed to make a *monthly* purchase, at the market rate, of 4.5 million *ounces* of silver. To pay for the bullion, he was to issue a new type of paper to be known as Treasury notes; these notes were to be redeemable *in either gold or silver* at the discretion of the Secretary. At silver prices prevailing in 1890, the new law authorized the purchase of almost double the monthly amount of silver taken in under the previous law. Almost at once, the market price of silver began a further sharp decline. Within three years, the *dollar amount* of silver being purchased was little more than it had been under the old act. In 1893, at the insistence of Democratic President Cleveland—a "sound-money" man at odds with his party on this issue—the Sherman Act was repealed. In over three years of purchasing under this law,

[4]By 1878, the market price of silver in New York averaged a little over $1.15 per ounce for the calendar year; the average market value of the silver contained in a dollar in that year was just over $.89. For the next 12 years, silver prices consistently fell. Two points ought to be made in passing: The market price of silver was bolstered by government purchases, and the government made quite a profit (about $70 million) on its silver purchases under the Act.

more than $150 million of the Treasury notes of 1890 were issued. Between 1878 and 1893, $500 million were added to the circulating medium by silver purchases—a consequential victory for the silver forces.

Gold and Gold Certificates

Nonetheless, between 1860 and 1914, gold provided the largest single increase in the nation's cash. During the Civil War and for a decade thereafter, gold was hoarded privately at home and abroad. After 1875, however, there was an almost uninterrupted increase in the monetary gold stock. In the 1880s, monetary gold doubled in quantity, and between 1890 and 1914 the gold stock tripled.[5] American mines poured forth their treasures at a stable rate; even in the years when the United States exported gold to make up adverse balances of payments, there were normally net additions to the total stock.

Although the silver acts of 1878 and 1890 made silver certificates redeemable in *either* gold *or* silver, in practice Treasury authorities redeemed them in gold if it were demanded. After 1879, Treasury secretaries felt that a minimum gold reserve of $100 million was necessary to back up the paper circulation. Just at the time when the Treasury notes of 1890 were authorized, the government's gold reserve began declining toward the $100 million mark as the public presented Treasury notes and greenbacks for payment in gold. To meet current expenses, the Treasury had to pay the paper money out again almost as soon as it was received. By early 1893, the gold drain had become serious, and the gold reserve actually dipped below the traditional minimum toward the middle of the year.

Several times during the next three years it appeared certain that the *de facto* gold standard would have to be abandoned. Two kinds of drains—"external" (foreign) and "internal" (domestic)—plagued the Treasury from 1891 to 1896. Today, abandonment of gold redemption hardly seems foreboding, but in the middle 1890s conservatives considered going off gold standard equivalent to declaring national bankruptcy. The difficulty was that when the danger of abandoning gold became apparent, people rushed to acquire gold, thus making it even more likely that the Treasury *would* have to abandon the gold standard. Chiefly by selling bonds for gold, the administration replenished the government's reserves whenever it appeared that the standard was about to be lost. The repeal of the Sherman Silver Purchase Law in 1893 reduced the number of Treasury notes, which, along with greenbacks, the public was presenting for redemption. Increasing exports at last brought an influx of gold from abroad in the summer of 1896, improving public confidence to the extent that the gold standard was saved.

The election of 1896 settled the matter of a monetary standard for nearly 40 years. The money issue was clearly drawn. The Democrats, under the lead-

[5] Included in these figures are *gold certificates.* In 1865, Congress provided that gold certificates might be issued by the Treasury in exchange for gold, simply as a convenience to those who had to make certain payments, such as customs duties, in gold. After 1879, gold certificates circulated freely and were used increasingly. The backs of the gold certificates in use until 1928 were a bright yellow, and they were commonly referred to as "yellowbacks."

ership of William Jennings Bryan, stood for free coinage of silver at a ratio of 16 to 1—even though the market ratio was then over 30 to 1. The Republicans, with McKinley as their candidate, stood solidly for the gold standard. The West and the South supported Bryan; the North and the East supported McKinley. Any attempt to stop the long years of deflation was anathema to the conservative East, and industrial employers—aided and abetted by the professional class (including Protestant clergy)—brought every possible pressure to bear on employee voters. Thus Bryan could not draw on the great urban vote, as Franklin Roosevelt was to do 36 years later, and when well-to-do farmers in the older agricultural states deserted him, the cause was lost. The Republican victory of 1896 was not followed immediately by legislation ending the controversy, because free silver advocates still had a majority membership in Congress. But the return of prosperity, encouraged by new gold discoveries, new methods of processing gold, and a rapid rate of investment, made Congress receptive to definitive gold legislation.

William Jennings Bryan on the political stump. Bryan was more than just a political leader; he also had a lively awareness of the need for economic and political reform. Although he was defeated on the money issue, Bryan's monetary prescriptions had a solid New Deal ring.

In 1900, the Gold Standard Act was passed. The dollar was defined solely in terms of gold, and all other forms of money were to be convertible into gold. The Secretary of the Treasury was directed to maintain a gold reserve of $150 million, which was not to be drawn on to meet current government expenses. To prevent a recurrence of the difficulties of the 1890s, a provision was made to keep redeemed silver certificates and greenbacks in the Treasury during times of stress for borrowing to meet deficits that might occur from time to time.[6] The United States had at last committed itself by law to the gold standard.

National-Bank Notes

National-bank notes were paper money issues of nationally chartered banks; they became important by 1865, grew steadily in amount for a decade, and then began to fluctuate. Originally, the total issue was limited to $300 million, this sum having been allotted among the states in proportion to the population and to the total national-bank capital within each state. Restrictions were removed by a clause in the Resumption Act of 1875, and from this year on national banks kept in circulation whatever amount of notes seemed profitable. The low point of notes outstanding was reached in the early 1890s. A slow rise followed that changed in the early years of the century to a sharp increase, a record high of more than $700 million was reached in 1914.

The decline of national-bank note circulation in the 1880s reflected the lessening importance of bank notes compared to bank deposits; this decrease in notes outstanding was greatest in the cities.[7] Also, as interest rates fell after 1873, the prices of bonds used as reserves to back up national-bank notes rose well above par, with the result that some banks found it did not pay to invest in these bonds whereas others sold their holdings for a profit. On the other hand, as bond prices dropped in the late 1880s, banks again found it profitable to buy eligible government bonds; in the 1890s, banks began to issue notes again. The Gold Standard Act of 1900 reduced the minimum capital requirements for national banks in small towns, making it more attractive for small banks (who would use the note-issue privilege) to become national banks. Finally, during the decade and a half before World War I, banks encountered an ever-increasing demand for currency as the dollar volume of business increased.

Summary of Changes in the Money Supply

By way of review, Figure 22-1 shows the absolute changes in the different kinds of currency in use. First greenbacks, then silver, and finally gold provided marked increases in the supply of hand-to-hand money, beginning at three successive points in time. These three types of currency provided, in order, the

[6] The Treasury notes of 1890 were retired by the Gold Standard Act.

[7] Some New York banks withdrew their circulation altogether.

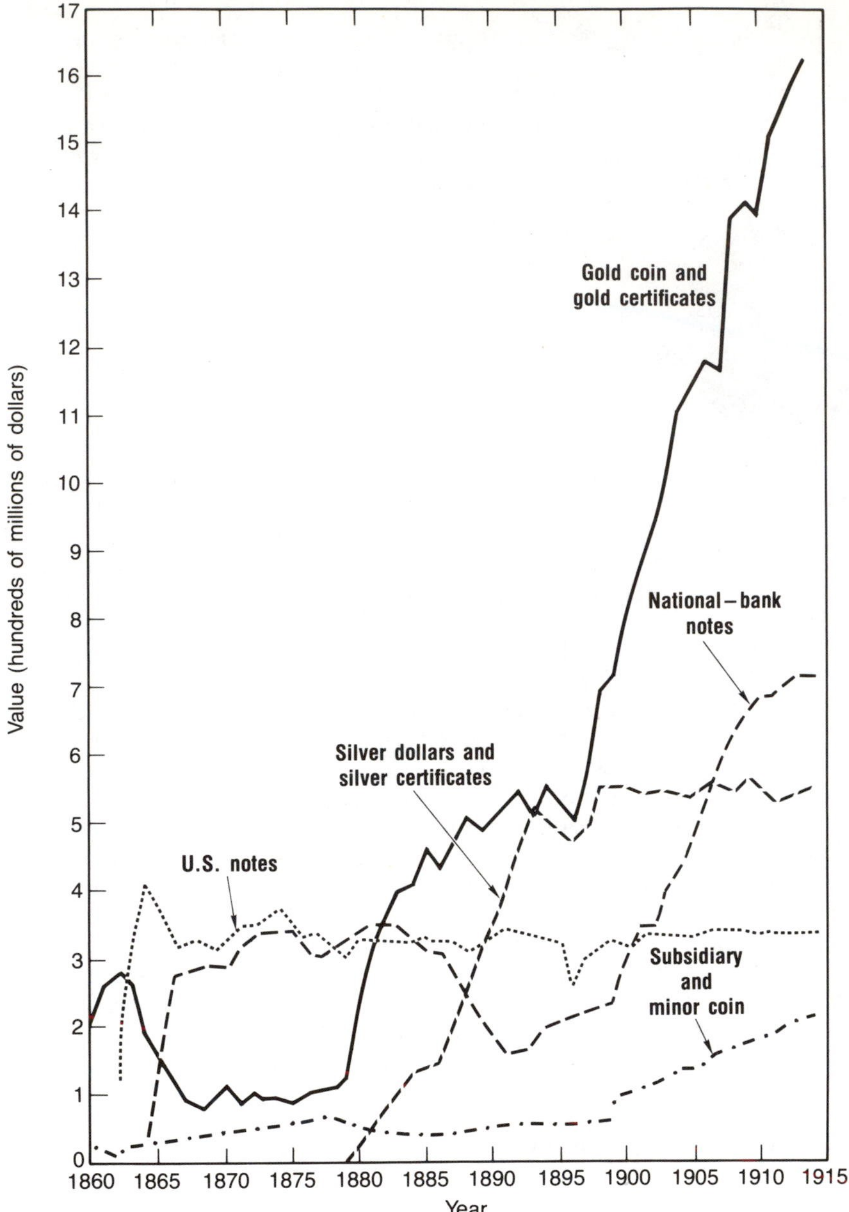

FIGURE 22–1

Forms of Money in the United States, 1860–1915: From the late 1870s to the early 1890s, there were substantial additions to the nation's monetary stocks of gold and silver, but the supply of paper money actually declined during these years.

Source: Board of Governors of the Federal Reserve System.

"dynamic" elements in the supply of money. Figure 22-2 shows the absolute changes in the total money supply and in the part of the money supply consisting of bank deposits. As Figure 22-2 indicates, the growth of bank deposits accounted for most of the increase in the total money supply. Cash, which (except for national-bank notes) constituted the reserves of the banking system, was sufficient to permit a rate of increase in bank deposits that was about equal to the rate of increase in physical production.

MONEY, PRICES, AND PRODUCTION

In view of the heated monetary controversies of the late nineteenth century, we might suspect that money was at the root of the price difficulties. Figure 22-3 indicates the changes in wholesale prices, nonagricultural production, and the money supply from 1860 to 1915. The most notable aspect of this graph is that the upward drifts of both the money supply and industrial production tend to be parallel, indicating about the same overall rate of increase for the 55-year period. We may therefore be inclined to rule money out entirely as a causal factor, because although the quantity of money grew with output throughout the *entire* period, prices fell for 30 years and then rose for 25 years. But closer inspection reveals that the money supply had either decreased or grown at an arrested rate before each of the major downturns in industrial production. Recoveries were accompanied by rapid and steady increases in the quantity of money. Moreover, after 1896, the money stock increased at a faster rate than in the preceding 30 years, and between 1896 and 1914 its growth was interrupted only once.

Specifically, Milton Friedman and Anna Jacobson Schwartz found that the growth rate of the money stock was "decidedly" smaller in the 1879–1897 period than in the 1897–1914 period, averaging about 6 percent per year in the former and 7½ percent per year in the latter. Their contention is that different rates of monetary growth were "associated" with corresponding differences in price behavior. Prices *fell* at an annual rate of over 1 percent between 1879 and 1897 and *rose* at an annual rate of over 2 percent between 1897 and 1914. Furthermore, the growth rate of the money supply was much more uneven in the first period than in the second—a fact that may account for the more unsteady pace of economic activity in the first period.[8]

Major Cycles

Of course, the uneven pace of progress was not achieved without setbacks that brought hardship and suffering to great numbers of people, especially the immigrants who swelled the white ghettos of the cities. In more peacetime years than not, employment and production were below 90 percent of a full-employment output.

[8] Milton Friedman and Anna Jacobson Schwartz, *A Monetary History of the United States, 1867–1960* (Princeton: Princeton University Press, 1963), pp. 91–92. Serious students of the period of U.S. monetary history lying between the Civil War and World War I will find Chapters 1–4 of this volume both taxing and rewarding.

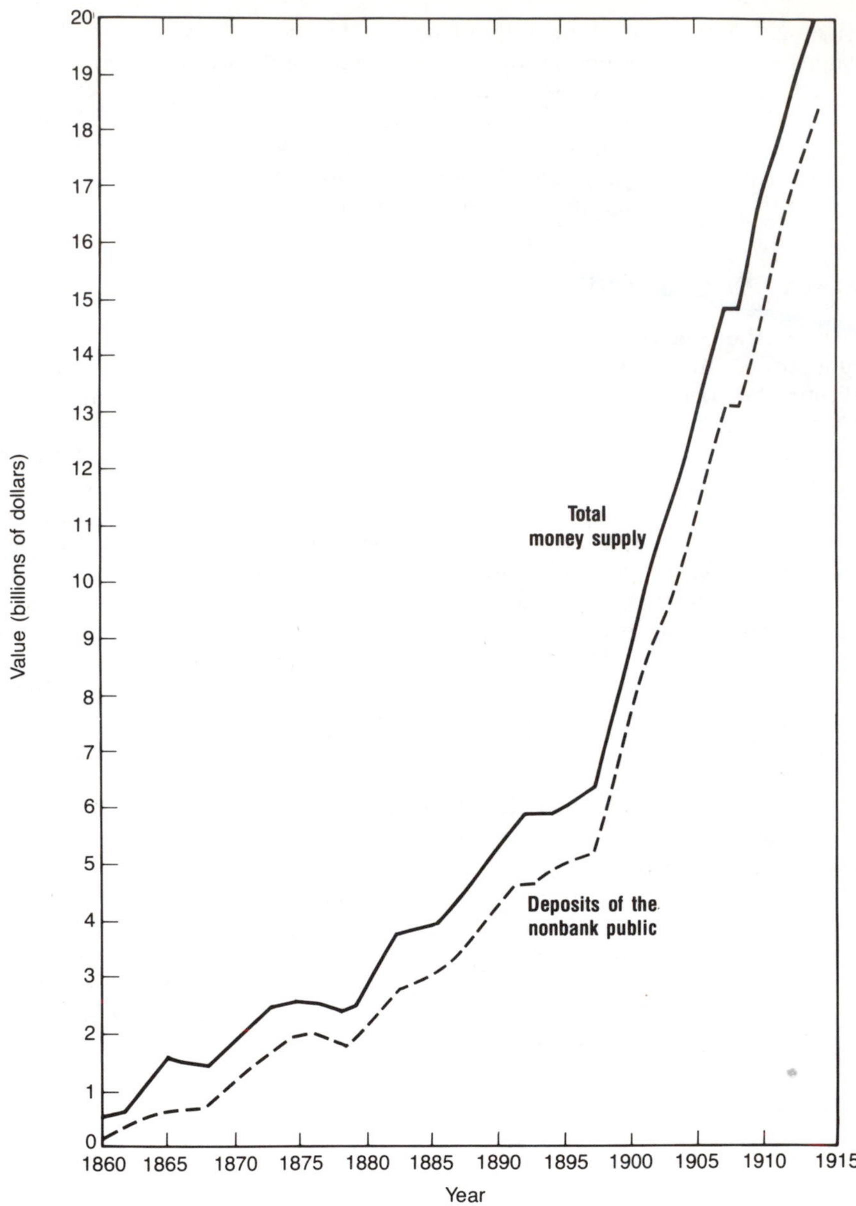

FIGURE 22–2

The U.S. Money Supply, 1860–1915: Although the total U.S. money supply, like the metallic money stock, grew during the decade and a half after specie resumption in 1879, the increase was insufficient to erase the forces of deflation.

Source: Albert G. Hart, *Money, Debt, and Economic Activity,* 1st Ed. (Englewood Cliffs, N.J.: Prentice-Hall, 1948).

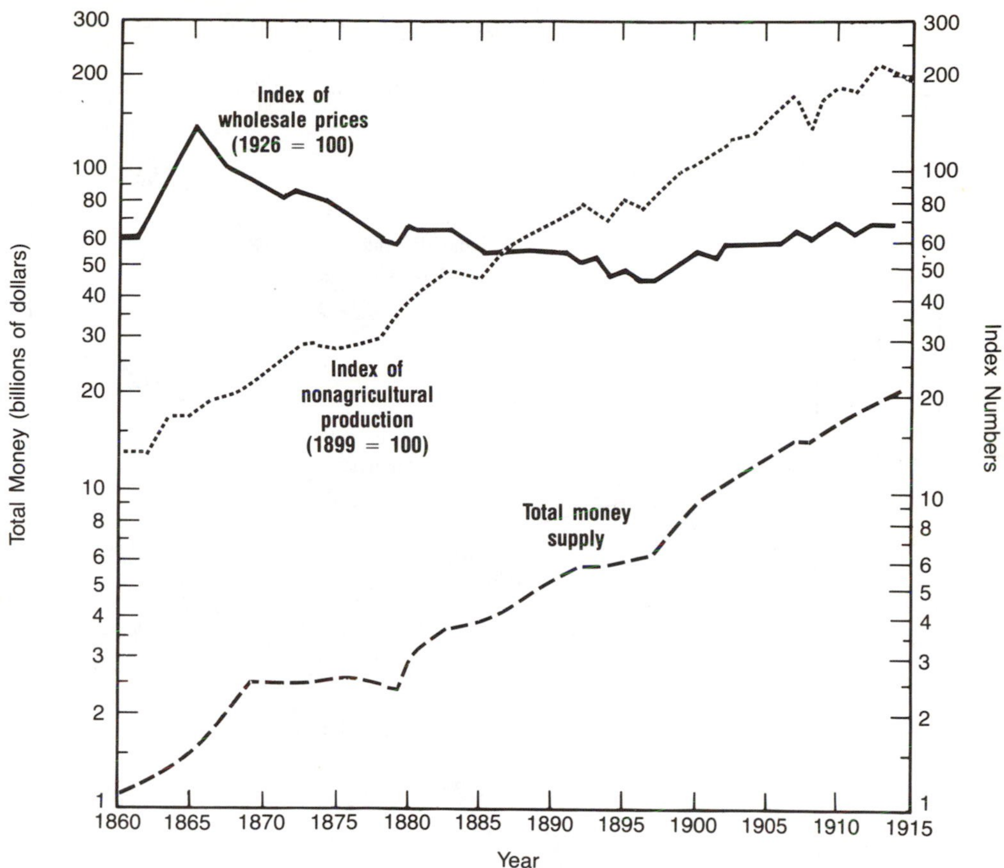

FIGURE 22–3

U.S. Prices, Production, and Money Supply, 1860–1915: The wholesale price index declined after the Civil War, while nonagricultural output increased dramatically and the money supply moved upward at a somewhat slower but still persistent rate.
Reprinted by permission of the publisher from Edwin Frickey, *Production in the United States, 1860–1914,* Cambridge: Harvard University Press, copyright © 1947, by the President and Fellows of Harvard College. Adapted by Albert G. Hart, *Money, Debt, and Economic Activity,* 1st Ed. (Englewood Cliffs, N.J.: Prentice-Hall, 1948).

Figure 22-4 shows industrial and commercial production, durable manufactures, and nondurable manufactures from 1865–1915 in the United States. If we connect the peaks of the curves in all three cases, we obtain very nearly straight lines that show growth trends.[9] Since the peaks indicate output when

[9]Because Figure 22–4 has a logarithmic vertical scale, the straight lines (trends) indicate constant rates of growth.

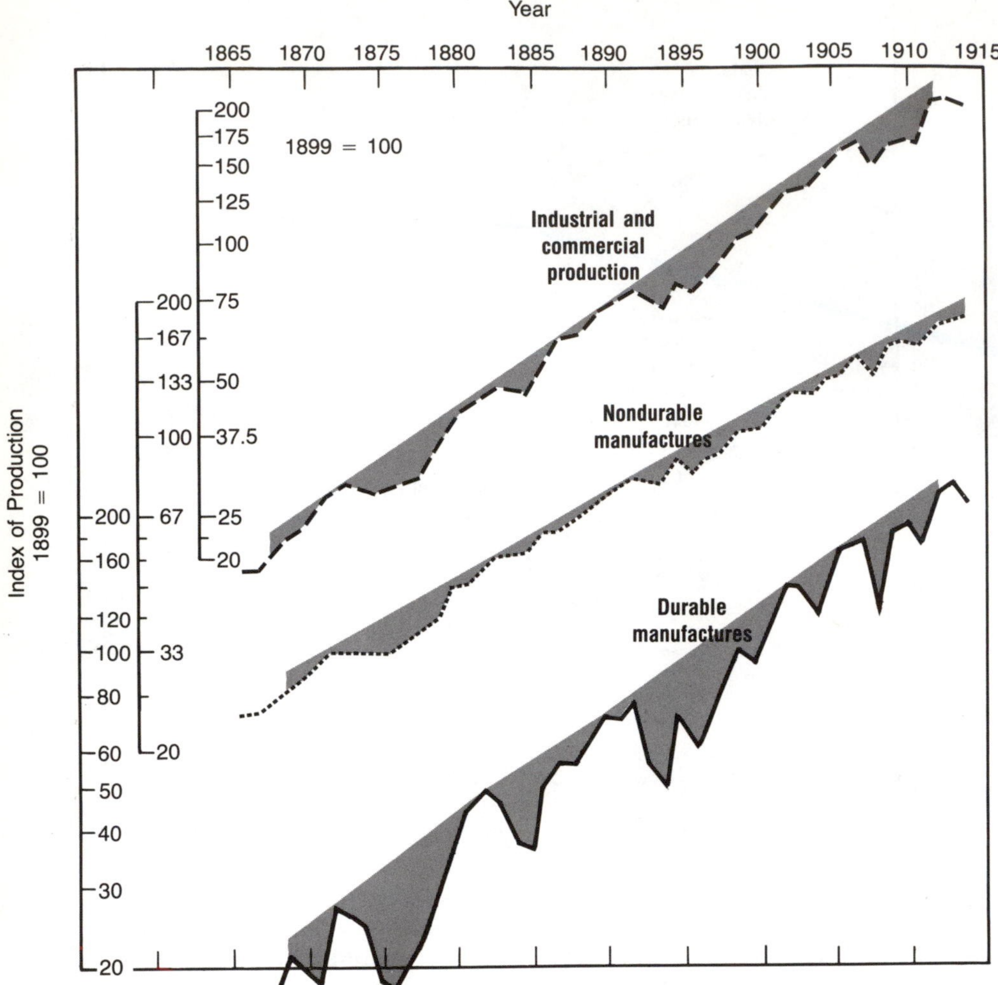

FIGURE 22–4

Indexes of U.S. Nonagricultural Production, 1865–1915: During the period of greatest industrial growth, the most volatile sector of production was durable goods, which expanded steeply—although erratically—after the Civil War.

Reprinted by permission of the publisher from Edwin Frickey, *Production in the United States, 1860–1914,* 1st Ed., Cambridge: Harvard University Press, copyright © 1942 by the President and Fellows of Harvard College. Adapted by Albert G. Hart, *Money, Debt, and Economic Activity,* 2nd Ed. (Englewood Cliffs, N.J.: Prentice-Hall, 1953).

resources were fully employed, the trend lines trace the production potential in each category. An inspection of all three curves reveals two extended periods—in the 1870s and 1890s—in which production was well below potential. In the 1880s and late in the first decade of the twentieth century, there were also slumps in activity that were not quite so pronounced but that were nonetheless serious. How far below potential the economy operated during these slumps can be judged by inspecting the shaded bands of Figure 22-4, each one tracing a shortfall of 10 percent. Thus, in 1876, production of durable goods was more than 40 percent below capacity output.

It should be noted that the amplitude of swings in durable-goods output was much greater than in nondurable goods output. During small slumps in durable-goods production, nondurable-goods output frequently did not drop at all, and year-to-year changes in durable-goods production were ordinarily several times greater than annual variations in nondurable-goods production. One reason for this difference is that durable goods, whether they belong to producers or consumers, yield their service flows over longer periods of time. Moreover, the replacement of durable goods can usually be postponed. A machine shop can ordinarily make an old lathe last another year, especially if business is bad. A household can put off buying a new car or a refrigerator if family income threatens to decline. But as entrepreneurs and household units postpone purchases of durables, those who service durables actually find the demand for their services increasing. The demand for food, residential utilities, tobacco, and cheaper forms of entertainment also falls slowly and in some instances may actually rise as incomes decline.

A closer inspection of these data would reveal several minor fluctuations or cycles in addition to the major ones. Yet we can obtain the clearest idea of the nature of economic fluctuations by focusing on the big swings. Alvin H. Hansen has described the four major cycles indicated by the curve of durable-goods output.[10]:

1. After an upward swing of seven years, production reached a peak in 1872 and then turned downward for four years. The trough was reached in 1876, and output of the previous peak year was not matched again until 1878—a year in which output was still far below potential. The length of the major cycle from trough to trough was 11 years, and the decline in output of durables from peak to trough was 33 percent.[11]
2. Durables production again reached a peak in 1882, after an upswing of six years. On the downswing, a trough was reached in three years, and after four years of depression there was recovery to the level of 1882. The length of the cycle from trough to trough was nine years, and the decline in output of durables from peak to trough was 25 percent.
3. The upswing of the cycle of 1892 was interrupted by two mild recessions, and the peak reached after seven years was below the curve of potential. The depression that began late in 1892 was extremely severe, but it was interrupted by a substantial recovery in 1895. If we count 1896 as the trough year, the length of the cycle from trough to trough was 11 years, and the decline in durables output was 34 percent.

[10] Alvin H. Hansen, *Business Cycles and National Income* (New York: W.W. Norton, 1951), pp. 22–31.

[11] Once again, the interested reader should refer to Figure 22-4 and note that, although the peak-to-trough decline in durables output was only 33 percent, the growth in *capacity* between 1872 and 1876 meant that durables manufacture was more than 40 percent below potential.

4. The upswing of the 1907 cycle was 11 years in length and was interrupted by two recessions, the recession of 1904 being so marked that some writers consider it a major depression. The contraction of 1907–08 amounted to a 29 percent decline in durables output, the drop occurring in so short a time that it gave an unusual shock to the economy. But recovery was quick, too—1907 output being reached again by 1909. The length of the cycle from trough to trough was 12 years. After the recovery of 1908 the economy started on a long upsurge of production that was interrupted in 1910 and 1914 and culminated in the war boom.

By way of explanation, it should be emphasized that the monetary contraction of the 1870s was aggravated by the resumption of specie payments. In 1873, gold was at a 10-percent premium in terms of greenbacks. By the end of 1878, the value of gold had fallen to par—rough evidence that the United States had been forced to deflate 10 percent more than the rest of the world to resume gold payments. The long and noisy debate over the silver question intensified the depression of the 1890s by creating some business uncertainty and by causing foreigners to withdraw funds (and thus bank reserves) at a most inopportune time. These incidents helped to make depressions longer and deeper, as did the banking crises that were the inevitable concomitants of pre-1920 panics. But for a better understanding of these events, we must turn to an analysis of the institutions that controlled the money supply.

CONTROLLING THE MONEY SUPPLY: THE INSTITUTIONS

From 1836 until 1914, the United States had no central bank. (We might place the earlier date at 1832, when Andrew Jackson began to withdraw government deposits from the second Bank of the United States.) Americans generally were fearful of centralized control of the money supply, and until the early years of the twentieth century it was politically impossible to reestablish a central bank. Yet some central-bank functions were necessarily performed; after 1850, the American economy was too complex to muddle along without any monetary guidance or assistance whatsoever. Such central-bank control as existed was developed by custom within the framework of the Independent Treasury Act of 1846 and the National Bank Act of 1864, as amended.

The Treasury and the Banking System

Ironically, monetary responsibilities were accepted by the U.S. Treasury shortly after the passage of the law that purported to make the Treasury independent of the money market. The main purpose of the Independent Treasury Act was to put the government on a strictly cash basis. Under it, banks periodically found their reserves reduced as people paid taxes, and replenished as the government made disbursements from one of the subtreasuries. Even before the Civil War, so much of the country's cash was locked up in Treasury vaults at inopportune times that to replenish the reserves of banks, the Secretary of the

Treasury found it necessary to purchase government bonds in the open market and prepay interest on bonds outstanding. From the close of the Civil War until the establishment of the Federal Reserve System, relations between the Treasury and the banks improved. Policies varied with different secretaries, but with few exceptions, there was a deep consciousness of the effect of Treasury policy on the money market and of the responsibility of the Treasury to the economy as a whole.

Treasury concern with central-bank functions was stimulated by Treasury surpluses, which were the rule from 1866 to 1915. The problem of getting the cash back into circulation that had been taken in by the government reached such proportions that the purchase of government securities and the prepayment of interest on the public debt were not sufficient solutions. By liberalizing the interpretation of laws permitting deposits of Treasury funds in national banks, successive secretaries developed a reliable technique of easing the money market. Leslie M. Shaw, who succeeded Lyman Gage as Secretary of the Treasury in 1902, demonstrated particularly remarkable ingenuity in developing control instruments. Shaw ruled that funds might be transferred from Treasury vaults to depositary banks and back again at the discretion of the Secretary. At the time, the greatest seasonal financial movement was at harvest time. Deliberately impounding funds during the summer months, Shaw released them where needed to finance crop movements to relieve autumn stringencies.[12] When, in 1911, Congress finally authorized the Treasury to accept certified checks drawn on commercial banks in payment of customs duties, the last hindrance to Treasury influence on the money market was removed.

The National Banking System

Even though the role of the Treasury grew increasingly important, it was to the commercial banking system itself that bankers looked for most of the services ordinarily performed by a central bank. To help finance the Civil War, to administrate the issue of national-bank notes, and to systematize and establish a uniform currency, the National Bank Act of 1864 was passed. This Act left a permanent imprint on the nation's economic system and provided the legal framework for national-bank charters that persists to the present day. The provisions of the National Bank Act can be summarized under three headings:

1. *Organization.* Five or more persons could form an "association"—really a corporation—for the purpose of carrying on a banking business.[13] Incorporators were to draw up articles of association and file them with the

[12] In his report of 1906, Shaw proposed that the Secretary of the Treasury be authorized to vary the required reserve ratios of national banks and that a fund of $100 million be made available for the sole purpose of easing and tightening bank reserves. However, Shaw argued against the establishment of a central bank on the grounds that government supervision of monetary operations would thereby be removed. *Annual Report of the Secretary of the Treasury,* 1906, pp. 41–50.

[13] The word *association* was used in this and much state-banking legislation to avoid the use of the word *corporation.* Few were deluded by the euphemism.

Comptroller of the Currency, who was to be the chief supervisor of all federally chartered banks. Associations in towns of less than 6,000 inhabitants had to have a minimum capital of $50,000; those in towns of more than 6,000 but less than 50,000, a capital of $100,000; and those in cities of 50,000 or more, a capital of $200,000. Strict rules required capital subscriptions to be paid in full, and all the old abuses associated with raising bank capitals were effectively prohibited.

2. *The basis of note issue.* To secure its note issue, each national bank was required to buy U.S. government bonds equal to one-third (later one-quarter) of the dollar amount of its paid-in capital stock, with the provision that no bank would have to buy more than $50,000 worth of bonds. Each bank was to deposit its bonds with the U.S. Treasurer and was to receive notes, engraved in a standard design but with the name of the issuing bank on the obverse side, in the amount of 90 percent of the par or market value (whichever was lower) of the bonds deposited. A national bank could have any amount of government bonds in its portfolio, but the amount of its notes outstanding could not exceed its *capital* in dollar amount.
3. *Reserves.* By 1860, several state laws required banks to keep cash reserves against their deposits and to note liabilities. In strict practice, reserves were kept as gold and silver in bank vaults, but as time went on the custom developed of maintaining deposits, known as *correspondent accounts,* with banks in other cities.[14] The National Bank Act recognized prevailing practice by permitting new national associations to keep their reserves in two forms—cash in their vaults or deposits with a national bank in one of 17 "redemption" cities. Banks located in New York City (later called a "central reserve" city) were exceptions in that they had to keep *all* their reserves as cash in vault.[15] Banks in the 16 other redemption cities (later redesignated "reserve" cities) had to keep half their reserves as cash in vault but could keep the other half as deposits with national banks in New York. Banks in all other cities and towns (country banks) had to keep two-fifths of their reserves as cash in vault but could deposit the remaining three-fifths in a national bank in a redemption city. Reserves, in whatever form they were maintained, were set at 25 percent for banks in redemption cities and at 15 percent for country banks. *Originally, reserves were to be calculated as a percentage of notes outstanding plus deposits.*

An important amendment affecting reserves was passed shortly after the panic of 1873. National banks were no longer required to keep reserves against *notes,* but they were required to keep a 5-percent redemption fund on deposit with the Treasury that could also be counted as part of reserves against deposits. After 1874, national banks calculated their minimum legal reserves *only as a percentage of deposits.*

[14] If a bank manager in Knoxville, Tennessee, knew that many checks drawn by depositors would be made payable to New York firms, the manager maintained funds in New York to meet these foreseeable obligations. In case of emergency, these deposits would serve just as well as cash in the Knoxville vault. They could be used to meet the bank's obligations in New York or the funds could be transferred for use at home.

[15] The law provided that the cash be "lawful money." In 1864, "lawful money" meant gold, silver, and greenbacks.

The National Bank Act of 1864 met several objectives. The objective of a uniform national currency was admirable, and a national charter might bring increased prestige and perhaps greater customer confidence. Yet it soon became apparent that there were few inducements to state banks to take out national charters. State bankers could see little reason for giving up comfortable (and sometimes nonexistent) supervision under state charters for the uncertainties of national regulation. The prospects of profits under national supervision seemed much slimmer than they did under state supervision.

Thus, to the disappointment of Secretary of the Treasury, Salmon Chase, and Comptroller of the Currency, Hugh McCulloch, growth of the system continued slowly through 1864. Especially vexing was the refusal of large, well-established banks in the East, which held a substantial proportion of the banking resources of the country, to leave the havens of state charters. Both Chase and McCulloch worked incessantly, but to little avail, to persuade established banks to convert. With the help of the influential banker, Jay Cooke and some subtle financial pressure, a few large state banks were persuaded to go national, and Cooke was instrumental in founding a $5 million bank—The Fourth National Bank of New York—a substantial institution for the time. But by early 1865, it was clear that if a national system were to emerge, existing institutions would for the most part have to be coerced into participation.

Since the beginning of the controversy over a uniform currency law, there had been considerable jockeying among members of Congress to place first national and then state banks at a tax disadvantage. After the passage and repeal of various statutes, this wrangling resulted in a tax for revenue purposes only that did not discriminate between national and state institutions. In the opinion of Secretary Chase and Comptroller McCulloch, it had become necessary to create a tax differential so severe that state banks would have to transfer to national status. On March 3, 1865, Congress imposed a tax of 10 percent on state-bank notes. Banks put their notes into circulation by lending them to borrowers. If the interest on a loan were 7 percent per annum and a bank were required to pay a tax of 10 percent per annum on the amount of its notes outstanding, the bank would obviously incur a loss on the transaction.

As Table 22-1 indicates, the tax was indeed effective. A majority of the state banks immediately shifted to federal jurisdiction; in 1866, less than 300 state banks remained. For the most part, these were large city banks that had long since discarded the practice of issuing notes when they extended loans. After the Civil War, deposits were far more important than notes in cities; by the mid-1870s, banks in all but the backwoods areas could extend loans simply by crediting the account of the borrower. Thus, after 1875, the tax on state-bank notes would no longer be a serious economic deterrent to operation under state charters.

By the early 1870s, then, it had become clear that a national charter was not essential to a profitable banking business. Moreover, for bank organizers who had no aspirations toward national or substantial regional operations, state charters had several positive advantages:[16]

[16] For a full discussion of the growing importance of state-bank charters in the late nineteenth century, see George E. Barnett, *State Banks and Trust Companies Since the Passage of the National-Bank Act* (Washington, D.C.: National Monetary Commission, 1911).

TABLE 22–1
Commercial Banks in the United States, 1860–1914

Year[a]	State banks[b]	National banks	Year[a]	State banks[b]	National banks
1860	1,562		1888	1,523	3,120
1861	1,601		1889	1,791	3,239
1862	1,492		1890	2,250	3,484
1863	1,466	66	1891	2,743	3,652
1864	1,089	467	1892	3,773	3,759
1865	349	1,294	1893	4,188	3,807
1866	297	1,634	1894	4,188	3,770
1867	272	1,636	1895	4,369	3,715
1868	247	1,640	1896	4,279	3,689
1869	259	1,619	1897	4,420	3,610
1870	325	1,612	1898	4,486	3,581
1871	452	1,723	1899	4,738	3,582
1872	566	1,853	1900	5,007	3,731
1873	277	1,968	1901	5,651	4,163
1874	368	1,983	1902	6,171	4,532
1875	586	2,076	1903	6,890	4,935
1876	671	2,091	1904	7,970	5,327
1877	631	2,078	1905	9,018	5,664
1878	510	2,056	1906	10,220	6,046
1879	648	2,048	1907	11,469	6,422
1880	650	2,076	1908	12,803	6,817
1881	683	2,115	1909	13,421	6,886
1882	704	2,239	1910	14,348	7,138
1883	788	2,417	1911	15,322	7,270
1884	852	2,625	1912	16,037	7,366
1885	1,015	2,689	1913	16,841	7,467
1886	891	2,809	1914	17,498	7,518
1887	1,471	3,014			

Source: *Banking Studies,* by members of the staff of the Board of Governors of the Federal Reserve System (Baltimore: Waverly Press, 1941), pp. 422–23. See also *Historical Statistics of the United States, Colonial Times to 1957,* esp. pp. 623–32.

[a] All figures as of June 30, or nearest available date.

[b] Excludes unincorporated banks and mutual savings banks.

1. Lower amounts of capital were required in most state jurisdictions and under nearly all circumstances. Until 1900, the minimum amount of capital required for a national bank was $50,000. In the West and South, state minimum capital requirements of $10,000 were frequent, and some states prescribed no capital minimums at all.
2. Reserves required against deposits were lower under most state banking laws than under the National Bank Act. Furthermore, national banks had to observe substantially stricter rules regarding the amount of cash held in reserve—and the Comptroller of the Currency was generally more severe in dealing with reserve deficiencies than were state counterparts. Finally, sev-

eral state laws distinguished between time and demand deposits, permitting lower reserves to be maintained against both.[17]

3. In general, national banks operated under much stricter lending and investment policies than did their state-chartered competitors.[18] Before 1913, the National Bank Act for all practical purposes prohibited loans on real estate, which in some areas constituted a major portion of competing banks' business. Until 1906, a national bank could not lend to a single borrower more than 10 percent of its paid-up capital—a limitation that became increasingly harmful in competing with other institutions. And although state banks and trust companies frequently had wide latitude in purchasing the stocks of banks and other corporations, national banks were barred from such activities.
4. Standards of bank supervision and examination were much higher in the national jurisdiction.

In summary, the rules governing the entry and operations of banks chartered by the states were far less onerous than those prescribed for national banks. From 1864 to 1914 (and, for that matter, to the present day), a dual banking system developed simply because one set of rules was easier than the other, and the data testify to the truth of the proposition.

As Table 22-1 shows, the revival of state banking began in the 1870s; by the early 1880s, the relative growth of the state-bank system was unmistakable. Between 1880 and 1900, the number of national banks increased from 2,076 to 3,731, while the number of state banks jumped from 650 to just over 5,000. In 1900, the resources of national banks were just less than double those of state banks. A few years later, in 1907, state banks outnumbered national banks by nearly two to one, and the resources of state banks were about the same as those of national banks.

State banks were apparently forging steadily ahead in the competition. National banks continued to enjoy a certain prestige, perhaps, but a large proportion of the state institutions gained growing public confidence. More significant than prestige to some banks was the attraction of the word "national" in a corporate title to correspondent banks and big companies. The rules governing national banks were uniform throughout the country, and anyone hesitant about making a commitment to a bank in another city could ordinarily reduce the risk by choosing a federally chartered institution. But these advantages, although real, were offset many times by the greater flexibility of state banks and trust companies, which often enabled them to accept business that national banks could not touch.

[17] Comptroller of the Currency, *Annual Report,* 1912, p. 11.

[18] We should not be so naive as to conclude that the prohibition of certain practices assured compliance on the part of national banks. A long-time official of the office testified in his memoirs, perhaps with some exaggeration, that at the turn of the century "probably 75 percent of the examiners' reports, and about the same percentage of reports of condition made by the banks, disclosed violations of law of one kind or another, making it necessary to write letters to that number of banks." See Thomas P. Kane, *The Romance and Tragedy of Banking* (New York: The Bankers' Publishing Company, 1930), p. 366. See also pp. 365–86 for a discussion of the most common types of violation.

23

Economic Change and New Dimensions of Government

We now pause to evaluate the performance of the American economy between 1860 and 1920. It seems fair to conclude that businesspeople, farmers, and laborers in general were better off at the end of this period than they were at the beginning. But, as we have seen, progress was interrupted from time to time by spells of declining economic activity with accompanying loss and hardship. Our problem now is to summarize the available data and comment on the efficiency and growth of the American economy. We will then observe how Americans began to ask their government for protection from the rigors of economic development and the competitive struggle.

THE PACE OF ECONOMIC GROWTH

In beginning, a few cautions should be recalled. Aside from the statistical difficulties of estimation, the value of the national-income yardstick is limited by the fact that the quality and variety of goods and services consumed change over time. Moreover, the national income must be stated in real or current dollars, and goods and services produced in the home (nonmarket output) are not included in the totals. Nevertheless, national-income estimates furnish the best indicator we have of the product that the people divided among themselves.

To date, the most complete estimates of early national income are those of Simon Kuznets. To "reduce detail, minimize error, and permit a clearer view of the longer-term changes," Professor Kuznets has put his estimates in decade averages. According to Table 23-1, the annual national income during the 1909 – 1918 decade,

TABLE 23–1
National Income in Current Dollars and Dollars of 1929 Purchasing Power, 1869–1918 (annual averages for overlapping decades)

	Total national income (billions of dollars)	
Decade	Current prices	1929 prices
1869–1878	6.5	9.4
1874–1883	8.4	13.7
1879–1888	9.9	17.9
1884–1893	10.9	21.0
1889–1898	11.7	24.2
1894–1903	14.5	30.1
1899–1908	19.8	37.5
1904–1913	26.1	44.8
1909–1918	36.3	50.3

Source: Simon Kuznets, "Changes in the National Income of the United States of America Since 1870," *Income and Wealth Series II* (London: Bowes & Bowes Ltd., 1952), p. 30. By permission of the publisher.

measured in 1929 prices, was more than five times what it was during the 1869–1878 decade. Over the years covered, changes from decade to decade averaged about 23 percent; but increases in the national income from year to year were by no means continuous or regular, although the table does not reveal the irregularities. Depressions, booms, deflation, and inflation were all reflected in fluctuations in income figures, although before 1920 these ups and downs were ordinarily not as marked as fluctuations in industrial production.

Table 23-2 provides information on per-capita growth in national income. On the average, per-capita income in real terms increased about 11 percent per decade. As the period progressed, there was a retardation in the rate of

TABLE 23–2
Population and National Income (1929 Prices) Per Capita, 1869–1918 (annual averages for overlapping decades)

Decade	Population (millions)	Percentage increase	National income per capita (dollars)	Percentage increase
1869–1878	43.5	—	216	—
1874–1883	48.8	12.2	281	30.1
1879–1888	54.9	12.5	326	16.0
1884–1893	61.2	11.5	343	5.2
1889–1898	67.6	10.5	358	4.4
1894–1903	74.0	9.5	406	13.4
1899–1908	81.3	9.9	461	13.5
1904–1913	89.6	10.2	500	8.5
1909–1918	97.6	8.9	515	3.0

Source: Simon Kuznets, "Changes in the National Income of the United States of America Since 1870," *Income and Wealth Series II* (London: Bowes & Bowes Ltd., 1952), p. 55. By permission of the publisher.

growth, but by World War I real per-capita income per year was nearly 2½ times as great as it was during the 1869–1878 decade.

According to Robert E. Gallman's estimate, real gross national product (GNP) grew at an average annual rate of somewhat more than 4 percent between 1865 and 1908—an increase of approximately eightfold for the period. A rate of real growth of this magnitude meant that per-capita output advanced at an average annual rate of 2 percent. So between the Civil War and World War I, real per-capita GNP more than doubled. These remarkable rates of growth were achieved in the heyday of capitalism when intervention by the federal government was minimal.

THE IMPETUS TO ECONOMIC GROWTH

American society was clearly an "achieving society," to use David C. McClelland's expression, and the drive to be successful was particularly strong among American entrepreneurs. Their efforts were reinforced by three sources of continually increasing productivity that assured a churning, throbbing economy.

1. *In the North and the West before 1860 and in the South after 1875, Americans were persuaded that investment in human capital—in education—paid big dividends.* From the beginning, the United States and its colonial predecessors had been at the forefront of the world in educating the populace. By 1840, more than 90 percent of all white American adults could read and write—an astoundingly high proportion relative to other countries. Popular education was originally supported by private funds, and public support steadily gained ground throughout the nineteenth century. Public expenditures rose from 47 percent of the total in 1850 to 79 percent in 1900. Thus, although public outlays to education rose dramatically, private support remained substantial, with Roman Catholic and Lutheran parochial schools accounting for a large portion of private expenditures.[1]

By 1900, an eighth-grade education was considered essential to success, and high school was rapidly coming within the reach of everyone. By 1920, a high-school education was considered the birthright of the majority of young Americans, and college was no longer just a distant dream. With something like a one-generation lag, America's investment in knowledge played a large part in the growth of the economy.

2. *The increasing size of the American market, which kept expanding until 1920, led to economies of scale in manufacturing that played a significant role in productivity changes.* By 1910, the advantages of a great common market were plain to see, and regional specialization largely offset the harm done by high protective tariffs and the consequent disruption to international trade.

The development of an efficient internal transportation system was crucial to the expansion of the original coastal settlement into an ever-widening hinterland that, with its rich soils, made possible the ultimate regionally specialized whole. The transportation system in turn depended on large in-

[1] Albert Fishlow, "Levels of Nineteenth-Century Investment in Education," *Journal of Economic History* **XXVI**:4 (December 1966), pp. 418–36.

vestments and the rapid adoption of newer and more efficient modes as they became available during the nineteenth century.

It was long customary in American historiography to accept the railroad as the overwhelmingly important innovation necessary to interregional development and specialization and thus to American economic growth. In one of the first major essays in econometric history, Robert W. Fogel shook the confidence of economic historians in this fundamental proposition.[2] In an attempt to assess the net effect of the railroad on American economic development, Fogel made a quantitative comparison between what actually happened and what would have happened if the United States had had to depend on wagons and the water system for its basic transportation network. Fogel's main conceptual device was the notion of "social saving," which he defined for any given year as ". . . the actual cost of shipping agricultural goods in that year and the alternative cost of shipping exactly the same collection of goods between exactly the same set of points without railroads."[3] Examining his counterfactual proposition, Fogel came up with the astonishing conclusion that for 1890 the social saving attributable to the railroad in the interregional shipment of agricultural products was about 1 percent of the gross national product in that year. Fogel subsequently raised this figure slightly to about 1.2 percent to include intraregional as well as long-distance agricultural shipments. Even if shipments other than agricultural were included, the Fogel investigation would yield a social saving of no more than 5 percent for 1890. Albert Fishlow, on the other hand, estimated the probable 1890 social saving at closer to 10 percent of that year's gross national product, and other estimates fall somewhere in between these two figures.[4] The thought that impresses us is that the great American common market would have emerged, more slowly to be sure, even in the absence of the railroad as a transportation mode and as a stimulus to the manufacture of steel and complicated capital equipment such as locomotives.

3. *More exciting in their short-run manifestations were the technological changes in manufacturing.* About 1900, the relationship between the business world and invention took a radical turn. Until this time, strategic inventions, which we have defined as the commercially successful ones, led to the establishment of business firms. As these firms manufactured the product made possible by invention, their engineering and technical staffs naturally made improvements and refinements in the basic product. But not until the electrical industry emerged in the 1890s did it become necessary for business firms to make a formal, systematic attempt to develop new products simply to keep ahead of other firms.

The electrical industry had had three main lines of development. The great pioneers in the arc-lighting industry—Edward Weston, Charles Brush, and Elihu Thomson—proved that lighting by electricity could be commercially

[2] Robert W. Fogel, "A Quantitative Approach to the Study of Railroads in American Economic Growth: A Report of Some Preliminary Findings," *Journal of Economic History,* **XXII:**2 (June 1962), pp. 163–97.

[3] Robert W. Fogel and Stanley L. Engerman (eds.), *The Reinterpretation of American Economic History* (New York: Harper & Row, 1971), p. 188.

[4] Davis, Easterlin, and Parker (eds.), *American Economic Growth* (New York: Harper & Row, 1972), p. 620.

successful. George Westinghouse, head of the firm bearing his name, pioneering with alternating current systems, ultimately won acceptance over the direct-current systems advocated by Thomas Edison. Edison and his firm, Edison General Electric, had been the pioneer innovator in incandescent lighting and had developed a good business in generating equipment for both isolated and central plants.

Largely to obtain each other's much needed patents, the firms of Thomson-Houston and Edison General Electric consolidated in 1892 to form a new company, General Electric. By 1894, the two dominant firms in the industry, Westinghouse and General Electric, possessed hundreds of patents; some were obtained directly from company engineers, some were purchased from outside inventors, and some were acquired from mergers with other firms. As the two leading firms expanded their lines to include nearly every type of electrical apparatus, they became more and more in conflict with one another, and by 1896 over 300 patent suits were pending between them. The result of their legal involvements was a cross-licensing agreement that, in effect, enabled the two companies to use all existing patentable ideas except those owned by the small independents in the business. Within a few years, many of these small firms had sold out to one or the other of the two giants.

In the 1890s, both of these major firms developed engineering staffs to systematize the search for new ideas. By 1900, as Harold Passer has remarked, "competition in reality was between the engineering staffs of two companies." We should not be surprised to learn, then, that in 1900 General Electric asked an MIT professor, Dr. Willis R. Whitney, to establish a Schenectady laboratory devoted to scientific research in applied physics. Needless to say, Westinghouse shortly established a competing laboratory in Pittsburgh.

Research and development began as a form of business strategy in an industry that to this day remains a leader in this kind of competitive effort. For 20 years or so after 1900, the research and development departments of General Electric and Westinghouse concentrated largely on improving processes and equipment in the power business (and, to a lesser extent, in the lamp business). But as electric-generating machinery became increasingly complex, both major companies assured themselves of a continuing flow of a multitude of parts by purchasing or establishing subsidiary companies to make parts and components. Because the end products of the companies did not require the entire output of switches, fuses, condensers, and so forth, company sales departments began to market these smaller items. Moreover, research aimed at producing better components often opened new vistas. Alfred D. Chandler, Jr., explains, for example, that dissatisfaction with its insulating materials brought General Electric into the plastics business, when its research laboratories began experimenting with resins in 1912.

But it was not until after World War I that General Electric and Westinghouse began the diversification of products that eventually affected even the organizational structures of the two firms. Two fundamental decisions led to the ultimate multiplicity of products. (1) It was decided to develop and manufacture consumer appliances to increase the demand for electricity and thus for the heavy power machinery that was the original output of the two firms. (2) As the research laboratories invented new alloys, new chemicals, and new electronic devices, it became an explicit business policy to expand the sale of these items whenever there was a prospect of long-term profitability. Consequently, General Electric formed one subsidiary to make and sell X-ray equipment and another (Carboloy, Inc.) to market the new metals that General Electric scientists first developed for use in generating and transmission equipment. Westinghouse, too, began the manufacture of X-ray equipment, but also went into the elevator business. Not until the early 1930s, however, were both companies irrevocably committed to the proposition that competition would forever take the form of systematically discovering, perfecting, and marketing new products and processes.

ECONOMIC CHANGE, SOCIAL JUSTICE, AND GOVERNMENT INTERFERENCE

Although the path of economic change was generally upward, the progress of the period was not without hardship and social reaction. As we have emphasized, the great downswing in prices after the Civil War spelled continual trouble for the agricultural South and West. During the major depressions, hardship also overtook the industrial East, where labor and small businesses bore the brunt of declining economic activity.

The depression of 1893 –1896 was the culmination of more than two decades of disconcerting cyclical fluctuations in the nation's economy. The physical suffering and spiritual degradation that accompanied it were unprecedented for the time and have only been equaled since by the Great Depression of the 1930s. During the harsh winter of 1893 –1894, the problem of relief reached enormous proportions in both large and small cities. Some communities limited their relief projects to soup kitchens and bread lines. New York, with the largest population, received the cooperation of charitable societies, the bread and clothing funds sponsored by newspapers, and the low-cost food centers run by philanthropists; nevertheless, the city had to provide millions of dollars of direct relief. There was a strong opinion in many cities that providing outright relief would contribute to a certain flabbiness of character in the poor, who would surely become used to getting something for nothing. Therefore, the municipality often required a day's labor in the public parks or on the streets in exchange for a weekly or daily family ration of food. Many argued for public-works projects on a statewide scale, but such proposals were not well received. Governor Roswell Pettibone Flower of New York, for example, rejected requests for a state public-works program in 1893 on the grounds that it was not the duty of government to support people and that public works for relief would lead to further paternal legislation and prodigal extravagance.[5]

Direct intervention of the federal government was proposed early in the emergency when the convention of the American Federation of Labor called for the issue of $500 million in paper money for the purpose of constructing

[5] For an absorbing discussion of the problem of relief, see Samuel Rezneck, "Unemployment, Unrest, and Relief in the United States During the Depression of 1893 –1897," *Journal of Political Economy,* **XLI** (August 1953), pp. 324– 45.

public works. The idea was picked up by Jacob Coxey; indeed, the objective of Coxey's Army and its march on Washington in the spring of 1894 was to petition Congress for a $500 million paper issue to be spent to improve existing roads or build new ones.[6] But such government interference with the private economy was unconscionable in the view of most propertied people, who were supported by the testimony of a large number of respected professors of economics and sociology.

People were more interested in discussing the causes and cures of the depression than they were in debating the merits of various relief plans. Most vociferous were the advocates of monetary reform, and the controversy between the "silver lunatics" and the "gold-bugs" reached heights of vituperation. Proponents of protection argued that the depression of 1893 had been brought on by business' fear of tariff reductions aroused by the Democratic victory of 1892, and advocates of low tariffs rejoined that this subsidy of the trusts was the very source of the oppression of the poor. Labor leaders attributed the workers' plight to the greed and selfishness of employers—particularly the managerial class because they promoted unrestricted immigration. On this question, surprisingly, labor had the backing of the dean of American economists, Francis A. Walker, who thundered that the American standard of living and the quality of American citizenship were being degraded by "vast throngs of ignorant and brutalized peasantry from the countries of eastern and southern Europe." A few obscure writers, who were not accepted members of the intellectual community, thought that deflation and depression might have been the result of government fiscal policy since the Civil War. Surpluses had been the rule, the federal debt having been reduced by nearly $2 billion between 1866 and 1893. But anyone who suggested deficit financing as a possible cure for depression was considered foolish, if not downright dangerous, because economic orthodoxy held that nothing was more damaging to business confidence than running a deficit.

No concrete proposal for mitigating slumps was enacted into law. As the decade of the 1890s dragged on toward revival and ultimate recovery, Americans seemed resigned to recurrent breakdowns of the economic machine with all the suffering they entailed. But a step was taken in the 1890s, seemingly almost by accident, that adumbrated the inclusion in the tax system of an automatic stabilizer and a more equitable division of the tax burden in good times and bad.

The Adoption of an Income Tax

In the campaign of 1892, Grover Cleveland and the Democrats had promised tariff reform; but as debate on a new tariff bill progressed, it appeared that a coalition of Republicans and conservative Democrats would succeed in preventing a downward revision of duties. Tariffs were then so high as to be significantly protective on dutiable goods, greatly restricting imports and therefore lowering ad valorem taxes on them. With practically no reduction in the

[6]*Ibid.*, pp. 327, 333.

previously existing high rates in sight, the Treasury was confronted with a continuation of the deficit that had begun late in 1892. An income tax provision was therefore inserted in the proposed tariff bill on the grounds that revenue from another source was necessary to compensate for the loss of revenue from customs duties. Conservative members of Congress bitterly fought the income tax provision, charging that the tax was unjust, inquisitorial, and ill-timed. William Jennings Bryan in the House and William V. Allen in the Senate defended the income-tax rider with fire and eloquence. Senator Allen pointed out that according to census statistics, 91 percent of the country's 12 million families owned 29 percent of the national wealth and that 9 percent of the families owned 71 percent.[7] Other Senators of the West and South urged, as they had been doing for 20 years, that a tax on income was fair because it was levied on individuals in proportion to their ability to pay and, with a part of income exempted, did not impinge on necessities. The most convincing argument of all was that the distress and unrest among low-income groups made it necessary for the rich to assume a larger proportion of the expenses of government if socialism were to be avoided.

The Wilson–Gorman Tariff Act of 1894, besides slightly reducing customs duties, provided for an income tax of 2 percent on personal incomes above $4,000 and for a tax of 2 percent on all corporate net income. The country was not without experience with this form of taxation; an income tax had been in effect from 1862 to 1872 as a Civil War finance measure. Nevertheless, the congressional action precipitated a storm of controversy exceeded in violence only by the debate over the silver question. The battle did not last any longer than it took for a test case to reach the Supreme Court. Despite a previous decision that a tax on income was an excise tax—and therefore not a direct tax—in 1895, the Court held that the income tax was a direct tax and therefore required by the Constitution to be apportioned among the states according to population. Since the Wilson–Gorman Act had not provided for apportionment among the states, the income tax legislation was declared unconstitutional.

This ruling of unconstitutionality did not permanently deter the advocates of an income tax. Within a decade, a majority of the electorate clearly wanted a more equitable basis of taxation. In his 1908 message to Congress, Theodore Roosevelt recommended both an income and an inheritance tax, and Roosevelt's successor, William Howard Taft, advocated a personal income tax in the campaign of 1908. Early in the Taft Administration, a tax of 1 percent was levied on corporate incomes of more than $5,000, and in 1909 Congress sent to the states for ratification a constitutional amendment providing for a tax on personal incomes.

With ratification of the Sixteenth Amendment early in 1913, the way was opened for an income tax law that could not be undone in the courts. Section II of the Underwood–Simmons Tariff Act of 1913 imposed a "normal" tax of 1 percent on the taxable income of every U.S. citizen, giving an exemption of $3,000 to each taxpayer plus an additional $1,000 to a married person living with spouse.[8] In addition to the normal tax, an additional tax, or *surtax*, was

[7] He did so despite the fact that income and wealth are two different things.

[8] No exemptions were allowed for minors. Interest on government bonds was exempted, as were interest on state and local bonds and the salaries of state and local officials.

TO BE FILLED IN BY COLLECTOR.

Form 1040.

TO BE FILLED IN BY INTERNAL REVENUE BUREAU.

List No. ....

File No. ....

INCOME TAX.

.... District of ....

Date received ....

THE PENALTY
FOR FAILURE TO HAVE THIS RETURN IN THE HANDS OF THE COLLECTOR OF INTERNAL REVENUE ON OR BEFORE MARCH 1 IS $20 TO $1,000.
(SEE INSTRUCTIONS ON PAGE 4.)

Assessment List ....

Page .... Line ....

UNITED STATES INTERNAL REVENUE.

RETURN OF ANNUAL NET INCOME OF INDIVIDUALS.

(As provided by Act of Congress, approved October 3, 1913.)

RETURN OF NET INCOME RECEIVED OR ACCRUED DURING THE YEAR ENDED DECEMBER 31, 191....
(FOR THE YEAR 1913, FROM MARCH 1, TO DECEMBER 31.)

Filed by (or for) .... of ....
(Full name of individual.) (Street and No.)

in the City, Town, or Post Office of .... State of ....
(Fill in pages 2 and 3 before making entries below.)

1. Gross Income (see page 2, line 12)		$
2. General Deductions (see page 3, line 7)		$
3. Net Income		$
Deductions and exemptions allowed in computing income subject to the normal tax of 1 per cent.		
4. Dividends and net earnings received or accrued, of corporations, etc., subject to like tax. (See page 2, line 11)	$	
5. Amount of income on which the normal tax has been deducted and withheld at the source. (See page 2, line 9, column A)		
6. Specific exemption of $3,000 or $4,000, as the case may be. (See Instructions 3 and 19)		
Total deductions and exemptions. (Items 4, 5, and 6)		$
7. Taxable Income on which the normal tax of 1 per cent is to be calculated. (See Instruction 3)		$

8. When the net income shown above on line 3 exceeds $20,000, the additional tax thereon must be calculated as per schedule below

	INCOME.	TAX.
1 per cent on amount over $20,000 and not exceeding $50,000	$	$
2 " " 50,000 " " 75,000		
3 " " 75,000 " " 100,000		
4 " " 100,000 " " 250,000		
5 " " 250,000 " " 500,000		
6 " " 500,000		
Total additional or super tax		$
Total normal tax (1 per cent of amount entered on line 7)		$
Total tax liability		$

levied progressively on income over $20,000. The maximum rate of 7 percent (1 percent normal plus 6 percent surtax) was applied to incomes of $500,000 or over. Adoption of the principle of progressive rather than proportional rates was hailed by reformers as a major step toward social justice, but propertied people and the conservative press spoke darkly of a first step toward the complete confiscation of private property.

Antitrust Enforcement and the Courts

When the Sherman Antitrust Act of 1890 was passed, it was heralded without fanfare or acclaim, largely because times had recently improved. But the problem of monopoly had been a source of great political turmoil—and was to be again. As the depression of 1893 deepened, monopolies in general and the trusts in particular were blamed. Nor did the trusts escape public wrath with the onset of prosperity in 1897, because the business upturn coincided with the beginning of a second combination movement. Journalists kept their readers informed of the nefarious conduct of large business firms and warned of the perils of concentration.

For nearly a decade after its passage, the Sherman Antitrust Act was as ineffective as the Interstate Commerce Act of 1887 had been. The statute seemed simple enough. It declared illegal "every contract, combination in the form of trust, or otherwise, or conspiracy in restraint of trade among the several states." It prescribed punishment of a fine or imprisonment or both for "every person who shall monopolize, or attempt to monopolize, or combine or conspire . . . to monopolize any part of the trade or commerce among the several states." The Attorney General was charged with enforcing the Act by bringing either civil or criminal proceedings in the federal courts. Thus, how the law should be interpreted was left to federal judges.

The Supreme Court did much to discourage enforcement by its decision, rendered in 1895, in the case of *United States* v. *E.C. Knight Company.* The American Sugar Refining Company had acquired the stock of the E.C. Knight Company, along with that of three other sugar refiners in the Philadelphia area, raising American's share of the refining market from 65 to 98 percent. The Attorney General brought an action against the sugar trust; but the Court would not apply the Sherman Act on the grounds that the company was engaged in manufacture—not in interstate commerce—and that Congress intended the prohibitions to apply only to interstate commerce. The business of sugar refining, the Court held, "bore no direct relation to commerce between the states or with foreign nations. . . . Commerce succeeds to manufacture, and is not a part of it." The Court further implied that the Sherman Antitrust Act did not preclude the growth of large firms by purchase of property—that is, by merger or consolidation.

(Opposite)

An unwelcome innovation to many Americans of upper-income status was the income tax. This early tax form barely hinted at the complexity of the contemporary Form 1040, still decades in the future.

In the case of *United States* v. *Addyston Pipe and Steel Company* (1899), the Court made it clear that the Sherman Act did apply to collusive agreements among firms supposed to be in competition with each other. And in 1904, in the *Northern Securities Company* case, the Court decided that the provisions of the Act also applied to holding companies, which came as a shock to corporate lawyers who thought that the holding company form of organization was immune to antitrust prosecution.[9]

As early as 1902, Theodore Roosevelt sensed the political value of trust-busting, and in the campaign of 1904 he promised vigorous prosecution of monopolies. During his administration, bills were filed against several great companies, the most important being against the American Tobacco Company and the Standard Oil Company of New Jersey. These firms were the archetypes of monopoly in the public mind, and the judgment of the Supreme Court in the cases against them would indicate the degree of enforcement that might be expected under the Sherman Act.

In decisions handed down in 1911, the Supreme Court found that unlawful monopoly power existed and ordered the dissolution of both the Standard Oil Company and the American Tobacco Company. But it did so on rather narrow grounds. First, it gave great weight to evidence of intent to monopolize. As an aid to discovering intent and purpose, the Court examined the predatory practices that had occurred during each company's growth period and the manner in which the companies exercised their monopoly power. The oil trust, so it was asserted, had achieved its powerful position in the market by unfairly obtaining rebates from the railroads and by acquiring refining companies brought to terms after price wars. Similarly, the tobacco trust was accused of bringing competing companies to heel by price wars, frequently closing them after acquisition by purchase. Moreover, the record showed that the old American Tobacco Company exerted a strong monopsonistic power, beating down the prices of tobacco farmers when the crop was sold at the annual auctions held throughout the tobacco-growing states. Second, the Court adopted a "rule of reason" with respect to restraints of trade; since action against all possible violators was obviously impossible, it became necessary for the Court to exercise judgment.

> Under this principle, combinations which restricted competition were held to be lawful as long as the restraint was not unreasonable. Since there is no precise economic standard by which the reasonableness of a restriction on competition can be measured, the courts examined the practices pursued by a corporate giant in achieving and maintaining its position in the market. Predatory practices were indicative of an intent to monopolize the market, and a corporate combination which achieved dominance by indulging in them

[9] Antitrust prosecution is full of ironies that suggest the tangled web that is woven when government intervenes on behalf of any group in society. In the *Northern Securities* case, the Supreme Court blocked the efforts of James J. Hill to create a great regional railroad system in the northwestern quadrant of the United States. More than half a century later, many transportation experts were urging the creation of such systems as the railroads' only hope of salvation, and in 1968 the ICC approved a merger of the very roads seeking to form an economical system in 1904 as well as other roads that added Chicago–Gulf Coast routes.

might be dissolved. Those which behaved in a more exemplary manner, even though their size gave them power over the market, did not transgress the law.[10]

Standard Oil and American Tobacco were the only companies that the Supreme Court dissolved, but even if the courts had continued ordering dissolution or divestiture, it is unlikely that competition in the classical sense would have been restored. The four major successor companies to the American Tobacco Company constituted a tight oligopoly with respect to cigarette manufacture.[11] Stock in the 33 successor companies of the Standard Oil Company was ordered distributed pro rata to the stockholders of the holding company, but whatever the benefits of dissolution, an increase in price competition was not an obvious outcome.[12]

In two decisions handed down at the close of World War I, large companies formed by merger were effectively freed from the threat of dissolution, provided that the actions of the dominant firm were not calculated to exclude competitors from the market. In the case of *United States* v. *United Shoe Machinery Company of New Jersey, et al.,* Justice Joseph McKenna took as the basis for his decision the finding of the trial court that the constituent companies had not been *competitors*—that they had performed supplementary rather than identical functions in making shoes. The Court did not deny the monopoly power of the United Shoe Machinery Company; it simply held that the company's power was not illegal, because the constituent companies had never been competitive. The decision in *United States* v. *United States Steel Corporation* made the position of merged companies even safer. Justice McKenna, who again spoke for the Court, found that the corporation possessed neither the power nor the intent to exert monopoly control. The majority of the Court was impressed by the fact that examination of the history of United States Steel revealed none of the predatory practices complained of in the oil and tobacco cases. The Court took cognizance of the splendid relations of the steel company with its rivals, noting that United States Steel's power "was efficient only when in cooperation with its competitors, and hence it concerted with them in the expedients of pools, associations, trade meetings, and finally in a system of dinners inaugurated in 1907 by the president of the company, E.H. Gary, and called 'The Gary Dinners.' "[13] But the corporation "resorted to none of the

[10] George W. Stocking, "The Rule of Reason, Workable Competition, and the Legality of Trade Association Activities," *University of Chicago Law Review,* **XXI**:4 (Summer 1954), pp. 532–33.

[11] There are ironies in the tobacco case, too. Before 1911, cigarettes were not nearly as important a commodity as they were to become after World War I changed men's smoking habits. Competitive advertising of the four successor companies unquestionably accounts for the rapid increase in women's smoking during the 1920s; institutional advertising of the staid old tobacco monopoly would almost certainly not have pushed the demand curve for cigarettes so sharply to the right. By bringing a successful antitrust suit against the producers of a trivial product, the do-gooders of one era took a long step toward making a nation of cigarette smokers in another.

[12] For an interesting account of growing price rigidity during these decades, see Austin H. Spencer, "Relative Downward Industrial Price Flexibility 1870–1921," *Explorations in Economic History* **14**:2, (January 1977), pp. 1–19.

[13] 40 Sup. Ct. 251 U.S. 417, p. 295.

brutalities or tyrannies that the cases illustrate of other combinations. . . . It did not have power in and of itself, and the control it exerted was only in and by association with its competitors. Its offense, therefore, such as it was, was not different from theirs and was distinguished from theirs only in the leadership it assumed in promulgating and perfecting the policy. This leadership it gave up and it had ceased to offend the law before this suit was brought."[14]

Justice McKenna held that United States Steel had not achieved monopoly power despite its control of 50 percent of the industry's output. He decided that the pattern of regular price changes over time, clearly shown by the evidence, could have emerged from a competitive market just as easily as from collusion. The government's assertion that the size of the corporation made it a potential threat to competition in the industry was denied. On the contrary, said the Court, "the law does not make mere size an offense, or the existence of unexerted power an offense." After such a decision, only the most optimistic Justice Department attorneys could see any point in bringing action against a firm simply because it was big.

In 1914, during Woodrow Wilson's first administration, Congress passed the Clayton Act, which was intended to remove ambiguities in existing antitrust law by making certain specific practices illegal. Price discrimination among buyers was forbidden, along with exclusive selling and tying contracts if their effect was to lessen competition. Firms could not acquire the stock of a competitor, and interlocking directorates among competing firms were forbidden—again, if the effect was to lessen competition. A newly established Federal Trade Commission of five appointive members was to enforce the Act, and decisions of the FTC were to be appealed to the circuit courts. The Commission could also carry out investigations, acting on its own initiative or on the complaint of an injured party. If a violation was found, the Commission could issue a "cease and desist" order; offenders then had the right to appeal to the federal courts.

The Clayton Act was so weakly drawn that it added little to the government's power to enforce competition. Once the existence of listed illegal practices was determined, the courts still had to decide whether their effect was to lessen competition or to promote monopoly. As we have just observed, by 1920 about the only practice the courts would consistently consider in restraint of trade was explicit collusion among independent producers or sellers. "Reasonable" monopoly practices of huge firms on one hand and "weak" forms of collusion on the other were not subject to punishment. The useful functions of the Federal Trade Commission became the compiling of a massive amount of data helpful to economists and the elevation of the ethics of competition by acting against misbranding and misleading advertising. Not until it could take action on the basis of injury to *consumers* instead of on the basis of injury to a *competitor* would the public gain much advantage from the FTC's efforts.

Thus, the one great pre-1920 experiment in the social control of business achieved little. By the time a vigorous enforcement of the antitrust laws was undertaken late in the 1930s, it was too late to do much about the problem of

[14] 40 Sup. Ct. 251 U.S. 417, pp. 295–96.

bigness in industry. But by then it was clear that a kind of competition not envisioned by the framers of the Sherman Act protected consumers. We will examine the effectiveness of this new competition in Chapter 27.

THE ESTABLISHMENT OF THE FEDERAL RESERVE SYSTEM

The depression of the mid-1890s was followed by the severe panic and ensuing depression of 1907. Once again, the American people were aroused to the need for basic reforms, which came within the next six years.

One of the most painful manifestations of economic crises in pre-World War I days was a scarcity of currency—of hand-to-hand money. As individuals and business firms became apprehensive about the economic future, they rushed to the banks to convert their deposits into cash. The banks, which operated on the "fractional reserve" principle, could not immediately meet the demands for their total deposit liabilities. A single bank could *gradually* convert its assets into cash; given time, any sound bank could even be liquidated in an orderly fashion, and its depositors and stockholders could be paid in full. But in periods of panic, an orderly shifting of assets into cash was difficult, if not impossible. Not only was there insufficient time, but as harried banks all tried to sell securities (their most liquid assets) at the same time, the prices of securities fell drastically. For some banks, the consequent losses on securities proved disastrous, even though "runs" were stopped. If, instead of selling its securities, a bank called its loans or refused to renew notes as they came due, pressure was transferred to the customers of the bank. And if these customers—business firms that had come to rely on the bank for loans in time of need—could not meet their obligations, they were forced into insolvency.

A common way of mitigating these difficulties was to "suspend" back payments during crises. Before the Civil War, suspension meant that banks temporarily refused to redeem their notes or to pay out deposits in specie. After the Civil War, suspension meant that banks ceased to pay out cash in any form—gold or gold certificates, silver or silver certificates, greenbacks, national-bank notes, or subsidiary coins. Instead of suspending payments, a bank might restrict cash payments to a certain maximum sum per day or per withdrawal. During the panic of 1907, such suspensions were more general and for longer time periods (over two months in some cities) than they had ever been before. In the Southeast and Midwest, the resulting shortage of cash was so serious that local clearing houses even issued "script" against collateral pledged by cooperating banks so that people could carry on business. These small-denomination "clearing-house certificates" were not issued much elsewhere, but large-denomination certificates were used by banks in cities all over the United States to make up balances due one another.

It is not surprising, then, that Americans became incensed over a recurring embarrassment that they felt was entirely the fault of existing laws, even though the banking community viewed the system as adequate and on the whole sound. The Aldrich–Vreeland Act, passed in 1908, provided for the organization of "national currency associations" to be composed of not less than ten banks in sound financial condition. The purpose of these associations was to enable the banks that formed them to issue emergency bank notes against the security of bonds and commercial paper in their portfolios. A secondary provision, which was really an attempt to postpone more positive action, established a National Monetary Commission. Made up of 18 members of Congress, nine from each house, the Commission sponsored voluminous studies that were recorded in a shelf of volumes ranging from compilations of data to superbly executed historical and analytical monographs. The report of the Commission in 1912 helped point out to the public the weaknesses of the American banking system.

The faults described by the Commission were the same ones that economists and businesspeople had been writing and talking about for years. A major defect was that the economy suffered from the harmful effects of an "inelastic" currency. By this, the Commission meant that the amount of coin and paper money in the economy did not expand and contract in accordance with the needs of the business community. It was argued that as business activity increased and decreased, the quantity of currency ought to increase and decrease. Since during the financial panics that always accompanied the onset of depressions, the cash demands of depositors could not be met by the banks without a resulting suspension of currency payments, the Commission felt that bank reserves should be "pooled" to make them readily available to all banks in times of stress. The Commission felt that what was needed was a central institution that could create reserves to stretch or contract the money supply.

Some contemporary writers thought the problem could be solved by simply putting cash reserves in a central place, from which they could be dispatched as required to various parts of the country. That is why we read so much in the literature of a half-century ago of the need for pooling reserves, although it should have been clear that reserves *were* pooled in New York.[15] But painful stringencies developed anyway, because New York banks could not create more cash. *A great central institution was needed with the authority to hold the reserves of the commercial banks and to increase their reserves through its own credit-granting powers.*

Fortunately, some problems described by the National Monetary Commission could be solved only by establishing a central bank. Both private firms and the U.S. government had to pay too much for routine services. The simple process of collecting checks was a complex and expensive procedure in post-Civil War days. There were extreme examples of checks being sent hundreds of miles through many banks to effect the collection of a sum drawn on a bank a short distance from the residence of the payee. Even normal banking procedures, however, were time-consuming and costly, since a bank always had to

[15] The concentration of reserves in New York City was tremendous. By the 1900s, six New York banks—with two-thirds of the resources of all the national banks in that city—held three-quarters of the reserve deposits of correspondent banks. During times of stress, the reserves of these banks slowly dropped below the 25-percent legal reserve ratio, falling as low as 19 percent during the crash of 1907. While permitting this violation of the rules, the Comptroller of the Currency, as well as the banks, viewed the practice with alarm.

depend on some other commercial bank to act as its collection agent. Because there was no national collection agency that could offset items the way that clearing houses did within local urban areas, there was much unnecessary remitting of cash, frequently over long distances. The transit departments of banks had to write innumerable letters and spend great amounts of time determining the most accurate and expedient way to collect an item, with consequent additions to operating expenses.

A central bank was also needed to help the Treasury. After the demise of the second Bank of the United States, the federal government had to maintain its own fiscal agent in the form of the Treasury, which was by law required to remain aloof from the banking system. Impossibly antiquated methods of handling government funds resulted. Even in the early years of the twentieth century, the government had a sizable amount of banking business to conduct. The Treasury continuously received and disbursed tax monies in all sections of the United States and needed an institution to carry its principal checking accounts. Furthermore, an official institution was required to handle the myriad physical details involved in government borrowing, to advise Treasury officials regarding management of the public debt, and to act as the agent of the Treasury in gold and foreign-exchange transactions. By 1910, the need for a modern, central fiscal agent was too great to be postponed further.

The National Monetary Commission placed undue emphasis on difficulties that were not of a crucial nature and failed to make explicit the need for establishing central control of the money supply. Nonetheless, its report of 1912 brought matters to a head. Even before the Commission issued its report, its chairman, Senator Nelson Wilmarth Aldrich of Rhode Island, published his *Suggested Plan for Monetary Legislation,* which he presented to Congress in 1912. The Aldrich bill provided for a weak central bank, with little government participation in its operations. It would have created a National Reserve Association with a central office in Washington and branches in important financial centers; direction of the National Reserve Association would have been in the hands of the officers of large banks. The association would have acted only in times of emergency, and there would have been no shifting of commercial-bank reserves to the central association. Control of the monetary system would have been exercised by bankers, and the public, through its elected officers, would have had little to say about monetary matters. Thus, the Aldrich bill bore little resemblance to the Federal Reserve plan that followed it, and the bill did not pass Congress for two reasons. To meet the demands of their constituents, the Congress that met in 1911 and 1912 insisted on public supervision of any proposed central bank. Moreover, the Democrats, confident that they would elect a national administration in 1912, probably wanted to delay action so that they would receive full credit for the establishment of a central banking institution.

Two days before Christmas in 1913, President Wilson signed the bill that established the Federal Reserve System. The act establishing the Federal Reserve System had not been arrived at easily; it represented a compromise between radical and conservative Democrats. Basically, the act was the work of Congressman Carter Glass, Chairman of the House Banking and Currency Committee, and Senator Robert L. Owen, Chairman of the Senate Committee on Banking and Currency.[16] Under its provisions, the United States was to be divided into not less than eight and not more than twelve districts, with a Federal Reserve Bank in each district. Twelve districts were decided on, and a city was selected for the location of the Federal Reserve Bank in each of these districts. Each district presumably enclosed an area of homogeneous economic activity that contained sufficient resources for the organization of a strong Reserve Bank. An unbelievable amount of wrangling and politicking ensued over the delineation of districts and the location of Federal Reserve Banks, and the cities that were not chosen could only hope that they might be the sites of branches to be organized in the future.[17]

The system was to be headed by a Federal Reserve Board composed of seven members, including the Secretary of the Treasury, the Comptroller of the Currency *ex officio,* and five appointees of the President. Each Federal Reserve Bank was to be run by a board of nine directors. Three of the directors, representing the "public," were to be appointed by the Federal Reserve Board; the remaining six were to be elected by the member banks of the district. Three of the six locally elected directors could be bankers; the remaining three were to represent business, industry, and agriculture. Thus, the banking community had a minority representation on the Reserve Bank directorates in each district.

The Federal Reserve Act made membership in the system compulsory for national banks; state banks, on compliance with federal requirements, might become members. To join the system a commercial bank had to purchase shares of the capital stock of the district Federal Reserve Bank in the amount of 3 percent of its combined capital and surplus. (Another 3 percent *might* be required.) Thus, the member banks nominally owned the Federal Reserve Banks, although the annual return they could receive on their stock was limited to a 6-percent cumulative dividend. A member bank also had to deposit with the district Federal Reserve Bank a large part of the cash it had previously held as reserves. The Act originally provided that member banks might retain a part of their reserves as cash in vault, but in 1917 the requirement was changed; after 1917, *all* the legal reserves of member banks were to be in the form of deposits with the Federal Reserve Bank.[18]

Because much of the final monetary chapter of history is concerned with the development of the Federal Reserve System, we can conclude our present discussion with three observations.

1. Although the majority opinion in the United States was strongly in favor of a central bank, there was real fear of one, as there had been in the days of the

[16] For details of the controversy over the framing of a bill to establish a central bank, see Ross M. Robertson, *The Comptroller and Bank Supervision* (Washington, D.C.: Office of the Comptroller of Currency, 1968) pp. 89–90. See also Gerald T. Dunne, "A Christmas Present for the President," *Business Horizons,* **6** (Winter 1963), esp. pp. 47–54.

[17] For more details, see Ross M. Robertson, "Branches of Federal Reserve Banks," *Monthly Review,* Federal Reserve Bank of St. Louis, **XXXVIII:**8 (August 1956), pp. 90–97.

[18] All required reserves were held on deposit with Federal Reserve Banks from June 21, 1917, until late 1959, when, after a series of transitional steps, member banks could once again count vault cash as reserves.

first and second U.S. banks. Consequently, twelve regional banks, centrally coordinated but presumably under a large measure of local control, were created.

2. Contrary to experience in other countries, where central banks were owned either by private individuals or by governments, Federal Reserve Banks were to be owned by the institutions having the privilege of membership. To be certain that decisions would not be based on profit motives, dividends to member banks were carefully limited.
3. It was expected that the Federal Reserve Banks would operate almost automatically and that, if the Federal Reserve Act were carefully followed, monetary disturbances would be very nearly eliminated. To most people, the elimination of monetary disturbances was synonymous with the elimination of business fluctuations. But as we will see in Part IV, monetary disturbances and business cycles were to reach a pinnacle in the modern era.

4

The Modern Era: 1915 to the Present

24

The Great Watershed of Modern Times

When World War I ended, the promising young song writer, Harry Donaldson, cast his lot with the just-organized Irving Berlin Music Company to begin a long and mutually profitable association. His smash 1919 hit was at once a question and a prophetic answer: "How ya gonna keep 'em down on the farm after they've seen Paree?" How indeed? Millions of young Americans had been wrested from the placid boredom of country life, marking the beginning of the end of an agrarian society. To be sure, only a fraction of them ever saw Paris, and some got no farther than Camp Funston. But country boy, small-town bookkeeper, and city millworker alike had a taste of travel that broke routine—although almost 100,000 of them died in battle and more than that succumbed to influenza.

The high pitch of wartime excitement had passed, of course, and there were signs that the old provincialism might return. Isolationist sentiment had prevailed in the congressional elections of 1918; and the press made it plain to all who could read that the intellectual in the White House would fight in vain for a genuine peace even if France and Britain could be dissuaded from their vengeful course. In a dreadful intrusion on the rights of the individual, a moralistic minority secured passage of the Eighteenth Amendment, which took away a basic comfort of field hands, factory workers, and others on the grounds that drinking was sinful and that poor people were not entitled to such a luxury anyway. A swell of religious fundamentalism was rising that would crest in the right-wing hate activities of the Ku Klux Klan, and by 1924 that wicked organization's anti-Negro, anti-Jew, and anti-Roman Catholic persecutions had become a national scandal.

The future nevertheless held a bright promise of prosperity and more leisure time for everybody. Women had at last gained an unequivocal right to vote, but their emancipation was broader than that. Young women in particular began to chisel away at the double standard of morality that had been typical of pre-1914 relations between the sexes; the flapper of the 1920s with her boyish bob and figure was already emerging in 1919 as the girl who could smoke men's cigarettes, drink men's whiskey, play men's games, and even work at men's jobs. There were many reasons why women gained their freedom, but a main one was that many men thought that life would be better that way. Not that freedom came easily or all at once! At least 50 years would go by before serious questions could be raised about the social wisdom of paying women less than men for the same work. In the meantime, productivity would suffer because bright women were not allowed to replace mediocre males in the workforce. The difficulties for women to move up into managerial or important administrative positions were particularly persistent.

The United States had entered World War I not so much as a result of provocation but because Americans spoke English and preserved an essentially English heritage. After all, the British blockade of Europe was actually more offensive and humiliating than the sinking of English and French vessels carrying American passengers and goods, and British propaganda about German atrocities should have been transparent even to prime specimens of H.L. Mencken's *homo boobiens.* What actually brought America into the war was the sudden agonized realization that German might would prevail in the absence of help from the United States.

America's entry on the side of the Allies clearly swung the tide of battle and assured victory to the exhausted French and British. Like the Civil War, World War I contributed little that was remarkable in the way of technological innovation, except in a few industries that produced strategic products like chemicals and machine tools. Indeed, the output response of the manufacturing industry on the whole was not spectacular. Unlike the Great War that was to follow a generation later, World War I did not induce radical changes in systems and processes that would overpoweringly affect American economic life.

Composer Donaldson's popular song implied that the upheaval of World War I was moral and social rather than technological and economic. With the peculiar insight vouchsafed only to artists, he foresaw the era of speak-easies and bathtub gin, of the Untouchables and the Capone mob, of Harding's Ohio gang and Coolidge's servants of big business. It would be impossible to keep the boys down on the farm, yet in the next two decades there would not really be a place for them in the city. For all their bright hopes, those who were young in 1919 would be the "lost generation" of Fitzgerald and Hemingway. The Great Depression would blight the most productive part of their lives, and the United States would not really enter the twentieth century until after World War II forced Americans to accept their international responsibilities. The events that ensued in the 2½ decades following World War I produced a great transformation in the U.S. economy—the great watershed of modern times.

PRELUDE TO DISASTER

In the uncommonly pleasant summer of 1929, Americans were congratulating themselves for having found a way to unending prosperity. The flow of U.S. goods and services had reached an all-time high, industrial production having risen 50 percent in a decade. Most businesses were satisfied with their profit positions, and workers were content with the moderate gains in wages and earnings that enabled them to enjoy the luxury of automobiles and household appliances. Farmers grumbled about price weaknesses in agricultural products, but it was traditional that they should; anyone could see that mechanical inventions had made life on the farm easier and more productive than ever before. Besides, anyone who really wanted to become rich had only to purchase the common stock of thriving enterprises and put the shares in safekeeping, secure in the knowledge that they would appreciate in value.

There was no reason to expect that prosperity and production would not continue to increase. The political climate was favorable to the business venturer, then held high in public esteem as the provider of material well-being. Herbert Hoover, a successful businessman and a distinguished public servant, had been elected to the Presidency, and although some people considered him a bit inclined to the liberal side, it was generally felt that he would be a temperate and judicious leader. Equally reassuring was the stability of the economies of western Europe. War damage had been repaired, the gold standard had been restored, and the problem of reparations seemed to be near solution. Hope was high for a return to the freer international movement of goods and capital that had characterized the rapid economic growth of the two decades before World War I.

But we all know how quickly the dream of lasting prosperity was broken. Even as the summer of 1929 passed, there were signs, for those who would read them, that all was not well. Toward fall, a perceptive few did read them, with the consequence that a wave of selling engulfed the stock market late in October. The psychological impact of falling securities prices alone would not have set the economy in a sharp downturn, but it unleashed other forces that had been gathering. Recession, then depression, and finally almost a complete breakdown of the entire economic system followed.

THE GREAT DEPRESSION

In the four years from 1929 to 1933, the American economy (and all other advanced economies as well) simply went to pot. The U.S. gross national product in current prices declined 46 percent, from $104.4 billion to $56 billion; in constant prices, the decline was 31 percent. Industrial production declined by more than one-half; wholesale prices dropped one-third and consumer prices one-quarter. But the most horrible statistics were those of employment and unemployment. Civilian employment dropped by almost 20 percent, and unemployment rose from 1.5 million to at least 13 million. Conservatively, one-quarter of the civilian workforce was unemployed, but extensive part-time

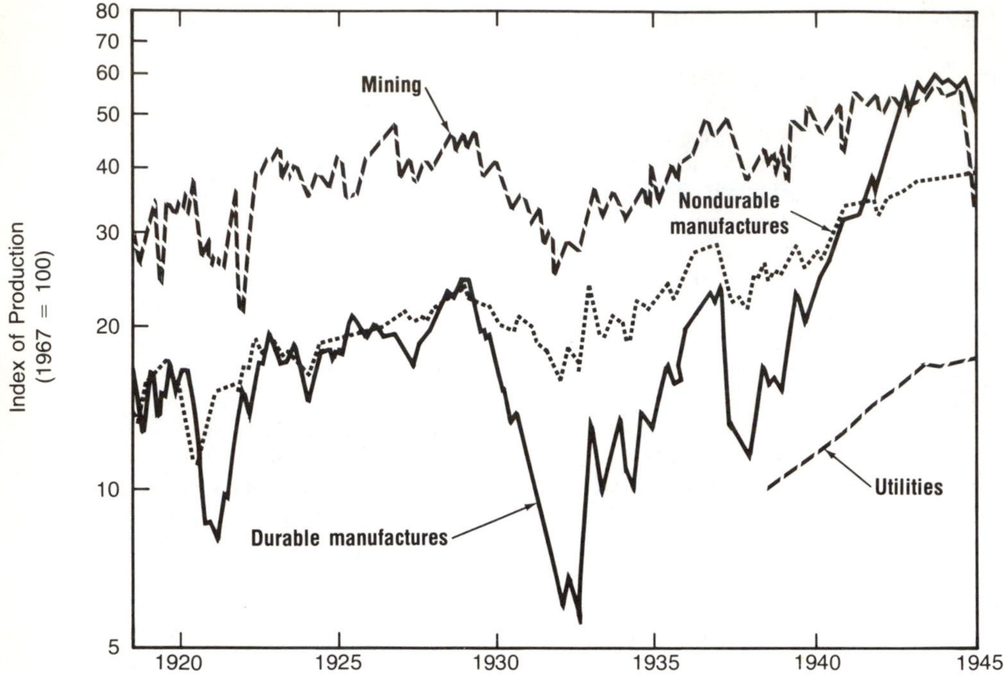

FIGURE 24–1
U.S. Industrial Production, 1920–1945.

employment and under-utilization of skills probably brought the real unemployment rate close to one-third. Fully one-half the nation's breadwinners were either out of work or in seriously reduced circumstances.

The profile of durable goods production since 1920 (shown in Figure 24-1) reveals more clearly than these words the magnitude of the decline in business in the early 1930s. From a peak of nearly 40 in 1929 (1967 = 100), the index of durable-goods output fell to 9 in 1932. At the trough of the Depression in March 1933, the durable-goods index stood at 8; output of durables had fallen 80 percent. Nondurables dropped much less—from an index of slightly over 40 to about 28.

The intensity of the Depression was distressing, but its seeming endlessness brought the frustration and despair. Forty years had passed since the long depression of the 1890s. The depression of 1920–1921 had been sharp and nasty, with a decline in durables output of 43 percent. But it had behaved as a depression should—it had come and gone quickly, with complete recovery of manufacturing production in less than two years. In the Great Depression, on the other hand, manufacturing output did not reach the 1929 level until late 1936; it stayed somewhat above the 1929 level for nearly a year but dropped again and did not climb back to the pre-Depression peak until late 1939. Durable-goods production did not regain the 1929 peak until August 1940, more than 11 years after the beginning of the Depression.

The Causes of Depression

For more than 30 years, economists have been asked to explain the greatest economic crisis to beset not only the United States but the entire world. A satisfactory explanation requires us to distinguish between the forces that brought a downturn in economic activity and those that turned a business recession into an utter disaster.

Hindsight enables us to detect two drags on the economy that prepared the way for a depression. The most important was the decline from 1925 onward in both residential and nonresidential construction. The boom in building activity that began in 1918 had doubtlessly helped the economy out of the slump of 1920–1921; the downward phase of the same building cycle, coinciding as it did with other economic weaknesses, was a major depressing influence. What was a gentle slide in construction from 1925 to 1927 became a marked decline in 1928.

The second drag on the economy came from the agricultural sector, which was still important enough in the 1920s to exert a powerful influence on the total economy. During the 1920s, the trend of world agricultural prices was downward. In the farm belts, where indebtedness incurred for the purchase of land remained high, there were widespread complaints among businesses that sales to farmers were falling. In the great agricultural midlands, few manifestations of boom psychology appeared after 1926.

A mild downturn in durables output in the spring of 1929 and a drop in nondurable production in the summer of that year could well have been expected. But nothing catastrophic was portended. The first emotional shock was the break in the stock market during the last week in October. Normally, economists do not consider fluctuations in the stock market to be a *cause* of business fluctuations, although many recognize the indirect effect of market swings on the attitudes of entrepreneurs and consumers; others consider the market an important leading indicator of the health of the economy. The 1929 break, however, must be viewed as an exception to the general rule due to the catastrophic magnitude of the decline. *The New York Times* index of 25 industrial stocks, which early in 1924 had stood at 110, by January 1929 had climbed to 338 and by September to 452. It was almost impossible to buy a common stock that did not rise rapidly in value, and investors quickly accumulated paper fortunes that many of them converted into real ones. The optimism engendered by these gains permeated the business community and led to the conclusion that permanent prosperity had been achieved. When the break came, the shock to the economy was indescribable. Paper fortunes disappeared; and so did a great many real ones, as people who had earned great profits on some issues were required to put up more collateral to save their other stockholdings. The terrible realization that a new era had not dawned—

Wall Street on Black Thursday, October 24, 1929: Investors and the curious milled around in confusion in the planked street (subway construction was going on) as the extent of the disaster inside the New York Stock Exchange (at right) became clear.

that American business was not infallible—engendered a pervasive pessimism that no amount of cheerful public statements could relieve. After falling to 275 within a week of the first drop, the market recovered only to slide another 50 points by mid-November. Whether the psychological trauma or the reduction in the supply of investment funds did the greater damage we do not know, but within a year of the stock-market crash, industrial production was down more than 25 percent.

In brief, the devastating impact of the stock-market collapse and other faltering aspects of the economy came in the early stages of the Depression. Public morale might have improved and the market and the economy might have regained some buoyancy if it had not been for the structural weaknesses of the banking system and the international economy. In particular, three waves of bank failures, each timed to have a particularly unsettling effect, shook the economy. The first came at the end of 1930 and the beginning of 1931, just when there were faint signs of an upturn. The second occurred late in 1931, after the Federal Reserve System had raised the rediscount rate to check an outward gold flow. The third, and most disastrous, began in mid-1932 and continued to the point of paralysis and breakdown in the late winter of 1932–1933. Each wave of failures resulted in the destruction of deposits in suspended banks and caused other banks to contract their loans as fast as they could. An equally important factor was that the wholesale breaking of trusted banks drove home to the public as nothing else could the terrible seriousness of the Depression. To some degree, the bank failures can be blamed on stupidity and gross neglect of duty on the part of the individual Federal Reserve Banks. As we will see, some blame should also be reserved for the shocking ignorance of the Federal Reserve Board late in 1931. A final difficulty lay in the faulty structure of the commercial banking system. Since early in the nineteenth century, Americans had insisted on a system of small, weak banking units that were largely required to provide their own liquidity; as values fell, these banks simply lacked the staying power that a few giant institutions, whose fortunes were not tied to any one community, would have had.

Most economists would agree that the forces examined so far played a major role in inducing the Depression of the 1930s. Other initiating influences have been given varying weights. One view, perhaps not as commonly held as it once was, is that the Federal Reserve System's allegedly easy-money episodes of 1924 and 1927 fed the flames of stock-market speculation and thus led to disaster. Another view is that a policy of restraint adopted in the late summer of 1929, precipitated the crisis by driving up interest rates and causing banks to turn away some borrowers. The Federal Reserve's odd reluctance to let the money supply increase more than a negligible amount in the last few years before mid-1929 unquestionably put a damper on income expansion, but far more startling was the disastrous period of inaction that followed. There is little doubt that Federal Reserve policies after the downturn significantly deepened the Depression. Let's examine why, in detail.

THE FEDERAL RESERVE: POLICIES AND DECISIONS

Beginning in the spring of 1923, open-market purchases and sales of the Federal Reserve Banks ceased to be a responsibility of the individual banks. Control over these operations was centralized, and the basis for making judgments about security purchases and sales changed. Henceforth, securities were purchased on account with the Federal Reserve System not to increase the earnings of the Federal Reserve Banks but to accommodate commerce and business. Between 1923 and 1929, open-market operations were occasionally used in conjunction with changes in the discount rate to employ the traditional "scissors" operation of central banks. When the desire was to decrease member-bank reserves, securities were sold on the open market. Banks, finding their reserves decreased, tended to borrow from the Federal Reserve Banks, where they were met with an increased discount rate and thus an increased cost of accommodation. To ease credit, on the other hand, open-market purchases were executed, and banks that did not find reserves increased sufficiently were encouraged to borrow from the Federal Reserve at a lower discount rate. As Federal Reserve holdings of securities declined, bills that had been discounted usually rose, and vice versa. Indeed, Federal Reserve authorities considered the response of commercial banks to open-market purchases or sales to be a "test" of monetary policy. If, for example, an injection of reserves was followed by an approximately equal reduction in member-bank borrowing, Reserve officials felt that the "right" amount of bank credit was outstanding.

When an incipient boom threatened inflationary pressures at the beginning of 1923, securities were sold and the discount rate was raised. A downturn in manufacturing production occurred in the summer of 1923 and continued into 1924, when discount rates were lowered and government securities were purchased. If Federal Reserve System policy was aimed at combatting the recession, it certainly came several months too late, and the monetary ease of 1924 is probably better explained by Governor Benjamin Strong's wish to keep interest rates down and thereby help England back onto the gold standard. In any event, business picked up in the fall of 1924; almost without effort, 1925 and 1926 were years of stable prices, output, and employment. But they were followed by the frustrating years of the late 1920s in which the Board was confronted with conflicting objectives. Rising real-estate prices and the rapidly growing volume of security credit concerned System authorities in early 1927. But late spring brought convincing evidence of a downturn in industrial production. According to Adolph Miller, the only economist on the Federal Reserve Board, European currencies were also exhibiting weaknesses—a turn that might interfere with agricultural sales abroad. So an easy-money policy, implemented by open-market purchases and a reduction in the discount rate, was begun in May. According to Miller, the policy "outlined by the New York Federal Reserve Bank, or more particularly by its distinguished governor," was brilliantly successful in the short run but allowed bank credit (always the touchstone of early System policy) to get out of hand. Despite restrictive efforts begun in 1928 by the Board, it was necessary to exert "moral suasion" early in 1929 in an effort to bring about a reduction in brokers' loans.[1] But direct pressure was largely ineffective because these loans were being made in great volume by lenders other than commercial banks. In the late summer of 1929, discount rates were raised to high levels—probably at just the right time to do the maximum amount of damage.

The general liquidation that began in the last week in October of 1929 was met by a lowering of the discount rate. Federal Reserve credit plummeted, but gold inflows steadied the volume of member-bank reserves after the first sharp drop. The Fed seemed content to let reserves stay at their 1929 levels throughout 1930 and the first half of 1931. Other than lowering the discount rate to 2 percent, the monetary authorities showed no signs of aggressive action or even of major concern.

[1] "Moral suasion" was the more elegant expression of an earlier day for the contemporary word "jawboning."

In September 1931, swamped by a wave of depression from the Continent, Great Britain went off the gold standard. Fearing that the United States would follow suit, foreign central banks and wealthy individuals transferred funds abroad, and U.S. gold reserves began to drop. Although American gold reserves were near an all-time peak, the Federal Reserve Bank of New York played the gold-standard game by raising the rediscount rate in an effort to increase interest rates in general and stop the external gold drain. But what was far worse, Fed officials allowed member-bank reserves to fall drastically, and the money supply continued its decline at an accelerated rate. Disaster befell the country as the Federal Reserve, figuratively wringing its hands, allowed banks to fail by the hundreds as its minions in the Reserve Banks actually attempted to collect on loans to failing banks before other creditors had their chance. By June of 1933, the money supply had dropped 30 percent from the June 1929 figure. In the 1932 Annual Report (*not* the 1931 report), the Board maintained that its use of open-market purchases in February 1932 was inhibited by the requirement that Federal Reserve notes be backed by either gold or eligible paper. Although discounts *secured* by government bonds were eligible collateral, the bonds themselves were not. The Board argued that if the Federal Reserve carried out open-market purchases, member banks would reduce their indebtedness and, consequently, the Reserve Bank's holdings of eligible paper. But this meant that more gold would be required as collateral for the notes at a time when only $416 million of gold was not committed to some legal reserve purpose. To substantiate its position, the Board remarked that the Glass–Steagall Act of February 1932 provided a remedy by permitting government securities to serve as collateral against Federal Reserve notes. The System began first moderate and then vigorous open-market purchases, and by mid-1932 System holdings of government bonds were over $1,800 million—a very large figure for the time. But it should never be forgotten that in 1931 Federal Reserve officials refused to inject reserves for far less technical reasons. In his diary entries during August 1931, Charles S. Hamlin, then a member of the Board, tells us that the Open Market Committee voted 11 to 1 against open-market purchases of $300 million, substituting $120 million instead. The governors of the several banks, who were still in control of monetary policy, simply could not comprehend the extent of the catastrophe, and Governor Meyer of the Federal Reserve Board was even worried about inflation.

Such distinguished authorities as Keynes and Harrod on the British side and Chandler, Friedman, and Schwartz on the American have given the Federal Reserve Board high marks for its management of the money supply during the 1922–1927 period. Then how can we account for the disastrous performance of the Board during the years 1928–1933? In a carefully documented, persuasive essay, Elmus R. Wicker has demonstrated that Federal Reserve policy remained consistent in both periods in that international considerations overshadowed domestic aims throughout the 1922–1932 decade and objectives of monetary policy were much narrower in the 1920s than monetary historians have acknowledged. At the risk of appearing blunt and unduly harsh in adverse criticism of our forebears, we can only conclude that the aim of the Federal Reserve authorities could not have been to achieve domestic economic stability. The modest results that appeared to be achieved in the years 1922–1927 were largely fortuitous, and the failures of 1928–1933 were essentially the consequence of a blatant ignorance of economic processes and a lack of strong and decisive leadership on the part of the Federal Reserve Board.[2]

As Americans suffered through the first two years of the Depression, they analyzed the causes of their troubles in everyday language, and suggested cures. Some of these analyses were astonishingly accurate, and many of the remedies proposed, had they been tried, might well have prevented the precipitate declines in income and employment that characterized the late stages of the Depression. But remedies potent enough to be very effective required a radically different approach to public finance and a revolutionary concept of the role of the federal government in times of economic crisis. The administration of Herbert Hoover, who was elected to office on promises of a safe, conservative program, was simply incapable of the radical, imaginative leadership that alone could have saved the day.

The common judgment that the Hoover Administration did nothing to combat the Depression is as erroneous as the notion that it was the cause of the Depression. Within the limits of economic orthodoxy, if not somewhat beyond, steps were taken to restore economic equilibrium. As we have said, monetary policy during the period of the Great Depression was idiotic, but the ignorance of the central bank was the ignorance of all but a few economists of the time. Although the Reconstruction Finance Corporation came chiefly to the assistance of large businesses, the very formation of such an agency marked a sharp break with tradition. Support of agricultural prices by the Federal Farm Board was equally revolutionary. The major deficiencies of the Hoover Administration were the persistent refusal to establish a federal program of work relief and the failure to carry out a fiscal policy of conscious and aggressive deficits financed by borrowing from the banking system.[3] Too much reliance was placed on maintaining confidence through the public testimonials of business and government leaders and not enough was placed on measures to raise incomes and correct the deflation.

For a while in the late summer of 1932, it looked as if the tide might turn. But banks continued to contract loans, and the deflation ground on. The Republican defeat in the fall may have frightened some conservatives, but more unsettling were the five leaderless months before the inauguration of Franklin D. Roosevelt on March 4, 1933. Bank runs spread to the largest institutions, and the leading banks in Detroit closed on February 14. In little more than two weeks, nearly half the states followed Michigan in declaring "bank holidays" or severely restricting banking operations. Industrial production was now at about

[2] Readers of this book who may be offended by such a strong historical judgment are urged to read Elmus R. Wicker, "Federal Reserve Monetary Policy, 1922–33: A Reinterpretation," *Journal of Political Economy,* **LXXIII** (August 1965), pp. 325–43. It can be said on behalf of Federal Reserve authorities that the ignorance of the Board and its staff was just a part of the ignorance of economists in general at this time.

[3] From the mid-1930s on, the Treasury ran a small deficit because tax revenues fell with declining incomes. But the deficit occurred despite efforts to prevent it. In fairness, it should be noted that Franklin D. Roosevelt promised during the campaign of 1932 to cut federal expenditures by 25 percent, thereby balancing the budget.

Grim hopelessness descended on the quarter of the population that was out of work and the two-thirds that occasionally went hungry as the Great Depression deepened. "Hoovervilles" like this one in New York's Central Park tarnished the countryside.

40 percent of full potential, one-quarter of the nation's breadwinners had no work, and unknown numbers of people were literally starving to death.

The New Deal

Under such circumstances, a change in administrations was bound to occur, and the vitality and self-confidence of Franklin D. Roosevelt were reassuring. The economy needed more, however, than a psychological uplift. The most pressing need was for the relief of destitute families. Scarcely less important was the necessity of reversing the declining price trend (of "reflating," in the current phraseology) and of raising incomes.

In later chapters, we will examine most of the legislative measures by which the President and Congress tried to achieve recovery. A federal program

Roosevelt's charm and buoyancy did much in itself to soften the Depression's psychological impact. His broad grin made his theme song, "Happy Days are Here Again," believable to a shaken nation.

of unemployment relief was put into effect immediately through the Federal Emergency Relief Administration (FERA) and the Civil Works Administration

(CWA), followed by the Public Works Administration (PWA), and mortgage relief prevented further loss of homes and farms by foreclosure. Runs on banks were stopped by first declaring a banking holiday and then reopening those banks that were certified to be sound.[4] Gold hoarding was ended by the simple device of requiring everyone to turn monetary gold over to the Treasury in exchange for some other form of currency. Late in 1933, the devaluation of the dollar was begun; by raising the Treasury's buying price of gold—that is, by lowering the gold content of the dollar—officials expected to make the dollars "cheaper" and to raise prices.[5]

These specific measures, plus a Federal Reserve policy of easy money, were intended to push the price level back up. But beyond these measures, the fundamental readjustment of farm income and the industrial wage–price structure was attempted in the two major agencies of the early New Deal—the Agricultural Adjustment Administration (AAA) and the National Recovery Administration (NRA). The policies of these agencies, rather than being geared to recovery, were primarily redistributive in character. The AAA plan for raising farm prices and incomes through acreage restrictions will be considered at length in Chapter 25. Here we will focus on the National Industrial Recovery Act, particularly those sections that established the Public Works Administration (PWA) and asserted the right of labor to bargain collectively. The chief purposes of the Act were to raise prices and wages, spread out work by reducing hours, and prevent price cutting by competitors trying to maintain volume. A National Recovery Administration under the direction of General Hugh Johnson supervised the preparation of a "code of fair practice" for each industry. Deputy administrators, presumably assisted by representatives of employers, labor, and consumers, prepared the codes, which were really agreements among sellers to set minimum prices, limit output, and establish minimum wages and maximum hours of work. Pending the approval of basic codes, the President issued a "blanket code" in July 1933. Sellers signing the blanket code agreed to raise wages, shorten the maximum workweek, and abstain from price cutting. In return, they could display a "blue eagle" and avoid being boycotted for not doing their part. By 1935, 557 basic codes had been approved. In practice, labor representatives participated in the construction of less than 10 percent of the codes, and consumer representation was negligible. Employer representatives found it convenient to work through their national trade associations and manufacturer's institutes, with the consequence that prices were set with a view toward profit maximization in the manner of a

[4] Milton Friedman and Anna J. Schwartz, *A Monetary History of the United States, 1867–1960* (Princeton: Princeton University Press, 1971), p. 330, point out that this was accomplished only at a tremendous cost:

> ... far from preventing further bank failures, it [the banking holiday] brought additional bank failures in its train. More than 5,000 banks still in operation when the holiday was declared did not reopen their doors when it ended, and of these over 2,000 never did thereafter. The 'cure' came close to being worse than the disease.

[5] Actually, only the most naïve monetary theorists thought that devaluation had any *direct* effect on domestic prices. But by making the dollar cheaper in terms of *foreign* currencies, it was hoped that American exports, particularly farm products, would be stimulated.

European cartel. The possibility of such an outcome was recognized in the National Industrial Recovery Act (NIRA), which suspended antitrust laws.

The effectiveness of the NIRA and other New Deal measures, especially in the early phase of development, will forever be debated. For the most part, however, they redistributed rather than expanded incomes. True, the gross national product rose from a low of $56 billion in 1933 to $72.5 billion in 1935, and the prices of all wholesale commodities increased by one-third in the same period, regaining the level of late 1930. But these improvements largely resulted from changes in the money supply and expansionary monetary policies. Manufacturing output jumped after the institution of NRA, as merchants added to their inventories in anticipation of price increases. But industrial production lapsed again, and by mid-summer of 1935 the index was no higher than it had been after the first NRA spurt. Unemployment, although reduced, was still incredibly high, and most manufacturing firms were operating at far less than capacity.

Early in 1935, there was a growing awareness that the lift the economy experienced had come chiefly from income injections via deficit spending and money creation. It was with little regret, then, that New Dealers saw the passing of NRA, which was declared unconstitutional by the Supreme Court on the grounds that Congress had illegally delegated legislative powers to the President. A marked rise in the index of physical production within a few months after the demise of NRA confirmed the view that an excess of government spending over government receipts—the difference made up by borrowing and expansion of the money supply—increased people's incomes. At this stage, however, the use of a budget deficit as an antidepression weapon had not become official administrative policy. There was much talk of "pump-priming" through expenditures for relief and public works, but the administration was reluctant to abandon Democratic campaign pledges of a balanced budget and an end to Republican "extravagance." Nevertheless, there was a deficit in the 1936 administrative budget of nearly $4.5 billion, by far the largest on record, and the cash deficit for the fiscal year was about $3.5 billion.[6]

The upswing that began in late 1935 continued through 1936. By early 1937, total manufacturing output exceeded that of 1929, and prices and wages were rising briskly. Although unemployment remained severe (between 7 million and 8 million at the peak of 1937 activity), government officials and

[6] The administrative or conventional budget of the United States records only receipts and expenditures of funds owned wholly by the federal government for the budget period (fiscal year) extending from July 1 to June 30. But to weigh the impact of Treasury surpluses and deficits on the economy, it is necessary to know how much will be taken away from people in taxes and how much will be turned back as cash expenditures. Economic analysts therefore find it convenient to prepare a "cash-consolidated" budget, which includes receipts and expenditures of trust funds (such as old-age and survivors insurance, unemployment insurance, and railroad retirement) but does *not* include expenditures not paid to the public (such as interest on the government securities in which the trust funds are invested). A third way of recording federal transactions is known as the *national income accounts budget,* which measures the impact of taxing and spending on U.S. income and output. Like the cash-consolidated budget, it includes trust-fund transactions; it excludes loans and repayments of loans, and records business taxes when they are accrued rather than when they are paid.

Agricultural poverty sent thousands fleeing from the Midwest to California, with belongings piled in the family jalopy. A nation that "drove to the poor house in an automobile," as Will Rogers said, had to change some of its babies' diapers on the miserable highways of the time.

economists were persuaded that prosperity had returned and that inflation loomed. Expenditures for relief and public works were cut; the cash deficit for the calendar year 1937 dropped almost to zero. Federal Reserve authorities, by raising the reserve requirements of member banks to maximums authorized by the Banking Act of 1935, drastically reduced the excess reserves of commercial banks, forcing a reduction in bank loans and investments of 1 billion dollars in 1937. The money supply in the calendar year 1937 dropped nearly $1.8 billion, or 3.4 percent.[7] It soon appeared that such policy decisions were ill-

[7] Milton Friedman and Anna J. Schwartz, *A Monetary History of the United States, 1867–1960* (Princeton: Princeton University Press, 1971), p. 715.

advised. Industrial production reached a post-1929 high in May 1937 and then turned downward. Commodity prices followed, and the weary process of deflation began again. Retail sales dropped off, unemployment increased, and payrolls declined substantially. Adding to the general gloom, the stock market started a long slide in August that brought stock prices in March 1938 to less than half the peak of the previous year.

In 1937, as now, many attributed the renewed onslaught of depression to the reform measures introduced and passed in 1935 and 1936. Social-Security legislation and the new freedom granted labor in 1935 received some hard words. But most of the criticism was directed toward the hostile political climate in which, it was asserted, vigorous business expansion was impossible. In his state of the union message of 1936, President Roosevelt had castigated "the royalists of the economic order" who, he said, opposed government intervention in economic affairs and received a disproportionate amount of the national income. Tax legislation of 1935 and 1936, directed toward preventing tax avoidance and making the tax structure more sharply progressive, was especially resented by people of means. In 1935, estate and gift taxes were increased as were individual surtaxes, and taxes on the incomes of large corporations were raised along with the excess profits tax. Most hated of all taxes was the undistributed profits tax of 1936—a surtax imposed on corporations to make them distribute profits instead of holding them so that individual stockholders could avoid personal taxation.

Distrust of New Deal reforms in general and of tax policies in particular may have weakened individual incentives to carry out real investment and thus contributed to the downturn of 1937–1938.[8] But the key move, which senselessly generated the reversal, was again made by the Federal Reserve Board. As already noted, in 1937, the Board—concerned over possible inflationary threats—raised reserve requirements, which sharply reduced excess reserves and contributed to the nasty recession of 1937–1938. Fortunately, this was later countered somewhat by the expansive policies of government beginning in April 1938, which helped to overcome the fears and reservations of business decision makers. Following an explicit recommendation of the President to increase the national income through fiscal policy, Congress provided increased appropriations for the Works Progress Administration (WPA). The Federal Reserve also helped by reverting to an easy-money policy, and the money supply soared in the latter half of 1938. No more tax reforms were introduced, and the only reform measure of any consequence passed in 1938 was the Fair Labor Standards Act. Business picked up in the summer of 1938, and recovery was well under way toward the close of the year.

Not until the end of 1939, however, was total industrial production back to 1937 peak levels, and the output of durables did not reach the 1937 level until well into 1940. After Hitler's success at Munich in September 1938, the threat of approaching war stimulated military buying, and the purchases of foreign governments, particularly Great Britain, grew steadily after the outbreak of war in

[8]As a result of the decrease in excess reserves brought on by the increase in reserve requirements, loans and investments of member banks declined from $33 billion on December 31, 1936, to $32 billion on December 31, 1937.

1939. Meanwhile the federal government had no scruples about providing adequate work relief. Net-income injection on government account—that is, the cash deficit—was nearly $3 billion in fiscal 1939 and again in 1940; in fiscal 1941, the cash deficit was almost $5 billion. During 1940, for the first time in more than a decade, the economy showed signs of achieving full recovery. Employment and payrolls rose with the rapid increase in industrial production. Prices remained stable through 1940, but at the close of the year wage rates were beginning to firm—a sign that full employment might once again be realized.

The Cure for Depression

The return of something like genuine prosperity in 1940 led a majority of the electorate to give the New Deal credit for the escape from mass unemployment and faltering production. There is no question that a program of positive action—any action—was sufficient to bring about an upturn in 1933 and 1934. From 1935 on, however, it was evident that output and incomes had risen due to net-income injections from government spending and increases in the money supply. Had these stimulations been made more vigorously from mid-1936 to mid-1938, despite fears of a rising national debt shared by most conservatives, the American economy would doubtlessly have rebounded much sooner.

Anyone who is unconvinced on this point only has to look at the budget, income, and production figures for the World War II period. In fiscal 1942 (from July 1941 through June 1942), cash outgo of the Treasury exceeded cash income by more than $19 billion. In the next fiscal year, the cash deficit was $54 billion; in succeeding years, it was $46 billion and $45 billion. Income-generating government expenditures of this magnitude, financed almost exclusively by selling government securities to commercial banks, accomplished what seven years of New Deal spending had not done. The gross national product—that is, the total value of output sold in the marketplace—more than doubled in five years from $100 billion in 1940 to $211 billion in 1944. In the same five years, industrial production almost doubled, the index rising from 67 in 1940 to 127 in 1944, and durables output increased more than 2½ times. To some extent, these gains were illusory, because prices rose moderately, many consumer durables disappeared from the market, and the quality of available durables and many nondurables declined. But the war itself also contributed to the disappearance of unemployment, which even during 1941 had *averaged* 5.5 million, or 10 percent of the civilian workforce. At the close of 1941, unemployment had been reduced to 3.5 million, and a year later it had dropped to 1.5 million. For two years during the war, unemployment from all causes never exceeded 1 million.

The rapid increase in federal expenditures, which during the war generated more than one-third of the gross national product, also led inevitably to great inflationary pressures. As output began to rise during 1940, so many people and manufacturing facilities were unemployed that goods were forthcoming without a rise in prices. Toward the end of the year, certain types of labor were

Compassionate concern for others was a special trait of first lady Eleanor Roosevelt, shown here at a Japanese–American relocation center in Arizona.

in short supply, and as the economy moved toward full employment in 1941, wages and other prices began to move upward. Informal price control during 1941 did not prove effective enough to check the inflation, and on January 30, 1942, the previously established Office of Price Administration (OPA) was given legal authority to put a rigid clamp on most prices. In April, OPA issued the first maximum price regulations, which froze prices at the level prevailing during March 1942. But ceilings could not be placed on food until agricultural prices reached 110 percent of parity, and wages were not yet under effective control. Consequently, prices continued their upward movement for several months after the first general regulation was imposed. In October, wages were placed under the control of the National War Labor Board, and by the spring of 1943 agricultural prices were so close to their maxima that a final "hold-the-line" regulation almost stopped further price increases for two years.

Contributing to the decline in unemployment and the rise in prices were policies of the Federal Reserve—policies that were not intentionally implemented for those purposes. The primary objective of Federal Reserve policy during World War II was to assure that Treasury funds were adequate to meet all government expenditures. On the day after Pearl Harbor, the Board of Governors announced that the Treasury would be supplied with sufficient money for war financing. In March 1942, the Federal Open Market Committee (FOMC) asserted its intention of preventing a rise in interest rates on government securities during the war and pledged the cooperation of the System. The chief instrument used to assure the success of Treasury financing and to keep interest rates from rising was open-market policy. The Federal Reserve stood willing to buy, without limitation, all government obligations offered at the established prices and yields. On long-term securities, this meant a maximum yield of 2.5 percent and yields ranged downward to a low of three-eighths of 1 percent on 90-day Treasury bills.

This wartime policy had two important consequences. The first was the virtual abandonment of controls over the System's holdings of government securities, the volume of bank reserves, and the money supply. To prevent yields from rising, the Federal Reserve had to buy all government securities that were offered to it at fixed prices. Thus, bank and nonbank investors alike could obtain cash for their government securities at will, and there was no effective upper limit to the monetization of the public debt. Second, large government deficits and restrictions on the availability of civilian goods sharply increased liquidity in the economy, and since anyone could shift out of government securities into cash, funds were readily available to private borrowers. As a result, the entire structure of interest rates remained low, and the upward pressure on prices remained high.

In summary, the extension of government controls in the post-World War I period was revolutionary in character. Government involvement in the economy was always apparent, to be sure, but the growth of government control during the Roosevelt years altered the American economy dramatically. First came the New Deal legislation; controls on prices and resource allocation followed during World War II. In combination, the many changes represented a true economic watershed in America's history. Certainly, the economic significance of the period abounds with evidence. In fairness, however, when assessing their impact, it should be recalled that the Roosevelt reforms were devised and introduced in an atmosphere of severe crisis. But they outlived the period of crisis, and as we will observe in the following chapters, the Roosevelt reforms have highly important implications, even today.[9]

[9] Also see Gary M. Walton (ed.), *Regulatory Change in an Atmosphere of Crisis: The Current-Day Implications of the Roosevelt Years* (New York: Academic Press, Inc., 1979).

25

Agriculture Turns to Government

THE ECONOMIC POSITION OF THE AMERICAN FARMER

For a quarter of a century before 1920, American agriculture was moving to a stronger position in the economy. Indeed, the 1896–1915 period—sometimes nostalgically referred to as "Agriculture's Golden Era"—was one of rapid improvement in the economic position of the American farmer. Farm production slackened its rate of increase, approximating one-half of 1 percent per annum over these years. Farm prices and gross farm income rose steadily. The agricultural population remained constant at 32 million, as the natural rate of increase of farm people (650,000 per year toward the close of the period) was offset by the movement of farmers to city occupations. Consequently, from 1911 to 1915, income per person employed in agriculture was approximately two-thirds that of those employed in industry—a remarkably favorable ratio that was not achieved again until World War II.[1] Moreover, farmers' assets—land, buildings, and livestock—continually appreciated in value.[2] Many people on the land were still abysmally poor, but the economic position of major producers was much improved. Then World War I abnormally stimulated farm production, boosted prices, and amplified the rise in incomes that had been underway for the previous 20 years.

[1] Due to the relatively favorable ratio of income per worker in agriculture to income per worker in industry, the quinquennium 1911–1915 has ever since been urged as the basis of computing "parity" income for agriculture.

[2] These figures are taken from Theodore W. Schultz, *Agriculture in an Unstable Economy* (New York: McGraw-Hill Book Co., 1945), pp. 114–16.

During 1919 and the early months of 1920, hopes for the future of farming were bright. But in mid-1920, farm prices bagan a precipitous drop. From an index of 234 in June 1920 (1909–1914 = 100), prices received by farmers fell to an index of 112 a year later. By the end of 1921, despite a slight recovery, wheat was selling for $0.93 a bushel that 18 months previously had sold for $2.58, and corn was down to $0.41 from $1.86. Many commodities did not suffer quite so severe a decline, but prices seriously decreased in all lines of production. A gradual recovery followed and the farm price index stood at 159 in August 1925. After a small decline during 1926 and 1927, prices remained stable until the end of 1929.

The deflation of 1920 and 1921 was severe in the industrial sector of the economy but was not as great as in the agriculture sector. Prices *paid* by farmers fell until the end of 1921 and then remained stable until the close of the decade. The terms of exchange (the ratio of the prices received by farmers to the prices they paid) ran against agriculture during the break in prices and then recovered, so that by 1925 they were not much below the figure of 1920. This index fell off a little during the next few years, but in 1929 it was still not far from the level of prosperous prewar years. On the whole, then, it does not seem that agriculture should have suffered much in the middle and late 1920s. Yet, as we will see later in this chapter, there was great agitation for remedial farm legislation during these years. Why?

The answer seems to lie in the fact that a large part of the farmers, especially in the Midwest, had incurred fixed indebtedness at what turned out to be the wrong time. During the decade 1910–1920, land values had risen sharply; at the height of the boom, the best lands in Iowa and Illinois sold for as much as $500 an acre—a fantastically high figure for the time. In those ten years, many high-grade farms doubled in value. To buy their high-priced properties farmers often borrowed heavily, and farm-mortgage debt increased rapidly. Long-term debt rose from $3.2 billion in 1910 to $8.4 billion in 1920 and, as a result of the distress that accompanied the deflation of the early 1920s, reached a high of nearly $11 billion in 1923. Although a majority of American farmers may not have been burdened with fixed charges during these years, such charges undoubtedly created difficulties for a large and extremely vocal minority.[3]

The troubles of the decade after World War I were mild compared with the debacle of the next decade. With the onset of the Great Depression, farm people began to suffer economic distress that only the old-timers would have believed was possible. First, let's consider what happened to farm prices. The break came in the first months of 1930 and continued until a low point was reached in February 1933. From a farm-price index of 147 in January 1930, there was a drop to 57 in February 1933 (1909–1914 = 100). Department of

[3] By fixed charges, we mean the payments of principal and interest that had to be met currently and at regular intervals. Farms, like business enterprises in general, have fixed costs that cannot be avoided, but these costs are certainly more burdensome when, because of thin equities, they must be met out of current income. It should be added that the balance sheets of all farms tended to change unfavorably during the 1920s, no matter what their debt positions may have been, because assets generally declined in value during the period. Thus, the equities of most farmers shrank.

Agriculture statistics show that in three years the average price of corn at central markets fell from \$0.77 to \$0.19 a bushel, and the average price of wheat dropped from \$1.08 to \$0.33 a bushel. Ten-cent corn and 25-cent wheat were common at local elevators, and 5-cent cotton was the burden of the southerner.

In terms of farm income and the disparity between agricultural and nonagricultural prices, the picture was just as bad. As we can see from Figure 25-1, gross farm income, which had reached a postwar high of almost \$14 billion in 1929, slipped to \$11 billion in 1930 and fell drastically to about \$6.5

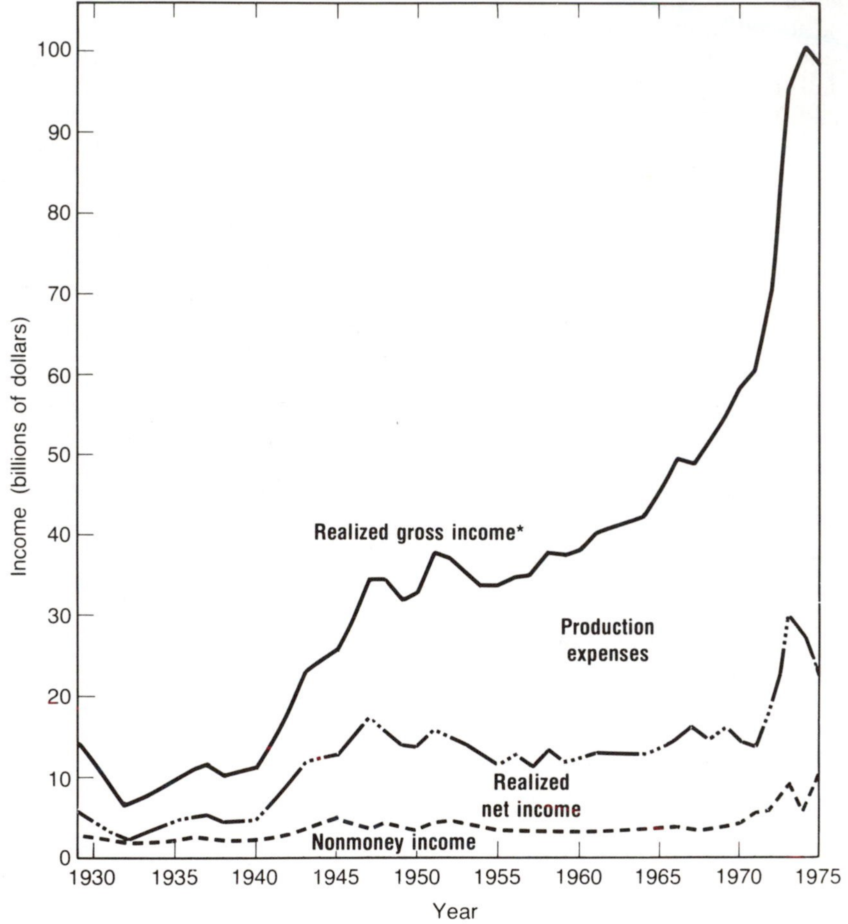

FIGURE 25–1

Farm Income: The growing gap between realized gross income in farming and the amount of cash left after heavy production expenses have been met reveals at a glance the source of much of the malaise in the American countryside, the sense of failing prospects on the family-size farm.

Source: United States Department of Agriculture.

billion in 1932. Production expenses also declined during this period, but not nearly as greatly as the gross-income figure. So in 1932, the *net* realized income from agriculture was just over $1.8 billion—*less than one-third of the 1929 figure and one-half of the figure for the bad year of 1921.* The agricultural terms of exchange had fallen by an almost unbelievable amount, having dropped by 1932 to a low of 54 percent of the level of 1920. Farmers with fixed indebtedness were unable to meet their obligations, and the threat of foreclosure marred the lives of rural people everywhere.[4]

Farm prices began to rise in April 1933, climbing to 131 early in 1937 (see Figure 25-2). The recession of 1937–1938 affected the agricultural sector, and the index of farm prices reverted back to 100, where it stood in both the first and last months of 1940. Meanwhile, prices *paid by* farmers recovered somewhat from a 1933 low and then remained almost stable throughout 1940; because farm prices recovered more than industrial prices, the terms of exchange were definitely improved. From the low of 1932, gross farm income moved steadily upward to $11 billion in 1937, declined slightly for two years, and then rebounded to the $11 billion mark in 1940—about where it had been a decade earlier.

American preparation for war, which began in 1940, did not affect agricultural markets until the next year. In 1941, the demand for farm products for both export and domestic consumption increased noticeably, and the United States' entrance into the war late in the year contributed a further impulse to this trend. During World War II, industrial production rose at a rate of 30 percent per year, and agricultural production, aided by exceptionally good weather, climbed at the remarkable rate of 5 percent per year.[5] Price controls during the war were purposely made less effective for agricultural than for nonagricultural commodities; consequently, the prices of farm products rose more rapidly during the war than the prices of the things that the farmer had to buy. Contrary to the predictions of many experts, the demand for food, feed, and fiber continued to be high after the war. The removal of price controls in the summer of 1946 permitted all prices to shoot up, but the rise in agricultural prices was steeper than the price rise in any other area. From a peak in January 1948, however, farm prices began to decline steadily, and by mid-1950 they were down about one-sixth from their high point. But even before the outbreak of war in Korea, the prices received by farmers began to rise again, soaring to an all-time high early in 1951. From February 1951, the trend of farm prices was generally downward, with a break in the latter part of 1952 that was great enough to cause consternation among farmers. In 1954, farm production was more than 40 percent greater than the 1935–1939 average, and the prices the farmers received were beginning to drift gently away from parity.

Favorable prices and a high level of farm output during the 1940s and early 1950s meant that the farmer's lot was much improved from what it had been in the dreary decade of the 1930s. From a peak of $16.8 billion in 1948, net agricultural income dropped to just over $13 billion in 1950. Half of this loss was regained in 1951, and a steady decline from 1952 to 1954 returned the

[4] In early 1933, 52 percent of all farm debts (45 percent of all farm debtors) were in default.

[5] These figures may be compared with the average World War I industrial rate of increase of 5.7 percent per annum and an agricultural rate of increase of 1.7 percent per annum.

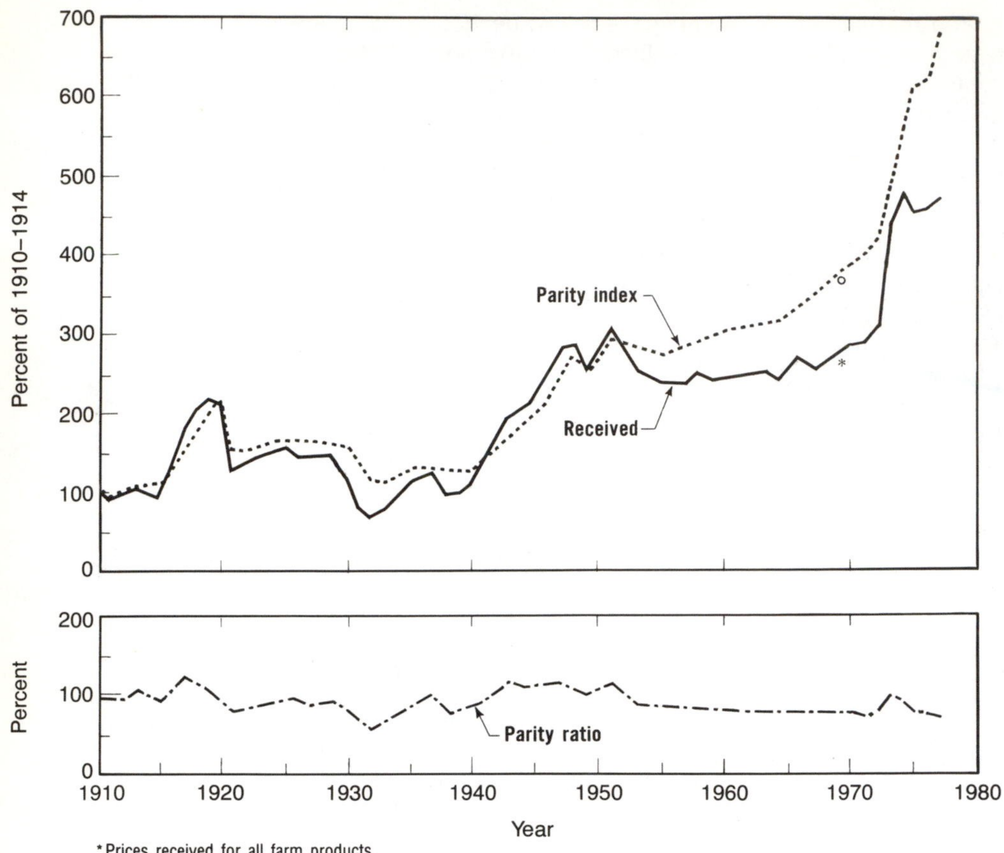

FIGURE 25–2

Outgo and Income: Since the early 1950s, prices received by farmers have not kept up with prices paid by farmers (upper chart) so that prices received have declined as a percentage of parity (lower chart). Parity is defined as the ratio of prices received by farmers to prices paid by them in the favorable years 1910–1914.

Source: United States Department of Agriculture.

net income to wartime levels. In 1950, the dollar income of farmers was three times as great as it had been in 1940, and because the general price level did not quite double during the period, real net income increased by 50 percent. But the dramatic improvement in the position of American agriculture did not signal an end to concern over the level of agricultural income. After sagging in the mid-1950s, gross farm income rose to more than $40 billion in 1962—an all-time record. Yet net income in that year stood at only $14.6 billion, 1 billion dollars below that of 1953 and $4 billion under the record high of 1947. As the chart of farm income components in Figure 25-1 shows, realized gross income maintained an almost uninterrupted rise until 1970. But production expenses rose even more rapidly, and only massive government payments kept realized net income from falling in the latter part of the 1960s.

FARM LEGISLATION

Pre-1920 attempts to help the farmer by federal legislation were not calculated to have a direct effect on prices and production. Over the past half-century, however, agricultural groups have succeeded in obtaining legislation that directly affects the prices received by the farmer and that consequently causes production to be different from what it would be in a "free" market. The acceptance by the American people of the principle that the government ought to bolster the economic fortunes of particular occupational groups or classes is of momentous importance. Farmers have not been the only beneficiaries of this emerging philosophy; but we cannot find a better example of the way in which legislation, passed at first in an effort to relieve emergency distress, has become accepted as a more or less permanent part of the economic mechanism. It is this monumental change in attitudes—away from reliance on markets and toward dependence on government—that marks the most significant characteristic of the period from the Great Depression to the present.

The farm program, in particular, has reached its present complexity in easy stages that are best analyzed by considering three subperiods. During the years from approximately 1921 to 1933, ideas were being formulated. From 1933 to 1941, farm legislation was designed to achieve recovery from economic depression. Then with the onset of World War II, new objectives developed. During the war, legislation was slanted toward the stimulation of certain kinds of farm output. In the postwar period, there has been a persistent attempt through subsidies to maintain agricultural income at an artificially high level in the vain hope that the inefficient "family-size" farm might be preserved as an American institution.

The First Efforts, 1921–1933

As early as 1919, Secretary of Agriculture, David Franklin Houston, who was not as optimistic as most agricultural leaders, called for a conference to discuss possible agricultural problems, but not until disaster struck in the form of sharply falling prices and incomes was this proposal seriously considered. Violent protests from farmers in the late months of 1920 led Congress to create a Joint Commission of Agricultural Inquiry in 1921. The Commission reported the obvious—that farm troubles were the result of general business depression and a decline in exports—and recommended measures to help cooperative marketing associations, improve credit facilities, and extend research activities by the Department of Agriculture. More important was the National Agricultural Conference, called early in 1922 by Secretary of Agriculture Henry C. Wallace. Despite the administration's attitude, expressed by President Harding, that "the farmer must be ready to help himself," many radical proposals were heard at this conference. In its report, the idea of parity for agriculture was first made explicit, and the slogan "Equality for Agriculture" was offered. There was recognition of the fact that in times of a decreasing demand for goods, manufacturers reduced production and lowered prices slowly, if at all, whereas farmers maintained or even increased production and took the consequences in the form of sharply falling prices. It was argued that agriculture as a whole was *entitled* to its fair share of the national income and that justice would be achieved if the ratio of the prices farmers received to the prices they paid were kept equal to the ratio that had prevailed from 1910 to 1914.

From 1923 to 1933, various ideas were proposed aimed at securing parity prices or "fair-exchange values" for agricultural products. Senator George Norris proposed a plan that proved unpopular with the Republican administration. Norris wanted to establish a government corporation that would actually handle the business of processing farm products, thereby eliminating the profits of middlemen. Then there was the plan of the National Grange to increase exports by the payment of export bounties. The bounties were to be paid, not in cash, but in negotiable certificates called *debentures,* which could be used to pay import duties and therefore would have a cash value. Toward the end of the period, a group of college professors developed a "domestic-allotment" plan, which introduced the concept of limiting the amount of products that farmers could produce and sell in the domestic market.

Most readily acceptable to professional farm supporters and politicians were the McNary–Haugen bills, considered by Congress between 1924 and 1928. They were well received because they made use of more or less traditional devices, including a high tariff on agricultural products. The fair-exchange value of each farm product was to be determined; the fair value was to be a price that would have pre-World War I purchasing power. This "fair" price was to be maintained in the domestic market in two ways. First, a tariff was to protect the home market from imports. Second, a private corporation chartered by the federal government was to buy a sufficient amount of each commodity to force its price up to the computed fair-value level. The corporation could in turn sell the acquired commodities. Obviously, if the purchases had been necessary to raise prices, the commodities could not be sold in the domestic market. Thus, it was proposed that they be sold abroad at the world price, which would presumably be lower than the supported American price. Administrative expenses and operating losses would be shared among the producing farmers. For every bale of cotton or bushel of wheat sold, a tax called an "equalization fee" would be charged to the grower. This tax would be used to defray all expenses of operating the price-support plan. The farmer would gain insofar as the additional amount of income resulting from higher prices exceeded the tax expense.

The McNary–Haugen bills were twice passed by Congress and twice vetoed by President Calvin Coolidge. But the agitation of the 1920s did secure special privileges for agriculture. For one, the Capper–Volstead law of 1922 exempted farmers' cooperatives from the threat of prosecution for violation of the antitrust laws. Also, the Federal Intermediate Credit Act of 1923 provided for 12 intermediate credit banks that would rediscount agricultural paper maturing within three years for commercial banks and other lending agencies.[6] To achieve the broader aims of price and income maintenance, there were two major efforts. A naïve belief in the tariff as a device to raise the prices of farm products, which had been traditionally exported *not* imported, led to "protection" for agriculture, culminating in the high duties of the Smoot–Hawley Act of 1929. More significant was the passage of the Agricultural Marketing Act of 1929, which was the outcome of Republican campaign promises of the previous year. The first law committing the federal government to a policy of stabilizing farm prices, the 1929 Act worked as much as possible through non-government institutions. The Act established a Federal Farm Board with the primary function of encouraging the formation of cooperative marketing associations. The board was also authorized to establish "stabilization corporations" to be owned by the cooperatives, which would use a $500 million fund to carry on price-support operations.

Had the economic conditions of the 1920s persisted, the law might have had fruitful results. With the onset of serious depression in 1930, the Federal Farm Board strove valiantly to support farm prices through its stabilization corporations, but between June 1929 and June 1932 the corporations bought surplus farm products only to suffer steadily increasing losses as prices continued to decline. The board itself took over the operation and accepted the losses, expending in three years some $676 million in stabilization operations and loans to cooperatives. While all this was going on, the individual farmer, faced with catastrophically falling prices, maintained or increased output. Obviously, a new approach was called for.

The Crystallization of a Farm Policy, 1933–1941

By the date of Franklin D. Roosevelt's inauguration, theories about farm policy had undergone fundamental changes. Proponents of dumping American farm products abroad were successful in securing the dollar devaluation of 1933–1934, which made dollars cheaper in terms of foreign currencies, thereby stimulating the demand for U.S. commodities traded in world markets. But this solution to the farmer's dilemma was not satisfactory because the worldwide depression was accompanied by extremely low world prices. American policymakers wished to devise a plan to raise farm prices substantially in the home market. It had become clear that supports through purchases and loans, like those attempted by the Federal Farm Board, would require enormous outlays and would probably be ineffectual unless the supply of products were restricted. As a consequence, a scheme evolved that took the central idea of the previously suggested domestic-allotment plan.

In May 1933, the Agricultural Adjustment Act was passed. One of the first major pieces of New Deal legislation, it provided for an Agricultural Adjustment Administration, popularly referred to as the AAA, which was given the respon-

[6] Nonemergency farm credit needs were pretty well taken care of with the passage of this act, for the Federal Farm Loan Act of 1916 had established twelve Federal Land Banks to provide long-term loans to farmers through cooperative borrowing groups.

sibility of raising farm prices by restricting the supply of farm commodities. The most important weapon of the AAA was the "acreage allotment." Taking into consideration prospective demand and carry-over from the previous season, the AAA would determine a total acreage of certain major crops to be planted in the next growing season. The total acreage would then be subdivided into state totals, which were in turn to be allotted to individual farms on the basis of each farm's recent crop history. For example, the base acreage for each wheat farm was to be the average acreage in wheat from 1928 to 1932. To secure the cooperation of the individual farmer, a direct "benefit payment," later called an "adjustment payment," was made. In the beginning, wheat farmers who restricted acreage received about $0.30 a bushel on 54 percent of their average production in the base period. The payment was made by check from the federal Treasury, but in these early New Deal days it still seemed a little too much to expect the general taxpayer to foot the bill—at least directly. The benefit payments were financed, therefore, by processing taxes paid by the first processor of any product (millers, for example, had to pay a tax for each bushel of wheat that was ground into flour), although it was not expected that the processor would bear the burden of the tax. It was assumed that the processing tax would be shifted forward and be paid by the consumer.

The original AAA scheme experienced a setback in 1936 when the Supreme Court, in the Hoosac Mills case, declared that the Agricultural Adjustment Act was unconstitutional because it attempted to regulate agricultural production—a power reserved to the several states. The processing tax was specifically declared invalid. The adverse decision did not force a discontinuance of acreage allotments, but only changed the *basis* on which these allotments were made to one that presumably encouraged soil conservation.

The drought of 1936, with its attendant dust-bowl conditions, focused attention on the need for vigorous soil-conservation measures and prompted passage of the Soil Conservation and Domestic Allotment Act of that year. Under this Act, the Secretary of Agriculture could replace the old type of specific contract between the government and the farmer with an open offer to make benefit payments to anyone who would reduce acreage of soil-depleting crops and take steps to conserve or rebuild the land withheld from production. But production in 1937 was very high, and there was pressure to supplement acreage reduction with even more vigorous measures.

The soil-conservation basis for acreage allotments was maintained. However, in 1938 Congress passed a new Agricultural Adjustment Act, which placed more emphasis than ever before on the principle of giving direct support to prices. Since 1933, the Commodity Credit Corporation (CCC) had operated as an independent agency, performing the minor function of "cushioning" the prices of corn, wheat, and cotton against adverse fluctuations in demand and supply. The CCC had carried out the cushioning process by making loans to farmers on the security of their crops. Most of these loans were made "without recourse." Nonrecourse loans were a heads-you-win, tails-I-lose proposition. If the CCC extended an advance against a commodity and the price of that commodity fell, the farmer could let the CCC take title to the stored product and cancel the debt together with the accumulated interest. If the price of the commodity against which the advance had been made rose, the farmer could

Adding to the farmer's woes during the depressed 1930s were several years of unprecedented heat and drought. The subsequent blowing of previously eroded land often left bleak landscapes, like this one in McClain County, Oklahoma.

sell the commodity, pay back the loan with interest, and keep any profit. Thus, loan rates became, in effect, minimum prices. From 1933 to 1937, CCC operations were carried out with reference to vague price objectives. In these early years, no loans were made on wheat because short crops kept wheat prices around $1 a bushel. Lending on corn and cotton was nominal due to reasonably low loan rates combined with a strong tendency for prices to move upward.

The Agricultural Adjustment Act of 1938 greatly increased the power of the CCC by making it mandatory that the directors extend loans on corn, wheat, and cotton at rates between 52 and 75 percent of parity. From this point on,

Congress was to specify support prices at a certain percentage of parity prices, parity prices being defined as farm prices having the same purchasing power as those prevailing in a favorable base period. In 1938 and for many years thereafter, the base period for most products was 1910–1914.

Mandatory supports went into effect after farm prices had dropped from their post-depression "recovery" highs of 1937. From 1939 to 1941, the CCC accumulated great quantities of wheat, corn, cotton, and tobacco. Strengthened demand following the outbreak of World War II enabled the government to sell these stocks at a profit, but large holdings of wheat were stored into the war years, and vast amounts of low-grade, short-staple cotton were not disposed of until even later.

Two other means of restricting the supply of farm products came into use during the 1930s. One of these, the *marketing agreement,* was tried in the early experimental years, then fell into disuse, and finally after 1937 became important in the production of certain fruits and vegetables and in the chief milk areas. Marketing agreements are contracts between an association of producers of a raw product and the processors of that product; the contractual agreement is referred by a Department of Agriculture representative. Producers and processors may set minimum prices, total quantities to be marketed, and allotments of marketings among processors. Milk producers and the city milk companies, in addition to controlling the amounts of milk marketed, have made a profitable enterprise by establishing different prices for milk uses with different elasticities of demand—that is, by becoming discriminating monopolists.

Marketing quotas—became important after 1936, when Congress empowered the Secretary of Agriculture to set an upper limit to the quantities that growers of certain crops could sell. Before such controls could be instituted, the Secretary had to determine that the current supply of a basic commodity exceeded a "reserve supply." A referendum was then held, and if two-thirds of the qualified producers approved, a quota was assigned to each grower. Any farmer who marketed amounts in excess of the quota was subject to a penalty or fine on the excess sold.

Most early efforts at raising farm prices were directed at reducing supply rather than increasing demand, but two ways of stimulating the dollar sales of food and fiber by federal subsidy were quickly devised. The more acceptable "surplus-removal" operation has been the nutrition or direct-distribution programs. Nutrition programs have taken the form of food-stamp plans, low-cost milk distribution plans, and school lunch programs. School lunch programs were so readily accepted by the public that they have since been authorized by separate legislation without any implications of furnishing relief. The Food Stamp Plan, in operation from 1939 to 1942, won enthusiastic supporters.[7] Stamps given to low-income families were (indeed, still are) used to purchase food from regular retail outlets; storekeepers, in turn, cashed the stamps in at

[7] In 1961, advocates finally secured reactivation of this program—first on a pilot basis in eight economically distressed areas, and then on a permanent basis nationwide. The fiscal 1971 appropriation for the national food-stamp program was just over $1.4 billion, roughly three times the amount budgeted for school lunch and special milk programs. Today the costs exceed $4 billion.

the Treasury. Thus, surplus commodities were given to those who presumably had the greatest need for them. The benefits to poor and undernourished people were more important than any influence such programs may have exerted on agricultural demand.

The second type of surplus-removal operation has been the *export subsidy.* This method of increasing the sales of farm commodities originated with the Agricultural Adjustment Act of 1933, but not until the passage of an amendment in 1935 (commonly referred to as Section 32) did sales become significant. In that year, the amendment provided that as much as 30 percent of annual customs revenues might be used to finance the disposal of farm surpluses at home and abroad.

The subsidization of exports by payments of bounties did not reach alarming proportions before World War II.[8] In the fiscal year 1939–1940, bounties for wheat and cotton amounted to $26 million and $38 million, respectively. As we will observe presently, expenditure of public funds on export subsidies would one day become an effective, if somewhat dubious, means of adding to American farm income.

Farm Policy During and After World War II

Early in 1941, the troubles that had plagued agriculture for so long began to disappear, as production expanded to meet lend-lease and growing domestic requirements. To encourage expansion, Congress passed three laws in May, July, and December of 1941. The first of these directed the CCC to support the basic crops of wheat, corn, cotton, tobacco, rice, and peanuts at 85 percent of parity. The second, the Steagall Amendment, gave the Secretary of Agriculture authority to support the price of any *nonbasic* commodity at *not less than* 85 percent of parity if, in the opinion of the Secretary, support was necessary to increase the production of a crop vital to the war effort. The third law guaranteed the 85-percent loan rate on basic crops for the years 1942–1946, inclusive, putting price floors into effect for six crops well into the future.

During 1942, administration thinking reflected two major concerns. Emphasis was placed on the necessity for stimulating particular *kinds* of output, notably meats and the oil-bearing crops, and avoiding a repetition of the price collapse that followed World War I. Legislation of October 1942 set final policy for the war period and for two postwar years. The 1942 act provided *minimum*

[8]An export bounty is a payment to exporters of so much per unit of commodity to offset losses incurred in the process of buying in the artificially supported home market and selling at lower world prices. This kind of interference with international trade, a form of dumping, can be defended on the grounds that it offers the rest of the world an enhancement of real income: Other countries can enjoy the goods that are dumped. But it adversely affects the income and marketing positions of producers of competing commodities, hurting friendly nations in a way the United States has always considered unfair. Matters of U.S. relationships with other countries aside, there are always other ways to give farmers as large an income as can be obtained with an export subsidy and taxes. For further details, see D. Gale Johnson, *Trade and Agriculture* (New York: John Wiley & Sons, 1950).

support rates of 90 percent of parity for both basic and Steagall commodities; the supports were to remain in effect for two full years, beginning with the first day of January following the official end of the war. Finally, price ceilings on farm products were set at a minimum of 110 percent of parity.[9]

Over the war period and during the first two postwar years, price supports were not generally required. Due to the great demand for most products, agricultural prices tended to push against their ceilings, but the Secretary found it necessary to set floors for some needed nonbasic commodities that were above minimum levels. Surplus supplies of eggs and certain grades of hogs created a problem for part of 1944, but farm prices on the whole were subject to upward pressure. For some meats and dairy products it was even necessary to roll back retail prices in an effort to "hold the line" against inflation. In such cases, to prevent a reduction in the floor prices received by farmers, meat packers and creameries were paid a Treasury subsidy equal to the amount of the rollback on each unit sold.

We have already noted that the war enabled the CCC to unload heavy inventories that had built up between 1939 and 1941. From 1944 to 1946, loans extended by the CCC were small. Beginning in 1944, however, egg purchases became so great as to cause embarrassment, and support to the production of eggs and potatoes received a fantastically unfavorable press in 1945 and 1946. But foreign demand through the United Nations Relief and Rehabilitation Administration (UNRRA) and military governments, an unexpectedly high domestic demand, and the removal of price ceilings led to highly favorable postwar prices and lightened CCC loan and purchase commitments. Most production restrictions on crops were canceled before or during World War II, and by the spring of 1948 only tobacco and potatoes were still controlled.

However, this state of affairs did not last long. Farm prices and income began a downward trend in July 1948. With the high support prices required by the Agricultural Acts of 1948 and 1949, price declines meant increases in loans and accumulation of inventories, for which the Commodity Credit Corporation was prepared. In June 1948, Congress had given the CCC a borrowing authorization of $4.75 billion and permanent status.[10] During fiscal years 1949 and 1950, price-support loans and inventories climbed to a total "investment" of over $3.5 billion. The seriousness of these increases was indicated by the concentration of support operations in the four great staples—corn, wheat, cotton, and tobacco. In fact, corn stocks owned by the CCC or pledged to it as

[9] There were two other provisions that some readers might wish to know about. Cotton supports were set at 92.5 percent of parity. The Secretary of Agriculture, at his discretion, could leave wheat and corn supports at 85 percent of parity if he felt that higher prices would limit available quantities of livestock feed.

[10] Under the War Food Administration, the CCC for a time had imported needed commodities such as coffee, tea, fats, and sugar. This foreign-purchase program was begun again after the war. In addition, the corporation in 1946 was charged with the responsibility of procuring large quantities of agricultural products to meet the requirements of both U.S. government agencies administering foreign relief and foreign governments and relief agencies. This "supply program" tapered off during the fiscal year ending in June 1950, largely as a result of the recovery of agriculture in western Europe. For further information, consult the *Report of the President of the Commodity Credit Corporation,* which appears at the end of each fiscal year.

collateral were greater than they had been at any previous time. Wheat inventories were about the same as those held in the previous high year of 1942. Although cotton holdings did not approach the inventories of 1939–1941, they were not far from those of 1942.

To understand why CCC inventories increased so markedly in years of mild recession, it is helpful to review postwar farm legislation. A presidential declaration that the war was officially over, made in December 1946, signaled the termination of rigid wartime supports at the end of 1948. Although it had been amended several times, the basic farm law was still the old Agricultural Adjustment Act of 1938, which was generally felt to be in need of revision. Consequently, extensive discussion of the whole farm problem went on during 1947 and the first half of 1948, and there was much talk of writing a permanent farm bill. Farm leaders, government experts, and university professors testified before the House Agricultural Committee. The result was the Agricultural Act of 1948—passed in haste in the last days of the congressional session—which maintained price-support levels through 1949 at the magical 90-percent figure for basic commodities and the principal Steagall commodities.

The contribution of the midwestern farm states to the Democratic victory of 1948 led to a lengthy reconsideration of the policy laid down by the Republican-controlled Eightieth Congress in the 1948 Act. Out of gratitude, the Democrats were determined to write a new law, and it seemed for a while that a novel and imaginative method of subsidizing agriculture might be devised. In the spring of 1949, Secretary of Agriculture, C.F. Brannan announced the plan of compensatory payments to which the press and public quickly attached his name, although its central ideas had been developing for many years in academic writings. The Brannan plan would have allowed the prices of certain perishable commodities to seek their own level in the marketplace, the difference between the market price and a "modernized" parity price to be paid to the farmer (up to a certain maximum number of "units") with a check from the Treasury. Secretary Brannan would have continued price supports for nonperishable (storable) products via the old device of extending nonrecourse loans to producers. After months of heated argument, during which the National Grange and the American Farm Bureau Federation aligned themselves against such an unconcealed payment of subsidies, the House of Representatives refused to give the Brannan plan a trial run on even three commodities. Opponents of the Brannan plan won the day by castigating such a straightforward subsidy as "socialism."

In the fall of the year, the Agricultural Act of 1949 was passed. The law distinguished among three groups of commodities: (1) the six "basics"—wheat, corn, cotton, tobacco, rice, and peanuts; (2) five "designated nonbasic" commodities—wool and mohair, tung nuts, honey, Irish potatoes, and milk and milk products; (3) and "other nonbasic" commodities—the rest of some 170 U.S. commodities. The Secretary of Agriculture was required to support the basic commodities, provided they were under production controls or marketing quotas, but a rigid support of 90 percent of parity was permanently mandatory only in the case of tobacco. After 1952, the other basic commodities were to be supported at between 75 and 90 percent of parity, the level of support depending on the supply of each commodity.[11] The 1949 Act, like the 1948 law before it, provided a new parity formula. The "modernized" method of computing parity prices took into consideration prices received and prices paid during the most recent ten-year period instead of the relationships prevailing during the 1910–1914 period. There were two exclusions in the new formula: No wartime subsidy payments were included on the "received" side, and no wages paid by farmers to hired hands were included on the "paid" side. However, parity prices computed under the new formula could not drop more than 5 percent per year below what they would have been under the old formula, and until the end of 1954, the parity price for any basic commodity could not be lower than it was under the old method of computation. In general, the new formula raised parity prices for livestock and livestock products, dairy products, poultry, and some fruits and vegetables and lowered parity prices for grains, cotton, citrus fruits, potatoes, and eggs.

The 1949 legislation thereby made use of methods devised in the preceding 17 years to restrict the supply of farm products. However, a decision was made in favor of *flexible* price supports and against the wartime *rigid* supports, tobacco being the one exception. And the new method of computing parity prices had the merit of basing the program (after 1954, at least) on a current experience that was no longer of another age and time.

Neither flexible supports nor the new parity formula became effective as planned. After the start of the Korean War, Congress amended the law to make 90 percent support of the basics mandatory, and the old method of computing parity prices remained more favorable to farmers than the new one. The war once again enabled the CCC to reduce embarrassingly high inventories and loans, and total "investment" fell to $2 billion in mid-1951. The crops of 1952 and 1953, however, required an inordinate amount of support, and by August 1954 CCC loans and inventories amounted to nearly $7 billion. Twice during 1954 it was necessary to increase CCC authority to borrow for support operations—the last change bringing total authority to $10 billion.

After procrastinating for more than a year, the Eighty-Third Congress at last came up with its version of a farm program in the Agricultural Act of 1954. The inner circle of Department of Agriculture officials strove valiantly to find a fresh approach to the problem of price maintenance, but in the end advocated making the major provisions of the 1949 Act effective.[12] Secretary of Agriculture Ezra Taft Benson was especially insistent on the restoration of flexible supports, which were finally set for five of the six basic commodities at 82.5 to 90 percent of parity.[13] The 1954 Act again postponed changing to the modern-

[11] The Secretary of Agriculture's support of the "designated nonbasic" commodities was also mandatory. Support levels were to be between 60 and 90 percent of parity, except for milk and milk products, which were to be between 75 and 90 percent. Support for the rest of the nonbasic commodities was permissive. If funds were available, the storable products were to be supported at between 75 and 90 percent of parity and the perishables at between 0 to 90 percent.

[12] Wool was singled out for experimental support on the compensatory-payment basis advocated by former Secretary Brannan.

[13] The support level of tobacco remained at 90 percent. Price supports on milk and milk products, tung nuts, and honey continued to be mandatory, but all other commodities, including Irish potatoes, were simply eligible for support.

ized parity price formula for basic commodities; the notion that the 1910–1914 period represented parity ("fairity") was too deeply ingrained to die easily. In an heroic attempt to "insulate" the massive stocks of the CCC from the market, Congress authorized that $2.5 billion of CCC stocks be set aside for donation or sale for enumerated worthy causes.

But feed grain and wheat carry-overs continued to swell, and other surpluses, although not as alarming, showed no signs of lessening. The Soil Bank Act of 1956 was devised to reduce supplies of the six basic commodities by achieving a 10–17 percent reduction in plowland through payments to farmers who "voluntarily" shifted land out of production in the "soil bank." The diversion payments were based on the old formula of *multiplying* a base unit rate ($1.20 for wheat, $0.90 for corn, and so on, in the beginning) *by* normal yield per acre *by* the numbers of acres withdrawn. The plan was disguised as a conservation program to avoid the appearance of controlling farm decisions. The results were unbelievable. Carry-overs went right on mounting, reaching astronomical heights in 1961 after nine consecutive years of increase. Benson appeared to put all his zeal into an effort to become the most unpopular Secretary of Agriculture in history.

The Kennedy Administration had no choice but to be hardboiled. Secretary of Agriculture Orville Freeman devised no new techniques. He simply made an honest approach to the problem by dropping any pretense of maintaining freedom and controls at the same time. The Emergency Feed Grain Bill of 1961 encouraged drastic reductions in acreages devoted to corn and grain sorghums by offering $1.20 a bushel in diversion payments to farmers who reduced their acreage by 20 percent. Even higher payments were offered for the diversion of an additional 20 percent of feed-crop acreage. On the whole, results in 1962 were good. Although a planned reduction of 23 percent of the 1959–1960 base acreage slipped to 18 percent, 20 million acres were finally diverted. For the first time in a decade, feed grain carry-over actually dropped, and in 1962, a continuing reduction was predicted. This modest success encouraged the administration to attack massive surpluses of wheat with a similar, but incredibly expensive, plan. Wealthy farmers and their organization, the Farm Bureau Federation, secured the defeat of the wheat program at the referendum in 1963, but even wealthy agrarians saw the error of their ways and joined wholeheartedly in forging the Food and Agriculture Act of 1965. A monstrous giveaway, this Act cost the American taxpayer $5–$6 billion a year to make rich farmers richer while allowing a little of the subsidy to trickle down to farmers with sales of less than $10,000 per annum.

Farmers, particularly in the Midwest, are predominantly Republican, although their prosperity has been assured largely by expensive Democratic farm programs. And just as surely as a Republican administration attains power with the help of the farm vote, the new Secretary of Agriculture will recommend a farm bill guaranteed to disenchant all but the wealthiest agricultural operators. The Nixon Administration was no exception to this general rule. Following the inauguration of Richard Nixon in 1969, Congress extended the 1965 Farm Act to December 31, 1970, and after lengthy consultation within the Department of Agriculture, Secretary Clifford M. Hardin produced the Agricultural Act of 1970. After congressional consideration, the Act was passed and signed by President Nixon in November 1970. Basically, the law suspended marketing quotas and acreage allotments for wheat, feed grains, and cotton, requiring farmers to "set aside" or divert from production a certain amount of acres previously devoted to *any* kind of crop. Great corporate operations were thereby given the right to grow as much of any *one* crop as they wished, provided they took sufficient *total* acres out of production. The 1970 Act *did* provide a $55,000 limit on the direct subsidy of any one crop, but a single grower could obtain the maximum subsidies for each of three crops.

A 1971 corn crop of more than 5 billion bushels, bringing corn prices down to less than $0.90 a bushel at local elevators, suggested that disaster might be in the offing. The Department of Agriculture's prediction that blight was expected to cut 1971 corn production did not mollify the farm constituency. Nor did the appointment of Purdue University Dean Earl Butz as Secretary of Agriculture to succeed the discredited Hardin reassure many farmers; Butz was obviously committed to agribusiness and the promotion of huge corporate farms. The family-size farm was no longer viable in America; but no politician who hoped to win a major election outside New England and the Middle Atlantic states would dare admit the fact, and Secretary Butz tried to demonstrate the administration's good faith by keeping farm prices free of the constraints of price controls.

POLICY ANALYSIS

Clearly, government agricultural policy has been based on an attempt to redistribute income to farmers. In doing so, food production has been curtailed, higher prices have been imposed, and taxes have been elevated. It is now routine procedure for farmers and their lobbyist representatives to ask for and receive help from government. But even this help has produced unexpected results for the farmers themselves.

Unquestionably, farm programs have helped operators who were well down on the income scale, but it is just as clearly true that the lion's share of assistance has gone to those who were already at the top of the heap. The biggest direct subsidies have gone to the biggest producers; when acreage restrictions were put into effect, those who were in a position to reduce acreage the most received the largest checks. As the government has supported commodity prices, those with the most bushels or bales to sell have received the chief benefits. Studies indicate that inequality of incomes in agriculture is greater today than it was three decades ago. There has been some recent improvement in the lot of the bottom half of the farm population, but only due to the relief afforded by outmigration.

As we know, in the absence of government subsidy, fluid outmigrations from agriculture or rapid expansions in industry are essential to a healthy farm economy. Full employment and rising incomes for workers in the nonfarm sector mean a strong and increasing demand for food and fiber. But more than this, a greater number of jobs in industry and commerce mean that those who cannot make an adequate living on the land will be able to earn a livelihood in the cities and towns. In a technically progressive economy—and certainly in one in which agricultural techniques are improving—the proportion of the total population that is gainfully employed in agriculture must continually fall. To put the matter another way, as our knowledge and intelligence grow, fewer and fewer resources must be devoted to obtaining the necessities of life and more and more resources may be devoted to obtaining conveniences and luxuries. This has been true throughout the entire economic history of the United States. In 1790, 90 percent of the workforce was employed in agriculture; in 1960, the figure was less than 10 percent.[14] At its peak in 1916, the farm population was 32.5 million; in 1954 it stood at 19 million, and in 1961 it was under 15 million, or 8.1 percent of the population. In 1977, the farm population stood at fewer than 10 million, or less than 5 percent of the total population, and farm employment of just over 4 million was about 5 percent of the workforce. Favorable as the exodus has been, there are still far too many people in agriculture, especially in the South. It is not inconceivable that 2 percent of the workforce could produce all the farm products that the United States and a large part of the rest of the world could use at profitable prices. And *within* agriculture, more resources must be devoted to the production of foods that are both nutritionally and gastronomically sound.

We can be sure that some kind of a federal farm program is going to be required for a long time. The question remains, is such interference with the price system wise or necessary? Farmers and economists have different, but not irreconcilable, answers.

In general, "commercial" farmers, represented by their organizations and by the farm block in Congress, continue to support federal legislation similar to the programs discussed here. Today's farmers know perfectly well that acreage restrictions are of little avail over a period of years; as soon as farmers receive acreage allotments, they remove their poorest land from production, leave the best acres planted in the restricted crop, and cultivate the remaining land more intensively. Farmers also know that price-support operations lead to tremendous stockpiles of commodities, which can be liquidated without lowering agricultural prices only in wartime or by dumping abroad. Responsible farm leaders are aware, too, that unfavorable press stories in conjunction with the accumulation of huge government-owned stocks of commodities excite public hostility to farm programs.

Yet a combination of acreage restrictions and CCC-type price supports has the unquestioned advantage of masking the amount and extent of the subsidy to agriculture. Tying price and income maintenance to conservation dilutes the element of subsidy in the public mind. Moreover, Department of Agriculture outlays on the subsidy program, great as they are, do not include the higher prices paid by consumers for food and fiber as a consequence of support operations. Finally, because the subsidy is provided by a market mechanism, it seems respectable, whereas subsidy checks paid at the end of a growing season to make up the amount of income deemed necessary seem too obvious to be tolerated. For these reasons, farmers generally support proven methods of government subsidy. Within agriculture, the only serious differences arising in recent years have been concerned with the question of rigorous versus mild

[14] Farm employment dropped from 13.5 million in 1910 to an average of 6.5 million in 1962.

controls over output. The American Farm Bureau Federation, which speaks for the more affluent farmers, wants lower support prices and greater freedom to plant, because Farm Bureau membership makes huge profits on large volume. Supporting sharp restrictions on acreage combined with astronomical support prices are the organizations of small farmers, chiefly the National Farmers Union, the National Farmers Organization, and the National Grange.

Although farm organizations, with the exception of the Farm Bureau Federation, are satisfied with recent attempts to solve their problems, economists, generally speaking, are not. Many agricultural economists who are definitely sympathetic to agriculture feel that policies established over the last four decades may, in the long run, prevent a satisfactory solution to the farm problem from being found. There has long been an objection to the ideal of "parity," partly on the ground that no group in society is entitled, by right, to a fixed portion of the real national income. But there is a stronger argument. Successful attempts to maintain prices of farm commodities in the same *relative* position over time may keep consumers from obtaining the supplies that they want most. Parity prices tend to keep agricultural resources employed in the production of products that people have wanted in the past. If some agricultural prices are not allowed to fall *relative* to others, the pattern of cultivation will remain too rigid, and the result will be chronic "surpluses" of some crops.

Although economists look with disfavor on present types of agricultural subsidies, they agree that *some* kind of a federal farm program is necessary. Due to the nature of competition in agriculture, farmers are peculiarly vulnerable to the ups and downs of economic fluctuations. Once a farm family is established, it becomes increasingly difficult to leave the farm, and there is substantial agreement that a legitimate aim of subsidy is to keep middle-aged farmers on the land until their retirement. Finally, nonagricultural firms react to falling demand in a way that farm units cannot. Agriculture meets recession by maintaining output and letting prices fall, whereas industry maintains prices and lets output (and employment) fall.[15] The approach of the agricultural sector is certainly better for consumers, but it is hard on farm people.[16] Incomes fall, and the terms of exchange are poor. Furthermore, many who would otherwise migrate to the towns and cities stay on the farms, and some return who have previously left the farm, because at least there is enough to eat on the old homestead. The net result is low per-capita farm incomes.

Most economists agree, therefore, that a farm program directed toward combating the evils of depression is necessary. It is one thing, however, to recommend measures that are primarily counter-cyclical in aim and an altogether different thing to advocate a permanent interference with the pricing system that is to be operative in good times as well as bad. A case can be made for braking the rate at which family farms disappear and for subsidizing the

[15] Not since the Great Depression has business activity fallen so drastically as to be met by widespread price reductions in the manufacturing industry. The chief reasons for resistance to downward price movements in the manufacturing sector are its oligopolistic structure and the vigorous opposition of strong unions to wage cuts.

[16] Of course, unemployment is also hard on the industrial worker, as we know. Indeed one agricultural economist, Peter Dorner, argues that farm-program costs and unemployment-compensation costs are incurred for precisely the same reason.

training of the displaced rural poor for urban pursuits. But no one familiar with the facts can advocate the artificial support of prices when a plan of compensatory payments would maintain farm incomes closer to agreed-on levels. To the $5 billion annual cost of subsidy programs ($1 billion for storage alone), in the early 1970s must be added higher consumer prices. Compensatory payments have worked well in the case of the one commodity for which they have been tried—wool. There seems to be little rationale to support U.S. subsidy of American wool producers who cannot begin to compete with their Australian counterparts. So the Department of Agriculture simply decides what Montana ranchers *should* receive and at the end of a growing season sends them a check for the difference between that figure and what they *did* receive for the number of pounds of wool they produced. A neat, tidy way of providing a subsidy at minimum administrative cost! And everyone knows who has their feet in the public trough and for how much. Unfortunately for consumers and taxpayers, the recommendations of social scientists as to what public policy ought to be carry less weight than the recommendations and lobbying of producers with vested interests.

26

Manufacturing and Automation

To many, industrial growth is both the wellspring of American progress and a source of despair for the future.[1] By nearly any measurement we choose to take, manufacturing continues to dominate the American economy. The manufacturing industries presently account for a greater share of both corporate profits and expenditures for new plant and equipment than any other class of industry (in the broader sense of the term). Despite a decline in manufacturing employment from 35 percent of all nonfarm wage and salary employment in 1947 to well under 25 percent by the mid-1970s, manufacturing still provides more jobs than any other category of goods- or service-producing industries.[2] Except for the years of the Great Depression, more than 25 percent of the national income has originated in manufacturing (see Table 26-1). If we include mining and construction, so-called industrial activity in recent times accounts for one-third or more of all national income received in any year.

In short, on the basis of income generated, manufacturing today is in about the same *relative* position as agriculture was 100 years ago. This position was very nearly attained by the end of World War I, and yet there have been many noticeable aspects of industrial change since the 1920s. In a single chapter, we cannot examine particular industries in great detail, but we will try to draw two generalizations from recent observations, namely typical growth patterns and technological developments.

[1] In this chapter, as in Chapters 13 and 19, the adjective *industrial* refers mainly to manufacturing and mining. Unavoidably, the word is sometimes used in a broader sense.

[2] *Manpower Report of the President* (Washington, D.C.: U.S. Government Printing Office, 1971), p. 12.

TABLE 26–1
National Income by Industrial Origin, Selected Years, 1929–1970
(in billions of dollars)

	1929	1933	1940	1950	1960	1970[b]	1976[c]
Agriculture, forestry, and fisheries	8.3	3.7	6.2	17.9	17.3	24.5	40.8
Mining	2.0	.6	1.9	5.0	5.2	49.4	19.4
Construction	3.8	.8	2.6	11.8	21.9		67.7
Manufacturing	21.9	7.6	22.3	74.3	122.0	217.7	365.0
Wholesale and retail trade	13.4	5.5	14.3	42.7	68.0	122.1	220.7
Finance, insurance, and real estate	12.7	5.7	8.2	21.8	42.5	87.0	160.8
Transportation	6.6	3.0	5.0	13.3	18.0	29.5	50.6
Communications and public utilities	2.9	2.0	3.0	7.2	16.7	31.3	56.8
Services	10.3	5.6	8.9	23.1	49.2	103.2	188.2
Government and government enterprises	5.1	5.3	8.8	23.5	52.5	126.5	214.9
All others	0.8	0.3	0.4	1.2	2.3	4.6	14.4
All industries total[a]	87.8	40.2	81.6	241.9	415.5	795.9	1399.3
Manufacturing as a percentage of total	24.9	18.9	27.3	30.7	29.4	27.4	26.1

[a] Items may not add to total due to rounding.
[b] *Survey of Current Business* (July 1971).
[c] *Statistical Abstract,* 1977, p. 434

RECENT GROWTH PATTERNS OF MANUFACTURING INDUSTRIES

In a well-known study published in 1934, the recent chairman of the Federal Reserve, Arthur F. Burns, reached some conclusions we now accept almost intuitively—that industries rise and decline and that at any moment in time some will be growing and others will be declining.[3] Two interesting additional facts emerged from Burns' study. One was that, contrary to popular belief, an industry does not seem to reach a maximum size and then level off; once it ceases to grow, it soon goes into a decline. A second, more significant fact is that individual industries exhibit a retardation in their growth rates as decades pass.

These characteristics of production trends seem to be borne out by other studies and by the testimony of those who make their living in the marketplace. When it is first introduced, a product normally goes through a brief period of slow growth while it is gaining acceptance. If it gains acceptance (and many products do not), output for a time increases at an accelerating rate. But as years pass, the growth rate of product output tends to decline, although retardation in expansion may be interrupted by sharp upward thrusts in demand resulting from such causes as an outbreak of war, stoppage of foreign supplies of the product, or an increase in consumer income.

At first it may appear that such a proposition is really just a mathematical truism—that an initial increase in production at a rate of, say, 100 percent per annum obviously cannot be maintained forever. But Burns sought less obvious

[3] Arthur F. Burns, *Production Trends in the United States Since 1870* (New York: National Bureau of Economic Research, 1934).

Massive capital equipment, such as the finishing stands shown here at a U.S. Steel Corporation hotstrip mill, for a time so increased the productivity of American industry that domestic producers could compete favorably with foreign manufacturers, who paid lower money wages. But foreign steelmakers have acquired new and advanced techniques and now pose a real threat to the American steel industry.

reasons and reached the following conclusions. Declines in the growth rates of particular industries are concomitants of rapid growth in total production. The continual introduction of new goods and services restricts the demand for older ones, and the faster the introduction of new commodities, the greater the restrictive influence on older ones.[4] Specifically, interindustry and interproduct competition (about which we will have more to say later) may have effects on a particular line of production, ranging from diversion of demand to the outright undoing of an established industry. Recent examples come readily to mind. The rapid acceptance of frozen foods has adversely affected the output of canned foods. Television has hurt the motion-picture industry badly, changed radio production altogether, raised problems in the spectator sports industry, and even affected book sales and the custom of restaurant dining. Nor is this all.

[4] Burns, p. xvi.

Besides the increase in the number and variety of commodities, the methods of producing a given commodity may also multiply over time. Thus, steel-reinforced aluminum cable, which is both stronger and lighter than an electrically equivalent copper cable, has captured the high-voltage transmission line business and is rapidly winning in the so-called secondary distribution field.

Finally, there is persistent competition between old and new industries for the factors of production as well as for customer favor. Indeed, the very existence of an economic system implies a bidding among entrepreneurs for the use of scarce resources. Technological advances can and do reduce the restrictions imposed by a scarcity of resources, but as we have just observed, the stimulation that one industry receives from technical developments is likely to lead to retardation in competing industries.

THE RISE AND FALL OF INDUSTRIES

Several years ago, U.S. Department of Commerce economists collected data on more than 160 industries and classified them, on the basis of their experience between 1940 and 1951, into three groups: fast growing, moderately or slowly growing, and declining.[5] Against the average annual growth rate of 5 percent during this period, industries were designated as rapidly growing if their average yearly rate of increase was 7.5 percent or more; industries or products having a growth rate of more than zero but less than 7.5 percent were considered to be moderately or slowly growing. Some industries and products, as we might surmise, showed declines.

More than 60 products fell in the rapidly growing category, including producer and consumer goods, both durable and nondurable, as well as services. Only about one-third of these rapidly growing items were new products; the remainder had long been on the market. Antibiotics exhibited the highest average growth rate—a phenomenal 118 percent per annum. Output of television sets was almost as great; home freezers and clothes dryers followed. But among the fast-growing industries, growth rates varied considerably toward the end of the period. Since 1948, for example, frozen foods and phosphoric acid exceeded their 1940–1951 average rate of growth, whereas tractors, locomotives, and rayon and acetate showed a definite tendency to slow down. Such abrupt changes in growth rates remind us that we must always be careful about inferring a *future* rate of growth from any average of past growth rates.

The intermediate group, as might be expected, was comprised predominately of older industries. The greater part of American industrial output lies in this category. Items such as shipping containers, glass containers, and truck and bus tires were at the top of the list, with increases above 5 percent but below 7.5 percent. Goods such as electric lamps, canned fruits and vegetables, lubricating oil, salt, and electric fans showed output increases approximately identical to that of the gross national product. Staple foods such as sugar and wheat flour and standard goods such as wool carpets and rugs, radios, and cigars had barely measurable annual rates of increase.

[5] For details, see Louis J. Paradiso and Francis L. Hirt, "Growth Trends in the Economy," *Survey of Current Business* (January 1953), pp. 5–10.

Paradiso and Hirt found that 17 industries studied showed a declining trend in output. Changes in consumer tastes accounted for some of these declines, as in the cases of pipe and chewing tobacco, and lamb and mutton. Average annual rates of decline in the production of men's suits and overcoats were accounted for partly by changes in taste and partly by the entry into military service of a large proportion of young males during the period studied. For the most part, however, the retrogressing industries had fallen victim to the competition of substitute or alternative products. Radiators, convectors, and mechanical stokers were rapidly displaced as more satisfactory heating systems became popular. Butter experienced an average annual decline in output of around 4 percent since 1940, not because oleomargarine was better but because it was so much cheaper. And so it was for windmill pumps, soap, steam locomotives, and wood shingles.

It is instructive to observe how growth patterns shift with the selection of a different time span. During the period 1948–1960, fast-growth products changed remarkably.[6] Of the more than 70 items in this group, 10 percent showed uninterrupted growth at a rate of over 15 percent per year. Outstanding examples included polyethylene and transistors. Some fast-growth products accelerated their rate of growth in the last six years of the period; some slowed their rate of growth, while others that averaged more than a 7.5 percent rate of increase for the whole period reached a leveling stage or actually declined.

Rapidly growing industries are important to development because they give impetus to the economy. One type of output that provides the economy with an undercurrent of great strength is the manufacture of household durables. For a while after its introduction, a new durable shows slowly increasing sales. Shortly, if it is to gain acceptance at all, the durable makes rapid gains—gains so great that they can affect incomes and employment in the entire economy. Before World War I, automobiles and washing machines gave the economy a boost. Electric refrigerators and radios got their start early in the 1920s and were a positive force through the 1930s. After World War II, automatic washing machines, television sets, home freezers, and, more recently, room air conditioners, dehumidifiers, clothes dryers, electric typewriters, and small digital computers made their mark. As the 1960s progressed, textile mill consumption of glass fibers soared, and knit cloth regained favor in many uses. Central air conditioning and electric heating systems, including heat pumps, vied with color television sets for a rapidly increasing share of household outlays. In the 1970s recreational and avocational expenditures on new designs of old products rose spectacularly, as families turned to cameras, stereophonic phonographs, and boats, airplanes, campers, and other leisure-time vehicles.

A final word needs to be said about individual growth rates and the relationship of these rates to business fluctuations. Some products and services—like cigarettes and telephone service—are affected only slightly by business downturns. Others, including consumer durables in general, feel the effects of falling income severely, although they may rebound quickly after a business upturn.

[6] For the average annual rates of growth of 304 products during 1948–1960, see Francis L. Hirt, "New Light on Patterns of Output Growth," *Survey of Current Business* (September 1961), pp. 14–15.

THE POSSIBILITY OF A SECOND INDUSTRIAL REVOLUTION

In our discussion of technological change between the Civil War and World War I in Chapter 19, we emphasized the mechanization of industry. From James Watt's first successful steam engine to the end of World War I, the story of technological advance was told in terms of larger and increasingly automated machines that became more and more dependent on the efficient use of inanimate energy derived primarily from fossil fuels.

A further examination of manufacturing techniques still requires us to pay attention to machines and power. Power-driven devices that performed feats of amazing dexterity on one hand and of great strength on the other were introduced at a particularly high rate during the 1920s and again during and after World War II. But two other forces have recently brought about important changes in technology: (1) recent applications of the discoveries of science to industrial processes and (2) the development of unified systems of automatic control. So great has been the impact of the scientist, who can now actually change molecules, and so fundamental have been the developments of control mechanisms that beginning in the early 1960s, commentators spoke of a "new technology" and a "second Industrial Revolution." A decade later, both physical and social scientists were still debating the aptness of these expressions.

First, it should be emphasized that mechanization is many-sided. Sometimes gains in mechanization result from the introduction of a completely new machine; sometimes they result from making old machines larger or faster. Not infrequently, the introduction of mechanical innovations will be combined with the removal of discontinuities in processing, and sometimes mechanization will take place because the materials being prepared have changed. This seems to be true presently in the construction industry, for example, where metal building-facings have gained acceptance. Sometimes, as in the case of the mechanization of coal mining, new and powerful devices employed to help workers perform essentially the same old jobs.

In the primary metals industries (see Map 26-1), almost unbelievable advances have been made in the physical handling of materials. The strip mining of coal, which furnishes so much of the energy needed for metals processing, has recently accounted for just under 40 percent of total bituminous output. The mechanical mining of ores and the mechanical charging of furnaces are almost universal. The continuous rolling of sheet metal, introduced in the steel industry in 1926, has become commonplace. More and more primary metals industries have achieved uninterrupted production in huge integrated plants. In the case of steel, this means that molten iron can be converted into steel beams, sheets, and plates without the great losses of heat that were usual until 1920. And throughout the process, heavy handling is done by all kinds of mechanical conveyors, from fork-lift trucks to giant cranes.

These types of changes are spectacular and are likely to be readily apparent. But improvements in mechanization have been taking place for nearly two centuries. The question that entrepreneurs as well as economists are now asking is this: Has there been any fundamental shift in the *way* innovation takes place and, consequently, in its social impact? During the 1920s and 1930s, as the mechanization of industry continued, we heard much about the problem of

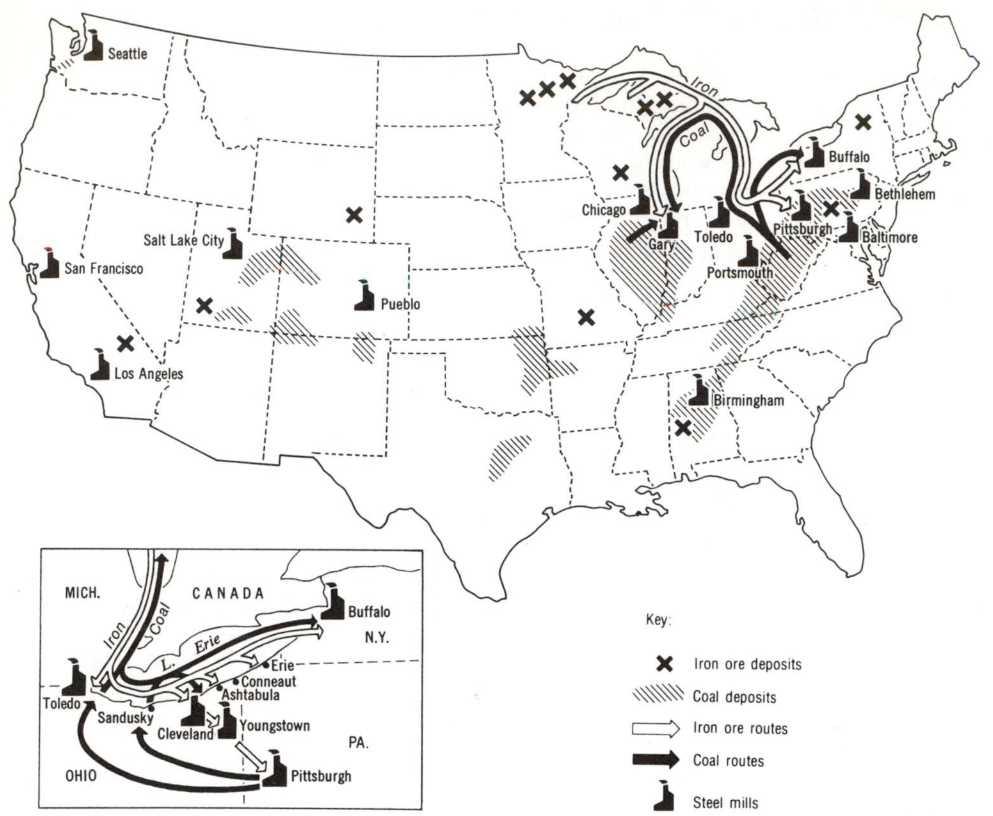

MAP 26–1

Heavy Industry: Major steel production is concentrated in centers that boast an abundance of either iron ore or coking coal or that have a favorable site (usually on a waterway) to which ore and coal can be transported cheaply.

"technological unemployment." Even in 1962, President Kennedy remarked that "the major domestic challenge of the sixties is to maintain full employment at a time when automation is replacing men." Although unemployment had returned as a problem a decade earlier, few knowledgeable economists or labor leaders were disposed to blame automation. Indeed, the vocal demands of young people and blue-collar workers to be relieved of unpleasant, routine jobs made it clear that automation was viewed as a boon instead of a burden.

SCIENCE, PRODUCTION, AND PRODUCTS

The Petrochemicals

The story of the impact of chemistry on economic life is essentially the story of the petrochemical industry. The beginnings of this industry can be traced from the early 1920s, when modern techniques of petroleum refining first came into use.

The catalytic cracking of petroleum takes place in these giant towers at Esso's refinery in Elizabeth, New Jersey. A gentle blizzard of platinum inside the towers promotes "fractional distillation," so that high-grade products like lighter fluid rise to the top while paraffin sinks to the bottom.

Crude petroleum is made up of various hydrocarbons—molecules of carbon and hydrogen atoms—in many different structural arrangements and hundreds of combinations. The process of petroleum refining separates the constituent molecules and, more recently, recombines the fractions in any manner desired. Refiners originally relied on the fact that the different hydrocarbons have different boiling points and therefore are passed off at different temperatures in the distillation process.

By "cracking" the crude oil, heavy molecules are broken up into lighter ones, and some of the remaining heavy molecules can then be treated further. So-called catalytic cracking, in which petroleum is subjected to heat under great pressure in the presence of a catalyst, began in the early 1920. Polymerization, whereby the chemist arranges light molecules in chains (polymers) and thus obtains physical properties that would never occur in a "natural" state, followed only a little later; this process is, in a sense, the opposite of cracking.

The scientific study of petroleum refining has resulted in a whole series of new products made from petrochemicals—that is, from compounds recovered from petroleum or natural gas. Many of the important basic chemicals, such as ammonia, methyl alcohol, ethyl alcohol, and glycerol, which were once derived from coal or agricultural products, are now in the petrochemical group. In 1967, petrochemicals accounted for more than 30 percent of total U.S. chemical production by weight and 60 percent of all U.S. chemical production by value. For 11 products (for example, benzene, butadiene, toluene, and comene), the proportions made by petroleum companies in the early 1970s exceeded 50 percent, and for five products (for example, ethylene and naphthalene), the proportion was between 25 and 50 percent. The most important end use for petrochemicals, measured on a tonnage basis, is synthetic rubber, followed by automobile and aviation antifreezes and antiknock compounds, and then by the synthetic fibers (cellulose acetate, nylon, dacron, and so on) and the various plastics.

To give us some idea of how new materials progress from the test-tube stage, we will consider the plastic polyethylene for a moment. This is the white, waxy substance familiar to everyone as the material used in squeeze bottles and semitransparent wrapping; it is also used as an alternate material for containers, primary insulators, piping, and so forth. Made by eight companies, including Du Pont, Union Carbide, and Monsanto, polyethylene remains ahead of the polyvinyls (shower curtains, seat covers, garden hose) and polystyrene (toys, bathroom tile, housewares) in total output. Polyethylene is made by the manipulation of ethylene—an invisible, light gas, which is obtained from natural gas or as a by-product of oil refining. Under great pressure, ethylene molecules are linked together, or polymerized, to form long chains of single molecules known as polymers. By regulating the size of the molecules, a plastic results that retains its flexibility at fairly low temperatures.

The New Metals

Science has also wrested from nature the secrets of processing metals of special importance in an age of great speed and unbelievably fine tolerances. Before 1900, only 14 metals were in common use, and two more—chromium and tungsten—were just gaining acceptance in steel alloys. During the past half-century, output of most of the old metals has increased greatly, and 30 or more new metals have emerged as valuable industrial materials. Public interest has been captured particularly by the increasing use of the light metals and the development of alloys and superalloys that can withstand high temperatures.

Aluminum had become a "tonnage" metal by the end of World War I. What Alcoa did with aluminum, Dow Chemical has since done with magnesium and, very recently, Du Pont has done with titanium. Although all three metals are now produced in significant amounts, aluminum is far ahead in quantity of output. Total annual U.S. production increased from about 85,000 tons in 1920 to nearly 300,000 tons in 1940. Since then aluminum output has increased to over 2 million tons. Compared with the 100 million tons per year produced by the steel industry, this seems a small quantity, but we should remember that steel is roughly three times as heavy as aluminum. And as aluminum researchers develop ever-stronger alloys that can actually compete in some uses with structural steel, the optimism of Alcoa, Reynolds, Kaiser, and Kennecott executives over their potential future markets expands.

Magnesium, the lightest of the structural metals, is now about where aluminum was in tonnage before World War II—but its present production is over 30 times what it was in 1940. Fabricators are learning how to handle magnesium, and its extreme lightness gives it such a decided advantage in some uses, particularly aircraft manufacture, that it may one day approach aluminum in sales volume. Whether titanium, which has been in production only a little more than 25 years, will ever achieve the status of aluminum is problematical, but it is now used in applications other than jet-engine manufacture.

Despite the glamour attached to the light metals, at least in part because they are used in aircraft and space vehicles, the metals (notably the steel alloys) that can withstand high temperatures have contributed much to economic progress. The development of steel alloys has been continuous since the end of the last century, largely due to their usefulness in making machine tools. But the last 35 years or so have produced a definite need for new alloys that will stand up under extremely high temperatures.

By the 1970s, power-plant boilers operated at steam temperatures of 1200° F. Alternatively, atomic reactors require sound parts that can withstand temperatures of 2000° F. Some chemical processing generates heat up to 4200° F, and the blaze of the arc in an electric-arc furnace reaches 6000° F. The reasons for the trend toward higher temperatures are many, but they may be summed up in the statement that (1) many processes are impossible without them and (2) modern engines of whatever type achieve efficiency as energy lost to the "sink" is reduced through higher inlet throttle temperatures.

AUTOMATION

Since shortly after World War II, there has been much excitement—and a little more than slight misapprehension—regarding extensions of automatic controls. The excitement is over the possibility that one day a few topnotch technicians and a skilled maintenance crew will be able to run factories that, under present techniques, are manned by hundreds or thousands of skilled and semiskilled workers. The misapprehension is experienced by people who feel that the automatic control of whole processes is no different from the automatic working of a single large machine or group of machines. However, such fears can be dispelled by recalling that automatic machines usually have been successfully introduced and operated without mass unemployment resulting.

For example, in 1912, it took 162 machines to finish the four flat faces of 108 cylinder heads in an hour; by 1946, six machines could do the same work, but they were still hand-fed. In 1953 a single, horizontal broach could outproduce the six machines of 1946. Why? Because castings were brought automatically to the broach, machining operations were automatic, and the completed heads were ejected automatically and sent by conveyor belt to the next operation. By the late 1950s, 42 automatic machines, linked together by automatic transfer devices for moving engine blocks through the process, could turn out finished six-cylinder blocks in 14.6 minutes, compared to nine hours in conventional manufacture.

This example reminds us that the automatic operation of a machine lessens the expenditure of human physical effort in a manufacturing process. Sometimes the reduction of effort is so pronounced, as in the case of the cylinder heads just mentioned, that it receives attention in the business press. The automatic loading and unloading of multistage machine tools and the movement of pieces in process from one machine to another by transfer machines and conveyor systems (so-called Detroit or "hard" automation) are certainly impressive. But, as one writer remarked in the early stages of automation, "automated" lines like these are but a step forward in the development of machine tools and production lines.[7]

How does automation differ intrinsically from improvements in production lines? In what sense is it a "new" technology? The easiest way to understand the principles involved is to recall the problems facing military officers charged with defending Britain against German planes early in World War II. The old methods of pointing antiaircraft guns by hand, taught to American ROTC students as late as 1940, were obviously of little avail against the extreme speeds of the enemy aircraft. Such speeds, according to Norbert Wiener, "made it necessary to give a predicting machine . . . communication functions which had previously been assigned to human beings. Thus, the problem of antiaircraft fire control made familiar the notion of a communication addressed to a machine rather than to a person."[8] A predicting *machine* had to be given communication functions, because human beings reacted too slowly. A machine, given certain instructions, had to point a gun at a target, and if the gun missed, had *itself* to make the correction that would enable the gun to hit the target on the next round.

Effective antiaircraft fire was really dependent on two advances. Some kind of self-correction had to be built into a closed system, and a way of amplifying small energy levels into high energy levels by other than mechanical means had to be devised. Operations were controlled by a device similar to a modern high-speed computer, and small energy levels were amplified by a vacuum tube or an electron valve rather than by complicated gears and other mechanical gadgets.

Thus was born an entirely new technology. This innovation was not simply an increase in mechanization, as some would argue, but an altogether novel concept of control in which a machine gives orders and directs its own operations. It can be argued that automation is simply the culminating innovation, the logical outcome, of the increasing mechanization of the workload. On the other hand, there is merit in the contention that transistors and integrated circuits are now replacing *thought* processes rather than muscle power and manual dexterity. To be sure, someone must program the computer. But the computer then goes on to perform what were once thought to be processes *beyond* addition, subtraction, multiplication, and division.

Modern oil refineries and some chemical plants have most closely ap-

[7] John Diebold, "Automation—The New Technology," *Harvard Business Review,* **XXXI**:6 (November–December 1953), p. 64.

[8] Norbert Wiener, *The Human Use of Human Beings* (Boston: Houghton Mifflin, 1950), p. 176.

proached the ideal of automation thus far, but more and more products that lend themselves to continuous-process manufacture and assembly-line techniques will be brought under complete automatic control. The computer that gives the orders for the entire process is fed its instructions on tape or punched cards. Since the system is based on the "feedback" principle, the control mechanism operates on a basis of *actual* performance instead of *expected* performance. If a part is turned out incorrectly, a sensory member tells the control mechanism, which either allows further time for machining or rejects the part. All feedback devices are tied together in a closed-loop system, so that the assembly or manufacture of a product or of multiple products can be performed without the intervention of a human hand. To repeat, the essence of automation is the giving of orders by machine in a self-correcting mechanism.

This revolutionary approach to manufacturing has required the redesign of products and machines—and even of entire processes. Redesign implies large additions to cost, but the computers that perform the logical tasks of control, although once inordinately expensive, are rapidly becoming less and less costly. As the new technology has become more familiar, broad principles of design have evolved, and something approaching quantity production of the control devices that have considerably similar parts has been achieved. Furthermore, flexibility of both materials-handling mechanisms and machine tools has been attained, so that a given automatic line can be shifted from the production of one product to another.

Perhaps the ultimate achievement of automation will be the large-scale innovation of what is presently being tried experimentally—robots that can not only perform routine production-line chores but that can also sense their environment (analyze the scene) sufficiently to make responses like the neurophysiological responses of human beings. If it is to increase productivity in the manufacturing industry greatly, automation ultimately must rely on the computer to link nearly all the processes of production, including office work. For, as Norbert Wiener remarked nearly a generation ago, to achieve true automatization, the white-collar operations connected with production also must be mechanized. The most modern office machines that perform cost accounting and other business functions must be controlled by the same mechanism that directs factory processes. The subjection of all the elements of production to computer control will almost certainly be a gradual development, so the problem of absorbing the workers who are displaced by the new technology will not become critical in the near future. Technological unemployment occurs in specific areas as the consequence of scientific progress, but this merely calls for the reallocation of inputs to other uses; mass unemployment does not occur.

Research and Development, Diversification, and Decentralization

Contrary to general opinion, the systematic application of science to product and process development through research and development (R&D) departments has not been widespread throughout American industry. By the early 1920s, only two other industries besides the electrical, chemical, and rubber industries made large outlays in this area. During the late 1920s and the 1930s, the petroleum industry, the farm implement industry, and the automobile industry also began to build large research organizations. In the years immediately preceding World War II, perhaps three-quarters of the personnel in organized industrial research worked in these six industries. To be sure, other industries—then, as now—were spending money searching for new products and processes. But the steel, nonferrous metals, paper, textiles, and food industries have employed well below 25 percent of the trained manpower in industrial laboratories, even since World War II.

In postwar years, two glamour industries have invested considerable resources in R&D. Partly due to its inevitable participation in the space race, the aircraft industry has spent a great amount of money on research. Yet aircraft manufacturers are in effect simply spending money for the government. Similarly, the federal government has provided well over half the funds that have been used in the development of scientific instruments, and at the same time has provided the largest market for these instruments. We might add that many of the newer products of the electrical companies have also been financed largely by government subsidy. However, with the exception of the scientific-instrument output of the electrical companies, the assembling and processing industries that were the original pioneers in research and development have continued to provide their own funds for this kind of investigation.

Both the changes in money expenditures on R&D in the postwar years and variations in the proportions of research expenditures financed by industry and the federal government are startling. From expenditures that averaged a little over $2 billion in 1946, R&D outlays rose to an average of nearly $14 billion in 1960, and to nearly $41 billion in 1977. Table 26-2 shows the amounts expended by the major spending units during this period.

The question of who ultimately foots the bill is a different one, as Table 26-3 shows. The federal government pays for much of the research done by industry and, through grants, for a good deal of academic research. Industry also finances research conducted by universities and nonprofit institutions. Although industry roughly doubled the amount of its expenditures on research and development during the 1955–1962 period, the federal government came

TABLE 26–2

Research: Who Spends the Money (in millions of dollars)

	1947	1960	1971	1977
Federal government	400	1,730	3,650	6,500
Industry	1,300	10,510	19,800	27,750
Colleges and universities	300	830	2,735	3,956
Nonprofit institutions	100	280	940	1,417
Federally funded university and college research centers	—	380	725	1,177
Total	2,100	13,710	27,850	40,800

Sources: Data for 1947–1960, *Statistical Abstract,* 1968, p. 525.
Data for 1971, *Statistical Abstract,* 1971, p. 508.
Data (estimated) for 1977, *Statistical Abstract,* 1977, p. 612.

TABLE 26–3
Research: Who Pays for It (in millions of dollars)

	1947	1960	1971	1977
Federal government	500	8,720	14,735	21,798
Industry	11,515	4,510	11,780	17,508
Colleges and universities	75	330	960	883
Nonprofit institutions	10	150	375	611
Total	12,100	13,710	27,850	40,800

Sources: Data for 1947–1960, *Statistical Abstract,* 1968, p. 525.
Data for 1971, *Statistical Abstract,* 1971, p. 508.
Data (estimated) for 1977, *Statistical Abstract,* 1977, p. 612.

close to tripling its outlays over the same span of years. Beginning in the late 1960s, however, government greatly slowed its annual rate of increase on R&D expenditures, while industry maintained yearly increases in such outlays. Although there appeared to be increases in the 1970s, in real terms of expenditures, the change was negligible, and was negative relative to other types of expenditures.

No one can say, of course, how these proportions will change in the future. Most informed estimates suggest that there will be a swing back toward a larger proportion of R&D outlays by industry and a somewhat smaller proportion of these outlays by the federal government. Since World War II, the nation's investment in research and development has been focused largely on defense and space technology. During the early 1960s, over one-half of national R&D expenditures were for this purpose; a decade later, the proportion had reached more than 40 percent. Just as government expenditures on research and development are concentrated in the few agencies involved with defense and space missions (the Department of Defense, the National Aeronautics and Space Administration, and the Atomic Energy Commission), industry's R&D expenditures are also concentrated in a few industries. In 1969, over 80 percent of industrial R&D outlays were accounted for by only five industries—aerospace, electrical equipment and communication, chemicals (including drugs), machinery, and motor vehicles. Moreover, industry expenditures are concentrated on products, not processes. Finally, American R&D investment emphasizes development, not research. This distinction may be ill defined, but nevertheless, a difference does exist between the search for new knowledge (research) and the application of research findings to practice (development).

It will be recalled that the typical American industrial corporation in the early 1900s manufactured a single line of products to be sold in a national market. The firm usually had an operating department to perform each major industrial function. Product diversification was not a business strategy, and output was uncomplicated. Organization was highly centralized: The functional departments were unified by an executive vice-president or an executive committee, who in turn reported to the president, who in turn might or might not report to the chairman of the board of directors.

But firms that adopted product diversification as a business strategy quickly found that their highly centralized structure did not work satisfactorily. These were firms primarily in the industries that were the chief participants in research and development. Thus, the General Electric Company, after two decades of experimenting with its organization, finally had to reorganize its activities along product lines. Just after World War II, the company accomplished its structural reorganization by setting up six major departments—apparatus, lamp, appliances, air conditioning, electronics, and chemicals. Each of these departments was headed by a senior executive who controlled all necessary operations and who was completely responsible for the profit performance of that department. The older functional departments, which remained at the head offices, in effect became advisory and planning departments that reported directly to the president and the chairman of the board. After 1950, General Electric carried this organizational plan even farther by subdividing its six main product departments into more than 70. Managers of these smaller departments presently have almost complete autonomy in directing production and in performing the marketing function. Although several smaller units are grouped under a general divisional manager, these division executives have no staff, presumably so that they will not interfere with the activities and responsibilities of their subordinates. Four new group vice-presidents at the top echelon were appointed to advise the division executives and to confer (as part of an executive committee) with the president and the chairman of the board.

As Alfred D. Chandler has demonstrated, a similar decentralization of structure has occurred in the other industries that have been active in diversifying products as a business strategy. On the other hand, companies in the metals- and agricultural-processing industries have been slow to adopt both the strategy and the organization of decentralization, although there are certainly exceptions to this rule.

Energy Sources

Of course, any discussion of technological change would be incomplete without a consideration of changing energy sources. Much of what has happened since 1920 in this area is summarized in Table 26-4.[9]

It is apparent that the American economy has depended for its energy almost entirely on the mineral fuels; but two developments of modern times stand out clearly. The first is that both crude petroleum and natural gas have become far more important than coal, traditionally the base fuel in an industrial civilization. The second is that coal—which reached its peak as an energy source during World War I, dropped markedly during the 1930s, and then increased to a new high right after World War II—suffered both relatively and absolutely in comparison to other mineral fuels until 1960 and since that time has just about held its own in percentage terms.

Coal has had a major role in world history—a role it will continue to have in the foreseeable future. Due to the probable earlier exhaustion of competing

[9] The table actually understates the growth of energy recovered from coal and other sources, because the unit heat values employed are constant whereas increasing efficiency of utilization has caused them to rise steadily over time. If we assume that the secular rise in efficiency for all mineral sources of energy has been about the same, Table 26-4 gives us a clear picture of the relative importance of the different sources.

TABLE 26–4
Energy Consumption—Total and Per Capita, 1920–1975
(total in trillions, per capita in millions, of British thermal units)

YEAR	ALL ENERGY[1]		NATURAL GAS[2]		COAL[3]		CRUDE PETROLEUM[4]	
	Total	Per capita	Total	Per capita	Total	Per capita	Total	Per capita
1920	19,782	186	827	8	15,504	146	2,634	25
1925	20,899	180	1,212	10	14,706	127	4,156	36
1930	22,288	181	1,969	16	13,639	111	5,652	46
1935	19,107	150	1,974	16	10,634	84	5,499	43
1940	23,908	181	2,726	21	12,535	95	7,487	57
1945	31,541	238	3,973	30	15,972	121	9,619	73
1950	33,992	223	6,150	40	12,913	85	13,489	88
1955	39,703	239	9,232	56	11,540	70	17,524	106
1960	44,569	247	12,699	70	10,140	56	20,067	111
1965	53,343	274	16,098	83	11,908	61	23,241	120
1970	67,143	328	22,029	108	12,698	62	29,537	144
1971	68,698	332	22,819	111	12,043	58	30,570	148
1972	71,946	346	23,025	111	12,426	60	32,966	158
1973	74,755	356	22,712	108	13,294	63	34,852	166
1974	72,933	344	21,733	103	13,182	62	33,467	158
1975[5]	71,078	333	20,173	95	13,376	63	32,701	153

[1] Includes electricity, not shown separately.
[2] Dry gas only. Marketed production minus shrinkage caused by liquids extraction (34 cubic feet per gallon produced).
[3] Includes bituminous coal and lignite and anthracite coal.
[4] Includes petroleum products and, beginning 1950, natural gas liquids.
[5] Estimated.
Source: *Statistical Abstract,* 1976, p. 549.

fossil fuels and the prospects of an economical process of the gasification of coal, some engineers and scientists even predict that one day we will again become more dependent on coal energy. The mechanization of mining operations and the favorable location of major U.S. deposits have kept the nation's per-ton coal costs lower than those of other countries. But as Erich W. Zimmermann once remarked, gasoline—the major petroleum product—"packs a much bigger punch" per pound or per cubic foot than coal does and has therefore become "the great mover."[10] In a vast country like the United States, where flexible transportation facilities are so important and where oil and natural gas are relatively abundant, it is not surprising that these hydrocarbons have gained the position that coal once held in the English economy.

[10] Erich W. Zimmermann, *World Resources and Industries,* Rev. Ed. (New York: Harper & Row, 1951), p. 495.

Although we hear much about the power output of the Tennessee Valley Authority and the great dams of the West, we should note that water power is relatively unimportant, accounting in the early 1960s for no more than 4 percent of the nation's annual supply of energy. The fact is that—although a certain glamour is attached to dams, reservoirs, turbogenerators, and long-distance transmission lines—water power has had difficulties competitively. Around 1880, water was disappearing as a power source but was rescued by the development of hydroelectric plants between 1880 and 1910. After 1900, however, the growing efficiency of fuel power plants appeared to threaten the water wheel and the water turbine. In fact, the number of pounds of coal required to generate a kilowatt-hour fell from 7.05 in 1899 to about 0.90 in the late 1950s.

In the meantime, it became apparent that hydropower was not free simply because it fell from heaven and rolled down steep, natural slopes. Expensive dams and equipment were required to utilize it. Nevertheless, certain forces at work during the last 35 years have enabled water power to develop modestly in competition with fuel power.[11] Old industries grew up where coal supplies were located, but certain new industries—the light metals, for example—have been established where cheap hydroelectric power is available. An increase in the distance of economical transmission—the maximum in the United States is now as great as 500 miles—has made it possible to bring existing urban centers within the orbit of hydroestablishments that were once too far from civilization to be used. For nearly 35 years, the actual quantity of fuel required to generate a kilowatt-hour has declined and the cost of the fuel has risen sharply. All these things have combined to keep water power in the running. Even more important, however, has been the political appeal—apparent even before the New Deal came to power—of the control of entire river systems or watersheds. Integrated watershed control implies multipurpose dams, which in turn represent hydroelectric output. But the number of dam sites is limited, and power plants that originally relied solely on water as an energy source have added steam and auxiliary power as their needs grow.

Of one thing we can be sure: An ever-increasing amount of coal, oil, gas, and water has been converted into electricity (see Map 26-2). At mid-century, more than one-quarter of the coal and practically all of the water power were used to produce electrical energy; roughly 10 percent of the available petroleum and natural gas were used for this purpose. For several decades, the quantity of electricity consumed by American households and business firms has approximately doubled each decade. The most recent estimates of future demand, prepared by regional committees of utility executives under Federal Power Commission auspices, indicate that consumption of electric energy will continue to double each decade at least until the year 1990. Tables 26-5 and 26-6 indicate the fantastic quantities projected as well as the proportions that will probably be accounted for by type of energy source.

Of course, the public-policy question of today is still what it has been since the turn of the twentieth century: Will the United States ultimately deplete its mineral sources of energy? By 1970, the vast tonnages of fuels used in energy production were 530 million tons of coal, 710 million tons of oil, and

[11] Zimmermann, pp. 470–71.

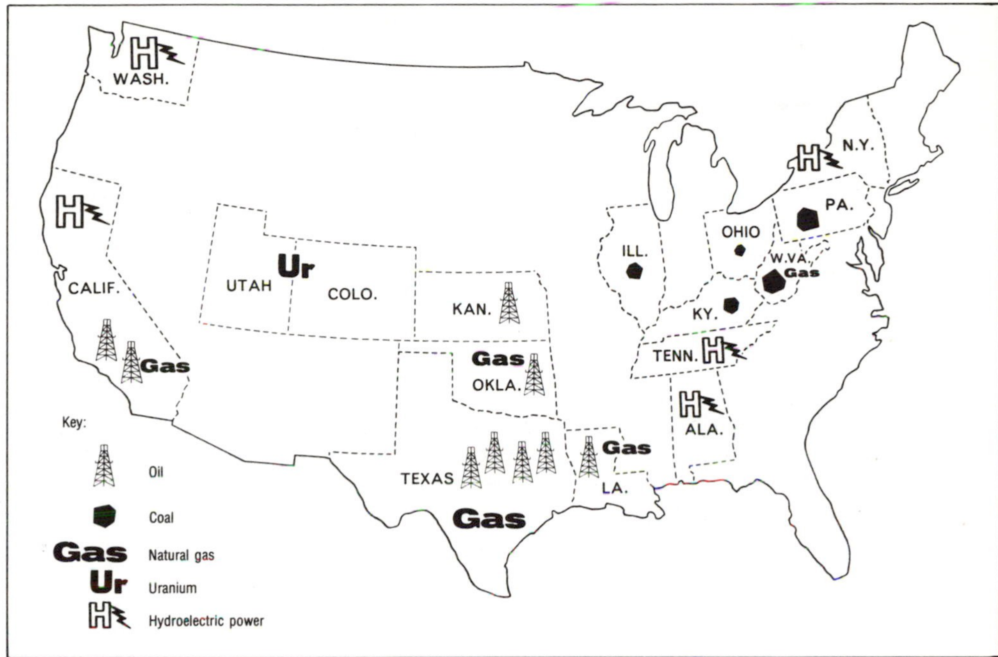

MAP 26–2

Power: Mineral and water sources of electric power fall into three main classes: hydroelectric, fossil fuel (including coal, natural gas, and oil), and nuclear. The map shows only the principal sources of such power.

500 million tons of natural gas. At such rates of usage, the possibility of the ultimate exhaustion of supplies remained a distant but nevertheless a real threat.

Such a possibility was distinctly accented when the Persian Gulf oil-producing nations effectively boycotted the United States in 1973. This not only

TABLE 26–5
Electric Generation by Type of Fuel and Hydropower
(billions of kilowatt-hours)

	Coal	Gas	Oil	Nuclear	Other	Thermal	Hydro	Total
1966	613.5	251.1	78.9	5.5	0.6	949.6	194.7	1,144.3
1970	807.7	325.7	76.9	67.8	3.3	1,281.4	236.1	1,517.5
1975	973.3	390.5	86.15	459.1	5.0	1,914.0	275.4	2,189.4
1980	1,049.1	439.8	79.5	1,210.9	7.3	2,786.6	295.8	3,082.4
1985	1,168.5	494.6	73.4	2,178.8	10.3	3,925.6	308.9	4,234.5
1990	1,309.3	606.2	69.45	3,521.7	12.8	5,519.4	311.9	5,831.3

Source: Federal Power Commission.

TABLE 26–6
Electric Generation by Type of Fuel and Hydropower
(percentage of total)

	Coal	Gas	Oil	Nuclear	Other	Thermal	Hydro
1966	53.6	22.0	6.9	0.48	—	83.0	17.0
1970	53.2	21.5	5.1	4.5	0.2	84.4	15.6
1975	44.5	17.8	3.9	21.0	0.2	87.4	12.6
1980	34.0	14.3	2.6	39.3	0.2	90.4	9.6
1985	27.6	11.7	1.7	51.4	0.2	92.7	7.1
1990	22.45	10.4	1.2	60.4	0.2	94.65	5.35

Source: Computed from data in Table 26-5.

disrupted the economy, but also raised the costs of environmental restrictions. "Conserve energy" immediately became the rallying cry of the American people, and our dependence on foreign sources of oil became painfully clear. Ironically, previous years of quotas and import restrictions—policies which were effected mainly during the 1950s under President Dwight D. Eisenhower—had backfired. Implemented to subsidize American oil producers, with the additional alleged intent of reducing dependence on foreign sources (for the sake of military preparedness), we simply used up our own oil reserves all the faster. After two decades of accelerated domestic production resulting from restrictions on foreign competition, the American economy ultimately faced increasing vulnerability.

When the foreign supply of petroleum was cut off in 1973, chaos was predicted but avoided. However, confusion and inconvenience were not. If prices had been free to move in an unrestricted manner, motorists would have escaped the long lines and hours of waiting and frustration precipitated by government gasoline rationing. Also avoided would have been the closing of schools in Denver and elsewhere for lack of heating fuel.

In general, however, the gasoline shortage proved more troublesome than the fuel-oil shortage, because at the outset the Federal Energy Office (now called the Federal Energy Administration) allowed the price of fuel oil to rise each month. As prices rose, consumers responded by using less fuel oil and tolerating lower temperatures in their homes and offices. Eventually, price adjustments also "corrected" the gasoline "shortage"—in reality, excess demand—but the Federal Energy Office did not allow gasoline prices to rise as sharply as fuel-oil prices. At artificially restrictive lower prices, suppliers held gasoline in reserve. Customers complained, and their frustrations grew; but the needed price adjustment was not permitted for nearly a year. When the price was finally raised, the queues rapidly disappeared in gasoline stations.

The role of prices in correcting such short-run rationing problems hopefully has become more apparent to the American people. What is not widely known, however, is that as the relative price of a key natural resource such as oil increases, the amount of global (proved) reserves also increases.[12] As prices

[12] Global reserves or proved reserves are based on the amounts of a resource that could be taken out of the earth, given the current state of the art, technology, and conditions of profitability.

rise, it becomes more profitable to discover and mine more remote reserves. We have consumed a tremendous quantity of petroleum since 1930, and yet we have more proved reserves available today than we did then. Consequently, as oil prices rise, greater sources of supply are activated; of course, higher prices discourage consumption and urge users to seek lower-cost alternative forms of energy.

In short, Americans are not likely to drastically reduce their demands for oil and other older energy sources. Although the prognosis of the late 1970s suggests a rapidly increasing reliance on nuclear-powered generators, a number of problems delayed nuclear-plant construction in the 1960s and have continued to increase the cost of nuclear power in the 1970s. Chief among these have been delays in licensing and siting problems near load centers, as some people raise the spectre of a nuclear "accident" and the consequent massive release of radioactive materials.

Even though evidence is overwhelming that a large nuclear plant produces no more radioactive emissions than a large light bulb, residents near a potential site often protest loudly against the construction. The same concern is endlessly expressed over leakage of fissionable materials into nearby streams. There is simply no solid evidence to substantiate the existence of these dangers under modern conditions of construction. Present estimates suggest that by 1990 nuclear power must supply more than 50 percent of U.S. electrical energy requirements. Restriction of expansion of capacity by environmentalists threatens economic breakdown in some communities.

The political battles over nuclear energy are not likely to subside in the near future, but clearly in the long run the hope of finding noncontroversial energy sources lies in technological advances.

27

Markets and Industrial Concentration

GOODS AND SERVICES

Earlier discussions of competition among manufacturers and other businesses suggest a kind of rivalry that is always present in the business world. Any business, when confronted with evidence of practices that limit competition or at least cushion its impact on competitors, inevitably rejoins that it "competes for the consumer's dollar." Economists have always recognized this proposition as having a certain validity, but it is wise to appraise the assertion carefully and acknowledge sources of monopoly.

Taking the broadest possible view, we can accept the idea that each entrepreneur does, in fact, contend with all other entrepreneurs for expenditures of household units. We know that consumers will make certain minimum outlays in several main categories of expenditures; that is, each family must spend part of its income on food, part on clothing, part on housing, and so on. But does a lack of competition for the consumer's dollar within categories of expenditure give the power to sellers to charge "monopoly" or "oligopoly" prices? Does a lack of competition within these categories permit sellers to market poor quality merchandise on unwary buyers?

Although the answer to both these questions appears to be "yes," close analysis suggests the opposite. For instance, both an electric refrigerator and a vacuum cleaner provide service flows that enable the members of a household unit to avoid expending energy. The refrigerator makes it unnecessary to empty water pans and chip ice with a pick; the vacuum makes it unnecessary

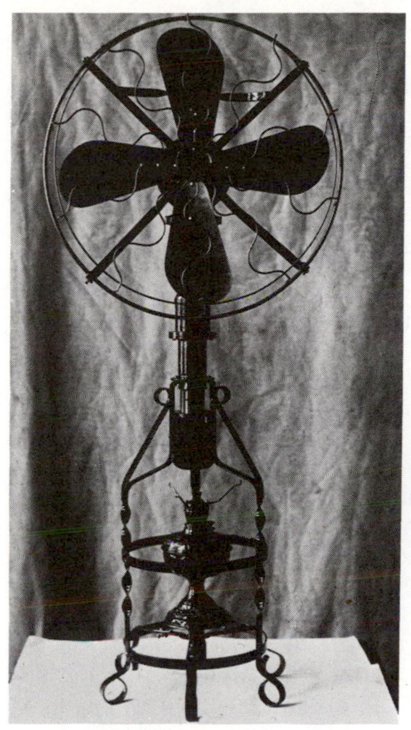

Air conditioning — BEFORE: ***Until electricity made its inroads in the 1890s, this kind of kerosene-powered fan cooled overheated Americans by redistributing rather than eliminating hot summer air.***

to wield a broom or a rug beater.[1] But the difference in the operations performed by the two appliances does not mean that there is no competition between them. From the point of view of the individual allocator of income, one way of conserving effort may be clearly preferable to the other. The fact remains that people have a wide range of alternatives to choose from. In this sense, there is a close, direct rivalry among producers of goods that seem to be widely separated in the scale of choices. Thus, a rough count shows more than 250 manufacturers of nationally sold household appliances in the so-called labor-saving category—enough to assure competition in the classical sense.[2]

[1] Some may contend that we consciously choose among certain labor-saving devices—for example, between kitchen blenders and electric drills for the home workshop—but that other devices such as refrigerators, stoves, washing machines, and vacuum cleaners are "necessities" and do not enter the consumer's economic calculus. Within the past two generations, such items have been taken for granted in a way our ancestors would have found incredible. Yet we in *this* generation can opt for more or less of these services; consider the family that debates the question of buying a new refrigerator with more freezer space, a no-frost freezer, and an ice-cube dispenser or a new cooking unit with a self-cleaning oven and thermostatically controlled burners. Economics is the study of rules governing endless choices.

[2] Over the past half-century, it appears that appliances have also competed with the manual labor of domestics, who formerly performed such household chores as washing, ironing, and rug-beating.

Also, we should not overlook the fact that the service flow from clothing satisfies not only obvious physiological needs, but helps to satisfy the "need" for recognition, exhibition, and status. Clearly, this explains the efforts of sellers to "differentiate" a product—that is, to create in the minds of buyers reasons for preferring *their* product over that of rival sellers. The concept of product differentiation is more meaningful if we think of differentiation as an attempt on the part of sellers to enlarge the constellation of wants toward which the service flow of a product is directed.

The readiness with which one service flow may be substituted for another therefore leads to much closer competition among functionally dissimilar goods than we would imagine at first. On the demand side of markets, another force exists that stimulates a vigorous, churning rivalry. The growth of the institution of consumer credit and of modern forms of urban residential credit have enabled the household unit to economize with greater precision than was possible before World War I. Since the early 1920s, more and more household units have become able to refine their immediate acceptance of service flows from durable goods in the present and to plan future acceptance of these flows with some precision—for the simple reason that durable goods do not have to be paid for in one lump sum. A much larger number of bidders consequently enters the market for manufactured goods and houses, thereby stimulating competition on the buyer's side.

Of course, ignorance of the choices available may lessen competition, but competition can exist despite a lack of consumer awareness. To be sure,

Air conditioning*—AFTER: *Modern air conditioning has made city living more tolerable. Originally promoted by electric utilities to smooth out the summer slump in the demand for electric current, air conditioning now leads to summer peak demands that threaten brownouts and even blackouts.

American manufacturers endlessly strive to develop new products and lodge them permanently in the marketplace—in the 1970s gambling as much as $15 billion a year on the outcome. But if anything is clear about product innovation it is that neither business firms nor households are likely to be convinced to buy something they do not want. Roughly five out of every six items introduced into supermarket channels each year fail to sell. Consequently, business emphasis has shifted away from technological efforts to make old products perform better and toward meeting the basic market demands of the consumer. Market testing alone can cost $30,000–$300,000 per item, and market-tested products can fail even when they are backed by massive advertising campaigns on national television.

On rare occasions, a totally new product is introduced. But Polaroid cameras, Wankel engines, and Xerox copiers are not commonplace. It is now clear that products like Gillette's Trac-II razor, Eastman Kodak's cartridge-loaded Instamatic camera, and General Foods Corporation's Maxim coffee have enjoyed rapid and continuing success largely because they are much more convenient to use than old forms of the same product. Yet more often than not, such attempts fail. The example of the Edsel is legendary. No less prestigious a

Domestic joy: Early radio appealed to listeners and had become the chief living-room entertainment by the late 1920s.

firm than duPont lost $100 million on Corfam, simply because people would not accept artificial leather shoes despite their porosity and low-care requirements. General Foods dropped an estimated $15 million on a cereal containing freeze-dried strawberries because children rejected the berries as "mushy and soggy."[3] There are those, of course, who argue that the rejection process is wasteful of resources and that it raises the costs of accepted products. The alternative is a system in which political commissars make choices for people, as is done in the Soviet Union; yet the Soviets envy the West primarily for its great array of attractive, well-made consumer goods.

MARKETING METHODS AND THE CONSUMER

No description of competition or monopoly would be complete without an account of the marketing institutions which bring consumers into contact with their alternative product choices. Before World War I, the dominance of the orthodox wholesaler in the marketing process was seriously threatened. "Large-scale retailing" had made its successful appearance, the independent retailer was already being pressed to operate more efficiently, and manufacturers were determining the best ways to present their products to a public with whom they had no direct contact. Pervading the entire distribution process was a growing respect for the effectiveness of advertising.

Wholesale Consumer Goods

In Chapter 21, we learned that manufacturers in the late nineteenth century began to disregard the wholesaler and to sell directly to retail outlets. The "general merchandise" wholesaler, with a warehouse of heterogeneous goods in many product lines, had declined rapidly before World War I and was no longer to be a significant figure in the marketing process. As of 1920, however, the full-service, full-line wholesale house that furnished goods in one particular line, such as hardware, groceries, or drugs, to retailers over great regions and even nationally, was still in a commanding position. Perhaps the major trend in wholesaling over the past 45 to 50 years has been the lessening relative importance of these great houses and the increasing relative importance of the specialty wholesaler, or "short-line" distributor. The specialty firm, which confines its selling activity to a portion of the products within a single line of merchandise, has fitted into the changing scene because it provides a high degree of expert knowledge from which small retailers can benefit.

We must not conclude that the decline in importance of the traditional wholesale house meant a reduction in the total flow of goods through wholesale channels. There has simply been a change in the way goods move from manufacturers (or from farm and mine) to the retailer. During the 1920s, there was a substantial change in the wholesale *structure* as the wholesalers lost ground to manufacturer's sales branches, agents and brokers, assemblers

[3] "New Products: The Push Is on Marketing," *Business Week* (March 4, 1972), pp. 72–77.

and rural buyers, bulk tank stations, and chain-store warehouses, in that order. Since 1929, the relative position of the different types of establishments has remained so nearly identical that for our purposes we need not trace the developmental changes. The total volume of wholesale trade has fluctuated with changes in business activity, moving secularly neither upward nor downward.

Wholesale houses have continued since 1929 to handle about two-fifths of the wholesale business as measured in net sales. This group is still the most important performer of wholesale functions, but within it the old order has disappeared from most product lines. A few of the great, traditional names remain, including Belknap and Simmons in hardware, Liggett and Reid, Murdock in groceries, and Butler Brothers and Rice-Stix in dry goods. In fact, the full-line wholesale houses have retained most of the hardware business and more than one-half of the drug business. But inroads have consistently been made into the full-line wholesaler's territory—to some extent by the limited-function companies (drop shippers, cash-and-carry wholesalers, and wagon distributors), but largely by the specialty firms that serve small geographic areas. The specialty wholesalers handle an assortment of items within one product line (coffee, tea, and condiments instead of "groceries"; cutlery instead of "hardware"). They can furnish fresh or new goods rapidly and they know their particular field of merchandising thoroughly.

The nature of wholesaling has been affected by the great structural shifts in retailing. It has been the growth in the size of the retail firm that has brought about the present-day orientation of the marketing process toward the manufacturer–retailer axis.

Large-scale Retailing

Department stores were well established by 1900 and were popularly accepted in the first decade of the century. Between 1910 and 1920, the mail-order companies began to make great gains. By 1919, the chain stores showed signs of being a potent marketing form, and in the 1920s they became a major force in retailing. How have these types of stores fared since?

It is all too easy to think of the department store as a fading institution, but we must not yet count "the big store" out as a merchandising forum. During the 1920s and 1930s, department stores maintained a constant proportion of retail sales, indicating that they were just about holding their own in the economy. World War II with its supply shortages restored some of the advantages of shopping under one roof, and department-store business increased to about 10 percent of retail sales—a gain of perhaps two percentage points. Since 1947, department stores, although not without a struggle, have moved slowly back to their pre-World War II position. Increasing traffic congestion in the downtown areas of cities, the rise of suburban shopping centers, and the expansion of variety chains and mail-order companies into broader fields have been the chief factors working against the independent department store. Yet many large stores have shown unexpected resilience in the face of changing competitive situations. Ownership groups have bought control of stores in several cities, thereby bringing the advantages of tremendous buying power to many of the independent stores that have continued to operate under their well-known old names. More recently, alert managements have followed the suburban trend by establishing branches, some of them rivaling the central-city store in volume. To fight the discount houses, with their emphasis on plain décor and a minimum of service, department stores have either met discount-house prices in their old locations or opened new and less pretentious outlets for the purpose of discounting. A final irony of this competition has been the opening of glossy, new central-city stores by the discounters; like every other major retailing form before them, they have finally succumbed to the compulsion to become respectable.

Mail-order houses, as such, have fared better in recent years than we might think, but only because they have changed their business methods to suit the times. Since 1929, the mail-order business has been fairly constant at roughly 1 percent of all retail sales, despite the disappearance of many of the reasons for ordering from a catalog. A number of companies specializing in a single line or a few items have sprung up. The application of new advertising techniques to catalog illustrations and the opening of "catalog stores" in small towns have helped the older houses maintain their sales volume. But the two great mail-order firms have also completely changed their sales methods to fit the time. In 1925, Montgomery Ward established its first retail store in Marysville, Kansas, and Sears, Roebuck quickly tried the same experiment. At the end of a decade and a half, these retail stores numbered in the hundreds, and more than one-half of the "mail-order" business was conducted over a counter. At the end of World War II, Sears boldly expanded by building great department stores in readily accessible sections of major cities. Montgomery Ward, because it was timorous in carrying out its expansion program, lost ground to such an extent that in 1950 its sales were less than one-half of the sales of its major competitor. During the ensuing decade, Sears, Roebuck and Company became the fifth largest employer in the United States, with a dollar volume of retailing of more than $4 billion a year—a retail sales figure exceeded only by A&P. In 1971, Sears was still the fifth largest employer in the country, and its sales of $10 billion were nearly twice the sales of A&P and Safeway, which were second and third on the retailer list, respectively.

Mention of the great grocery chain reminds us that the past 35 years have witnessed a widespread acceptance of the chain principle of merchandising. Between 1919 and 1929, chain sales rose from an estimated 4 percent of retail sales to slightly less than 25 percent—a proportion that has not varied much since in good times or bad. Since 1929, however, the number of retail units in chain organizations has declined, possibly by as much as one-third, as the trend has been toward fewer stores and greater volume. There has also been some shift in the use of the chain form in various lines of business. The opening of department stores by Sears, Roebuck and Montgomery Ward has been reflected statistically in a definite spread of chains to the department-store, dry-goods, and general-merchandise fields. Chain-store growth has been especially marked in drugs, shoes, women's ready-to-wear, and jewelry, whereas only moderate gains have been made in variety merchandise, food, and automobile accessories and equipment. At the same time, a high degree of concentration has developed within chain-store groups, as the six largest concerns in each field have attained a preponderance of chain sales in the general merchandise (department store), variety, grocery, and drug lines.

Chains have unquestionably found a place in American economic life from which they will not soon be dislodged. The principle of the chain has been adopted by some independent retailers. In an effort to obtain some of the advantages of vertical integration, independent retailers in most lines pioneered by the chains have achieved some success in establishing informal buying pools and voluntary chains. Nevertheless, the historical trend toward distributor integration was slowed greatly, if not actually halted, 30 years ago. In concentrating on the spectacular growth in *absolute* volume of the big merchandisers, we should not forget that their *relative* strength has not changed much since before the Great Depression.

Limited-line stores, widely varying in size and under independent ownership, have continued to conduct more than one-half of the retail business in the United States. Independents have located in the suburban shopping centers and malls that have sprung up so conspicuously since World War II. Although the chains were pioneers in the development of the supermarket, independents have competed successfully as supermarkets in the grocery business, and their success has often led to expansion into a local group of several stores. Supermarket merchandising has also been successful in metropolitan-area stores selling higher-priced goods such as clothing, appliances, and even automobiles. In an age in which deference is paid to the specialist, specialists in the retail field have been able to hold their own, because they—like the large-scale retailers—can successfully differentiate their product.

Product Differentiation

At the beginning of this chapter, it was suggested that products are sometimes differentiated to enlarge the constellation of service flows they provide. Differentiation may be achieved by adjusting the conditions surrounding the sale of the product or by varying the quality or appearance of the product itself.

Thus, a good is differentiated spatially if prospective customers are able to economize physical effort to obtain it. Independent retailers have traditionally operated neighborhood stores to reap the rewards of spatial differentiation, and they are still able to do so in suburban shopping centers and malls, which contain parking space for thousands of automobiles. In other respects, retailers may be equally successful in differentiating their establishment and the products they sell. They can give "tone" to their establishment; carry the goods of nationally known manufacturers or "private" lines; and appeal to customers who prefer a certain personal quality when dealing with merchants or who simply wish to be waited on in anonymity.

The successful differentiation of a product sold in the nationwide market ordinarily requires large advertising outlays. Consumers must be persuaded that there is a good reason to buy one brand of cigarettes, cornflakes or washing machines rather than another. Advertising is profitable to the firm if it convinces buyers that one brand of any item is clearly preferable to another. Whether this is socially beneficial or wasteful is another matter, but as early as

1910 the annual volume of advertising expenditure reached $1 billion. By 1920, this figure was $2 billion; by 1929, the estimated outlay had passed $2.5 billion. Advertising declined greatly during the 1930s to an annual average of perhaps $1.7 billion, only to rise rapidly in the 1940s and early 1950s to nearly $8 billion in 1953. A decade later, advertising outlays passed the $12 billion mark, and in 1976 they reached over $33 billion.

One of the advantages of large size to a manufacturing firm is that the firm can afford to spend great sums on advertising to gain acceptance of its product on a national or regional scale. The requirement to advertise is therefore an inducement to a firm to achieve optimum size.

But this very fact also makes it possible for small retailers to compete successfully with large ones. Much of the impact on buyer consciousness has been made through the manufacturer's efforts; the items that the retailer sells have been largely differentiated by high-powered national advertising. Independent retailers need only inform the public of their existence and depend on their location and the tone of their establishment to bring them a profitable volume of trade. Thus, the successful differentiation of products by the largest firms in oligopolistic industries helps to account for the unexpected strength of the small outlet in its recent competitive struggle with the large retailers.

CONCENTRATION IN INDUSTRY

Judging from the amount of space devoted to the subject in economic journals, monographs, and textbooks, the concentration of industry continues to be regarded as a major social problem. Especially during the 1930s, when the characteristics of American capitalism were being examined with unusual intensity, professional economists were in almost unanimous agreement about the growing evils of monopoly power.[4]

It is understandable that observers of the Depression era became concerned about the "decline of competition." In the first place, the decade of the 1920s had brought a wave of business consolidation that was comparable in some respects to the merger movement of 1897–1904. Second, the best figures available indicated that a startlingly large proportion of corporate wealth was concentrated in the hands of a few firms. One study concluded that in 1933, 57 percent of all corporate wealth outside the financial field was controlled by 200 firms. Third, new and subtle ways of reducing the pangs of price competition seemed to be gaining popularity. Among these, the most effective was to organize all the producers in a field into manufacturers' institutes or trade associations. Finally, and most importantly, it was apparent during the Depression that prices were stickier and output declines were more severe in those industries where a few firms were dominant.

[4] During the first flurry of excitement over growing monopoly power, which came at the turn of the century, the most respected economists considered the combination movement a normal step toward achieving economies of scale. It was the popular journalists who feared the new corporate giants who alerted their readers to the danger of monopoly.

"Merger for Oligopoly" instead of "Merger for Monopoly"

In Chapter 19, we discussed several ways of achieving and maintaining a measure of monopoly power. In practice, largely as a consequence of the Sherman Law, the *safest* way of gaining market power has been to grow big by consolidation. In addition, consolidation has almost always been a highly effective way of achieving market supremacy. The third great wave of mergers, which began toward the end of World War I, had largely exhausted itself by 1929. Only a few important combinations were to be formed in the 1930s; the market structures of the major industries were almost completely determined.

George J. Stigler has pointed out a fundamental characteristic of this third merger movement that will help us to place it in proper historical perspective.[5] He has shown that during the first two waves of combination, the resulting firms attained very high percentages—seldom less than 50 percent—of the output of their industries. The major objective of such combinations was a high degree of market control, although pure monopolies rarely resulted.[6] In post-World War I years, most of the merged firms secured much smaller percentages of an industry's output, because mergers usually took place among companies that were smaller than the dominant company in the industry. In the meantime, the dominant firm, which had frequently held a partial monopolistic position, gradually came to control a smaller share of the industry's production. The steel industry best exemplified this trend. United States Steel's share of ingot capacity dropped as Bethlehem and Republic sharply increased their shares through mergers. The shift from partial monopoly markets to oligopolies was also notable in cement, cans, petroleum, agricultural instruments, and glass.[7]

Some industries that had approached the competitive norm, in that they had been composed of large numbers of firms, became oligopolies during the third merger movement. Dairy products and packaged foods were the outstanding examples of this kind of rapid change in market structure, but liquors and beverages, paper and printing, machinery and machine tools, and even motion pictures were also eventually priced in markets characterized by "few" sellers.

Oligopoly and the "New" Competition

"Merger for oligopoly" had achieved unquestioned success in major industries. Yet even as the nation's economists viewed the problem with alarm some 35 years ago, progressively greater industrial concentration had come to at least a temporary halt. A new crop of mergers in the 1950s, however, again brought cries of alarm from academic halls and courtrooms, but the rate of

[5] George J. Stigler, "Monopoly and Oligopoly by Merger," *American Economic Review,* **XL**:2 (May 1950), pp. 23–33.

[6] Recalling the reasons given for the first and second combination movements in Chapter 19, readers should be sure that they understand why such high degrees of control were considered necessary.

[7] Stigler, "Monopoly and Oligopoly," p. 31.

merger leveled off in the early and mid-1960s, easing the concern of professional antitrusters.

Contrary to widely held beliefs, there is no overpowering evidence that monopoly power has increased over the past three decades. Large firms have grown larger, to be sure, but in an expanding economy small firms have grown larger, too, and may even have increased their relative share of their respective markets to some degree.

But the change from monopolistic to oligopolistic markets and the arrest of the trend toward concentration of productive capacity in a few firms may nonetheless have left us with an economy tethered by monopolistic restrictions. Consider the findings presented in a report prepared by the U.S. Bureau of the Census, *Concentration Ratios in Manufacturing Industry,* 1967. Table 27-1 lists 16 industries in which 61 percent or more of total shipments in 1967 were concentrated in four firms. Nevertheless, in general, the concentration ratios in these industries have drifted downward.

Yet even as observers were becoming sanguine about the combination movement in America, a new creation of the U.S. economy—the conglomerate—was emerging. As we have seen, product diversification as a business strategy has long characterized certain major industries, and multiproduct firms were well-established long before. But in the past, diversification had usually resulted from the logical extension of product lines either to create new demands for existing products or to make new uses of materials developed for existing products. The conglomerate of the 1960s and 1970s was *finan-*

TABLE 27–1

Percentage of Value of Shipments Accounted for by the Four Largest U.S. Companies in 1947, 1958, and 1967

Industry	1947	1958	1967
Primary aluminum	100	[a]	91
Locomotives and parts	91	95	[a]
Electric lamps (bulbs)	92	92	88
Telephone and telegraph equipment	—	92	[a]
Flat glass	—	92	[b]
Soap and detergents	79	90	64
Gypsum products	85	88	78
Steam engines and turbines	88	87	78
Cereal breakfast foods	79	83	82
Metal cans	78	80	70
Cigarettes	90	79	[a]
Aluminum rolling and drawing	94	78	64
Synthetic fibers	78	78	79
Computing and related machines	69	77	[b]
Motor vehicles and parts	56	75	61
Tires and inner tubes	77	74	71

Source: *Concentration Ratios in Manufacturing Industry,* 1958 (Washington, D.C.: U.S. Government Printing Office, 1962, 1966). 1967 Census of Manufactures, U.S. Department of Commerce, February 1971.

[a]Withheld to avoid disclosing figures for individual companies.

[b]Not available.

cially motivated and *financially* oriented: Its fundamental purpose was to maximize the value of the common stock of a firm intent on acquiring, through merger, companies with equity securities felt to be underpriced in the market. Thus, conglomerate merger is the merger of firms in noncompeting lines of endeavor with no apparent horizontal or vertical economic relationships. A characteristic of the conglomerate is its management organization. A small, elite headquarters staff attends to such general matters as financial planning, capital allocations, legal and accounting tasks, and operations research. Operating managers, motivated by handsome stock options, are usually given wide latitude in regulating their subsidiaries.

Thus, Ling-Temco-Vought, one of the first and most successful companies of its type, began in 1958 as a small firm called Ling Electronic, with annual sales of less than $7 million. During the next ten years, Ling acquired or merged with Temco Aircraft, Chance-Vought, Okonite, Wilson and Company, Wilson Sporting Goods Company, the Greatamerica Corporation, and some 24 other companies. Its revenues in 1968 were close to $3 billion. When LTV acquired the Jones and Laughlin Steel Company in 1969, the merger meant that two corporations in the list of the nation's 100 largest companies were combining to make LTV the fourteenth largest company in the United States.[8] Comparably spectacular results have been achieved by other conglomerates, such as Gulf and Western Industries, International Telephone and Telegraph, Litton Industries, Boise Cascade, and the "Automatic" Sprinkler Corporation. Although each conglomerate has been plagued with both financial and managerial difficulties from time to time, as a group they have maintained much of the glamour and excitement associated with fast-paced financial action. Yet images of ruthless capitalism and irresponsible financing continue to crop up, and some business people are trying to replace the pejorative word "conglomerate" with the more neutral term "congeneric."

Whatever we call them, conglomerates have not simplified the problem of antitrust in the United States. They unquestionably add to the concentration of business assets in the hands of progressively fewer companies. Thus, in 1969, 31 companies disappeared from *Fortune*'s list of the top 500 corporations; 26 of these were absorbed by other companies. Conglomeration was a major cause of the growing concentration of head offices; today, over 80 percent of the assets of the top 200 manufacturing firms are concentrated in only six states: New York, California, Michigan, Pennsylvania, Ohio, and Illinois. Yet a persuasive case, supported by the data in Table 27-1, can be made for the proposition that the creative energy of the conglomerates has actually stimulated and revised competition in many industries. Conglomerates often pick up marginal producers and fuse them with new capital, new ideas, and forward-looking management. Moreover, the threat of takeover unquestionably motivates the managers of some sleepy, near-moribund companies to reactivate their own people and enter into competition more vigorously.

[8] Richard W. McLaren, then Assistant Attorney General for antitrust, obtained an injunction against LTV halting the final merger of the two companies. In 1971, pursuant to a consent decree, LTV agreed to divest itself of Braniff Airlines and other assets as a condition of merger with Jones and Laughlin.

There is simply no doubt that sufficient concentration exists in manufacturing industries of key importance to permit oligopolistic power, as orthodox economic theory defines it. How serious a problem of public policy confronts us? The answer to this question depends on the reply to a further question. Granted the high degree of concentration, is there still effective competition among producers? Classical economists have concluded that, except in unusual circumstances, consumers need not fear the power of any seller, because they will always be protected by the inexorable forces of the marketplace. However, the implication of much of the recent literature on imperfectly competitive markets is that the built-in protective mechanism of the competitive process is very weak.

So we are confronted with a paradox. By any measure we choose to take, the American consumer's position has progressively improved over the past half-century. But how *can* this be true in an economy weighted down with monopolistic restrictions? Despite the prevalence of oligopoly, how have more and more of the world's goods and services been made available to consumers? Part of the answer has already been alluded to in the discussion of retailing, but basically the answer to this question appears to rest on the fact that—especially since 1939—interindustry competition and, to a lesser extent, competition among products and processes *within* certain industries has caused oligopolistic power to wane. The demand for a firm's products today is not as stable as it used to be, because the alternative (substitute) products of firms in *other* industries are becoming a greater part of the competition.[9] So, counting only the firms within a particular "industry" tells us very little. Instead, we must count *categories of uses* for the output of an industry, considering the products of other industries that directly compete within these categories. This is a more complicated process because it requires an understanding of many varied technologies.

INDUSTRY: 1921 TO THE PRESENT

Intercompetition: The Aluminum Case

Before World War II, the Aluminum Company of America was the classroom example of monopoly in a nationwide market. Since World War II, this industry has been the most definitive example of an oligopoly.

It is possible to speak of a demand for "primary aluminum," but primary aluminum includes over 100 wrought and casting alloys in many different shapes and innumerable lengths and thicknesses. In comparing the demand for these alloys with the demands for the other metals, we must first specify

[9] The question of interproduct and interindustry competition received considerable attention in the early 1950s. See David E. Lilienthal, *Big Business: A New Era* (New York: Harper & Row, 1952), pp. 47–94; Sumner H. Slichter, "The Growth of Competition," *Atlantic Monthly* (November 1953), pp. 66–70; A.D.H. Kaplan, *Big Enterprise in the Competitive System* (Washington, D.C.: Brookings Institution, 1953); and Edward S. Mason, "The New Competition," *The Yale Review* (Autumn 1953), pp. 37–48.

categories of uses. To be specific about the competition of aluminum with other metals in terms of uses, we will consider the category of electrical cable and conductors. It is well known that aluminum and copper compete in this use, but it is not enough simply to observe this fact. The essence of the competition lies in the "bundle of properties" of each of the two metals. The two bundles have marked likenesses and differences.[10] Both copper and aluminum exhibit high electrical conductivity, but the specific gravity of aluminum is slightly less than one-third that of copper, so the mass conductivity of aluminum is twice that of copper. Thus, a steel-reinforced aluminum cable, both stronger and lighter than an electrically equivalent copper cable, can be used in longer spans with fewer supporting structures. On the basis of aluminum and copper prices prevalent in the last two decades, copper has lost the high-voltage, transmission-line business. At the other extreme, copper with its higher electrical conductivity still has a decided advantage over aluminum where wire of fine sizes is used and space must be conserved. Between the two extremes, there is a vigorous, persistent competition on a pure cost basis—the costs of product design, investment in tools and dies, and so on. Large motor windings, power and feeder cable, and bus bars in central power stations are alternatively made from either material. In this use, four firms in the copper industry and their copper and brass fabricating subsidiaries are direct rivals of the four major aluminum companies.

Now we will consider another use category. In the field of die castings, aluminum alloys have greatly supplanted zinc castings, which have long been dominant. In this field, there is also competition with the brasses and, more and more, with alloys of magnesium and the plastics. If we add sand and permanent-mold castings to this use category, we must include almost any metal that can be melted—gray and malleable iron and cast steel being the chief additions to the competition, which is decided (once weight, strength, and finish have been considered) on a basis of costs, including those of dies and machining.

The rivalry between aluminum and the steels is keen in the manufacture of truck, van, and trailer bodies (where magnesium and wood are also alternative materials) and in certain construction uses. In making truck bodies, the competition beween aluminum and steel involves a balancing of manufacturing costs and costs in use; the higher cost of aluminum bodies is generally much more than offset by the greater average pay loads, reduced license fees, and increased tire mileage that result from the lower weight of the product. In construction uses, the cost advantage may turn on savings in maintenance, as in the case of industrial windows.

As we proceed to examine the main use categories of aluminum, the other metals appear and reappear; as unlikely a competitor as lead is an alternate material for at least two uses (collapsible tubes and cable coverings). The plastics also reappear; wood, rubber, fiberglass, and even conventional building facings like brick and stone enter the system of alternatives.

In sum, if we consider interindustry competition, the number of competing firms rapidly moves from "few" to "many," but two exceptions should be

[10] Kaplan, *Big Enterprise,* p. 19.

noted. First, even after interindustry competition has been taken into account, rivalry may be limited to a few firms. For one use—for instance, castings—the competition is with 100 or more producers of primary materials outside the aluminum industry, but for another use—such as conductors—the number of competitors may be reduced to four outside the industry. It appears, however, that as we cut across industry lines, the conditions of rivalry differ greatly from those of intraindustry competition. The managers of firms usually cannot have the technological or accounting knowledge that enables them to predict the reactions of other-industry rivals as well as they can predict those of rivals within the industry.

A further objection may be that after all such considerations, the aluminum industry is left with a hard monopolistic core. Although there is an ever-growing list of alternative materials, aluminum is still economically necessary in the manufacture of structural parts for aircraft. Many of the alloys commonly employed in aircraft manufacture have a host of applications; but the high-strength alloy that is used for the skin of an airplane has few other uses, and there is no feasible alternative material for airplane skins. It is conceivable that the companies in the industry could collude, tacitly or explicitly, in discriminating against airplane manufacturing companies, especially in view of the fact that aluminum from the secondary (used) market is not suitable for aircraft. It seems unlikely that discrimination to maintain a monopolistic position in such a small market would be worthwhile, but this is a fact that has to be ascertained. To say the least, the problem of monopoly in the aluminum industry has been narrowed to manageable proportions.

Although we could trace similar examples in industry after industry and arrive at similar conclusions, we still could not assert with complete assurance that interproduct and interindustry competition provide adequate protection against monopolistic power. *The point is that simply counting the number of producers within an industry is a poor way to evaluate the degree of competition in a market.*

Two final comments are in order. First, competitive forces, such as the ones we have just examined, work over long periods of time. It may require years for a change to be made from one process to another or from one material to another. In assessing the merits of a competitive system, we cannot base our judgment on the possibility of temporary abnormal profits. Second, after making allowances for interindustry and interproduct competition, it is possible that the monopolistic core remaining in some industries may still be large. Again it is a question of the facts. For nearly a century, the steels have had no close competition for a large number of applications in which weight, strength, and durability are of primary importance; rails, heavy structural members, pressure vessels, and heavy machinery are some examples. Even today, the marginal effect of competition on the steel industry is much smaller than the effect on the competing industries. For example, if all automobile license plates presently made of steel were to be made of another material, the loss to the steel industry would be approximately 0.02 percent of average annual output in recent years. But if aluminum were to gain this business for any one year, it would mean an increase in output of nearly 1 percent.

Recent Antitrust Policy

If the previous argument makes sense, a reevaluation of American antitrust policy is in order. It may be that we have paid too much attention to the bogey of concentration and not enough attention to the necessity of finding hard cores of monopoly and excising them.

Since 1937, the courts have taken the view expressed in the preceding section in only one major case. After Thurman W. Arnold became head of the antitrust division of the Justice Department, a vigorous program of antitrust prosecution was instituted that continued after Arnold's resignation. Between 1937 and 1948, more prosecutions were begun than in the entire history of the Sherman Act before 1937, and the cases instituted were largely directed toward established oligopolies. Emphasis was placed on dissolution, divorcement, and divestiture cases—that is, on the actual breaking up of industrial concentration in the old "trust busting" sense.[11] But although the government won most of its major cases, the penalties imposed by the courts were mild — for the simple reason that drastic penalties would have resulted in units of uneconomic size.

The case against the Aluminum Company of America provides the best example of the perplexities that have confronted the courts in modern antitrust actions. In 1937, a complaint was instituted against ALCOA alleging that it monopolized the manufacture and sale of virgin aluminum and fabricated shapes. In 1942, the District Court found the defendant company not guilty, but in March 1945, this decision was reversed by the Circuit Court of Appeals, Judge Learned Hand giving the opinion.[12] Judge Hand ruled that ALCOA, which at the time of the trial made and fabricated over 90 percent of the virgin aluminum manufactured in the United States, was a monopoly. Turning away from the old dictum that "mere size is no offense," Judge Hand ruled that size, in the sense of market control, was the very essence of the offense. Even though the company had engaged in no immoral or predatory competitive practices, it was still in violation of the Sherman Act if, through normal business methods, it controlled most of the output of the industry. But having pronounced ALCOA a monopoly, the court refused to order dissolution of the company or divestiture of its assets. Instead, the court recommended that remedial measures be withheld until the effect on competition of the government disposal of war-surplus aluminum plants could be determined. Further attempts by the government to force ALCOA to divest itself of assets met with little more success. In 1950, with Kaiser and Reynolds firmly established in the industry, the Court held that competition had not been established in the aluminum industry; but the only relief granted was to require persons who held stock in both ALCOA and ALTED, the Canadian subsidiary, to divest themselves of the stock of one corporation or the other.

[11] Walter Adams, "The Aluminum Case: Legal Victory–Economic Defeat," *American Economic Review,* **XLI:** 5 (December 1951), p. 915.

[12] On appeal to the Supreme Court, a quorum could not be obtained because some justices had been previously involved in the case. Consequently, the Circuit Court decision stood.

In the case of *United States* v. *United Shoe Machinery Corporation,* the courts concluded that United's control of the shoe machinery market was indisputable and found further that the company's practices had been neither predatory nor discriminatory between different customers. Judge C.E. Wyzanski held that the United Shoe Machinery case fell "within the main thrust of the doctrine applied in the *Aluminum* and subsequent cases" and that United had violated the Sherman Act.[13] But he refused to dissolve the company and ordered three forms of relief that would do little to weaken United's monopoly.

By this time, the courts appeared to have brought the legal concern of monopoly into line by establishing the concept that size alone determines a company's power to affect prices by varying output. To be sure, in *United States* v. *Columbia Steel Company, et al.,* a 1948 case, the Supreme Court had flirted once again with the rule of reason in deciding that Columbia Steel, a subsidiary of United States Steel, had not violated the Sherman Act in purchasing the Consolidated Steel Corporation, the largest independent steel fabricator on the West Coast. In *United States* v. *Paramount Pictures, Inc., et al.,* another 1948 case, the Court ordered major motion picture producers to divest themselves of exhibitors on the ground that separating the functions of the production and the distribution of films did not produce higher production costs for the firms. And in the Cellophane Case (*United States* v. *E.I. duPont de Nemours and Company,* 1953), it seemed that the Supreme Court would move in the direction of considering interproduct competition in determining the extent of monopolistic power when the Court defined the relevant market to include all the wrap that competed with cellophane—from brown paper to polyethylene film. By the mid-1950s, the judiciary had apparently accepted the propositions that modern productive methods leave no economic alternative to concentration to a few large firms in most manufacturing and extractive industries and that breaking up large firms could well lead to inefficient production.

Yet in the field of antitrust, we can be sure that once the law seems reasonably certain, the Supreme Court will change direction and chart a new course via "judicial legislation." Just four years after the Cellophane decree, pursuant to an action brought against the same company, the Court reversed itself, narrowly defining the market for finishes and fabrics to include not the *entire* market but only the *automobile* market. Moreover, this second duPont case produced the startling realization that any large corporation that has achieved size through stock acquisitions since 1914—the year of passage of the Clayton Act—can be required to divest itself of those holdings, no matter what the cost to the firm or how complicated the proceedings. But it was in the landmark case of *Brown Shoe Company* v. *United States* in 1962 that the Supreme Court greatly strengthened the hand of the Justice Department in merger cases. The Brown Shoe Company and the G.R. Kinney Company were both engaged in the manufacture and retail marketing of shoes. Brown accounted for about 4 percent of the national output of shoes; Kinney, for about 1.5 percent. Together, these two companies could not have controlled more than 6 percent of the production of *retail* shoe sales. But the government argued that the relevant lines of commerce were not just "footwear" but, alterna-

[13] *United States* v. *United Shoe Machinery Corp.,* 110 F. Supp. 295.

tively, men's, women's, and children's shoes. The Court also ruled that the "section of the country" within which the anticompetitive effect of a merger is to be judged is the nation as a whole and, alternatively, every city with a population of 10,000 or more in which Brown or Kinney shoes were sold. Thus, in Dodge City, Kansas, the combined share of the market was over 57 percent for women's shoes and 49 percent for children's shoes—a dangerous horizontal concentration. Oddly, this was followed by the assertion that it was the intent of Congress when passing the Celler–Kefauver Amendments to the Clayton Act in 1950 to stop "incipient" oligopoly on a national scale.

The same contrived definition of markets was successfully attempted in other cases. Yet due to a lack of resources or the vacillation of succeeding Attorney General, little effort was made to arrest the tide of mergers that marked the late 1960s. Another explanation for so little force on the part of the Justice Department lies in the fact that most recent mergers have been of the conglomerate type (see Table 27-2). Donald F. Turner, Assistant Attorney General for Antitrust in the Johnson Administration and a legal scholar with degrees in both economics and law, took the view that the Clayton Act could not be applied against conglomerate mergers unless the government could demonstrate that anticompetitive results occurred in a specific market. William H. Rehnquist, Turner's successor under Nixon, took the tougher stance that major conglomerate acquisitions (such as LTV's purchase of Jones and Laughlin) must be offset by the spinoff of an approximately equal amount of other assets. The consequence has been that attacks on "product extension," such as the one initiated by the Federal Trade Commission against Procter & Gamble's acquisition of the assets of the Chlorox Chemical Company, have been trivial. In this particular case, Procter & Gamble (by no means a conglomerate) was required to divest itself of Chlorox on the grounds that P&G's tremendous marketing power would give the product a great advantage over the three major competing products and keep Procter & Gamble from entering the market as a separate competitor.

If, as suggested earlier, interindustry competition affords effective protection to consumers for most categories of goods, many economists feel that the Justice Department would be well advised to stop trying to add one or two more firms to industries that must always remain oligopolistic—and, for that

TABLE 27–2
Percentage Distribution of Mergers by Type and Period, 1926–1968

Type of Merger	1926–1930	1940–1947	1951–1955	1956–1960	1961–1965	1966–1968
Horizontal	75.9	62.0	39.2	30.1	22.5	8.6
Vertical	4.8	17.0	12.2	14.9	17.5	9.8
Conglomerate	19.3	21.0	48.6	55.0	60.0	81.6
Total	100.0	100.0	100.0	100.0	100.0	100.0

Source: Staff Report of the Federal Trade Commission, *Economic Report on Corporate Mergers,* Hearings on Economic Concentration, Subcommittee on Antitrust and Monopoly, U.S. Senate, 91st Congress, 1st Session, Washington, 1969. Adapted from Table 1–6, p. 63.

matter, to stop worrying about the purchase of one company by another *when market structure does not change after the acquisition.* Instead, the Department might concentrate on detecting products for which there are few alternative suppliers, within or without the "industry," and bring actions in these relatively few cases. Such a course would enable the Justice Department to root out genuine instances of monopoly, negotiate downward price adjustments, and avoid much useless and costly negotiation.

28

Labor's Progress in Modern Times

Despite deterioration in the union movement between 1920 and 1932, the economic position of the average worker had improved sharply before 1929. Advances came in the form of higher earnings, improved safety and work conditions, and somewhat greater job security. Of course, as we well know, the events of the Great Depression brought widespread unemployment and grief to many people. But these events also initiated legislation that propelled organized labor into a position of unprecedented influence, not only in matters of work and earnings but also in politics generally. In 1933, labor leaders acquired government assistance in achieving their objectives, especially the right to strike. Thereafter, organized labor began a period of almost uninterrupted advances on all fronts. Some of these advances were common to all workers, including nonunion workers; other union gains were limited to members only. Some union measures were achieved at the expense of nonunion workers and consumers in general.

In viewing these differential gains, we must recognize that the progress of labor has not been identical to the progress of *organized* labor. Moreover, great regional differences in labor type, race, sex, and age have existed. With these cautions in mind, we can proceed to examine the aggregate data that reveal the average changes and general trends in work conditions in America.

HOURS AND WAGES

Let's begin by considering the length of the standard workweek. During World War I, the 48-hour workweek was accepted in many manufacturing industries, and by 1920 some agreements

TABLE 28–1
Real Average Weekly Earnings of Production Workers in Manufacturing (1967 = 100)

Year	(1) Index of average weekly earnings of production workers in manufacturing	(2) Index of real average weekly earnings of production workers in manufacturing
1919	19.2	37.6
1920	22.9	38.7
1921	19.3	36.6
1922	18.7	37.9
1923	20.7	41.2
1924	20.8	41.3
1925	21.2	41.0
1926	21.5	41.1
1927	21.5	42.0
1928	21.7	42.9
1929	21.8	43.0
1930	20.2	41.1
1931	18.2	40.5
1932	14.8	36.8
1933	14.6	38.2
1934	16.0	40.5
1935	17.5	43.3
1936	19.0	46.4
1937	20.9	49.4
1938	19.4	46.7
1939	20.8	50.6
1940	21.9	53.1
1941	25.8	59.3
1942	31.9	66.3
1943	37.6	73.5
1944	40.1	77.3
1945	38.6	72.8
1946	38.2	66.2
1947	43.5	66.0
1948	47.1	66.4

granted a half-holiday on Saturday. Not until 1930, however, was a 48-hour week standard for most occupations. Pressures to "share the work" helped to shorten the standard workweek during the 1930s. The Fair Labor Standards Act of 1938, covering industries engaged in interstate commerce, set a maximum standard workweek of 40 hours and authorized "time and a half" rates for

Table 28 – 1 *(continued)*

Year	(1) Index of average weekly earnings of production workers in manufacturing	(2) Index of real average weekly earnings of production workers in manufacturing
1949	47.8	68.0
1950	51.6	72.8
1951	56.3	73.5
1952	59.2	75.5
1953	62.4	79.0
1954	62.6	78.9
1955	66.4	84.3
1956	69.6	86.8
1957	71.7	86.4
1958	72.7	85.2
1959	76.8	89.3
1960	78.1	89.5
1961	80.4	91.1
1962	84.0	92.7
1963	86.7	94.5
1964	89.6	96.4
1965	93.6	99.1
1966	97.8	100.5
1967	100.0	100.0
1968	106.7	102.2
1969	112.8	102.5
1970	116.4	100.1
1971	142.4	117.4
1972	154.7	123.5
1973	165.7	124.5
1974	176.4	119.4
1975	189.5	117.6
1976	207.6	121.8
1977	220.8	122.9

Sources: *Historical Statistics of the United States, Colonial Times to 1957, Statistical Abstract of the United States, 1962–1971,* and (for 1971–1977 data) *Statistical Abstract of the United States,* p. 412.

overtime work. In 1940, half a day's work on Saturday was still not uncommon, but the end of World War II saw its virtual disappearance. By 1950, the 40-hour week was standard, and in some industries and in offices many workers were becoming accustomed to a 35-hour week.

Nearly all workers had higher incomes as well as more leisure time at this point. Table 28-1 enables us to estimate the improvement in manufacturing income. The base year is 1967. Between 1926 and 1974, the average weekly income of wage earners in manufacturing increased almost six times. Consumer prices more than doubled during the same period. If we take into account the rising cost of living, this represents increases in real weekly earnings in manufacturing of more than 140 percent (see Column 2), meaning that real weekly earnings more than doubled in the nearly 50-year period. Moreover, wages and earnings figures understate labor's material gains, because workers in the post-World War II period have received "fringe benefits," such as paid vacations and company pension plans, that have an ascertainable money value.[1]

A closer inspection of Table 28-1 reveals interesting relationships in three short periods. During the Great Depression, wages fell moderately; earnings dropped more severely due to the great reduction in number of hours worked. But because consumers' prices decreased, real wages declined only slightly in one year (1932) and average real earnings fell only moderately. Of course, such figures do not reflect the great burden imposed on the unemployed, who had no earnings at all. The sharp inflation that occurred between 1945 and 1948 was accompanied by a 25-percent increase in money wages, but real wages fell drastically and then remained nearly constant for several years as the cost of living rose even more. Again, despite handsome increases in average weekly earnings in the late 1960s and 1970s, inflation seriously eroded gains in real earnings.

We will now compare changes in money earnings for major classes of workers.[2] Before 1929, salaried workers were much better paid than wage earners, but the earnings of a second great white-collar group—employees in the retail and wholesale trade and in the telephone industry—were only slightly higher than the income of wage earners. The depression of the 1930s hit the wage earners hardest: Their money earnings dropped by 30 percent. Trade and telephone workers suffered a drop of about 25 percent in earnings, and the earnings of salaried workers declined 15 percent. At the trough of the depression, the earnings of salaried employees were 60 percent greater than those of wage earners, and the earnings of the trade and telephone employees were 17 percent greater. But with recovery, the salaried employees' advantage began to disappear, and by 1939 the relationships of 1929 were approximately restored. By 1943, the wartime demand for production workers had increased wage earners' weekly incomes to the point that they were ahead of the incomes of salaried workers. Postwar increases put salaried employees in the lead again in 1946, but the boom years of 1947 and 1948 brought the manual-earnings figure nearly to equality. The high level of industrial production in

[1] Not counting paid holidays and paid vacations, the value of fringe-benefit payments rose from an estimated $3.8 billion in 1946 to $20.6 billion in 1962–an increase of 700 percent. By the end of 1970, the value of such benefits had passed well beyond the $30 billion mark. A large portion of these benefits, however, are extended to salaried personnel as distinguished from wage earners.

[2] The following passage draws heavily on Robert K. Burns, "The Comparative Economic Position of Manual and White-Collar Employees," *Journal of Business,* **XXVII:** 4 (October 1954), pp. 257–67.

1951 and 1952 once again put the wage earners ahead. In the meantime, although the money earnings of the trade and telephone employees had advanced at a higher rate since 1943 than those of the other two groups, the average income of manual workers exceeded that of the trade workers by 20 percent. More recent evidence suggests no substantial change in these relationships.

Thus since the depths of the depression, wage earners have overcome the income superiority of salaried workers that existed before 1929. Many influences have favored the manual worker. The expansion of public educational facilities at all levels has made training for white-collar positions available to an ever-larger proportion of the labor force, and the increase in competition for white-collar jobs has naturally kept salaries down. The increasing entry of women into the workforce has further swelled the ranks of clerical and sales personnel, particularly at lower-paid levels. Immigration restrictions since the early 1920s and a desire on the part of parents to deter their children from blue-collar occupations doubtlessly have reduced the relative supply of manual workers.

White-collar employees continue to hold an advantage over manual workers in two respects. The earnings of white-collar workers are more stable because their workweek—unlike the wage earner's—does not fluctuate with the firm's production schedule. Moreover, the incidence of unemployment is not nearly as great in the salaried occupations as it is in the wage occupations. Manual workers, despite their remarkable improvement in earnings, remain peculiarly vulnerable to economic fluctuations, as the economic slump of 1969–1970 demonstrated.

THE THREAT OF UNEMPLOYMENT[3]

Turning to the record of unemployment, it is important to note that excessive unemployment, actual or threatened, has been a source of grave concern in about one-half of the peacetime years since World War I. The 1920s were fairly free of this cyclical unemployment after the depression years of 1921 and 1922, when unemployment may have peaked at 11 percent of the labor force. But the 1930s were dismal years of joblessness. No two estimates of the extent of unemployment during this period agree. Bureau of Labor Statistics data, which are considered conservative, show that one-quarter of the civilian workforce of

[3] People are said to be "involuntarily unemployed" when they are willing and able to work but cannot find a job for which they are trained. Some kinds of involuntary unemployment, often referred to as "frictional unemployment," are unavoidable in a free economy. People constantly change jobs, and firms go out of business or move their plants and warehouses. Some businesses have seasonal ups and downs in employment. Technological unemployment occurs as innovations throw people out of work, and older people so separated from their jobs may never make another permanent connection. And there are always marginal workers who, due to approaching old age or mental or physical disabilities, find themselves continually moving into and out of the workforce. Frictional unemployment cannot be lightly dismissed, but it is not an economic malfunction. Serious unemployment is the mass unemployment that results from sudden, drastic declines in economic activity.

TABLE 28–2
Estimated Unemployment, 1929–1943

Year	Average annual number unemployed (in thousands)	Percentage of civilian labor force
1929	1,550	3.2
1930	4,340	8.7
1931	8,020	15.9
1932	12,060	23.6
1933	12,830	24.9
1934	11,340	21.7
1935	10,610	20.1
1936	9,030	16.9
1937	7,700	14.3
1938	10,390	19.0
1939	9,480	17.2
1940	8,120	14.6
1941	5,560	9.9
1942	2,660	4.7
1943	1,070	1.9

Source: U.S. Bureau of Labor Statistics.

approximately 48 million were without jobs at the trough of the Great Depression. For ten straight years (1931–1940), more than one-tenth of the civilian labor force was unemployed, and for most of these years the ratio was one-sixth or more (see Table 28-2). Such figures do not, of course, take into account the severe amount of underemployment that resulted from short work-weeks and work-sharing plans, nor do they reflect the great numbers of people who worked far below their appropriate levels of ability and training. At least one-half of the people in the workforce were unemployed or desperately disadvantaged by underemployment at one time or another during the 1930s.

Unemployment of such magnitude urged the administration of Franklin D. Roosevelt to devise a massive program of relief. No other activity except the sweep of regulations that developed so clearly typified the New Deal, and the remedies prescribed were the object of conservative scorn. As hastily devised and poorly administered as some of them were, they nevertheless marked a sharp change from the grudging Reconstruction Finance Corporation loans and the "trickle-down" theories of the Hoover Administration and were approved by the great majority of the electorate.

The Federal Emergency Relief Administration (FERA) was established in May 1933 to make grants to state and local agencies for direct relief and work projects on public property. A few months later, the Civil Works Administration (CWA) was created under the FERA to undertake the first large-scale work program. CWA workers repaired streets, painted buildings, and improved parks under the supervision of public officials. The first "permanent" plan of relief was provided by the National Industrial Recovery Act, which created the Public Works Administration (PWA). Administered by Harold L. Ickes, Secretary of the

Unemployment was of little public concern throughout the 1960s but had become a significant social problem by the 1970s, as these applicants for public-service jobs in Chicago in 1975 vividly attest.

Interior, the PWA granted funds and made loans to states and municipalities for the construction of such public works as highways, post offices, and school buildings. Work under PWA programs was performed by private contractors, who were not required to hire laborers from the ranks of the unemployed. It was felt that even though the program might not help unemployment directly, large expenditures (amounting to more than $3 billion) would stimulate the economy and at least indirectly provide employment.

The national work-relief program came to full flower in 1935 with the establishment of the Works Progress Administration (WPA) under Harry Hopkins. The object of the WPA was to provide work directly to the unemployed. In an effort to avoid a "dole," the WPA created projects that used the services of painters, authors, sculptors, and musicians, as well as manual workers. More than one-half of total WPA expenditures were on public works. Because it operated under its own administrative staff rather than through private contractors, the WPA was accused of competing with private industry, and its projects were viewed with derision. Nonetheless, WPA provided an enormous amount of relief in a way that allowed people to maintain their self-respect.[4] Not until 1942 was the agency dissolved.

The problem of unemployment vanished during World War II and, to the relief of national administrations, did not reappear until several years after the war had ended. But as the recession of 1949 deepened, unemployment passed the 4 million mark, dropped seasonally, and came uncomfortably close to 5 million—7.5 percent of the labor force—in February 1950. A decrease in unemployment before the outbreak of the Korean conflict was encouraging, coming as it did without the stimulus of a rearmament program. But a rather serious decline in industrial production beginning in July 1953 again resulted in increasing joblessness, and by March 1954 unemployment exceeded 3.75 million—nearly 6 percent of the civilian labor force. From the middle 1950s on, economic policymakers were concerned with the stickiness of the unemployment rate during economic expansions (see Figure 28-1). In the boom of 1955, 19 months after the trough of the 1953–1954 recession, unemployment was 3.4 percent of the civilian workforce. In 1959, 14 months after the trough of the 1957–1958 recession, the unemployment rate was still 5.6 percent, and in early 1964, 36 months out of the trough of the 1960–1961 recession, the figure was a sticky 5.5 percent. The frustrating fact is that the unemployment rate has continued to hover near the 6-percent mark throughout the 1970s. As the economy emerged from the recession of 1969–1971, restoration of full employment did not occur.

Economists, employers, union leaders, and government officials disagree as to what constitutes a tolerable amount of unemployment. The long-held, substantial opinion regards unemployment of about 4 percent of the labor force as unavoidable during peacetime. The amount of unemployment from "accepted and normal" causes is no less hard on the workers who are affected than cyclical unemployment, but it is possible to mitigate its short-run impact

[4] At the peak of its activity in 1938, the WPA employed about 3.3 million workers on its projects. Employment on undertakings supervised by PWA, the Civilian Conservation Corps, and the National Youth Administration brought the total number of government "relief" jobs to well over 4 million in 1938.

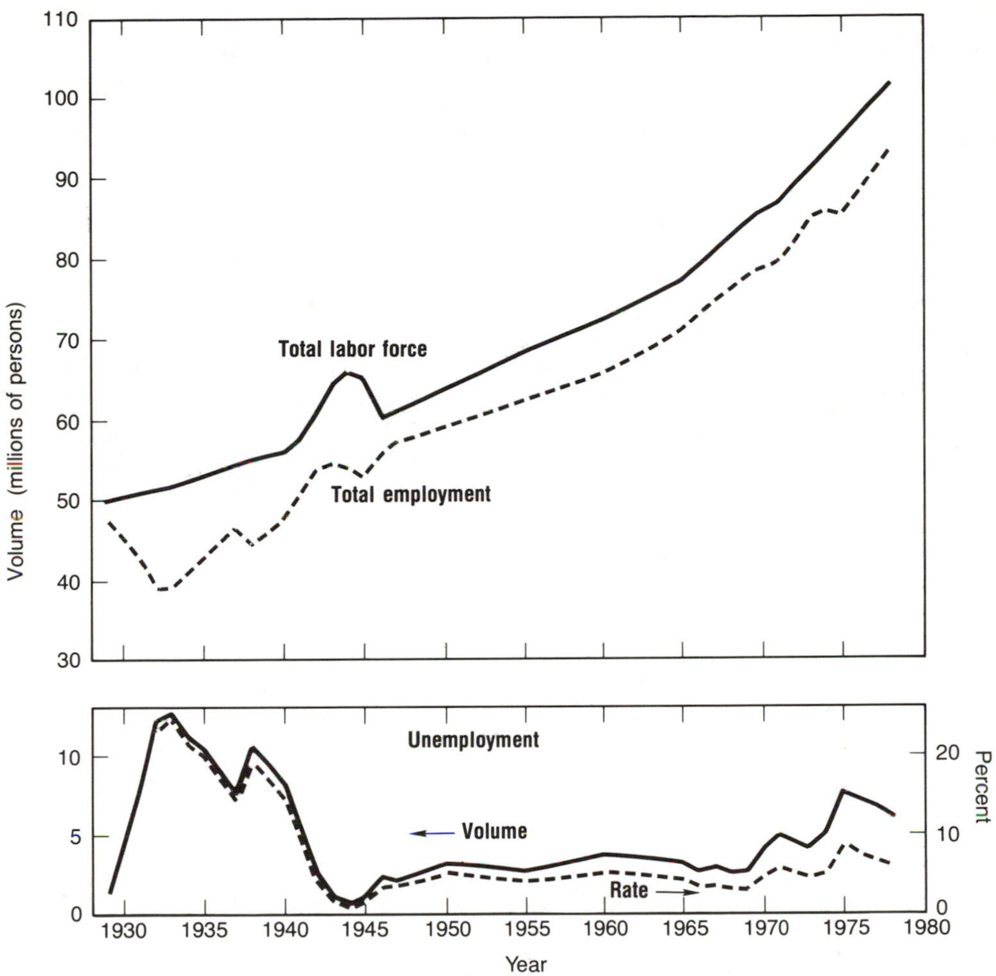

FIGURE 28–1

Employment and Unemployment in the United States, 1930–1978: Since World War II, the total labor force has increased almost without interruption, and since 1963 total employment has moved steadily upward. But unemployment that went over the 5 percent mark in the recession of 1969–1970 remained throughout the decade.

Source: Board of Governors of the Federal Reserve System.

through social insurance. But when unemployment reaches or passes the 5-percent mark, chronic joblessness appears in the durable-goods industries, and political pressures for remedies build up in urban areas.

In 1970, unemployment averaged 4.1 million, and employment increased by 725,000. In 1971, the number of unemployed Americans averaged 5 million, even though the number of jobs rose about 1.6 million. The average duration of joblessness rose to more than 12 weeks in 1971 from about 9 weeks in 1970. Yet the total figures mask the incidence of heaviest unemployment. The unemployment rate for married men stood at only 3.2 percent during 1971, whereas the rate for teen-agers was 17 percent. Unemployment among blacks and members of other minority groups averaged nearly 10 percent, and the jobless rate of Vietnam veterans stood at 8.8 percent.

Labor analysts have argued that over the decade between the 1960–1961 recession and the 1969–1971 recession, the composition of the civilian labor force changed substantially. In 1960, women and teen-agers accounted for 37.4 percent of the civilian labor force, whereas a decade later this proportion had risen to 43.1 percent. In 1971, these two groups comprised 58 percent of the unemployed in contrast with 44 percent during May 1961—the peak month of joblessness in the 1960–1961 recession. During this interval, the proportion of the unemployed consisting of married men dropped from 37 percent to 27.3 percent. On the assumption that a considerably higher proportion of married men than women and teen-agers are the chief breadwinners of families, a 6-percent unemployment rate in 1971 was less burdensome than the same rate would have been a decade previously. Indeed, the research department of the Mellon National Bank has calculated that if the age and sex composition of the labor force in 1971 had been the same as it was in 1961, the total rate of unemployment would have been 4.1 percent, rather than 6.1 percent.

Unemployment is an issue of grave importance even today. And appropriate remedies to erase unwanted idleness still elude us. If anything, the 1970s have provided some new and more troublesome lessons. Recent attempts to drive down the unemployment rate through expansionary monetary policies have only resulted in renewed inflationary pressures. Whereas politicians and economic advisors once considered it possible to trade off inflation for unemployment, it now appears that this is possible only in the very short run.

THE LABOR MOVEMENT AND GOVERNMENT INTERVENTION

The Growth of Labor Unions

Membership in labor unions, which in 1920 exceeded 5 million, dropped precipitously to 3.5 million in 1923 and remained nearly constant at that figure until 1929. Even the depression brought no further great losses; total membership amounted to just under 3 million in 1933. In the meantime, membership in the American Federation of Labor (AFL) fell from about 4 million to 2.2 million.[5]

The depression of 1920–1921, unsuccessful postwar strikes, and a renewed wave of employer antagonism contributed to the first sharp drop in union membership. Equally devastating to union progress and union morale was labor's support of company welfare programs that were designed to entice workers away from their own organizations and into company unions. But the

[5] Irving Bernstein, "The Growth of American Unions," *American Economic Review,* **XLIV**:3 (June 1954), pp. 301–18.

inertia of the 1924–1929 period must be attributed primarily to two other causes. The price level remained almost constant as money wages rose moderately, so that the greater part of labor felt comfortable and generally grateful toward business, big and small. More importantly, the powerful AFL unions, whose members especially benefited during the building boom, took no interest in organizing the growing mass-production industries. Added to this was a generally feeble and unimaginative leadership.

A sign of the low level to which union energies had declined was the apparent resignation of workers at the onset of the depression to the national disgrace of depression unemployment. But before the new administration had been in power a year, the more vigorous union leaders sensed that the government would encourage organization and that the attitude of the nation toward unions had changed as people became disillusioned with business. Especially successful in their organizational efforts were the powerful and able leaders of the industrial unions that had evolved within the AFL: John L. Lewis of the United Mine Workers, Sidney Hillman of the Amalgamated Clothing Workers, and David Dubinsky of the International Ladies Garment Workers.

By the mid-1930s, a conflict within labor over the question of proper union structure had grown to major proportions. The move to organize the new mass-production industries (steel, automobiles, rubber, and electrical equipment) was inevitable; but the older unions hampered such organization by insisting that their craft jurisdiction remain inviolate and by raiding the membership of the new industrial unions. In 1935, eight industrial unions formed the Committee for Industrial Organization within the AFL, and in 1936 these unions were suspended from the federation. Three years later, the CIO became a separate entity, the Congress of Industrial Organization.

Conflict continued between these two great federations, but the competition seemed only to spur membership growth. There was defection, to be sure. After interminable controversy over policy, John L. Lewis resigned from the presidency of the CIO and withdrew the United Mine Workers from it. After unsuccessfully attempting to attract other unions to coalesce about him, Lewis rejoined the AFL in 1946 only to disaffiliate the next year. Meanwhile, CIO leaders made no secret of their contempt for the AFL's lack of militancy and its failure to participate aggressively in political activities, and AFL leaders viewed the CIO's violent break with conservative unionism with concern. But complacency and inertia no longer beset the labor movement. In 1955, the AFL and the CIO, prodded into unity by hostile public opinion and punitive labor legislation, merged to form the AFL–CIO.

Estimates of union membership since 1920 are shown in Table 28-3. The periods of the New Deal and World War II brought rapid growth, and membership continued to increase steadily in the early 1950s. A membership in 1953 of nearly 17 million, or 28 percent of the civilian labor force, was in itself an impressive statistic.[6] It seems even more so when we reflect that 75 percent or more of the employees in manufacturing, mining, construction, and transportation and public utilities were working under collective-bargaining agreements.

[6]Roughly 50 percent of the total membership was in AFL affiliates, 30 percent in CIO unions, and the remainder in unaffiliated unions.

TABLE 28–3
Union Membership, 1920–1971 (in thousands)

Year	Number	Year	Number	Year	Number
1920	5,048	1937	7,001	1956	17,490
		1938	8,034	1957	17,300
1921	4,781	1939	8,763	1958	17,029
1922	4,027	1940	8,717	1959	17,100
1923	3,622			1960	17,049
1924	3,536	1941	10,201		
1925	3,519	1942	10,380	1961	17,328
		1943	13,213	1962	17,630
1926	3,502	1944	14,146	1963	17,586
1927	3,546	1945	14,322	1964	17,976
1928	3,480			1965	18,519
1929	3,461	1946	14,395		
1930	3,401	1947	14,787	1966	19,181
		1948	14,300	1967	19,712
1931	3,310	1949	14,300	1968	20,258
1932	3,050	1950	14,300	1969	19,000
1933	2,689			1970	19,400
1934	3,088	1951	15,900		
1935	3,584	1952	15,900	1971	20,582
		1953	16,948	1972	20,894
1936	3,989	1954	17,022	1973	21,294
		1955	16,802	1974	21,643

Sources: U.S. Bureau of Labor Statistics, "Handbook of Labor Statistics 1971," *Monthly Labor Review* (January 1972), and "Handbook of Labor Statistics 1977."

Yet as it turned out, 1953 membership was close to the peak membership of that decade, and in the early 1960s there was little reason to be sanguine about a near-term upward movement from labor's "organizational plateau."

There were many reasons why phenomenal growth should have occurred in the unions between 1933 and 1953.[7] An addition of 15 million people to the civilian labor force represented a rising "organizable potential." Joining a union became socially acceptable in many geographical areas where formerly it had not been. The increasing homogeneity of the labor force made the job of union organizers easier; differences in language, religion, and educational background did not sharply separate American workers as they once had. But the main force was that the pro-labor attitude of government in the 1930s broke down the barriers to organization in the new mass-production industries and hastened the growth of trade unionism.

Since the early 1950s, there has been a reversal of these trends. In the peak year of 1953, slightly more than 25 percent of the labor force was enrolled in labor unions, and this percentage has fluctuated around 22 percent throughout the later 1970s.

[7] Bernstein, "The Growth of American Unions," pp. 313–15.

Mass labor meetings like this one are becoming less and less typical of American labor strategy.

This failure to increase can be attributed largely to the rapid growth of the nonmanufacturing sector, particularly services, where employee groups are usually small and difficult to organize. Moreover, for two decades within the goods-producing sector there has been a steady shift from blue-collar to white-collar employment that has resulted in a constant or slightly falling organizable potential. Forces that once produced homogeneity in the workforce have been working recently to move the children and grandchildren of labor's former partisans into the upper middle class, which, with some obvious exceptions, is not sympathetic to labor's cause. Intralabor squabbles, such as the 1968

United Automobile Workers (UAW) disaffiliation from the AFL–CIO resulting from policy differences between UAW President Walter Reuther and AFL–CIO President George Meany, have weakened the organizational cause. Recent public misapprehension of the complex relationships between prices and wages, together with press and legislative exaggeration of union corruption, have created suspicion and resulted in declining support at the polls. Changes in national labor policy beginning in 1947 have hurt organizational efforts by making it difficult to organize unions in smaller firms, in the retail and service trades, and in the South. We will now turn to the subject of post-1930 labor policy.

Federal Intercession

Throughout the 1920s, employers continued their effective use of the anti-union instruments developed before World War I. They discriminated, in hiring and firing, against employees who joined or organized unions. The hated yellow-dog contract, judged constitutional by the Supreme Court, was commonly employed to prevent union membership and to serve as a basis of civil suits against unions that persuaded employees to violate the contract. But the most useful weapon was the injunction, by which a court could forbid, at least temporarily, such practices as picketing, secondary boycotts, and the feeding of strikers by the union.

Except for legislation that applied only to the railroad industry, Congress refused to interfere by statute with labor relations until 1932. The Norris–La Guardia Act of 1932 was a first great step toward removing the barriers to free organization. Largely procedural in character, the Act had the effect of eliminating or modifying the worst abuses of the labor injunction. The yellow-dog contract was eliminated by making it nonenforceable in the federal courts, and the issuance of injunctions was greatly restricted. Moreover, as a result of a liberal definition of the term *labor dispute,* unions were freed to engage in organizational activity. Specifically, the term was defined in such a way as to permit *secondary* activity in the form of boycotting and picketing by nonemployees as distinguished from the narrower concept of *primary* activity only. By the Act, the government granted the *opportunity* to organize to workers but did not positively intercede to assure that they could secure the benefits of collective bargaining.

The first positive assertion of the right of labor to bargain collectively was contained in Section 7a of the National Industrial Recovery Act, but no means of enforcing the statement of principle were provided. Two years later, the NIRA was declared unconstitutional on grounds that had nothing to do with the labor section, and Congress replaced Section 7a with a much more elaborate law of labor relations. This was the National Labor Relations Act, usually referred to as the Wagner Act after its sponsor, Senator Robert F. Wagner of New York.

The Wagner Act proceeded from the explicit premises that inequality of bargaining power between individual employees and large business units depresses "the purchasing power of wage earners in industry" and prevents "stabilization of competitive wage rates and working conditions," and that denial of the right to self-organization creates industrial strife. The Act established the principle of collective bargaining as the cornerstone of industrial relations in the United States and stated that it was management's obligation to recognize and deal with a bona fide labor organization in good faith. The Act further guaranteed workers the right to form and join a labor organization, to engage in collective bargaining, to select representatives of their own choosing, and to engage in concerted activity. In addition, the Wagner Act outlawed a list of "unfair" managerial practices that had had the effect of denying worker rights. Henceforth, employers could *not:*

1. interfere with, restrain, or coerce employees in the exercise of their rights of self-organization and collective bargaining.
2. dominate or interfere with the formation or administration of any labor organization or contribute financial or other support to it.
3. encourage or discourage union membership by discrimination in regard to hiring or tenure of employment or condition of work, except such discrimination as might be involved in a closed-shop agreement with a bona fide union enjoying majority status.
4. discharge or otherwise discriminate against an employee for filing charges or testifying under the Act.
5. refuse to bargain collectively.

The Wagner Act was no mere statement of principles. It established a National Labor Relations Board (NLRB), composed of three members with genuine powers of enforcement. After hearings regarding a union complaint, the Board could issue cease-and-desist orders to employers who were judged guilty of unfair labor practices. If employers did not comply with these orders, the NLRB could turn to a U.S. Circuit Court of Appeals for enforcement. The Board also had the power, on its own initiative or at the request of a union, to supervise a free, secret election among a company's employees to determine which union, if any, should represent the workers.

Labor hailed the Wagner Act as its Magna Charta. When the Supreme Court declared the law constitutional in 1937, there were no remaining barriers to the rapid organization of labor. But before the question of constitutionality was settled, many employers openly violated the Act, producing increasing turbulence in labor relations. Animosity between the suspended CIO unions and the AFL grew, leading to jurisdictional conflicts that the NLRB had to spend much time settling. As industrial strife seemed to be increasing rather than decreasing, there were public demands for amendments to the Act, and employers complained bitterly of the one-sidedness of the law.

The Wagner Act was never intended to be a comprehensive code of labor relations. It did not even define "collective bargaining," nor did it cover the problems of jurisdictional disputes, "national emergency" disputes, and secondary boycotts. If World War II had not intervened, basic amendments to the Act would doubtlessly have been made sooner, but the war placed the national problem of labor relations almost in abeyance. Through the National War Labor Board, established in 1942, wage rates were stabilized; wages rose about 13 percent during the war, or a little less than other controlled prices. With financial pressures removed, labor and management were persuaded to give up strikes and lockouts in exchange for representation on the War Labor Board. Work stoppages occurred, particularly in 1944; but the workdays lost were only a small percentage of total working time, and presidential seizures of struck industries, although well publicized, were few. Normal two-party collective bargaining procedures were often circumvented by reliance on the cooperative decisions of regional offices of the board.

With the end of the war, much overtime disappeared, and earnings fell as prices held firm or edged up. Labor leaders were under pressure to secure wage increases, which were not to be forthcoming without a struggle. The widespread work stoppages of 1945 and 1946 alienated large segments of the electorate. Employers complained loudly that they were being caught in the jurisdictional disputes of rival unions and that labor itself was guilty of unfair practices. There was a growing belief that union power was being used to infringe on the rights of individual workers. After the Republicans won control of Congress in 1946, they lost no time in drawing up a long, technical bill that significantly amended the Wagner Act. The new law, passed in 1947 over President Harry S. Truman's veto, was called the Labor–Management Relations Act and became known familiarly as the Taft–Hartley Act.

The Taft–Hartley Act reflected the belief that individual workers should be protected by public policy not only in their right to join a labor organization but also in their right to refrain from joining. The closed-shop agreement, under which the employer hires only union members, was outlawed. Union-shop agreements, which permit nonunion members to be employed but require them to join the union within a certain time period after starting to work, were permitted. However, the enforcement of union-security provisions was limited to cases of nonpayment of dues, and, more importantly, the law permitted the states to outlaw *all* forms of union security, including the union shop.

The Taft–Hartley Act, unlike the Wagner Act, further assumed that the interests of the union and individuals in the union are not identical, taking the view that many union members are "captives" of the "labor bosses"—a position especially offensive to a great part of organized labor. For example, the Act provided that a union could not negotiate a union-shop provision in collective-bargaining agreements unless a majority of workers in the unit voted for it. In 1951, after 46,000 separate polls in which security provisions won 97 percent of the time, the requirement of NLRB-conducted union-security elections was dropped, and a large number of doubters became convinced that union leaders commonly reflect the wishes of their memberships.

The most important features of the Taft–Hartley Act were those purporting to regulate unions in the "public" interest. A union seeking certification or requesting an investigation of unfair labor practices had to submit to a scrutiny of its internal affairs by filing financial statements, and its officers were required to sign affidavits stating that they were not Communists. The right to strike was modified by providing a "cooling-off period" after notice of termination of contract, and the President was given authority to postpone strikes for 80 days by injunction. More significant in "evening up" the one-sidedness of the Wagner Act was the outlawing of certain unfair union practices. Since 1947, it has been unfair for a union:

1. to restrain or coerce *employees* regarding their right to join or refrain from joining a labor organization, or to restrain or coerce *employers* in the selection of employer representatives for purposes of collective bargaining or adjustment of grievances.
2. to cause or attempt to cause an *employer* to discriminate against an employee.
3. to charge, under a valid union-shop agreement, an "excessive" initiation fee.
4. to refuse to bargain collectively with an employer when the union involved is the certified bargaining agent.
5. to "featherbed" the job—that is, to cause an employer to pay for services that are not performed.[8]
6. to engage in, or encourage employees to engage in, a strike where the object is to force one employer to cease doing business with another employer. This provision banned the secondary boycott.

After 12 years of almost complete freedom, labor found the Taft–Hartley Act harshly restrictive. Dire warnings were voiced about the coming decline of trade unionism in America. Labor's leadership was incensed at the offensive language and punitive spirit of the Act. But many of the provisions looked worse in print than they proved in practice. The injunction clause, for example, stirred memories of the days when the courts granted injunctions at the request of private parties; in the hands of a President of the United States, acting in an emergency, however, the injunction was no longer a destructive weapon. Regulation of internal union affairs was only a nuisance and an interference with private business.

However, some of the new requirements for rigorously admissible evidence of unfair employer practices doubtlessly retarded union organization, especially in the South. By 1963, 19 states had passed anti-labor legislation in the form of "right-to-work" laws." By making it illegal to enforce the union-shop provisions of an agreement within the state concerned, "right-to-work" legislation kept efforts to unionize in a continuous state of reorganization and were a source of friction among union and nonunion workers.[9] American labor would continue to fight for revision of the Taft–Hartley Act.

As the decade of the 1950s closed, labor's public relations showed no signs of improvement. Indeed, the Labor–Management Reporting and Disclosure Act of 1959 (the Landrum–Griffin Act) suggested that Congress would discipline the whole of labor to protect the public against the manipulations of a few corrupt leaders. In any case, the law tightened restrictions on secondary boycotting and organized picketing, required detailed reports of all financial transactions between unions and their officers and members, and provided for secret-ballot elections of union officers, whose terms of office were carefully restricted. Few could object to the provision preventing felons and

[8] Featherbedding continued to be a scandal in the railroad industry, which is not subject to the Taft–Hartley Act.

[9] The only "right-to-work" states with serious pretensions to consideration as industrial states were Indiana and Texas, and Indiana repealed its "right-to-work" statute in 1965. In general, managerial fear of union-security provisions is a fairly accurate indication of an inept and insecure managerial corps.

Communist-party members from being union officers for five years after conviction, nor could there be serious reservations about the new rules restricting the freewheeling use of union funds. But in the so-called bill of rights for union members, it was once again clear that Congress viewed the interests of union leaders and the rank-and-file as irreconcilable—a view scarcely supported by overwhelming evidence of union workers loyalty to their leadership.

If the unions had lost political potency in recent national elections, it was not due to a lack of political activity. The AFL–CIO, with its political arm, was trying vigorously to reward labor's friends and defeat its enemies. The federation had assembled a large staff of trained economists to test labor's economic gains against changes in productivity and to formulate clever arguments to substantiate new demands on managerial prerogatives. Indeed, labor's economists seemed to have an increasing penchant for specious arguments, particularly under the pressures generated by the recession of 1969–1971 and the continuing intractability of inflation.

They were arguing, for example, that it was unfair for 1971 corporate profits to rise more than 50 percent from lows of the recession year 1970 while compensation for workers went up only a little more than 7 percent. Yet it is commonly known that profits are much more volatile than wage rates (and earnings) and may fall to zero or less, whereas reductions in wage rates are almost unheard of in modern times. Labor was also pressing for a $2.20-per-hour minimum wage for all workers covered by the Fair Labor Standards Act of 1966 as well as a new group of state and local government employees, retail store workers in smaller businesses, domestics, and certain seasonal farm workers. Yet such a law could only keep unemployment artificially high among the very sectors of the labor market in which it was a problem, particularly among the unskilled young and old. And labor economists were contending in all seriousness that 1971 wage (and benefits) increases in the neighborhood of 30 percent over a three-year period, many with escalator or cost-of-living clauses, were not inflationary. With productivity increases for the year in the 3–4 percent range, it was clear that increases in compensation of as much as 15 percent in the first of the three-year contract periods could only raise unit labor costs (and ultimately consumer prices) substantially.

Moreover, labor's leadership, by taking a public posture that seemed to be uncooperative with the administration's attempts to control wages and prices, received a bad press and continued the process of alienation from nonorganized labor (as well as businesspeople and professionals) that was characteristic of the 1950s and 1960s. When in early 1972, George Meany, autocratic boss of the AFL–CIO, left the Pay Board with Presidents I.W. Abel of the Steelworkers, Floyd Smith of the Machinists, and Leonard Woodcock of the Auto Workers (leaving only Teamster President Frank Fitzsimmons to represent labor), the average householder was more receptive than ever to irresponsible allegations that big labor had *caused* the inflation.[10]

[10] Secretary of Agriculture Earl Butz, for example, told a news conference that "the nation's union members should get new leaders ... who will rise to the call of greatness." At the time, Secretary Butz was busy boosting subsidies on farm products to raise farmers' incomes, but such charges against labor appeared to be eroding labor's public support.

Clearly, these events emphasize the important characteristics of the conflict not just between worker and employer but between organized and nonorganized workers as well. When union power succeeds in raising wages above those that would prevail in the absence of a union, this generally causes reductions in employment. Facing higher wages, employers tend to substitute more capital for labor. And nonunion workers must be prevented from eroding the unusually high contracted wages. Barriers to union entry have taken many forms; where successful, these measures have maintained favorable labor earnings, resulting in excessive labor supplies in nonunion pursuits and lower wages there.

THE QUEST FOR SECURITY

In some regards, however, union and nonunion labor have experienced common changes. Before 1932, loss of income from any cause other than industrial accident posed a great hardship, because workers had no economic protection except the buffer of their savings, organized charity, and payments from the relief agencies of states and their subdivisions. The burden of relief during the Great Depression soon overwhelmed charitable organizations and local government units, and the federal government, largely through the PWA and the WPA, took over the job. This experience with federal relief convinced the majority of Americans, on both economic and ethical grounds, of the necessity of a permanent plan for coping with severe losses in income.

A few leaders in government, business, and the universities had long argued that a comprehensive program of social security was requisite to the adequate functioning of a modern industrial economy. Yet as late as 1930, there was little public sentiment in favor of social-security legislation. Americans believed that the individual ought to be self-reliant and objected to compulsory supportive action by the government. In agriculture, where the need for social insurance was not so pronounced, there was understandable opposition to additional taxes for such insurance. The astonishing fact is that organized labor itself did not support social insurance (except worker compensation) before 1930; as late as 1931, a national AFL convention refused to endorse unemployment-insurance legislation. Not inconsequential opposition was also voiced by private insurance companies, which sought to prevent, or at least modify, government insurance of social risks.

Four years of economic disaster removed all serious obstacles to major legislation. Whatever the philosophical objection to a social-security program may have been, certain hard facts of life were undeniable. Almost four out of every five income receivers depended on paid employment for their livelihood. There were many hazards to continuity of income, some of which seemed to be increasing in severity as the economy became more specialized. Income interruptions included being laid off, getting sick, being injured on the job, and becoming too old to meet the demands of modern industrial life. Finally, the *incidence* of income interruptions, although uncertain and uneven, fell most heavily on low-income people, who were the least able to prepare for them.

New Deal Legislation

The Social Security Act of 1935, which has since been amended, has attacked social risks through application of the *insurance* principle and the *assistance* principle. Under social-insurance programs, the individual acquires a *right* to income because he or she has paid premiums and premiums have been paid by an employer.[11] The Social Security Act of 1935 provided for a federal old-age and survivors insurance program and for a federal–state system of unemployment insurance. It further provided for *assistance* to the needy aged, needy and dependent children, and the needy blind; recent amendments have added other groups. Assistance programs involve grants-in-aid to the states; the federal government meets one-half of the administrative costs and somewhat more than one-half of the assistance payments. Federal assistance programs still involve relief; although the programs are on a more just basis of payment than in former days, the individual who is dependent on them must demonstrate need and is always a supplicant rather than an applicant.

Social insurance has emancipated millions of workers from the fear of one day being "on the county." Originally, the only strictly federal part of the Social Security system was the old-age and survivors program. Under it, until 1950, workers contributed 1 percent of their first $3,600 of wages, and the employer paid an equal amount (again, see footnote 11). In the 1950s, the rate was raised to 1½ percent and in 1954 the first $4,200 of an individual's income was taxable. Subsequent legislation raised the contributions of both employer and employee. Effective January 1, 1972, the first $9,000 of yearly income was subject to Social Security contributions. Under continuing pressure for ever-higher employee benefits, Congress has further increased both individual and employer contributions and benefits substantially.

Equally gratifying to supporters of strong social-insurance programs have been recent increases in coverage. By 1950, 35 million persons, or about 60 percent of the workforce, were covered by old-age and survivor's insurance. Amendments in 1950 incorporated another 10 million workers in the program, including previously excluded regular agricultural and household employees and most of the urban self-employed; in 1954, a second 10 million workers were added. Since 1964, more than 90 percent of the labor force has been covered by Social Security benefits.

Partly due to increased coverage, but also due to a declining ratio of premium payers (employed workers) to benefit receivers (retired workers), the Social Security system as it is budgeted today faces peril. Indeed, the recent increases in Social Security rates have been necessary to maintain benefit payments. Further rate advances will be required in the future, given the current trends in the age profile of the population—unless, of course, past guarantees are weakened or payments are derived from general tax revenues.

[11] It should be emphasized that the premium payment by the employer is part of the wage cost to the employer. Therefore, this results in a lower wage being paid to the worker. It is an unfortunate but common misconception that the employer pays half the premiums; actually, the worker pays almost the entire amount.

The program of unemployment insurance is less extensive in its aim than Social Security, but it is a powerful short-run help to discharged workers. Largely to circumvent legal difficulties, unemployment insurance is provided through state systems. The Social Security Act of 1935 secured state action by levying a 3-percent tax on the first $3,000 of wages paid by employers in all except a few business occupations. Similar to changes in Social Security, recent trends have been to make unemployment insurance laws more liberal—largely in recognition of the fact that unemployment compensation is a highly dependable automatic stabilizer. In 1970, Congress enacted the Employment Security Amendments, which required most of the states to make changes effective January 1, 1972. The federal unemployment taxable wage base was raised to $4,200, requiring over half the states to raise the taxable wage base for the first time since 1935. Coverage was increased to include workers in certain state government jobs (including state hospitals and institutions of higher learning), nonprofit organizations, and small business establishments. Perhaps most importantly, the law automatically extended the duration of benefits in periods of high unemployment, so that persons who exhausted their regular claims could be covered for as many as 39 weeks.

Until 1954, the only major income hazard not increasingly covered by social insurance was nonoccupational sickness and nonoccupational accident. Since the mid-1950s, disability protection has been expanded and improved several times. Provided that sufficient work credits have been earned, monthly benefits can be made to (1) disabled workers under 65 and their families, (2) persons disabled before the age of 18 who continue to be disabled, and (3) disabled widows, dependent widowers, and (under certain conditions) disabled surviving divorced wives of workers who were insured at death. In general, a disability must be expected to last at least 12 months or result in death; benefits for a disabled worker under 65 may be as high as the maximum benefits for a retired worker who is 65 or older. Nonoccupational sicknesses and accidents of a temporary nature are still not covered by any kind of federal plan for workers under 65, despite frequent proposals for some type of federally sponsored national health insurance plan. But for people who are 65 or older, both Medicare and Medicaid provide protection for temporary disability due to sickness or injury. Medicare hospital insurance is financed by a separate payroll contribution and defrays the costs of in-patient hospital care and post-hospital extended care. Medicare medical insurance must be elected by the insured and is financed by monthly premiums. Half of these premiums are paid by the federal government; half, by the insured. Medicaid is an assistance program jointly financed by the federal government and almost all the states. In general, Medicaid pays the hospital and medical bills of needy, low-income people who are aged, blind, disabled, or members of families with dependent children.

Age and Sex

Finally, measures have also been taken to assure particular conditions of employment according to age and sex. Indeed, as we noted earlier, one of the primary measures of labor's progress before World War I was the enactment by various states of laws regulating child labor and women's work. In recent decades, such legislation has lost much of its protective significance, as compulsory education laws have kept children in school longer and federal legislation has regulated the employment of firms engaged in interstate commerce. Since 1936, federal law has set minimum ages for children working on public contracts and, by the Fair Labor Standards Act of 1938, has prohibited the shipment in interstate commerce or to foreign countries of goods produced by companies employing "oppressive child labor." In general, oppressive child labor means the employment of minors under 16 years of age, except in hazardous occupations, where 18 is the lower limit.

Laws regulating women at work purportedly were directed toward protecting the health of present or prospective mothers rather than toward abolishing women from the workforce. These laws were intended first to reduce the number of hours in the working day. By 1920, some states had passed statutes requiring a weekly day of rest, prohibiting or reducing night work, and limiting home work. By 1940, 43 states and the District of Columbia had made some attempt to limit daily or weekly work hours for women, and the number of protective states remained unchanged a decade later. The laws vary so in their provisions that they defy classification. Half the states and the District of Columbia have set a maximum of eight hours a day and/or 48 hours a week in one or more industries. Most of the industrial states in the East have provided the 48-hour standard, but in seven states and Puerto Rico there is no limit to the workweek and in 12 more states a 54–60-hour week is possible. Especially in the Southeast, excessive hours and onerous working conditions have remained a problem in service and other establishments clearly functioning in intrastate trade.

The fact is, however, that laws restricting women's employment have also come under increasing scrutiny, and state enactments barring sex discrimination have passed the legislatures of most states. More and more courts are outlawing statutes or work rules that discriminate against women, including prohibitions against working long hours, lifting heavy loads, and engaging in hazardous occupations. Consistently, the Federal Occupational Safety and Health Act of 1970, which took effect in April 1971, puts pressure on the states to develop and enforce standards of job safety and healthful working environments for *all* members of the workforce, regardless of age or sex.

29

Government in the Transportation Business

The title of this chapter was not chosen carelessly. Most companies in the several transportation industries of the United States are privately owned by individuals who receive profits and presumably incur losses. Yet for reasons we will examine shortly, the federal government has intruded far into the transportation business. Americans have generously voted tax monies to build facilities for all the new and one of the old transportation industries. And the regulatory function, undertaken at the national level in 1887, has expanded to such an extent that no firm can make a major decision to invest or disinvest without the approval of a regulatory agency.

Government subsidy of agriculture has been a small operation compared with the subsidy of transportation. This interference with private enterprise is the result of the most remarkable feature of recent transportation history—the rapid change from older to newer transportation modes. As each new transportation form proved itself, Americans were eager to benefit from it. But under the market system, resources would have been directed only to those geographical areas that showed promise of earning at least the going rate of return, and less favored areas would have been ignored. So government subsidy was sought. In an age of increasing speed, the town, city, or state with access to only inferior (older) transportation facilities pressed for improvements and contributed funds to stay abreast of the economic competition. National considerations also led to strong congressional support for investment at the federal level. Canals, then railroads, and finally highways, airways, and natural waterways have therefore received subsidies from the federal government. Subsidy of the different industries has been granted without much regard for interindustry competition and with little consideration for maintaining the balance of the system as a whole.

Canals were falling rapidly into disuse before the outbreak of World War I. Almost everywhere, except on the upper Ohio River and the Great Lakes, traffic on the natural waterways was dwindling. The electric street railway showed unmistakable signs of decay before 1920, as did the foreign merchant marine until wartime activity revived it. Until the end of World War I, railroads were the dominant means of transportation. As we look back, we can see that the industry had reached maturity via nearly every type of test.

Since 1920, the shift from railroad to highway has had the most important influence on the transportation industry. Trucks and buses have taken business away from the railroads—trucks especially hurting the railroads by winning the short-haul, high-tariff traffic. The airlines began to compete with the railroads for passenger traffic in 1930 and by 1940 were capturing much of the long-distance, first-class passenger business. Between the two World Wars, the foreign merchant marine once again shrank as the coastal trade and the Great Lakes bulk traffic continued to expand.

World War II reversed the fortunes of both the railroads and the foreign merchant marine. Gasoline and rubber shortages enabled the railroads to win back passenger and freight traffic that had seemed to be irrevocably lost to truck lines and automobiles. The foreign merchant marine was suddenly stimulated, and coastal shipping was reduced due to the menace of submarines. Airlines, despite the difficulties of enlarging their fleets, continued their prewar growth, and technological advances in military aviation promised a golden future when the equipment became available. Although the older forms of transportation were given a new lease on life and achieved record-high volumes of traffic in this period, it was apparent that after the war the automobile and the airplane would again be damaging competitors.

THE FEDERAL GOVERNMENT AND NEW FORMS OF TRANSPORTATION

The Highways

For financial rather than technical reasons, progress in highway building long lagged behind progress in vehicle manufacture. Thus, the early use of cars and trucks was limited mostly to city streets due to the inadequacy of interurban roads. During World War I, the private motor car ceased to be used exclusively for social purposes and for sport, the omnibus appeared on city streets, and motor trucks replaced horse-drawn drays. But intercity bus travel and intercity motor-truck transport did not become important until the 1920s.

Until the advent of the automobile, responsibility for the roads was delegated to local governments. During the first 15 years of the twentieth century, states became aware of the need for supervision and coordination of the old road districts and the somewhat more modern country systems. Yet only a few states were financially able to provide a basic statewide road network, let alone make adequate provisions for country roads. And there remained the problem of developing an interstate system. Clearly, some kind of federal program was necessary.

The movement for better-quality roads received its impetus from many groups. One group was the auto clubs. The first automobile show was held in 1900 in the old Madison Square Garden, and it was not long before social clubs, such as the American Automobile Club of New York and the Automobile Club of Southern California, were formed.[1] When the local clubs federated to form the American Automobile Club in 1902, auto enthusiasts could speak with a loud voice. They were soon joined in their demands by the American Road Builders Association and its lobby and by the American Association of State Highway officials. Between 1910 and 1915, national conventions and congresses met at length to urge an integrated interstate highway system. Promoters set up booster organizations in towns along the route of the proposed coast-to-coast Lincoln Highway. But it was the farmers who pressed hardest to get out of the mud, and legislators with heavily rural constituencies—Congressman Shackleford of Missouri and Senator Bankhead of Alabama—piloted the first federal highway legislation through Congress.

With the passage of the Federal Aid Road Act of 1916, the development of a national highway system began in halting, timorous fashion. The government committed itself to spending $75 million to build rural post roads; the money was to be expended by the Department of Agriculture over a period of five years. The national contribution was not to exceed 50 percent of the total construction cost, exclusive of bridges and other major structures, and was conditional on the organization of state highway departments with adequate personnel authority and sufficient equipment for initial work and subsequent maintenance. The Federal Highway Act of 1921 amended the original law by requiring that the Secretary of Agriculture, in dispensing aid, give preference to states that had designated a system of highways to receive federal aid. A designated state system was to constitute the "primary" roads of the state and was not to exceed 7 percent of the state's total highway mileage. Incidentally, in the Act of 1921, Congress appropriated as much money for a single year's construction (1922) as it had for all of the preceding five years.

Despite such a promising beginning, more than a decade of frustration was to meet the efforts of those who had "seen the light and carried the fight" for better roads. State legislative appropriations were sporadic and uneven. The traveler of the 1920s often found a smooth strip of concrete ending suddenly in a sea of mud or terminating at a stream that lacked a ferry or a bridge. Within the states, the most densely populated areas naturally tended to receive the "primary" road designations and consequently the good roads. In the great agricultural midlands, highways remained in unbelievably poor condition as late as the early 1930s. In Kansas, for example, long after the cities of Kansas City, Topeka, and Wichita were connected by a concrete slab, travelers along the old Pike's Peak Ocean-to-Ocean Highway, designated U.S. Highway 36, were frequently stranded hubcap deep in mud. The dirt roads of Kansas were connected to Nebraska's major highways, then topped with a magnificent layer of

[1] F.L. Paxon, "The Highway Movement, 1916–1935," *American Historical Review,* **LI** (1946), pp. 236–53.

gravel, and the county and township roads had not been noticeably improved for 50 years. Under such conditions, a trip of only a few miles could not be undertaken until favorable weather was certain.

One blessing of the Depression was the impetus given road programs by relief and recovery agencies. Roads properly received a large share of public expenditures undertaken to escape economic doldrums. Before 1932, federal funds had not amounted to as much as 10 percent of total revenues for highways. In 1932, they rose to 30 percent and climbed to over 40 percent the next year. Federal participation, as a percentage of expenditures, did not drop to pre-depression levels until the beginning of World War II. Meanwhile, the concept of federal aid had expanded. After 1933, "secondary" roads—that is, roads outside the primary 7 percent—were included in the assistance program, and money was authorized to improve portions of highways that ran through cities and to eliminate grade crossings.

During the war years, proper highway maintenance was not possible, and some major routes deteriorated rapidly. In anticipation of a rebuilding program, Congress passed the Federal-Aid Highway Act of 1944, making $1.5 billion available for expenditure in the three fiscal years following the end of the war. The law provided for the designation of an interstate highway system of not over 40,000 miles; this system was to receive the largest single portion of the appropriated funds. Secondary and feeder routes, including farm-to-market roads, received specific appropriations. Recognizing the seriousness of the growing congestion in urban areas, the law set aside monies for use exclusively on those segments of the basic interstate system lying within the limits of cities of 5,000 or more.

Within a decade after the end of World War II, it became apparent that the narrow, two-lane highways that constituted most of the U.S. highway network could no longer meet the nation's transportation needs. Spurred by the "highway lobby," Congress authorized the Interstate and Defense Highway System in 1956.[2] Designed to provide some 41,000 miles of limited-access, multilane mileage connecting the principal centers of the United States, the project was scheduled for completion in 13 years and was estimated to cost $27 billion. Fifteen years later, 42,500 miles had been completed at a cost of $43 billion, and 10,500 additional miles were completed by 1977. The interstate system was financed on the familiar grant-in-aid basis; the federal government contributed 90 percent of the money and the states provided 10 percent.[3] Additional excise taxes on petroleum products, tires, and trucks were to be placed in a highway trust fund to finance the new system on a pay-as-you-go basis, grumblingly called a "paid-before-you-go" basis by critics. Into this trust fund poured an

[2] The highway lobby includes the American Association of State Highway Officials, the American Automobile Association, American Trucking Association, Automobile Manufacturers Association, American Road Builders Association, and many other organizations, which reputedly spend more than $100 million a year to influence highway legislation.

[3] Originally, states barring advertising within 600 feet of the right of way qualified for an extra federal grant of ½ percent. The Highway Beautification Act of 1965 directed that after January 1, 1968, a state would be penalized 10 percent of its federal-aid highway funds for noncompliance with billboard and junkyard controls, but in the 1970s the outdoor advertising lobby still thwarted the intent of Congress.

Superhighways such as these compete with houses for room to grow. Complex highway systems have revolutionized the inventory policies of some companies by making truck transportation rapid and dependable.

increasing stream of earmarked user taxes, which amounted to more than $5 billion per year in the 1970s.

Airways and Airports

Before 1920, the airplane had practically no economic significance. For more than a decade after the first flight of a heaver-than-air craft in 1903, the new machines were the playthings of eccentric sports enthusiasts and scientists. World War I gave impetus to the development of airplane engines and structures, but major improvements lay in the future. In 1918, a military airplane was used for a commercial purpose when the Post Office Department and the War Department jointly sponsored an airmail route between Washington and New York. The project was soon dropped, but in the early 1920s the Post Office Department established airmail service between major cities. In 1925, when it appeared that airmail was practical, Congress ordered that all contracts be let to privately owned airlines. The Air Commerce Act of 1926 marked the first federal attempt to promote civil aviation. Funds were provided for a civil airways system as well as for improvements in navigation facilities. Meanwhile, sensational long-distance flights, financed by the rich, caught the

Fast domestic and foreign air travel has made airports more dependent on long runways and nearby residents painfully aware of the screech of jet engines. Drastically shortened travel time has greatly increased the productivity of business and professional people and has changed the character of many service trades as well.

public imagination and furnished evidence of the great future of commercial aviation.

The U.S. government was expected to assist this infant industry. Its first direct contribution, aside from subsidies granted through airmail payments, was the establishment of marked routes, equipped at first with beacon lights and then with radio markers and radio-range beacons. With the growth of the private airline companies, route mileage rose from less than 2,000 miles in 1926 to 22,000 miles in 1935, when plans to modernize and improve the airways were drawn up in the interest of airline safety. In 1949, there were 57,000 miles of federally owned air routes operating in the United States and its territories; by 1960, this figure had soared to 220,000. The system, made up largely of "VHF" airways and "superskyways" above the 17,000-foot level, was equipped with navigational aids, instrumental approach systems, air-route traffic-control centers, an extensive weather-reporting service, and traffic control towers at major airports. From 1925 to 1961, government expenditures on the construction, maintenance, and operation of airways amounted to approximately $3 billion. These contributions to the airways system were made without recovering any funds from the users of the system.

Long after the beginning of commercial aviation in 1926, the federal government assumed no responsibility for airport construction except for the provision of emergency landing fields, which were considered part of the airways system. Until 1933, airports were built as private business ventures or as projects of municipalities wishing to grasp the opportunities of a coming air age. Municipal financial troubles accompanying the depression made investment in such long-range projects progressively more difficult, and the federal government then began to participate in these ventures as a part of the relief program. Between 1933 and 1940, the federal government contributed just over 70 percent of the funds for airport construction, and municipalities furnished most of the rest. Because the main object of government expenditure was unemployment relief, no comprehensive plan of location and design was followed, and much of the construction was wasted. In 1940, Congress provided for a systematic extension of airport facilities, but the war intervened before it could go into effect. During the war years, practically all activity occurred at the federal level, and military objectives were the primary factor in all investment decisions. The result was that by the end of World War II the government had provided about three-quarters of the money for all airport construction.

The 1946 Federal Airport Act attempted to infuse order and consistent long-range planning into airport construction. Of the available funds, 75 percent were to be apportioned among the states based on population and area; the remainder was to constitute a discretionary fund. Federal participation in small airports was limited to 50 percent of construction costs, discounting land acquisition; in large airports, federal participation might be less than 50 percent. Applications for federal aid could be made by any public agency at a local level, but to be approved projects had to be included in the current National Airport Plan of the Civil Aeronautics Administrator. The 1946 Act worked well through the 1950s, but in 1958 the Eisenhower Administration tried to prevent its extension beyond June 30, 1959. However, Congress did not concur in the view that the government should "begin an orderly withdrawal from the airport grant program," and continued to grant federal aid.

Throughout the 1960s, federal aid to airports averaged $75 million a year, dwindling to $30 million in fiscal 1969. In that year, several airports were so congested at peak traffic hours that controllers staged slowdowns, and the Federal Aviation Administration imposed air-traffic quotas on the nation's five busiest airports. With administration urging, Congress passed the Airport and Airway Development Act of 1970, which established an "Airport and Airway Trust Fund" to be fed by user tax revenues over the decade of the 1970s. Although the law required expenditures on airports and airways of no less than $500 million per annum until 1980, the user taxes were estimated to generate 1 billion dollars of revenue annually by 1975 and not far short of twice that amount by 1980. Experience with the highway trust fund suggests that whatever the Airport and Airway Trust Fund receives will be spent.

As late as 1940, most airports did not earn sufficient revenues to meet operating expenses, let alone capital costs. With the great increase in air passenger traffic in wartime and postwar years, users paid a much greater share of airport expenses, and almost all major air terminals, if properly managed, began to cover their maintenance and operating costs; a few actually covered *all* their costs, including rental payments, landing fees, aviation fuel sales, and restaurant and other concessions. Airports in small cities often failed to meet their operating expenses. Yet a national system of air transport required federal planning of minimum facilities, and the government got something else for its subsidy—free use of the airports by military aircraft and space for air traffic control and weather observers.

FEDERAL REGULATION OF TRANSPORTATION

The Railroads

Federal regulation of the transportation industries began with the railroads and acquired a complexity there that is not found in water, air, or highway transportation. Before 1920, the chief emphasis was on protecting the public from discriminatory railroad rates. After 1920, the competition of trucks and automobiles brought a complete turnabout in the objectives of government control; since then, the railroads—not the public—have obtained the protection of the regulatory authority.

The great debate after World War I over the return of the railroads to private ownership made it clear that adjustments in the financial structure of the railroads would be required if a large number of companies were to survive. Even before competing industries made their inroads on rail traffic, the railroad industry was in poor financial health, and many companies, large and small, were in desperate circumstances. Inept and sometimes fraudulent managements had settled large, funded, interest-earning debts on many roads, and restrictive rate-setting by the Interstate Commerce Commission often kept companies from obtaining legitimate rate increases. In 1920, when the return of the railroads to their owners was imminent, additional financial problems appeared. The government had to be reimbursed for improvements to the railroads made during government seizure, funds had to be raised for modern-

The railroad still accounted for more intercity freight traffic than any other mode of transportation by 1970. One of the few postwar technological innovations in railroading —the "piggybacking" of long-distance truck cargoes—is shown here.

ization, and money had to be found to bring together scattered employees and equipment.

The Transportation Act of 1920 was a heroic effort to solve both the transitional and long-run problems. The Act guaranteed that for six months after the return of the railroads to private operation, railroad owners would receive a net income equal to that of the best six-month period under federal control. The carriers were permitted to fund the debt owed for government improvements at 6 percent interest. For loans with maturities up to 15 years, $300 million was provided, and financial help was extended to short lines that had been especially hurt by war-time losses of traffic volume. It was felt that if the railroads were given this much assistance during the transitional period, permanent policy decisions regarding rates and the consolidation of companies into systems could be made to produce a sound, healthy industry.

Section 15a of the Act outlined a rule of rate-making for the Interstate Commerce Commission. The Commission was instructed to set rates that would enable the railroads, as a whole or in certain groups, to earn "under honest, efficient and economical management a fair return upon the aggregate value of the railway property." The rule, we note, applied to the railroads as a whole or in groups, not to individual carriers. A perplexing problem therefore arose. Some roads were high-cost carriers, and others were low-cost carriers. A rate that would yield a handsome profit to one road might net a loss to another road, and there was no guarantee that the government would make up the deficits. Also, different rates for the same class of service would remove some lines from competition or discriminate unfairly against certain users of the service. What was the solution?

The answer was given in the "recapture clause" of the Act, which required that one-half of the earnings of any railroad in excess of a fair return on the fair value of its property should be paid to the Interstate Commerce Commission. These earnings were to be placed in a contingent fund from which loans could be made to weak lines for capital expenditures or to refund maturing obligations. Carriers fortunate enough to earn more than the allowed rate of return were to retain the other half of the excess in a reserve fund from which they could pay interest, dividends, and rentals in bad years.

Another provision of the Act reversed a previously settled policy toward pooling agreements—devices (discussed previously) for splitting either traffic or profits among colluding companies in some predetermined way. Long considered a monopolistic practice, pooling was henceforth not regarded as restrictive of competition if it was in the "public interest" and was carried out under ICC regulation. Legalization of the practice reflected congressional feeling that highway competition would effectively protect the consumer from monopolistic restrictions of the railroads.

The guide to rate-making, the recapture clause, and permissive pooling were more than transitional measures, but they were not considered final solutions. To achieve effective control of the entire railroad industry, the Commission was granted the authority to consolidate roads into systems and to control the rate of investment and disinvestment. Great hopes were placed in the concept of consolidation. The Commission was instructed to devise a plan whereby each individual line would be assigned to a system, and each system would be set up so that a uniform rate scale would yield approximately the same return on the fair value of the property. After the system plans were established, hearings were to be held at which stockholders and shippers could express their views. The ICC was then to publish a final plan and assist in proposed consolidations. Any two companies could combine properties, provided that the merger was in accordance with the master plan and was agreeable to the stockholders and to the Commission.

The grandiose consolidation scheme was supported by provisions giving the Commission "exclusive and plenary" jurisdiction over the issuance of railroad securities. To this financial power was added absolute control over abandonments; after 1920, no railroad line could cease operation without the permission of the ICC. Furthermore, the Commission could require the construction of new lines where traffic justified extensions and could compel the owner of a terminal to allow the use of the facility to another carrier upon payment of just compensation.

After 1920, passenger business began to decline. Freight revenues held up well during the general prosperity of the 1920s; even so, the financial position of the roads as a whole was not good. In only one year was the "fair-return" standard of 5.5 percent on the "fair value" of properties actually reached by the railroads as a whole. With the onset of depression in 1929, the financial position of all the companies deteriorated rapidly. By 1931, railroad managements were demanding rate increases, just when shippers could least afford them and when competing agencies were striving desperately to take away business. The Commission could offer only a little relief. With 60 percent of their total capitalization in bonds, on which interest was payable regardless of earnings, the railroads were in a critical position. Many were saved from outright collapse only by loans from the Reconstruction Finance Corporation. Deficits in 1932 and the failure to recover in the first half of the next year led to the Emergency Transportation Act of 1933.

The emergency Act contained two parts. One was designed to relieve the railroads of immediate financial pressure; the other made important amendments to the Interstate Commerce Act. The emergency provisions tried to promote cooperation among the lines through three large regional committees to be guided by a Federal Coordinator of Transportation. Joint use of facilities, elimination of "wasteful competitive practices," and financial reorganizations to reduce fixed charges were suggested as necessary economy measures, but in the years of severe strain not even temporary relief was secured by these means.

Changes in the Interstate Commerce Act marked the passing of two cherished notions. The 1920 rule of rate-making was abandoned. Instead of fixing rates on the old "fair-return" standard, which had proved so difficult and expensive to enforce, the Commission was directed to consider the carriers need for sufficient revenues to provide an adequate transportation service. Further, the highly controversial "recapture" clause was repealed. Railroads with high earnings had continuously resisted efforts to take away their excesses over a "fair-return" standard, and weak roads that needed loans from recaptured funds could not meet the stringent mortgage requirements. No one argued to retain this foolish law.

The 1933 Act tenaciously clung to the idea of consolidation, which by then had lost its universal appeal. The combination of strong and weak roads to form large rail systems was resisted, for obvious reasons, by the stockholders of the money-making lines. Labor feared such consolidations because they would mean a reduction in jobs. Shippers believed consolidations would result in higher rates. Yet those who dealt with the problem of the financial deterioration of the railroads could cling only to this one hope. They felt that failure to accept the ICC's final plan of consolidation, published in 1929, could be partially explained by the technical difficulties of bringing properties together. When these difficulties were removed by the 1933 legislation, it was hoped that consolidation would begin in earnest.

The severity and length of the depression in railroading was bewildering. Ton-miles of freight and passenger-miles fell disproportionately compared to those of competing transportation modes. What was worse, recovery in the railroad industry lagged far behind the rest of the economy. In 1936, net income was about 1 percent of capital, and the recession of 1937–1938 brought another bad deficit in the latter year. In 1938, roads controlling one-third of total mileage were in receivership, and only the threat of war in Europe created enough business to keep many lines from bankruptcy. The chief source of difficulty was the depression, because it bore down heavily on industries that furnished the greater part of revenue-yielding traffic. Yet the failure of the railroads to respond to the general improvement in the economy must be blamed on other causes. Competition from the trucking industry and the private automobile, as well as from pipelines and water carriers, had produced devastating effects. Coal, the principal commodity carried by the railroads, was losing ground to other energy sources, and shipments of building materials—also an important source of railroad revenue—did not recover to predepression levels. The decline of foreign trade eliminated much long-haul business from the interior to the coasts. And heavy, long-term indebtedness precluded substantial cost reductions that could have been gained through the purchase of efficient, modern equipment.

The railroads were buoyed up by World War II; to the credit of the railroad industry, it must be said that the handling of traffic was as admirable as it had been sorry during World War I. Facilities for handling traffic were about the same. Cars and locomotives were fewer in number, but their capacities were greater; railroad mileage was less in 1941 than it was in 1916, but there were more sidings and more double track. The roads were helped by the fact that traffic did not all flow to one coast, by much more commodious port facilities, and by the efficient use of equipment through the care-service division of the American Association of Railroads. An incentive to cooperative effort was the fearsome specter of immediate and probably permanent nationalization of the railroads in the event of a breakdown comparable to that of World War I. Finally, the Office of Defense Transportation, headed by Joseph B. Eastman, did a masterful job of coordinating the entire effort. The expeditious handling of a volume of rail traffic almost twice that of World War I stood as a first-class achievement.

Yet only a little while after the war, it became apparent that the railroads were in serious and continuing trouble. The Korean War slowed the decline in percentage of freight and passenger traffic carried, but the downward trend continued into the early 1960s. From carrying two-thirds of all intercity freight traffic in 1946, the roads slid to little more than two-fifths in 1961; in the meantime, rail passenger traffic dropped from just under 20 percent to less than 3 percent of all passenger-miles. In 1961, the industry earned a minuscule 1.9 percent on its total investment of $27 billion, and railroad employment on Class I lines was only 664,000, less than one-third of the total employed in 1921. In the decade of the 1960s, the railroads maintained a nearly unchanging proportion of intercity freight business, but intercity passenger revenues almost vanished.

The railroad industry's difficulties were readily attributable to a relative, even absolute, decline in the demand for railroad services in a period of almost uninterrupted growth in business generally. But what caused this catastrophic drop in demand? In part, it resulted from a continuing erosion of the bulk-commodity traffic—the bread-and-butter cargo the railroads had always carried with an "inherent advantage." Much of the coal business, for example, disappeared as the transmission of electricity over long-distance, high-voltage lines made it possible to burn coal at a mine site or at a generating station along the Ohio River. The St. Lawrence Seaway has diverted enormous ton-

Despite new modes of travel, the canal remains charmingly inexpensive, particularly to bulk-cargo shippers. Here an oil tanker clears a lock in the Erie Canal near Waterford, New York, with its usual few inches to spare.

nages of grain from the eastern trunk lines to waterways, and iron ore can now be shipped from foreign countries to salt water's edge instead of traveling cross-country and adding to domestic ton-miles. Water transport by river and canal has chewed away at the carriage of bulk goods at one extreme, and motor carriers have skimmed much of the traffic cream by moving high-tariff items swiftly across an ever-improving highway network. It was not just *how much* the trucks hauled but *what* they hauled that mattered.

Recent public policy has showed some signs of recognizing the problem of the railroad industry as one of tremendous excess capacity, made worse by the exciting technological innovation of the most progressive railroad companies. An industry that could handle 75 percent more traffic with little addition to variable costs obviously needs more business, and more business will come only with substantial rate reductions. By stating a new rule of rate-making in the Transportation Act of 1958, Congress encouraged the Interstate Commerce Commission to stimulate weakened business with rates that would bring lost business back. Section 15a was amended by the following paragraph:

> In a proceeding involving competition between carriers of different modes of transportation subject to this Act, the Commission, in determining whether a rate is lower than a reasonable minimum rate, shall consider the facts and circumstances attending the movement of the traffic by the carrier or carriers to which the rate is applicable. Rates of a carrier shall not be held up to a particular level to protect the traffic of any other mode of transportation, giving due consideration to the objectives of the national transportation policy declared in this Act.

Presumably it would be difficult for a competitor to complain about a railroad rate so low that it produces an adverse effect on competition. Yet the last clause in the new rule would give a commissioner or a judge an excuse to keep a railroad from competing on a price basis—on the ground that such competition conflicted with the objectives of "national transportation policy." And yet government's recent connection to Amtrack and its financial involvement with Penn Central are legends of contemporary history.

Motor Carriers

Improved highways, better trucks, and the large pneumatic tire were responsible for the commercial success of a new form of transportation—the truck line. It was not hard to get into the trucking business. A few hundred dollars would make the down payment on a truck, and one truck was the only piece of equipment many of the early operators owned. When the depression came, many unemployed truck drivers, who were formerly draymen, gravel-haulers, or businesspeople, purchased a truck on credit and started an intercity truck "line." In this way, they bought themselves a job that would last as long as they could pay out-of-pocket expenses like gas and oil and meet the equipment payments. These shoestring operators did not keep books or take out insurance, and few worried about covering all their costs. Thousands of them hauled freight, and the mushrooming industry began to suffer all the pangs of competition.

Since Americans have always been enthusiastic about the virtues of competition, it seems odd that this development in the trucking industry should have caused concern. Indeed, there were those who argued that truck lines ought to compete freely among themselves and that competition should be carried further to permit all of the various transportation modes to strive in any way to take business away from rivals. But there were many sources of opposition to such a policy. The large, well-established operators in the trucking industry felt their profits being reduced by the undercutting of a mass of small-scale common and contract carriers. The market, as they put it, was "chaotic" and needed the quick restoration of order.[4] By 1933, the railroads were aware of the dangers of an uncontrolled trucking industry, and their executives

[4] To this day, the first argument for regulation advanced by large trucking interests is that a regulatory authority prevents "chaos," meaning that the big companies are thereby spared certain of the less pleasant manifestations of a competitive industry.

pressed Congress for a tough law. Meanwhile, a number of trade associations and the United States Chamber of Commerce became interested, as did the New Dealers in Washington. Some of the last even proposed that all the competing transportation industries should be welded into rational systems, and that each type of carrier should perform the service for which it was best suited.

But the idea of forming great regional transportational systems comprised of all different types of carriers was abandoned in favor of a plan of interindustry competition. Each new transportation industry was nevertheless to be regulated in Washington as it approached maturity. The Motor Carrier Act of 1935 was the first major attempt to bring an industry other than the railroads under almost total regulation.

This Act became Part II of the Interstate Commerce Act (everything having to do with the railroads was included in Part I). The law exempted certain types of motor carriers, such as vehicles used to carry agricultural products, trucks used by farmers in the course of their operations, and vehicles employed by railroads and airlines. Private trucks and buses—those owned and operated by firms that were not in the transport business—were not entirely exempted from ICC regulation but were subject to only minor supervision.[5] The two major categories covered by the Act were "common" and "contract" carriers.[6]

Economic regulation of any transportation facility implies the power of an authority to grant the right to operate in specified territories or over certain routes, to control rates, and to determine the kinds of services to be rendered to shippers or travelers. Thus, the Motor Carrier Act of 1935 directed the Interstate Commerce Commission to issue "certificates of public convenience and necessity" to common carriers and "permits" to contract carriers. In general, rates were to be "just and reasonable" and nondiscriminatory, but the rule of rate-making, like the one applying to the railroads, allowed the Commission to exercise wide discretion. The Commission *might* fix both maximum and minimum rates for common carriers; for contract carriers, only minimum rates might be prescribed, and no undue advantage over any common carriers was to be granted. Tariffs had to be published, and 30 days' notice of changes in rates or classifications was required. Services had to be safe and adequate. Although these were the basic conditions imposed by the Act, other provisions were included to assure *total* regulation of interstate motor carriers, like that of the railroads. Records and accounts were to be kept and reports made as prescribed. Securities issues of large lines were placed under the scrutiny of the Commission. All of the provisions governing intercorporate relationships

[5] Both exempted carriers and private carriers must observe certain requirements regarding safety equipment, qualifications of drivers, and maximum hours that personnel may work. Private carriers, in addition, are subject to the requirements of accounting, submitting reports, and marking vehicles.

[6] Common carriers stand ready to accept the business of anyone who ships commodities that they are equipped to carry. Contract carriers take shipments only by specific agreement and presumably do not serve the general public. In practice, the distinction between common and contract carriage is unclear, because contract carriers may keep on accepting contracts until for all practical purposes, they are common carriers.

of the railroads—the control of consolidations, pooling, and the like—applied to motor carriers as well.

For a while after 1935, it appeared that the hand of the regulatory authority would weigh as heavily on the trucking industry as it had on the railroads. But after a desperate time during World War II due to tire and gasoline rationing, the motor-carrier industry expanded tremendously, and the greatest growth was that of private trucks rather than common carriers. The Interstate Highway System, by adding speed and flexibility and thereby permitting refinements of scheduling, may have encouraged the expansion of private trucking, because from this point inventories could be largely carried in transit. Yet the relatively slower growth of the common motor carrier meant that from the early 1960s on only one third of all truck traffic has been regulated. Why? By keeping new competitors out of the business and setting rates that protect the least efficient common carriers, the ICC encourages shippers to maintain their own transportation facilities. Even though private carriers are fully loaded in both directions little more than 7 percent of the time, it is apparently cheaper for companies to own their own fleets than to hire specialists who are granted monopoly rates by the ICC. Something *must* be wrong with the economics of common carriage.

The Airlines

During the 1930s, people were still thrilling to the new speed records that were being set by aviators. As multi-engined aircraft provided safer and more economical flights, people began to travel by air. The early airlines did not fail to take advantage of the adventuresome appeal of their service. They were clever enough to capitalize on the concept of the luxury and glamour of air travel. Hostesses were also registered nurses, meals were served on a complimentary basis, and attention was lavished on the traveler. Such treatment eased the qualms of passengers who reflected on the unenviable safety records of airlines in the early years of commercial air transportation.

Regulation of the growing air transportation industry had long been under consideration by the government. By the mid-1930s, three administrative agencies were rivals for regulatory authority: the Department of Commerce, the Interstate Commerce Commission, and the Post Office Department, the last by virtue of its power to fix rates for airmail. In 1937, legislation was proposed that would have placed commercial air transportation, along with the railroads and the motor carriers, under the jurisdiction of the ICC. This legislation was not enacted, partly because President Roosevelt, himself an aviation enthusiast, wanted a separate commission to be created that had promotional as well as regulatory powers. Bills to this end were drawn up, and at the hearings a fourth agency—the Maritime Commission—unsuccessfully asserted its claim to control overseas lines.

The Civil Aeronautics Act of 1938 established the first real economic regulation of commercial air transport. We do not need to go into the details of the original Act, because only two years later the Civil Aeronautics Authority created under the original law was reorganized. At this time, Congress established within the authority (then an agency in the Department of Commerce) the Civil Aeronautics Administration and the Civil Aeronautics Board. The CAA was to handle all matters pertaining to the airways system, enforcement of safety rules laid down by the CAB, and promotion of airline traffic. The CAB was to be in charge of economic regulation and the determination and issuance of all rules relating to safety.

From its inception, the Civil Aeronautics Board has exercised authority over the airlines similar to the authority exercised by the ICC over land carriers. CAB has issued certificates of public convenience and necessity to domestic carriers and permits to lines operating between the United States and foreign countries. It sets minimum and maximum tariffs. Control over intercompany relationships has been complete and final. Provisions of the law have permitted a tighter regulation than that exercised over any other kind of transportation facility. Moreover, the CAB was directed to do everything in its power to further the progress of commercial aviation. This provision has resulted in a rate-making policy that until recently protected the airlines from continuing losses and in a paternalism that has neglected the welfare of competing transportation industries altogether.

For more than a decade, the CAB assured the airlines of profitable operations by means of an airmail subsidy. Although the Postmaster-General paid for the transportation of airmail, charges for the service were determined by the CAB under its authority to fix just and reasonable rates. The Civil Aeronautics Act directed the CAB, in fixing rates, to consider "the need of each such carrier for compensation for the transportation of mail sufficient to ensure the performance of such service and, together with all other revenue of the air carrier under honest, economical, and efficient management, to maintain and continue the development of air transportation to the extent and of the character and quality required for the commerce of the United States, the Postal Service, and the United States." The Board interpreted the "need" of the airlines in a sense most favorable to them. Any company that was not run dishonestly or inefficiently could obtain sufficient airmail payments to make up any operating losses and provide stockholders with a "fair" return on their investment. Under this system, of course, there was no way to be sure what portion of payments was a proper reimbursement for carrying the mail and what portion was pure subsidy.

Congress had said, in effect, that the airlines could operate on a cost-plus basis. The possibility of incurring a loss within any accounting period was not precluded, but adjustments could quickly be made to remove any loss. Each company's "need" was considered separately, the result being that the large, money-making lines, such as the four transcontinentals, received low "service" payments per mail-ton-mile after a time while other companies received high "need" payments. In 1948, these rates varied from 60 cents to $70 a mail-ton-mile.

In 1951, the CAB began to divide payments into two parts, separating airmail pay from subsidy, and the Federal Aviation Act of 1958 made this procedure mandatory. Both feeder and major lines have since received a service rate based on line-haul and terminal charges, and feeder lines and helicopter companies have enjoyed substantial direct subsidies. The apportionment of costs among passenger, express, freight, and airmail services implies arbitrary judgments on which complete agreement would be unlikely, but there appears to be a consensus among transportation economists that airmail payments are greater than the costs justify and so involve some subsidy.

Due to the growing complexity of air traffic, the Federal Aviation Act of 1958 established a Federal Aviation Agency to exercise control over the physical facilities of civil aviation, including the safety regulatory functions of the Civil Aeronautics Board. The agency's administrator, who reported directly to the President, coordinated the requirements of national defense and commercial aviation and in effect had complete charge of the total aviation system. Functions previously performed by the Secretary of Commerce under the Federal Airport Act of 1946 were turned over to the agency's administrator, as were responsibility for the National Airport Plan and expenditures of federal aid for airport construction. The Transportation Act of 1966, which established a Department of Transportation, kept the acronym FAA while redesignating the agency the Federal Aviation Administration. Although air-traffic control is the agency's most time-consuming function, it also conducts an aggressive program of research and development in the interest of improving air safety, maintains training and mechanical facilities, and works in cooperation with the International Civil Aviation Organization (ICAO) to achieve uniformity of standards, practices, and safety rules throughout the world.

As an independent agency, the CAB has historically tended to maintain high air fares to keep total returns up, and at the same time has freely awarded new operating rights on trunk routes. For example, *Fortune* magazine reports that in 1967–1968, the CAB allowed American, Trans World Airlines, and United to increase the number of daily nonstop flights between New York and Chicago from 102 to 135. Introducing larger planes, the carriers increased average aircraft capacity by 4.4 seats at the same time. Although air traffic rose 10 percent, total capacity increased so much that the average load factor (percentage of seats occupied) dropped from 59 to 47. As load factors and profits dropped, the three companies appealed to the CAB for fare increases, which the obliging agency granted.[7] Perhaps for these reasons—and certainly as a result of the efforts of Alfred Kahn—new laws are soon to take effect, eliminating CAB's very existence.

Domestic Water Carriers

In our earlier discussion of water carriage, we ended on a doubtful note about the future of this mode of transportation. By 1915, watter carrier traffic flourished only on the Great Lakes, the Ohio River, and the coastal lanes. Yet the belief persisted (and still persists) that water transport was inherently cheap and that great industrial and commercial development awaited communities, especially those in the Midwest, that could gain access to a navigable

[7] That CAB-approved rates are on the high side is evidenced by the California experience, where state-regulated fares are 40 percent below those elsewhere in the United States and traffic between Los Angeles and San Francisco is phenomenally high.

channel. Proponents of inland water transportation have been indefatigable. With the Army Corps of Engineers to abet them, they have succeeded in persuading Congress to provide large funds to create avenues for water-borne commerce. For the last 30–45 years, the rivers and harbors bill has typified pork-barrel legislation.

Water transport of bulk goods *is* cheap—to the shippers who pay nothing in the way of user charges for the canals and rivers that are their roadways. In 1972, shipping by barge averaged 0.3 cents a ton-mile, compared with 1.4 cents for rail shipping and 7.7 cents for trucking. Only 10 percent of the volume carried by barges is subject to ICC control, with the result that practically no monopoly pricing elements have been injected into water shipping by government. But someone is literally paying the freight.

In addition to traffic on inland rivers and canals, domestic water transportation includes shipping on the Great Lakes and on coastal and intercoastal routes. Some public expenditures have been required on the Lakes, chiefly to improve connecting channels, and on the coasts for harbor work and deep-water channels. The really significant sums, however, have been expended on the river systems and on the intracoastal canals along the Atlantic and Gulf coasts. By 1960, the Corps of Engineers had spent more than $5 billion on dredging channels to minimum depths, building dams and locks to maintain water depths, dredging harbors, and constructing revetments. Annual expenditure levels reached one-third of a billion dollars in the early 1960s and kept on rising; the federal government had invested $10 billion or more in the Corps by 1972, and almost $2½ billion was spent in 1977.

Like all other transportation agencies, domestic water carriers eventually fell under federal regulation. During the 1930s, there was agitation for unified government control over inland water carriers, although the reasons for regulation were less compelling than in the cases of the motor carriers and the airlines. By 1938, common carriers in the intercoastal, coastal, and Great Lakes trade were required under Maritime Commission authority to fix rates, but contract carriers were excluded from regulation. The ICC had jurisdiction over the common ship carriers owned by the railroads. Thus, there were two regulatory authorities concerned with inland water transportation, and the railroads complained that their lines were much more severely restricted than those under Maritime Commission control. Furthermore, the railroads were beginning to feel the pinch of unrestrained canal and river competition and lobbied steadily for their inclusion in a comprehensive regulatory act.

Sentiment among transportation experts and members of Congress was generally favorable toward unifying legislation. The Transportation Act of 1940 transferred jurisdiction over all water carriers engaged in interstate commerce from the Maritime Commission to the ICC. Control provisions with regard to water carriers were similar to those previously applied to railroads and motor carriers, and these provisions became Part III of the Interstate Commerce Act. However, so many exemptions were granted that in 1943 the ICC reported its control was limited to a small proportion of all water-borne commerce. If a carrier transported no more than three commodities in bulk or if the cargo were liquid in bulk, no regulation could be imposed. Furthermore, all private carriers were exempt. Since most tonnage carried by water moved in exempt categories or in private fleets, there was little left to regulate; as already noted, not more than 10 percent of inland-waterway traffic was under ICC jurisdiction in the 1970s.

The Merchant Marine

The Merchant Marine Act of 1920 was designed to remove the federal government from the foreign shipping business. Government-owned vessels were to be sold at low prices to shipping companies, which were to receive tax advantages and construction loans on favorable terms. But even though these ships moved into private hands, the merchant marine continued to dwindle. An act of 1928, which attempted to bolster the merchant marine by increasing indirect subsidies, especially through mail payments, was of no avail. Tonnage in the foreign trade dropped from 11 million in 1920 to 7 million in 1929; a decade later, tonnage was down to about 3.3 million. By 1935, only one-third of U.S. exports and imports and a negligible portion of the remainder of world trade was carried in American ships. Although in the late 1930s the American merchant fleet was still second only to that of Britain in tonnage, it was slow and old; within another few years, it would have been almost entirely obsolete.

For reasons of national defense, in 1936 Congress reversed the long-standing policy of not granting direct subsidies to carriers in the foreign service. The Merchant Marine Act of 1936 established a new body, the United States Maritime Commission, which was authorized to grant "construction differential" and "operating differential" subsidies. The purpose of the Act was to put American shipbuilders and ship operators on an equal footing with their lower-cost foreign competitors, so that the American merchant fleet would carry a substantial part of U.S. foreign commerce. On application by a qualified concern, the Commission would undertake construction of a vessel in an American shipyard, at the same time contracting to sell it to the applicant for a price equal to the cost of building the vessel abroad. The difference between the actual cost and the estimated foreign cost was the amount of the "construction differential" subsidy, which was supposed to be no more than 50 percent of the cost of construction in an American shipyard. If, however, certain features especially useful for national defense were incorporated in the ship, the government would absorb their costs.[8]

The principle of the operational subsidy was the same; the Commission would make up the difference between the cost of operation under U.S. ownership and the cost of operation under a foreign flag. A recapture clause in the contracts enabled the government to claim half of any profits in excess of 10 percent per year over a ten-year period.

The Commission experienced difficulty in determining the foreign costs of construction and operation, but the directive of Congress in this respect was

[8] Through this device, the liner *United States,* which cost an estimated $70 million, was made available to the United States Lines for only $28 million. Unfortunately, the great liner was retired in 1969 because it could not cover costs despite the receipt of both construction and operating subsidies.

clear. The mandate to promote the merchant marine to the extent that it would carry a "substantial" portion of U.S. foreign commerce was not so clear. In practice, the Commission interpreted "substantial" to mean 50 percent of the trade *taken as a whole.* Although an effort was made to place American carriers on all the important trade routes between the United States and foreign countries, it was not considered necessary to have one-half the commerce of *each* route handled by U.S. operators.

The assistance rendered to the shipping industry between 1936 and 1941 did not produce a merchant fleet large enough to transport troops and supplies to the fighting fronts in World War II. The Liberty ships and Victory ships of the World War II years were built on government account, so the construction and operating programs under the Maritime Commission were interrupted. After Pearl Harbor, shipyards that had been acres of weeds, rotting timbers, and rusting iron were refurbished, and new shipyards sprang up on inland waterways, in back channels, and on the Great Lakes. For the first time in the history of shipbuilding, component parts were fabricated at inland points and assembled on the coasts.

Since World War II, the merchant marine has enjoyed indirect benefits that are of greater monetary value than the amounts it has received for construction and operational differential subsidies. In the Merchant Ship Sales Act of 1946, Congress provided for the sale of hundreds of high-quality ships on terms especially favorable to American-flag operators. Several hundred first-rate dry-cargo vessels were sold for as low as one-third their prewar cost. Other indirect benefits have included the charter of government-owned vessels under favorable terms, assured loans at low interest rates for ship-construction programs, and the guarantee to U.S. operators of half the business shipped under the European Recovery Program and the military-aid program. Direct subsidy payments have been resumed under the Federal Maritime Commission—an independent agency that performs the standard regulatory functions of determining the rates, services, and practices of seagoing vessels that serve as common carriers and that actually executes the subsidy contracts with shipping companies.

In the intensely competitive world of international ocean shipping, the United States lost its leadership more than a century ago, largely because American labor was relatively less productive in this industry. Or stated another way, foreign-built and foreign-operated ships produced a service at lower cost per ton-mile than American-built and -operated ships did. Beginning in the mid-1960s, there were signs of a possible revival of American leadership in this field. The innovation was the container ship, with its containers loaded six deep in the holds and three deep above deck. Specially designed vessels, such as the Lancer and the SL-7, with top speeds of 24–33 knots, have tremendous competitive advantages, but the United States' primary advantage is the drastic reduction in labor costs that result from container loading. The United States does not have a monopoly in container shipping, which constitutes 60 percent of the shipping on the North Atlantic run, but such companies as Sea Land Service, Incorporated, and United States Lines, Incorporated, at least can compete for business outside the constraints of the primitive labor relations that nearly destroyed the American shipping industry.

FEDERAL GOVERNMENT INVOLVEMENT IN REVIEW

The transportation problem in the United States can best be brought into focus by considering the tremendous government outlays that have been made since World War I to subsidize the various modes of transportation. A good part of this expenditure was a legitimate charge against the public Treasury for social-overhead capital that could not have been provided in any other way. It is hard to believe, though, that a substantial proportion of proposed outlays (see Table 29-1) can be explained except as boodle for those who lobby most effectively in Washington.

The Conflict between Regulation and Promotion

The logical inconsistencies of many of the developments recounted in this chapter are apparent without further discussion. Americans have created a transportation system in which all the major modes except railroads and pipelines are subsidized by the government. Furthermore, government officials pour public funds into all forms of transportation facilities without attempting to coordinate these expenditures by some accepted principle.

TABLE 29–1
Summary of Federal Program Funds in Direct Aid of Transportation (in millions, rounded)

Subject	Program magnitude 1917 (or later) through 1960	Program magnitude 1961–1975
Corps of Engineers expenditures for navigation improvements	$ 5,080	$ 9,000[e]
Tennessee Valley Authority expenditure for navigation	219[a]	91
Coast Guard expenditures related to navigation	1,687[b]	4,787
Coast and Geodetic Survey expenditures for surveys and charts to aid navigation	158	198
Federal-aid highway authorization	20,659	60,000[e]
Federal aviation program	4,489[c]	30,000[e]
Merchant marine subsidies:		
Operational differential subsidy	969[d]	2,000[e]
Construction and reconstruction subsidy	306[f]	500[e]
Total	$33,567	$106,576

Source: *National Transportation Policy* (Doyle Report), Preliminary Draft of a Report to the Senate Committee on Interstate Commerce, Eighty-Seventh Congress, First Session (Washington, D.C.: U.S. Government Printing Office, 1961), p. 172.

[a] Beginning in 1935.
[b] Beginning in 1952; data for prior years was not furnished.
[c] Beginning in 1927.
[d] Beginning in 1947.
[e] Changed from Doyle Report estimates to reflect recent statutory changes.
[f] This construction differential subsidy program started in 1936, and the reconstruction subsidy program started in 1955.

One half-hearted effort to bring order into the confusion was the Transportation Act of 1940. This law, as we have seen, placed domestic water transport partially under the control of the ICC. The Act made improvements in ICC procedures for handling the growing burden of work. Moreover, it instituted major changes in certain matters of policy that directly affected the railroads. The 20-year-old plan to consolidate the rail lines according to an ICC plan was abandoned, and the Commission was directed to fix rates without regard to protecting certain carriers. But the 1940 Act was basically a statement of national transportation policy. The Commission was directed to provide "fair and impartial regulation of all modes of transportation" and to administer the law so as "to recognize and preserve the inherent advantages of each." But air transport is outside the jurisdiction of the ICC, and much water and highway traffic also lies outside its control. The ICC has nothing to say about how many airports are to be constructed, how many miles of highway are to be built, or how many miles of channel are to be dredged. Finally, the Interstate Commerce Commission has appeared to set rates that have, in fact, protected the railroads against other competing forms of transportation.

Indeed, both motor and water carrier lobbyists have complained that the Commission approves extremely low rail rates when it is likely that traffic will be diverted to trucks or barges. In this way, they have argued, the agency that has an inherent advantage in furnishing a certain type of service is shut out of the competition by the below-cost rates of the railroads. To such contentions, the railroads retort that neither motor nor water carriers pay amounts comparable to the fees that they should for the use of waterways and highways and that without this subsidy their charges for the service in question would be much higher. The trucking companies assert in turn that they pay through license fees and gasoline taxes for their use of the highways—a contention hardly supported by tests indicating that heavy vehicles are destructive to the roads. Representatives of railroad interests offer a final plea of unfair treatment with the argument that, as railroads are common carriers, their freight is entirely subject to regulatory authority, whereas the greater part of truck and water freight escapes regulation.

A solution to the problem of conflict between regulation and promotion was suggested in a 1949 report by former Secretary of Commerce Charles Sawyer. The government, he stated,

> . . . should consider continuing its various promotional programs along lines which call for payments by the user for the various facilities. Government regulatory agencies should simultaneously consider the elimination of rates which are not closely related to the fully distributed cost of rendering the service. If action along both lines were to proceed at the same time, most of the legitimate complaints which the railroads have against their competing carriers would be eliminated and most of the legitimate complaints which water and motor carriers have against the rail carriers would be disposed of. The net result would be a more effective use of transport resources, with each type of carrier performing the various services in which it had a cost advantage.

In the quarter-century following Secretary Sawyer's statement, there seemed to be an increasing sentiment in support of imposing realistic user charges. There was also a growing belief that less regulation and more market discipline would achieve a healthier set of transportation industries. As L.L. Waters has remarked, the growth of private transportation, while leaving a few pockets of monopoly, has removed much of the need for conventional regulation; the greatest measure of consumer and customer protection now lies in the power of individuals to move themselves and their goods by *private* vehicle over public highways, waterways, and air routes. Government can exercise its most effective control by the determination of public expenditures on public transportation routes. Traditional regulatory agencies have therefore become a poor third in providing user protection. It follows that greater reliance can be placed on the price system by allowing the forces of competition to determine rates of investment and output in the transportation industries. Responsible commentators of the 1970s have even suggested that the traditional regulatory agencies of the ICC and the CAB be abolished. By 1978, significant steps had been taken toward deregulation of the airlines, and the CAB was to be dismantled.

Yet common sense and experience tell us that advocates of the various forms of transportation will continue to compete for public funds—and therefore for resources—without much regard to social need. A genuine coordinating agency should be placed in charge of *all* promotional activity, so that resource allocation could be justified on other than political grounds. During the 1960s, there was great pressure to establish a Department of Transportation, (DOT) under the supervision of a secretary of cabinet rank who could face the combined problems of promotion, investment, and regulation. The legislation establishing the DOT was a disappointment to those who wished the Secretary of Transportation to have more than a vague coordinating authority; the regulatory agencies were left with their powers intact. Yet the potential influence of a strong cabinet officer was suggested by the highway lobby's startled and hostile reaction to Secretary John A. Volpe's 1971 suggestion that urban transit as well as the interstate transportation system participate in the highway trust fund.

A different approach to transportation policy should not be anticipated in the near future, because the outcome of complete control by a government commission is that the commission eventually identifies itself with the controlled industry. As long as shippers and the traveling public receive reasonably good service without patently discriminatory rates, there will probably be no insistence on a coordinated, rational system. Only economists and a few government legislators will press for change, and there is little reason to believe that they will make a successful case against the combined opposition of both the regulators and the regulated—who have usually agreed that the status quo is preferable to any sweeping change. Yet President Kennedy's 1962 plea for a greater reliance on "unsubsidized privately owned facilities, operating under the incentives of private profit and the checks of competition" elicited some legislative response from Congress. Perhaps Americans will decide that they can no longer tolerate the cartel pricing of transportation services under the auspices of a federal bureaucracy.[9]

[9] For persuasive arguments on the side of eliminating regulatory authorities, see George W. Hilton, "The Basic Behavior of Regulatory Commissions," *American Economic Review,* **LXII:**2 (May 1972), pp. 47–54.

30

Today's Economic Issues in Historical Perspective

PROTECTION OF SPECIAL INTERESTS

Economic forecasters of the early 1970s cheerfully predicted a gross national product for 1980 of over $2 trillion. Such an assurance for the future was both comforting and gratifying. But it is not ordinarily the business of either the economist or the historian to make long-range quantitative predictions, as human beings are not gifted with prescience. War, inflation, unforeseen innovations, changes in levels of investment, the degree of international cooperation, improved birth-control practices—these and many other influences have altered the course of economic growth. Indeed, the belief that world economic growth at 1950–1978 rates implies global doom within a century has led some to advocate a slowing of economic growth as the very center of a new public policy.

Yet our study of economic history would be something less than satisfying if it did not help us to judge the kind of organization and performance of the economy that Americans will face in the future. It has been our special concern to observe the growing demands of different groups for government protection of their special interests. We have emphasized the sweep of forces that explain the abandonment of the nineteenth-century liberal ideal of the least possible amount of government interference in private affairs. If changes in the concept of the role of the state in economic affairs had only been manifestations of the economic and political unrest of the 1930s, we would have anticipated some lessening of federal controls. But demands for much of the New Deal legislation had been long in developing. The first spur-of-the-moment, experimental laws have been modified and recast, but they have been retained, and their purpose of solving problems rooted deeply in the past is still the same.

The farm problem, for example, did not appear suddenly in 1930. Farmers have always been peculiarly vulnerable to shifts in economic conditions. In part, their troubles are the result of a liberal land policy that they themselves were largely instrumental in securing. But long-time adverse influences on the supply of and the demand for agricultural products are not the fault of the farmers, and they have generally been able to win price supports to bolster their incomes. The continuation of price guarantees in 1978 is typical of the historic support for the farm bloc. Stronger consumer response in the face of general inflation (propelled in part by annual increases in food prices that had reached 8.9 percent in early 1978) undoubtedly contributed to the political difficulty of passing the farm aid bill. In addition, it is now generally recognized that price-support mechanisms only help make rich farmers richer but do little to maintain the family-size farm or relieve agrarian poverty. But, despite general opposition, the views of strong, articulate vested interests have again prevailed. One day perhaps we will see the adoption of a farm plan that is primarily contracyclical in purpose, and the old concept of maintaining parity prices and incomes will disappear as a structure of very large farms tied to equally large food-, feed-, and animal-processing firms emerges.

Similarly, the labor problem that has existed for two centuries will persist as long as the United States maintains a reasonably free capitalistic economy. There is simply no way to avoid disagreements between labor and management as long as they are both permitted to bargain. The argument that trade unionism has not been as successful in improving wages, hours, and working conditions as union members and leaders commonly have supposed carries little weight with organized labor, and we can anticipate continuing efforts to increase union membership in unorganized occupations. But the conflict between powerful unions and large companies seems likely to abate as the level of economic understanding improves. Labor leaders, advised by competent professional staffs, are aware that they can demand only such gains as increasing productivity will permit, unless they are willing to force short-run increases in unit labor costs that would result in both inflation and a noncompetitive status for American products in world markets. Employers, equally well advised, are likely to become more willing to pass on the benefits of increased productivity to employees, which, as tight labor markets recur, the forces of competition assure to labor anyway.[1]

There are signs, however, that the public is tired of being at the mercy of these two contending giants who, while testing each other's strength, can bring the economic machine to a standstill. The coal strike in early 1978 is a classic example of monopoly labor power in conflict with the general welfare of the country. Disruptions of businesses and social services, such as the closing of Indiana University and other institutions due to a lack of coal for heating, significantly raised the public scorn. Nor will the public continue to tolerate violence, whether it takes the form of gangsterism in a few union leaderships or

[1]As noted in Chapter 28, real product per man-hour in the private economy and real hourly earnings in manufacturing have increased at nearly the same rate since 1910.

an employer's use of armed force to resist an organizing drive. This side of the millennium, we can expect government to remain the arbiter of the continuing contest between big labor and big business, according to rules that favor one side or the other as the nation's political complexion shifts.

The future of government intercession as a tool to control the monopolistic practices of large firms is not quite so clear. As we have observed, the restoration of competition in the sense of "atomizing" an industry that is composed of one or a few firms is physically impossible and, even if it were possible, economically undesirable. And it does little good to increase the number of firms from, say, one to four, as in the case of the aluminum industry, because prices and outputs are determined by very similar rules when there are "few" competing firms as they are when there is one firm. Dissolution is no more effective a remedy today than it was half a century ago, as Judge Wyzanski's decision in the *United Shoe Machinery* case affirms. As we argued at length in Chapter 27, the courts and the Justice Department can effectively root out socially objectionable cases of monopoly control only by defining use categories and searching out those categories in which there is no interindustry or interproduct competition. For a long time to come, however, the orthodox view will prevail. Many people believe that monopolistic behavior has been inhibited simply by the threat of antitrust prosecution. Moreover, there is evidence that collusion in industries composed of many firms has sometimes been prevented by Justice Department action. The decision in *Brown Shoe Company* v. *United States* (1962) suggests that the Supreme Court will stand in the way of some mergers, even though oligopoly is only "incipient" in an industry plagued by the ills of competition. But thus far the problem of conglomerate mergers has proved intractable; as we observed in Chapter 27, competition in the classical sense is probably promoted by conglomerates, but such huge concentrations of business assets are frightening and disturbing to those who are afraid of bigness.

If we were to continue to enumerate the instances in which the federal government has intervened in the private sector of the economy, we would find almost no exceptions. There is no longer any serious objection to old-age and survivors insurance, unemployment insurance, federal insurance of bank deposits and savings and loan shares, federally underwritten residential mortgages, and rural electrification. On the question of public power, national opinion vacillates with swings in political sentiment, but in the regions that are directly affected, the legislator who opposes federal multipurpose dams, steam-plant construction, and power preference to municipalities and REA cooperatives enjoys a brief career. Today, scarcely a voice is raised against federal supervision of the issuance of securities.[2]

To recall, the major thrust of New Deal economic policy was to assure protection for all sectors of the economy. The policies fell into two general categories: economic stabilization and income maintenance. Consequently, the goal of protecting and maintaining incomes for various groups such as farmers,

[2] The swell of government activity may be abating, however. Several important voices have recently questioned the advisability of federally subsidizing the air, truck, and bus lines, and deregulation of these industries is an increasing possibility.

laborers, businesses, and others, was added to the goal of eliminating wide fluctuations in economic activity. These were the objectives of the generation of economists who are now moving into retirement.

GUARANTEEING ECONOMIC STABILITY

From the founding of the first Bank of the United States in 1791 to the establishment of the Federal Reserve in 1913, there were attempts to mitigate the effects of business fluctuations by manipulating the money supply. But during the first two decades of the Federal Reserve System's history, the money managers had no clear concept of a monetary policy aimed at broad stabilization objectives. The failure of the System to prevent the Great Depression and, worse, its inability to bring about an economic revival disillusioned economists and laymen alike. People began to wonder if they had not been wise to attribute so much importance to money as a causal factor in economic fluctuations.

The prosperity of the World War II years convinced almost everyone that the secret of permanent prosperity lay in a fiscal policy directed toward preventing unemployment. In 1945, Congress even considered a bill that would guarantee full employment by placing a $40 billion "annual investment fund" at the disposal of the Secretary of Commerce. Senator Murray, its author, said that the bill was a "legal acknowledgment that the national government assumes the responsibility for prosperity in peacetime. The federal government is the instrument through which we can all work to accomplish full employment and high annual income." After much argument and semantic juggling, a revised version of the original "full-employment" bill was passed as the "Employment Act of 1946." Full employment was no longer explicitly required; instead it was to be the federal government's responsibility to "promote maximum employment, production and purchasing power." The adjective *maximum* was purposely ambiguous, but the entire statement was generally understood to mean that the government would act quickly to shore up the economy if a severe recession threatened. A Council of Economic Advisers, with an adequate professional staff, was added to the Executive Office of the President. The President, assisted by the Council, was directed to submit to Congress at least annually a report on current economic conditions, with recommendations for legislative action. The statute further provided that the House and the Senate were to form a standing Joint Committee on the Economic Report (later simplified to the Joint Economic Committee), which would study the report of the President and the Council of Economic Advisers, hold hearings, and report in turn to Congress. Although no "investment fund" was provided, a watchdog agency was established to keep Congress and the President systematically informed of economic change.

Despite the Employment Act of 1946, inflation and unemployment have recurred in the Post World War II period, as shown graphically in Figures 30-1 and 30-2. As we can see, the fears of a major postwar depression proved groundless; instead, inflation proved to be the problem. The recession of 1948–1949 caused uneasiness as industrial production dropped 10 percent, and the gross national product fell $11 billion, or 4 percent. The Truman ad-

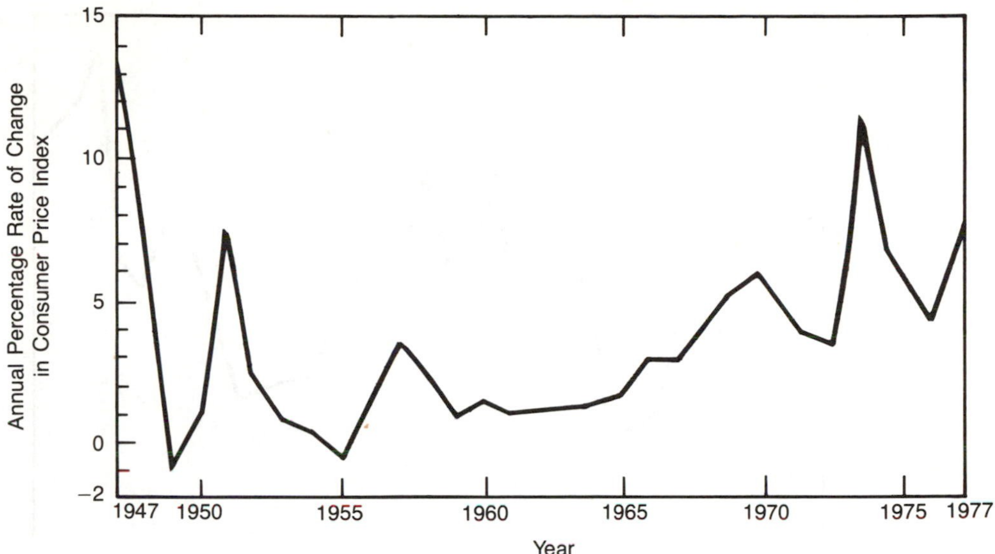

FIGURE 30–1
The Rate of Inflation in the United States, 1947–1977
Source: U.S. Bureau of Labor Statistics

ministration moved quickly, however, to award military contracts in "distressed areas," and although unemployment rose above 5 percent of the workforce for several months, revival came so quickly that public clamor for action never reached much of a pitch. The growth of spending during the Korean War assured the nation of at least three more years of prosperity, although there was a slump in consumer durables sales in 1951.

During 1953, the key indicators of economic well-being took an unfavorable turn. Industrial production, the gross national product, construction contracts, and manufacturers' new orders dropped and unemployment jumped in the last quarter of the year. Because these changes did not occur all at once and were not precipitate, their impact on income earners was neither sudden nor severe. But as the throbbing boom of the early 1950s faded, a pessimism that had not shown itself in 1949 pervaded the country. The magnitude of the drop was approximately the same as the first post World War II turndown. In about nine months, industrial production fell 10 percent, the gross national product declined 4 percent, and manufacturing employment dropped 10 percent. There was much talk of another "inventory recession" like the one in 1949, but it was clear that entrepreneurs had some good reason for reducing inventories. This widely forecasted recession was plainly triggered by a drop in national-defense spending and therefore in total government spending, which declined $11 billion between the second quarter of 1953 and the second quarter of 1954. In short, the federal government caused the recession; since there was a $10 billion drop in gross investment—mostly in inventories—the gross

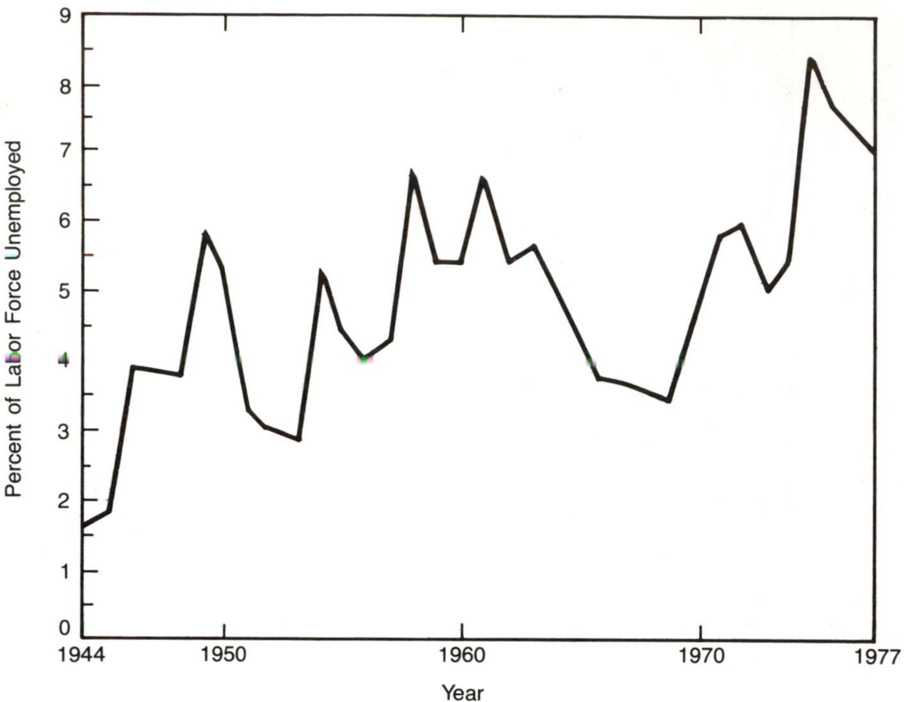

FIGURE 30–2
Unemployment in the United States, 1944–1977
Source: U.S. Bureau of Labor Statistics

product would have declined more than $21 billion if there had not been offsetting expenditures. Fortunately, state and local governments spent more during the year, exports exceeded imports, and personal consumption expenditures increased; the total offset amounted to a little over $7 billion.

Now this was far from a serious decline. Compared to the full-blown depressions of former years, the 1953–1954 recession seemed small indeed. Nevertheless, it aroused great concern. Unemployment in several areas of manufacturing exceeded 10 percent of the local workforce, and many families exhausted their unemployment insurance benefits before any clear signs of economic improvement were visible. The fact that the economy leveled off for several months during the summer and fall of 1954 was far from comforting to those who knew that output could not stand still if net additions to the workforce of about 750,000 people a year were to be absorbed.

The administration, reassured by the Council of Economic Advisers, took no drastic steps to combat the recession by fiscal means. A moderate cash deficit, partly the result of a reduction in federal personal income-tax rates effective January 1, 1954, had a stimulating effect. A Federal Reserve policy of "active ease" was adopted before most informed people were aware that the business indicators had taken a turn for the worse. Nevertheless, as Dean John P. Lewis has remarked, "In the days of routine instability, this would have been just the sort of situation calculated to launch the various downward cumulators in the economy—the multiplier, the accelerator, self-confirming price expectations, and credit contraction—into a progressive, interacting erosion of demand."[3] It was apparent that there were strong sustaining forces in the economy. A continuing rapid increase in population and a substantial rate of household formation created a demand for consumer goods; indeed, the most important resistance to this recession was consumption, as personal income remained insulated from the general decline in spending and income. Even the distribution of the population among age groups was favorable: The babies born in the postwar boom were growing up to eat more food and wear more clothing. To such long-term natural supports were added the automatic stabilizers, which almost immediately operated to counteract the downward movement in economic activity. Unemployment insurance payments, a reduction in the total tax bill as the incomes of individuals and corporations declined, the support of falling agricultural prices, and even some increase in Social Security payments all acted in an essential way to cushion the decline in aggregate spending and keep it from falling in proportion to gross income.

After a four-year respite from inflationary pressures, prices began a steady rise in mid-1955 that continued until early 1957; the increase amounted to about 8.5 percent during this brief period. Inflation became the pressing domestic problem of the day, and Federal Reserve authorities doubtlessly increased public annoyance by intemperate references to both the causes and the dangers of inflation. Even worse, the Fed continued its tight-money policy until well past the point of economic downturn in the late summer of 1957, not reversing itself until November. A recession of unnecessarily substantial proportions followed—the deepest of the postwar period. By the spring of 1958, the gap between output and capacity had reached $40 billion, and unemployment at 7.5 percent of the civilian labor force was burdensome and frightening.

The remarkable resilience of the American economy was once again evidenced by a rebound that began in April 1958. But the recovery through 1959 was halting and disappointing, and when the indicators took another adverse turn at the end of the year, the frustration of policymakers knew no bounds. Once again, the recession was short-lived, and after a trough reached in February 1961, the economy began its longest sustained rise in the post-Korean war years. Not until the fourth quarter of 1969 was there more than a brief hesitation in the rate of advance of the economy. The ensuing recession was technically brief, the major indicators showing a trough in the fourth quarter of 1970.

Shortly thereafter, in 1971, the pace of inflation stabilized near the 4-percent rate, but the unemployment rate also remained above the 6-percent mark. Propelled to action by these conditions, President Nixon embarked on an unusual peacetime economic venture: He imposed wage and price controls. With the intention of stopping inflation, controls were imposed on the critical prices and wages of all major industries in the economy. Although shortages in these industries were soon experienced, the major disappointment was a *rise* in the inflation rate during the middle and end phases of the control period.

[3] John P. Lewis, *Business Conditions Analysis* (New York: McGraw-Hill Book Company, 1959), p. 331.

And, of course, once controls were lifted, prices lunged upward, showing that—except for timing—controls are not effective. With few professional opinions to the contrary, it is widely recognized that price and wage controls always failed; indeed, abandoning controls in 1974 proved to be a positive step in that shortages were eliminated in various sectors of the economy. Nevertheless, because of their political popularity and bureaucratic support, price and wage controls frequently resurface—as testified by President Jimmy Carter's 1978 inflation plan for voluntary controls.

As Figures 30-1 and 30-2 emphasize, the 1970s have been filled with economic and political paradoxes. Compared to other peacetime periods, the United States has experienced exceptionally high rates of inflation in the 1970s. Even more paradoxically, however, the persistent inflation has been accompanied by high levels of unemployment. The combination of high rates of inflation and unemployment (each about 6 percent) is unique to the mid- and late 1970s. This problem has been recently dubbed "stagflation." Policymakers straining to find the appropriate mix of monetary and fiscal policy to reduce inflation and unemployment simultaneously have not yet been successful. Some economists claim that these traditional tools are not longer sufficient to cure such unique ills. Opposing views run the gamut from insisting on additional government planning to greatly reducing government intervention. Naturally, which course we will take in the future is beyond the powers of economic science to predict.

CONSERVATION AND THE ENVIRONMENT: CONCEPTUAL ISSUES

Another deep American concern today—as it was in the 1930s and even earlier—is the environment and the issue of industrial, mining, and consumer waste. In many ways, current environmentalists are very similar to conservationists of an earlier day. The central issue both to today's environmentalists and to earlier conservationists is how to best use our natural resources—broadly defined—on a long-term basis. Conservation and preservation (or repair) of the environment refers to some "proper" allocation of resource uses over time. Therefore, the aim of a true conservation or environmental program ought to be to preserve the future productivity of a soil area, a stand of timber, or a mineral deposit or to protect a natural beauty spot or the quality of life in urban areas. Moreover, to conserve a natural resource or location for future use it is usually necessary to make a current expenditure of capital and labor, rather than simply to withdraw what is to be preserved from use.[4]

Some public expenditures of capital and labor, rationalized on the grounds that they are made in the interests of conservation or the environment, actually amount to nothing more than outlays to increase *present* production. These outlays could be made now or 100 years from now and produce no deterioration in our natural resources. Thus, irrigation and drainage projects do not ordinarily prevent diminution of future production. Speaking generally, a piece of Arizona desert land can be irrigated at any time in the future

[4]For a more technical exposition of such matters, see Earl O. Heady, "Soil-Conservation Programs," *Journal of Political Economy,* **LIX:**1 (February 1951), p. 48 ff.

Conservation and the careful nurturing of fields have also increased farm productivity—and unintentionally exacerbated the farm problem in the process.

and the resultant increase in production will be just as great as it would if the improvement were made now. *Reclamation is not the same thing as conservation.* Similarly, the application of fertilizers to level land may only increase short-run production and do nothing to prevent permanent soil deterioration.

Like all other economic problems, conservation and environmental change involve making choices, either through the private market system or government intervention. If an expenditure is to be made for the purpose of increasing the income stream from a given resource, a complete calculation of benefits versus costs may require a consideration of "income" (for example, natural beauty) for which no private entrepreneur would pay anything. The conflict between development and preserving nature erupts because some values can be protected only through social action. Moreover, the problem of allocating resources for conservation objectives is simplified if we consider the *natural* resource base as part of the *total* capital base of the economy. J.W. Milliman has remarked, "Natural resources are only part of the total stock of capital and . . . there is no a priori reason for believing that natural resource capital is any more productive than other types of capital. It is not the *origin* of capital that is important, man-made or natural, but rather its total amount and the relative productivity at the margin of alternative forms of capital."[5]

Conservation in Twentieth-Century Perspective

Between the administrations of Woodrow Wilson and Franklin D. Roosevelt, the cause of conservation suffered under the public management of natural resources. The first blow to enthusiasm for public measures was dealt in the Presidency of Warren G. Harding. In 1915, President Wilson had set aside Naval Oil Reserve No. 3 in Wyoming. The reserve was named Teapot Dome after a butte located on it, and its supervision and that of the previously established California reserves were entrusted to the Secretary of the Navy. President Harding illegally transferred the administration of these reserves to Secretary of the Interior Albert B. Fall—a confirmed enemy of the conservation movement. Fall granted contracts to private oil companies, allowing them to take oil from the naval reserves to the point of exhaustion in exchange for the construction of storage tanks on both coasts. When the fraud became known, control of the oil reserves was restored to the Secretary of the Navy, but "Teapot Dome" became a rallying cry for those who wished to oppose government ownership and control of natural resources.

The trend away from federal conservation activities that became established during the early 1920s was not lessened under Herbert Hoover. Both the President and his Secretary of the Interior, Ray Lyman Wilbur, flatly supported the transfer of all unappropriated and unreserved lands to the western states. A commission—appointed by President Hoover to make recommendations regarding future land policies—supported the proposal of ceding the remaining public domain to the states. But even westerners, including those with powerful livestock interests, were opposed to the idea, and Congress refused to enact a bill containing the Commission's recommendations.

The development of the Forest Service gained impetus during the 1920s. The policy was to cut and sell only mature timber from the national forests. Efforts were made to introduce the most up-to-date methods of cutting and planting, so that a substantial future supply of timber would be assured. There was a remarkable improvement in the administration of the range lands within the national forests. Essentially, however, nothing new was added to the conservation policy of Theodore Roosevelt that had been enunciated and practiced early in the twentieth century.

There was an upward surge in the movement under the administrations of Franklin D. Roosevelt. Old methods were carried out with renewed vigor, and

[5] J.W. Milliman, "Can People Be Trusted with Natural Resources?" *Land Economics,* **XXXVIII:** 3 (August 1962), p. 201.

two innovations marked a new approach. First, the government took steps to conserve the soil owned by *private* individuals. Second, it insisted that a meaningful program of conservation required the simultaneous protection of many resources within an entire region.

Along lines of traditional policy, perhaps the most important step was the withdrawal from entry of the remaining public domain—nearly 175 million acres—until the land could be classified as to its best use. A small portion of the public domain was later made available for private entry, but most of it was organized into grazing districts under the Taylor Grazing Act of 1934. Before the passage of this Act, stockmen let their animals feed on the great public ranges without restraint. Under the new system, permits were issued that limited the number of grazing animals to the amount that a given range could accommodate without depleting the forage. By 1950, there were 59 grazing districts that included 145 million acres, and in addition, grazing leases were issued on scattered public domain lands and on Indian reservations. A generation after passage of the original Act, controversy still smolders over the proper disposition of these lands. Among westerners, there is substantial opinion that the federal government should reserve and oversee those areas that are suitable for recreation, national forests, wildlife refuges, and reclamation and power projects and sell remainders of the public domain to the highest bidders; but in the populous areas on the East and West Coast, there is resistance to the sale of any part of the public domain.

During the Depression, the government made great expenditures in conservation work. Late in 1933, Harold Ickes could remark, with truth, that the Civilian Conservation Corps had accomplished more reforestation in six months than all the federal agencies had in the preceding 15 years. More importantly, funds were obtained to expand the national forests by purchasing poorly kept private forest lands, located for the most part in the Southeast. By 1950, national forest acreage had risen to 180 million, and the government controlled some 200 million acres of additional forested land in Indian reservations, wildlife refuges, national parks, and other public holdings. However, by no means did all of this land contain first-rate timber.

About 116 million acres, or one-quarter of the U.S. total, was publicly owned commercial forest land divided between federal agencies, which managed 89 million acres, and state and local agencies, which controlled 27 million acres. The very best timber owned by the federal government was located in the West, far from markets and in inaccessible areas, so that investments in roads would be necessary before it could be used. But much of the noncommercial forest land owned by the government was to become merchantable—far sooner than it would have in private hands.

Old-line conservation efforts included some incidental preservation of the soil. Not until New Deal days, however, were serious efforts made to systematically conserve agricultural land. These efforts began with the establishment of the Soil Erosion Service in 1933 in the Department of the Interior. In 1935, the Soil Conservation Service became an agency of the Department of Agriculture. Originally, contracts were made with individual farmers; the Service furnished technical assistance and some materials, and the farmers furnished labor and the remaining materials. Early in 1937, President Roosevelt wrote the governors of the states requesting that their legislatures pass acts enabling landowners and occupiers to form soil-conservation districts. A model state law was enclosed, which the states followed rather closely. By May 1947, all the states, as well as Hawaii and Alaska (soon to be admitted) and Puerto Rico and the Virgin Islands, had passed laws permitting the establishment of soil-conservation districts when they were approved by a vote of the farmers within a proposed area. By 1954, about 2,500 soil-conservation districts, including 80 percent of all U.S. farms, had been organized.

Any discussion of new concepts of conservation must contain some mention of what may constitute the ultimate solution to the whole problem—the inclusion of water control and of major valleys in programs of great scope. Some advocates argue that nothing less can produce permanently successful conservation. The evidence is not conclusive, although the Tennessee Valley Authority (TVA)—one outstanding example—has unquestionably done a remarkable job of upgrading an entire region (see Map 30-1). Two judgments about the TVA may be safely made. First, major floods are a thing of the past in the Tennessee Valley; this means that much of the bottom land in the valley is protected from the periodic dumping of erosion debris.[6] Second, the TVA has done much to prevent upland erosion. Although a unified system of dams and reservoirs can prevent *major* floods and their consequent destruction of bottom land, the problem of erosion on the uplands remains. Silting from the uplands is the enemy of the reservoirs and the navigable channel; it must be stopped at the source—where the raindrop strikes the ground. Thus, TVA authorities have had no choice but to work hard to secure the general adoption of conservation practices. Their program includes reforestation and afforestation, the substitution of cover crops for row crops, contour plowing, and the building of check dams to prevent rapid runoff. Technical assistance and demonstration, in cooperation with other federal agencies and with state universities, has been the chief help to the landowner, but free seedlings and fertilizers have frequently swung the balance in securing the farmers' cooperation.

There will certainly be enough cropland to spare for another quarter-century, although prudence suggests the maintenance of a soil area sufficient to meet possible explosive demands as the twenty-first century nears. If we have limited funds to spend on conservation, they must be used to conserve, not simply to raise short-run productivity. Expenditures for irrigation, drainage, better crop rotation on level land, and the like, cannot be justifiably included in a conservation program unless these practices do indeed save the soil. And there is a further point to be considered. Soils in different geographical areas vary greatly in quality. With limited funds, it is more advantageous from society's point of view to give priority to the conservation of the better soils. This sounds like hard doctrine, and it is. And conservation policy tends to neglect such realistic considerations, partly because the execution of such a policy is fraught with political difficulties; it is easy to point out that the farmer who owns poor land needs assistance more than the farmer who owns good land.

[6] Such dumping can be devastating. The old farm of Ross Robertson's grandparents, flooded in the 1930s by the Kansas River, was a complete loss, with as much as 30 feet of sand covering what was once highly productive land.

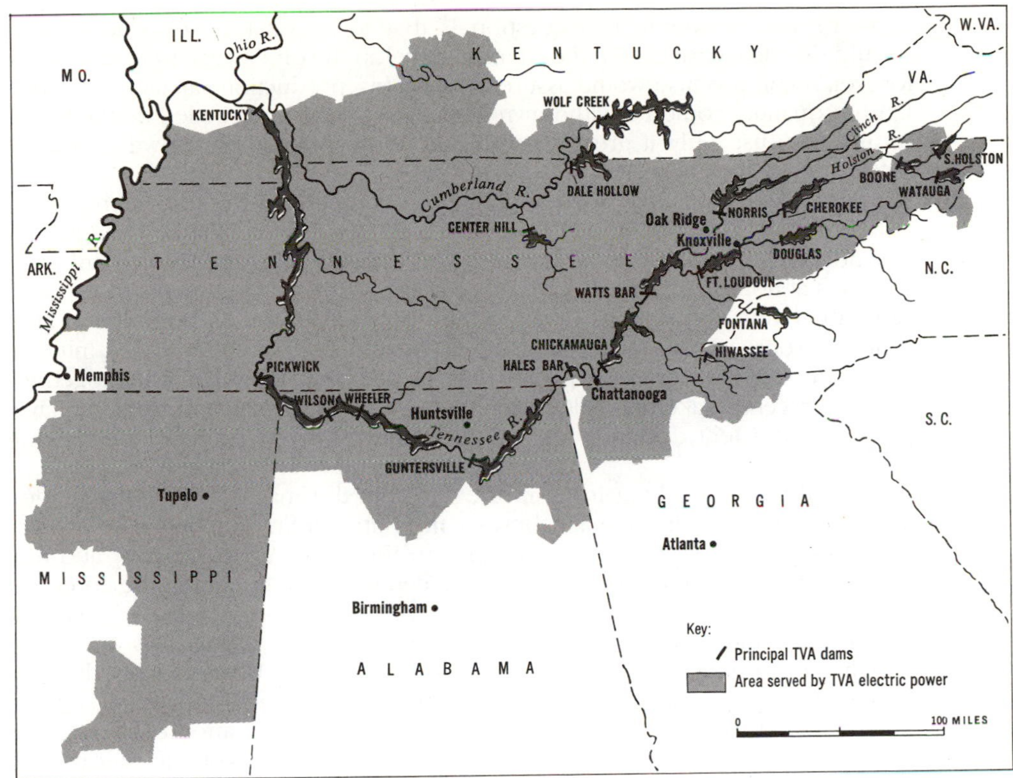

MAP 30–1

Public Power: The Tennessee Valley Authority—the New Deal's major experiment in publically financed power—ranges through portions of six states. Its supporters call the TVA a splendid monument to "regional planning"; its foes denounce it as a noxious example of "creeping socialism."

Technical advances have made possible the reclamation of arid land that was once considered certain waste. Only water is needed to transform most desert into croplands. Pumps driven by 65,000 horsepower motors have been installed at the Grand Coulee Dam to lift water 280 feet from the Columbia River into the Coulee, from which it can then be diverted to irrigate vast areas. For instance, by means of complex systems of dams, reservoirs, pumps and tunnels, water from northern California has been diverted to southern California. The Bureau of Reclamation estimates that eventually 50 million acres west of the Rockies can be converted to fertile land. Such developments lead us to ask whether the whole problem of soil conservation should not be closely related to reclamation (that is, soil-development) programs. Would it be possible to increase future output to a greater degree by investing a given amount in, say, irrigation than by investing the same amount in the prevention of soil erosion? The answer to this question is that to be on the *safe* side society should decide to preserve rather than to develop. If soil erodes away, it is gone forever. A compromise would assure a "stand-by" production capacity. Marginal land in quantity could be withdrawn from production and seeded down, to be returned to use only if great domestic or world population growth one day made such a step necessary.[7]

Such reflections may seem mundane in comparison to the contemporary concerns we face about the natural world around us. Rapid changes in technology, improvements in transportation, and the discovery of new mineral deposits at home and abroad have made some of the old arguments in support of conservation seem trivial. In short, the depletion of soil and of mineral and timber resources is no longer the main focus of conservationists. Today, intense conservationist concern is apparent only in the area of energy. This, together with the recent awakening epitomized by the environmentalist movement, have produced insistent demands for new legislation at both the state and federal levels.

Yet there is mocking irony in the fact that the major federal statute designed to rectify environmental abuses—the National Environmental Policy Act of 1969—consists largely of amendments to the Clean Air Act of 1894 and the Refuse Act of 1899. For three-quarters of a century, despite laws to the contrary, American business had socialized the costs of disposing of wastes. Now efforts are being made to have those costs paid by the firms themselves and then largely passed on to consumers through price increases. Unfortunately, the fact is that energy problems are intensified by environmental concerns. For instance, to obtain cleaner air in urban places, we impose smog controls, ban low-grade fuels, and take similar actions. This raises the costs of energy and more rapidly depletes vital energy sources. Again, it is a matter of choices.

THE DILUTION OF ECONOMIC PROGRESS

Economic progress implies that its beneficiaries can obtain the things they want more readily than they or their ancestors could previously. However much some may long for a golden age long past—for the charm of candles and coaches instead of electric lights and automobiles—Americans today are demonstrably better off materially than our forebearers were a century ago. Moreover, Americans have made greater strides out of the past than any other people. With little more than 6 percent of the world's population and less than 7 percent of its land area, the United States produces and consumes more than one-third of the world's annual production of goods and services. American factories turn out almost half of the world's annual output of manufactured goods. The incomes of Americans probably exceed the combined incomes of everyone living in western Europe. Combined U.S. income is certainly greater than that of Asia and the Soviet Union.

[7] There are apparent exceptions to this generalization. For example, it may be necessary to stop the erosion of hopeless upland areas to prevent sand from being carried into lowland areas where it can be deposited on highly productive land. But of course the object in such a case is to save the better, not the worse, soil.

One way to measure the economic achievement of the United States is to compare what an hour's work will buy in America with what it will buy in other countries of the world. In this regard, the United States has an edge on Canada, a considerable advantage over Great Britain, and a tremendous advantage over the Soviet Union. If we wish to compare present-day output with our own past output, equally impressive figures are available. U.S. productivity has increased so fast that on the average American workers produce more than 10 times as much per hour than their great-grandparents did in 1860. And work is clearly less burdensome than it has ever been. With power-driven mechanical equipment, one person can do as much work in a 40-hour week today as three people could do in the 70-hour workweek that was common 100 years ago. Leisure time has at least doubled since 1910; in the past half-century or more, American workers have taken about two-thirds of national productivity gains in the form of goods and services and about one-third in the form of increased leisure.

Some of the benefits of increasing mechanization have spread to the home and are available to almost the entire spectrum of income groupings. Nearly every American house is now wired for electricity, and more than 90 percent of them are equipped with electric refrigerators, electric washing machines, and television sets. Other appliances and, perhaps more importantly, private baths or showers and private flush toilets are found in more than three out of four American homes. Over three-quarters of all U.S. families own at least one automobile, and one-sixth own two or more. The number of weeks of vacations had doubled in the post–World War II period to more than 80 million weeks a year by 1960. Americans who did not spend their leisure time traveling could add to their real income by engaging in do-it-yourself projects at home or they could read, play musical instruments, participate in organized sports, listen to phonograph records sold in astronomical numbers, ride recreation vehicles ranging from boats and airplanes to snowmobiles, or they could simply restore vitality by loafing on a patio or in air-conditioned comfort.

Life in America in the early 1960s was becoming less arduous, was spent in better physical health and was certainly longer. When the United States became a going concern in 1789, the life expectancy of a white baby at birth was a little more than 30 years. By 1900, a white male child could be expected to live 48.2 years; by 1975, life expectancy for the same baby had risen to over 69 years. The change for female babies was even more dramatic; women could expect to live a few years longer than men in both 1900 and 1979—three years longer in 1900 and about 7.8 years longer in 1979. Nonwhite babies did not have the same life expectancy, but their gains since 1900 have been greater than those for whites. It is reasonable to expect that life expectancy for nonwhites will continue to make relatively large increases.

Yet as these differences in life expectancy suggest, we would be naïve, if not dishonest, if we failed to note those factors that dilute gains in economic progress. At this juncture, we border on the province of the applied economist, whose business it is to resolve economic problems and thereby make life easier for us to live. Yet economic historians a generation from now will judge the total performance of the American economy on the basis of the success with which private enterprisers and public officials make the benefits of capitalistic progress accessible to the disadvantaged.

TABLE 30–1
Distribution of U.S. Income of Families, 1952, 1962, 1972

Families	Percentage of Money Income Share			Percentage of Total Income Share (Adjusted)		
	1952	1962	1972	1952	1962	1972
Top 20 percent	42.2%	41.3%	41.4%	35.3%	34.0%	31.9%
Fourth 20 percent	23.5	24.0	23.9	23.3	22.9	20.9
Third 20 percent	17.1	17.6	17.5	18.8	19.1	18.4
Second 20 percent	12.2	12.1	11.9	14.8	15.1	16.1
Bottom 20 percent	4.9	5.0	5.4	7.8	9.0	12.6

Source: Edgar K. Browning, "The Trend Toward Equality in the Distribution of Net Income," *Southern Economic Journal,* **43** (July 1976), pages 913 and 919.

Largely because sheer luck and competence are so unequally distributed, it is inevitable that some people will not fair well under the pressures of competition. The consequence is the frustrating problem of poverty. The existence of both rural and urban poverty in the United States remains despite the diffusion of higher standards of living. It is hard to identify the poor precisely; some people attach more importance to worldly goods than others do, and no one can say with certainty that a family earning $4,000 a year is less happy than a family earning $6,000.

During the 1960s, the number of families with incomes below the poverty line decreased sharply. At the beginning of the 1970s, 10 percent of all American families were still officially below that line, which was set for a family of four at about $3,800. Table 30-1 shows the distribution of money income as used by government officials in their assessment of poverty levels. According to official estimates in 1977, 26 million Americans still lived below the federal poverty line. More than one-half of the rural blacks and one-quarter of the rural whites were poor; in the metropolitan areas, these ratios were, respectively, one-seventh and one-twelfth.

As we have seen, the stresses and tensions of low-income households have been increasingly mitigated by the intervention of government. It has become an accepted role of government to modify the impact of competitive forces. This intervention, as we know, spans the whole of economic life, but nowhere has it been as remarkable as it has in its direct outlays for public welfare. In 1890, total social-welfare expenditures were an estimated $318 million, or 2.4 percent of the gross national product. By 1913, the figure was $1 billion, or 2.8 percent of the gross national product; by 1929, it had risen to $4.3 billion, or 4.1 percent of the gross national product.[8] The common impression that the

[8]These data are taken from Series N 1-29, "Social Welfare Expenditures Under Civilian Public Programs: 1890–1956," U.S. Bureau of the Census, *Historical Statistics of the United States, Colonial Times to 1957,* pp. 189, 193. Included in the category of social-welfare expenditures are all social-insurance programs, public aid, health and medical programs, vocational rehabilitation, institutional care, school lunch programs, child welfare, public housing, and education. A definition of welfare programs that includes education may seem too broad, but the use of this concept is dictated by the need for a generally accepted and continuous time series.

Three Presidents and a President to be—Truman, Eisenhower, Kennedy, and Johnson—at the 1962 preburial services for the Speaker of the House, Sam Rayburn.

"welfare state" began in the 1930s is borne out by the data. Social-welfare programs in 1935 required a $6.7 billion outlay—9.8 percent of that year's GNP and slightly more than one-half of government expenditures at all levels for all purposes in 1935. Although such expenditures declined both absolutely and relatively during World War II, they rose steadily after the war—amounting to $58 billion, or approximately 11.5 percent of GNP, in 1961. In the ensuing decade, federal welfare expenditures soared to $198.3 billion and state welfare funds rose to $133 billion, which together represented 19.6 percent of the 1976 GNP. Public outlays for social-welfare spending in 1971 at all levels of government represented 51 percent of total government spending for all purposes, compared with the 38 percent recorded in both 1950 and 1960. Measured in constant prices, social-welfare expenditures rose slightly more than 80 percent between 1965 and 1971 and continued to climb throughout the 1970s.

A large number of articulate welfare supporters advocate much greater public expenditures than are presently undertaken. On the other hand, an equally vocal group insists that growing welfare expenditures serve not to buttress a capitalistic economy but to weaken it. The uncontested fact is that over 20 percent of the U.S. gross national product is currently appropriated for public and private philanthropy. In fact, the tremendous rise in welfare expenditures in recent decades strongly suggests that the guidelines used to measure poverty should be reassessed. Economists are now reconsidering the official methods of measuring poverty and, in so doing, are altering our concept of the extent of poverty measured by the U.S. Bureau of the Census, as Table 30-1 shows. If we consider more than mere money income and include rent supplements, Medicare, Medicaid, food stamps, and other factors as income, some households—especially the poorer ones—would have much greater incomes than their money incomes alone imply. The effects of including these types of transfers or supplements is shown in Table 30-1 for three years of comparison, 1952, 1962 and 1972. The role of income redistribution by government was still modest in 1952, but since then government intervention has significantly altered the after-tax and after-transfer distribution of income. According to Congressional Budget Office Director, Alice M. Rivlin, "The nation has come a lot closer to eliminating poverty than most people realize." Whether or not we can go as far as George Washington University economist Sar A. Levitan, who stated that "if poverty is defined as a lack of basic need, it's almost been eliminated," is an open question. But clearly, this new perspective on poverty in America is enabling key officials to make some bold statements about the economics of social welfare that would have been considered unthinkable only a few years ago.

IN CONCLUSION

Whatever particular methods are chosen to resolve the vital problems of today, the larger questions of freedom and equality remain. On matters of justice and the role of special interests, on matters of employment, inflation, the environment, energy, poverty, and in other areas the larger issue is the appropriate mix of individual initiative and government control. Since the Great Depression, the American people seem to have lost faith in the capabilities of business and the private sector to resolve social ills. Today, according to the polls, and as expressed politically in the current tax revolt, Americans have also lost faith in other elements of leadership—expecially in government. What recourse is left is unclear. A return to solving economic problems through market forces may be a matter of default rather than deliberate choice. We cannot predict whether or not this will happen. But it should be remembered that since the settlement at Jamestown, the American market system has performed its allocating function with a high degree of efficiency. Americans generally have admired this impersonal mechanism—partly because freedom of economic choice is consistent with freedom of political choice and partly because freedom of choice assures more rapid advancement over a wide range of economic activities than an authoritarian system of resource allocation does—however efficient such a system might sometimes appear to be in achieving specific, short-run goals. For one of the scarcest of all resources is administrative ability of high order, and the market mechanism is often a better guide to action than conscious administrative decisions. There is much evidence that markets do not make mistakes in allocating resources as often as fallible human beings do, and there is even more evidence that the market mechanism assures creative innovation of a high order.

Glossary

In each edition of *History of the American Economy,* we have made every effort to define in context words and expressions from the vocabulary of economics. But as the narrative proceeds, technical words recur that were first introduced many pages or even chapters earlier, and it is bothersome to leaf through a book to find a first definition. Users of this text have suggested that we append a glossary of terms for ready reference and to elucidate definitions encountered previously. Although this list is limited in scope, we hope that it will prove useful.

Absolute advantage. If country A produces good X with less factor inputs than country B, country A is said to have an absolute advantage in the production of good X.

Acceleration (accelerator) principle. A given percentage change in the rate of sales of consumer products causes a greater percentage change in the demand for the capital goods used to produce the consumer goods.

Aggregate demand. The total dollar expenditure on goods and services generated in an accounting period by the four sources of final demand: government purchases of goods and services, investment, consumption expenditures, and net exports.

Aggregate supply. The total dollar output of goods and services produced in an accounting period by private firms and public agencies.

Automatic stabilizers. Arrangements that yield changes in the shares of government revenues and transfers as existing tax and transfer programs respond to changes in business conditions.

Bank, central. A central bank is the official financial institution of a sovereign government, routinely performing the function of fiscal agent for that government's treasury and dominating the check-collection process. More importantly, the central bank supervises the creation of a country's money supply and intervenes in foreign exchange markets to affect the value of the domestic currency in international markets.

Bank, commercial. The financial intermediary that people ordinarily think of in connection with the word *bank.* It receives funds as deposits from both households and business firms and puts these funds to use in the form of loans to firms and households and in the form of other financial assets, such as government and corporate bonds and short-term Treasury issues. A commercial bank is unique among financial intermediaries in that it receives demand deposits subject to check. Under present laws, other financial intermediaries do not participate in the payments mechanism, although there are political pressures to allow them to do so.

Bank, mutual savings. A financial intermediary that receives true savings deposits, primarily from households, and invests them in a carefully restricted list of financial assets. Recently, mutual savings banks have been given most of the powers of commercial banks, including checking-account functions.

Capital account. The part of an international balance-of-payments statement that reports the capital transactions, both private and public, between one country and the rest of the world. To be distinguished from the *current account.*

Capital consumption allowances. The approximate value of the capital consumed in producing a year's current output of goods and services. The difference between gross national product and net national product is equal to capital consumption allowances.

Capital good. A good in an intermediate stage of production; one of the produced means of production.

Checkoff. The payroll deduction of dues by an employer on behalf of a recognized union.

Closed shop. A place of employment operating under an agreement between management and a recognized union whereby membership in the union is a condition of employment.

Collusion. The act of agreement among sellers or buyers in a market, ordinarily to affect total output or purchases and therefore to affect prices. Collusion was once explicit and even contractual, but in the United States in recent decades it has usually been tacit.

Comparative advantage. Country A may have an absolute advantage over country B in the production of goods X and Y; that is, country A may be able to produce *both* goods with less factor inputs than those of country B. Yet trade in goods X and Y may take place between the two countries if country A specializes in the production of good X, in which it has a *greater absolute* or *comparative* advantage.

Competition, monopolistic. The market type characterized by a large number of buyers and sellers trading in a differentiated rather than a homogeneous product. A product is said to be "differentiated" when *any* reason exists in the minds of buyers for preferring the product of one seller over that of another.

Competition, perfect. A normative market type characterized by a large number of buyers, a large number of sellers, and a homogeneous product. A theoretically perfect market would also be characterized by completely disseminated (costless) information and free entry of resources.

Consumer good. A good in the possession of a household unit that yields a flow of services. The service flow may be short in the case of products that are ingested and long in the case of appliances. Houses are the one exception to this definition. In the income-and-product accounts, an expenditure on a new house is considered to be an investment rather than a consumption expenditure.

Corporation. A form of business organization formed in the United States under a charter from one of the states and, in a few instances, under federal charter. The corporation is recognized as a legal entity (person) apart from its shareholders or owners.

Costs. The expenses of a firm incurred in the employment of all the factors of production. Costs include outlays on materials in process, wages, rent, interest, depreciation, and a return for undertaking the risks of a venture. *Average cost* is the total cost of a given output *divided by* the number of units of output. *Fixed costs* are those costs that remain unchanged as output changes. *Variable costs* are those costs that change as output changes and that are no longer incurred when production ceases.

Current account. The part of an international balance-of-payments statement that reports the total exports and imports of goods and services. To be distinguished from the *capital account.*

Deficit. A Treasury deficit is an excess of total payments over total tax receipts. A balance-of-payments deficit is the excess of a country's outpayments to foreigners over its inpayments from foreigners.

Deflation. A decline in the average level of prices; a rise in the value (purchasing power) of money.

Demand. The quantity of a good or service that buyers are willing to purchase during a given time period at a range of alternative prices.

Demand, law of. The quantity of a good or service demanded varies inversely with its price, if the nominal prices of other goods and the nominal income remain constant.

Diminishing returns, law of. As the quantity of one productive input is increased, the quantities of other productive services remaining constant, a point is reached beyond which the marginal product of the variable input declines.

Disposable personal income (DPI). Personal income minus personal taxes and nontax payments to government.

Distributive shares. The shares of the total value of production earned by the several factors of production.

Dumping. The sale of goods in international trade at prices to foreigners that are lower than the full costs of production in the exporting country.

Durables. Products used by firms and households (usually buildings or machinery or other apparatus) that have an expected service life of several years.

Economic aggregate. The total of some economic quantity relevant to analysis. For example, the total money supply, gross national product, and industrial output are aggregates.

Economics. The study of the way scarce resources are allocated among alternative ends.

Elasticity, cross. The relative responsiveness of the quantity of good X demanded to a change in the price of good Y.

Elasticity, demand. The responsiveness of the quantity of good X demanded to a change in the price of good X. When the price change is small, price elasticity of demand is approximately indicated by the formula

$$\frac{\text{Percentage change in quantity of X demanded}}{\text{Percentage change in price of X}}$$

Elasticity, income. The responsiveness of the quantity of good X demanded to a change in income. When the income change is small, income elasticity of demand is approximately indicated by the formula

$$\frac{\text{Percentage change in quantity of X demanded}}{\text{Percentage change in income}}$$

Elasticity, supply. The responsiveness of the quantity of good X supplied by producers to a change in the price of good X.

Entrepreneur. One who undertakes the risk of starting a new venture or expanding an old one. Ordinarily, the entrepreneur assumes administrative responsibilities in addition to those of risk-taking.

Equilibrium. A term borrowed from physics that denotes a state of balance between opposing forces or actions. Thus, an equilibrium price is one brought to a state of balance or rest by the many forces of supply and demand.

Equilibrium, general. The type of economic analysis that considers each variable in the system to be a function of all other variables in the system.

Equilibrium, partial. The type of economic analysis that examines the forces determining price and output behavior for a single commodity, assuming all other prices and quantities are constant. Changes in markets other than the one being examined are assumed to be inconsequential relative to other markets in the total system.

Eurodollars. Deposits denominated in U.S. dollars in banks outside the United States, including foreign branches of U.S. banks.

Expansion of credit. The process by which banks create money, through the execution of their lending and investment functions.

Exploitation. In a technical sense, exploitation of labor occurs when the wage of labor is less than the value of its marginal physical product. Two types of exploitation are ordinarily distinguished. *Monopolistic exploitation* occurs when the demand curve for the commodity produced is not perfectly elastic for the individual firm; *monopsonistic exploitation* occurs when the supply curve of labor is not perfectly elastic for the individual firm.

Export. Most obviously, the sale of goods and services by domestic nationals to foreign nationals. Exports are credits in the balance-of-payment accounts and require that payment must ultimately be made by converting foreign currencies into the domestic currency.

Externality. A side consequence of the operation of a business (or household) that injures or benefits other businesses (or households). Thus, pollutants dumped into air and streams represent a cost that is external to the operations of the offending firm. Society is presently insisting that firms "internalize" these costs.

Factor of production. A resource used in the production of final goods and services that is normally placed in one of four main categories: land, labor, capital, or entrepreneurial (venturing) ability.

Firm. The basic decision-making unit of the business sector. The firm may be organized as a sole proprietorship, a partnership, or a corporation; large firms may consist of several constituent plants.

Fiscal drag. The tendency of an economy with a given fiscal plan to develop increasing surpluses (or decreasing deficits) at full employment over time, thereby making the attainment of full employment increasingly difficult.

Gross national product (GNP). The value at market prices of the total output of the final goods and services of an economy in a given time period.

Household unit. A single person or a combination of two or more persons residing in a single domicile with a single budget. The basic decision-making unit of the consumer sector.

Hypothesis. A formal proposition to the effect that if such and such conditions are met, certain consequences will follow. Such propositions are used to guide the theorist through alternative concepts and, to be useful, must be subject to scientific refutation.

Import. Most obviously, a good or service purchased by a domestic national from a foreign national. Imports are debits in the balance-of-payment accounts and require that payment ultimately be made by converting the domestic currency into a foreign currency.

Industry. Formally, a group of firms producing the same product or a set of closely similar products. Practically, the definition of an industry presents serious empirical problems, largely due to the difficulty of defining and classifying "products."

Inflation. A rise in the average level of prices; a decline in the value (purchasing power) of money.

Interest. The price paid for the use of borrowed funds. In classical economic theory, interest was considered to be the return to capital in the long run; the revival and current popularity of many classical economic concepts has brought this definition back into some contemporary usage.

Intermediary, financial. A financial institution that receives liquid funds from households and business firms and puts them to income-earning use.

Intermediary, nonbank. All financial intermediaries except commercial banks. The nonbank intermediaries include savings and loan associations, mutual savings banks, life insurance companies, credit unions, noninsured pension funds, and many others.

International reserves. Any liquid asset that may be used by a country to make up a deficit in its balance of payments. Practically, gold and the so-called "hard" currencies (the most important of these being U.S. dollars) constitute today's international reserves. In recent years, Special Drawing Rights in the International Monetary Fund (paper gold) have been artificially created to increase international reserves.

Investment. Outlays for new capital goods only; includes business fixed investment, residential construction and change in inventories.

Labor. Any activity performed by human beings to meet some objective other than the pleasure of the activity itself.

Land. Any free gift of nature.

Long run. A period of time sufficient in length to enable a firm to adjust all its inputs. (In the long run, all costs are variable.)

Macroeconomics. The prefix *macro-* is from the Greek word meaning "large." That part of the study of economics that treats aggregate or economywide variables.

Marginal cost. The increase in total cost dependent on a unit increment of total output.

Marginal efficiency of capital. That rate of discount that would make the present value of the series of annuities expected from a capital asset exactly equal to its supply price.

Marginal product. The difference in rate of output of a good or service resulting from a unit change in the rate of input of one factor in the production process, if the inputs of all other factors are held constant.

Market. A set of sellers and buyers, usually subject to some geographical constraint, who exchange goods and services, securities, or money (including foreign currencies). Sometimes the reference is to aggregates, such as the consumer-goods market or the producer-goods market. The outcome of market activity is the determination of prices and quantities.

Microeconomics. The prefix *micro-* is from the Greek word meaning "small." That part of the study of economics that analyzes the behavior of decision-making units such as the household and the firm. Microeconomics provides the theoretical foundation for the study of macroeconomics.

Mint par of exchange. Under a gold standard, the official exchange rate arrived at by *dividing* the gold content of one unit of account (say, the pound sterling) *by* the gold content of another (say, the U.S. dollar).

Model. Loosely, synonymous with a theory. More generally, a highly abstract system of economic variables and parameters linked together to make a "working" apparatus by a set of "principles" or theorems that presumably express tendencies operative in the real world.

Money. Whatever is customarily used to discharge economic obligations. Two Federal Reserve definitions are:

M_1 = Currency outside banks *plus* demand deposits adjusted (narrow definition).
M_2 = M_1 *plus* time deposits of commercial banks *minus* certificates of deposit of $100,000 or more (broad definition).

Monetary base. The net monetary liabilities of the treasury and the central bank of a sovereign government that are held by commercial banks and the nonbank public. In modern economies, the monetary base is used in conjunction with estimated multipliers to predict changes in the money stock.

Monopoly. A market in which there is a single seller of a good for which there is a gap in the chain of substitutes.

Monopoly power. Some freedom on the part of a seller to restrict output and raise prices as a pure monopolist can do.

Monopsony. A market in which there is a single buyer of a good or service for which there is a gap in the chain of substitutes.

Multiplier. The word is used in two main senses: (1) the factor by which an increase in aggregate demand is multiplied to give a total increase in income; (2) the factor by which an increase in the monetary base is multiplied to give a total increase in the money stock.

National income (NI). Earnings of the privately owned factors of production arising from current production; includes compensation of employees, proprietors' income, rental income of individuals, corporate profits (plus inventory valuation adjustment), and net interest paid by businesses.

Net national product (NNP). The gross national product *minus* capital consumption allowances.

Oligopoly. An industry characterized by a few sellers and many buyers of a product that is ordinarily differentiated but may be homogeneous.

Oligopsony. An industry characterized by few buyers of a product that is usually homogeneous but may be differentiated.

Open shop. A place of employment where union membership is not a condition of employment.

Opportunity cost. The income (earnings) foregone to put energies or property to work in an alternative pursuit. Thus, a high-school graduate who takes a four-year college course must consider as a cost of education, in addition to out-of-pocket expenses, the income he or she would have earned in full-time employment as a high-school graduate.

Optimum firm. The "best" size of firm in the sense of being the most efficient or lowest cost firm in the long run.

Partnership. A business organization in which all of the firm's assets are owned and controlled by two or more persons. Each partner is liable for all the debts of the business to the full extent of his or her own property, and profits are ordinarily divided evenly among partners unless there is an express agreement to the contrary.

Parity. A term used in the special context of American agricultural policy. A parity index of 100 is defined as the ratio of the prices received by farmers to the prices paid by farmers in the quinquennium 1910–1914. Other base periods have been proposed, but the farm lobby has successfully resisted attempts to make the parity concept less rigid.

Personal income (PI). All income and income-like payments actually received by persons. Personal income is equal to national income *minus* corporate profits and Social Security taxes *plus* dividends paid by corporations and transfer payments.

Personal outlays (PO). Outlays for (1) personal consumption expenditures, (2) interest paid by consumers, and (3) net foreign transfers by persons.

Productivity of labor. Output per man-hour.

Profit, accounting. The excess of a firm's receipts over its expenditures.

Profit, economic. The part of a firm's net income that exceeds all costs of land, labor, capital, and management. Essentially, the reward for venturing or risk-taking.

Proprietorship. A business organization in which all the firm's assets are owned and controlled by one person. The sole proprietor assumes all the risk and receives the profits or suffers the losses of the business. The entire return of the business is treated as personal income under federal income tax laws.

Public good. A "social" good that, once produced, may be used by one person without diminishing the amount available for other people.

Quota. A nontariff barrier to international trade in the form of a restriction on imports by total value or by quantity.

Rent. In classical economic theory, the return paid for the use of land. More generally, rent is the portion of the price of a good that does not influence the amount of it in existence.

Required reserves. The assets, usually "cash" and "due from banks," that a commercial bank must hold as a proportion of demand and time deposits. Member banks of the Federal Reserve System must hold reserves in the form of cash in vault or deposits with Federal Reserve Banks.

Required reserve ratio. The percentage of demand and time deposits that a commercial bank is required by the monetary authority to keep as required reserves.

Savings, business. The gross retained earnings of business or, approximately, undistributed corporate profits *plus* capital consumption allowances.

Savings, personal. The allocation of disposable personal income to nonpersonal outlays.

Savings. The stock of accumulated financial assets resulting from the act of saving.

Short run. A period of time insufficient in length to enable a firm to adjust all its inputs. (One or more factors of production is fixed in the short run.)

Subsidy. A monetary grant by government to private business, including the farm sector.

Supply. The quantity of a good or service that sellers are willing to offer during a given time period at a range of alternative prices.

Surplus. A treasury surplus is an excess of total tax receipts over total payments. A balance-of-payments surplus is the excess of a country's inpayments from foreigners over its outpayments to foreigners.

Surtax. A tax, usually temporary, that is computed as a percentage of a preexisting or "normal" tax and then added to it.

Tariff. A tax on imports usually designated as a percentage of the value of the goods *(ad valorem);* a tariff may also be expressed as a specific money amount per unit of goods.

Tax, direct. A tax is direct if the burden of the tax actually falls on the person or business from which it is collected. The personal income tax is the archetype of direct tax.

Tax, indirect. A tax is indirect if the burden of the tax can be shifted from the unit (household or business) on which it is levied. Thus, sales and excise taxes are usually indirect.

Taxes, proportional, progressive, and regressive. A tax is *proportional* if its rate *remains the same,* whatever the size of the tax base. A tax is *progressive* if its rate *increases* as the tax base increases. A tax is *regressive* if its rate *decreases* as the tax base increases. Because all taxes, no matter what their base, ultimately are deducted from income, income is the base ordinarily used to determine the social effects of a given tax. Thus, although a sales tax is proportional if the base is considered to be retail sales, it is regressive with respect to income.

Theory. Compare the definitions of *model* and *hypothesis.* A formal statement, subject to qualifying conditions, of forces perceived to govern the relationships among variables in a system. More generally, the body of, say, economic theory consists of a set of such statements that are continually subject to empirical testing.

Transfer payments. Payments to persons in return for which no services are currently performed.

Unemployed. A person is said to be unemployed when he or she is willing to work and is actively seeking work but cannot find a job within a reasonable geographical distance from home.

Unemployment, cyclical. Any unemployment over and above seasonal, frictional, and structural unemployment. Cyclical unemployment is therefore the result of slumping economic activity.

Unemployment, frictional. Temporary unemployment resulting from a search for a first job or a transitional period between jobs.

Unemployment, seasonal. Unemployment related to changes in weather and holidays with accompanying swings in agricultural and construction activity, retail trade, and the like.

Unemployment, structural. Unemployment resulting from deep-seated and relatively permanent changes in the locations of demand for certain grades and kinds of labor.

Union shop. A place of employment operating under an agreement between management and a recognized union whereby membership in the union is required within a stipulated time period (say, 30 days) as a condition of employment.

Unit-labor cost. Average compensation per man-hour *divided by* output per man-hour.

Utility. The capacity of a good to satisfy a human want.

Wages. The price paid for the use of labor. *Money wages* are the amount of money received by a worker per unit of time. *Real wages* are the quantity of goods and services that can be obtained with money wages.

Suggested Readings

HISTORY

Altick, Richard D., *The Scholar Adventurers,* New York: Macmillan, 1950.
Becker, C.L., *Everyman His Own Historian,* New York: Appleton-Century-Crofts, 1935.
Cheyney, E.P., *Law in History and Other Essays,* New York: Alfred A. Knopf, 1927.
Cook, Edward M., *The Fathers of the Towns: Leadership and Community Structure in Eighteenth-Century New England,* Baltimore: Johns Hopkins University Press, 1976.
Henretta, James A., *The Evolution of American Society, 1700–1815: An Interdisciplinary Analysis,* Lexington, Mass.: D.C. Heath, 1973.
Johnson, Allen, *The Historian and Historical Evidence,* New York: Charles Scribner's Sons, 1926.
Langlois, C.V., and Seignobos, C., *Introduction to the Study of History,* translated by G.G. Berry, New York: Holt, Rinehart & Winston, 1909.
Malin, James C., *Essays on Historiography,* privately published, Lawrence, Kan., 1946.
Mathews, Shailer, *The Spiritual Interpretation of History,* Cambridge: Harvard University Press, 1916.
Nevins, Allan, *The Gateway to History,* New York: Appleton-Century-Crofts, 1938.
Robinson, James Harvey, *The Mind in the Making,* New York: Harper & Row, 1921.
Rogers, J.E. Thorold, *The Economic Interpretation of History,* New York: G.P. Putnam's Sons, 1909.
Salmon, Lucy M., *Why Is History Rewritten?* New York: Oxford University Press, 1929.
Sée, Henri, *The Economic Interpretation of History,* New York: Adelphi, 1929.
Seligman, E.R.A., *The Economic Interpretation of History,* 2nd ed., New York: Columbia University Press, 1924.
Taylor, Hugh, *History as a Science,* London: Methuen, 1933.

Teggart, Frederick F., *Theory and Processes of History,* Berkeley and Los Angeles: University of California Press, 1960.

Trevelyan, George Macaulay, *Clio: A Muse,* New York: Longmans, Green, 1913.

ECONOMICS

Alchian, Armen and Allen, William R., *Exchange and Production: Competition, Coordination, and Control,* 2nd ed., Belmont, Calif.: Wadsworth, 1977.

Crouch, Robert L., *Macroeconomics,* New York: Harcourt Brace Jovanovich, Inc., 1972.

Dernburg, Thomas F. and McDougall, Duncan M., *Macroeconomics,* 4th ed., New York: McGraw-Hill Book Co., 1972.

Knight, Frank H., *The Economic Organization,* New York: Kelley, 1951.

Kreinin, Mordechai E., *International Economics: A Policy Approach,* 3rd ed., New York: Harcourt Brace Jovanovich, Inc., 1979.

Leftwich, Richard H., *The Price System and Resource Allocation,* New York: Holt, Rinehart & Winston, 1961.

Lindbeck, Assar, *The Political Economy of the New Left: An Outsider's View,* New York: Harper & Row, 1971.

Marshall, Alfred, *Principles of Economics,* 8th ed., New York: Macmillan, 1949.

Miller, Roger L., *Economics Today,* 3rd ed., New York: Harper & Row, 1979.

Noyes, C. Reinold, *Economic Man in Relation to His Natural Environment,* Vols. I and II, New York: Columbia University Press, 1948.

Robinson, E.A.G., *The Structure of Competitive Industry,* New York: Harcourt Brace Jovanovich, Inc., 1932; rev. ed., Chicago: University of Chicago Press, 1959.

Schumpeter, Joseph A., *The Theory of Economic Development,* Cambridge: Harvard University Press, 1949.

Veblen, Thorstein, *The Theory of Business Enterprise,* New York: Charles Scribner's Sons, 1904.

EARLY MODERN AND COLONIAL HISTORY

Andrews, Charles M., *The Colonial Period of American History,* New Haven: Yale University Press, 1934.

Bailyn, Bernard, *The Ideological Origins of the American Revolution,* Cambridge: Belknap Press of Harvard University Press, 1967.

Beatty, Richmond C., *William Byrd of Westover,* Boston: Houghton Mifflin, 1930.

Beer, George L., *British Colonial Policy, 1754–1765,* Gloucester, Mass.: Peter Smith, 1958.

——— *Commercial Policy of England Toward the American Colonies,* New York: Columbia University Press, 1893 (Studies in History, Economics, and Public Law, Vol. III, No. 2).

——— *The Old Colonial System, 1660–1754,* Gloucester, Mass.: Peter Smith, 1958.

——— *The Origins of the British Colonial System, 1578–1660,* New York: Macmillan, 1908.

Boorstin, Daniel J., *The Americans: The Colonial Experience,* New York: Random House, 1958.

Bridenbaugh, Carl, *Cities in Revolt: Urban Life in America, 1743*–1776, New York: Alfred A. Knopf, 1955.

——— *Cities in the Wilderness: The First Century of Urban Life in America, 1625–1742,* New York: Alfred A. Knopf, 1955.

——— *Myths and Realities: Societies of the Colonial South,* Baton Rouge: Louisiana State University Press, 1952.

——— *Rebels and Gentlemen: Philadelphia in the Age of Franklin,* New York: Reynal and Hitchcock, 1942.

Brock, Leslie V., *The Currency of the American Colonies, 1700–1764: A Study in Colonial Finance and Imperial Relations,* New York: Arno Press, 1975.

Bruce, Phillip A., *Economic History of Virginia in the Seventeenth Century,* New York: Smith, 1935.

Bruchey, Stuart, *The Colonial Merchant: Sources and Readings,* New York: Harcourt Brace Jovanovich, Inc., 1966.

Chitwood, Oliver P., *A History of Colonial America,* New York: Harper & Row, 1948.

Clapham, J.H., and Power, Eileen, (eds.), *Cambridge Economic History of Europe from the Decline of the Roman Empire,* Vols. I and II, Cambridge, England: Cambridge University Press, 1941–1952.

de Roover, Raymond, *The Rise and Decline of the Medici Bank, 1397–1494,* New York: W.W. Norton, 1966.

Ernst, Joseph Albert, *Money and Politics in America 1755–1775: A Study in the Currency Act of 1764, and the Political Economy of Revolution,* Chapel Hill: University of North Carolina Press, 1974.

Fiske, John, *Old Virginia and Her Neighbours,* Vols. I and II, Boston: Houghton Mifflin, 1897.

Hamilton, Earl J., *American Treasure and the Price Revolution in Spain, 1501–1650,* Cambridge: Harvard University Press, 1934.

Hoskins, Halford L., *British Routes to India,* Philadelphia: Longmans, Green, 1928.

Jensen, Merrill, *The New Nation: A History of the United States During Confederation, 1781–1789,* New York: Alfred A. Knopf, 1958.

Latouche, Robert, *The Birth of Western Economy: Economic Aspects of the Dark Ages,* New York: Barnes & Noble, 1961.

Lopez, Robert S., and Raymond, Irving W., (eds.), *Medieval Trade in the Mediterranean World,* New York: Columbia University Press, 1955.

Miller, John C., *Triumph of Freedom, 1775–1783,* Boston: Little, Brown, 1948.

Morris, Richard B., *The American Revolution Reconsidered,* New York: Harper & Row, 1967.

Morrison, Samuel Eliot, *The European Discovery of America: The Northern Voyages,* New York: Oxford University Press, 1971.

Musson, A.E. and Robinson, Eric, *Science and Technology in the Industrial Revolution,* Manchester, England: Manchester University Press, 1969.

Nettles, Curtis, *The Roots of American Civilization,* New York: Appleton-Century-Crofts, 1938.

Pohl, Frederick J., *Atlantic Crossings Before Columbus,* New York: W.W. Norton, 1961.

Power, Eileen, *Medieval People,* Garden City: Doubleday, 1954.

Richards, Gertrude R.B., *Florentine Merchants in the Age of the Medici,* Cambridge: Harvard University Press, 1932.

Saltzman, L.F., *Building in England Down to 1540,* Oxford: Clarendon Press, 1952.

Scott, William R., *The Constitution and Finance of English, Scottish, and Irish Joint Stock Companies to 1720,* Vols. I, II, and III, Cambridge, England: Cambridge University Press, 1912.

Scoville, Warren Candler, *The Persecution of Huguenots and French Economic Development, 1680–1720,* Berkeley: University of California Press, 1960.

Shepherd, James F. and Walton, Gary M., *Shipping, Maritime Trade, and the Economic Development of Colonial North America,* Cambridge, England: Cambridge University Press, 1972.

Twaney, R.H., *Religion and the Rise of Capitalism,* New York: Harcourt Brace Jovanovich, Inc., 1952.

Walton, Gary M., and Shepherd, James F., *The Economic Rise of Early America,* New York and London: Cambridge University Press, 1979.

Weber, Max, *The Protestant Ethic and the Spirit of Capitalism,* New York: Charles Scribner's Sons, 1930.

AGRICULTURAL HISTORY, THE WESTWARD MOVEMENT, AND THE PLANTATION ECONOMY

Agricultural History

Barger, Harold, and Landsberg, H.H., *American Agriculture, 1899–1939: A Study of Output, Employment, and Productivity,* New York: National Bureau of Economic Research, 1942 (Publication No. 42).

Bidwell, P.W., and Falconer, J.I., *A History of Agriculture in the Northern United States, 1620–1860,* Washington, D.C.: Carnegie Institution of Washington, 1925 (Publication No. 358).

Edwards, E.E., "American Agriculture—The First 300 Years," *1940 Yearbook of Agriculture,* Washington, D.C.: U.S. Government Printing Office.

Gates, Paul W., *The Farmer's Age: Agriculture 1815–1860,* New York: Holt, Rinehart & Winston, 1960.

Gray, Lewis C., *History of Agriculture in the Southern United States to 1860,* Vols. I and II, Washington, D.C.: Carnegie Institution of Washington, 1933.

Heimann, Robert, *Tobacco and Americans,* New York: McGraw-Hill Book Co., 1960.

Hulbert, A.B., *Soil: Its Influence on the History of the United States,* New Haven: Yale University Press, 1930.

Johnson, D. Gale, *Trade and Agriculture,* New York: John Wiley & Sons, 1950.

Kelsey, Darwin P. (ed.), *Farming in the New Nation: Interpreting American Agriculture, 1790–1840,* Washington, D.C.: Agricultural History Society, 1972.

McCormick, Cyrus, *The Century of the Reaper,* Boston: Houghton Mifflin, 1931.

National Advisory Commission on Food and Fiber, *Food and Fiber for the Future,* Washington, D.C.: U.S. Government Printing Office, 1967.

Rasmussen, Wayne D., *Readings in the History of American Agriculture,* Urbana: University of Illinois Press, 1960.

Rogin, Leo, *The Introduction of Farm Machinery in Its Relation to the Productivity of Labor in the Agriculture of the United States During the Nineteenth Century,* Berkeley: University of California Press, 1931 (Publications in Economics, Vol. IX).

Schlebecker, John T., *Whereby We Thrive: A History of American Farming,* Ames: Iowa State University Press, 1975.

Schultz, Theodore W., *Agriculture in an Unstable Economy,* New York: McGraw-Hill Book Co., 1945.

——— *The Economic Organization of Agriculture,* New York: McGraw-Hill Book Co., 1953.

Shannon, Fred A., *Economic History of the United States,* Vol. V, *The Farmer's Last Frontier: Agriculture 1860–1879,* New York: Farrar and Rinehart, 1945.

Shepherd, Geoffrey S., *Agricultural Price and Income Policy,* 3rd ed., Ames: Iowa State University Press, 1952.

Tostlebe, Alvin S., *The Growth of Physical Capital in Agriculture,* New York: National Bureau of Economic Research, 1954 (Studies in Capital Formation and Financing, Occasional Paper 44).

The Westward Movement

Abernethy, T.P., *Western Lands and the American Revolution,* New York: Appleton-Century-Crofts, 1937 (Virginia University Institute for Research in the Social Sciences, Institute Monograph No. 25).

Adams, Ramon, *The Old-Time Cowhand,* New York: Macmillan, 1961.

Atherton, Lewis E., *The Cattle Kings,* Bloomington: Indiana University Press, 1962.

——— *Main Street on the Middle Border,* Bloomington: Indiana University Press, 1954.

——— *The Pioneer Merchant in Mid-America,* Columbia: University of Missouri Press, 1939.

——— *The Southern Country Store, 1800–1860,* Baton Rouge: Louisiana State University Press, 1949.

Billington, Ray A., *Westward Expansion,* 2nd ed., New York: Macmillan, 1960.

Chittenden, Hiram Martin, *The American Fur Trade of the Far West,* Vols. I and II, Stanford: Stanford University Academic Reprint, 1954.

Clark, Dan E., *The West in American History,* New York: Crowell, 1937.

Clark, T.D., *Pills, Petticoats and Plows: The Southern Country Store,* Indianapolis: Bobbs-Merrill, 1944.

Coman, Katherine, *Economic Beginnings of the Far West,* New York: Macmillan, 1925.

Dale, E.E., *Cow Country,* Norman: University of Oklahoma Press, 1942.

——— *The Range Cattle Industry,* Norman: University of Oklahoma Press, 1930.

Defebaugh, J.E., *History of the Lumber Industry of America,* Chicago: American Lumberman, 1906–1907.

Dick, Everett N., *The Sod-House Frontier, 1854–1890,* New York: Appleton-Century-Crofts, 1937.

Hibbard, B.H., *A History of the Public Land Policies,* New York: Macmillan, 1924 (Land Economics Series).

Hulbert, A.B., *Soil: Its Influence on the History of the United States,* New Haven: Yale University Press, 1930.

Innis, H.A., *The Fur Trade in Canada,* rev. ed., Toronto: University of Toronto Press, 1956.

Ise, John, *Our National Park Policy: A Critical History,* published for Resources for the Future, Inc., Baltimore: Johns Hopkins University Press, 1961.

——— *United States Forest Policy,* New Haven: Yale University Press, 1920.

——— *United States Oil Policy,* New Haven: Yale University Press, 1926.

Jackson, Curtis E., and Galli, Marcia J., *A History of The Bureau of Indian Affairs and Its Activities Among Indians,* San Francisco: R & E Research Associates, 1977.

Lavender, David, *Bent's Fort,* Garden City: Doubleday, 1954.

McFarland, R., *A History of the New England Fisheries,* Philadelphia: University of Pennsylvania Press, 1911 (Publications in Political Economy and Public Law No. 24).

Otis, D.S., *The Dawes Act and the Allotment of Indian Lands,* Norman: University of Oklahoma Press, 1973.

Paxson, F.L., *History of the American Frontier, 1763–1893,* Boston: Houghton Mifflin, 1924.

Prucha, Francis Paul, S.J., *American Indian Policy in the Formative Years: The Indian Trade and Intercourse Acts, 1780–1834,* Cambridge: Harvard University Press, 1962.

Robbins, R.M., *Our Landed Heritage: The Public Domain 1776–1936,* Princeton: Princeton University Press, 1942.

Tower, W.S., *A History of American Whale Fishery,* Philadelphia: University of Pennsylvania Publication, 1907.

Treat, P.J., *The National Land System, 1785–1820,* New York: Treat, 1910.

Turner, F.J., *The Frontier in American History,* New York: Holt, Rinehart & Winston, 1921.

——— *The Significance of Sections in American History,* New York: Holt, Rinehart & Winston, 1932.

The Plantation Economy

Bancroft, Frederic, *Slave Trading in the Old South,* Baltimore: Furst, 1931.
Cairnes, J.E., *The Slave Power,* 2nd ed., New York: Carleton, 1862.
David, Paul A. et al., *Reckoning with Slavery,* New York: Oxford University Press, 1976.
Dow, G.F., *Slave Ships and Slaving,* Salem, Mass.: Marine Research Society, 1927.
Elkins, Stanley M., *Slavery: A Problem in American Institutional and Intellectual Life,* Chicago: University of Chicago Press, 1959.
Engerman, Stanley L. and Genovese, Eugene D., *Race and Slavery in the Western Hemisphere: Quantitative Studies,* Princeton: Princeton University Press, 1975.
Fogel, Robert W. and Engerman, Stanley L., *Time on The Cross,* Vols. I and II, Boston: Little, Brown, 1974.
Genovese, Eugene D., *The Political Economy of Slavery,* New York: Pantheon Books, 1965.
Hart, A.B., *Slavery and Abolition,* New York: Harper & Row, 1906.
Hedges, James B., *The Browns of Providence Plantations: Colonial Years,* Cambridge: Harvard University Press, 1952.
Olmsted, Frederick L., *The Cotton Kingdom,* 1861, A.M. Schlesinger (ed.), New York: Alfred A. Knopf, 1953.
Phillips, U.B., *American Negro Slavery,* New York: Appleton-Century-Crofts, 1918.
——— *Life and Labor in the Old South,* Boston: Little, Brown, 1929.
Stampp, Kenneth M., *The Peculiar Institution: Slavery in the Ante-Bellum South,* New York: Alfred A. Knopf, 1956.

TRANSPORTATION AND COMMUNICATION

Abbot, W.J., *The Story of Our Merchant Marine,* New York: Dodd, Mead, 1919.
Barger, Harold, *The Transportation Industries 1889–1946,* New York: National Bureau of Economic Research, 1951 (Publication No. 51).
Barker, T.C., and Robbins, Michael, *A History of London Transport,* London: Allen and Unwin, 1963.
Chandler, Alfred D. Jr., *The Railroads—The Nation's First Big Business,* New York: Harcourt Brace Jovanovich, Inc., 1965.
Clark. A.H., *The Clipper Ship Era, 1843–1849,* New York: G.P. Putnam's Sons, 1910.
Cochran, Thomas C., *Railroad Leaders, 1845–1890, The Business Mind in Action,* Cambridge: Harvard University Press, 1953.
Dearing. C.L., *American Highway Policy,* Washington, D.C.: Brookings Institution, 1941.
Dearing, C.L., and Owen, Wilfred, *National Transportation Policy,* Washington, D.C.: Brookings Institution, 1949.
Duffus, R.L., *The Santa Fe Trail,* New York: Longmans, Green, 1930.
Fishlow, Albert, *American Railroads and the Transformation of the Antebellum Economy,* Cambridge: Harvard University Press, 1965.
Fogel, Robert William, *The Union Pacific Railroad,* Baltimore: Johns Hopkins University Press, 1960.
——— *The Union Pacific Railroad: A Case in Premature Enterprise,* Baltimore: Johns Hopkins University Press, 1964.
——— *Railroads and American Economic Growth: Essays in Economic History,* Baltimore: Johns Hopkins University Press, 1964.
Goodrich, Carter (ed.), *Canals and American Development,* New York: Columbia University Press, 1961.

Grodinsky, Julius, *Transcontinental Railway Strategy, 1869–1893,* Philadelphia: University of Pennsylvania Press, 1962.

Haites, Erik, Mak, James, and Walton, Gary, *Western River Transportation: The Era of Early Internal Development, 1810–1860,* Baltimore: Johns Hopkins University Press, 1975.

Harlow, A.F., *Old Towpaths,* New York: Appleton-Century-Crofts, 1926.

Hilton, George, and Due, John, *The Electric Interurban Railways in America,* Stanford: Stanford University Press, 1960.

Hoyt, Edwin P., *The Vanderbilts and Their Fortunes,* Garden City: Doubleday, 1962.

Hulbert, A.B., *Paths of Inland Commerce,* New Haven: Yale University Press, 1920.

Kirkland, E.C., *Men, Cities, and Transportation,* Vols. I and II, Cambridge: Harvard University Press, 1948.

Leonard, W.N., *Railroad Consolidation Under the Transportation Act of 1920,* New York: Columbia University Press, 1946 (Studies in History, Economics, and Public Law No. 522).

MacGill, C.E. et al., *History of Transportation in the United States Before 1860,* Washington, D.C.: Carnegie Institution of Washington, 1917.

Martin, Albro, *Enterprise Denied: Origins of the Decline of American Railroads, 1897–1917,* New York and London: Columbia University Press, 1971.

McKee, M.M., *Ship Subsidy Question in United States Politics,* Northampton, Mass.: Smith College, 1922 (Studies in History, Vol. VIII, No. 1).

Morrison, John H., *American Steam Navigation,* New York: Sametz, 1903.

Puffer, C.E., *Air Transportation,* Philadelphia: Blakiston, 1941.

Ringwalt, J.L., *Development of Transportation Systems in the United States,* Philadelphia: J.L. Ringwalt, 1888.

Ripley, W.Z., *Railroads: Rates and Regulations,* New York: Longmans, Green, 1912.

Rosskam, Edwin, and Rosskam, Louise, *Towboat River,* New York: Duell, Sloan and Pearce, 1948.

Scheele, Carl H., *A Short History of the Mail Service,* Washington, D.C.: Smithsonian Institution Press, 1970.

Ulmer, Melville J., *Trends and Cycles in Capital Formation by United States Railroads, 1870–1950,* New York: National Bureau of Economic Research, 1954.

FINANCIAL HISTORY

Alhadeff, David A., *Monopoly and Competition in Banking,* Berkeley: University of California Press, 1954.

Allen, Frederick Lewis, *The Great Pierpont Morgan,* New York: Bantam Books, 1949.

Behrens, Kathryn L., *Paper Money in Maryland, 1727–1789,* Baltimore: Johns Hopkins University Press, 1923.

Bolles, Albert Sidney, *Financial History of the United States,* Vols. I, II, and III, New York: Appleton-Century-Crofts, 1885.

Bourne, Edward G., *The History of the Surplus Revenue of 1837,* New York: G.P. Putnam's Sons, 1885.

Bray, Hammond, *Banks and Politics in America from the Revolution to the Civil War,* Princeton: Princeton University Press, 1957.

Bullock, C.J., *Essays on the Monetary History of the United States,* New York: Macmillan, 1900.

Cagan, Phillip, *Determinants and Effects of Changes in the U.S. Money Stock, 1875–1960,* New York: National Bureau of Economic Research, 1965.

Carson, Deane (ed.), *Banking and Monetary Studies,* Homewood, Ill.: Richard D. Irwin, 1963.

Catterall, Ralph C.H., *The Second Bank of the United States,* Chicago: University of Chicago Press, 1903.

Chaddock, Robert E., *The Safety Fund Banking System in New York, 1829–1866,* Washington, D.C.: U.S. Government Printing Office, 1910.

Conant, Charles A., *A History of Modern Banks of Issue,* New York: G.P. Putnam's Sons, 1896.

Davis, A.M., *The Origin of the National Banking System,* Washington, D.C.: U.S. Government Printing Office, 1910–1911.

——— *Colonial Currency Reprints, 1682–1751,* Boston: Prince Society, 1910.

Dewey, D.R., *Financial History of the United States,* New York: Longmans, Green, 1934.

——— *State Banking Before the Civil War,* Washington, D.C.: U.S. Government Printing Office, 1910.

Dillistin, William H., *Bank Note Reporters and Counterfeit Detectors, 1826–1866, with a Discourse on Wildcat Banks and Wildcat Bank Notes,* New York: American Numismatic Society, 1949.

Dunbar, Charles F., *The Theory and History of Banking,* New York: G.P. Putnam's Sons, 1922.

Dunne, Gerald T., *Monetary Decisions of the Supreme Court,* New Brunswick, N.J.: Rutgers University Press, 1960.

Fforde, J.S., *The Federal Reserve System, 1945–1949,* New York: Oxford University Press, 1954.

Fischer, Gerald C., *American Banking Structure: Its Evolution and Regulation,* New York: Columbia University Press, 1967.

——— *Bank Holding Companies,* New York: Columbia University Press, 1961.

Friedman, Milton, and Schwartz, Anna J., *A Monetary History of the United States, 1867–1960,* Princeton: Princeton University Press, 1963 (National Bureau of Economic Research, Studies in Business Cycles 12).

Gibbons, James S., *The Banks of New York, Their Dealers, the Clearing House, and the Panic of 1857,* New York: Appleton-Century-Crofts, 1858.

Goldenweiser, E.A., *American Monetary Policy,* New York: McGraw-Hill Book Co., 1951.

Goldsmith, Raymond W., *The Share of Financial Intermediaries in National Wealth and National Assets, 1900–1949,* New York: National Bureau of Economics Research, 1954 (Studies in Capital Formation and Financing, Occasional Paper).

Golembe, Carter H., *State Banks and the Economic Development of the West, 1830–1844,* New York: Columbia University Press, 1952.

Gouge, William M., *A Short History of Paper Money and Banking in the United States, Including an Account of Provincial and Continental Paper Money,* Philadelphia: Usbick, 1883.

Govan, Thomas Payne, *Nicholas Biddle,* Chicago: University of Chicago Press, 1959.

Grayson, Theodore J., *Leaders and Periods of American Finance,* New York: John Wiley & Sons, 1932.

Greef, Albert O., *The Commercial Paper House in the United States,* Cambridge: Harvard University Press, 1938.

Green, George D., *Finance and Economic Development in the Old South: Louisiana Banking, 1804–1861,* Stanford: Stanford University Press, 1972.

Hacker, Louis M., *Alexander Hamilton in the American Tradition,* New York: McGraw-Hill Book Co., 1957.

Hardy, C.O., *Credit Policies of the Federal Reserve System,* Washington, D.C.: Brookings Institution, 1932 (Institute of Economics Publication No. 45).

Harris, S.E., *Twenty Years of Federal Reserve Policy,* Cambridge: Harvard University Press, 1933 (Harvard Economic Studies, Vol. XLI).

Hart, Albert Gailord, *Debts and Recovery,* New York: Twentieth Century Fund, 1938.

——— *Money, Debt, and Economic Activity,* 2nd ed., New York: Prentice-Hall, 1953.

Hedges, Joseph Edward, *Commercial Banking and the Stock Market Before 1863,* Baltimore: Johns Hopkins University Press, 1938.

Helderman, Leonard C., *National and State Banks,* Boston: Houghton Mifflin, 1931.

Hepburn, A.B., *History of Currency in the United States,* rev. ed., New York: Macmillan, 1924.

Holdsworth, John Thom, and Dewey, Davis R., *The First and Second Banks of the United States,* Washington, D.C.: U.S. Government Printing Office, 1910.

Howe, Frederic C., *Taxation and Taxes in the United States Under the Internal Revenue System, 1791–1895,* New York: Crowell, 1896.

Huntington, A.T., and Mawhinney, Robert J., *Laws of the United States Concerning Money, Banking, and Loans, 1778–1909,* Washington, D.C.: U.S. Government Printing Office, 1910.

James, Frank C., *The Economics of Money, Credit, and Banking,* 3rd ed., New York: Ronald, 1940.

Klebaner, Benjamin J., *Commercial Banking in the United States: A History,* Hinsdale, Ill.: Dryden Press, 1974.

Krooss, Herman E., and Blyn, Martin R., *A History of Financial Intermediaries,* New York: Random House, 1971.

Larson, Henrietta, *Jay Cooke, Private Banker,* Cambridge: Harvard University Press, 1936 (Harvard Studies in Business History, Vol. II).

Laughlin, J.L., *History of Bimetallism in the United States,* 4th ed., New York: Appleton-Century-Crofts, 1897.

Lester, Richard Allen, *Monetary Experiments: Early American and Recent Scandinavian,* Princeton: Princeton University Press, 1939.

Levinson, Leonard Lewis, *Wall Street, A Pictorial History,* New York: Ziff-Davis, 1961.

Linderman, Henry R., *Money and Legal Tender in the United States,* New York: G.P. Putnam's Sons, 1878.

McKee, Samuel, Jr., *Alexander Hamilton: Papers on Public Credit, Commerce, and Finance,* New York: Columbia University Press, 1934.

Miller, Harry E., *Banking Theories in the United States Before 1860,* Cambridge: Harvard University Press, 1927 (Harvard Economic Studies).

Mints, Lloyd W., *A History of Banking Theory in Great Britain and the United States,* Chicago: University of Chicago Press, 1945.

Mitchell, Wesley, *A History of Greenbacks,* Chicago: University of Chicago Press, 1903.

Nettels, C.P., *The Money Supply of the American Colonies Before 1720,* Madison: University of Wisconsin Press, 1934 (Studies in the Social Sciences and History No. 20).

Noyes, Alexander D., *Thirty Years of American Finance (1865–1896),* New York: G.P. Putnam's Sons, 1898.

—— *The War Period of American Finance (1908–1925)*, New York, G.P. Putnam's Sons, 1926.

O'Connor, James F.T., *The Banking Crisis and Recovery Under the Roosevelt Administration,* Chicago: Callaghan, 1938.

Pollard, Sidney (ed.), *The Gold Standard and Employment Policies,* London: Methuen, 1970.

Ratchford, B.U., *American State Debts,* Durham, N.C.: Duke University Press, 1941.

Ratner, Sidney, *American Taxation,* New York: W.W. Norton, 1942.

Redlich, Fritz, *The Molding of American Banking: Men and Ideas,* New York: Hafner, 1947 (Part I), 1951 (Part II).

Riefler, Winfield W., *Money Rates and Money Markets in the United States,* New York: Harper & Row, 1930.

Ripley, William Z., *The Financial History of Virginia, 1609–1776,* New York: Columbia University Press, 1893.

Robertson, Ross M., *The Comptroller and Bank Supervision,* Washington, D.C.: Office of the Comptroller of the Currency, 1968.

Shultz, W.J., and Caine, M.R., *Financial Development of the United States,* New York: Prentice-Hall, 1937.

Smith, Walter B., *Economic Aspects of the Second Bank of the United States,* Cambridge: Harvard University Press, 1953 (Studies in Economic History Series).

Sumner, William G., *The Financier and the Finances of the American Revolution,* Vols. I and II, New York: Dodd, Mead, 1891.

——— *A History of American Currency,* New York: G.P. Putnam's Sons, 1878.

Taus, Esther Rogoff, *Central Banking Functions of the U.S. Treasury, 1789–1941,* New York: Columbia University Press, 1943.

Taylor, George R. (ed.), *Jackson vs. Biddle: The Struggle Over the Second Bank of the United States,* Boston: D.C. Heath, 1949 (Problems in American Civilization, Vol. 3).

Upham, Cyril B., and Lamke, Edwin, *Closed and Distressed Banks,* Washington, D.C.: Brookings Institution, 1934 (Institute of Economics Publication No. 58).

Walters, Raymond, Jr., *Albert Gallatin: Jeffersonian Financier and Diplomat,* New York: Macmillan, 1957.

Watson, David K., *History of American Coinage,* New York: G.P. Putnam's Sons, 1899.

Wilburn, Jean Alexander, *Biddle's Bank—The Crucial Years,* New York: Columbia University Press, 1967.

INDUSTRY AND COMMERCE

Industrial Development

Alderfer, E.B., and Michl, H.E., *Economics of American Industry,* 2nd ed., New York: McGraw-Hill Book Co., 1957.

Allen, Frederick Lewis, *Lords of Creation,* New York: Harper & Row, 1935.

Ashton, T.S., *The Industrial Revolution, 1760–1830,* London: Oxford University Press, 1961.

Barger, Harold, and Schurr, S.H., *Mining Industries, 1899–1939: A Study of Output, Employment, and Productivity,* New York: National Bureau of Economic Research, 1944.

Berglund, Abraham, *The United States Steel Corporation,* New York: Columbia University Press, 1907.

Binder, Frederick Moore, *Coal-Age Empire: Pennsylvania Coal and Its Utilization to 1860,* Harrisburg: Pennsylvania Historical and Museum Commission, 1974.

Bining, A.C., *British Regulation of the Colonial Iron Industry,* Philadelphia: University of Pennsylvania Press, 1933.

Bishop, James Leander, *A History of American Manufacturers from 1608–1860,* Vols. I and II, Philadelphia: Young, 1868.

Bolles, Albert S., *Industrial History of the United States,* Norwich, Conn.: Henry Bill, 1881.

Borenstein, Israel, *Capital and Output Trends in Mining Industries, 1870–1948,* New York: National Bureau of Economic Research, 1954.

Bowden, Witt, *The Industrial History of the United States,* New York: Adelphi, 1930.

Bridenbaugh, Carl, *The Colonial Craftsman,* New York: New York University Press, 1950.

Burns, A.F., *Production Trends in the United States Since 1870,* New York: National Bureau of Economic Research, 1934.

Chandler, Alfred D., Jr. (ed.), *Giant Enterprise: Ford, General Motors, and the American Automobile Industry,* New York: Harcourt Brace Jovanovich, Inc., 1964.

Clark, John G., *Towns and Minerals in Southeastern Kansas: A Study in Regional Industrialization, 1890–1930,* Topeka, Kansas: State Geological Survey of Kansas, 1970.

Clark, V.S., *History of Manufacturers in the United States, 1607–1914,* Vols. I and II, Washington, D.C.: Carnegie Institution of Washington, 1916–*28.*

Clow, Archibald, *The Chemical Revolution,* London: Batchworth Press, 1952.

Cole, Arthur Harrison, *The American Wool Manufacture,* Vols. I and II, Cambridge: Harvard University Press, 1926.

Copeland, M.T., *The Cotton Manufacturing Industry of the United States,* Cambridge: Harvard University Press, 1912 (Harvard Economic Studies, Vol. VIII).

Copp, Anthony E., *Regulating Competition in Oil: Government Intervention in the U.S. Refining Industry, 1948–1975,* College Station: Texas A & M University Press, 1976.

Creamer, Daniel B., *Capital and Output Trends in Manufacturing Industries, 1880–1948,* New York: National Bureau of Economic Research, 1954 (Studies in Capital Formation and Financing, Occasional Paper No. 41).

Defebaugh, J.E., *History of the Lumber Industry of America,* Vols. I and II, Chicago: American Lumberman, 1906–1907.

Frickey, Edwin, *Production in the United States, 1860–1914,* Cambridge: Harvard University Press, 1947 (Harvard Economic Studies, Vol. LXXXII).

Gras, N.S.B., *Industrial Evolution,* Cambridge: Harvard University Press, 1930.

Habakkuk, H.J., *American and British Technology in the Nineteenth Century,* London: Cambridge University Press, 1962.

Hazard, B.E., *The Organization of the Boot and Shoe Industry in Massachusetts Before 1873,* Cambridge: Harvard University Press, 1921 (Harvard Economic Studies, Vol. XXIII).

Hendrick, B.J., *Life of Andrew Carnegie,* Vols. I and II, Garden City: Doubleday, 1932.

Jerome, Harry, *Mechanization in Industry,* New York: National Bureau of Economic Research, 1934.

Kennedy, E.D., *The Automobile Industry,* New York: Reynal and Hitchcock, 1941.

Kuhlmann, C.B., *Development of the Flour-Milling Industry in the United States,* Boston: Houghton Mifflin, 1929.

Landes, David S., *The Unbound Prometheus,* London: Cambridge University Press, 1969.

MacLaren, Malcolm, *The Rise of the Electric Industry During the Nineteenth Century,* Princeton: Princeton University Press, 1943.

Mantoux, Paul J., *The Industrial Revolution in the Eighteenth Century,* New York: Harcourt Brace Jovanovich, Inc., 1935.

Mee, John F., *Management Thought in a Dynamic Economy,* New York: New York University Press, 1963.

Musson, A.E., and Robinson, Eric, *Science and Technology in the Industrial Revolution,* Manchester, England: Manchester University Press, 1969.

Neimi, Albert W., *State and Regional Patterns in American Manufacturing, 1860–1900,* Westport, Conn.: Greenwood Press, 1974.

Rae, John B., *The American Automobile,* Chicago: University of Chicago Press, 1965.

——— *American Automobile Manufacturers,* New York: Chilton, 1959.

Roll, Erich, *An Early Experiment in Industrial Organization, Being a History of the Firm of Boulton and Watt, 1775–1805,* New York: Longmans, Green, 1930.

Rosen, S. McKee, and Rosen, Laura, *Technology and Society: The Influence of Machines in the United States,* New York: Macmillan, 1941.

Rosenberg, Nathan, *Technology and American Economic Growth,* New York: Harper & Row, 1972.

Shaw, William Howard, *Value of Commodity Output Since 1869,* New York: National Bureau of Economic Research, 1947 (Publication No. 48).

Thompson, Holland, *The Age of Invention,* New Haven: Yale University Press, 1921.

Tryon, Rolla M., *Household Manufacturers in the United States, 1640–1860,* Chicago: University of Chicago Press, 1917.

Usher, A.P., *History of Mechanical Invention,* New York: McGraw-Hill Book Co., 1929.
Vatter, Harold G., *The Drive to Industrial Maturity: The U.S. Economy, 1860–1914,* Westport, Conn.: Greenwood Press, 1975.
Walsh, Margaret, *The Manufacturing Frontier: Pioneer Industry in Antebellum Wisconsin, 1830–1860,* Madison: State Historical Society of Wisconsin, 1972.
Ware, Caroline F., *The Early New England Cotton Manufacture: A Study in Industrial Beginnings,* New York: Houghton Mifflin, 1931.
Williamson, Harold F., *Winchester, The Gun That Won the West,* Washington, D.C.: Combat Forces Press, 1952.
Williamson, Harold F., and Daum, Arnold R., *The American Petroleum Industry: The Age of Illumination, 1859–1899,* Evanston, Ill.: Northwestern University Press, 1959.
Woodworth, J.V., *American Tool Making and Interchangeable Manufacturing,* 2nd ed., New York: Henley, 1911.

Foreign and Domestic Commerce

Ashworth, William, *A Short History of the International Economy, 1850–1950,* New York: Longmans, Green, 1952.
Bailyn, Bernard, *The New England Merchants in the Seventeenth Century,* Cambridge: Harvard University Press, 1955.
Baxter, William T., *The House of Hancock; Business in Boston, 1724–1775,* Cambridge: Harvard University Press, 1945.
Beckman, Theodore N., and Engle, Nathanael H., *Wholesaling,* 3rd ed., New York: Ronald, 1959.
Beer, G.L., *Commercial Policy of England Toward the American Colonies,* New York: Columbia University Press, 1893 (Studies in History, Economics, and Public Law, Vol. III, No. 2).
Bloomfield, Arthur I., *Capital Imports and the American Balance of Payments, 1934–1939,* Chicago: University of Chicago Press, 1950.
Buck, Norman S., *The Development of the Organization of Anglo-American Trade, 1800–1850,* New Haven: Yale University Press, 1925.
Clark, T.D., *Pills, Petticoats, and Plows: The Southern Country Store,* Indianapolis: Bobbs-Merrill, 1944.
Condliffe, J.B., *The Commerce of Nations,* New York: W.W. Norton, 1950.
Craven, Wesley F., *Dissolution of the Virginia Company: The Failure of a Colonial Experiment,* New York: Oxford University Press, 1932.
Depew, D.M. (ed.), *One Hundred Years of American Commerce,* Vols. I and II, New York: Haynes, 1895.
East, R.A., *Business Enterprise in the American Revolutionary Era,* New York: Columbia University Press, 1938 (Studies in History, Economics, and Public Law No. 439).
Einzig, Paul, *The History of Foreign Exchange,* New York: St. Martin's Press, 1962.
Gibb, George Sweet, *The Whitesmiths of Taunton,* Cambridge: Harvard University Press, 1946.
Hall, A.R., *The Export of Capital from Britain, 1870–1914,* London: Methuen, 1968.
Harrington, Virginia D., *The New York Merchant on the Eve of the Revolution,* New York: Columbia University Press, 1935.
Hidy, Ralph W., *The House of Baring in American Trade and Finance: English Merchant Bankers at Work, 1763–1861,* Cambridge: Harvard University Press, 1949.
Hill, H.C., *Roosevelt and the Caribbean,* Chicago: University of Chicago Press, 1927.
Hotchkiss, George Burton, *Milestones of Marketing,* New York: Macmillan, 1938.
Hughes, J.R.T., *Fluctuations in Trade, Industry, and Finance: A Study of British Economic Developments, 1850–1860,* Oxford: Oxford University Press, 1960.

Johnson, Emory R. et al., *History of Domestic and Foreign Commerce of the United States,* 2nd ed., Pittsburgh: Carnegie Press, 1915.

Knight, M.M., *The Americans in Santo Domingo,* New York: Vanguard, 1928 (Studies in American Imperialism).

Krause, Lawrence B., *Sequel to Bretton Woods: A Proposal to Reform the World Monetary System,* Washington, D.C.: Brookings Institution, 1971.

McCain, W.D., *The United States and the Republic of Panama,* Durham, N.C.: Duke University Press, 1937.

McMaster, John B., *The Life and Times of Stephen Girard,* Philadelphia: J.B. Lippincott, 1918.

Mikesell, Raymond F., *Foreign Exchange in the Postwar World,* New York: Twentieth Century Fund, 1954.

Nearing, Scott, and Freeman, Joseph, *Dollar Diplomacy,* New York: Viking Press, 1925.

Pares, Richard, *Yankees and Creoles: The Trade Between North America and the West Indies Before the American Revolution,* Cambridge: Harvard University Press, 1956.

Pincus, Jonathan J., *Pressure Groups and Politics in Antebellum Tariffs,* New York: Columbia University Press, 1977.

Porter, Kenneth W., *The Jacksons and the Lees: Two Generations of Massachusetts Merchants, 1765–1844,* Vol. I, Cambridge: Harvard University Press, 1937.

——— *John Jacob Astor, Business Man,* Cambridge: Harvard University Press, 1931.

Presbrey, Frank S., *The History and Development of Advertising,* Garden City: Doubleday, 1929.

Ratner, Sidney, *The Tariff in American History,* New York: Van Nostrand, 1972.

Rippy, J.F., *Latin America and the Industrial Age,* New York: G.P. Putnam's Sons, 1944.

Roosa, Robert V., *The Dollar and World Liquidity,* New York: Random House, 1967.

Schlesinger, A.M., *The Colonial Merchants and the American Revolution,* New York: Columbia University Press, 1918 (Studies in History, Economics, and Public Law, No. 182).

Sellers, Leila, *Charleston Business on the Eve of the American Revolution,* Chapel Hill: University of North Carolina Press, 1934.

Stuart, G.H., *Latin America and the United States,* 4th ed., New York: Appleton-Century-Crofts, 1943.

Taussig, F.W., *Tariff History of the United States,* 7th ed., New York: G.P. Putnam's Sons, 1923.

Thorp, Willard H., *Trade, Aid, or What?* Baltimore: Johns Hopkins University Press, 1954.

Triffin, Robert, *Our International Monetary System,* New York: Random House, 1968.

Monopoly and Concentration of Industry

Alhadeff, David A., *Monopoly and Competition in Banking,* Berkeley: University of California Press, 1954 (Bureau of Business and Economic Research Publications).

Allen, F.L., *Lords of Creation,* New York: Harper & Row, 1935.

Asch, Peter, *Economic Theory and the Antitrust Dilemma,* New York: John Wiley & Sons, 1970.

Berle, Adolf A., Jr., *The 20th Century Capitalist Revolution,* New York: Harcourt Brace Jovanovich, Inc., 1954.

Berle, Adolf A., Jr., and Means, G.C., *The Modern Corporation and Private Property,* Chicago: Commerce Clearing House, 1932.

Blair, John M., *Economic Concentration,* New York: Harcourt Brace Jovanovich, Inc., 1972.

Bonbright, J.C., and Means, G.C., *The Holding Company,* New York: McGraw-Hill Book Co., 1932.

Burns, A.R., *The Decline of Competition,* Columbia University Council for Research in the Social Sciences, New York: McGraw-Hill Book Co., 1936.
Chandler, Alfred D., Jr., *Strategy and Structure,* Cambridge: Massachusetts Institute of Technology Press, 1962.
——— *Giant Enterprise: Ford, General Motors, and the Automobile Industry,* New York: Harcourt Brace Jovanovich, Inc., 1964.
Davis, Joseph S., *Essays in the Earlier History of American Corporations,* Cambridge: Harvard University Press, 1917.
Fetter, Frank A., *The Masquerade of Monopoly,* New York: Harcourt Brace Jovanovich, Inc., 1931.
Fusilier, H. Lee, and Darnell, Jerome C., *Competition and Public Policy: Cases in Antitrust,* Englewood Cliffs, N.J.: Prentice-Hall, 1971.
Galambos, Louis, *The Public Image of Big Business in America, 1880–1940: A Change,* Baltimore: Johns Hopkins University Press, 1975.
Himmelberg, Robert F., *The Origins of the National Recovery Administration: Business, Government, and Trade Association Issue, 1921–1933,* New York: Fordham University Press, 1976.
Josephson, Matthew, *Robber Barons: The Great American Capitalists, 1861–1901,* New York: Harcourt Brace Jovanovich, Inc., 1934.
Kaplan, A.D.H., *Big Enterprise in a Competitive System,* Washington, D.C.: Brookings Institution, 1954.
Knapp, Joseph G., *The Advance of American Cooperative Enterprise: 1920–1945,* Danville, Ill.: Interstate Printers and Publishers Incorporated, 1973.
Machlup, Fritz, *The Political Economy of Monopoly,* Baltimore: Johns Hopkins University Press, 1952.
Martin, David D., *Mergers and the Clayton Act,* Berkeley and Los Angeles: University of California Press, 1959.
Moody, John, *The Truth About the Trusts,* New York: Moody, 1904.
Myers, Gustavus, *History of Great American Fortunes,* Vols. I, II, and III, Chicago: Kerr, 1910.
Nevins, Allan, *John D. Rockefeller: The Heroic Age of American Business,* Vols. I and II, New York: Charles Scribner's Sons, 1940.
Regier, C.C., *The Era of the Muckrakers,* Chapel Hill: University of North Carolina Press, 1932.
Sobel, Robert, *The Age of Giant Corporations: A Microeconomic History of American Business, 1914–1970,* Westport, Conn.: Greenwood Press, 1972.
Steffens, Joseph Lincoln, *Autobiography of Lincoln Steffens,* Vols. I and II, New York: Harcourt Brace Jovanovich, Inc., 1931.
Stocking, George W., and Watkins, Myron W., *Monopoly and Free Enterprise,* New York: Twentieth Century Fund, 1951.
Tarbell, Ida M., *History of the Standard Oil Company,* Vols. I and II, New York: Macmillan, 1925.

LABOR

Abbott, Edith, *Historical Aspects of the Immigration Problem,* Chicago: University of Chicago Press, 1926 (University of Chicago Social Service Series).
Ahearn, Daniel J., *The Wages of Farm and Factory Laborers, 1914–1944,* New York: Columbia University Press, 1945 (Studies in History, Economics, and Public Law, No. 518).
Beard, Mary, *A Short History of the American Labor Movement,* New York: Macmillan, 1927.

Bell, Spurgeon, *Productivity, Wages, and National Income,* Washington, D.C.: Brookings Institution, 1940 (Institute of Economics Publication, No. 81).

Brandes, Stuart D., *American Welfare Capitalism, 1880–1940,* Chicago: University of Chicago Press, 1976.

Brissenden, P.F., *The I.W.W.: A Study of American Syndicalism,* 2nd ed., New York: Columbia University Press, 1920 (Studies in History, Economics, and Public Law, No. 193).

Bureau of Labor Statistics, *History of Wages in the United States from the Colonial Times to 1928,* Washington, D.C.: U.S. Government Printing Office, 1929.

Clark, M.R., and Simon, S.F., *The Labor Movement in America,* New York: W.W. Norton, 1938.

Coalson, G.O., *The Development of the Migratory Farm Labor System in Texas: 1900–1954,* San Francisco: R and E Research Associates, 1977.

Commons, J.R., *Documentary History of American Industrial Society,* Vols. I–X, J.R. Commons et al. (eds.), Cleveland: Clark, 1910 11.

Commons, J.R. et al., *History of Labor in the United States,* Vols. I–IV, New York: Macmillan, 1918.

Daugherty, Carroll R., *Labor Problems in American Industry,* 5th ed., Boston: Houghton Mifflin, 1941.

David, Henry, *History of the Haymarket Affair,* 2nd ed., New York: Russell & Russell, 1958.

Dempsey, Bernard W., *The Frontier Wage: The Economic Organization of Free Agents,* Chicago: Loyola University Press, 1960.

Douglas, Paul H., *Real Wages in the United States, 1890–1926,* Boston: Houghton Mifflin, 1930 (Pollak Foundation Publication No. 9).

——— *The Theory of Wages,* New York: Macmillan, 1934.

Ely, R.T., *The Labor Movement in America,* New York: Crowell, 1886.

Foner, Philip S., *History of the Labor Movement in the United States,* Vol. I, New York: International Publishers, 1947.

Foner, Phillip S., *Labor and the American Revolution,* Westport, Conn.: Greenwood Press, 1976.

Gutman, Herbert G., *Work, Culture, and Society in Industrializing America,* New York: Alfred A. Knopf, 1976.

Higgs, Robert, *Competition and Coercion,* New York: Cambridge University Press, 1977.

Jenks, J.W., and Lauck, W.J., *The Immigration Problem,* New York: Funk & Wagnalls, 1912.

Kuznets, Simon, and Rubin, Ernest, *Immigration and the Foreign Born,* New York: National Bureau of Economic Research, 1954.

McLaurin, Melton A., *Paternalism and Protest: Southern Cotton Mill Workers and Organized Labor, 1875–1905,* Westport, Conn.: Greenwood Press, 1971.

Millis, Harry A., and Brown, Emily C., *From the Wagner Act to Taft–Hartley,* Chicago: University of Chicago Press, 1950.

Millis, Harry A., and Montgomery, Royal E., *Economics of Labor,* Vol. III: *Organized Labor,* New York: McGraw-Hill Book Co., 1945.

Mills, Frederick C., *Productivity and Economic Progress,* New York: National Bureau of Economic Research, 1952.

Nelson, Daniel, *Managers and Workers: Origins of the New Factory System in the United States, 1880–1920,* Madison: University of Wisconsin Press, 1975.

Perlman, Selig, *A History of Trade Unionism in the United States,* New York: Macmillan, 1922.

Ranson, Roger, and Sutch, Richard, *One Kind of Freedom,* New York: Cambridge University Press, 1977.

Rees, Albert, *Real Wages in Manufacturing, 1890–1914,* Princeton: Princeton University Press, 1961.

Saposs, D.J., and Saposs, B.T., *Readings in Trade Unionism,* New York: Macmillan, 1927.

Smith, Abbot Emerson, *Colonists in Bondage,* Chapel Hill: University of North Carolina Press, 1947.

Solomon, Barbara M., *Ancestors and Immigrants: A Changing New England Tradition,* Cambridge: Harvard University Press, 1956.

Stephenson, G.M., *History of American Immigration, 1820–1924,* Boston: Ginn & Company, 1926.

Ware, Norman H., *The Industrial Worker, 1840–1860,* Boston: Houghton Mifflin, 1924.

—— *The Labor Movement in the United States,* New York: Appleton-Century-Crofts, 1929.

Wolman, Leo, *Growth of American Trade Unions 1880–1923,* New York: National Bureau of Economic Research, 1924 (Publication No. 6).

Woytinsky, W.S. et al., *Employment and Wages in the United States,* New York: Twentieth Century Fund, 1953.

Wright, David McCord (ed.), *The Impact of the Union,* New York: Harcourt Brace Jovanovich, Inc., 1951.

ECONOMIC GROWTH AND FLUCTUATIONS

Armstrong, Ellis L., *History of Public Works in the United States,* Chicago: American Public Works Association, 1976.

Bellush, Bernard, *The Failure of the NRA,* New York: W.W. Norton, 1975.

Bruchey, Stuart, *Cotton and the Growth of the American Economy: 1790–1860,* New York: Harcourt Brace Jovanovich, Inc., 1967.

Cole, A.H., *Wholesale Commodity Prices in the United States, 1700–1861,* Vols. I and II, Cambridge: Harvard University Press, 1938 (International Scientific Commission on Price History).

Collman, Charles A., *Our Mysterious Panics, 1830–1930,* New York: William Morrow, 1931.

David, Paul A., *Technical Choice Innovation and Economic Growth,* New York: Cambridge University Press, 1975.

Davis, Lance E., and North, Douglass C., *Institutional Change and American Economic Growth,* New York: Cambridge University Press, 1971.

Davis, Lance E., Easterlin, Richard A., Parker, William N., et al., *American Economic Growth: An Economist's History of the United States,* New York: Harper & Row, 1972.

Fellner, William J., *Trends and Cycles in Economic Activity: An Introduction to Problems of Economic Growth,* New York: Holt, Rinehart & Winston, 1956.

Fels, Rendigs, *American Business Cycles, 1865–1897,* Chapel Hill: University of North Carolina Press, 1959.

Frickey, Edwin, *Economic Fluctuations in the United States,* Cambridge: Harvard University Press, 1942 (Harvard Economic Studies, Vol. LXXIII).

—— *Production in the United States, 1860–1914,* Cambridge: Harvard University Press, 1947 (Harvard Economic Studies, Vol. LXXXII).

Galbraith, John Kenneth, *The Great Crash,* Boston: Houghton Mifflin, 1955.

Goldsmith, Raymond W., *Income and Wealth of the United States: Trends and Structure,* Cambridge, England: Bowes & Bowes, 1952.

—— *A Study of Savings in the United States,* Princeton: Princeton University Press, 1955.

Hansen, Alvin H., *Business Cycles and National Income,* New York: W.W. Norton, 1951.

Harris, Seymour E., *Inflation and the American Economy,* New York: McGraw-Hill Book Co., 1945.

Kuznets, Simon, *Cyclical Fluctuations,* New York: Greenberg, 1926.

——— *National Income: A Summary of Findings,* New York: National Bureau of Economic Research, 1946 (Twenty-fifth Anniversary Series No. 1).

——— *National Product in Wartime,* New York: National Bureau of Economic Research, 1945 (Publication No. 44).

Jenks, Leland H., *The Migration of British Capital to 1875,* New York: Alfred A. Knopf, 1927.

Kendrick, John W., *Productivity Trends in the United States,* Princeton: Princeton University Press, 1961.

Lewis, W. Arthur, *The Theory of Economic Growth,* London: Allen and Unwin, 1955.

Matthews, R.C.O., *A Study in Trade Cycle History: Economic Fluctuations in Great Britain, 1833–1842,* Cambridge, England: Cambridge University Press, 1954.

McGrane, R.C., *The Panic of 1837,* Chicago: University of Chicago Press, 1924.

Mills, Frederick C., *Productivity and Economic Progress,* New York: National Bureau of Economic Research, 1952.

Mitchell, Wesley, *Business Cycles: the Problem and Its Setting,* New York: National Bureau of Economic Research, 1927 (Publication No. 10).

Morris, Bruce R., *The Problems of American Economic Growth,* New York: Oxford University Press, 1961

National Bureau of Economic Research, *Output, Employment, and Productivity in the United States After 1800: Studies in Income and Wealth,* Vol. 30, New York: Columbia University Press, 1966.

——— *Trends in the American Economy in the Nineteenth Century: Studies in Income and Wealth,* Vol. 24, Princeton: Princeton University Press, 1960.

North, Douglass C., *The Economic Growth of the United States, 1790 to 1860,* Englewood Cliffs, N.J.: Prentice-Hall, 1961.

Primm, James N., *Economic Policy in the Development of a Western State: Missouri, 1820–1860,* Cambridge: Harvard University Press, 1954.

Robbins, Lionel, *The Great Depression,* Toronto: Macmillan, 1934.

Roland, Charles P., *The Improbable Era: The South Since World War II,* Lexington: University Press of Kentucky, 1975.

Rosenberg, Nathan, *Technology and American Economic Growth,* New York: Harper & Row, 1973.

Rosenof, Theodore, *Dogma, Depression and the New Deal: The Debate of Political Leaders Over Economic Recovery,* New York: Kennikat Press, 1975.

Rostow, W.W., *The Process of Economic Growth,* New York: W.W. Norton, 1952.

——— *The Stages of Economic Growth,* Cambridge, England: Cambridge University Press, 1960.

Schumpeter, Joseph A., *Business Cycles,* Vols. I and II, New York: McGraw-Hill Book Co., 1939.

Slichter, Sumner H., *Economic Growth in the United States,* Baton Rouge: Louisiana State University Press, 1962.

Smith, Walter B., *Fluctuations in American Business, 1790–1860,* Cambridge: Harvard University Press, 1935.

Sprague, O.M.W., *History of Crises Under the National Banking System,* Washington, D.C.: U.S. Government Printing Office, 1910.

Temin, Peter, *Did Monetary Forces Cause the Great Depression?,* New York: W.W. Norton, 1976.

Thomas, Brinley, *Migration and Urban Development: A Reappraisal of British and American Long Cycles,* London: Methuen, 1972.

Thorp, W.L., and Thorp, H.E., *Business Annals,* New York: National Bureau of Economic Research, 1926 (Publication No. 8).

Van Vleck, G.W., *The Panic of 1857,* New York: Columbia University Press, 1943.

GENERAL

Aitken, Hugh G.J. (ed.), *The State and Economic Growth,* New York: Social Science Research Council, 1959.

Andreano, Ralph (ed.), *The Economic Impact of the Civil War,* Cambridge, England: Schenkman, 1962.

Barkley, Paul W., and Seckler, David W., *Economic Growth and Environmental Decay: The Solution Becomes the Problem,* New York: Harcourt Brace Jovanovich, Inc., 1972.

Beard, C.A., *An Economic Interpretation of the Constitution of the United States,* New York: Macmillan, 1913.

Beard, Miriam, *A History of the Business Man,* Vols. I and II, Ann Arbor: Ann Arbor Paperbacks, University of Michigan Press, 1962.

Berle, Adolf A., Jr., *The 20th Century Capitalist Revolution,* New York: Harcourt Brace Jovanovich, Inc., 1954.

Bogart, E.L., and Thompson, C.M., *Readings in the Economic History of the United States,* New York: Longmans, Green, 1916.

Bonjean, Charles M., Louis Schneider and Lineberry, Robert L. (eds.), *Social Science in America: The First Two Hundred Years,* Austin: University of Texas Press, 1976.

Borcherding, Thomas (ed.), *Budgets and Bureaucrats: The Sources of Government Growth,* Durham, N.C.: Duke University Press, 1977.

Brown, Ralph H., *Historical Geography of the United States,* New York: Harcourt Brace Jovanovich, Inc., 1948 (Yale Institute of International Studies).

Brown, Robert E., *Charles Beard and the Constitution: A Critical Analysis of "An Economic Interpretation of the Constitution,"* Princeton: Princeton University Press, 1956.

Bunke, Harvey C., *The Liberal Dilemma,* Englewood Cliffs, N.J.: Prentice-Hall, 1964.

Callendar, G.S., *Selections from the Economic History of the United States, 1765–1860,* Boston: Ginn & Company, 1909.

Cameron, Rondo E., *France and the Economic Development of Europe, 1800–1914,* Princeton: Princeton University Press, 1961.

Carus-Wilson, E.M., *Essays in Economic History,* London: Edward Arnold, 1954 (Vol. 1), 1962 (Vols. 2–3).

Clark, Colin, *The Conditions of Economic Progress,* 2nd ed., New York: Macmillan, 1951.

Clough, Shepard B., *The Economic Development of Western Civilization,* New York: McGraw-Hill Book Co., 1959.

Clough, Shepard B., and Cole, Charles W., *Economic History of Europe,* rev. ed., Boston: D.C. Heath, 1946.

Coats, A.W., Robertson, Ross M. (eds.), *Essays in American Economic History,* London: Edward Arnold, 1969.

Cochran, Thomas C., *American Business in the Twentieth Century,* Cambridge: Harvard University Press, 1972.

Cochran, Thomas C., and Miller, William, *The Age of Enterprise,* New York: Macmillan, 1942.

Coleman, Peter J., *Debtors and Creditors in America: Insolvency, Imprisonment for Debt, and Bankruptcy, 1607–1900,* Madison: The Historical Society of Wisconsin, 1974.

Crenson, Mathew A., *The Federal Machine: Beginnings of Bureaucracy in Jacksonian America,* New York: Dodd, Mead, 1975.

Deane, Phyllis, and W.A. Cole, *British Economic Growth, 1688–1959,* Cambridge, England: Cambridge University Press, 1962.

Dunne, Gerald T., *Justice Joseph Story and the Rise of the Supreme Court,* New York: Simon & Schuster, 1970.

Editors of Fortune, *U.S.A.—The Permanent Revolution,* Englewood Cliffs, N.J.: Prentice-Hall, 1951.

Flügel, F., and Faulkner, H.U., *Readings in the Economic and Social History of the United States, 1773–1829,* New York: Harper & Row, 1929.
Fogel, Robert W., and Engerman, Stanley (eds.), *The Reinterpretation of American Economic History,* New York: Harper & Row, 1971.
Freeman, Ralph E., *Postwar Economic Trends in the United States,* New York: Harper & Row, 1960.
Freeman, Roger A., *The Growth of American Government,* Stanford: Hoover Institution Press, 1975.
Gras, N.S.B., *Industrial Evolution,* Cambridge: Harvard University Press, 1930.
——— *An Introduction to Economic History,* New York: Harper & Row, 1922.
Gras, N.S.B., and Larson, Henrietta, *Casebook in American Business History,* New York: Appleton-Century-Crofts, 1939.
Hacker, Louis M., *Major Documents in American Economic History,* Vols. I and II, New York: Van Nostrand, 1961.
——— *The Triumph of American Capitalism,* New York: Simon & Schuster, 1940.
Heaton, Herbert, *Economic History of Europe,* New York: Harper & Row, 1936.
Holmes, Graeme M., *Britain and America: A Comparative Economic History, 1850–1939,* New York: Barnes & Noble, 1976.
Hopkins, J.G.E., and Robinson, Florett, *Album of American History,* New York: Charles Scribner's Sons, 1960.
Hughes, Jonathan, *The Vital Few,* Boston: Houghton Mifflin, 1966.
Hughes, J.R.T., *Industrialization and Economic History: Theses and Conjectures,* New York: McGraw-Hill Book Co., 1970.
Jewkes, John, Sawyers, D., and Stillerman, R., *The Sources of Invention,* London: Macmillan, 1958.
Josephson, Matthew, *The Robber Barons,* New York: Harcourt Brace Jovanovich, Inc., 1962.
Kirkland, E.C., *A History of American Economic Life,* rev. ed., New York: Appleton-Century-Crofts, 1939.
Kuznets, Simon, *Economic Change*, New York: W.W. Norton, 1953.
——— *National Product Since 1869,* New York: National Bureau of Economic Research, 1946 (Publication No. 46).
Lane, Frederic C. (ed.), *Enterprise and Secular Change,* Homestead, Ill.: Richard D. Irwin, 1953.
Leech, Margaret, *In the Days of McKinley,* New York: Harper & Row, 1959.
Leontieff, W., *The Structure of the American Economy, 1919–1929,* Cambridge: Harvard University Press, 1941.
Lord, Walter, *The Good Years,* New York: Harper & Row, 1960.
Martineau, Harriet, *Society in America,* Vols. I, II, and III, 2nd ed., London: Saunders and Otley, 1839.
Mathias, Peter, *The First Industrial Nation: An Economic History of Britain, 1700–1914,* London: Methuen, 1969.
McDonald, Forrest, *We The People,* Chicago: University of Chicago Press, 1958.
Miller, William (ed.), *Men In Business,* New York and Evanston: Harper & Row, 1962.
Morison, Samuel Eliot, *The Oxford History of the American People,* New York: Oxford University Press, 1965.
Mumford, Lewis, *The City in History: Its Origins, Its Transformations, and Its Prospects,* New York: Harcourt Brace Jovanovich, Inc., 1961.
Nevins, Allan, *Ordeal of the Union,* Vols. I and II, New York: Charles Scribner's Sons, 1947.
Perkins, Edwin J., *Men and Organizations: The American Economy in the Twentieth Century,* New York: G.P. Putnam's Sons, 1977.
Postan, M.M., *An Economic History of Western Europe, 1945–1964,* London: Methuen, 1967.

Reeves, Dorothea D., *Resources for the Study of Economic History,* Boston: Harvard Graduate School of Business, 1961.

Robertson, Ross M., and Pate, James L., *Readings in United States Economic and Business History,* Boston: Houghton Mifflin, 1966.

Roosevelt, Franklin Delano, *The Public Papers and Addresses of Franklin D. Roosevelt,* Vols. I–IV, S.I. Rosenman (ed.), New York: Harper & Row, 1941–1945.

Saul, S.B., *The Myth of the Great Depression, 1873–1896,* London: Macmillan, 1969.

Schlesinger, A.M., Jr., *The Age of Jackson,* Boston: Little, Brown, 1945.

Schumpeter, Joseph A., *The Theory of Economic Development,* Cambridge: Harvard University Press, 1934.

Shannon, F.A., *America's Economic Growth,* 3rd ed., New York: Macmillan, 1951.

Slichter, Sumner H., *The American Economy,* New York: Alfred A. Knopf, 1938.

Sombart, Werner, *The Quintessence of Capitalism: A Study of the History and Psychology of the Modern Business Man,* New York: E.P. Dutton, 1915.

Soule, George, *Economic Forces in American History,* New York: Dryden, 1952.

——— *Economic History of the United States,* Vol. VIII, *Prosperity Decade from War to Depression, 1917–1929,* New York: Holt, Rinehart & Winston, 1947.

Steiner, George A., *Government's Role in Economic Life,* New York: McGraw-Hill, 1953.

Tunnard, Christopher, and Henry Rope Reed, *American Skyline: The Growth and Forms of Our Cities and Towns,* Boston: Houghton Mifflin, 1955.

Walton, Gary M., and Miller, Roger L., *Economic Issues in American History,* San Francisco: Canfield Press, 1978.

Ward, Barbara and Dubos, Rene, *Only One Earth,* New York: W.W. Norton, 1972.

Williamson, Harold F., *The Growth of the American Economy,* 2nd ed., Englewood Cliffs, N.J.: Prentice-Hall, 1951.

Williamson, Harold F., and Buttrick, John A. (eds.), *Economic Development: Principles and Patterns,* Englewood Cliffs, N.J.: Prentice-Hall, 1954.

Wright, Chester W., *Economic History of the United States,* 2nd ed., New York: McGraw-Hill Book Co., 1949.

Sources of Illustrations

Alinari/Art Reference Bureau, 19; Brown Brothers, 20; Courtesy New York Central System, 23; Charleston Historical Society, 52; Library of Congress, 52; The Whaling Museum, New Bedford, Massachusetts, 59; The Bettmann Archive, Inc., 65; Museum of the City of New York, 70; Library of Congress, 74; Henry E. Huntington Library and Art Gallery, 91; The Bettmann Archive, Inc., 99; The Library of Congress, 110; Independence National Historical Park Collection, 136; Yale University Art Gallery (one of the paintings deposited by John Trumbull at Yale before his death), 138; Courtesy of the Chase Manhattan Bank Money Museum, 140; The Bettmann Archive, Inc., 143; Courtesy of the New York Historical Society, New York City, 146; Culver Pictures, Inc., 155; Association of American Railroads, 162; U.S. Department of the Interior, Bureau of Land Management, 163; U.S. Dept. of the Interior, 173; The Public Library of Cincinnati and Hamilton County, 174; Courtesy of the New York Historical Society, New York City, 180; Courtesy of the New York Historical Society, New York City, 186; Courtesy Chicago Historical Society, 190; The Bettmann Archive, Inc., 200; The Bettmann Archive, Inc., 200; The Bettmann Archive, Inc., 215; Library of Congress, 215; Library of Congress, 234; Library of Congress, 236; Library of Congress, 237; Library of Congress, 239; Chicago Historical Society, 243; Brown Brothers, 254; Courtesy Union–Pacific Railroad, 257; Harper's Magazine, 259; Courtesy Illinois Central Railroad, 261; Historical Society of Montana, Helena, 276; Library of Congress, 279; Brown Brothers, 281; Library of Congress, 288; The Bettmann Archive, Inc., 300; Library of Congress, 304; Culver Pictures, Inc., 315; Brown Brothers, 319; Library of Congress, 325; Culver Pictures, Inc., 328; The Bettmann Archive, Inc., 330; George Eastman House, Inc. Photograph, 336; Culver Pictures, Inc., 336; AFL–CIO, 337; Brown Brothers, 338; The Bettmann Archive, Inc., 340; The Bettmann Archive, Inc., 345; Courtesy Levi Strauss and Co., 346; F. W. Woolworth Co., 347; Culver Pictures, Inc., 349; Harper's Magazine, 364; Culver Pictures, Inc., 365; Brown Brothers, 368; Internal Revenue Service, Treasury Department, 390; Brown Brothers, 408; Culver Pictures, Inc., 412; The Bettmann Archive, Inc., 414; Culver Pictures, Inc., 420; Library of Congress, 417; USDA–Soil Conservation Service, 431; Rotkin, pfi, 444; Rotkin, pfi, 449; UPI, 463; Fedder's Air Conditioning Co., 464; Brown Brothers, 465; UPI, 487; AFL–CIO, 493; Bob Burroughs (© 1978)/Jeroboam, 507; British Airways, 508; American Association of Railroads, 511; Standard Oil Company (New Jersey), 514; USDA–Soil Conservation Service, 535; UPI, 543.

Index

A

B

C

D

E

N

O

P

Q

R

S

A 9
B 0
C 1
D 2
E 3
F 4
G 5
H 6
I 7
J 8